Prentice Hall

GRAMMAR AND COMPOSITION

SERIES CONSULTANTS

Grade 6
Joleen Johnson
Curriculum Writer, Office of Secondary Instruction
San Bernardino City Unified Schools
San Bernardino, California

Grade 7
Ellen G. Manhire
English Consultant Coordinator
Fresno, California

Grade 8
Elizabeth A. Nace
Supervisor, Language Arts
Akron, Ohio

Grade 9
Jerry Reynolds
Supervisor, Language Arts
Rochester, Minnesota

Grade 10
Marlene Corbett
Chairperson, Department of English
Charlotte, North Carolina

Grade 11
Gilbert Hunt
Chairperson, Department of English
Manchester, Connecticut

Grade 12
Margherite LaPota
Curriculum Specialist
Tulsa, Oklahoma

CRITIC READERS

Hugh B. Cassell
Jefferson County Public Schools
Louisville, KY

Mary Demarest
St. Mary's Dominican High School
New Orleans, LA

Judy Luehm Junecko
Leesburg High School
Leesburg, FL

Ruth E. Loeffler
Norman High School
Norman, OK

D. Gay Masters
Salem-Keizer Public Schools
Salem, OR

Laura Moyer
Gloversville High School
Gloversville, NY

Avis Satterfield
Virgil I. Grissom High School
Huntsville, AL

Bonnie Scott
St. Augustine High School
St. Augustine, FL

Margie M. Spencer
S. R. Butler High School
Huntsville, AL

Jeanne Bussiere-Stephens
Phillips Academy
Andover, MA

Marvin Zimmerman
Little Rock School District
Little Rock, AR

George Comer
Gary Public Schools
Gary, IN

Prentice Hall
GRAMMAR AND COMPOSITION

SERIES AUTHORS

Gary Forlini — **Senior Author**
Pelham High School, Pelham, New York

Mary Beth Bauer — Harris County Department of Education, Houston, Texas

Lawrence Biener — Locust Valley Junior-Senior High School, Locust Valley, New York

Linda Capo — Pelham Junior High School, Pelham, New York

Karen Moore Kenyon — Saratoga High School, Saratoga, California

Darla H. Shaw — Ridgefield School System, Ridgefield, Connecticut

Zenobia Verner — University of Houston, Houston, Texas

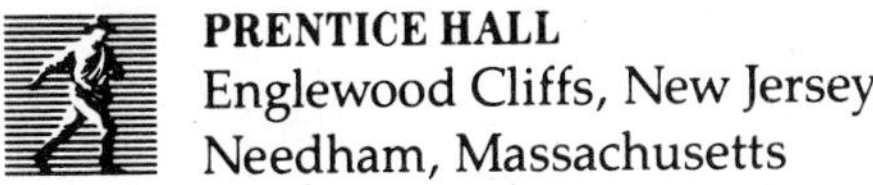

PRENTICE HALL
Englewood Cliffs, New Jersey
Needham, Massachusetts

SUPPLEMENTARY MATERIALS

Annotated Teacher's Edition
Teacher's Resource Book
Computer Exercise Bank
Writing Model Transparencies

Acknowledgments: page 862

PRENTICE HALL **Grammar and Composition**
Fourth Edition

© 1990, 1987, 1985, 1982 by Prentice-Hall, Inc., Englewood Cliffs, New Jersey 07632. All rights reserved. No part of this book may be reproduced in any form or by any means without permission in writing from the publisher.
Printed in the United States of America.

ISBN 0-13-711854-6

10 9 8 7 6 5

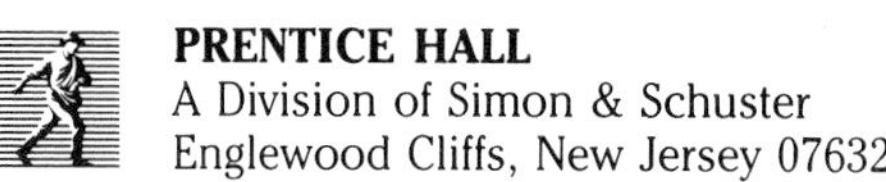
PRENTICE HALL
A Division of Simon & Schuster
Englewood Cliffs, New Jersey 07632

Contents

Grammar Usage Mechanics

Composition and Allied Skills

V Composition–Forms and Process of Writing 471

UNIT I

Grammar

1 Nouns, Pronouns, and Verbs
2 Adjectives and Adverbs
3 Prepositions, Conjunctions, and Interjections
4 Reviewing Parts of Speech
5 Basic Sentence Parts and Patterns
6 Phrases
7 Clauses
8 Avoiding Sentence Errors

Chapter 1

Nouns, Pronouns, and Verbs

Each word you use can be classified as one of the eight *parts of speech:* nouns, pronouns, verbs, adjectives, adverbs, prepositions, conjunctions, and interjections.

In English, *nouns* and *pronouns* are the two parts of speech used to name things. Nouns name people, places, and things. Pronouns stand for nouns. *Verbs* tell something about nouns and pronouns, often by expressing some kind of action. The next three sections will explain these three parts of speech.

1.1 Nouns

In grammar, the names people give to themselves and others, to the places they live, and to the things that surround them are called *nouns*.

A noun is the name of a person, place, or thing.

Nouns as Names

Although there are three basic categories of nouns, the category of things can be expanded greatly.

Nouns name things that can be seen and touched as well as those that cannot be seen and touched.

The last five categories of nouns in the following chart all name things.

CATEGORIES OF NOUNS			
People	Mark	citizen	Aunt Jo
Places	beach	hotel	Europe
Visible Things	moose	tree	lightning
Ideas	freedom	religion	friendship
Actions	decision	treatment	punishment
Conditions	health	dismay	happiness
Qualities	wisdom	strength	courage

Nouns that name people, places, or things that can be seen or recognized through any of the five senses are called *concrete nouns*. Nouns that name other things such as ideas, actions, conditions, and qualities are called *abstract nouns*.

Another special type of noun is used to name *groups* of people or things. Nouns of this type are called *collective nouns*.

COLLECTIVE NOUNS: community household team flock

EXERCISE A: Identifying Nouns. Write the two nouns in each sentence, labeling one *concrete* and one *abstract*.

EXAMPLE: My mother admired your honesty.
mother (concrete) honesty (abstract)

1. An inventor must have a good imagination.
2. Their excitement at the zoo was expected.
3. The election was held in the auditorium.
4. Poor health kept the frail child indoors.
5. Wild animals in captivity often seem pathetic.
6. The artist thought about her plan.
7. The young boy wanted to know about his future.
8. The average of his tests was not satisfactory.
9. Amazingly, our team won the championship.
10. Her memories of Italy were fading.

Compound Nouns

Some nouns, such as *Aunt Liz, son-in-law,* and *baseball,* consist of two or more words acting as a unit.

A compound noun is a noun that is made up of more than one word.

Notice the three ways *compound nouns* are formed.

TYPES OF COMPOUND NOUNS		
Separated	**Hyphenated**	**Combined**
fire engine soap opera	commander-in-chief jack-of-all-trades	toothbrush dishwasher

EXERCISE B: Recognizing Compound Nouns. Write the three nouns in each sentence. Circle each compound noun.

EXAMPLE: Smoke from the campfire drifted toward the trees.
Smoke (campfire) trees

1. The maid-of-honor at the wedding cried during the ceremony.
2. The back of the station wagon was loaded with luggage.
3. The gardener and his son filled the trash bags.
4. Ed enjoyed his visit with his mother-in-law.
5. Three planes awaited the signal for takeoff.
6. In the attic the children found a lampshade.
7. The fisherman wore a red feather in his hat.
8. Most families still have an ironing board and iron.
9. The old cook put too much salt on the lima beans.
10. Laura held the position of editor-in-chief.

Common and Proper Nouns

All nouns are either *common nouns* or *proper nouns*.

A common noun names any one of a class of people, places, or things.

A proper noun names a specific person, place, or thing.

Proper nouns always begin with capital letters.

Common Nouns	Proper Nouns
novelist	Willa Cather, Henry James
continent	North America, Africa
city	Atlanta, Portland
planet	Mercury, Venus

NOTE ABOUT NAMES OF FAMILY MEMBERS: A noun used to describe a person's role in a family may be either common or proper, depending on how it is used. A name used simply to indicate a person's role is a common noun. A name used as a title before a personal name is part of a compound proper noun.

COMMON: My best friend is my *uncle*.

PROPER: My best friend is *Uncle* Barry.

A *noun of direct address*—that is, the name of a person to whom you are speaking—is always proper.

DIRECT ADDRESS: Please, *Dad*, may I go out tonight?

EXERCISE C: Distinguishing Between Common and Proper Nouns. Determine which words are common nouns and which are proper. If a word is a common noun, write a proper noun that falls into the same category. If a word is a proper noun, write a common noun of the same category.

EXAMPLE: language
French

1. town
2. dog
3. author
4. Labor Day
5. state
6. woman
7. Sahara
8. river
9. George III
10. organization
11. boy
12. planet
13. relative
14. building
15. Asia
16. toothpaste
17. mountain
18. United States
19. animal
20, country

DEVELOPING WRITING SKILLS: Writing Sentences with Nouns. Use the following instructions to write five sentences of your own.

EXAMPLE: Write a sentence about plants that includes two common nouns.

Crocuses bloom in the early spring.

1. Write a sentence about school activities that includes one common noun and one compound common noun.
2. Write a sentence about a city or town that includes one common noun and one compound proper noun.
3. Write a sentence about a person that includes one concrete noun and one abstract noun.
4. Write a sentence about food that includes one common noun and one compound common noun.
5. Write a sentence about another country that includes one proper noun and one collective noun.

1.2 Pronouns

Repeating the same noun over and over in writing or speaking would result in awkward choppy sentences. Instead of repeating the same noun many times, speakers and writers use substitutes called *pronouns*.

Pronouns are words that stand for nouns or for words that take the place of nouns.

Antecedents of Pronouns

Pronouns get their meaning from the words they stand for. These words are called *antecedents*.

Antecedents are nouns (or words that take the place of nouns) for which pronouns stand.

In the examples at the top of the next page, the arrows point from the pronouns to the words they stand for. In the first sentence, the pronouns *you* and *your* stand for the noun *Tom*. In the second sentence, the pronoun *it* stands for a group of words that takes the place of a noun, *Making lasagna for dinner*.

EXAMPLES: Tom, did *you* submit *your* article on tennis?

Making lasagna for dinner was easy, and *it* will be fun to do again.

Antecedents usually come before their pronouns, as in the examples above. Sometimes, however, this pattern is reversed.

EXAMPLE: *That* is the best book I have ever read.

Pronouns usually have specific antecedents; some do not.

EXERCISE A: Recognizing Antecedents. Write the antecedent of each underlined pronoun.

EXAMPLE: My brothers cooked all of the food by themselves.
food brothers

1. Betty accomplished all of this work herself.
2. The doll was one that had been made in England. It was painted by hand.
3. Mr. Jenkins gave a bonus to all of the employees and to himself as well.
4. The audience was disappointed with the play, and many left before it was over.
5. Magnolias are trees that grow in the South. They produce beautiful white blossoms.
6. The class gave their petitions to the senator, who was glad to receive them.
7. Joe, these are great potatoes. Where did you buy them?
8. Many of the people rose from their seats.
9. The group gave themselves credit for their hard work.
10. How could Matt prove he wrote that paper himself?

Personal, Reflexive, and Intensive Pronouns

The pronouns you use most often to refer to yourself, to other people, and to things are called *personal pronouns*. *Reflexive* and *intensive pronouns* are formed by adding *-self* or *-selves* to some of the personal pronouns.

Personal Pronouns. *Personal pronouns* are used more often than any other type of pronoun.

Personal pronouns refer to (1) the person speaking, (2) the person spoken to, or (3) the person, place, or thing spoken about.

First-person pronouns refer to the person who is speaking. *Second-person pronouns* refer to the person spoken to. *Third-person pronouns* refer to the person, place, or thing spoken about.

PERSONAL PRONOUNS		
	Singular	**Plural**
First Person	I, me, my, mine	we, us, our, ours
Second Person	you, your, yours	you, your, yours
Third Person	he, him, his, she, her, hers, it, its	they, them, their, theirs

In the first example below, the antecedent of the personal pronoun is the person speaking. In the second, the antecedent of the personal pronoun is the person being spoken to. In the last example, the antecedent of the personal pronoun is the thing spoken about.

FIRST PERSON: *My* name is not George.

SECOND PERSON: When *you* left for school, *you* forgot *your* lunch.

THIRD PERSON: Don't judge a book by *its* cover.

Reflexive and Intensive Pronouns. Pronouns that end in *-self* or *-selves* are either *reflexive pronouns* or *intensive pronouns*.

A reflexive pronoun ends in *-self* or *-selves* and adds information to a sentence by pointing back to a noun or pronoun earlier in the sentence.

An intensive pronoun ends in *-self* or *-selves* and simply adds emphasis to a noun or pronoun in the same sentence.

The reflexive and intensive pronouns are shown in the following chart.

REFLEXIVE AND INTENSIVE PRONOUNS		
	Singular	**Plural**
First Person	myself	ourselves
Second Person	yourself	yourselves
Third Person	himself, herself, itself	themselves

A reflexive pronoun always adds information to a sentence. It cannot be left out without changing the meaning. In the first example, *himself* tells whom Michael taught. In the second, *herself* tells for whom the jeans were bought.

REFLEXIVE: Michael taught *himself* to play the piano.

Gloria bought *herself* a new pair of jeans.

An intensive pronoun emphasizes its antecedent but does not add information to a sentence. If an intensive pronoun is removed, a sentence will still have the same meaning.

Usually, an intensive pronoun follows immediately after its antecedent, as shown in the first of the following examples. Sometimes, however, an intensive pronoun is located in another part of the sentence, as shown in the second example.

INTENSIVE: The President *himself* attended the gala opening.

We spliced the film *ourselves*.

EXERCISE B: Identifying Personal, Reflexive, and Intensive Pronouns. Write the pronoun in each sentence. Then label each as *personal, reflexive,* or *intensive*.

EXAMPLE: Abby taught herself to play the piano.

herself (reflexive)

1. Grandfather wrote you a letter yesterday.
2. Laura made herself a white dress for the dance.
3. I can't study while the radio is playing.

4. If the bus does not arrive soon, we will be late.
5. The Queen herself is coming to launch the ship.
6. Jim promised himself a reward for working so hard.
7. A flying squirrel uses its tail as a rudder.
8. The family harvested the wheat themselves.
9. Louise's good judgment saved their lives.
10. The sun itself provides energy, light, and warmth.

Demonstrative, Relative, and Interrogative Pronouns

Three other kinds of pronouns, called *demonstrative, relative,* and *interrogative pronouns,* have very special uses.

Pronouns That Point Out. Pronouns that direct attention to one or more nouns are called *demonstrative pronouns.*

Demonstrative pronouns direct attention to specific people, places, or things.

The following chart shows the four demonstrative pronouns.

DEMONSTRATIVE PRONOUNS	
Singular	**Plural**
this, that	these, those

Demonstrative pronouns may be located before or after their antecedents.

BEFORE: *That* is the house I would like to own.

Are *these* the colors I selected?

AFTER: The girl asked for pie. *This* was her favorite dessert.

I planted tulips and roses, but *those* did not bloom.

Pronouns That Relate. One of the demonstrative pronouns, *that,* can also be used as a *relative pronoun.*

A relative pronoun begins a subordinate clause and connects it to another idea in the sentence.

Chapter 7 tells about clauses. The following chart shows the five relative pronouns that are used to introduce many clauses.

RELATIVE PRONOUNS				
that	which	who	whom	whose

The sentences in the following chart show relative pronouns used to connect one group of words, a subordinate clause, to another group of words, an independent clause.

Independent Clauses	Subordinate Clauses
He found the money	*that* he had lost.
Carl is the secretary	*whom* the class elected.

Pronouns That Ask Questions. All relative pronouns except *that* can also be *interrogative pronouns*.

An interrogative pronoun is used to begin a question.

The following chart shows the five interrogative pronouns.

INTERROGATIVE PRONOUNS				
what	which	who	whom	whose

In the following examples, notice that interrogative pronouns do not always have specific antecedents.

EXAMPLES: *What* did you say? *Which* of the answers is best?
Who is on the telephone?
With *whom* did you wish to speak?
Mine is blue. *Whose* is red?

EXERCISE C: Recognizing Demonstrative, Relative, and Interrogative Pronouns. Write the pronoun in each of the following sentences. Then label each as *demonstrative, relative*, or *interrogative*.

EXAMPLE: What is known about planetary rings?
What (interrogative)

(1) Who first discovered rings around a planet? (2) In the early 1600's, Galileo, who was an Italian astronomer, first saw rings around Saturn. (3) With a small telescope, Galileo could not see clearly and thought the things that appeared were satellites. (4) Later, other astronomers, using more powerful telescopes, saw these were rings. (5) In 1980 scientists discovered the true nature of the rings, which are actually made up of thousands of pieces of ice. (6) Which of the other planets are known to have rings? (7) Uranus has nine thin rings, fainter than those of Saturn. (8) Jupiter's one thin ring, which appears to be made of rock fragments, was discovered by the *Jupiter I* space probe in 1980. (9) Who knows why the rings around planets are always parallel to the planets' equators? (10) This and other questions may be answered by future space probes.

Indefinite Pronouns

Indefinite pronouns also often lack specific antecedents.

Indefinite pronouns refer to people, places, or things, often without specifying which ones.

Some of the most frequently used indefinite pronouns are shown in the following chart.

INDEFINITE PRONOUNS			
Singular		**Plural**	**Singular or Plural**
another	much	both	all
anybody	neither	few	any
anyone	nobody	many	more
anything	no one	others	most
each	nothing	several	none
either	one		some
everybody	other		
everyone	somebody		
everything	someone		
little	something		

Indefinite pronouns may or may not have antecedents.

SPECIFIC ANTECEDENT: *Several* of the guests were late.

NO SPECIFIC ANTECEDENT: *Everyone* ate *everything* offered.

EXERCISE D: Supplying Indefinite Pronouns. Write each sentence, adding one indefinite pronoun for each blank.

EXAMPLE: Did you eat _______ of the apples?
Did you eat any of the apples?

1. Jonathan has forgotten _______ he learned.
2. _______ has been done to inform _______.
3. Does _______ know where the supplies are?
4. You may take _______ of the packages.
5. We sent _______ of the invitations to our friends.
6. As a visitor to this country, she knew _______ of the customs but _______ of the language.
7. Are _______ of the guests here yet?
8. Rebecca has lost _______ of her charm.
9. He shares his ideas with _______.
10. _______ of the boys looks a lot like his father.

DEVELOPING WRITING SKILLS: Writing Sentences with Pronouns. Use the following instructions to write five sentences of your own.

EXAMPLE: Write a sentence that includes two personal pronouns.
I have finished my homework.

1. Write a sentence that includes a demonstrative pronoun followed by the word *were* and a personal pronoun.
2. Write a sentence that includes an interrogative pronoun followed by the word *is* and a personal pronoun.
3. Write a sentence that includes a personal pronoun and an intensive pronoun.
4. Write a sentence that includes an indefinite pronoun followed by the word *of* and a personal pronoun.
5. Write a sentence that includes a reflexive pronoun and a relative pronoun.

1.3 Action Verbs and Linking Verbs

Nouns are necessary to name all people, places, and things. *Verbs* are also necessary. They give life to nouns by allowing people to make statements about them.

A verb is a word that expresses time while showing an action, a condition, or the fact that something exists.

In the sentence *Sue threw the ball,* the verb *threw* expresses action. In the sentence *The puppy is sick,* the verb *is* expresses a condition. In the sentence *They were here,* the verb *were* shows existence.

This section will discuss the two main kinds of verbs: *action verbs* (verbs that express action) and *linking verbs* (verbs that express condition).

Action Verbs

Verbs that tell what someone or something does, did, or will do are called *action verbs*.

An action verb is a verb that tells what action someone or something is performing.

In the following examples, the verbs tell what actions have been or are being performed by Hank and the parakeet.

ACTION VERBS: Hank *painted* the tool shed.

The parakeet *swings* back and forth.

The person or thing that performs the action is called the *subject* of the verb. In the above examples, *Hank* and *parakeet* are the subjects.

Verbs such as *painted, swings, shouted,* and *moves* represent visible action. Some action verbs, however, represent mental actions. When people *forget* or *believe,* they are performing mental actions.

MENTAL ACTION: Jefferson *thought* about the problem.

Other verbs such as *sleep* or *relax* also seem to show little action, but they are still action verbs.

EXERCISE A: Supplying Action Verbs. Write each sentence, adding an action verb for each blank. Then label each verb as *visible* or *mental.*

EXAMPLE: The stars ______ in the dark sky.

The stars twinkled in the dark sky. (visible)

1. They ______ about life on the planet Mars.
2. Someone ______ it was almost midnight.
3. The ping-pong ball ______ off the table.
4. A dog house ______ its occupant from the rain.
5. The witches ______ their terrible brew.
6. Why don't you ______ for a few minutes?
7. No one ______ the dismal weather.
8. The carpenter ______ the pine boards.
9. The waitress ______ at the soggy mess.
10. How did the pilot ______ where to land?

Transitive and Intransitive Verbs

An action verb may be *transitive* or *intransitive* depending on whether or not it transfers its action to another word in the sentence.

An action verb is transitive if it directs action toward someone or something named in the same sentence.

An action verb is intransitive if it does not direct action toward someone or something named in the same sentence.

The word that receives the action of a transitive verb is called the *object* of the verb. In the following examples, *pictures* is the object of *took,* and *something* is the object of *baked.*

TRANSITIVE VERBS: The camera *took* clear pictures.

Irene *baked* something for the bake sale.

Intransitive verbs do not have objects. The action is not directed toward any noun or pronoun in the sentence. The examples at the top of the next page show intransitive verbs.

INTRANSITIVE VERBS: The hurricane *blew* over the mainland.
Sandy *smiled* happily.

To find out whether a verb in a sentence is transitive or intransitive, ask *Whom?* or *What?* after the verb. If there is an answer, the verb is transitive. If there is no answer, the verb is intransitive.

TRANSITIVE: Robert *polished* his shoes.
(Polished *what?* shoes)

INTRANSITIVE: Linda *waited* for the bus.
(Waited *what?* no answer)

Most action verbs can be transitive or intransitive, depending on their use in the sentence. Some action verbs, however, can only be transitive while others can only be intransitive.

TRANSITIVE OR INTRANSITIVE: I *wrote* that letter.
The secretary *wrote* quickly.

ALWAYS TRANSITIVE: California wines *rival* those of France.

ALWAYS INTRANSITIVE: She *winced* at the sound of his voice.

Consult a dictionary if you are uncertain about whether an action verb should have an object.

EXERCISE B: Distinguishing Between Transitive and Intransitive Verbs. Write the verb in each sentence. Then, label each as *transitive* or *intransitive*. Finally, write the object of each transitive verb.

EXAMPLE: We prepared sandwiches for our lunch
prepared (transitive) sandwiches

1. The bird cage swung from a golden chain.
2. Margaret angrily crumpled her letter in her fist.
3. Someone answered that question.
4. He shuddered with fright during the scary movie.
5. The rats chewed their way into the old house.
6. Acorns drop from the trees every fall.
7. Charlie combed his hair before the dance.
8. We made lemonade for the picnic.

9. Zelda smiled gleefully at the thought of a parade.
10. Fish and potatoes sizzled in the pan.

Linking Verbs

Linking verbs link, or join, two or more words in a sentence.

A linking verb is a verb that connects a word at or near the beginning of a sentence with a word at or near the end.

In the following examples, *was* connects the subject *Victoria* with the word *Queen* and *is* connects the subject *child* with the word *miserable*. The verbs allow *Queen* and *miserable* to help identify or describe the subjects.

LINKING VERBS: Victoria *was* Queen from 1837 to 1901.

The feverish child *is* miserable.

Forms of *Be*. The above examples both use verbs that are forms of *be*, the most common linking verb. *Be* has many different forms, as shown in the following chart.

THE FORMS OF *BE*			
am	am being	can be	have been
are	are being	could be	has been
is	is being	may be	had been
was	was being	might be	could have been
were	were being	must be	may have been
		shall be	might have been
		should be	must have been
		will be	shall have been
		would be	should have been
			will have been
			would have been

NOTE ABOUT VERBS EXPRESSING EXISTENCE: The forms of *be* do not always function as linking verbs. Instead, they may express existence, usually by showing where something is located. At the top of the next page are forms of *be* expressing existence.

EXAMPLES: Your shirt *is* in the closet.

There *are* several mistakes in that article.

Other Verbs That Link. Twelve other verbs may also act as linking verbs.

OTHER LINKING VERBS					
appear	feel	look	seem	sound	taste
become	grow	remain	smell	stay	turn

These verbs also allow other words in the sentences to name or describe the subjects of the sentences.

EXAMPLES: He *remained* a hermit for many years.

The music *sounded* tuneless to her.

EXERCISE C: Recognizing Forms of *Be* Used as Linking Verbs. Write each sentence, underlining the linking verb. Then draw a double-headed arrow to show which words are linked by the verb.

EXAMPLE: We should have been the champions.

1. Poodles can be excellent pets.
2. Albert was being gentle with the newborn kittens.
3. A chef should be creative in the kitchen.
4. The sharp knife is the one on the counter.
5. She should have been an Olympic star.
6. This doughnut is not very fresh.
7. They are being very prompt with their payments.
8. At sunset the sky was a soft pink.
9. We will be the first customers in the door.
10. It had been a long and difficult day.

EXERCISE D: Identifying Other Linking Verbs. Write each sentence, underlining the linking verb. Then draw a double-headed arrow to show which words are linked by the verb.

1. She turned blue from the cold.
2. The foghorn sounded strange in the darkness.

3. Those apples on the ground taste bitter.
4. After years of studying, he finally became a doctor.
5. They remained cheerful in spite of their hardships.
6. Some people stay business partners for years.
7. This rose smells different from that one.
8. They appeared older after their terrifying ordeal.
9. The baby's hair felt sticky from the candy.
10. This coat looks too small for you.

Linking Verb or Action Verb?

Most of the verbs in the chart on page 36 can be either linking or action verbs. To see if a verb is a linking verb, substitute *am, are,* or *is* for it. If the substitution makes sense and connects two words, then the original is a linking verb. Otherwise, the original is an action verb.

***Am, are,* or *is* will make sense when substituted for another linking verb in a sentence.**

Notice how each of the verbs in the following examples has been tested to see whether it is an action verb or a linking verb. Notice also that the linking verb connects two words.

EXAMPLES: The breeze *felt* cool.
(The breeze *is* cool? linking)

Henry *felt* the sand.
(Henry *is* the sand? action)

EXERCISE E: Distinguishing Between Linking Verbs and Action Verbs. Write each sentence, filling in the blank with one of the following verbs: *feel, grow, look, sound,* or *taste*. Then label each verb as *linking* or *action*.

EXAMPLE: The puppy ______ hungry all the time.
The puppy looks hungry all the time. (linking)

1. His voice ______ peculiar on the phone.
2. In their garden they ______ tomatoes.
3. Marion's clam sauce ______ slightly sweet.
4. If Jeff ______ sick, he should stay home.
5. His face ______ pale when he thinks about his debts.

6. Mr. Blake could ______ a bump on his forehead.
7. Our furniture ______ new after being reupholstered.
8. The boy on horseback ______ the alarm.
9. We must ______ for a birthday card after school.
10. Craig ______ the lobster stew.

DEVELOPING WRITING SKILLS: Writing Sentences with Linking Verbs and Action Verbs. Use each verb in two sentences, first as a linking verb, then as an action verb.

EXAMPLE: turn

He turned purple in anger.
He turned the page and found the answer.

1. appear 2. feel 3. grow 4. look 5. smell

1.4 Helping Verbs

One verb may consist of as many as four words. Acting as a unit, these words form a *verb phrase*.

Helping verbs are verbs that can be added to another verb to make a single verb phrase.

Recognizing Helping Verbs

All the forms of *be* listed on page 35 as well as a few other verbs function as *helping verbs*.

Any of the many forms of *be* as well as some other verbs can be used as helping verbs.

Below are other verbs that can be used as helping verbs.

HELPING VERBS OTHER THAN *BE*			
do	have	shall	can
does	has	should	could
did	had	will	may
		would	might
			must

Helping verbs are sometimes called *auxiliary verbs* or *auxiliaries* because they help add meaning to other verbs. Notice how helping verbs change the meaning of the sentences in the following chart.

Without Helping Verbs	With Helping Verbs
I *talk* on the telephone.	I *will talk* on the telephone.
He *returned* that book.	He *should have returned* that book.

EXERCISE A: Supplying Helping Verbs. Write each sentence, adding one helping verb for each blank

EXAMPLE: The sun _______ _______ set by six o'clock.
The sun will have set by six o'clock.

1. A shark _______ swimming in the water.
2. Todd's car _______ _______ repaired at the gas station on the corner.
3. Our driveway _______ _______ plowed after a snowfall.
4. _______ we _______ studying enough?
5. The woodcutter _______ _______ sawing carefully.
6. Carol _______ not _______ going with us.
7. Poodles _______ be the smartest of the canines.
8. Sandals _______ not considered appropriate for a vacation in Siberia.
9. How many planets _______ we _______ discovered by the year 2000?
10. No species of insect _______ yet become extinct.

Finding Helping Verbs in Sentences

A verb and its helping verbs are often interrupted by other words, especially in questions.

Other words may sometimes separate helping verbs from key verbs in sentences.

The examples at the top of the next page show the words of a verb phrase together and verb phrases interrupted by other words.

UNINTERRUPTED VERB PHRASE:	The groundhog *will see* its shadow.
INTERRUPTED VERB PHRASES:	The groundhog *will* probably not *see* its shadow.
	Will the groundhog *see* its shadow?

EXERCISE B: Locating Helping Verbs. Write the verb phrase or verb phrases in each sentence.

EXAMPLE: Contact lenses are quickly becoming more popular.

are becoming

(1) Many people are finding contact lenses very convenient. (2) They can be bought almost anywhere glasses are sold. (3) If you are presently considering whether or not you should invest in contacts, you should definitely know this fact. (4) More contacts have been lost down the drain as they were being inserted than while the lenses were actually being worn. (5) Therefore, lenses should be inserted carefully. (6) If you do drop a lens, you must remember that if you should step on it, you will probably scratch it; then replacement of the lens would be necessary, for a scratch on the lens might seriously damage your eye. (7) Precautions must also be taken so that all protein deposits are removed because even a thin film of protein build-up can impair your vision. (8) Will you be happy with contact lenses? (9) Will the benefits outweigh the problems? (10) Will you be of the successful wearers?

DEVELOPING WRITING SKILLS: Writing Sentences with Helping Verbs. Use the following instructions to write five sentences of your own.

EXAMPLE: Interrupt the verb phrase *have seen* with *never*.

I have never seen an aardvark.

1. Use the verb phrase *has been talking* in a question.
2. Interrupt the verb phrase *might know* with *not*.
3. Interrupt the verb phrase *could have sold* with *never*.
4. Use the verb phrase *will have left* in a question.
5. Interrupt the verb phrase *can be used* with *hardly ever*.

Skills Review and Writing Workshop

Nouns, Pronouns, and Verbs

CHECKING YOUR SKILLS

Identify each underlined item as a *noun*, *pronoun*, or *verb*. Label each noun *concrete* or *abstract* and each pronoun *personal*, *reflexive*, *intensive*, *demonstrative*, *relative*, *interrogative*, or *indefinite*. Label each verb *action* or *linking*.

Located in (1) Italy, Pompeii (2) was a (3) city (4) that vanished after (5) Mount Vesuvius erupted in 20 A.D. Although (6) many of its citizens saved (7) themselves, over a thousand of (8) them (9) had died. (10) What could have been done to avoid (11) this? The people of (12) Pompeii (13) should have heeded the warnings of the volcano (14) itself. Sixteen years earlier, an (15) earthquake (16) had damaged Pompeii. Afterwards, the (17) crater still (18) appeared active, but (19) no one paid any (20) attention.

USING GRAMMAR SKILLS IN WRITING
Writing a Letter

Imagine you have entered a letter-writing contest. You are going to write to a famous person explaining why that person would enjoy meeting you. Follow the steps below to write a winning letter.

Prewriting: Select the person you want to meet. Decide which qualities, talents, and abilities you have that will make that person want to meet you. Remember a famous person is a person first and has probably shared some of your thoughts and feelings, so there is a basis for friendship.

Writing: Organize your presentation clearly. Save your strongest point or points for the end.

Revising: Have you expressed your thoughts clearly. Are your nouns specific and your pronouns clear? Do your verbs say what you want to say in an interesting way? Look for improvements you can make. Proofread carefully.

Chapter **2**

Adjectives and Adverbs

Nouns, pronouns, and verbs make simple communication possible. These three parts of speech can express essential ideas, such as *I need food,* but for more descriptive and detailed communication two other parts of speech are necessary: *adjectives* and *adverbs*. With adjectives you can describe, for example, what kind of food you need (*fresh, hot,* and so on) or how much *(enough, little, much)*. Moreover, with adverbs you can indicate, for example, when food is needed *(now, soon, daily)*.

These two parts of speech that add description and detail to your written and spoken words are called *modifiers*. How adjectives and adverbs modify other words will be shown in the next two sections.

2.1 Adjectives

Whenever you want to create a clearer picture of a person, place, or thing, you are likely to use an *adjective*.

An adjective is a word used to describe a noun or pronoun or to give a noun or pronoun a more specific meaning.

The way an adjective describes a word or makes it more specific is called *modification*.

The Process of Modification

Modification is the act of changing something slightly. An adjective modifies a noun or pronoun by adding information that answers any of four questions about the noun or pronoun.

Adjectives answer the question *What kind? Which one? How many?* or *How much?* about the nouns and pronouns they modify.

In the following chart, the examples show adjectives that answer the four questions about nouns or pronouns.

What Kind?	
large couch	*lost* boy
metallic gleam	*purple* sage
Which One?	
that necklace	*any* number
other door	*last* opportunity
How Many?	
both apples	*some* possibilities
five dollars	*frequent* interruptions
How Much?	
enough homework	*more* fun
less effort	*adequate* pay

An adjective may come before or after the noun or pronoun it modifies.

BEFORE: The *silver* ornament was in the window.

AFTER: The ornament in the window was *silver.*

Two or more adjectives can modify one word, as in the following example.

EXAMPLE: *Several large shaggy* dogs were running on the beach.

NOTE ABOUT *A, AN,* AND *THE:* Three adjectives—*a, an,* and *the*—are called *articles. The* is called a *definite article* because it refers to a specific noun. *A* and *an* are called *indefinite articles* because they refer to any one of a class of nouns. In the examples below, *the* refers to a specific book, while *a* and *an* refer to any kind of *car* and *answer.*

DEFINITE: Let me see *the* book.

INDEFINITE: We would like *a* new car.

Lynn wants *an* answer.

EXERCISE A: Recognizing Adjectives. Write the adjectives in each sentence.

EXAMPLE: A loud roar greeted the victorious team.

A loud the victorious

1. The dull walls and dingy carpet give the room a somber atmosphere.
2. The lonesome howl of a coyote came from the woods.
3. With gray faces and hesitant steps, they approached the haunted house.
4. After a major collision, there may be few survivors.
5. On the last day of the month, you have an important medical appointment.
6. There wasn't enough money in the wallet to pay the bill.
7. If you add milk to the eggs, a dozen eggs will be plenty.
8. Bluefish give fishermen a good fight.
9. The brilliant diamonds decorated red and calloused hands.
10. The knife was silvery in the dim shadows.

Nouns Used as Adjectives

Many nouns can be used as adjectives. They become adjectives when they modify other nouns and answer one of two questions about the nouns they are modifying.

A noun used as an adjective answers the question *What kind?* or *Which one?* about a noun that follows it.

Nouns	Adjectives
pineapple	*pineapple* juice (*What kind* of juice?)
summer	*summer* vacation (*Which* vacation?)

EXERCISE B: Recognizing Nouns Used as Adjectives. Write the noun or nouns used as adjectives in each sentence.

EXAMPLE: Betty put on her red winter coat.
winter

(1) Betty glanced at the storm clouds. (2) She wished she had worn her leather gloves and her fur hat. (3) She waited impatiently at the bus stop. (4) Finally, the school bus arrived, and Betty got on. (5) As the bus stopped at the school door, Betty noticed that tiny snowflakes had begun to fall. (6) If it snowed hard, Betty and her friends could go to the ski slope outside of town on their next vacation day. (7) She wished she had listened to the weather report this morning. (8) Betty thought about the jacket she had seen in a store window yesterday. (9) She remembered the money her aunt had sent her for a birthday present. (10) Perhaps a new ski jacket would be just the thing to spend it on.

Proper and Compound Adjectives

Two other types of adjectives are *proper adjectives* and *compound adjectives.*

Proper Adjectives. Sometimes, proper nouns are used as adjectives.

A proper adjective is a proper noun used as an adjective or an adjective formed from a proper noun.

Notice in the following chart that *proper adjectives* modify nouns by answering the questions *What kind?* or *Which one?*

Proper Nouns	Proper Adjectives
Vermont	*Vermont* cheddar (*What kind* of cheddar?)
Brahms	the *Brahms* symphony (*Which symphony?*)

Sometimes, proper nouns change their form when they are used as proper adjectives.

Proper Nouns	Proper Adjectives
Shakespeare	*Shakespearean* play (*What kind of* play?)
Germany	*Germanic* tribes (*Which* tribes?)

Proper adjectives generally begin with a capital letter.

Compound Adjectives. Adjectives can also be compound.

A compound adjective is an adjective that is made up of more than one word.

Most *compound adjectives* are hyphenated, but some are written as combined words.

Hyphenated	Combined
freeze-dried coffee	*farsighted* planner
heavy-duty boots	*underpaid* staff

If you are uncertain about the spelling of a compound adjective, consult a dictionary.

EXERCISE C: Recognizing Proper and Compound Adjectives. Write the proper and compound adjectives in each sentence.

EXAMPLE: Please pass me the Swiss cheese.
Swiss

1. The red-cheeked girl ate Turkish taffy.
2. The foolishness of their actions was self-evident.
3. She caught a wide-mouthed bass this morning.
4. Well-qualified surgeons do open-heart surgery.
5. In combat the horse remained steadfast.
6. We bought the Victorian table for the hallway.
7. Phil, who was well-liked, lived in an out-of-the-way place.
8. Although he lived in Utah, Al kept his Bostonian accent.
9. He wore a waterproof Icelandic parka.
10. The hostess served a Scandinavian meal.

Pronouns Used as Adjectives

Just as nouns can be used as adjectives, so can certain pronouns. In fact, some personal pronouns, known as *possessive pronouns* or *possessive adjectives,* act as both pronouns *and* adjectives. Others act as either pronouns *or* adjectives.

A pronoun is used as an adjective if it modifies a noun.

Possessive Pronouns or Adjectives. Seven personal pronouns are known as *possessive pronouns* or *possessive adjectives.* They are pronouns because they have antecedents. They are adjectives because they modify nouns and answer the question *Which one?*

POSSESSIVE PRONOUNS OR ADJECTIVES						
my	your	his	her	its	our	their

ANTECEDENT WORD MODIFIED

The *team* found *their* long-lost *mascot.*

Whether you think of these words as adjectives or as pronouns, remember the essential word is *possessive.*

Demonstrative Adjectives. All four of the demonstrative pronouns can be used as adjectives. Unlike the personal pronouns above, they become *demonstrative adjectives* instead of pronouns. As adjectives, they always come before the nouns they modify. They never come directly before a verb.

DEMONSTRATIVE ADJECTIVES			
this	that	these	those

Demonstrative Pronouns	Demonstrative Adjectives
Did you buy *this*?	Did you buy *this* book?
Those are fresh peaches.	*Those* peaches are fresh.

Interrogative Adjectives. Three of the interrogative pronouns become *interrogative adjectives* when they modify a noun.

INTERROGATIVE ADJECTIVES	
which what whose	
Interrogative Pronouns	**Interrogative Adjectives**
What happened?	*What* color looks best?
Whose is that?	*Whose* scarf is orange?

Indefinite Adjectives. Many indefinite pronouns become *indefinite adjectives* when they modify nouns. The chart below shows whether they modify singular or plural nouns.

INDEFINITE ADJECTIVES				
Singular		**Plural**	**Singular or Plural**	
another	much	both	all	other
each	neither	few	any	some
either	one	many	more	
little		several	most	

Indefinite Pronouns	Indefinite Adjectives
She will choose *one.*	Andy sent only *one* letter.
Few remembered the event.	Very *few* people will come.
They needed *some* for today.	He will think of *some* excuse.
	Mary wants *some* new pencils.

In the last two sentences on the right, *some* first modifies a singular noun, *excuse,* and then a plural noun, *pencils.*

EXERCISE D: Supplying Pronouns Used as Adjectives. Write the kind of adjective needed to complete each sentence.

EXAMPLE: We picked (demonstrative) flowers from the garden.
those

1. (Indefinite) player was cheered by the crowd.
2. (Possessive) bus never came, and we were late for work.
3. Harvey will never wear (demonstrative) ties.
4. (Interrogative) human being could endure such a climate?
5. Max told (possessive) son to be quiet.
6. I misplaced (possessive) keys, and I can't open the door.
7. (Interrogative) mail was placed in our mailbox?
8. (Indefinite) children were jumping rope.
9. Sue declared that (indefinite) candidate was qualified.
10. She paid too much for (demonstrative) coat.

Verbs Used as Adjectives

Many verbs can also be used as adjectives.

Some verbs, especially those ending in *-ing* and *-ed,* may sometimes be used as adjectives.

Below are verbs used first as verbs and then as adjectives.

Verbs	Adjectives
The bell *was ringing* loudly.	The *ringing* bell was loud.
The ice *melted* in the sun.	The *melted* ice was in the sun.

EXERCISE E: Recognizing Verbs Used as Adjectives. Write the verb used as an adjective in each sentence.

EXAMPLE: They waited an hour in the pouring rain.
pouring

1. The frightened mouse was scurrying around the room.
2. The milk was spilled by the hurrying waiter.
3. The meeting room will be available on Tuesday.
4. We handed Mrs. Howard our completed assignments.
5. Are you planning to take swimming lessons?
6. The cheering crowd inspired the team.
7. Did you find the gardening tools?
8. The exhausted baby finally fell asleep.
9. Our grandparents met us in the waiting room.
10. I found the lost keys under my bed.

DEVELOPING WRITING SKILLS: Writing Sentences with Adjectives. Write each sentence, adding two or more adjectives. Include at least one noun used as an adjective, one proper adjective, one compound adjective, one pronoun used as an adjective, and one verb used as an adjective.

EXAMPLE: The skater entered the arena.

The champion skater entered the crowded arena.

1. He could not swallow the food.
2. Mickey bought a sweater and a pair of pants.
3. The seagull's wing trailed on the sand.
4. She grew plants with berries.
5. Snow covered the branches and ground.
6. Donald finally selected a toy for his sister.
7. They made posters to announce the carnival.
8. A stream flowed past the fence.
9. In the evening, fireflies flashed in the darkness.
10. At the zoo they saw seals begging for fish.

2.2 Adverbs

Like adjectives, *adverbs* are used to describe or add information about other words.

An adverb is a word that modifies a verb, an adjective, or another adverb.

Adverbs Modifying Verbs, Adjectives, and Other Adverbs

Just as adjectives answer questions about nouns and pronouns, adverbs answer questions about words they modify.

An adverb answers one of four questions about the word it modifies: *Where? When? In what manner? To what extent?*

An adverb modifying a verb can answer any of the four questions. An adverb modifying an adjective or another adverb, however, will only answer one of the questions: *To what extent?*

The chart below shows adverbs answering each of the four questions. Notice the positions of the adverbs. When an adverb modifies a verb or verb phrase, it may come after or before the verb or verb phrase. Frequently, it comes within the verb phrase. If an adverb modifies an adjective or another adverb, it generally comes immediately before the adjective or other adverb.

Adverbs Modifying Verbs	
Where? slide *under* move *near* sit *there* slipped *between*	**When?** *often* asks sails *daily* should have answered *promptly* *soon* will depart
In What Manner? reacted *positively* *silently* nodded left *quickly* *rudely* laughed was *cheerfully* humming	**To What Extent?** *widely* read *barely* walks arrived *unexpectedly* had *just* started must *not* have finished
Adverbs Modifying Adjectives	**Adverbs Modifying Adverbs**
To What Extent? *very* tall *somewhat* satisfied *frequently* absent *not* sad	**To What Extent?** *very* thoroughly *not* exactly *more* quickly *quite* definitely

EXERCISE A: Recognizing Adverbs. Write the adverb or adverbs in each sentence.

EXAMPLE: The otter swam very rapidly.
very rapidly

1. We will be leaving for the movie soon.
2. The starving refugees needed much more food.
3. Will you definitely move to Ohio?
4. Everyone thought the movie was too violent.

5. He frowned rather sternly at the boy's antics.
6. Our cat does not like cat food.
7. The multicolored balloons floated away.
8. Some students have nearly completed their papers.
9. Todd accepted the suggestion surprisingly quickly.
10. Sharon was remarkably indifferent.

Nouns Used as Adverbs

A few words that are usually nouns can also act as adverbs.

Nouns used as adverbs answer the question *Where?* or *When?* about a verb.

Some of the nouns that can be used as adverbs are *home, yesterday,* and *today.*

Nouns	Adverbs
Our *home* is in Lubbock.	Let's go *home.* (Go *where?*)
The summer *nights* have been humid.	My father works *nights.* (Works *when?*)

EXERCISE B: Recognizing Nouns Used as Adverbs. Write the two adverbs in each sentence. Then circle each noun used as an adverb.

EXAMPLE: Yesterday, I took a very difficult test.

(Yesterday) very

1. Evenings my parents and grandparents would loudly discuss politics.
2. I was sent home because I had a very high fever.
3. Tuesday was an extremely bad day, but the things that happened Wednesday were worse.
4. You must definitely see a doctor today.
5. If you decide to visit tomorrow, please come early.
6. Saturdays I usually babysit for my brother.
7. I did not see her yesterday.
8. I ran approximately two miles Friday.
9. She works days and attends school nights.
10. Winters are always dreadfully cold in that province.

Adverb or Adjective?

Sometimes, the same word can be either an adverb or an adjective, depending upon how it is used in a sentence.

Remember that an adverb modifies a verb, an adjective, or another adverb; an adjective modifies a noun or a pronoun.

Notice in the following examples that the adverb modifies a verb. The adjective, on the other hand, modifies a noun.

ADVERB: He walked *straight* down the path.

ADJECTIVE: The path was *straight*

Generally, adverbs and adjectives have different forms. Many adverbs, in fact, are formed by adding *-ly* to an adjective.

Adjectives	Adverbs with *-ly* Endings
honest response	responded *honestly*
awkward movement	moved *awkwardly*

A few words ending in *-ly*, however, are adjectives.

ADJECTIVE: Carla's *weekly* allowance was not much.

EXERCISE C: Distinguishing Between Adverbs and Adjectives. Identify each underlined word as an *adverb* or *adjective*.

EXAMPLE: His room was very neat.
adjective

1. The mounted moose head looked real.
2. I really believed the weather forecast.
3. Bertram walks to the office daily.
4. Our office runs ads in the daily newspaper.
5. Matilda spoke darkly of her husband's past.
6. No light filtered into the dark cell.
7. Immigrants worked hard to build the railroads.
8. Sandstone is not a hard rock.
9. Zack is an early riser.

10. Mildred starts the day early and finishes late.
11. I will gladly finish the dishes.
12. We are glad to have you as a friend.
13. When his aunt died, he was suddenly rich.
14. The musketeer was richly dressed in velvet.
15. After scrubbing the floor, his hands were rough.
16. He roughly stroked the German shepherd.
17. He stared dismally at the destruction.
18. Her outlook on life is dismal.
19. Today's high cost of living causes people to be thrifty.
20. His past employer spoke highly of him.

DEVELOPING WRITING SKILLS: Writing Sentences with Adverbs. Write each sentence, adding one or more adverbs. Include at least one noun used as an adverb.

EXAMPLE: Kathleen entered the room.

Kathleen quietly entered the room.

1. Tony will go to the grocery store for us.
2. Barn swallows are helpful because they eat insects.
3. His poor posture made him seem shorter than he was.
4. The sorcerer cast a terrible spell upon the town.
5. We were sad about the end of summer.
6. Many people think snails are delicious.
7. The boat docked and lowered its sails.
8. Their enthusiasm faded.
9. Night fell and the celebration began.
10. Can a helicopter rescue those men?

Skills Review and Writing Workshop

Adjectives and Adverbs

CHECKING YOUR SKILLS

Write and label the adjectives and adverbs in the following sentences. Do not include articles.

(1) The old, wooden rowboat drifted quietly. (2) The Kelly sisters, its two occupants, fished and occasionally chatted. (3) Several hours passed. (4) Suddenly, a huge, black cloud appeared overhead. (5) Surprised, one girl grabbed the oars and rowed rapidly. (6) She rowed hard but soon noticed that the faraway shore did not seem much closer. (7) Booming thunder startled both worried girls. (8) Little time had passed, but that thunderstorm was very steadily advancing. (9) What one question did they ask? (10) Would they reach the shore safely?

USING GRAMMAR SKILLS IN WRITING

Writing an Invitation

To write persuasively, your message must be appealing to your readers. Suppose you belong to a committee that is working to convert a dump site to a community vegetable garden. Write an invitation asking everyone in the neighborhood to come to a meeting. Follow the steps below to write an invitation that will be hard to refuse.

Prewriting: People will agree that a vegetable garden is better than a dump site. But they may not want to do the necessary work. Therefore, you need to convince them by answering the question, what's in it for me?

Writing: Vividly describe the pleasures of eating fresh vegetables, using sensory descriptions—sight, smell, taste, touch. Remind people they will also save money.

Revising: Read your invitation. Would it persuade you to come to the meeting? Is the time and place of the meeting clear? After you have revised, proofread carefully.

Chapter 3

Prepositions, Conjunctions, and Interjections

The next two sections cover the last three parts of speech. As you will see, *prepositions* relate words, *conjunctions* join words, and *interjections* serve as attention-getters.

3.1 Prepositions

There are fewer *prepositions* than there are nouns, verbs, and modifiers. The role they play, however, is important.

A preposition is a word that relates a noun or pronoun that appears with it to another word in the sentence.

Words Used as Prepositions

A preposition can affect the entire meaning of a sentence.

The choice of preposition affects the way the other words in a sentence relate to each other.

3.1 Prepositions

Sixty of the words most often used as prepositions are listed in the following chart.

FREQUENTLY USED PREPOSITIONS				
aboard	before	despite	off	throughout
about	behind	down	on	till
above	below	during	onto	to
across	beneath	except	opposite	toward
after	beside	for	out	under
against	besides	from	outside	underneath
along	between	in	over	until
amid	beyond	inside	past	up
among	but	into	regarding	upon
around	by	like	round	with
at	concerning	near	since	within
barring	considering	of	through	without

Some prepositions consist of more than one word and are called *compound prepositions*.

COMPOUND PREPOSITIONS			
according to	because of	in place of	next to
ahead of	by means of	in regard to	on account of
apart from	in addition to	in spite of	out of
aside from	in back of	instead of	owing to
as of	in front of	in view of	prior to

Notice how the choice of preposition affects the relationship between the word following the preposition and the word before it. By changing this relationship, different prepositions give each sentence different meanings.

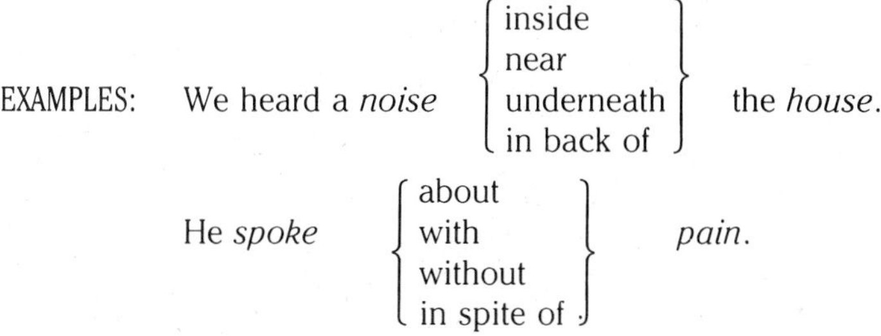

EXAMPLES: We heard a *noise* {inside / near / underneath / in back of} the *house*.

He *spoke* {about / with / without / in spite of} *pain*.

EXERCISE A: Supplying Prepositions. Write each sentence, adding a preposition for each blank. Use at least three compound prepositions.

EXAMPLE: _______ apples, we had raisins.

Instead of apples, we had raisins.

1. Every store _______ this one is having a sale.
2. Water lilies floated _______ the surface of the pond.
3. Some dwarf fruit trees grew _______ the house.
4. _______ the authorities, the alleged robbers were caught.
5. A lantern's gleam could be seen _______ the tunnel.
6. Please buy construction paper _______ scissors and glue.
7. Wonder Woman jumped _______ the balcony.
8. He looked _______ the room.
9. _______ the water shortage, we will be careful.
10. His ancestors left Ireland _______ the potato famine.

Prepositional Phrases

Within a sentence a preposition is almost always followed by a noun or pronoun.

A prepositional phrase is a group of words that includes a preposition and a noun or pronoun.

The noun or pronoun generally found after a preposition is called the *object of the preposition.* One preposition can have two or more objects, as the last example in the chart shows.

PREPOSITIONAL PHRASES	
Prepositions	**Objects of Prepositions**
for	*you*
throughout	the *school*
between	*you* and *me*

A prepositional phrase usually is only two or three words long; it can, however, be much longer. As the examples on the next page show, length depends on the number of modifiers before the object of the preposition, the number of objects, and the length of the preposition itself.

EXAMPLES: *in* a *community*
in a small agricultural *community*
because of her *temper* and *irritability*
because of her terribly vicious, totally unpredictable *temper* and general *irritability*

EXERCISE B: Identifying Prepositional Phrases. Write each prepositional phrase. Then underline each preposition and circle each object.

EXAMPLE: We admire the beauty of animals' tails.
of animals' (tails)

(1) The tails of birds and animals can also be useful appendages to their bodies. (2) Because of their tails, beavers can transmit a warning regarding impending danger. (3) With its rattle, a rattlesnake warns those around that they should watch where they are stepping. (4) Apart from protective use, tails also help animals with the more practical side of life. (5) Kangaroos and lizards would not move with such agility without their tails for balance. (6) With their long tails, wagtails, a kind of bird, disturb insects in the grass and thus secure their food. (7) In addition to these uses, tails also help many animals communicate during courtship. (8) A coyote holding his tail high above him is expressing interest in his mate. (9) Similarly, by means of his tail feathers, a male peacock displays his interest in front of the hen. (10) The swordtail, a fish often found in home aquariums, also uses his tail in a courtship dance.

Preposition or Adverb?

Many of the words listed as prepositions in the charts on page 57 can also be adverbs, depending on how they are used in sentences.

Remember that prepositions always have objects. Adverbs do not.

Notice in the chart at the top of the next page that prepositions are always part of a phrase.

Prepositions	Adverbs
The smoke drifted *up* the chimney.	The dark, ugly smoke drifted *up*.
Flowers grew *along* the path.	Won't you come *along* with us.
The park is *near* our house.	We knew help was *near*.

EXERCISE C: Distinguishing Between Prepositions and Adverbs. Identify each underlined word as a *preposition* or *adverb*.

EXAMPLE: The spider sat down beside her.
adverb

1. Hang on and don't let go!
2. The snoring told him someone slept within.
3. No one can make that horse go over a bridge.
4. The snail crept along the bottom of the fish tank.
5. On account of lateness, you have fallen behind.
6. Walk right in if you don't find us at home.
7. She put her work aside and talked with me.
8. The balloon floated up, rising higher and higher.
9. Beneath our house is the cellar of an old cabin.
10. We searched around carefully for the lost money.

DEVELOPING WRITING SKILLS: Writing Sentences with Prepositions. Use each prepositional phrase in a sentence of your own.

EXAMPLE: across the street
We walked across the street to the library.

1. down the mountain path
2. during English class
3. about six o'clock
4. according to my father
5. by means of hard work
6. in spite of their sorrow
7. throughout the day
8. after school
9. despite the cold
10. instead of spaghetti

Conjunctions and Interjections 3.2

The last two parts of speech are *conjunctions* and *interjections*. Conjunctions are more important than interjections.

Different Kinds of Conjunctions

Unlike prepositions, which show relationships between words, conjunctions make direct connections between words.

A conjunction is a word used to connect other words or groups of words.

In English three main kinds of conjunctions connect words: *coordinating conjunctions, correlative conjunctions,* and *subordinating conjunctions.*

Coordinating Conjunctions. The seven *coordinating conjunctions* connect similar kinds of words or groups of words that are grammatically alike.

COORDINATING CONJUNCTIONS						
and	but	for	nor	or	so	yet

In the following examples, coordinating conjunctions are used to connect similar kinds of words.

NOUNS AND PRONOUNS: Joaquin *and* I are good friends.

VERBS: Amos trembled *yet* continued on his way.

ADVERBS: Meg churned the butter slowly *but* skillfully.

Coordinating conjunctions can also be used to connect groups of words that are grammatically alike.

PREPOSITIONAL PHRASES: The dog ran out the door *and* across the field.

SUBORDINATE IDEAS: Karen wrote that she was enjoying London *but* that she had caught a cold.

COMPLETE IDEAS: The bear slept, *for* winter had come.

Correlative Conjunctions. *Correlative conjunctions* are similar to coordinating conjunctions. They differ only in that correlative conjunctions are always used in pairs.

CORRELATIVE CONJUNCTIONS		
both . . . and	neither . . . nor	whether . . . or
either . . . or	not only . . . but also	

See how these conjunctions can be used to connect similar kinds of words and groups of words that are grammatically alike.

NOUNS: He owned *neither* a coat *nor* a hat.

NOUNS AND PRONOUNS: Sue asked *whether* Liz *or* I had left.

ADJECTIVES: *Both* gold *and* beige carpets were considered.

PREPOSITIONAL PHRASES: The guilt was shared *not only* by him *but also* by us.

COMPLETE IDEAS: *Either* Brenda forgot about the meeting, *or* she is sick.

Subordinating Conjunctions. *Subordinating conjunctions* connect two complete ideas by making one of the ideas subordinate to or less important than the other.

FREQUENTLY USED SUBORDINATING CONJUNCTIONS			
after	because	now that	until
although	before	since	when
as	even if	so that	whenever
as if	even though	than	where
as long as	if	though	wherever
as soon as	in order that	till	while
as though	lest	unless	

The following examples show how subordinating conjunctions are used to begin subordinate ideas.

EXAMPLES: *Because* Carol practices, [SUBORDINATE IDEA] she is a good musician. [MAIN IDEA]

He ran steadily [MAIN IDEA] *as though* wolves were after him. [SUBORDINATE IDEA]

EXERCISE A: Identifying Conjunctions. Write the conjunction in each sentence. Then label each as *coordinating, correlative*, or *subordinating*.

EXAMPLE: We ran for shelter when the rain started.
when (subordinating)

1. During his fast he neither ate food nor drank liquids.
2. They promised to return, for everyone had a good time.
3. Gordon bit his nails whenever he was nervous.
4. The judge listened to the explanation in order that he might decide fairly.
5. Evan's joke was not only silly but also too long.
6. Already ten inches of rain had fallen, yet the downpour continued.
7. Since Ben refuses to vote, he shouldn't complain about our country's leadership.
8. Was the opossum actually dead or just pretending?
9. Belinda had not succeeded before, nor was she likely to succeed now.
10. Buffalo are scarce today because people in the last century recklessly slaughtered them.

Conjunction, Preposition, or Adverb?

After, before, since, till, and *until* can be subordinating conjunctions or prepositions. *After, before,* and *since* can also be adverbs. *When* and *where* can be subordinating conjunctions or adverbs. The part of speech of these words depends on their use within a sentence.

Remember that subordinating conjunctions connect complete ideas.

The following examples show the word *before* used in three different ways.

SUBORDINATING CONJUNCTION: He started to run *before* the signal was given.

PREPOSITION: Dennis never speaks *before* breakfast.

ADVERB: Haven't you ever been here *before*?

EXERCISE B: Identifying Words as Conjunctions, Prepositions, or Adverbs. Identify each underlined word as a *subordinating conjunction, preposition,* or *adverb*.

EXAMPLE: I have not seen him since Thursday.
preposition

1. Their house will be vacant till next summer.
2. The child had never ridden a horse before.
3. Never stand under a tree when there is lightning.
4. Tin is rarely used for foil since aluminum is cheaper.
5. Where are you going at this late hour?
6. The band did not play until it reached the town.
7. Don't stop working before noon.
8. Dolores always brushes her teeth after meals.
9. Crops grow where once there was only desert.
10. They never rise till the rooster crows.

Conjunctive Adverbs

Some words act as both conjunctions and adverbs at the same time. These words are called *conjunctive adverbs*. Since their primary function is to connect words, they are classified as conjunctions.

A conjunctive adverb is an adverb that acts as a conjunction to connect complete ideas.

Conjunctive adverbs are often used as *transitions*, words that serve as links between different ideas. They help, for example, to contrast or compare ideas or to show a result.

FREQUENTLY USED CONJUNCTIVE ADVERBS		
accordingly	finally	nevertheless
again	furthermore	otherwise
also	however	then
besides	indeed	therefore
consequently	moreover	thus

Notice how conjunctive adverbs work to make different kinds of transitions between related ideas.

EXAMPLES: It rained until the field was soggy; *consequently*, the game was canceled.

They had never been in a large city before. *Indeed*, they had never been away from home.

Notice the punctuation in the sentences containing conjunctive adverbs. In the first sentence, a semicolon is used with a conjunctive adverb to tie two closely related ideas together. In the second, a period is used so that the conjunctive adverb, *indeed,* will add extra emphasis to the second idea. Notice also that when a semicolon or period precedes a conjunctive adverb, the conjunctive adverb is followed by a comma.

EXERCISE C: Supplying Conjunctive Adverbs. Write a conjunctive adverb that could be used to tie together the ideas in each pair of sentences.

EXAMPLE: Snow fell steadily. We trudged onward.
nevertheless

1. His plane was delayed in Dallas. It arrived two hours late.
2. I have listened long enough to your excuses. I am tired of your lack of originality.
3. Some materials are more expensive than others. Wool and linen are often quite costly.
4. Fewer people bought new cars this year. There was less profit for the automotive industry.
5. First Frank smiled. He laughed heartily.
6. Raymond can be demanding and impatient. He is sometimes very helpful and understanding.
7. Please bring paper cups and napkins. Bring something to drink.
8. The general instructed the soldiers to move ahead. They advanced several paces.
9. Blanche has a beautiful voice. She is often asked to sing at weddings.
10. Rosemary has many trophies over the fireplace. I assumed she had won them.

Interjections

Interjections are used mainly in speaking, not writing.

An interjection is a word that expresses feeling or emotion and functions independently of a sentence.

Many feelings can be expressed by interjections, such as *ah, darn, goodness, hey, oh, ouch, tsk, uh, well,* or *wow*. The following examples show other interjections being used to express several different emotions.

JOY: *Hurray!* We won!

EXHAUSTION: *Whew!* That was hard.

SURPRISE: *Aha!* I found it.

SORROW: She knew, *alas*, the truth.

Since interjections are independent from other words, they are set off by exclamation marks or commas.

EXERCISE D: Supplying Interjections. Write five sentences, each using an interjection to show the indicated emotion.

EXAMPLE: disapproval
Tsk, tsk, you have spilled your milk.

1. anger
2. pain
3. pleasure
4. hesitation
5. fear

DEVELOPING WRITING SKILLS: Using Conjunctions and Conjunctive Adverbs to Combine Sentences. Turn each pair of sentences into a single sentence by using the kind of conjunction or conjunctive adverb indicated.

EXAMPLE: Gil went to the movies. I went to the movies. (coordinating conjunction)
Gil and I went to the movies.

1. Rhoda rescued a small boy from a tree. She was afraid of heights. (subordinating conjunction)
2. The puppy might be hiding in the closet. He might be hiding under the bed. (coordinating conjunction)
3. Paula will take the job as a cashier. She will take classes in the evenings. (correlative conjunction)
4. Goldilocks slept soundly. The three bears came home. (subordinating conjunction)
5. We had warned him not to swim in that river. He was devoured by crocodiles. (conjunctive adverb)

Skills Review and Writing Workshop

Prepositions, Conjunctions and Interjections

CHECKING YOUR SKILLS

Write and label the prepositional phrases, conjunctions, and interjections in the following sentences. Identify each conjunction as *coordinating, correlative,* or *subordinating.*

(1) Calendars measure and record the passage of time. (2) People have been designing picture calendars for centuries. (3) At first picture calendars were each painted by hand, so only extremely wealthy people could own one. (4) After the invention of the printing press, many more calendars could be produced. (5) Either wood-block or copper-plate illustrations were used. (6) The most common subjects for illustrations were signs of the zodiac, saints, and the weather. (7) Over the years calendars have changed not only because people's tastes have changed but also because new printing processes have been developed. (8) Now color photographs and fine art are reproduced on many calendars. (9) Printing and selling them has become a big business. (10) Oh, how times and calendars have changed!

USING GRAMMAR SKILLS IN WRITING

Writing a Job Application

Write a short essay telling a prospective employer why you want a particular job.

Prewriting: Ask yourself not only why you want—and deserve—the job, but why your prospective employer will benefit from your services. Include both sets of reasons.

Writing: Be specific. Stress reliability by referring to your attendance record at school. Mention your skills. Talk about future goals if they relate to his job.

Revising: Are your sentences varied enough? Have you used prepositional phrases and conjunctions effectively? Proofread carefully.

Chapter **4**

Reviewing Parts of Speech

You should now be familiar with all eight parts of speech. Here you will have a chance to practice categorizing them.

4.1 Words as Different Parts of Speech

Never assume you know a word's part of speech until you examine how it is used in its sentence.

Identifying Parts of Speech

Remember the following rule when you attempt to identify the part of speech of a word.

The way a word is used in a sentence determines what part of speech it is.

Notice how the part of speech of the word *left* changes according to the way it is used.

AS A NOUN: Our house is the one on the *left*.

AS A VERB: We *left* shortly after midnight.

AS AN ADJECTIVE: Susan's *left* shoe is untied.

4.1 Words as Different Parts of Speech

The column of questions in the middle of the following charts will help you identify the parts of speech.

Nouns, Pronouns, and Verbs. A noun names a person, place, or thing. A pronoun stands for a noun. A verb shows action, condition, or existence.

Parts of Speech	Questions to Ask Yourself	Examples
Noun	Does the word name a person, place, or thing?	*Cliff* rode a *camel* in *Egypt*.
Pronoun	Does the word stand for a noun?	*We* bought *several* of *them*.
Verb	Does the word tell what someone or something did?	They *raised* the flag.
	Does the word connect one word with another word that identifies or describes it?	Pat *is* president. She *will be* angry.
	Does the word merely show that something exists?	Here I *am*.

Modifiers. Adjectives modify nouns or pronouns. Adverbs modify verbs, adjectives, or other adverbs.

Parts of Speech	Questions to Ask Yourself	Examples
Adjective	Does the word tell what kind, which one, how many, or how much?	A game like *this* one is *difficult*.
Adverb	Does the word tell where, when, in what manner, or to what extent?	Papers blew *around*. Leave *now*. She smiled *sadly*. Jim *just* left.

Prepositions, Conjunctions, and Interjections. A preposition relates a noun or pronoun that appears with it to another word. A conjunction connects words or groups of words. An interjection expresses feeling or emotion.

Parts of Speech	Questions to Ask Yourself	Examples
Preposition	Is the word part of a phrase that includes a noun or pronoun?	The pony ran *beside* the train. Buy pens *in addition to* paper.
Conjunction	Does the word connect other words in the sentence?	He wants to go, *but* he can't. We will *either* win *or* lose.
Interjection	Does the word express feeling or emotion and function independently?	*Wow!* That's amazing.

EXERCISE A: Identifying Nouns, Verbs, and Adjectives. Identify each underlined word as a *noun, verb,* or *adjective.*

EXAMPLE: Beethoven composed nine symphonies.
adjective

1. This restaurant serves delicious green salad.
2. Put some greens in the vase with the flowers.
3. Spring sunshine will quickly green the lawns.
4. The grammar test will be easy.
5. The lawyers say the trial will be a test case.
6. This machine tests blood for anemia.
7. A mattress should give good back support.
8. They painted a mural on the back of the barn.
9. We promised we would look for the lost child.
10. A wistful look appeared on the lonely boy's face.

EXERCISE B: Identifying Pronouns and Adjectives. Identify each underlined word as a *pronoun* or *adjective.*

1. If Julie makes apple pie, you should have some.
2. Some fragments of Indian arrowheads were found.
3. Which is harder, a diamond or an emerald?
4. Please decide which hat is the most flattering.
5. The museum uses these soft overhead lights.
6. Throw these out with the rest of the trash.
7. The hostess asked everyone to eat more.
8. She keeps adding more clocks to her collection.

9. I will try to entertain this little monster for you.
10. She sang a lullaby, and this put the baby to sleep.

EXERCISE C: Identifying Nouns, Prepositions, and Adverbs. Identify each underlined word as a *noun, preposition,* or *adverb*.

1. Our cat is deaf and cannot go outside.
2. On the outside the house was drab.
3. Arnold's parrot sometimes flies outside the house.
4. Virginia was curious about her new friend's past.
5. Larry cannot see past his actions to their results.
6. You can drive past without seeing the tiny cabin.
7. These warm comforters are filled with down.
8. Don't look down if you are afraid of heights.
9. Most people believe in life beyond death.
10. She gazed in horror at what lay beyond.

EXERCISE D: Identifying Conjunctions, Prepositions, and Adverbs. Identify each underlined word as a *conjunction, preposition,* or *adverb*.

1. He ran about, shouting for help.
2. We are concerned about your health.
3. Always harvest wheat before the rainy season.
4. He stepped into the road before the light changed.
5. I never saw that man before.
6. I sleep with a pillow underneath my head.
7. The door will be locked, so slip my mail underneath.
8. After the factories closed, the town seemed empty.
9. Wendy usually goes straight home after school.
10. The boys remained after and picked up the papers.

DEVELOPING WRITING SKILLS: Using Words as Different Parts of Speech. Use each word in two sentences of your own, first as one part of speech, then as another.

EXAMPLE: cake

My boots are caked with mud.
Did you bake this delicious carrot cake?

1. past 2. turn 3. fast 4. look 5. beyond

Skills Review and Writing Workshop

Reviewing Parts of Speech

CHECKING YOUR SKILLS

Identify the parts of speech of the underlined words in each sentence.

(1) Icebergs are (2) huge masses of ice that (3) break from the ends of glaciers and float (4) into the sea. The tall ones can extend over four hundred feet (5) above the surface of the ocean. (6) Amazingly, (7) this (8) constitutes only one tenth of an iceberg's mass. The rest sits (9) below the surface, a menace to ships in these cold and (10) icy regions. The biggest iceberg that has (11) ever been charted had a diameter of (12) sixty miles and a (13) length of well over two hundred miles. The North American iceberg (14) usually originates in (15) Greenland, (16) but icebergs often (17) move many miles from their area of (18) birth. Today, the International Ice Patrol reports the position of icebergs and (19) charts their migration. (20) Alas, the Ice Patrol, which came into (21) existence in 1914, arrived (22) too late to help the (23) victims of (24) early disasters, but (25) they do prevent many accidents from occurring today.

USING GRAMMAR SKILLS IN WRITING

Writing a Summary of an Article

Imagine you are working for a foreign government. It is your job to write a summary of an important article from a U.S. newspaper.

Prewriting: Select an article from your local newspaper. Be sure the article contains a complete account of an event. Underline the most important facts in the article.

Writing: Put the main fact in your first sentence. Put the supporting facts in the following sentences and paragraphs.

Revising: Check your summary to make sure that your sentences are clear and that they include all the information needed to summarize the article well. Proofread carefully.

Chapter **5**

Basic Sentence Parts and Patterns

You use sentences every time you speak or write, yet you may not be aware of their essential parts. Knowing how the parts of speech work to form sentences will give you a better understanding of how words communicate ideas.

Subjects and Verbs 5.1

Language is a tool that people use to communicate. Many things can go wrong with this process, preventing a listener or reader from understanding the intended idea. A writer may use words that the reader cannot understand. A dictionary solves this problem easily enough. A more serious problem occurs when a writer writes in patterns that do not make sense to readers. The result is a short circuit, and communication comes to a dead stop. Recognizing that every sentence must have two key parts will help you avoid this problem in your own writing.

Complete Subjects and Predicates

Every *sentence* that is grammatically correct consists of two parts: a *complete subject* and a *complete predicate.*

A sentence is a group of words with two main parts: a complete subject and a complete predicate. Together these parts express a complete thought.

The complete subject includes a noun or pronoun that names the person, place, or thing that the sentence is about. The complete predicate includes a verb or verb phrase that tells something about the complete subject. In the following examples, you can see that a complete subject or complete predicate may have only a single essential word (a noun or pronoun for the complete subject, a verb for the complete predicate). Often, however, a complete subject or complete predicate may have many words that modify and expand upon the essential words.

EXAMPLES: *They* | *were stumbling* through the briars.

COMPLETE SUBJECT	COMPLETE PREDICATE
They	*were stumbling* through the briars.

COMPLETE SUBJECT	COMPLETE PREDICATE
The three *students* at the podium	*spoke.*

EXERCISE A: Recognizing Complete Subjects and Predicates. Make two columns as shown in the example. Then write each complete subject in the first column and each complete predicate in the second column.

EXAMPLE: The fluffy squirrel chattered at us.

Complete Subject	Complete Predicate
The fluffy squirrel	chattered at us.

1. The new puppy won't leave the older dog alone.
2. An old-fashioned spinning wheel sat in the corner of the room.
3. Seasonal winds in India are called monsoons.
4. New skin was grafted onto his burned leg.
5. We should have been on the road before now.
6. Anyone could have made a mistake like that.
7. My umbrella handle is carved from wood.
8. The Sons of Liberty was a secret society.
9. Mink oil is excellent for conditioning leather shoes, boots, and baseball mitts.
10. Her stationery is always simple but elegant.

Sentence or Fragment?

A group of words lacking a complete subject or a complete predicate, or both, is called a *fragment.*

A fragment is a group of words that does not express a complete thought.

The following chart contrasts fragments with the sentences they become after the italicized words are added. Notice how the fragments pose problems for a reader because they leave out essential ideas.

Fragments	Complete Sentences
Wild Bill Hickok, a famous frontiersman.	Wild Bill Hickok, a famous frontiersman, *was an honest marshall.*
Shot several men in the line of duty.	*He* shot several men in the line of duty.
In a saloon in Dakota.	*Hickok died* in a saloon in Dakota.

In the first sentence, the italicized words form the complete predicate. In the second, one word has been added to make up the complete subject. In the last, a complete subject, *Hickok,* and the essential part of a complete predicate, *died,* have been added.

Though fragments, such as those in the above chart, are confusing to a reader, they sometimes can express complete thoughts to a listener in a conversation.

Conversational Fragments. In conversation, you can often express clear ideas in fragments. Repetition, the tone of your voice, your gestures, and your facial expressions all help add meaning to your words.

The following conversation, consisting of both sentences and fragments, is easily understood.

SENTENCE: "When did you last see Jane?"

FRAGMENT: "Yesterday."

SENTENCE: "I thought she had already left for her vacation."

FRAGMENT: "No, not yet."

Written Fragments. Although fragments can sometimes be acceptable in conversation, you should generally avoid fragments in your writing. One permissible use of fragments in writing is to represent speech. Another use is the *elliptical sentence,* in which the missing word or words are obvious and can easily be understood. Even these elliptical sentences should be used sparingly, especially in formal writing.

ELLIPTICAL SENTENCES: [I] Thank you.
Why [are you] so sad?

EXERCISE B: Distinguishing Between Sentences and Fragments. Decide whether each item is a sentence or a fragment. If it is a sentence, write *sentence*. If it is a fragment, rewrite it to make it a sentence.

EXAMPLE: By the swimming pool.
They met by the swimming pool

1. A sewing machine with all the frills.
2. Stories about creatures in the ocean's depths.
3. Jan did not finish her breakfast.
4. Jumped higher and higher on the trampoline.
5. Few, if any.
6. Basketball, the most popular spectator sport.
7. Wearing a white, heavy knit sweater.
8. A stitch in time saves nine.
9. Trembled and shook with fear.
10. Beside the pool, soaking up the sunshine.

Simple Subjects and Predicates

Every complete subject and complete predicate contains a word or group of words that is essential to the sentence.

The simple subject is the essential noun, pronoun, or group of words acting as a noun that cannot be left out of the complete subject.

The simple predicate is the essential verb or verb phrase that cannot be left out of the complete predicate.

In the following examples, notice that all the other words in the complete subject modify or add information to the *simple subject*. In the same manner, all the other words in the complete predicate either modify the *simple predicate* or help it complete the meaning of the sentence.

	SIMPLE SUBJECT	SIMPLE PREDICATE
EXAMPLES:	*Jugs* of sweet cider	*covered* the table.
	COMPLETE SUBJECT	COMPLETE PREDICATE

SIMPLE SUBJECT	SIMPLE PREDICATE
Some *flowers*	*will* not *bloom* in the shade.
COMPLETE SUBJECT	COMPLETE PREDICATE

Notice in the first example that the simple subject of the sentence is *jugs,* not *cider*. The object of a preposition can never be a simple subject. Notice also that in the last example, the verb phrase *will bloom* is split by an adverb, *not*.

NOTE ABOUT THE TERMS *SUBJECT* AND *VERB:* From this point on in this book, the word *subject* will refer to the simple subject, and the word *verb* will refer to the simple predicate.

Knowing how to find the subject and verb in the sentences you write will help you to write more clearly. The same skill will also help you understand more difficult sentence patterns.

If you prefer to find the subject of a sentence before the verb, ask yourself, "What word is the sentence about?" Then, ask yourself, "What did the subject *do*?" The answer will be an action verb. If there is no answer to the last question, look for a linking verb.

EXAMPLE: The stream trickled slowly down the ravine.

Subject: stream

Question: What did the stream *do*?

Answer: trickled

On the other hand, you may find it easier to locate the verb before the subject. In that case, first look for an action verb or a linking verb. Then, ask *Who?* or *What?* before the verb. The answer will be the subject.

EXAMPLE: A wasp's nest was hanging above the porch.

Verb: was hanging

Question: *What* was hanging?

Answer: nest

EXERCISE C: Recognizing Subjects and Verbs. Write each subject and verb, underlining the subject once and the verb twice.

EXAMPLE: Ancient legends continue to be fascinating.

legends continue

(1) Greek literature contains many stories about Amazons. (2) Supposedly living near the Black Sea, the Amazons were a nation of women warriors noted for their strength. (3) Not enjoying the presence of men, the Amazons lived apart in their own cities. (4) Ares, the god of war, was worshipped in their temples. (5) They fought against the Greeks during the Trojan War. (6) They were also fearless hunters. (7) Their bravery made them famous. (8) Many Greek statues of Amazons with bows and arrows can be seen today in museums. (9) These women never really existed, however, according to some scholars. (10) They are merely the product of the Greeks' imagination.

Compound Subjects and Verbs

The word *compound* describes a noun, adjective, or preposition with more than one part. *Airport,* for example is a compound noun. *Compound* also describes subjects or verbs connected by conjunctions.

Compound Subjects. The complete subject of a sentence may contain two or more subjects.

A compound subject is two or more subjects that have the same verb and are joined by a conjunction such as *and* or *or*.

In the example at the top of the next page, the parts of the *compound subject* are underlined once and the verb is underlined twice.

EXAMPLE: Parsley, sage, dill, and rosemary were growing there.

Compound Verbs. Sentences may also contain two or more verbs in the complete predicate.

A compound verb is two or more verbs that have the same subject and are joined by a conjunction such as *and* or *or*.

In the example, the *compound verb* has three parts.

EXAMPLE: The star signed autograph books, smiled at her fans, and then departed in a limousine.

Sentences may also have both compound subjects and compound verbs.

EXAMPLE: Mr. Willis and his neighbors argued and shouted.

NOTE ABOUT COMPOUND VERBS: When a compound verb consists of two or more verb phrases with the same helping verb, the helping verb is often used only with the first verb.

AWKWARD REPETITION: The banjo player was strumming his banjo, was stomping his feet, and was singing enthusiastically.

HELPING VERB NOT REPEATED: The banjo player was strumming his banjo, stomping his feet, and singing enthusiastically.

EXERCISE D: Recognizing Compound Subjects and Verbs. Write the words that make up the subject and verb in each sentence, underlining the subjects once and the verbs twice.

EXAMPLE: A hummingbird can hover and then fly straight up.
hummingbird can hover fly

1. A hat, gloves, and warm coat should be worn in this weather.
2. Our aunt and uncle visit us every year and bring many gifts.
3. Both salt and pepper are used as seasonings.

4. In the summer my friends and I swim and ride our bicycles on country roads.
5. Moles have very poor eyesight and therefore burrow in dark tunnels underground.
6. The team not only had a perfect season but also won the tournament.
7. Hair dyes and lipsticks come in almost every shade.
8. The mother cat and her kittens mewed pitifully and rubbed against our legs.
9. A Piper Cub was gliding and spiraling above us.
10. Moths cluster on the screen and beat their wings.

EXERCISE E: Finding Simple and Compound Subjects and Verbs. Make two columns as shown in the example. Then write the words that make up the subject and verb in each sentence in the correct columns.

EXAMPLE: After school the band met and practiced.

Subject	Verb
band	met practiced

1. The nozzle of the garden hose was clogged with dirt.
2. Many people have trouble with the high note of "The Star-Spangled Banner."
3. Rats and mice eat huge amounts of valuable grains.
4. Today Aunt Jennie and Uncle Nick will fly in from Hawaii and bring us crates of pineapples.
5. Miners and their families do not lead easy lives.
6. Max can hear a tune once and whistle it perfectly.
7. Remedies for colds usually do not help much.
8. During the dry season, campfires and carelessly tossed matches can cause raging forest fires.
9. Phoebe's hard work and honesty won our respect.
10. Hilary, Miranda, and their cousin could dance, sing, and play musical instruments.

DEVELOPING WRITING SKILLS: Using Subjects and Verbs to Write Sentences. Combine the ten simple and compound subjects and the ten simple and compound verbs in the following items to make ten logical sentences.

1. child
2. people
3. painting
4. water
5. colt
6. Alma Gilbert
7. iron copper
8. ketchup mustard
9. sand gravel
10. knife fork
11. grew
12. poured
13. were placed
14. are required
15. go
16. cried laughed
17. played entertained
18. was torn ripped
19. can be used may provide
20. was running jumping

Hard-To-Find Subjects 5.2

In most English sentences, a subject is followed by a verb. This section will present sentences with subjects that are not so easily found.

Subjects in Orders and Directions

In sentences that give orders or directions, the subject is usually not expressed.

In sentences that give orders or directions, the subject is understood to be *you*.

The following chart contrasts sentences with and without the understood *you*. The subjects are underlined once and the verbs twice. Notice in the last sentence that even when a person is addressed, the subject is still understood to be *you*.

Orders or Directions	With Understood *You* Added
Dust the furniture and then wax the floor.	[You] dust the furniture and then wax the floor.
Kim, give me an apple.	Kim, [you] give me an apple.

EXERCISE A: Creating Sentences with Understood Subjects. Use each verb in a sentence that gives an order or direction. Add the understood subject in parentheses in each sentence.

EXAMPLE: lend

Joe, (you) lend me your pencil.

1. give
2. wipe
3. speak
4. wash
5. step
6. drive
7. clean
8. brush
9. rake
10. mix

Subjects in Inverted Sentences

In some sentences the usual subject-verb order is *inverted*—that is, reversed. Sentences that may be inverted in English include questions and sentences beginning with *there* or *here*. In addition, some sentences are inverted for emphasis.

Subjects in Questions. Questions are often inverted.

In questions the subject often follows the verb.

An inverted question can begin with a verb, a helping verb, or one of the following words: *how, what, when, where, who, whose,* or *why*.

To find the subject in an inverted question rephrase the question mentally as a statement. Then the subject and verb will fall into the usual order.

Questions	Reworded as Statements
Are we ready?	We are ready.
Do you like raisins?	You do like raisins.
Where was the car parked?	The car was parked where.

NOTE ABOUT QUESTIONS: Some questions are not inverted. Those beginning with an interrogative adjective or pronoun may be in the usual subject-verb order.

EXAMPLES: Which poet won the Pulitzer Prize this year?

Who cares about such nonsense?

Sentences Beginning with *There* or *Here*. Two words often used to begin inverted sentences are *there* and *here*.

The subject of a sentence is never *there* or *here*.

When *there* or *here* begins a sentence, the subject usually follows the verb. As with inverted questions, mentally rephrase the sentence to find the subject.

Sentences Beginning with *There* or *Here*	Reworded with Subjects Before Verbs
There is my old, battered suitcase.	My old, battered suitcase is there.
Here is a patch for your sleeve.	A patch for your sleeve is here.

In the sentences in the chart, *there* and *here* are adverbs; they modify the verbs and tell where. Occasionally, *there* is merely used to help the sentence get started and does *not* modify the verb. When *there* is used in this manner, it is not an adverb but an *expletive*.

EXAMPLES: There is no bridge across this river.

There will be a drastic change in the weather.

In sentences where *there* is an expletive, rephrasing to find the subject may not work. To find the subject in this situation, mentally drop *there* and ask *Who?* or *What?* before the verb.

Sentences with Expletive *There*	Questions for Finding Subjects	
There are some crumbs on your chin.	*Question:*	*What* are?
	Answer:	crumbs
There may not be any logical answer to that question.	*Question:*	*What* may be?
	Answer:	answer

NOTE ABOUT SENTENCES BEGINNING WITH *THERE* OR *HERE*: Some sentences beginning with *there* or *here* are not in inverted order.

EXAMPLE: There you are!

Inverted Order for Emphasis. Sometimes, the subject-verb order is deliberately inverted to emphasize the last words.

In some sentences the subject is placed after the verb in order to receive greater emphasis.

Inverted subject-verb order directs attention to the subject at the end of the sentence. Rephrased in normal subject-verb order, the sentence is less dramatic.

Inverted Word Order for Emphasis	Reworded with Subject Before Verb
Beneath the ruined temple waited the deadly cobra.	The deadly cobra waited beneath the ruined temple.

EXERCISE B: Finding Subjects in Questions. Write the subject and verb in each sentence, underlining the subject once and the verb twice.

EXAMPLE: Who knocked on the door?
Who knocked

1. Is a tomato a fruit or a vegetable?
2. Where did you put the buttered rolls?
3. Which shade of blue looks best?
4. Should a murderer ever be released from prison?
5. Who won the prize for the silliest costume?
6. May we have a little peace and quiet?
7. Was the key under the mat?
8. How long will you take to decide?
9. Whose honor was at stake?
10. Can we climb these mountains safely?

EXERCISE C: Finding Subjects in Sentences Beginning with *There* or *Here*. Write the subject and verb in each sentence, underlining the subject once and the verb twice.

1. Here are your gloves.
2. There was the leaky pipe.
3. There he was, with no bus fare.
4. Here are some suggestions for your composition.

5. There are two possible answers to that question.
6. There were the lost documents.
7. Here is a new slant on that topic.
8. Here comes Megan.
9. Here is your change from the dollar bill.
10. There are no mistakes in this needlepoint sampler.

EXERCISE D: Finding Subjects in Sentences Inverted for Emphasis. Write the subject and verb in each sentence, underlining the subject once and the verb twice.

1. Into the valley of death rode the warriors.
2. On the top of a mountain lived the bitter recluse.
3. In the woods lay the rusted musket.
4. With understanding comes compassion for others.
5. From the kitchen drifted the smell of baking bread.
6. Beside the trail grew raspberry bushes.
7. With the rain came strong, gusty winds.
8. At the head of the line stood my sister.
9. In the exhibit were several paintings by Picasso.
10. From one branch to another fluttered the baby bird.

DEVELOPING WRITING SKILLS: Writing Sentences with Hard-to-Find Subjects. Use the following instructions to write five sentences of your own.

1. Write a sentence with an understood subject.
2. Write a question that begins with a helping verb.
3. Write a question that begins with *where*.
4. Write an inverted sentence with *there* used as an expletive.
5. Write an inverted sentence that emphasizes the subject.

Direct Objects, Indirect Objects, and Objective Complements 5.3

With a verb, a complete predicate may also have a *complement*.

A complement is a word or group of words that completes the meaning of the predicate of a sentence.

This section presents three different kinds of complements used in sentences with action verbs: *direct objects, indirect objects,* and *objective complements*.

The Direct Object

Direct objects usually follow action verbs.

A direct object is a noun or pronoun that receives the action of a transitive action verb.

To find a direct object, ask *Whom?* or *What?* after an action verb. In the following, subjects are underlined once, action verbs twice, and direct objects are boxed and labeled. Notice how the direct objects answer the questions *Whom?* and *What?*

EXAMPLES: The army blanket covered the old [soldier] (DO).
(Covered *whom*? *Answer:* soldier)

The carpenter is sanding the [bookcase] (DO).
(Is sanding *what*? *Answer:* bookcase)

Only transitive action verbs direct their action toward someone or something—the direct object. Intransitive verbs have no direct objects.

TRANSITIVE: The tidal wave sank the [ship] (DO).
(Sank *what*? *Answer:* ship)

INTRANSITIVE: The wheels sank into the mud.
(Sank *what*? *Answer:* none)

Direct Objects in Questions. When a question follows the normal subject-verb order, you can still find the direct object by asking *Whom?* or *What?* after an action verb.

EXAMPLE: Who wrote that [story] (DO)?

When a question is inverted, however, the direct object will sometimes appear near the beginning, before the verb. To find the direct object, reword the question as a statement in normal word order as shown in the examples on the next page.

INVERTED QUESTION: Which book did you read?

REWORDED AS A STATEMENT: You did read which book. (DO: book)

Compound Direct Objects. When an action verb directs action toward more than one direct object, the result is a *compound direct object.* If there is a compound direct object in a sentence, asking *Whom?* or *What?* after the verb will give you two or more answers.

EXAMPLE: The carpenter is sanding the table and chairs. (DO: table; DO: chairs)

Direct Object or Object of a Preposition? A direct object is never the noun or pronoun at the end of a prepositional phrase. Do not confuse these two sentence parts.

EXAMPLES: I photographed the woman with the children. (DO: woman; PREP PHRASE: with the children)
(Photographed *whom?* *Answer:* woman)

We walked with the children through the zoo. (PREP PHRASE: with the children; PREP PHRASE: through the zoo)
(Walked *what?* *Answer:* none)

EXERCISE A: Recognizing Direct Objects. Write the direct object in each sentence, including all parts of any compound direct objects.

EXAMPLE: You can save energy and money through conservation of electricity.
energy money

(1) You should never use unnecessary lights. (2) In daylight hours, the sun can often provide enough light. (3) You can also use bulbs of lower wattage in some areas of a home or business. (4) These use less energy. (5) Some areas, however, require lots of light. (6) You should usually use one larger bulb there. (7) You can also install dimmer switches and three-way bulbs in your home. (8) These will control the amount of light from your lighting fixtures. (9) Fluorescent fixtures in contrast to incandescent bulbs give more light at less cost. (10) Everyone should regularly practice these methods of energy conservation in their homes and places of business.

The Indirect Object

Sentences with direct objects may have *indirect objects* too.

An indirect object is a noun or pronoun that appears with a direct object and names the person or thing that something is given to or done for.

To find an indirect object, first be certain that the sentence has a direct object. Then, having found the direct object, ask *To or for whom?* or *To or for what?* after the action verb.

EXAMPLES: Liz promised her sister (IO) a reward (DO) for good behavior.

(Promised *to whom*? *Answer:* sister)

We should give Fred's idea (IO) a chance (DO).

(Should give *to what*? *Answer:* idea)

Compound Indirect Objects. When there is a compound indirect object in a sentence, asking *To or for whom?* or *To or for what?* after the verb will lead to two or more answers.

EXAMPLES: Liz promised her sister (IO) and brother (IO) a reward (DO).

(Promised *to whom*? *Answer:* sister and brother)

We should give Fred's idea (IO) and effort (IO) a chance (DO).

(Should give *to what*? *Answer:* idea and effort)

Indirect Object or Direct Object? To avoid confusing an indirect object with a direct object, remember that an indirect object almost always comes between the verb and the direct object. In a sentence in normal subject-verb order, the pattern is always verb-indirect object-direct object.

EXAMPLE: Uncle Charlie handed the bellhop (IO) a tip (DO).

Asking the questions for direct and indirect objects will also help you distinguish between the two kinds of complements. In the above example, the question for direct objects—Handed *what*?—gives the answer *tip*. The question for indirect objects—Handed *to whom*?—leads to the indirect object *bellhop*.

Indirect Object or Object of a Preposition? Do not confuse an indirect object with an object of a preposition. An indirect object is never preceded by the word *to* or *for*. Moreover, it almost never follows the direct object. In the first example below, *friends* is the object of a preposition and is located *after* the direct object. In the second, there is no preposition and *friends* comes before the direct object.

EXAMPLES: Angela told the news (DO) to her friends (PREP PHRASE).

Angela told her friends (IO) the news (DO).

EXERCISE B: Recognizing Indirect Objects. Write each indirect object, including all parts of any compound indirect objects. If a sentence has no indirect object, write *none*.

EXAMPLE: They gave Mark and Elizabeth a puppy.
Mark Elizabeth

1. Trading vessels brought people exotic spices.
2. Our committee distributed fliers to our neighbors.
3. Mr. Hinkle taught Harriet and Alberta a good lesson.
4. Please bring the children and me some ice cream.
5. The Constitution guarantees freedom to all.
6. She sold her home for very little profit.
7. When will Lena tell him the truth?
8. Education gives men and women more opportunities.
9. Lucille made herself some hot chocolate.
10. The article had a warning for cigarette smokers.

The Objective Complement

A third kind of complement, one that generally comes after a direct object, is called an *objective complement*.

An objective complement is an adjective or noun that appears with a direct object and describes or renames it.

Objective complements do not occur often. They are used only with verbs such as *appoint, name, make, think,* or *call.*

An objective complement can be found only in a sentence that has a direct object. To determine whether a word is an objective complement, say the verb and the direct object, and then ask *What?* The following examples illustrate the method you should use to locate objective complements.

EXAMPLES: Ben called his dog (DO) Rover (OC).
(Called dog *What?* *Answer:* Rover)

The beautician made Ann's hair (DO) short (OC) and curly (OC).
(Made hair *what?* *Answer:* short and curly)

The objective complement in the last example is compound.

EXERCISE C: Recognizing Objective Complements. Write the objective complement in each sentence, including all parts of any compound objective complements.

EXAMPLE: Mr. Montes made his reply very short.
short

1. The neighborhood bully considered Martin a sissy.
2. A card for Father's Day makes my dad very happy.
3. That pleasant woman called me kind and helpful.
4. A stubborn man, Mr. Fenston thinks other people obstinate.
5. John's uncle makes everyone welcome.
6. Her friends nominated Jane president.
7. The ointment made the wound less red and sore.
8. Impulsively, she painted the doors to the dining room pink.
9. The boss appointed Ms. Brady chairwoman.
10. Such experiences make life worthwhile.

DEVELOPING WRITING SKILLS: Writing Sentences with Direct Objects, Indirect Objects, and Objective Complements. Use the following instructions to write five sentences of your own.

1. Write a sentence with a direct object. Use *Alice* as the subject and *described* as the verb.
2. Write a sentence with a compound direct object. Use *electrician* and *plumber* as the subject and *checked* as the verb.

3. Write a sentence with a direct object and an indirect object. Use *catcher* as the subject and *tossed* as the verb.
4. Write a sentence with a direct object and a compound indirect object. Use *Sid* as the subject and *owes* as the verb.
5. Write a sentence with an objective complement, including a direct object. Use *I* as the subject and *called* as the verb.

Subject Complements 5.4

In this section, you will see linking verbs followed by other kinds of complements, called *subject complements*.

A subject complement is a noun, pronoun, or adjective that appears with a linking verb and tells something about the subject of the sentence.

A subject complement, which will almost always be found *after* a linking verb, may be either a *predicate nominative* or a *predicate adjective*.

The Predicate Nominative

The word *nominative* comes from the Latin word *nomen* meaning "name." The words *noun* and *pronoun* are also derived from *nomen*.

A predicate nominative is a noun or pronoun that appears with a linking verb and renames, identifies, or explains the subject of the sentence.

A subject and a *predicate nominative* are two different words for the same person, place, or thing. Acting as an equal sign, the linking verb joins these two parts and equates them.

In the following examples, subjects are underlined once, linking verbs twice, and predicate nominatives are labeled.

EXAMPLES: Emily Bronte became a famous author. (PN: author)

The best person for the job is you. (PN: you)

Like other sentence parts, predicate nominatives may be *compound*.

EXAMPLES: Two of spring's flowers are crocuses and tulips. (PN: crocuses, PN: tulips)

Our nominee might be either Dean or Julie. (PN: Dean, PN: Julie)

EXERCISE A: Recognizing Predicate Nominatives. Write the predicate nominative in each sentence, including all parts of any compound predicate nominatives.

EXAMPLE: Gwendolyn was a lawyer and a mother.
lawyer mother

1. The girl in the green sweater is she.
2. Bill's favorite sports were hockey and football.
3. Good sources of protein are eggs, meat, or beans.
4. Agatha remained an athlete in spite of her illness.
5. The winning essay will be the one with the most originality.
6. Audubon was an American naturalist and artist.
7. Gold and silver are valuable metals.
8. Peace of mind and a clear conscience are everything.
9. Bob's idea for the assembly seems the best.
10. My best friends are you and he.

The Predicate Adjective

The second kind of subject complement is the *predicate adjective*.

A predicate adjective is an adjective that appears with a linking verb and describes the subject of the sentence.

In sentences with predicate adjectives, the linking verb joins the subject and the predicate adjective. Notice in the examples how the predicate adjectives refer to the subjects.

EXAMPLES: The design on the vase was intricate. (PA: intricate)

This tomato soup tastes too salty. (PA: salty)

Like predicate nominatives, predicate adjectives may also be compound.

EXAMPLES: The kite was light but sturdy. (PA: light, sturdy)

Your hands look grimy and dirty. (PA: grimy, dirty)

EXERCISE B: Recognizing Predicate Adjectives. Write the predicate adjective in each sentence, including all parts of any compound predicate adjectives.

EXAMPLE: That soup smells delicious.
delicious

1. Her voice on the telephone sounded muffled.
2. After work Eugene's muscles felt stiff and sore.
3. The mayor's policy is important to our city.
4. My sandwich at the beach was gritty and inedible.
5. Joan grew kinder and more understanding.
6. A crossword puzzle should be fairly difficult.
7. This item on the list appears unnecessary.
8. The sergeant's criticism was harsh yet impersonal.
9. Because of fright Ted's face looked drawn and pale.
10. Janice became successful overnight.

DEVELOPING WRITING SKILLS: Writing Sentences with Subject Complements. Use the following instructions to write five sentences of your own.

1. Write a sentence with a noun as a predicate nominative. Use *Adam* as the subject and *became* as the verb.
2. Write a sentence with a noun as a predicate nominative. Use *Beth* as the subject and *remained* as the verb.
3. Write a sentence with two or more nouns as a compound predicate nominative. Use *insects* as the subject and *are* as the verb.
4. Write a sentence with a predicate adjective. Use *friends* as the subject and *were* as the verb.
5. Write a sentence with a compound predicate adjective. Use *plants* as the subject and *looked* as the verb.

5.5 Basic Sentence Patterns

English sentences fall into certain patterns. The most basic pattern is a *subject* followed by a *verb*. If you say, "It is over there," you are using the S-V pattern. The subject is *it* and the verb is the word *is*. The other words are modifiers.

This section will explain several other basic patterns.

Five Basic Patterns with Complements

Sentences with complements follow predictable patterns.

In the English language, subjects, verbs, and complements follow five basic sentence patterns.

The following charts show different kinds of complements. There are five basic patterns for sentences with complements. Three make use of transitive action verbs. Two make use of linking verbs. Subjects in all of the charts are underlined once, verbs twice, and complements are boxed and labeled.

Patterns with Transitive Verbs. Transitive action verbs are generally followed by direct objects. They may also be followed by indirect objects or objective complements.

Patterns	Examples
S-AV-DO	Bill presented a formal [speech (DO)].
	They chose [me (DO)].
S-AV-IO-DO	His teacher wrote [him (IO)] a [letter (DO)].
S-AV-DO-OC	My parents named the [baby (DO)] [Jenny (OC)].
	The team's victory made [him (DO)] [happy (OC)].

Patterns with Linking Verbs. Linking verbs are generally followed by either a predicate nominative or a predicate adjective, as the chart on the next page shows.

Patterns	Examples
S-LV-PN	A pit viper is a poisonous snake. (PN: snake)
	The winner is she. (PN: she)
S-LV-PA	She is ill today. (PA: ill)

Compound Patterns. Any of the five sentence patterns can be expanded by making any of the sentence parts compound.

EXAMPLE: S-S-AV-DO-DO-DO

Both Herman Melville and James Joyce wrote poetry (DO), short stories (DO), and novels (DO).

Experimenting with these patterns will give your writing variety and style.

EXERCISE A: Recognizing Basic Sentence Patterns. Write each sentence, underlining the subject once, underlining the verb twice, and circling each complement. Then write the pattern of each sentence, using the abbreviations in the charts.

EXAMPLE: Molly handed (me) her (report) on antiques.

S-AV-IO-DO

1. Warren repeated the message slowly.
2. Dennis nicknamed me Buzzy.
3. This lamb stew is hearty and delicious.
4. Phyllis sent Mike and me a wonderful surprise.
5. Paul offered the most helpful suggestions.
6. Jill dyed her hair bright orange.
7. After years of exile, Nolan felt desperate for news about his country.
8. A powerful telescope gives astronomers a better look at the universe.
9. Pileated woodpeckers are large, red-crested birds.
10. Hubert covered the walls with peanut butter.

Inverted Patterns

The five basic patterns used with complements are not the only ones you can use. Inverted patterns can also be used.

In an inverted sentence pattern, the subject is never first.

Inverted patterns are used for three types of sentences.

Patterns for Inverted Questions. Questions beginning with interrogative adjectives or pronouns are not always inverted, but most questions are. In a question with a single form of the verb *be*, the subject often follows the verb.

Pattern	Examples
V-S	Are the peaches from California?
	Why are they here?

Another inverted pattern is found in questions containing verb phrases. The subject often comes between a helping verb and the main verb.

Pattern	Examples
HV-S-V	Will Joe arrive today?
	Where is he going?

Complements usually follow the verb and subject in inverted questions. However, a complement may begin a sentence.

Patterns	Examples
V-S-COMP	Was Robert delirious (PA)?
HV-S-V-COMP	Are you reading that novel (DO)?
COMP-HV-S-V	Which necklace (DO) did the jeweler sell?

Pattern for Sentences Beginning with *There* or *Here*. Sentences beginning with *there* or *here* are almost always inverted: The subject follows the verb.

Pattern	Example
V-S	There is an owl in the barn.

Pattern for Sentences Inverted for Emphasis. In sentences inverted to emphasize the subject, the subject again follows the verb.

Pattern	Example
V-S	Above the dying animal, soared a dozen vultures.

An inverted sentence may also emphasize, not the subject at the end, but a complement at the beginning.

Patterns	Examples
COMP-S-V	What a victory (DO) we had!
COMP-V-S	How fragile (PA) was that peace!

EXERCISE B: Recognizing Inverted Sentence Patterns. Write each sentence, underlining the subject once, underlining the verb twice, and circling each complement. Then write the pattern of each sentence.

EXAMPLE: Which (movie) did you see?
COMP-HV-S-V

1. Why does everyone always suspect the butler?
2. Back and forth paced the anxious father.
3. "What a piece of work is man!"
4. How many trees will they plant?
5. Deep under the sea lay the ancient Spanish ship.
6. Was Marlene trapped in the broken elevator?

7. When was De Gaulle the president of France?
8. Is this frayed wire dangerous?
9. What beautiful weather we had!
10. Could you imagine such a spectacular sight?

DEVELOPING WRITING SKILLS: Writing Sentences with a Variety of Patterns. Use each pattern in a sentence of your own. Then underline each subject once, underline each verb twice, and circle each complement.

1. S-V
2. S-AV-IO-DO
3. S-AV-DO-OC
4. S-LV-PN
5. HV-S-V
6. V-S-COMP
7. HV-S-V-COMP
8. COMP-HV-S-V
9. V-S
10. S-S-AV-IO-IO-DO

5.6 Diagraming Basic Sentence Parts

Diagraming is a way of seeing how all of the many different parts of a sentence relate to each other. Like a blueprint, a diagram can make a fuzzy mental picture of a sentence clear and logical.

Subjects, Verbs, and Modifiers

To diagram a sentence with just a subject and a verb, draw a horizontal line, place the subject on the left, the verb on the right, and then draw a vertical line to separate the subject from the verb.

EXAMPLE: Kathleen (S) laughed (V).

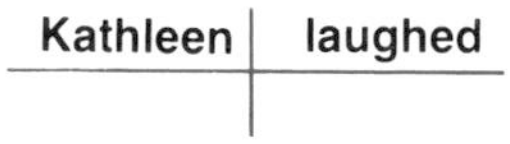

Kathleen | laughed

When you diagram adjectives, place them on slanted lines directly below the nouns or pronouns that they modify. Similarly, place adverbs on slanted lines directly below the verbs, adjectives, or other adverbs that they modify. The example at the top of the next page illustrates how this is done.

EXAMPLE: Quite hesitant, my sister did not answer quickly.
(ADV: Quite; ADJ: hesitant; ADJ: my; ADV: not; ADV: quickly)

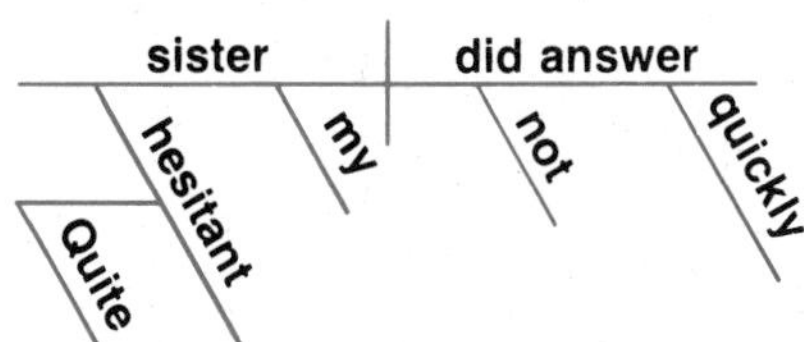

Orders and directions whose subjects are understood to be *you* are diagramed in the usual way with parentheses around the understood subject. Inverted sentences also follow the usual subject-verb order in a diagram. The capital letter shows which word begins the sentence.

EXAMPLES: ORDER: Stand up. QUESTION: How are you?

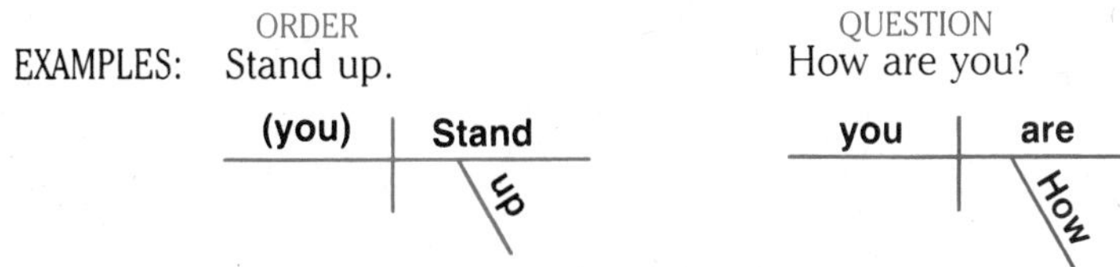

Usually when *there* or *here* begins a sentence, it will function as an adverb modifying the verb. It will then be diagramed on a slanted line below the verb. Sometimes, however, *there* is used simply to get the sentence started. In this case it is an expletive. Diagram an expletive by placing it on a short horizontal line above the subject. Diagram interjections and nouns of direct address in exactly the same way.

EXAMPLES: There was a storm. (EXP: There) Alas, my friend, you lost. (INT: Alas; N OF DA: friend)

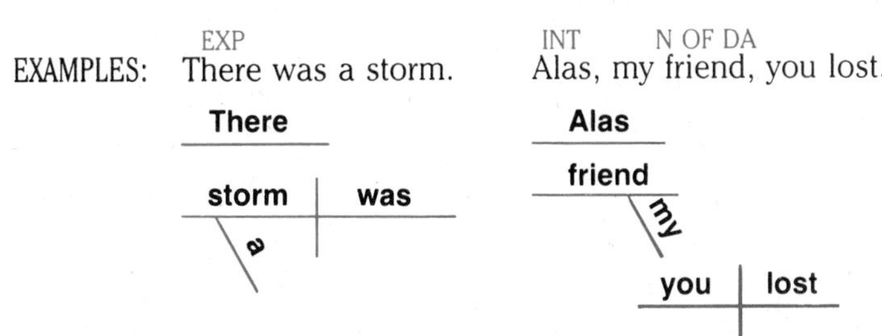

EXERCISE A: Diagraming Subjects, Verbs, and Modifiers. Correctly diagram each sentence.

1. Mr. Ricardo, come here.
2. The ship wandered quite aimlessly.

3. Swallows soared overhead.
4. The beautiful white waterfall thunderously cascaded down.
5. There should be a parade today.

Adding Conjunctions

Conjunctions are diagramed on dotted lines drawn between the words they connect. In the example, coordinating conjunctions are used to join both adjectives and adverbs.

EXAMPLE: The small but (CONJ) fierce dog barked loudly and (CONJ) steadily.

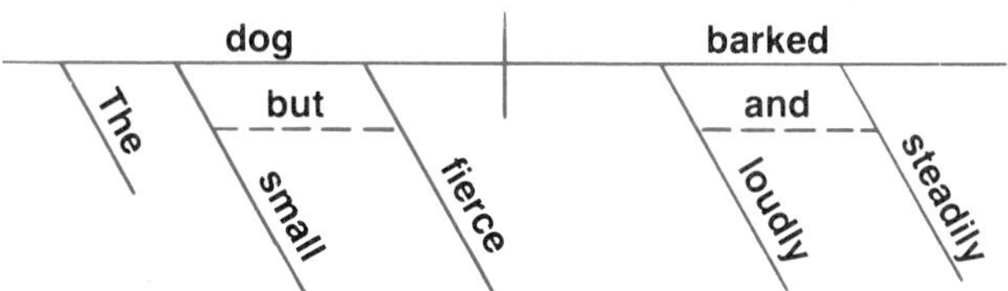

Conjunctions that connect compound subjects and compound verbs are also written on dotted lines drawn between the words they connect. Notice in the following example how the horizontal line of the diagram is split so that each part of a compound subject or verb appears on a line of its own. Notice also the position of the correlative conjunction *neither . . . nor.*

EXAMPLE: Neither (CONJ) Amanda nor (CONJ) Lisa wrote or (CONJ) called.

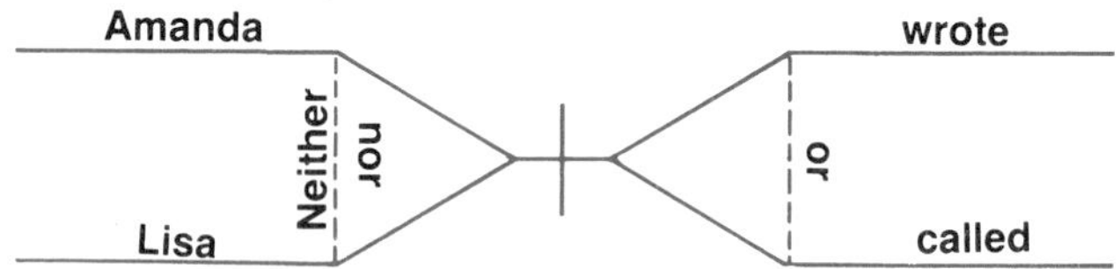

Notice in the example at the top of the next page that modifiers are placed under the part of the sentence they modify. When a modifier modifies both parts of a compound subject or verb, however, it is placed under the main line of the diagram. In the example the adverb *confidently* modifies both parts of the compound verb, so it is placed under the main line.

EXAMPLE: Confidently (ADV), the (ADJ) children and their (ADJ) parents walked in (ADV) and sat down (ADV).

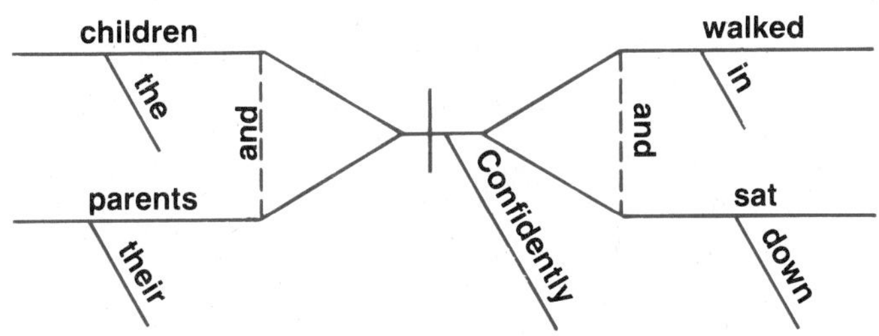

If each part of a compound verb has its own helping verb, each is placed on the line with its verb. When a helping verb is shared by both parts of a compound verb, however, the helping verb is placed on the main line of the diagram.

EXAMPLE: This idea will (HV) be (HV) either accepted or rejected.

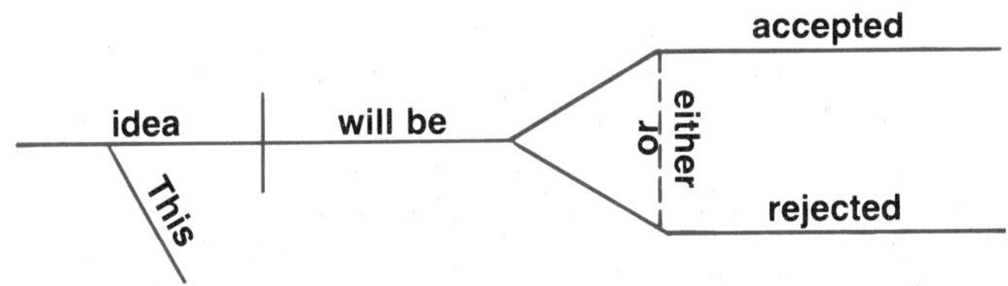

EXERCISE B: Diagraming Sentences with Conjunctions. Correctly diagram each sentence.

1. Wood can be painted or varnished.
2. Must pork and bacon be cooked thoroughly?
3. The unusual and colorful kite soared gracefully and slowly dipped.
4. Two obviously unhappy children and their desperately uncomfortable parents fidgeted anxiously and waited very impatiently.
5. The mechanical toy frog can not only croak but also jump far.

Complements

In a diagram a direct object is positioned on the main horizontal line after the verb. A short vertical line is added to separate it from the verb. An indirect object is placed on a horizontal line extending from a slanted line directly below the verb.

EXAMPLES: Sue wore a gold chain. (DO: chain) I gave Ted advice. (IO: Ted; DO: advice)

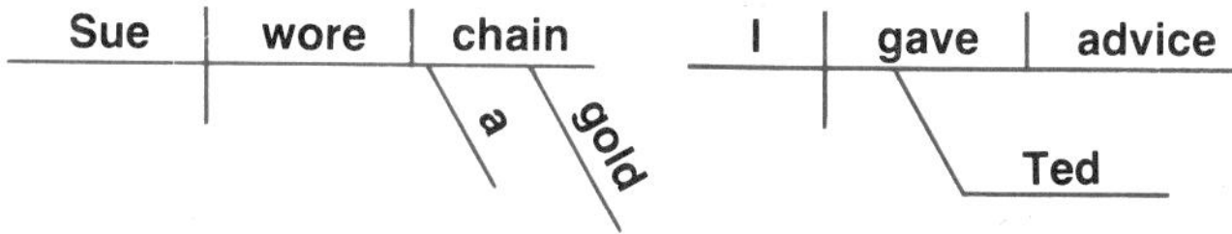

Since an objective complement helps complete the meaning of a direct object, they are placed side by side. A short slanted line is added to separate the direct object from the objective complement.

EXAMPLE: The President named him Chief-of-Staff. (DO: him; OC: Chief-of-Staff)

In a sentence diagram, both predicate nominatives and predicate adjectives are placed on the main horizontal line after the verb. A short, slanted line is used to separate them from the verb.

EXAMPLES: My dog is a spaniel. (PN: spaniel) We felt grouchy. (PA: grouchy)

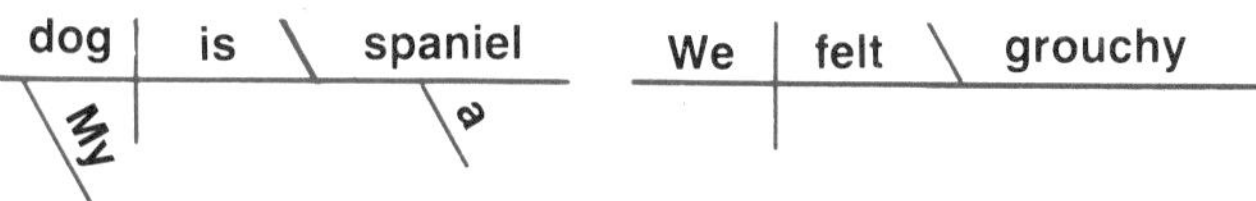

As the example at the top of the next page shows, compound complements are diagramed by splitting the lines on which they appear. Conjunctions are placed on dotted lines drawn between the words they connect.

EXAMPLE: We showed Ellie (IO) and Tom (IO) the zoo (DO) and the museum (DO).

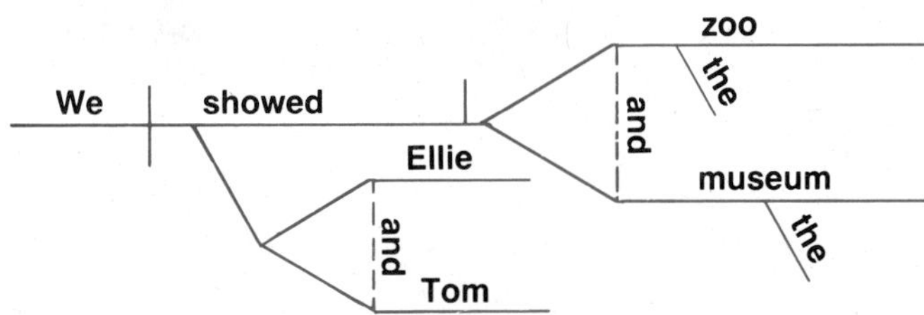

EXERCISE C: Diagraming Complements. Correctly diagram each sentence.

1. The irritable little boy pushed his food away.
2. This remarkable but true story taught Sally and me something.
3. Henry, do not call me Abigail!
4. Many good mechanics can fix both cars and bicycles.
5. His shy and cautious manner gave June and me courage.
6. That painting is a masterpiece.
7. The fresh, clean mountain air felt wonderful.
8. Her husband is a friend and a companion.
9. Their pie crusts are light and flaky.
10. Domestic turkeys are dull-witted but delicious.

DEVELOPING WRITING SKILLS: Writing and Diagraming Sentences. Use the following patterns to write five sentences of your own. Then correctly diagram each sentence. Keep your sentences simple but be sure to include appropriate adjectives and adverbs.

EXAMPLE: Subject-Subject-Linking Verb-Predicate Adjective

Jim and David were classmates.

1. Subject-Action Verb-Action Verb
2. Subject-Action Verb-Direct Object
3. Subject-Action Verb-Indirect Object-Direct Object-Direct Object
4. Subject-Action Verb-Direct Object-Objective Complement
5. Subject-Linking Verb-Predicate Nominative

Skills Review and Writing Workshop

Basic Sentence Parts and Patterns

CHECKING YOUR SKILLS

Identify each underlined item as a *subject, verb, direct object, indirect object, objective complement, predicate nominative,* or *predicate adjective.*

(1) People named certain animals porcupines. (2) The name comes from words meaning "spiny pig" in Latin. (3) Strong, stiff quills covering porcupines' bodies give them protection from their enemies. (4) The quills of some types of porcupines are tiny barbs. (5) They have tiny, backward-pointing tips. (6) An animal stuck with a barbed quill often cannot remove it. (7) Infection or damage to a vital organ may occur. (8) Porcupines are slow-moving creatures. (9) They look quite strange. (10) Their quills, however, usually keep them safe.

USING GRAMMAR SKILLS IN WRITING

Writing Instructions

Instructions must be written with perfect clarity because readers cannot ask questions. Imagine you have invented a machine. Now write operating instructions explaining how your machine works. Follow these steps.

Prewriting: Does the person who is going to operate your machine need something you have not provided? Does your machine operate outside or inside? Note special needs.

Writing: State the purpose of the machine. Number the steps that must be followed to operate the machine properly.

Revising: Check the steps you have outlined. Are they clear? Are the directions numbered logically? Are your sentences grammatically correct? After you have revised, proofread carefully.

Chapter 6

Phrases

A verb phrase, consisting of two or more words, functions just as a single verb would. Prepositional phrases and other kinds of phrases, as you will see in this chapter, function similarly.

A phrase is a group of words, without a subject and verb, that functions in a sentence as one part of speech.

There are several kinds of *phrases,* among them prepositional phrases, appositive phrases, participial phrases, gerund phrases, and infinitive phrases. The last three types of phrases may be grouped together as verbal phrases. In this chapter you will learn how phrases can be used to add meaning and variety to your sentences.

Prepositional Phrases 6.1

A *prepositional phrase* is a group of words made up of a preposition and a noun or pronoun, called the object of the preposition. *Over their heads, until dark, in addition to the surprise birthday party,* and *after the baseball game* are all examples of prepositional phrases. Sometimes, a single prepositional phrase may have two or more objects joined by a conjunction. *Between the window and the wall* and *because of the wind and freezing rain* are examples of prepositions followed by compound objects. (See Section 3.1 to review prepositions.)

In this section you will learn how prepositional phrases modify other words by functioning either as adjectives or as adverbs within sentences.

Adjective Phrases

A prepositional phrase that acts as an adjective is called an *adjective phrase*.

An adjective phrase is a prepositional phrase that modifies a noun or pronoun by telling what kind or which one.

The following chart contrasts adjectives with adjective phrases.

Adjectives	Adjective Phrases
A *beautiful* painting hung in the hall.	A painting *of great beauty* hung in the hall.
Mary took a *boxed* lunch.	Mary took lunch *in a box*.

A prepositional phrase that answers the adjective questions *What kind?* or *Which one?* will be an adjective phrase. In the first sentence on the right in the chart, for example, the question *What kind of painting?* is answered by *of great beauty*.

Adjective phrases usually modify nouns functioning as subjects, direct objects, indirect objects, or predicate nominatives.

MODIFYING A SUBJECT: The mansion *across the road* has been abandoned.

MODIFYING A DIRECT OBJECT: Mary quickly erased the poem *on the blackboard*.

MODIFYING AN INDIRECT OBJECT: A realtor sold the noisy neighbors *above us* a new house.

MODIFYING A PREDICATE NOMINATIVE: A unicorn is a gentle white creature *with a single horn*.

A sentence may often have a series of two or more adjective phrases. When this happens, each succeeding phrase may modify the object of the preceding phrase.

EXAMPLE: The wind blew down the tree *on the corner of the block*.

The adjective phrase *on the corner* describes *tree*. The adjective phrase *of the block* modifies *corner*.

In other situations, more than one adjective phrase may describe the same noun.

EXAMPLE: The old barn was filled with many things, including patches *with bright colors for a quilting bee*.

Both phrases tell what kind of *patches*.

EXERCISE A: Identifying Adjective Phrases. Write each sentence, underlining the adjective phrase or adjective phrases in each. Then draw an arrow from each phrase to the word it modifies.

EXAMPLE: Tom's mother wrote a note for her son's absence.

1. Agatha Christie was a widely read writer of mysteries.
2. The article about Indian folklore is fascinating.
3. My uncle designed the props for the play by Ibsen.
4. Her masterpiece is a book with three parts.
5. A trellis near the door supported the climbing vines.
6. We painted the ceilings throughout the house and shampooed the carpeting on the stairs and floors.
7. Bring me the wagon beside the door of the barn.
8. A rendezvous at the outdoor cafe was canceled.
9. Some of the students in the class showed interest in mechanical drawing.
10. The Danish ballet dancers made a favorable impression upon the audience.

Adverb Phrases

A prepositional phrase can also act as an adverb.

An adverb phrase is a prepositional phrase that modifies a verb, adjective, or adverb by pointing out where, when, in what manner, or to what extent.

The following chart shows that adverb phrases function in a manner similar to single-word adverbs.

Adverbs	Adverb Phrases
She ran *swiftly.*	She ran *with speed.*
They were happy *there.*	They were happy *at the picnic.*

If a prepositional phrase is an adverb phrase, it will answer one of the adverb questions: *Where? When? In what manner?* or *To what extent?* In the first example on the right in the chart, the question *Ran in what manner?* is answered by *with speed,* an adverb phrase.

Unlike an adjective phrase, which almost always follows the word it modifies, an adverb phrase may either follow the word it modifies or be located elsewhere in the sentence.

EXAMPLES: The village vanished *during the avalanche.*

During the avalanche the village vanished.

Like single-word adverbs, adverb phrases can modify either verbs, adjectives, or adverbs.

MODIFYING A VERB: The runner dashed *past the spectators.*

MODIFYING AN ADJECTIVE: The forest was quiet *before dawn.*

MODIFYING AN ADVERB: He arrived late *for class.*

Like adjective phrases, two or more adverb phrases may modify the same word.

EXAMPLE: *In the evening* we walked *to the movies.*

EXERCISE B: Identifying Adverb Phrases. Write each sentence, underlining the adverb phrase or adverb phrases in each. Then draw an arrow from each phrase to the word it modifies.

EXAMPLE: He quietly rapped upon the door.

1. The Pied Piper lured the children from the village.
2. Calcium is essential for strong bones and teeth.
3. The crab was fairly safe inside its skeleton.
4. After the ceremony the bride left with the groom.
5. The whale died in silent agony on the beach.
6. After the lecture she spoke about her military experience.
7. In a flash the mischievous child plucked all the flowers.
8. During the afternoon the crowd drifted to the shady spots.
9. The editorial is rich in sarcasm.
10. When she worked at the foundry, she rose at dawn.

DEVELOPING WRITING SKILLS: Writing Sentences with Adjective and Adverb Phrases. Use each prepositional phrase in two sentences of your own, first as an adjective phrase, then as an adverb phrase.

EXAMPLE: about trout fishing

I read an article about trout fishing.
I have been thinking about trout fishing all day.

1. on the train
2. before school
3. in the attic
4. in front of the store
5. during the night

Appositives and Appositive Phrases 6.2

Using *appositives* in your writing is an easy way to give additional meaning to nouns and pronouns.

Appositives

The term *appositive* comes from a Latin verb meaning "to put near or next to."

An appositive is a noun or pronoun placed next to another noun or pronoun to identify, rename, or explain it.

As the chart on the next page shows, appositives generally follow immediately after words they identify, rename, or explain.

APPOSITIVES
Her greatest attribute, *charm,* was not enough.
Some villagers, the *old-timers,* prefer the dirt roads.

Notice that both the examples in the chart are set off by commas. The punctuation is used because these appositives are *nonessential*. In other words, they could be omitted from the sentences without altering the sentences' basic meaning.

Some appositives, however, are not set off by any punctuation because they are *essential* to the meaning of the sentence.

EXAMPLES: The artist *Van Gogh* cut off his ear.

That scene is from the movie *Star Wars*.

See Section 16.2 for more about punctuating appositives.

NOTE ABOUT TERMS: Sometimes the terms *nonrestrictive* and *restrictive* are used in place of *nonessential* and *essential*.

EXERCISE A: Identifying Appositives. Write the appositive in each sentence. Then write the word each appositive renames.

EXAMPLE: The view, a sunset, was spectacular.

sunset view

1. Edna discussed her favorite topic, food.
2. My cousin Phyllis will spend this summer with us.
3. We thought he would give Cara, a girlfriend, something for Valentine's Day.
4. *Moby Dick* was written by the American writer Herman Melville.
5. Our cat, a Manx, has free run of the house.
6. The poem "Snow Fall" is my favorite.
7. Douglas looks good in his favorite color, blue.
8. We remembered one important item, a flashlight, as we set up camp on the mountainside.
9. She played a woodwind instrument, the clarinet.
10. The inventor Frankenstein created a monster.

Appositive Phrases

When an appositive is accompanied by its own modifiers, it forms an *appositive phrase.*

An appositive phrase is a noun or pronoun with modifiers, placed next to a noun or pronoun to add information and details.

The modifiers within an appositive phrase can be adjectives, adjective phrases, or other groups of words functioning as adjectives.

APPOSITIVE PHRASES
Amethyst, *a purple birthstone,* is the gem for February.
Fred explained numismatics, *the hobby of coin collecting.*
The sailor had scurvy, *a disease caused by a lack of vitamin C.*

Appositives and appositive phrases may follow nouns or pronouns used in almost any role within a sentence. The following examples show a few of the positions in which appositives may be found.

WITH A SUBJECT: Ernest Hemingway, *a famous author,* wrote in a terse style.

WITH A DIRECT OBJECT: Eve wore high boots, *the latest fad.*

WITH AN INDIRECT OBJECT: I bought my brother, *a boy of six,* a pet turtle.

WITH AN OBJECTIVE COMPLEMENT: I chose the color purple, *an unusual color for a house.*

WITH A PREDICATE NOMINATIVE: A porcupine's best defense is its quills—*sharp, barbed spines.*

WITH THE OBJECT OF A PREPOSITION: We store onions, potatoes, carrots, and apples in the cellar, *a cool, dry room.*

Appositives and appositive phrases may also be compound. In the following, notice that the compound parts of the appositives are joined by the conjunctions *and* and *both . . . and.*

EXAMPLES: We visited two Hawaiian islands: *Oahu* and *Maui.*

Armand, both *his schoolmate* and *his confidant,* was always welcome in the house.

When appositives or appositive phrases are used to combine sentences, they help to eliminate unnecessary words. The following examples show how two sentences may be joined.

TWO SENTENCES: Jules Verne wrote about submarines before they were invented. He was a remarkable man.

COMBINED: Jules Verne, *a remarkable man,* wrote about submarines before they were invented.

TWO SENTENCES: Vermont is a state with breathtaking scenery. It has brilliant foliage in the fall.

COMBINED: Vermont, *a state with breathtaking scenery,* has brilliant foliage in the fall.

NOTE ABOUT APPOSITIVE PHRASES WITH *NOT:* Sometimes an appositive phrase may begin with the word *not.* Its effect is to set up a sharp contrast.

EXAMPLE: He spoke of the good old days, *not the bad old days.*

EXERCISE B: Identifying Appositive Phrases. Write the appositive phrase in each sentence, including all parts of any compound appositive phrases. Then write the word each appositive phrase renames.

EXAMPLE: The dogs, an old hound and a tiny poodle, were very friendly.

an old hound a tiny poodle dogs

1. Tammy learned a new safety measure, a technique for saving people from choking.
2. The bobcat, an endangered species, has been hunted as a pest in the East.

3. At the circus the clown rode a dromedary, a one-humped camel, rapidly around the ring.
4. He was proud of owning his first car, an old jalopy.
5. She named Don Jones chairman, a well-deserved title.
6. I will tell you, my good friend, an intriguing story.
7. Herb will read anything: old matchbooks, junk mail, or the backs of cereal boxes.
8. Marsha gave the baby two stuffed animals: a white, woolly lamb and a huggable teddy bear.
9. My family took our guests to a French restaurant, one of the best places in the city.
10. Bill excelled in two outdoor sports, cross-country skiing and ice hockey.

DEVELOPING WRITING SKILLS: Using Appositives and Appositive Phrases to Combine Sentences. Turn each pair of sentences into a single sentence with an appositive or appositive phrase.

EXAMPLE: They lived in India. India is a huge country.

They lived in India, a huge country.

1. The ostrich is a native of Africa and parts of Asia. The ostrich is the largest of all birds.
2. Mrs. Gordon always kept a melodeon in her parlor. Her parlor was a room for special guests.
3. The restaurant serves lobster in a delicious Newburg sauce. Newburg sauce is a creamy sauce with butter and wine.
4. Marjorie is one of the most interesting people I know. She is a gourmet, an expert ventriloquist, and a very good poet.
5. Donny's father is a neurologist. He is a specialist on the nervous system.

Participles and Participial Phrases 6.3

When a verb is used as a noun, adjective, or adverb, it is called a *verbal*. Although a verbal does not function as a verb, it still retains two characteristics of verbs. It can be modified in different ways and it can have one or more complements. A verbal with modifiers or a complement is a *verbal phrase*.

This section will explain the kind of verbal that functions as an adjective—the *participle*.

Participles

Many of the adjectives you use are actually verbals known as *participles*.

A participle is a form of a verb that can act as an adjective.

There are two kinds of participles: *present participles* and *past participles*. These two kinds of participles can be distinguished from each other by their endings. Present participles end in *-ing (frightening, entertaining)*. Past participles usually end in *-ed (frightened, entertained),* but many have irregular endings such as *-t* or *-en (burst, written)*. (See Section 10.1 for more information on irregular verb endings.)

The following chart shows participles modifying nouns within sentences.

Present Participles	Past Participles
Limping, the hiker favored his *aching* ankle.	*Confused,* Nan returned to her *interrupted* work.

Notice that participles answer the adjective questions *What kind?* or *Which one?* about the nouns or pronouns that they modify.

EXAMPLES: Irma's *shining* eyes betrayed her excitement.
(*What kind* of eyes? *Answer: shining* eyes)

The *shattered* window needs replacement.
(*Which* window? *Answer:* the *shattered* window)

NOTE ABOUT *BEING* AND *HAVING:* The present participles *being* and *having* may be followed by a past participle.

EXAMPLES: *Being informed,* I knew what to expect.

Having decided, Adele acted quickly.

EXERCISE A: Identifying Present and Past Participles. Write the participle in each sentence. Then label each as *present* or *past*.

EXAMPLE: The returning players had a story to tell.
returning (present)

1. Mrs. Jefferson's fractured hip is very painful.
2. A fluttering white flag appeared in the distance.
3. Water surged over the banks of the swollen river.
4. This arsonist has an established pattern for fires.
5. Drizzling rain kept us all in the house.
6. We sat and listened to the pounding waves and the cry of seagulls.
7. The handyman left splattered paint all over the floor.
8. Lisping, the child told us about the Tooth Fairy.
9. During the storm a broken branch fell onto the roof of our house.
10. Disgusted, his mother glowered at the mess.

Verb or Participle?

It is easy to confuse a verb and a participle acting as an adjective since they often share the endings *-ing* and *-ed*.

A verb shows an action, a condition, or the fact that something exists. A participle acting as an adjective modifies a noun or a pronoun.

The following chart shows words used first as verbs and then as participles. Notice that as verbs the words tell what someone or something does or did. As participles, however, the same words describe someone or something.

Verbs	Participles
The dog is *snarling* at the plumber. (What is the dog *doing*?)	The *snarling* dog attacked the plumber. (*Which* dog?)
The singers *delighted* their audience. (What did the singers *do*?)	*Delighted*, the audience applauded. (*What kind* of audience?)

EXERCISE B: Distinguishing Between Verbs and Participles. Identify each underlined word as a *verb* or *participle*. If the word is a participle, also write the word it modifies.

EXAMPLE: The 1984 Olympics added an exciting new event.
participle event

(1) In the Los Angeles Memorial Coliseum, 77,000 people waited. (2) Through the streets tired runners raced toward the Coliseum. (3) The cheering crowd rose as Joan Benoit, a member of the U.S. Olympic team, entered. (4) She ran around the track easily and crossed the finish line. (5) Smiling, Joan waved to the spectators as they cheered her. (6) About four months before the race, Joan underwent surgery on her right knee. (7) Training, she had wondered whether or not she would be able to compete. (8) When the race was over, Joan learned that she had run the third-fastest marathon ever run by a woman. (9) She ran the 26 miles and 385 yards of the exhausting race in 2 hours, 24 minutes, and 52 seconds. (10) Pleased, Joan accepted her gold medal as the winner of the first women's marathon in Olympic history.

Participial Phrases

Participles may be part of *participial phrases*.

A participial phrase is a participle modified by an adverb or adverb phrase or accompanied by a complement. The entire phrase acts as an adjective.

The following examples show different ways that participles may be expanded into phrases.

EXAMPLES: *Jumping high,* Brad hit his head on the ceiling.

The chemist, *blinded by smoky fumes,* stumbled.

Scanning the book, Ann spotted the answer.

In the first sentence above, an adverb modifies the participle *jumping*. In the second sentence, an adverb phrase modifies *blinded*. In the third sentence, *scanning* has a direct object.

Participial phrases are punctuated according to their use within a sentence. The following chart contrasts nonessential and essential participial phrases. In the sentences on the left, the participial phrases could be removed without altering the sentences' basic meaning. However, if you remove the participial phrases from the sentences on the right, the sentences' meaning will not be the same.

Nonessential Phrases	Essential Phrases
There is Craig, *standing by the bus stop*.	The boy *standing by the bus stop* is Craig.
Painted in 1497, the mural is Leonardo's masterpiece.	The mural *painted in 1497* is almost beyond repair.

In the first sentence on the left in the chart, *standing by the bus stop* merely adds information about *Craig,* who has already been identified. In a similar sentence on the right, however, the same phrase is essential for the identification of *boy* since there could be many different boys in view. In the second sentence on the left, *painted in 1497* is an additional description of *mural*. In the sentence on the right, the phrase is essential. It identifies the mural that is being discussed. (See Section 16.2 for more about punctuating participial phrases.)

Participial phrases can often be used to combine information from two sentences into one.

TWO SENTENCES: We were exhausted by the climb. We rested by the side of the trail.

COMBINED: Exhausted by the climb, we rested by the side of the trail.

EXERCISE C: Recognizing Participial Phrases. Write the participial phrase in each sentence. Then, write the word the participial phrase modifies. Finally, label the phrase as *nonessential* or *essential*.

EXAMPLE: The box wrapped in orange is for you.
wrapped in orange box (essential)

1. Andrea, waking from a dream, cried fearfully.
2. Slumped over a chair, I could think only of sleep.
3. The boat, making large waves, overturned our canoe.
4. She picked up debris thrown by a careless motorist.
5. Feeling jaunty in his borrowed tuxedo, Barney sauntered into the room.
6. We stared at the horizon, broken only by sails.
7. As Zack fell, he grabbed a branch jutting out from the cliff.
8. Shivering in anticipation, I could hardly wait for the conclusion to Poe's "The Pit and the Pendulum."
9. She ordered a plate piled high with flapjacks.
10. She saw in the mirror a face streaked with tears.

Nominative Absolutes

Sometimes, the noun or pronoun modified by a participle or participial phrase belongs neither to the complete subject nor to the complete predicate of the sentence. Such constructions are called *nominative absolutes*.

A nominative absolute is a noun or pronoun followed by a participle or participial phrase that functions independently of the rest of the sentence.

Although a nominative absolute is grammatically separate from the rest of the sentence, it is still closely related because it indicates time, reason, or circumstance for the rest of the sentence.

TIME: *Three hours having passed,* we could wait no longer.

REASON: *His task completed,* Andy asked for payment.

CIRCUMSTANCE: The car stopped, *its tires sinking quickly.*

NOTE ABOUT *BEING:* Sometimes, the participle *being* is left out of the nominative absolute. In the following example, *being* is added in brackets.

EXAMPLE: Lenny was caught in the act, *his hand* [*being*] *in the cookie jar.*

EXERCISE D: Recognizing Nominative Absolutes. Write the nominative absolute in each sentence.

EXAMPLE: The play having ended, we left.
The play having ended

1. Her smile vanishing from her face, Julia listened in stunned silence.
2. Six huskies pulled the sled, its runners skimming over the ice.
3. The furnace broken, we huddled under blankets throughout the cold night.
4. Several minutes having gone by, the bank teller finally pushed the alarm button.
5. Roger carefully whittled a stick, his dog Briar lying at his feet.
6. A bonnet tied around her head, Lisa resembled a Puritan woman.
7. Candles and flowers on every table, the room looked inviting.
8. Several delays being unavoidable, our guests finally departed.
9. Midnight striking, she hurried down the steps toward her carriage.
10. His glasses at home, Mr. Owens squinted at the paper with bleary eyes.

DEVELOPING WRITING SKILLS: Writing Sentences with Participial Phrases. Use the following instructions to write five sentences with participial phrases.

1. Use *tell* as a present participle.
2. Use *cook* as a past participle.
3. Use *toss* as a past participle.
4. Use *work* as a present participle.
5. Use *having left* in a nominative absolute.

Gerunds and Gerund Phrases 6.4

Many nouns ending in *-ing* are actually verbals known as *gerunds*.

Gerunds

Gerunds are not difficult to recognize once you realize that they always end in *-ing* and always function as nouns.

A gerund is a form of a verb that acts as a noun.

The following examples show some of the ways gerunds may be used just as nouns would be.

GERUNDS
Subject: *Sailing* is my favorite sport.
Direct object: They make *visiting* a pleasure.
Indirect object: Mr. Mendoza's lecture gave *traveling* a new dimension.
Predicate nominative: Walter's most annoying habit is *interrupting*.
Object of a preposition: Their well-behaved dog showed signs of *training*.
Appositive: Brady's profession, *advertising*, is very competitive.

EXERCISE A: Identifying Gerunds. Write the gerund in each sentence. Label each one as a *subject, direct object, indirect object, predicate nominative, object of a preposition,* or *appositive*.

EXAMPLE: She gave skiing her best effort.
skiing (indirect object)

1. Gardening can be enjoyable and profitable.
2. The school offered classes in weaving.
3. To arrive on time for his appointment, Fred started running.
4. The man's crime was counterfeiting.
5. Milking was one of Wilbur's chores.
6. Denise's hobby, sky-diving, is a thrilling one.
7. Esther's favorite occupation, eavesdropping, can be most unpleasant.
8. My father enjoys the art of fencing.
9. Jogging can be very satisfying.
10. With this machine, vacuuming seems easy.

Verb, Participle, or Gerund?

Words ending in *-ing* may be either verbs, participles, or gerunds.

Words ending in *-ing* that act as nouns are gerunds. They do not have helping verbs as verbs ending in *-ing* do nor do they act as adjectives as participles do.

The following chart shows the same word functioning in sentences as a verb, a participle, and a gerund.

Verb	Participle	Gerund
Kevin is *yawning* at his desk.	The *yawning* boy was very tired.	*Yawning* is contagious.

EXERCISE B: Distinguishing Between Verbs, Participles, and Gerunds. Identify each underlined word as a *verb, participle,* or *gerund.*

EXAMPLE: They are *quitting* early today.
verb

1. Do we have any wrapping paper left?
2. The detective was wrapping up the case.
3. Wrapping the gifts took longer than expected.
4. Ann must have been dreaming about her future.
5. The dreaming boy stared absently out the window.
6. Rarely do I remember dreaming.
7. Many athletes use running as a means of exercise.
8. Our summer cabin has running water in the kitchen.
9. Shopping can become tiresome after a few hours.
10. Lou is shopping for a new trenchcoat.

Gerund Phrases

Like participles, gerunds may be joined by other words to make *gerund phrases*.

A gerund phrase is a gerund with modifiers or a complement, all acting together as a noun.

The following examples show just a few of the ways that gerunds may be expanded into gerund phrases.

GERUND PHRASES
With adjectives: *His constant, angry frowning* made wrinkles in his face.
With an adjective phrase: *Arguing about grades* will get you nowhere.
With an adverb: *Answering quickly* is not always a good idea.
With an adverb phrase: The park prohibits *walking on the grass*.
With a direct object: Russell was incapable of *recovering the ball*.
With indirect and direct objects: Mrs. Jeffries tries *giving them praise*.

NOTE ABOUT GERUNDS AND POSSESSIVE PRONOUNS: You should always use the possessive form of a personal pronoun in front of a gerund.

INCORRECT: We never listen to *him boasting*.

CORRECT: We never listen to *his boasting*.

EXERCISE C: Identifying Gerund Phrases. Write the gerund phrase or gerund phrases in each sentence. Label each one as a *subject, direct object, predicate nominative, object of a preposition,* or *appositive*.

EXAMPLE: Swimming before dawn was forbidden.
Swimming before dawn (subject)

1. She is good at remembering trivia.
2. The most amusing event, catching a greased pig, was the highlight of the fair.
3. As a child, his household tasks were setting the table before dinner and washing the dishes afterwards.
4. Caring for pets is a good way of earning money.
5. During the summer Hal taught deep-sea diving and horseback riding.

6. Drying fruits and vegetables for winter use is good for cutting down expenses.
7. Morris's worst habits are complaining about everyone's faults and worrying unceasingly.
8. After the football game was over, we enjoyed trading stories.
9. To me, summer, fall, and winter are just times for mowing grass, raking leaves, and shoveling snow.
10. Hoarding money under the mattress is not the best way to beat inflation.

DEVELOPING WRITING SKILLS: Writing Sentences with Gerund Phrases. Use the following instructions to write five sentences with gerund phrases. Then, underline the gerund phrase in each.

1. Use *cooking* as a direct object.
2. Use *preparing* as a predicate nominative.
3. Use *explaining* as the object of a preposition.
4. Use *traveling* as a subject.
5. Use *directing* as a predicate nominative.

Infinitives and Infinitive Phrases 6.5

This section will present the third and last kind of verbal, the *infinitive*.

Infinitives

Infinitives can function in sentences as nouns, as adjectives, or as adverbs.

An infinitive is a form of a verb that generally appears with the word *to* and acts as a noun, adjective, or adverb.

The chart at the top of the next page shows examples of infinitives acting as nouns. When infinitives function as nouns in sentences, they can be used in almost as many ways as gerunds.

INFINITIVES USED AS NOUNS

Subject: *To understand* required maturity and acceptance.

Direct object: Working hard at her new job, Brenda hoped *to succeed*.

Predicate nominative: The hunter's only defense against the bear was *to run*.

Object of a preposition: With his muscles tensed, the inexperienced parachuter was about *to jump*.

Appositive: You have only one choice, *to go*.

Unlike gerunds, infinitives can also act as adjectives and adverbs.

INFINITIVES USED AS MODIFIERS

Adjective: The children showed a willingness *to cooperate*.

Adverb: They struggled *to resist*.

Some people are unable *to adjust*.

EXERCISE A: Identifying Infinitives. Write the infinitive in each sentence. Then, label each as a *subject, direct object, predicate nominative, object of a preposition, appositive, adjective,* or *adverb*.

EXAMPLE: Her goal is to sing.
to sing (predicate nominative)

1. To fantasize was his only way out of a dreary life.
2. We were reluctant to leave.
3. Worried by my decision, I decided to reconsider.
4. Seth had only one alternative, to flee.
5. The teacher assigned us too many pages to read.
6. Our best tactic is to watch.
7. To build was the architect's fondest dream.
8. To escape, the cat clawed at the top of the box.
9. Hated by the people, the king was about to abdicate.
10. They produced one of the first airplanes to fly.

Prepositional Phrase or Infinitive?

The difference between a preposition and an infinitive is easy to recognize once you are aware of it.

A prepositional phrase always ends with a noun or pronoun. An infinitive always ends with a verb.

Notice the difference between the prepositional phrase and the infinitive in the following chart.

Prepositional Phrase	Infinitive
The soldier listened *to the command.*	A general's purpose in the army is *to command.*

EXERCISE B: Distinguishing Between Prepositional Phrases and Infinitives. Write the infinitive or the prepositional phrase beginning with *to* in each sentence. Then label each as a *prepositional phrase* or *infinitive.*

EXAMPLE: When I am in New York, I like to shop.
to shop (infinitive)

1. At the outdoor market, my grandmother likes to bargain.
2. Would you try to explain?
3. Give an explanation to Glenn.
4. To believe took considerable faith.
5. Lindsey wrote letters to friends.
6. After working so hard, he wanted to rest.
7. Our trip to China was filled with surprises.
8. Baxter's gift to me was too extravagant.
9. When do you plan to graduate?
10. On Vicky's way to town, she had a flat tire.

Infinitive Phrases

Infinitives also can be joined with other words to form phrases.

An infinitive phrase is an infinitive with modifiers, complements, or a subject, all acting together as a single part of speech.

The following examples show just a few of the ways infinitives can be expanded into phrases.

INFINITIVE PHRASES	
With an adverb:	Jeffrey's entire family likes *to rise early*.
With adverb phrases:	*To skate on the ice without falling* was not easy for him.
With a direct object:	He hated *to discuss emotions*.
With indirect and direct objects:	They promised *to show us their slides*.
With subject and complement:	I would like *her to determine her own goals*

NOTE ABOUT INFINITIVES WITHOUT *TO*: Sometimes infinitives do not include the word *to*. When an infinitive follows one of the eight verbs listed here, the *to* is generally omitted.

dare	help	make	see
hear	let	please	watch

EXAMPLES: She doesn't dare *go* without permission.

They heard the canary *sing* its song.

Let's *be* on our way.

EXERCISE C: Identifying Infinitive Phrases. Write the infinitive phrase or infinitive phrases in each sentence. Label each one as a *subject, direct object, predicate nominative, object of a preposition, appositive, adjective,* or *adverb*.

EXAMPLE: I have an assignment to finish before tomorrow.

to finish before tomorrow (adjective)

1. To describe the hockey game in an understandable manner required gestures.
2. The birdwatcher's ambition was to see one hundred different species during one weekend.
3. My friends and I went to see the exhibit on Indian art and to gather material for our reports.
4. Huck and Tom swore to keep the secret about Injun Joe.

5. To inhale these fumes is to die instantly.
6. With no money to pay our bill, we had no choice except to wash dishes.
7. To heed his warning was to be prepared for anything.
8. Ray hopes to become a veterinarian.
9. They made plans to meet on Friday night.
10. Since we were about to sink in the leaky boat, the only answer was to bail it out.

DEVELOPING WRITING SKILLS: Writing Sentences with Infinitive Phrases. Use the following instructions to write ten sentences with infinitive phrases. Then underline the infinitive phrase in each.

1. Use *to erase* as a subject.
2. Use *to draw* as a predicate nominative.
3. Use *to read* as an adjective.
4. Use *to show* as a direct object.
5. Use *to begin* as the object of a preposition.
6. Use *to work* as an adverb.
7. Use *to wander* as a subject.
8. Use *to mail* as a direct object.
9. Use *to fly* as an appositive.
10. Use *to assist* as a direct object.

Diagraming Phrases 6.6

In this section you will see how prepositional phrases, appositives, appositive phrases, verbals, and verbal phrases are diagramed. Keep in mind that phrases are never diagramed on a single straight horizontal or vertical line.

Prepositional Phrases

The diagram for a prepositional phrase has a slanted line for the preposition and a horizontal line for the object of the preposition. Modifiers are placed on slanted lines below the horizontal line. Adjective phrases are placed directly below the noun or pronoun they modify. Adverb phrases are placed directly below the verb, adjective, or adverb they modify.

EXAMPLE: The child *with the red ball* skipped *up the hill.* (PREP PHRASE: *with the red ball*; PREP PHRASE: *up the hill*)

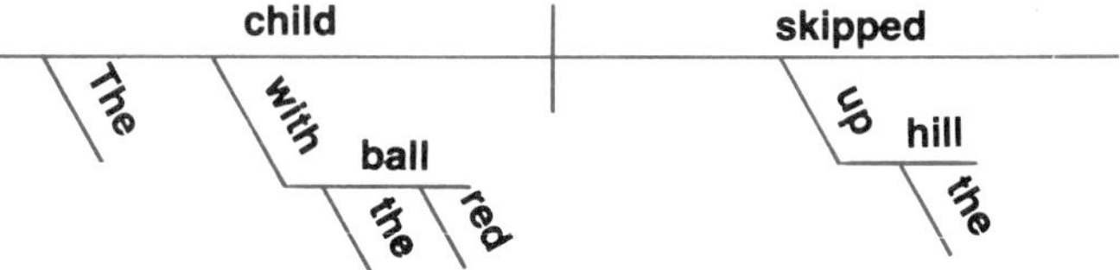

An adjective phrase that modifies the object of the preposition of another prepositional phrase goes below the other phrase as shown in the first diagram below. When an adverb phrase modifies an adverb or an adjective, the diagram for the adverb phrase changes slightly, as shown in the second example below.

EXAMPLES: I had salad *with pineapple in it.* (PREP PHRASE: *with pineapple*; PREP PHRASE: *in it*)

We arrived yesterday *after midnight.* (ADV: yesterday; PREP PHRASE: *after midnight*)

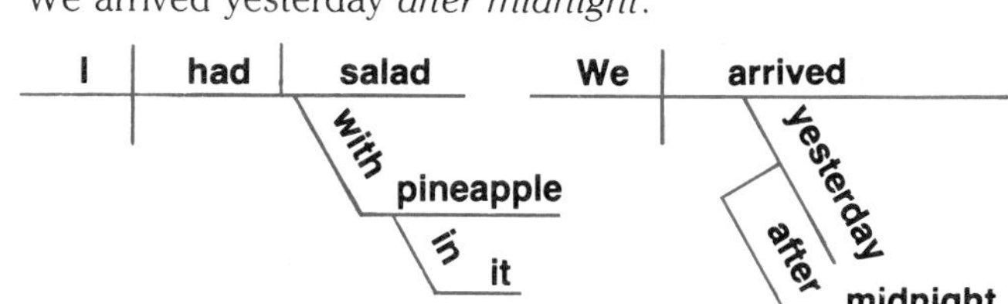

A prepositional phrase with a compound object is diagramed in the same way as the other compound parts of a sentence. The following example shows an adjective phrase that modifies a direct object.

EXAMPLE: We need a house *with three bedrooms and a den.* (PREP PHRASE: *with three bedrooms and a den*)

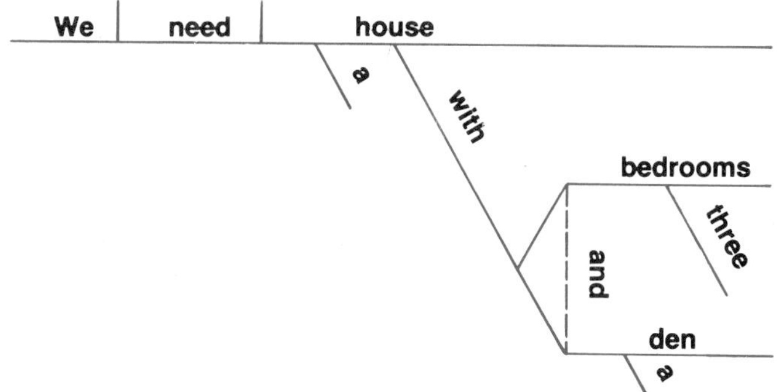

EXERCISE A: Diagraming Prepositional Phrases. Correctly diagram each sentence.

1. They flew in a private airplane across the Rockies.
2. Water trickled down Mark's neck.
3. Select a detergent for clothing with greasy stains and ground-in dirt.
4. Without much hope, Becky argued for more time.
5. Corina lives in an apartment with a balcony.

Appositives and Appositive Phrases

An appositive is placed in parentheses beside the noun or pronoun it identifies, renames, or explains. Any adjectives or adjective phrases included in an appositive phrase are placed directly beneath the appositive.

APPOSITIVE PHRASE

EXAMPLE: Harriet Danby, *her friend for many years,* is a lawyer.

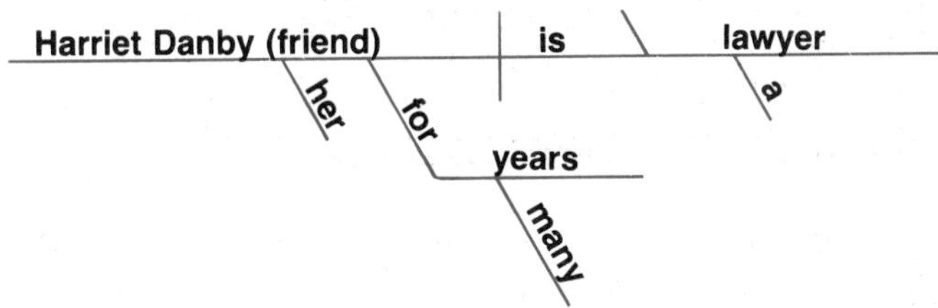

EXERCISE B: Diagraming Appositives and Appositive Phrases. Correctly diagram each sentence.

1. Gladys was a pianist, a very talented performer.
2. I know the author of that book, one of the top bestsellers.
3. The rat, a rodent, has one pair of upper incisors.
4. Mario prepared the meal, a lavish feast with six courses.
5. Their staircase, a spiral flight of steps, connects the two floors.

Participles and Participial Phrases

Since participles act as adjectives, they are placed directly beneath the noun or pronoun they modify. Unlike adjectives, however, participles are positioned partly on a slanted line and partly on a horizontal line that extends from the slanted line. An adverb or adverb phrase that modifies a participle is placed below it. When a participle has a complement, the complement is also placed in its normal position, on the horizontal line with the participle, separated from the participle by a short vertical line.

PARTICIPIAL PHRASE
EXAMPLE: *Carefully reviewing books for children,* Russell stays busy.

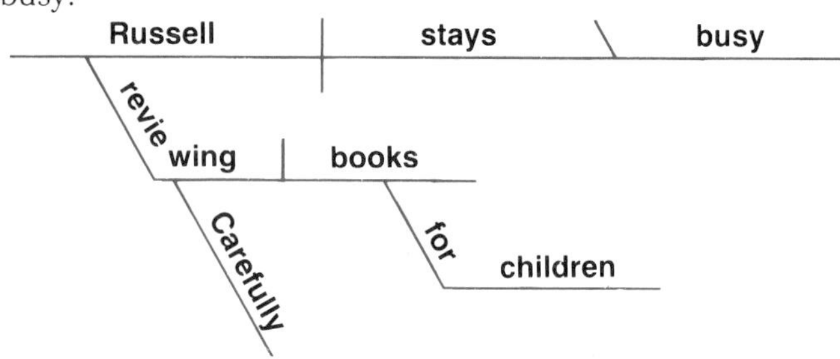

A nominative absolute is diagramed in the same way an expletive is.

NOMINATIVE ABSOLUTE
EXAMPLE: *His speech finished,* everyone applauded.

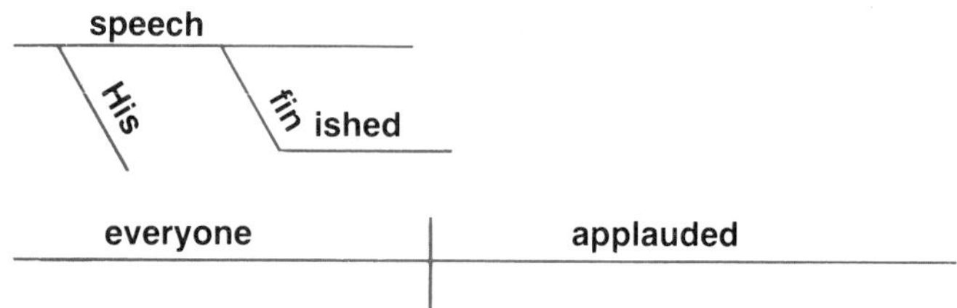

EXERCISE C: Diagraming Participles and Participial Phrases. Correctly diagram each sentence.

1. He held a basket brimming with goodies.
2. The small town destroyed, many volunteers worked into the night.
3. This deserted island offers peace and tranquillity.
4. From the beehive came a loud buzzing noise.
5. Its engine stalled, the car caused a traffic jam.

Gerunds and Gerund Phrases

Since all gerunds function as nouns, they can be subjects, complements, objects of prepositions, or appositives. A gerund that acts as a subject, direct object, or predicate nominative is diagramed on a pedestal above the main horizontal line of the diagram. Modifiers and complements that are part of a gerund phrase are added to the diagram in the usual way. Notice the shape of the line on which the gerund rests.

GERUND PHRASE

EXAMPLE: The lease forbids *keeping any pets on the premises.*

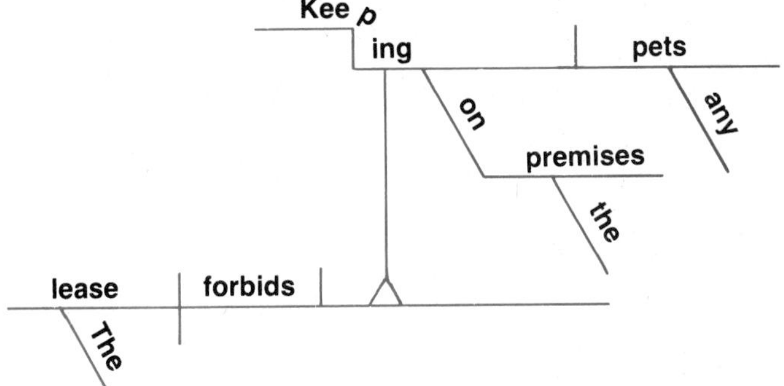

A gerund or gerund phrase that acts as an indirect object or an object of a preposition is placed on a line slanting down from the main horizontal line.

GERUND PHRASE

EXAMPLE: His lecture gave *traveling to South America* new dimensions.

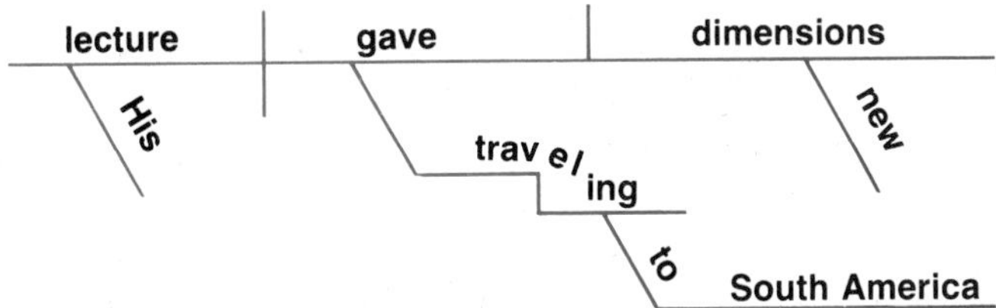

A gerund or gerund phrase that acts as an appositive is placed on a pedestal, in parentheses, next to the noun or pronoun it accompanies. The example at the top of the next page shows a diagram containing an appositive modifying a direct object.

GERUND PHRASE
EXAMPLE: We mastered one sport, *playing tennis.*

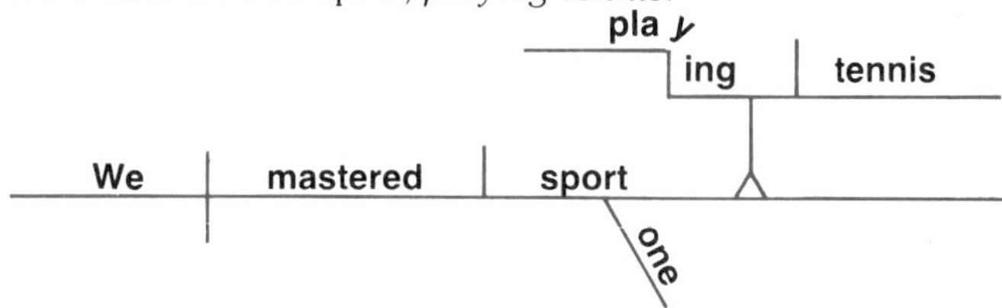

EXERCISE D: Diagraming Gerunds and Gerund Phrases. Correctly diagram each sentence.

1. His favorite activity was hiking through the woods.
2. Achieving the position of senator will be very difficult.
3. Their immoral values gave stealing respectability.
4. Clark's fear, injuring his elbow, kept him on the bench.
5. All of Jill's friends like helping her with her projects.

Infinitives and Infinitive Phrases

Infinitives and infinitive phrases can act as nouns, adjectives, or adverbs. An infinitive acting as a noun is generally diagramed on a pedestal just as a gerund is, but the line on which the infinitive rests is simpler.

INFINITIVE PHRASE
EXAMPLE: She wanted *to show us her stamp collection.*

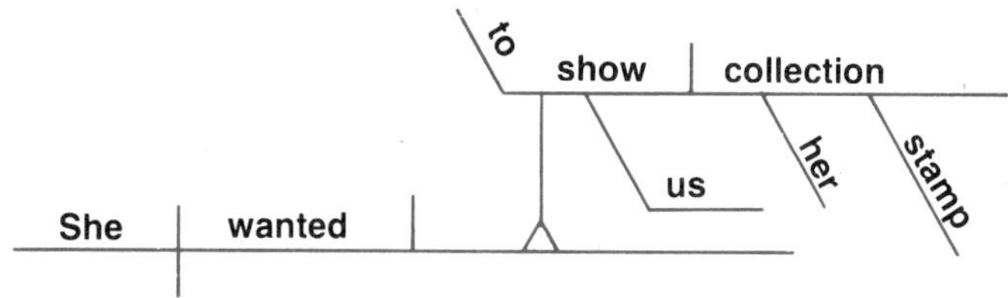

If an infinitive phrase has a subject, add it at the left.

INFINITIVE PHRASE
EXAMPLE: We asked *her to stay.*

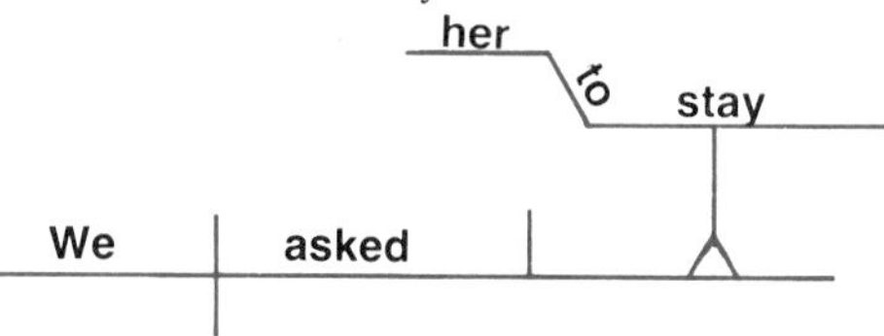

An infinitive acting as an adjective or adverb is diagramed much as a prepositional phrase is.

INFINITIVE
EXAMPLE: Beth was proud *to try.*

Beth | was \ proud
to try

When an infinitive in a sentence does not include the word *to,* add it to the sentence diagram in parentheses.

INFINITIVE PHRASE
EXAMPLE: Clancy helped *me climb the ladder to the attic.*

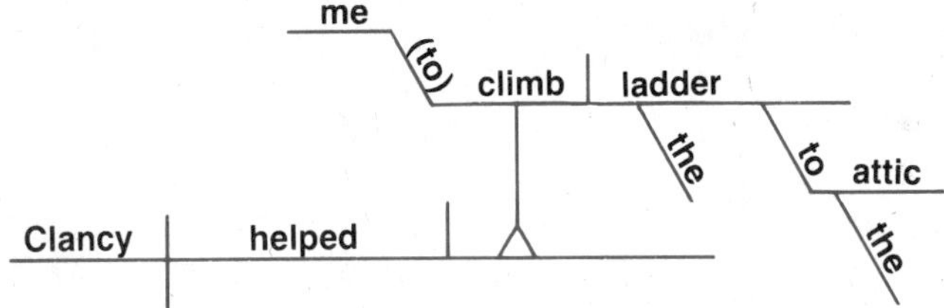

EXERCISE E: Diagraming Infinitives and Infinitive Phrases. Correctly diagram each sentence.

1. Gordon's greatest accomplishment was to write a novel about etiquette during the sixteenth century.
2. Her mother let Susan go to the movies.
3. To focus on just one problem would be advisable.
4. Her inclination was to tell him the truth about his idea.
5. The person to see about tickets has left.

DEVELOPING WRITING SKILLS: Writing and Diagraming Sentences with Phrases. Use the following instructions to write five sentences of your own. Then correctly diagram each sentence.

EXAMPLE: Write a sentence that includes an adjective phrase.

The jacket with the fur collar is my favorite.

1. Write a sentence that includes an adverb phrase.
2. Write a sentence that includes an appositive.
3. Write a sentence that includes a participial phrase.
4. Write a sentence that includes a gerund phrase.
5. Write a sentence that includes an infinitive.

Skills Review and Writing Workshop

Phrases

CHECKING YOUR SKILLS

Identify each underlined phrase as *prepositional*, *appositive*, *participial*, *nominative absolute*, *gerund*, or *infinitive*.

(1) Early motorists had to deal not only with unreliable machines, but also with some amazing laws. (2) Being informed, they knew what to expect. (3) As early as 1895 the city of Chicago had a regulation banning automobiles on public streets. (4) In those days policemen were on foot or rode bicycles. (5) One law required a motorist to stop his car and fire a Roman candle when a horse-drawn vehicle approached. (6) Around 1905 a bill requiring cars to ring a bell for each wheel revolution was passed. (7) Fortunately for all concerned the idea found few backers. (8) Driving an automobile was difficult enough without worrying about absurd laws. (9) Early roads being muddy ruts, drivers often became stuck. (10) To travel anywhere by automobile was difficult.

USING GRAMMAR SKILLS IN WRITING

Writing a Review

The more complicated your subject, the more grammar you need to understand. Writing a review of a record album is complicated because you must discuss many elements. Follow the steps below to write a review of an album.

Prewriting: What elements do you want to discuss: style, lyrics, sound? Try to limit your choice of elements, so you can be specific about those you choose to discuss.

Writing: You may want to quote from a review of the group's last album or single. That review might be used to substantiate your evaluation of the album under discussion.

Revising: Make your writing vivid enough to interest or to discourage a prospective buyer. After you have revised, proofread carefully.

Chapter 7

Clauses

Chapter 6 shows how a phrase functions within a sentence. Chapter 7 presents a similar but more complex structure called a *clause*.

A clause is a group of words with its own subject and verb.

The two basic kinds of clauses are the *independent clause* and the *subordinate clause*.

An independent clause can stand by itself as a complete sentence.

Independent clauses are used in several different ways. *That girl teaches sign language* is an example of an independent clause standing alone. *Mud slides will engulf these hillside homes, and some will be ruined* is an example of one independent clause added to another. *Brian asked to be excused from class because he was ill* is an example of an independent clause followed by a subordinate clause. Each of the independent clauses that you have read could be written by itself as a complete sentence.

The basic difference between a subordinate clause and an independent clause is that a subordinate clause, even though it also has a subject and a verb, does not express a complete thought. Therefore, a subordinate clause cannot stand alone as a sentence. A subordinate clause must be part of a sentence that contains at least one independent clause if it is to express its meaning.

A subordinate clause, although it has a subject and verb, cannot stand by itself as a complete sentence; it can only be part of a sentence.

The girl to whom I introduced you teaches sign language contains a subordinate clause *to whom I introduced you* that appears in the middle of an independent clause. *Unless the rain stops soon, mud slides will engulf these hillside homes* contains a subordinate clause *unless the rain stops soon* followed by an independent clause. *Brian asked that he be excused* contains a subordinate clause *that he be excused* that follows an independent clause. No matter where a subordinate clause appears, remember that it must always be attached to an independent clause.

Like phrases, subordinate clauses can function as adjectives, adverbs, and nouns in sentences. The following sections will discuss clauses and how they can help you improve your writing.

7.1 Adjective Clauses

One way to add description and detail to a sentence is by using an *adjective clause*.

An adjective clause is a subordinate clause that modifies a noun or pronoun by telling what kind or which one.

The Adjective Clause

Most often *adjective clauses* begin with one of the relative pronouns: *that, which, who, whom,* or *whose*. (See Section 1.2 for a review of relative pronouns.) Sometimes, however, adjective clauses may begin with a *relative adverb,* such as *before, since, when, where,* or *why*. All of these words relate the clause to the word it modifies.

Adjective clauses begin with relative pronouns or relative adverbs.

In the chart on the next page, the adjective clauses are italicized. Arrows indicate the noun or pronoun modified by each clause. These are adjective clauses because they answer the questions *What kind?* and *Which one?* Notice also that the first three clauses begin with relative pronouns, the last two with relative adverbs.

ADJECTIVE CLAUSES

Anyone *who remains calm* will probably be good in an emergency.

I finished reading the book *that you loaned me*.

We gave the stray mutt, *which we found,* a hearty meal.

Spring is the time *when peepers make their shrill evening sound.*

Our trip to Holland ended with a visit to the town *where my parents were born*.

Notice in the chart the different parts of sentences that are modified by adjective clauses. In the first sentence, the subject is modified. In the second and third, a direct object and then an indirect object are modified. In the fourth, a predicate nominative is modified. In the last sentence, the object of a preposition is modified.

Like appositives and participial phrases, adjective clauses can often be used to combine information from two sentences into one. Using adjective clauses to combine sentences can indicate the relationship between ideas as well as add detail to a sentence.

TWO SENTENCES: Thomas Jefferson was the third President of the United States. He wrote the Declaration of Independence.

COMBINED: Thomas Jefferson, who wrote the Declaration of Independence, was the third President of the United States.

Adjective clauses, like appositive and participial phrases, are set off by punctuation only when they are not essential to a sentence's meaning. The chart at the top of the next page contrasts nonessential and essential adjective clauses. In the sentences on the left, omitting the adjective clauses would not change the basic message. However, if you were to take away the adjective clauses on the right, the sentences' message would not be complete. (See Section 16.2 for more about punctuating adjective clauses.)

Nonessential Clauses	Essential Clauses
One of Dickens' best characters is Charles Darnay, *who appears in Dickens' novel about the French Revolution*.	The novel *that everyone must read by Monday afternoon* promises to be very exciting.
Jean McCurdy, *who studied three hours each evening for a month,* won the statewide competition.	A student *who studies regularly* usually finds test-taking easy.

In the sentences on the left, the commas indicate that the clauses give additional information. In the sentences on the right, the lack of commas shows that the clauses are needed to define the words they modify. Read the contrasting sentences aloud. Notice that you naturally pause before and after the nonessential clauses and that your voice drops as you read them. Realizing this should help you recognize clauses in your own writing that need to be set off with commas.

EXERCISE A: Identifying Adjective Clauses and the Words They Modify. Write the adjective clause in each sentence. Then, write the word the adjective clause modifies. Finally, label the clause as *nonessential* or *essential.*

EXAMPLE: James, who plays the flute, joined our band.
who plays the flute James (nonessential)

1. The student whom Mr. Stein chose was first in her class.
2. Is this the year when the planets will align?
3. Henry VIII was a king whose many wives fared badly.
4. It has been years since I visited my aunt in Miami.
5. Our school play, which lasted two hours, was enjoyed by everyone.
6. Books that deal with current events in an exciting way often become bestsellers.
7. My father works in an office where everyone helps each other.
8. People still remember June's last letter, which arrived twenty years ago.
9. The position that Jackie wanted was already filled.
10. The man whose playing you admired is an internationally recognized chess champion.

Introductory Words

Relative pronouns or relative adverbs begin adjective clauses.

Relative Pronouns. *Relative pronouns* function in two ways.

Relative pronouns connect adjective clauses to the words they modify and act as subjects, direct objects, objects of prepositions, or adjectives in the clauses.

To tell how a relative pronoun is used within a clause, separate the clause from the rest of the sentence and find the subject and verb in the clause.

THE USES OF RELATIVE PRONOUNS WITHIN CLAUSES
As a Subject
A house *that is built on a good foundation* is built to last. *Clause:* that is built on a good foundation. *Subject:* that *Verb:* is built *Use of relative pronoun:* subject
As a Direct Object
My brother-in-law, *whom my sister met at college,* is a poet. *Clause:* whom my sister met at college *Reworded clause:* my sister met whom at college *Subject:* sister *Verb:* met *Use of relative pronoun:* direct object
As an Object of a Preposition
This is the book *about which I read enthusiastic reviews.* *Clause:* about which I read enthusiastic reviews. *Reworded clause:* I read enthusiastic reviews about which *Subject:* I *Verb:* read *Use of relative pronoun:* object of a preposition
As an Adjective
The senator *whose opinion was in question* spoke to the press. *Clause:* whose opinion was in question *Subject:* opinion *Verb:* was *Use of relative pronoun:* adjective

NOTE ABOUT UNDERSTOOD WORDS: Sometimes in writing and in speech, a relative pronoun is left out of an adjective clause. The omitted word, though simply understood, still functions in the sentence.

EXAMPLES: The suggestions [*that*] *they made* were ignored.

The legendary heroes [*whom*] *we studied* were great men and women.

Relative Adverbs. Unlike a relative pronoun, a relative adverb has only one use within a clause.

Relative abverbs connect adjective clauses to the words they modify and act as adverbs in the clauses.

The following chart shows an adjective clause introduced by a relative adverb.

THE USE OF RELATIVE ADVERBS WITHIN CLAUSES
Pat yearned for the day *when she could walk without crutches.*
Clause: when she could walk without crutches
Reworded clause: she could walk when without crutches
Subject: she *Verb:* could walk
Use of relative adverb: adverb

EXERCISE B: Recognizing the Uses of Relative Pronouns and Relative Adverbs. Write the adjective clause in each sentence, circling the relative pronoun or relative adverb. Then label the use of the circled word within the clause as *subject, direct object, object of a preposition, adjective,* or *adverb*.

EXAMPLE: Gina, who likes to travel, is a flight attendant.

(who) likes to travel (subject)

1. We look forward to a weekend when we can rest.
2. A sales representative whose approach is too insistent may anger potential customers.
3. The person with whom you spoke is my father.
4. In the time since Maria returned, she has talked only about her trip.

5. My friend whom you admired liked you also.
6. The play featured too many actors who had not learned their lines.
7. In the centuries before the car was invented, people relied on horses for transportation.
8. An historian who knows the facts can compare the past with the probable future.
9. Physics is a subject about which I know nothing.
10. The first person on the moon walked on land where no one had ever walked before.

DEVELOPING WRITING SKILLS: Using Adjective Clauses to Combine Sentences. Turn each pair of sentences into a single sentence with an adjective clause. Then underline each adjective clause and draw an arrow from it to the word or words it modifies.

EXAMPLE: Dr. Perone is a good veterinarian. I always take our dog to Dr. Perone.

I always take our dog to Dr. Perone, <u>who is a good veterinarian</u>.

1. This store sells a wide variety of crafts. These crafts were made by Navajo artists.
2. Fall is a time for fresh starts. It is my favorite time of year.
3. Their apartment is in the city. Their apartment has all the modern conveniences.
4. Mr. Hart spoke kindly of his worst enemy. Mr. Hart always saw good instead of evil.
5. These old photographs recall happy moments. My father took the photographs.
6. We walked silently through the forest. In the forest great pines gave us a sense of peace.
7. Our dog is like a member of the family. Our dog's tail never stops wagging.
8. Our summer house is on a lake. We once swam and paddled our canoe in the lake.
9. The highway went straight through the desert. We saw no signs of life in the desert.
10. Colleen has a terrific record collection. Sometimes Colleen lets me borrow records.

7.2 Adverb Clauses

Subordinate clauses can also act as adverbs.

Subordinate adverb clauses modify verbs, adjectives, adverbs, or verbals by telling where, when, in what manner, to what extent, under what condition, or why.

The Adverb Clause

You will find that every *adverb clause* begins with a subordinating conjunction.

All adverb clauses begin with subordinating conjunctions.

The following chart shows some of the most common subordinating conjunctions. (See Section 3.2 for a more complete list.)

SUBORDINATING CONJUNCTIONS		
after	even though	unless
although	if	until
as	in order that	when
as if	since	whenever
as long as	so that	where
because	than	wherever
before	though	while

Recognizing these subordinate conjunctions will help you identify adverb clauses. In the chart on the next page, the adverb clauses are italicized. Arrows point to the words modified by each clause. Note that each clause answers a question for adverbs. The first adverb clause answers the question *When?*. The second adverb clause answers the question *Where?*, and so on. The last two adverb clauses are different because they provide information that a single adverb cannot. The next to last adverb clause answers the question *Under what condition?* and the question *Why?* is answered by the last adverb clause in the chart.

ADVERB CLAUSES
Modifying a Verb
When the fog is dense, you should use low beams.
Modifying an Adjective
Tricia seemed happy *wherever she was.*
Modifying an Adverb
Faster *than the eye could follow,* the race car sped away.
Modifying a Participle
Laughing *until he gasped for breath,* Fred could not speak.
Modifying a Gerund
Driving a car *if you do not have a license* is illegal.
Modifying an Infinitive
We decided to remain in our seats *so that we could watch the movie again.*

Whether an adverb clause appears at the beginning, middle, or end of a sentence can sometimes affect the meaning.

EXAMPLE: *Before the day was over,* I made plans to see Ed.

I made plans to see Ed *before the day was over.*

Like adjective clauses, adverb clauses can be used to combine the information from two sentences into one. The combined sentence shows a close relationship between the ideas.

TWO SENTENCES: It was raining. We did not go to the lake.

COMBINED: *Because it was raining,* we did not go to the lake.

EXERCISE A: Identifying Adverb Clauses and the Words They Modify. Write the adverb clause in each sentence. Then write the word or words each adverb clause modifies.

EXAMPLE: While you were out, someone telephoned you.

While you were out telephoned

1. Before she gave the assignment, Miss Martin explained the method for review.
2. Mark looks gloomy whenever that topic is discussed.
3. After the sun goes down, the temperature drops several degrees.
4. We wanted to stop so that we could enjoy the scenery.
5. The Petersons have lived in Seattle since I was young.
6. Miserable unless there is work, my father aimlessly putters in his workshop.
7. Picked when they are ripe, fresh strawberries have a luscious taste.
8. The treasure was buried deeper than we had thought.
9. Winking as if he knew a secret, Mr. Bumble departed.
10. Susan planned to remain in the country until her visa expired.

Elliptical Adverb Clauses

Sometimes, words are omitted in adverb clauses, especially in those clauses that begin with *as* or *than* and are used to express comparisons. Such clauses are said to be *elliptical*.

An elliptical clause is a clause in which the verb or subject and verb are understood but not actually stated.

Even though the subject or the subject and the verb have been left out of an elliptical clause, they still function to make the clause express a complete thought. In the following examples, the understood words have been added in brackets. The sentences are alike except for the words *he* and *him*. In the first sentence, *he* is a subject. In the second sentence, *him* functions as a direct object. The use of each word is easy to see when the omitted words are added.

VERB UNDERSTOOD: She resembles their father more *than he* [*does*].

SUBJECT AND VERB UNDERSTOOD: She resembles their father more than [*she resembles*] *him*.

When you read or write elliptical clauses, mentally include the omitted words. Doing this should help clarify the meaning you intend.

EXERCISE B: Recognizing Elliptical Adverb Clauses. Write each sentence, adding the missing words in any elliptical clause. Then underline the complete adverb clause in each sentence and circle any words you have added.

EXAMPLE: I am as angry as you.

I am as angry as you are.

1. We think our cheerleaders are better than theirs.
2. Blake is happier working with people than he is working by himself.
3. My younger brother is as tall as I.
4. Small children sometimes appreciate classical music more than nursery jingles.
5. In Riley's backyard you can find junk heaped wherever there is an inch of space.
6. Joe pitches better than she.
7. Professor Horton likes ancient history more than current events.
8. I like green beans better than he.
9. Everyone else was as disappointed with the test scores as I was.
10. We needed her help more than his.

DEVELOPING WRITING SKILLS: Using Adverb Clauses to Combine Sentences. Turn each pair of sentences into a single sentence with an adverb clause. Then underline each adverb clause.

EXAMPLE: Livia is unhappy. Her parakeet died.

Livia is unhappy because her parakeet died.

1. The mother called the doctor in the middle of the night. Her child's temperature was abnormally high.
2. The crowd looked up in wonder. Another brilliant display of fireworks went off.
3. We toasted marshmallows over the dying embers. We silently shared a feeling of closeness.

4. Randolph will never learn to study. He learns to concentrate.
5. Give me some more ideas. I can think of a topic.
6. Everyone reported to class late. The bell had rung.
7. The settlers chose that area for their homestead. A nearby stream provided fresh water.
8. Our trip to Washington, D.C., will be canceled. We are not able to raise sufficient funds.
9. She had a bad cough. She still insisted upon going to work.
10. You find the time. Write your uncle a get-well note.

7.3 Noun Clauses

Subordinate clauses can also act as nouns.

A noun clause is a subordinate clause that acts as a noun.

The Noun Clause

A *noun clause* acts in almost the same way as a single-word noun does in a sentence.

In a sentence a noun clause may act as a subject, direct object, indirect object, predicate nominative, object of a preposition, or appositive.

Notice the various functions that noun clauses may have.

NOUN CLAUSES
Subject: *Whoever is last* must pay a penalty.
Direct object: Please invite *whomever you want*.
Indirect object: His manner gave *whoever met him* a shock.
Predicate nominative: Our problem is *whether we should stay here or leave*.
Object of a preposition: Use the money for *whatever purpose you choose*.
Appositive: The occupied country rejected our plea, *that orphans be cared for by the Red Cross*.

EXERCISE A: Identifying Noun Clauses. Write the noun clause in each sentence. Then label the clause as a *subject, direct object, indirect object, predicate nominative, object of a preposition,* or *appositive*.

EXAMPLE: I made whoever was hungry a sandwich.
whoever was hungry (indirect object)

1. Whoever is interested in the past will like the book *Foxfire*.
2. The governor's dilemma, how it would be possible to please both factions, required hard thinking.
3. Everyone wants to hear about what you wore to the party.
4. That the play is a financial success is the result of the critics' reviews.
5. Leon discusses politics with whoever is unfortunate enough to sit next to him.
6. The planning committee needed more suggestions, whatever ideas people thought would be workable.
7. The brochure describes what a tourist can see in Kenya.
8. Tell Ms. Cato when she should expect you to arrive.
9. Carmella's selection of fabrics will be whichever ones she orders from the retailer.
10. Mr. James gave whoever came into his store a warm greeting.

Introductory Words

Noun clauses frequently begin with the words *that, which, who, whom,* or *whose,* or the same words that are used to begin adjective clauses. *Whichever, whoever,* or *whomever* may also be used as introductory words in noun clauses. Other noun clauses begin with the words *how, if, what, whatever, where, when, whether,* or *why*.

Introductory words may act as subjects, direct objects, objects of prepositions, adjectives, or adverbs in noun clauses, or they may simply introduce the clauses.

The examples in the chart on the next page show two of the possible uses of introductory words in noun clauses. Note that the introductory word *that* in the last example has no function except to introduce the clause.

A FEW USES OF INTRODUCTORY WORDS WITHIN NOUN CLAUSES	
Direct object:	*Whatever he accomplished* would be satisfactory.
Adjective:	The little girl could not decide *which flavor of ice cream she would like.*
No function in clause:	The officials determined *that the polls had been rigged.*

Most words that begin noun clauses may also introduce adjective or adverb clauses. To decide if a clause acts as a noun, look at the clause's role in the sentence. In the following examples, all three subordinating clauses begin with *where,* but only the first is a noun clause because it functions in the sentence as a direct object.

NOUN CLAUSE: The advertisement told people *where they should call for information.*

ADJECTIVE CLAUSE: They took him to the emergency ward, *where a doctor examined his cut.*

ADVERB CLAUSE: Sue lives *where the weather is warm all year.*

NOTE ABOUT INTRODUCTORY WORDS: The introductory word *that* is often omitted from a noun clause. In the following example, the understood *that* is in brackets.

EXAMPLE: The secretary suggested [*that*] *you leave your name.*

EXERCISE B: Recognizing the Uses of Introductory Words. Write the introductory word from each noun clause in Exercise A. Then label the use of each within the clause as a *subject, direct object, object of a preposition, adjective, adverb,* or a word with *no function.*

EXAMPLE: I made whoever was hungry a sandwich.

whoever (subject)

DEVELOPING WRITING SKILLS: Writing Sentences with Noun Clauses. Use the following instructions to write ten sentences with noun clauses.

1. Use *which* as an introductory word; the clause should function as the subject of the sentence.
2. Use *how* as an introductory word; the clause should function as the subject of the sentence.
3. Use *what* as an introductory word; the clause should function as a direct object in the sentence.
4. Use *that* as an introductory word; the clause should function as a direct object in the sentence.
5. Use *whichever* as an introductory word; the clause should function as an object of a preposition in the sentence.
6. Use *wherever* as an introductory word; the clause should function as an object of a preposition in the sentence.
7. Use *whatever* as an introductory word; the clause should function as an object of a preposition in the sentence.
8. Use *whether* as an introductory word; the clause should function as a predicate nominative in the sentence.
9. Use *where* as an introductory word; the clause should function as a predicate nominative in the sentence.
10. Use *that* as an introductory word; the clause should function as an appositive in the sentence.

Sentences Classified by Structure and Function 7.4

Sentences can be classified by structure and by function.

The Four Structures of Sentences

The four basic sentence structures are *simple, compound, complex,* and *compound-complex*.

A simple sentence consists of a single independent clause.

A compound sentence consists of two or more independent clauses joined by a comma and a coordinating conjunction or by a semicolon.

A complex sentence consists of one independent clause and one or more subordinate clauses.

A compound-complex sentence consists of two or more independent clauses and one or more subordinate clauses.

The subjects in the chart are underlined once and the verbs twice.

FOUR STRUCTURES OF SENTENCES
Simple Sentences
The big day arrived early.
Both Mom and Dad saw the accident and reported it.
Struck by the novelty of the idea, Pat grinned with pleasure.
Compound Sentences
We went to an auction yesterday, but we did not buy anything.
Sue is a night owl; therefore, she sleeps late in the morning.
Complex Sentences
MAIN CLAUSE / SUBORDINATE CLAUSE Your boa constrictor was the culprit that ate my white mice.
MAIN / SUBORDINATE CLAUSE / CLAUSE The Red Cross, which gives invaluable aid, was flown in to SUBORDINATE CLAUSE help people who were made homeless by the flood.
MAIN CLAUSE SUBORDINATE CLAUSE Whoever wants this job can have it.
Compound-Complex Sentences
INDEPENDENT CLAUSE The truck dropped its load of gravel onto the driveway SUBORDINATE CLAUSE / INDEPENDENT CLAUSE where the car was parked, and then the truck drove off.
SUBORDINATE CLAUSE / INDEPENDENT CLAUSE When the lights went out, we felt extremely uneasy, INDEPENDENT CLAUSE / SUBORDINATE CLAUSE but we always knew that morning would eventually come.

Notice in the chart that even a simple sentence, one independent clause, may have a compound subject, compound verb, or both.

Notice also that in complex sentences independent clauses are often called *main clauses* to distinguish them from subordinate clauses. The subject and verb of a main clause, in turn, are usually called the *subject of the sentence* and the *main verb*. Sometimes, in such a sentence, a subordinate clause may fall between the subject and verb of the main clause, as in the second complex sentence in the chart. Other times, an entire noun clause may be the subject of the sentence, as in the third complex sentence in the chart.

EXERCISE A: Identifying the Structure of Sentences. Identify each sentence as *simple, compound, complex,* or *compound-complex*.

EXAMPLE: Before Matthew went to school, he fed the puppy.
complex

(1) Matthew had always wanted a dog of his own. (2) One day he went to an animal shelter that offered all kinds of dogs for adoption. (3) As he entered, Matthew remembered his parents' asking if he was sure that he had time in his busy schedule for a dog. (4) Matthew put the question out of his mind; he was intent on picking out his dog. (5) Matthew finally chose a small brown bundle of fluff with sparkling eyes and a wagging tail. (6) In the weeks that followed, Matthew sometimes felt that days were too short to do all that had to be done, but somehow he managed. (7) He found that he needed to organize his time carefully. (8) He kept his grades up, played soccer, and wrote articles for the school newspaper. (9) Giving the puppy plenty of water, food, exercise, and attention took time, but every minute was well spent. (10) As Matthew worked at his desk every evening, a small brown chin often rested on his foot, and two floppy ears perked up whenever he spoke.

The Four Functions of Sentences

Sentences may also be classified by *function*. A sentence may be *declarative, interrogative, imperative,* or *exclamatory*.

A declarative sentence states an idea and ends with a period.

An interrogative sentence asks a question and ends with a question mark.

An imperative sentence gives an order or a direction and ends with a period or an exclamation mark.

An exclamatory sentence conveys strong emotion and ends with an exclamation mark.

The type of sentence most often used in both writing and speaking is the declarative sentence. All questions that actually demand answers, either spoken or unspoken, are interrogative sentences. Sentences that are meant to give orders or directions are imperative. Sentences that are meant to show emotion are exclamatory.

FOUR FUNCTIONS OF SENTENCES
Declarative Sentences
She is an expert in karate.
Icarus fell into the sea when the sun melted his wax wings.
Interrogative Sentences
When did Hannibal cross the Alps?
Did you renew your magazine subscription?
Imperative Sentences
Brush the crumbs off the table.
Run!
Will someone please take these packages into the house before I drop them.
Exclamatory Sentences
The roof is collapsing!
Would you look at that!
An avalanche!
Late again!

As you can see in the chart, the subject of most imperative sentences is understood to be *you*. The third imperative sentence in the chart does contain a subject. It is still an imperative sentence, however, because it gives an order or direction.

The first exclamatory sentences would be declarative and interrogative except that they show strong feeling. Exclamatory sentences may also have understood subjects, verbs, or both, as shown in the last two examples in the chart.

EXERCISE B: Identifying the Function of Sentences. Identify each sentence as *declarative, interrogative, imperative,* or *exclamatory*. Then write the end mark for each sentence.

EXAMPLE: I must return this overdue book to the library.
declarative

1. Look carefully in both directions before crossing the street
2. When the alarm sounds, it summons firefighters
3. Your dress is absolutely ruined
4. All of my tires are new
5. Is there any way to tell when the corn is ripe
6. Will you please turn off the light before you leave
7. Should we whitewash this wall or leave it as it is
8. The toast
9. Oil the hinges and this door will no longer squeak
10. If you look in that tree, you will see a bird's nest

DEVELOPING WRITING SKILLS: Writing Sentences with Different Structures and Functions. Use the following instructions to write ten sentences of your own.

1. Write a simple declarative sentence.
2. Write a simple imperative sentence.
3. Write a compound declarative sentence.
4. Write a simple interrogative sentence.
5. Write a compound interrogative sentence.
6. Write a simple exclamatory sentence.
7. Write a complex declarative sentence.
8. Write a complex interrogative sentence.
9. Write a compound-complex declarative sentence.
10. Write a compound-complex interrogative sentence.

7.5 Diagraming Clauses

Diagrams of simple sentences are placed on one main horizontal line. Diagrams of more complicated sentence structures need more than one main horizontal line.

Compound Sentences

To diagram a compound sentence, just diagram each independent clause separately. Then join them at the verbs with a dotted line on which the conjunction or semicolon is placed.

EXAMPLE: INDEPENDENT CLAUSE: *A gentle breeze blew across the lake,* and INDEPENDENT CLAUSE: *the raft floated inland.*

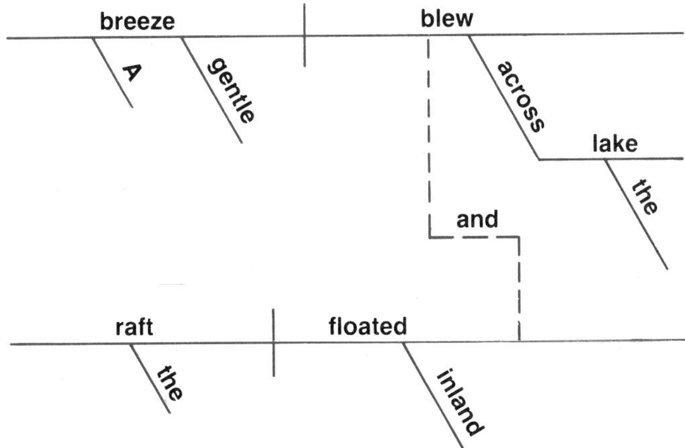

EXERCISE A: Diagraming Compound Sentences. Correctly diagram each sentence.

1. His temperature is high, but he remains alert.
2. Should I plant this cherry tree in that corner, or would you prefer it near the fence?
3. The steak was perfect, and the salad was excellent, but the dessert was too sweet.
4. Joan has little sense of her own worth; she never asserts herself.
5. Yesterday, we cleaned the attic and filled boxes with useless items; later, we went to the dump.

Complex Sentences

Complex sentences have an independent clause and one or more adjective, adverb, or noun subordinate clauses. Each clause is placed on a separate horizontal line.

Adjective Clauses. To diagram a sentence with an adjective clause, first diagram the independent clause. Then diagram the adjective clause beneath it. Connect the two clauses with a dotted line that extends from the modified noun or pronoun in the independent clause to the relative pronoun or relative adverb in the adjective clause. The position of the relative pronoun changes depending on its function in the adjective clause. In the following example, the relative pronoun is acting as the direct object of the adjective clause.

ADJECTIVE CLAUSE
EXAMPLE: My friend *whom you met yesterday* just called.

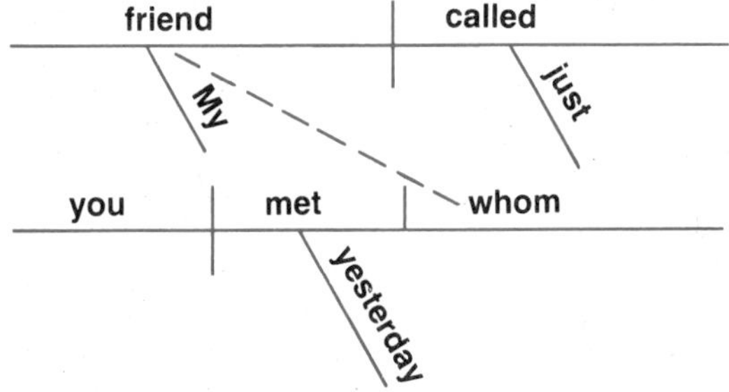

When a relative pronoun acts as an object of a preposition or as an adjective or a clause is introduced by a relative adverb, the dotted line must be bent to connect the clauses properly.

ADJECTIVE CLAUSE
EXAMPLE: I need time *when I can study.*

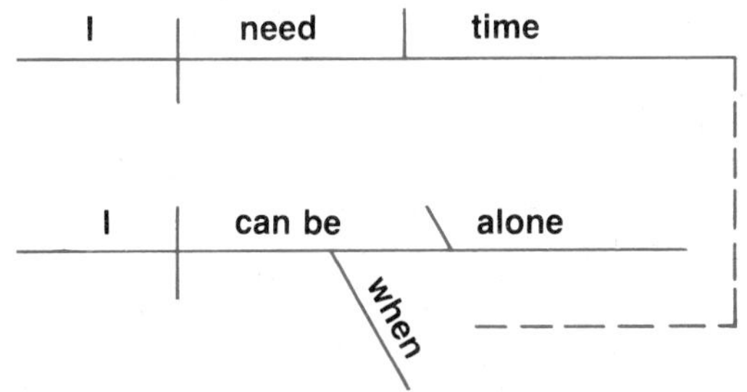

Adverb Clauses. The main difference between a diagram for an adjective clause and one for an adverb clause is that the subordinating conjunction for an adverb clause is written on the dotted line. This line extends from the modified verb, adjective, adverb, or verbal in the main clause to the verb in the adverb clause.

ADVERB CLAUSE

EXAMPLE: To look *before you leap* is good advice.

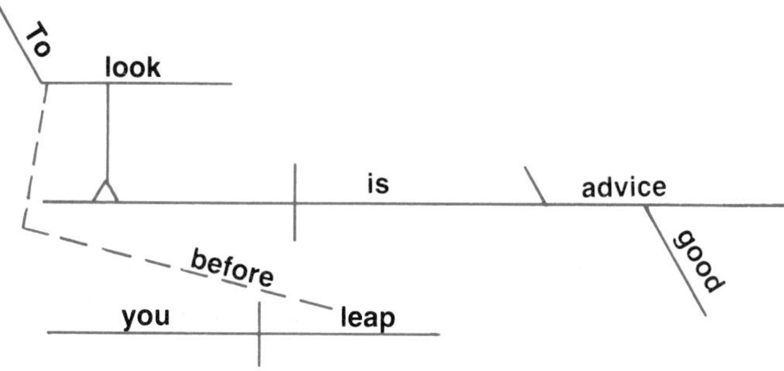

If the adverb clause is elliptical, the understood words are placed in the diagram in parentheses, as shown in the following example.

ADVERB CLAUSE

EXAMPLE: Barbara seems more tense *than before the accident.*

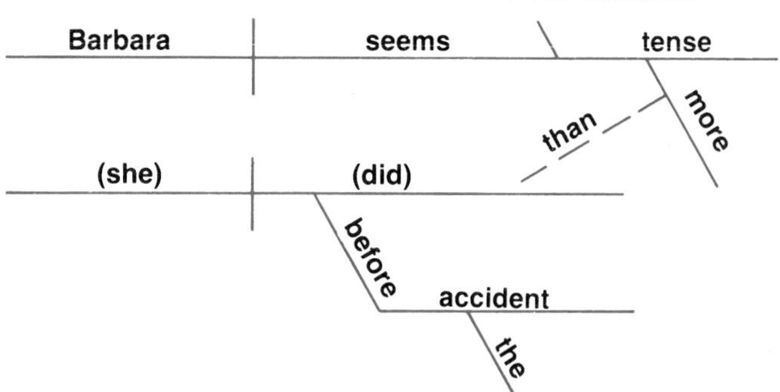

Noun Clauses. When diagraming a sentence with a noun clause, first diagram the independent clause. Then place the entire noun clause on a pedestal extending upwards from the position the noun clause fills in the independent clause. Notice that the pedestal meets the noun clause at the verb.

NOUN CLAUSE
EXAMPLE: *Whatever you decide* is fine with me.

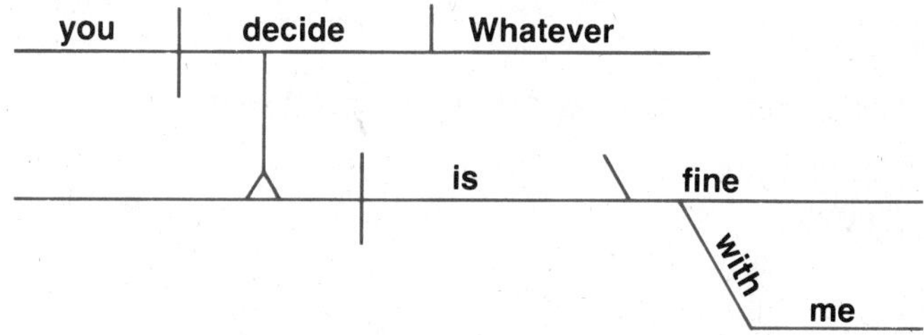

When an introductory word in a noun clause has no function in the clause, it is written alongside the pedestal.

NOUN CLAUSE
EXAMPLE: The question, *whether Jonas is truly sorry,* will be revealed in the next episode.

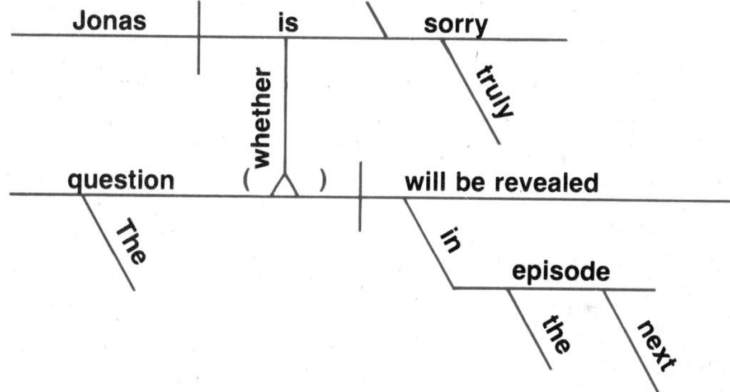

EXERCISE B: Diagraming Complex Sentences. Correctly diagram each sentence.

1. Barbara McClintock is a scientist whom I greatly admire.
2. He drives as if he were in a race.
3. They told us that they would be late.
4. We hope to complete this job while time remains.
5. The side lawn is the place where we always played croquet.
6. The sleuth suspected that the killer was living on the west side of town.
7. The Persians lost because Alexander's troops had superior military skill.
8. In the movies, sit behind someone whose hat is off.

9. Before we bought our house, we rented an apartment.
10. He has hiccups more than you.

Compound-Complex Sentences

To diagram a compound-complex sentence, begin by diagraming and connecting each of the independent clauses just as you would if you were diagraming a compound sentence. Then diagram and connect each subordinate clause.

EXAMPLE: *When we bought our microwave oven,* (ADVERB CLAUSE) we considered that brand, but we decided *that it was too expensive.* (NOUN CLAUSE)

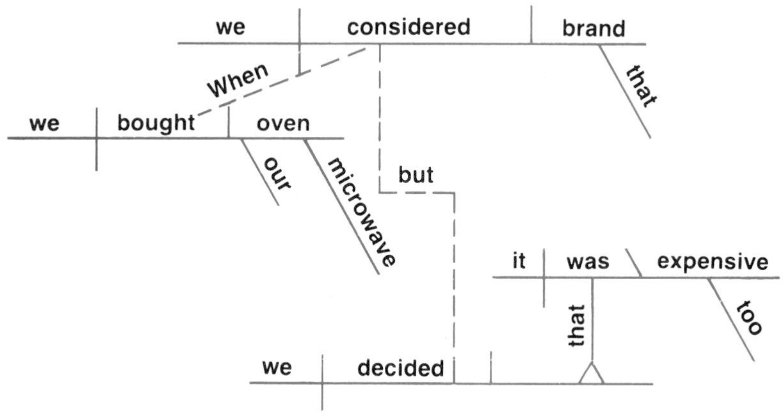

EXERCISE C: Diagraming Compound-Complex Sentences. Correctly diagram each sentence.

1. Because it rained, we missed the game that had been scheduled, but we still had a good time.
2. We waited until the plane landed, and then we rushed to the gate where the passengers would enter.

DEVELOPING WRITING SKILLS: Writing and Diagraming Various Sentence Structures. Write four sentences: one simple, one compound, one complex, and one compound-complex. Then correctly diagram each sentence.

Skills Review and Writing Workshop

Clauses

CHECKING YOUR SKILLS

Write the subordinate clause in each sentence. Identify each as an *adjective clause, adverb clause,* or *noun clause.*

(1) Salt, whose chemical name is sodium chloride, is used to flavor and preserve food. (2) Because salt is vital to human life, some ancient countries even used it as money. (3) In some other countries, whoever bought salt had to pay a tax on it. (4) Years ago most of the salt that people needed was obtained from sea coasts. (5) Several important early trade routes were established by people who bought and sold salt. (6) Mines that are located under the earth also produce salt. (7) Many scientists believe that most people eat too much salt. (8) Most salt, however, is used by companies that make various chemicals. (9) A large amount of this important mineral is also spread on roads where it melts the ice. (10) Although eating too much salt may be unwise, it still plays an important part in our lives.

USING GRAMMAR SKILLS IN WRITING

Writing an Essay

An essay must be well organized to capture the reader's attention. Follow the steps below to write an essay explaining what you do to stay healthy.

Prewriting: How do you take care of yourself? Think about the aspects of the health program you want to discuss.

Writing: Organize your essay according to subtopic. Write an introduction, a conclusion, and supporting paragraphs.

Revising: An essay is like a one-way conversation. People cannot interrupt, but they can stop reading. Have you varied the structure of your sentences to make them interesting? Check your clauses. Are they structured correctly? When you have revised, proofread carefully.

Chapter 8

Avoiding Sentence Errors

Once you understand the makeup of sentences, you will be better able to recognize errors in your own writing. This chapter will help you find and fix a number of these errors.

8.1 Fragments and Run-ons

Fragments and run-ons are two errors commonly found in writing. Section 5.1 deals briefly with fragments. This section will give you more practice with them and show you several ways to correct them. You will also practice correcting run-ons.

Fragments

A *fragment,* a group of words that does not express a complete thought, is generally considered an error in writing.

Do not capitalize and punctuate phrases, subordinate clauses, or words in a series as if they were complete sentences.

Fragments in writing are usually the result of carelessness and haste. If you find you are having a problem with fragments, take the time to check your work. Read it aloud, listening to the natural pauses and stops. You should hear where your sentences actually begin and end. Be sure that every sentence you have written contains a subject and a verb and expresses a complete thought.

Often you will find that a fragment should simply be linked up with words that come before or after it. Fragments of this sort are generally the result of errors in capitalization and punctuation. Sometimes, however, you will need to add words to a fragment in order to make it into a complete sentence, one that has both a subject and a verb.

In the next few pages, you will have a chance to look more closely at common types of fragments and ways of correcting them.

Phrase Fragments. *Phrase fragments* may consist of modified nouns without verbs, modified verbs without subjects, or prepositional, appositive, or verbal phrases. You may be able to correct many phrase fragments by adding them to nearby sentences.

APPOSITIVE FRAGMENT: A box of chocolates.

ADDED TO NEARBY SENTENCE: Bill handed Sue her gift, *a box of chocolates.*

Often, however, you will have to add missing sentence parts to correct phrase fragments. A noun fragment will need a verb and whatever other sentence parts you wish to add.

NOUN FRAGMENT: A single long-stemmed rose.

COMPLETED SENTENCES: *A single long-stemmed rose* stood in a crystal bud vase.

Andy selected *a single long-stemmed rose.*

In the first completed sentence, the noun fragment was used as a subject. Therefore, a verb was added. In the second completed sentence, the noun fragment was used as a complement and a subject and a verb were added.

If a noun fragment contains a noun modified by a participial phrase, you can turn the participle into a verb by adding a helping verb.

NOUN FRAGMENT: The ball thrown by the pitcher.

COMPLETED SENTENCE: *The ball* was *thrown by the pitcher.*

Just as a noun with its modifiers cannot stand alone as a sentence, a verb with its modifiers and complements cannot stand alone. Always make sure your verbs have subjects.

VERB FRAGMENT: Soon will be ready for restoration.

COMPLETED SENTENCE: The turn-of-the-century house *soon will be ready for restoration.*

A prepositional fragment will need both a subject and a verb.

PREPOSITIONAL FRAGMENT: By the roadside.

COMPLETED SENTENCE: Wild blackberries grew *by the roadside.*

A participial fragment will need a subject and a verb or a subject and one or more helping verbs.

PARTICIPIAL FRAGMENT: Washed clean by the rain.

COMPLETED SENTENCES: *Washed clean by the rain,* the car looked new.

The car had been *washed clean by the rain.*

A gerund fragment will need a verb, a subject and a verb, or a subject and one or more helping verbs.

GERUND FRAGMENT: Winding my watch.

COMPLETED SENTENCES: *Winding my watch* is a daily habit.

I dislike *winding my watch.*

I am *winding my watch.*

An infinitive fragment will need a verb or a subject and a verb.

INFINITIVE FRAGMENT: To walk to school in good weather.

COMPLETED SENTENCE: Mike likes *to walk to school in good weather.*

Clause Fragments. Subordinate clauses are another construction that should not be capitalized and punctuated as sentences. Instead, you should connect them to nearby independent clauses or supply the missing sentence parts yourself.

ADJECTIVE CLAUSE FRAGMENT: Which I enjoyed.

COMPLETED SENTENCE: I read a book, *which I enjoyed.*

ADVERB CLAUSE FRAGMENT: Where the ice is thin.

COMPLETED SENTENCE: Do not skate *where the ice is thin*.

NOUN CLAUSE FRAGMENT: Whoever needs a ride.

COMPLETED SENTENCE: *Whoever needs a ride* may come with us.

Series Fragments. Sometimes, a series of words or phrases may be so long that it fools you into thinking it is a sentence. To avoid writing series fragments, be sure that each of your sentences has a subject and a verb.

SERIES FRAGMENT: A flowering pink cherry tree near the fence, red and yellow primroses along the border, and neat rectangular beds of orange and yellow tulips.

COMPLETED SENTENCE: *A flowering pink cherry tree* blooms *near the fence, red and yellow primroses* dot *the borders, and neat rectangular beds* blaze *with orange and yellow tulips.*

As you can see, sentence fragments can be corrected in many different ways. Which method you use to correct a fragment will depend on what kind of fragment it is.

EXERCISE A: Correcting Fragments. Identify each item as a *phrase fragment, clause fragment,* or *series fragment*. Then use each fragment in a complete sentence.

EXAMPLE: A terrible case of poison ivy.

phrase fragment I had a terrible case of poison ivy.

1. Laughed, shouted, and romped.
2. While she was running after the bus.
3. Frequent loud interruptions.
4. Petrified dinosaur bones.
5. Where cattails and reeds grew high.
6. Sometimes downcast, depressed, or just unhappy.
7. Watching, stalking, and pouncing.
8. Which recalled a time of carefree days.
9. Must have been abandoned by someone.
10. Whomever he invites.

Run-ons

Another kind of sentence error is the *run-on sentence,* often called simply a *run-on.* A run-on sentence is two or more complete sentences that are capitalized and punctuated as if they were one.

Use punctuation, conjunctions, or other means to join or separate the parts of a run-on sentence.

There are two common kinds of run-ons. One kind consists of sentences that are not separated or joined by any punctuation at all. The other kind is made up of sentences with only a comma between them.

WITH NO PUNCTUATION: He rushed down the subway steps an angry woman followed close behind.

WITH ONLY A COMMA: This is a very belated birthday card, my birthday was three months ago.

Like fragments, run-ons are usually the result of carelessness and haste. Avoid them by rereading your work, aloud if necessary. Listen for the natural stops that indicate where your sentences end. If you find run-ons in your writing, you can correct them in the following ways.

Correcting Run-ons with Punctuation and Conjunctions. The following chart shows three ways that run-ons may be corrected with punctuation and conjunctions.

USING PUNCTUATION AND CONJUNCTIONS	
Run-ons	**Sentences with End Marks**
Will summer ever come we doubt it very much	Will summer ever come? We doubt it very much.
Edith slumped into a chair, the worst had happened.	Edith slumped into a chair. The worst had happened.
Run-ons	**Sentences with Commas**
Storm clouds gathered lightning lit up the sky.	Storm clouds gathered, and lightning lit up the sky.
They may have stopped to eat, they may be lost.	They may have stopped to eat, or they may be lost.

Run-ons	Sentences with Semicolons
He doesn't merely like fishing, he adores it.	He doesn't merely like fishing; he adores it.
Charlene hates cooking, therefore, she never invites anyone for dinner.	Charlene hates cooking; therefore, she never invites anyone for dinner.

In the last example, notice that when a semicolon is placed before a conjunctive adverb a comma must be placed after it.

Correcting Run-ons by Rewriting. Sometimes the best way to correct a run-on sentence is by rewriting. The following show run-ons rewritten to form parts of simple sentences.

RUN-ON: Julie sometimes comes over to visit us, her little brother comes too.

SENTENCE WITH COMPOUND SUBJECT: *Julie and her little brother* sometimes come over to visit us.

RUN-ON: Leaping from behind the chair, the kitten batted the yarn, then she dashed across the rug.

SENTENCE WITH COMPOUND VERB: Leaping from behind the chair, the kitten *batted the yarn and then dashed across the rug.*

RUN-ON: The restaurant was well-known for its pastry, sauces, and patés, it was a small French cafe.

SENTENCE WITH APPOSITIVE PHRASE: The restaurant, *a small French cafe,* was well-known for its pastry, sauces, and patés.

Run-ons can also be rewritten to form complex sentences. In the following the second clause in the run-on is already subordinate to the other clause—it implies a condition.

RUN-ON: The picnic may be canceled, it may rain all afternoon.

SENTENCE WITH SUBORDINATE CLAUSE: The picnic may be canceled *if it rains all afternoon.*

Sometimes, a run-on may be corrected by rewriting it as a complex sentence even though neither clause seems subordinate to the other.

RUN-ON: I like to watch a good movie twice, I do this every time I can.

SENTENCE WITH SUBORDINATE CLAUSE: I like to watch a good movie twice *whenever I can.*

EXERCISE B: Correcting Run-ons. Use an end mark, a comma and a coordinating conjunction, or a semicolon to correct each of the first five run-ons. Form a simple or complex sentence to correct each of the last five run-ons.

EXAMPLE: Davy Crockett was a frontiersman, he was also a congressman.

Davy Crockett was a frontiersman. He was also a congressman.

1. Every year at this time the snow melts and the creek flows, in six months, however, it will be dry.
2. They bought an old mill, eventually they were able to make it into a unique and beautiful home.
3. Jody dropped out of school in her junior year, she received a diploma years later.
4. Days turned into years, the years seemed endless.
5. Will he leave his job and its security to try his luck at farming it seems unlikely.
6. Sir Winston Churchill was a brilliant man he was the English Prime Minister during World War II.
7. Catherine II was a Russian empress, she was called Catherine the Great.
8. Marty was afraid of bees, he had a severe allergic reaction to their stings.
9. In the spring cardinals come to our bird feeder, an occasional blue jay also makes an appearance.
10. Rapunzel let her long hair fall to the ground, her name means "lettuce."

DEVELOPING WRITING SKILLS: Correcting Fragments and Run-ons. Rewrite the following paragraphs, correcting all fragments and run-ons.

(1) The storm had suddenly come upon them. (2) Surprising the two boys. (3) Their jackets offered little protection from the

rain. (4) Jack led the way to the cabin, it was almost hidden by the trees. (5) Within minutes they stood on the porch. (6) The door opened, they entered, throwing their backpacks onto the floor. (7) They shivered. (8) The room was cold, it was damp.

(9) They could not see in the darkness, Jack felt for the lantern. (10) Which he knew was on the table. (11) If they had started out earlier, they would not have been caught in the rain. (12) Unable to reach the cabin before night. (13) A warm fire and supper would certainly help.

(14) When the lantern was lit, Jack gasped, the doors to the cupboard which his father had filled were opened, revealing empty shelves. (15) Walking back onto the porch. (16) He stared at the empty place where wood had been stacked. (17) Obviously, someone had been warm and well-fed at their expense. (18) Phil, he knew, would accept his apology, that was a small consolation for the uncomfortable night they would have. (19) At least a lesson had been learned, next time he would prepare for any emergency. (20) That might occur.

Misplaced and Dangling Modifiers 8.2

The correct placement of phrase and clause modifiers is an essential ingredient of clear writing.

A modifier should be placed as close as possible to the word it modifies.

Recognizing Misplaced and Dangling Modifiers

A modifier may be placed too far from the word it modifies.

Misplaced Modifiers. A *misplaced modifier* can cause confusion for the reader.

A misplaced modifier appears to modify the wrong word in a sentence.

In the following example, notice how the italicized modifier can confuse the reader.

MISPLACED MODIFIER: *Growing wild in the forest,* we picked the tiny blossoms.

Although *growing wild in the forest* logically should modify *blossoms,* the modifier is positioned as though it modified *we.* The sentence should be rewritten so that the modifier is closer to the modified word.

CORRECTED SENTENCE: We picked the tiny blossoms *growing wild in the forest.*

Dangling Modifiers. Another common sentence error occurs when a modified word appears to be missing entirely.

A dangling modifier appears to modify either the wrong word or no word at all because the word it should logically modify is missing.

To understand a sentence with a *dangling modifier,* the reader must pause and guess what the missing word should be, as in the following example.

DANGLING MODIFIER: *Pausing to congratulate Barbara,* the conversation continued.

The italicized dangling modifier appears to describe *conversation,* which, according to the sentence, paused to congratulate Barbara. The sentence can be rewritten logically to include the missing word.

CORRECTED SENTENCE: *Pausing to congratulate Barbara,* we continued the conversation.

EXERCISE A: Identifying Misplaced and Dangling Modifiers. Identify each underlined phrase or clause as *misplaced, dangling,* or *correct.*

EXAMPLE: He ran to the car with arms full of boxes.
misplaced

1. Grinning happily, the prize for first place was accepted.
2. Wait for the bus that stops at the corner.
3. They planned to win before the game started.
4. Hoping to succeed in the interview, long hours were spent in preparation.
5. She flew in a small aircraft trembling with fear.
6. Jumping out of his seat, Milton shouted with surprise.

7. Reading the directions carefully, the test was quite easy.
8. This letter, which I found behind a drawer, was written over a century ago.
9. She fearfully pointed to the spider over her head that hung from a transparent web.
10. We joined the crowd in cheering the winner with enthusiasm.

Correcting Misplaced Modifiers

A misplaced modifier is usually a prepositional phrase, a participial phrase, or an adjective clause.

Correct a misplaced modifier by moving the phrase or clause closer to the word it should logically modify.

Notice how the misplaced modifiers were corrected.

MISPLACED PREPOSITIONAL PHRASE: The lake attracted many birds *with gentle waves*.

CORRECTED SENTENCE: The lake *with gentle waves* attracted many birds.

MISPLACED PARTICIPIAL PHRASE: *Balanced on one leg,* the boys stared at the flamingo.

CORRECTED SENTENCE: The boys stared at the flamingo *balanced on one leg*.

MISPLACED ADJECTIVE CLAUSE: Gazing upwards at the bats, the spelunkers shone their flashlights *that hung by the thousands from the roof of the cave*.

CORRECTED SENTENCE: Gazing upwards, the spelunkers shone their flashlights at the bats *that hung by the thousands from the roof of the cave*.

EXERCISE B: Recognizing and Correcting Misplaced Modifiers. Write each sentence, correcting the misplaced modifier. Then underline the corrected modifier and draw an arrow from it to the word it modifies.

EXAMPLE: He ran to the car with arms full of boxes.

With arms full of boxes, he ran to the car.

1. The watch was his favorite gift that broke.
2. Lionel sold his bicycle to a friend with four speeds.
3. The zoo keeper captured the escaped iguana brandishing a net in his upraised hand.
4. The boys ran from the haunted house noticeably trembling.
5. Brenda put oranges into the punch that came from California.
6. The deer bounded into the woods shaking in panic.
7. Jed ordered a steak and a salad cooked rare.
8. The fish were photographed at the pier that we caught.
9. Perched on top of the counter in a red dress, the child sat.
10. Leaving the party after midnight, we waved farewell to our happy guests.

Correcting Dangling Modifiers

A dangling modifier is usually a participial phrase or an adverb clause.

Correct a dangling modifier by rewriting the sentence to include the missing word.

If the dangling modifier is a participial phrase, the missing word or words can be added after the phrase, or the phrase can be rewritten as a clause containing the missing word or words.

DANGLING PARTICIPIAL PHRASE: *Looking at the stars,* a meteor flashed across the sky.

CORRECTED SENTENCES: *Looking at the stars,* we saw a meteor flash across the sky.

As we were looking at the stars, a meteor flashed across the sky.

If the dangling modifier is a clause,. the problem will often involve the use of pronouns. In the following example, the adverb clause dangles because of a confusion between *Sarah* and *Sarah's mother*. The sentence is corrected by making clear exactly who "was a baby."

DANGLING ADVERB CLAUSE: *When she was a baby,* Sarah's mother was very strict.

CORRECTED SENTENCE: *When Sarah was a baby,* her mother was very strict.

EXERCISE C: Recognizing and Correcting Dangling Modifiers. Write each sentence, correcting the dangling modifier. Then underline the corrected modifier and draw an arrow from it to the word it modifies.

EXAMPLE: Folding laundry, the phone rang.

Folding laundry, we heard the phone ring.

1. Researching that topic, three new ideas were found.
2. Picketing for improved working conditions, the strike continued.
3. Searching for the missing diamond ring, every possible nook and cranny was explored.
4. Swallowing the bitter medicine, a cold was avoided.
5. Lost in a daydream, my words went unheard.
6. When he was nine months old, Jeremy's father decided that the family should move to Alaska.
7. Driving into Santa Fe, the desert looked like the moon.
8. Winning the race, the losers applauded loudly.
9. When they misbehaved, the boys' parents complained.
10. Returning the wallet, the owner gave a reward.

DEVELOPING WRITING SKILLS: Correcting Misplaced and Dangling Modifiers. Rewrite the following paragraph, correcting all misplaced or dangling modifiers.

(1) Sue is a successful architect and interior designer whose custom-built homes stagger the imagination. (2) Priced beyond what the average person can afford, you can see her houses in many expensive neighborhoods. (3) The front of one house is made entirely of glass. (4) Extending outward from the second floor, potted flowers grow on an elaborate balcony. (5) Within the center of the house, a huge tropical aquarium rests on a marble floor with exotic fish. (6) A wrought iron staircase winds its way around the aquarium connecting the first and

second stories. (7) Recessed in the ceilings, each room is softly lit by fluorescent lights. (8) Turning a dial in any room, your favorite kind of music can be heard. (9) In the winter, fireplaces provide warmth; in the summer, cool air is circulated by fans. (10) With enough money, the house can become yours.

8.3 Faulty Parallelism

Another type of sentence error that can confuse a listener or reader is faulty parallelism.

Recognizing the Correct Use of Parallelism

Parallelism is a big word for a simple, logical idea.

Parallelism is the placement of equal ideas in words, phrases, or clauses of similar types.

Checking your sentences for parallelism can ensure that your ideas are clear and logical.

Correct Use of Parallelism. Whenever you present a comparison or a series of ideas that are equal in importance, you should express them in equal—that is, parallel—grammatical structures. Parallel structures can be two or more words of the same part of speech, two or more phrases of the same type, or two or more clauses of the same type. A coordinating conjunction such as *and* or *or* usually helps link parallel structures.

PARALLEL WORDS: The board reviewed several aspects of the plan: *social, educational,* and *financial.*

PARALLEL PHRASES: She loves *to swim in the ocean* and *to water ski at the lake.*

PARALLEL CLAUSES: We wondered *what was in the box, where it came from, who had sent it,* and *why it had not been unwrapped.*

Parallel structures may also be written with an understood word that is omitted after the first item in a series. In the following example, notice that the word *by* begins the first phrase but has been omitted in the second and third phrases. The understood word is shown in brackets.

PARALLEL PHRASES: You can improve your chances of making the team *by eating properly,* [*by*] *sleeping regularly,* and [*by*] *exercising daily.*

Sometimes, the conjunction may also be omitted between parallel structures.

PARALLEL CLAUSES: *If you do no homework,* [*and*] *if you show no interest in the classroom,* you may fail the course.

Faulty Use of Parallelism. Faulty parallelism results when ideas of equal importance are not expressed in equal grammatical structures. The last idea in the following sentence, for example, is not parallel to the others.

FAULTY PARALLELISM: The waiter suggested *lamb chops, green beans,* and *that we try the sweet potatoes.*

The direct objects in the sentence above are not parallel: The first two are nouns; the third is a noun clause. The easiest way to correct the faulty parallelism is to make all three direct object nouns.

CORRECTED SENTENCE: The waiter suggested *lamb chops, green beans,* and *sweet potatoes.*

EXERCISE A: Recognizing Parallel Ideas. Write the two or more parallel ideas in each sentence. Then label each set as *correct parallelism* or *faulty parallelism*.

EXAMPLE: In her lecture the professor discussed migration, courtship, and how birds establish nesting territories.

migration courtship how birds establish nesting territories (faulty parallelism)

1. Good speech must be audible, logical, and have clarity.
2. My paper received a high grade for originality and for neatness.
3. Claire likes hiking for great distances and to climb mountains.
4. You can adjust the swing by lengthening one rope or you can shorten the other rope.

5. The insurance agent sold my parents a homeowners' policy and a life insurance policy.
6. The clock is compact, silent, and runs accurately.
7. The dolls were Russian, Italian, and one from England.
8. We interviewed the principal, a teacher, and with the nurse.
9. The football sailed across the yard, over the fence, and into our neighbor's prize dahlias.
10. In India we saw neither the Ganges nor went to Calcutta.

Correcting Faulty Parallelism

To correct a sentence containing faulty parallelism usually takes only a few moments of thinking and rewriting.

Correct a sentence containing faulty parallelism by rewriting it so that each parallel idea is expressed in the same grammatical structure.

As you will see, faulty parallelism can involve not only words, phrases, or clauses in a series but also words, phrases, or clauses in a comparison.

Nonparallel Words. In a series of words, each word should be the same part of speech. You should also be careful not to match a series of words with a phrase or a clause.

CORRECTING NONPARALLEL WORDS	
Nouns and Phrase	**Nouns**
The qualities of a good scout are *loyalty, honesty,* and *being brave*.	The qualities of a good scout are *loyalty, honesty,* and *bravery.*
Adverbs and Phrase	**Adverbs**
A well-trained dog obeys *willingly, completely,* and *with speed.*	A well-trained dog obeys *willingly, completely,* and *quickly.*
Verbs and Clause	**Verbs**
The class *analyzed, discussed* and *we raised questions about the new rules.*	The class *analyzed, discussed,* and *questioned* the new rules.

Nonparallel Phrases. When ideas are presented in a series of phrases, make sure each phrase is the same type: prepositional, participial, gerund, or infinitive. In addition, make sure the series contains nothing but phrases.

CORRECTING NONPARALLEL PHRASES	
Gerund and Infinitive Phrases	**Gerund Phrases**
You should always find time for *doing your chores, enjoying leisure time,* and *to think of others.*	You should always find time for *doing your chores, enjoying leisure time,* and *thinking of others.*
Prepositional Phrases and Verb with Complement	**Prepositional Phrases**
They traveled *to Oregon, to California,* and *visited Mexico.*	They traveled *to Oregon, to California,* and *to Mexico.*
Participial Phrase and Clause	**Participial Phrases**
Jared faced his trial, *believing in his own innocence* and *he desired the truth.*	Jared faced his trial, *believing in his own innocence* and *desiring the truth.*

Nonparallel Clauses. When a series of subordinate clauses is presented, each clause should be of the same type.

CORRECTING NONPARALLEL SUBORDINATE CLAUSES	
Adjective and Adverb Clauses	**Adjective Clauses**
Our lawyer accepts cases *that are worthy* and *if she thinks she will win.*	Our lawyer accepts cases *that are worthy* and *that she thinks she will win.*

Nonparallel Comparisons. A common saying warns, "Don't compare apples with oranges." This saying can easily be applied to sentences that compare two things: A comparison should not be worded so that one grammatical structure is compared to another.

CORRECTING NONPARALLEL COMPARISONS	
Phrase and Clause	**Prepositional Phrases**
My report received a low grade more *for its grammatical mistakes* than *what was said in it.*	My report received a low grade more *for its grammatical mistakes* than *for its content.*
Gerund and Infinitive Phrases	**Gerund Phrases**
Giving an oral presentation can require more preparation than *to write a term paper.*	*Giving an oral presentation* can require more preparation than *writing a term paper.*
Noun and Gerund Phrase	**Gerund Phrases**
I like *television* as much as *going to movies.*	I like *watching television* as much as *going to movies.*

EXERCISE B: Correcting Faulty Parallelism of Words, Phrases, and Clauses. Write each sentence, correcting the faulty parallelism.

EXAMPLE: Joel likes imitating people and to tell jokes.
Joel likes imitating people and telling jokes.

1. We were happy to hear the good news and for being the first to congratulate them.
2. The florist arranged the flowers, placing a few ferns here and there and then added a ribbon.
3. Searching for buried treasure was fun, but to find real pirate booty was astounding.
4. We talk to one another, not talking about one another.
5. By thinking clearly and with being patient, you can unscramble an anagram.
6. The man and his wife were served soup that offended them, a main course that sickened them, and the dessert made them nauseated.

7. My desires were to visit the museum and seeing everything in the displays.
8. These plants need water and looking after.
9. In the pond small beetles darted to and fro, pollywogs wriggling, and snails climbing up stems.
10. He agreed to participate in the talent show but refused singing without a microphone.

EXERCISE C: Correcting Faulty Parallelism in Comparisons. Write each sentence, correcting the faulty parallelism.

EXAMPLE: Joel likes imitating people better than to tell jokes.
Joel likes imitating people better than telling jokes.

1. Swimming in the lake during the summer is more fun than to skate on it in the winter.
2. They prefer to see the sights rather than shopping all day.
3. I like listening to music less than a good game of chess with a friend.
4. Sailing the boat well is more important to them than to win the regatta.
5. She prefers staying at home to parties.
6. We judge people for what they do rather than for their words.
7. Eating a balanced diet is more healthful than junk food.
8. He was pleased less by the reward than what he had accomplished.
9. We decided to walk home rather than waiting for the school bus.
10. He was chosen to play the part because of his red hair rather than that he was a skilled actor.

DEVELOPING WRITING SKILLS: Writing Sentences with Parallel Structures. Use the following instructions to write five sentences of your own.

1. Use *and* to join two parallel prepositional phrases.
2. Use *and* to join two parallel gerund phrases.
3. Use *either* and *or* to join parallel infinitive phrases.
4. Use *and* to join two parallel subordinate clauses.
5. Write a comparison beginning "Listening to the radio is often more interesting than . . ."

Skills Review and Writing Workshop

Avoiding Sentence Errors

CHECKING YOUR SKILLS

Rewrite the following paragraph correcting each fragment, run-on, misplaced sentence, dangling modifier, or use of faulty parallelism.

(1) American popular music changed a great deal in the years that followed World War II, major changes began in the 1950's. (2) The Big Band sound was still popular right after the war which had come into style in the 1930's. (3) Later, a group of recording artists created a sound different from the Big Band sound. (4) The group included Perry Como, Patti Page, Rosemary Clooney, and Jo Stafford. (5) Singing Broadway songs and other ballads, their music in the early 1950's was slick, sweet, and cool. (6) Then, in 1956, an explosion named Elvis Presley hit American popular music. (7) Borrowing the rhythm and blues music of the South. (8) Doing new dances, his records were bought by millions of teenagers. (9) A new style was born in popular music. (10) Which was to lead to the rapid rise of rock music in the 1960's.

USING GRAMMAR SKILLS IN WRITING

Writing a Report from Your Notes

Taking notes involves getting facts and information on paper. Listen to a panel discussion on TV. Take notes. Follow the steps below to write a report of that discussion.

Prewriting: Review your notes, looking for main ideas and major details.

Writing: Use your notes to write your report. The discussion may have been repetitive. Your report should not be.

Revising: Check the facts. Be sure you are accurate. After you have revised, proofread carefully.

UNIT II

Usage

Chapter **9**

Levels of Usage

The customary manner in which people use language is referred to as usage. As you know, customs differ from place to place and according to the occasion. Correct usage is that which is appropriate for the time, the place, and the occasion.

In this chapter you will study the two main levels of usage: *standard* and *nonstandard*. Standard English is used by most educated people. Nonstandard English is used by certain social, regional, or ethnic groups for a variety of reasons.

9.1 The Varieties of English

Both standard and nonstandard English have more than one variation. In this section you will learn that standard English can be either formal or informal. You will also learn that nonstandard English includes dialect and slang.

Standard English

If you were asked to deliver an important speech to a large audience, you would probably use a kind of standard English different from the kind you would use on a picnic with your friends. For a serious speech, you would probably use *formal* English. For casual conversation, you would more likely use *informal* English.

Formal English. Formal English is appropriate for most serious writing and speaking. It is used with more accuracy and precision than informal English. This unit will stress formal English to help you develop a command of it in the circumstances that require formal use of the language.

Formal English uses traditional standards of correctness. It is characterized by complex sentence structures and an extensive vocabulary.

Notice in the following passage that even though the author uses a long and sophisticated sentence structure the content is not difficult to understand.

EXAMPLE: Great literature, past or present, is the expression of great knowledge of the human heart; great art is the expression of a solution of the conflict between the demands of the world without and that within. —Edith Hamilton

Informal English. It is informal English that you most often use during the course of your daily activities. It is the appropriate kind of language for casual conversation and personal letters.

Informal English is conversational in tone. It uses a smaller vocabulary than formal English and generally shorter sentences.

In the example below the author uses contractions, exclamations, informal expressions, and looser grammatical constructions than would be found in formal English.

EXAMPLE: It was my first experience with pure hysteria and I hadn't the foggiest notion of what to do. I tried comforting, I tried cajoling. I even tried to exert some authority. But she continued to carry on, *all night*! —Avis Carlson

EXERCISE A: Recognizing Formal and Informal English. Label each sentence as *formal* or *informal*.

EXAMPLE: I was pretty sure Jim'd show up just in the nick of time for the big game.
informal

1. After careful consideration, the committee decided to accept the new measures for environmental protection.
2. We kids were just playing in the backyard.
3. The ordeal was sufficiently taxing to encourage him to consider his actions more carefully in the future.
4. She kept jumping up and down when they called her name.
5. Despite the skepticism of her audience, the woman held tenaciously to her views.
6. Dinner will be served promptly at eight.
7. In a pinch Lou can fix the gas pump for you.
8. The committee will be pleased to review your application.
9. The fans went wild when the team scored the winning shot.
10. Pull up a chair and join the party.

Nonstandard English

Nonstandard English is used by certain groups of people who do not follow all the conventions of standard English. Nonstandard English is not considered appropriate in most situations that require serious writing and speaking.

Dialect. A nonstandard *dialect* is mainly spoken language used by people in a specific social, regional, or ethnic group. The vocabulary, pronunciations, and grammatical constructions are considered nonstandard because they are not used by the general population of educated people.

A nonstandard dialect is a form of English that makes use of words, pronunciations, and sentence structures not used in standard English.

The regional dialect below is spoken by a character in a short story by Hamlin Garland. Some regional dialects can be difficult to understand. The passage below is easier to understand if you read it aloud.

EXAMPLE: I'm a gettin' purty heavy t' be on m' laigs all day, but we can't afford t' hire, so I keep rackin' around somehow, like a foundered horse. S' lame—I tell Council he can't tell how lame I am f'r I'm jest as lame in one laig as t' other. —Hamlin Garland

Slang. *Slang* is a kind of nonstandard English that is rarely used by the general population. Some slang words are used by small groups of people. Airline pilots, for example, might refer to passengers as *geese*. Other slang words are used by larger groups. Young people of the 1960's, for example, sometimes used the word *heavy* to mean "deep" or "meaningful."

Slang is a nonstandard form of English that is colorful and expressive but short-lived.

The following passage contains dated expressions such as *big shot* and *dope*. Notice also that the general tone is casual.

EXAMPLE: Trying to act like a big shot, he'd already shown himself up for a dope. No wonder they were laughing at him, the way he had let Merle cheat him. —Henry George Felsen

EXERCISE B: Recognizing Dialect and Slang. Label each sentence as *dialect* or *slang*.

EXAMPLE: Unless you come, we ain't gonna have no party.
dialect

1. Remember that dude who came to town last week? Well, the cat turned out to be a real clip-artist.
2. Aye, there be a storm brewing, but we seen herself keening down by the sea.
3. Her outfit was like far-out, man.
4. That dog he hollerin' and carryin' on like the world gone and ended.
5. Are yous guys gonna set on the stoop all night?
6. I tell you, that guy's such a space cadet he'd never be able to organize the get-together.
7. She don't let nobody in the kitchen when she cookin'.
8. The pad is dullsville without you.
9. By midnight the juke joint was jiving.
10. Y'all come again real soon, y'hear.

DEVELOPING WRITING SKILLS: Changing Nonstandard English into Standard English. Rewrite the ten sentences in Exercise B using formal English.

EXAMPLE: Unless you come, we ain't gonna have no party.
Unless you come, we are not going to have a party.

Skills Review and Writing Workshop

Levels of Usage

CHECKING YOUR SKILLS

Rewrite the following paragraph using standard English.

(1) All members of the Acting Society are invited to a meeting this afternoon at 3:00. (2) All you aspiring actors, don't be scared, just show up! (3) Ah hope you'all can use a southern belle. (4) Mebbe they'll be after wantin a bloke from Ireland as well. (5) Man, that carpenter role sure turns me on. (6) I'm looking for an acting gig, too. (7) Think we'll have a good turnout? (8) Are you kidding? This is the big show of the year. (9) The play, which combines elements of humor with great sadness, will have its first performance in March. (10) I guess that means it's important.

USING USAGE SKILLS IN WRITING

Writing Dialogue

In order to write believable dialogue you must spend some time thinking about your characters. Do they have accents? Do they use slang? Follow the steps below to create dialogue that sounds real.

Prewriting: Invent two characters who are very different from each other. One of them speaks standard English; the other uses slang. Have them argue. End the argument in a friendly way or by having one of the characters leave the scene abruptly.

Writing: Don't give your characters long speeches. Short exchanges are more powerful, and more natural too, when people argue.

Revising: Read the dialogue aloud and listen to the rhythm of the words. Does each character's speech sound natural? Check the slang. Be sure it is appropriate and easily understood. Does the argument move along? Try not to be be repetitive. After you have revised, proofread carefully.

Chapter 10

Verb Usage

Your command of standard English requires a thorough understanding of how verbs are used. Even the best speakers and writers sometimes have trouble choosing the correct form of a verb. For instance, how often have you heard "I sung the song" instead of "I sang the song"?

In this chapter you will study the variety of verb forms, the way verbs are used to express time, and the difference between the active and passive voice.

Verb Tenses 10.1

An important use of the verb is to indicate when something happens. It is the *tense* of a verb that tells you if something is happening now, was happening at some time in the past, or will be happening at some time in the future.

A tense is a form of a verb that shows the time of an action or a condition.

The Six Tenses of Verbs

The time of an action or condition can be expressed by six tenses, each of which can be formed in at least two ways.

Each tense has a basic and a progressive form.

The first chart on the next page gives examples of the six tenses in their *basic forms*.

THE BASIC FORMS OF THE SIX TENSES	
Present	He *studies* hard all the time.
Past	He *studied* adverbs last week.
Future	He *will study* pronouns next week.
Present Perfect	He *has studied* adjectives already.
Past Perfect	He *has studied* nouns before he studied adjectives.
Future Perfect	He *will have studied* all the parts of speech by the end of next week.

The chart below illustrates the six *progressive forms*. Notice that all the forms end in *-ing*.

THE PROGRESSIVE FORMS OF THE SIX TENSES	
Present Progressive	He *is studying* verbs today.
Past Progressive	H *was studying* yesterday also.
Future Progressive	He *will be studying* while he babysits tonight.
Present Perfect Progressive	He *has been studying* verbs since early this morning.
Past Perfect Progressive	He *had been studying* nouns when he became interested in grammar.
Future Perfect Progressive	He *will have been studying* for four weeks when we take the test.

A third form, the *emphatic,* exists only for the present and past tenses. The present emphatic is formed by using the helping verbs *do* and *does*. The past emphatic is formed with *did*.

THE EMPHATIC FORMS OF THE PRESENT AND THE PAST	
Present Emphatic	He certainly *does study* intensely.
Past Emphatic	He *did study* even more last year.

As you can see, the basic forms are identified by their tense names. The progressive and emphatic forms are identified by their tense names plus the words *progressive* and *emphatic*.

EXERCISE A: Recognizing Basic, Progressive, and Emphatic Forms. Identify the form of each verb as *basic, progressive,* or *emphatic.*

EXAMPLE: She had been exercising.
progressive

1. He is trying.
2. I had forgotten.
3. It will sink.
4. She was relaxing.
5. They had been dancing.
6. He promises.
7. She does understand.
8. They had finished.
9. We lost.
10. I will have been waiting.

EXERCISE B: Recognizing the Six Tenses. Write the tense of each verb in Exercise A. If the form is not basic, add the name of the form.

EXAMPLE: She had been exercising.
past perfect progressive

The Four Principal Parts of Verbs

Each tense of a verb is formed from one of the verb's four *principal parts*. Except in the basic forms of the present and past tenses, a helping verb is used with the principal part.

A verb has four principal parts: the present, the present participle, the past, and the past participle.

The chart below shows the principal parts of two common verbs.

THE FOUR PRINCIPAL PARTS			
Present	**Present Participle**	**Past**	**Past Participle**
use	using	used	used
take	taking	took	taken

The first principal part is used for the basic forms of the present and future tenses as well as the emphatic forms. To form the present, an *-s* or *-es* is added whenever the subject is *he, she, it,* or a singular noun *(I use, Rita takes)*. To form the future tense, the helping verb *will* is added *(I will use, Rita will take)*. To form the present emphatic, the helping verbs *do* or *does* are added *(I do use, Rita does take)*. To form the past emphatic, *did* is added *(I did use, Rita did take)*.

The second principal part is used with various helping verbs to produce all six of the progressive forms (*I am using, Rita was taking,* and so on).

The third principal part is used to form the past tense *(I used, Rita took)*.

The fourth principal part is used with helping verbs for the three perfect tenses (*I have used, Rita had taken,* and so on).

EXERCISE C: Recognizing Principal Parts. Identify the principal part used to form each verb in Exercise A.

EXAMPLE: She had been exercising.
present participle

Regular and Irregular Verbs

Depending on their principal parts, verbs are classified into two types: *regular* and *irregular*. The principal parts of regular verbs follow a set pattern. The third and fourth principal parts of irregular verbs, however, differ from verb to verb and must be learned individually.

Regular Verbs. Most verbs, including *use*, are regular.

A regular verb is one whose past and past participle are formed by adding *-ed* or *-d* to the present form.

The past and past participle of regular verbs always have the same form. In the chart on the next page, *have* is in parentheses in front of the past participle to remind you that this verb form is a past participle only if it is used with a helping verb.

Notice that a final consonant is sometimes doubled to form the present participle (sli*pp*ing) as well as the past and past participle (sli*pp*ed). Notice also that a final *e* may be dropped in forming the present participle (lov*i*ng).

PRINCIPAL PARTS OF REGULAR VERBS			
Present	**Present Participle**	**Past**	**Past Participle**
ask	asking	asked	(have) asked
slip	slipping	slipped	(have) slipped
love	loving	loved	(have) loved

Irregular Verbs. Some of the most common verbs, including *take,* are irregular.

An irregular verb is one whose past and past participle are not formed by adding *-ed* or *-d* to the present form.

Irregular verbs form their past and past participle in various ways. The three charts on pages 189–192 show the most common ways. In the first two charts, the verbs have the same past and past participle. The verbs in the third chart deserve special attention because the past and past participle are formed in unpredictable ways.

There are three main usage problems people have with irregular verbs. The first problem is using a principal part that is nonstandard (for example, *catched* instead of *caught*). The second problem is confusing the past and past participle when they are different (for example, "I drunk" instead of "I drank"). The third problem is spelling. As with regular verbs, the final consonant is sometimes doubled to form both the present participle (ge*tt*ing) and the past participle (go*tt*en). A final *e* may also be dropped in forming the present participle (leav*i*ng). Keep these problems in mind as you read the following charts.

IRREGULAR VERBS WITH THE SAME PRESENT, PAST, AND PAST PARTICIPLE			
Present	**Present Participle**	**Past**	**Past Participle**
bid	bidding	bid	(have) bid
burst	bursting	burst	(have) burst
cost	costing	cost	(have) cost
cut	cutting	cut	(have) cut
hit	hitting	hit	(have) hit
hurt	hurting	hurt	(have) hurt

let	letting	let	(have) let
put	putting	put	(have) put
set	setting	set	(have) set
shut	shutting	shut	(have) shut
split	splitting	split	(have) split
spread	spreading	spread	(have) spread
thrust	thrusting	thrust	(have) thrust

IRREGULAR VERBS WITH THE SAME PAST AND PAST PARTICIPLE

Present	Present Participle	Past	Past Participle
bind	binding	bound	(have) bound
bring	bringing	brought	(have) brought
build	building	built	(have) built
buy	buying	bought	(have) bought
catch	catching	caught	(have) caught
fight	fighting	fought	(have) fought
find	finding	found	(have) found
get	getting	got	(have) got *or* gotten
grind	grinding	ground	(have) ground
hang	hanging	hung	(have) hung
hold	holding	held	(have) held
keep	keeping	kept	(have) kept
lay	laying	laid	(have) laid
lead	leading	led	(have) led
leave	leaving	left	(have) left
lose	losing	lost	(have) lost
pay	paying	paid	(have) paid
say	saying	said	(have) said
sell	selling	sold	(have) sold
send	sending	sent	(have) sent
sit	sitting	sat	(have) sat
sleep	sleeping	slept	(have) slept
spend	spending	spent	(have) spent
spin	spinning	spun	(have) spun
stand	standing	stood	(have) stood
stick	sticking	stuck	(have) stuck
strike	striking	struck	(have) struck

swing	swinging	swung	(have) swung
teach	teaching	taught	(have) taught
win	winning	won	(have) won
wind	winding	wound	(have) wound
wring	wringing	wrung	(have) wrung

IRREGULAR VERBS THAT CHANGE IN OTHER WAYS

Present	Present Participle	Past	Past Participle
arise	arising	arose	(have) arisen
begin	beginning	began	(have) begun
blow	blowing	blew	(have) blown
break	breaking	broke	(have) broken
choose	choosing	chose	(have) chosen
come	coming	came	(have) come
do	doing	did	(have) done
draw	drawing	drew	(have) drawn
drink	drinking	drank	(have) drunk
drive	driving	drove	(have) driven
eat	eating	ate	(have) eaten
fall	falling	fell	(have) fallen
fly	flying	flew	(have) flown
freeze	freezing	froze	(have) frozen
give	giving	gave	(have) given
go	going	went	(have) gone
grow	growing	grew	(have) grown
know	knowing	knew	(have) known
lie	lying	lay	(have) lain
ride	riding	rode	(have) ridden
ring	ringing	rang	(have) rung
rise	rising	rose	(have) risen
run	running	ran	(have) run
see	seeing	saw	(have) seen
shake	shaking	shook	(have) shaken
shrink	shrinking	shrank	(have) shrunk
sing	singing	sang	(have) sung
sink	sinking	sank	(have) sunk
slay	slaying	slew	(have) slain
speak	speaking	spoke	(have) spoken
spring	springing	sprang	(have) sprung

steal	stealing	stole	(have) stolen
stride	striding	strode	(have) stridden
strive	striving	strove	(have) striven
swear	swearing	swore	(have) sworn
swim	swimming	swam	(have) swum
take	taking	took	(have) taken
tear	tearing	tore	(have) torn
throw	throwing	threw	(have) thrown
wear	wearing	wore	(have) worn
write	writing	wrote	(have) written

The best way to learn these irregular verbs is to study the charts. If you are in doubt about the principal parts of an irregular verb, check your dictionary. Dictionaries usually list the principal parts of irregular verbs after part-of-speech labels.

EXERCISE D: Learning the Principal Parts of Irregular Verbs. Write the present participle, the past, and the past participle of each verb.

EXAMPLE: ride

riding rode ridden

1. fight	6. catch	11. sit	16. teach
2. let	7. sell	12. freeze	17. sing
3. split	8. slay	13. swim	18. win
4. shrink	9. cost	14. draw	19. tear
5. arise	10. hang	15. stick	20. lay

EXERCISE E: Recognizing Principal Parts in Sentences. Choose the correct form of the verb in parentheses.

EXAMPLE: She (throwed, threw) the ball over the fence.

threw

1. The child (knowed, knew) the answer.
2. The customers (payed, paid) the bill promptly.
3. Grandfather (taught, teached) us how to whittle.
4. The high winds (blew, blowed) all night on the open sea.
5. The audience thought the judges (choosed, chose) the wrong contestant as the winner.
6. Jennifer (layed, laid) the package on the table.

7. Alice (wore, weared) a different blouse every day last week.
8. The bellboy (leaded, led) us to our rooms.
9. On Christmas morning, the eager child (tore, teared) the wrapping paper to pieces.
10. No one knew who had (stealed, stolen) the money.

EXERCISE F: Choosing Between the Past and Past Participle. Choose the correct form of the verb in parentheses. Remember that the past participle is used with a helping verb.

(1) As early as 3000 B.C., the Egyptians had already (began, begun) keeping cats as pets. (2) Over the years cats (grew, grown) very valuable. (3) In particular, the Egyptians (gave, given) cats the job of keeping rats out of their grain supplies. (4) Egyptians (saw, seen) cats as so important that they embalmed them along with Pharaohs! (5) Archaeologists have found cat mummies in tombs where they have (lay, lain) for centuries. (6) Eventually, the Egyptians (came, come) to worship a cat-god called Bast. (7) According to legend, the defeat of the Egyptian army in 525 B.C. (arose, arisen) because of Bast. (8) The Persian enemy (knew, known) of Egyptian cat worship. (9) So the Persian general had (came, come) to battle with a row of cats in front of his troops. (10) Because Egyptian archers refused to shoot toward the sacred animals, victory (gone, went) to the Persians.

Conjugating the Tenses

One very good way to learn all of the forms of either a regular or irregular verb is through *conjugation*.

A conjugation is a complete list of the singular and plural forms of a verb in a particular tense.

The singular and plural forms of a verb correspond to the singular and plural forms of the first-, second-, and third-person personal pronouns.

In the charts on the next three pages, the irregular verb *take* is conjugated in the basic, progressive, and emphatic forms. To conjugate a verb, you need various helping verbs such as *has, do, will,* and so on. You also need the principal parts: the present (*take*), the present participle (*taking*), the past (*took*), and the past participle (*taken*).

The chart below conjugates *take* in the basic forms of the six tenses. Notice that only three principal parts—the present, the past, and the past participle—are used to conjugate the six basic forms.

CONJUGATION OF THE BASIC FORMS OF *TAKE*		
Present	**Singular**	**Plural**
First Person	I take	we take
Second Person	you take	you take
Third Person	he, she, it takes	they take
Past		
First Person	I took	we took
Second Person	you took	you took
Third Person	he, she, it took	they took
Future		
First Person	I will take	we will take
Second Person	you will take	you will take
Third Person	he, she, it will take	they will take
Present Perfect		
First Person	I have taken	we have taken
Second Person	you have taken	you have taken
Third Person	he, she, it has taken	they have taken
Past Perfect		
First Person	I had taken	we had taken
Second Person	you had taken	you had taken
Third Person	he, she, it had taken	they had taken
Future Perfect		
First Person	I will have taken	we will have taken
Second Person	you will have taken	you will have taken
Third Person	he, she, it will have taken	they will have taken

Only one principal part, the present participle, is used to conjugate the six progressive forms.

CONJUGATION OF THE PROGRESSIVE FORMS OF *TAKE*		
Present Progressive	**Singular**	**Plural**
First Person	I am taking	we are taking
Second Person	you are taking	you are taking
Third Person	he, she, it is taking	they are taking
Past Progressive		
First Person	I was taking	we were taking
Second Person	you were taking	you were taking
Third Person	he, she, it was taking	they were taking
Future Progressive		
First Person	I will be taking	we will be taking
Second Person	you will be taking	you will be taking
Third Person	he, she, it will be taking	they will be taking
Present Perfect Progressive		
First Person	I have been taking	we have been taking
Second Person	you have been taking	you have been taking
Third Person	he, she, it has been taking	they have been taking
Past Perfect Progressive		
First Person	I had been taking	we had been taking
Second Person	you had been taking	you had been taking
Third Person	he, she, it had been taking	they had been taking

Future Perfect Progressive		
First Person	I will have been taking	we will have been taking
Second Person	you will have been taking	you will have been taking
Third Person	he, she, it will have been taking	they will have been taking

To conjugate the emphatic forms, one principal part, the present, is used with the helping verbs *do, does,* and *did*.

CONJUGATION OF THE EMPHATIC FORMS OF *TAKE*

Present Emphatic	**Singular**	**Plural**
First Person	I do take	we do take
Second Person	you do take	you do take
Third Person	he, she, it does take	they do take
Past Emphatic		
First Person	I did take	we did take
Second Person	you did take	you did take
Third Person	he, she, it did take	they did take

NOTE ABOUT *BE: Be* is one of the most irregular verbs in its principal parts. The present participle is *being*. The past participle is *been*. The present and the past, however, vary depending on the subject of the verb and the tense, as can be seen in the conjugation of the first three tenses.

PRESENT:	I am	we are
	you are	you are
	he, she, it is	they are
PAST:	I was	we were
	you were	you were
	he, she, it was	they were

FUTURE:	I will be	we will be
	you will be	you will be
	he, she, it will be	they will be

EXERCISE G: Conjugating the Basic Forms of Verbs. Conjugate the basic forms of the two verbs below in the manner shown in the example.

EXAMPLE: choose (conjugated with *I*)

Present: I choose
Past: I chose
Future: I will choose
Present Perfect: I have chosen
Past Perfect: I had chosen
Future Perfect: I will have chosen

1. climb (conjugated with *we*) 2. say (conjugated with *they*)

EXERCISE H: Conjugating the Progressive Forms of Verbs. Conjugate the progressive forms of the two verbs below in the manner shown in the example.

EXAMPLE: choose (conjugated with *I*)

Present Progressive: I am choosing
Past Progressive: I was choosing
Future Progressive: I will be choosing
Present Perfect Progressive: I have been choosing
Past Perfect Progressive: I had been choosing
Future Perfect Progressive: I will have been choosing

1. talk (conjugated with *he*) 2. sing (conjugated with *we*)

EXERCISE I: Conjugating the Emphatic Forms of Verbs. Conjugate the emphatic forms of the two verbs below in the manner shown in the example.

EXAMPLE: choose (conjugated with *I*)

Present Emphatic: I do choose
Past Emphatic: I did choose

1. own (conjugated with *she*) 2. sell (conjugated with *they*)

EXERCISE J: Identifying the Tenses of Verbs in Sentences. Write the tense of each underlined verb and its form if the form is not basic.

EXAMPLE: We have lived in the same house for years.
present perfect

1. I almost froze after walking two hours in the storm.
2. Surprisingly, Betty has written a beautiful poem.
3. This year my parents are spending a lot of money to renovate the house.
4. Juan Carlos rises at dawn to do his exercises.
5. My mother had shut all the windows before leaving.
6. In an hour we will have arrived at the airport.
7. We will be going to Mexico this summer for our vacation.
8. Much to our amazement, my brother ate the entire cake.
9. The documents were lying under the desk all the time.
10. Mr. Williams did try to explain the importance of the test.
11. Who is driving to town for the supplies?
12. By the end of the term, we will have moved to a small town in northern California.
13. Several people have already swum across the lake.
14. Last year our hockey team strove to improve its record.
15. My grandmother was standing at the bus stop for over an hour before the bus came.
16. For the last time, I will explain the rules of the game.
17. As part of my job, I fly to London twice a year.
18. Disappointed, our fullback burst into the locker room.
19. The criminal has paid his debt to society.
20. Charles does expect to be accepted to law school.
21. Will you be speaking to your mother this evening?
22. The villagers were wringing their hands in dismay.
23. The committee has been in session all morning.
24. What did the volunteers hope to achieve?
25. The rude woman thrust herself in front of the line.

DEVELOPING WRITING SKILLS: Using Different Tenses. Use each verb in a sentence of your own.

EXAMPLE: Future perfect of *finish*
We will have finished the painting by dinner time.

1. Present progressive of *go*
2. Past of *wring*
3. Future perfect of *keep*
4. Past emphatic of *wait*
5. Present of *slay*
6. Present perfect of *talk*
7. Past progressive of *take*
8. Present emphatic of *eat*
9. Future of *spend*
10. Present of *lie*
11. Past of *fly*
12. Present progressive of *play*
13. Past perfect of *put*
14. Future of *be*
15. Past of *shrink*
16. Past emphatic of *belong*
17. Present perfect of *bring*
18. Future progressive of *open*
19. Past perfect of *win*
20. Future perfect of *raise*

Expressing Time Through Tense 10.2

In speaking and writing, there are three main categories of time: *present*, *past*, and *future*. The tenses of verbs allow you to express time within these categories in a variety of ways. The basic and progressive forms of the six tenses express time in all three categories. The two emphatic forms, however, express time only in the present and the past.

Uses of Tense in Present Time

Present time can be expressed in a basic form, a progressive form, and an emphatic form.

The three forms of the present tense show present actions or conditions as well as various continuous actions or conditions.

The chart below provides an example of each of these three forms.

FORMS EXPRESSING PRESENT TIME	
Present	She speaks.
Present Progressive	She is speaking.
Present Emphatic	She does speak.

The chart at the top of the next page shows the chief uses of the present tense in its basic form.

USES OF THE PRESENT
Present action: Here they *come.*
Present condition: The air in the room *is* stale.
Regularly occurring action: Grandfather *sings* in the shower.
Regularly occurring condition: I *am* most alert in the morning.
Constant action: Animals *need* air to breathe.
Constant condition: The heart *is* a pump.

The present progressive is used to express continuous actions or conditions taking place now. Notice in the chart below that the actions may be of a long duration or a short duration.

USES OF THE PRESENT PROGRESSIVE
Long continuing action: My uncle *is building* a sailboat.
Short continuing action: I *am whistling* a tune from *Oklahoma.*
Continuing condition: Gloria *is being* extra helpful this week.

The two main uses of the present emphatic are shown in the chart below.

USES OF THE PRESENT EMPHATIC
Emphasizing a statement: I *do believe* you dropped this.
Denying a contrary assertion: Despite the review's claim, that diner *does bake* its own pies.

EXERCISE A: Identifying the Uses of Tense in Present Time. Identify the use of the underlined verb in each sentence, using the labels in the charts above.

EXAMPLE: Carl <u>drives</u> his mother to church every Sunday.
regularly occurring action

1. My brother <u>is picking</u> up Father at the station.
2. I <u>hear</u> loud noises next door.
3. Now the president <u>approaches</u> the podium.
4. I <u>jog</u> three miles every morning.

5. In spite of warnings, my sister still <u>chews</u> her nails.
6. The weather <u>is</u> bad along the entire East Coast today.
7. The members of the club <u>are raising</u> funds through many different activities this year.
8. Mumps and measles <u>are</u> widespread this year.
9. My old aunt <u>walks</u> to town almost every morning at the same time.
10. I <u>do see</u> a ship in the distance.

Uses of Tense in Past Time

Past time can be expressed in seven different forms.

The seven forms that express past time show actions and conditions beginning in the past.

The following chart gives an example of each form.

FORMS EXPRESSING PAST TIME	
Past	She spoke.
Present Perfect	She has spoken.
Past Perfect	She had spoken.
Past Progressive	She was speaking.
Present Perfect Progressive	She has been speaking.
Past Perfect Progressive	She had been speaking.
Past Emphatic	She did speak.

The uses of the most common form, the past, are shown in the following chart.

USES OF THE PAST
Completed action: Judy *finished* her science project.
Completed condition: Father *was* terribly depressed.

Notice that these verbs show completed actions or conditions that took place at some indefinite time. The time could be made definite by adding such words as *last year* or *yesterday*.

The present perfect differs from the past in that the present perfect cannot be made definite by adding such words as *last year* or *yesterday*. It also differs in that it can be used to show actions or conditions continuing to the present time.

USES OF THE PRESENT PERFECT
Completed action (indefinite time): Sue *has washed* her hair.
Completed condition (indefinite time): She *has been* ill.
Action continuing to present: I *have worked* here a year.
Condition continuing to present: She *has been* here since May.

The past perfect shows a connection between two past events. It is used to show an action or condition completed before another action or condition began.

USES OF THE PAST PERFECT
Action completed before another past action: Bob *had studied* all the college catalogs before he filled out any applications.
Condition completed before another past condition: I *had been* a member of the club long before you were.

The three progressive forms expressing past time are used to show continuous actions and conditions.

USES OF PROGRESSIVE TO EXPRESS PAST TIME	
Past Progressive	*Long continuing action in the past:* Last summer my brother *was working* in Florida. *Short continuing action in the past:* I *was making* omelets this morning. *Continuing condition in the past:* Frank *was being* careful with the pesticide.
Present Perfect Progressive	*Action continuing to the present:* Bob *has been studying* college catalogs.
Past Perfect Progressive	*Continuing action interrupted by another:* The wheat crop *had been thriving* until it was attacked by locusts.

The past emphatic is used to emphasize a statement or to deny a statement about something in the past.

USES OF THE PAST EMPHATIC	
Emphasizing a statement:	I *did favor* his candidacy until he changed his platform.
Denying a contrary assertion:	But I *did finish* my homework!

EXERCISE B: Using the Past, the Present Perfect, and the Past Perfect. Choose the correct form of the verb in parentheses.

EXAMPLE: Marie (came, has come) home yesterday.
came

1. Joshua (has been reading, had read) all of the book before the quiz yesterday.
2. The train (pulled, has pulled) into the station hours ago.
3. Katherine (had been working, has been working) on that poem for a month, and it's still not finished.
4. Every day last week the mail carrier (brought, has brought) me at least one letter.
5. When we drank the soda, we noticed it (has lost, had lost) its fizz.
6. Before he spoke, the demonstrators (rushed, have rushed) down the aisle.
7. The young children never (have seen, had seen) a bald eagle before yesterday.
8. I (developed, have developed) this process a week ago.
9. The judge (has granted, granted) the lawyer's request for leniency yesterday.
10. Mr. Suarez (was working, worked) when a thunderstorm suddenly began.

EXERCISE C: Identifying the Uses of Tense in Past Time. Identify the use of each underlined verb, using the labels in the charts on pages 201–203.

EXAMPLE: He <u>has been</u> in Miami for a year now.
condition continuing to present

1. I have seen that movie.
2. Lou finished his assignment this morning.
3. The actors have been rehearsing the new play for three months.
4. I had read the book before it was assigned to the class.
5. Keith has finished three paintings.
6. Mother was very happy.
7. We have never been very lucky.
8. Bill had reached Albuquerque before the roads were closed.
9. Linda had been working until she broke her leg.
10. Although she began slowly, Marian did win.

Uses of Tense in Future Time

Future time can be expressed in four forms.

The four forms that express future time show future actions or conditions.

The chart below gives an example of each form.

FORMS EXPRESSING FUTURE TIME	
Future	She will speak.
Future Perfect	She will have spoken.
Future Progressive	She will be speaking.
Future Perfect Progressive	She will have been speaking.

The uses of the basic forms are shown in the chart below.

USES OF THE FUTURE AND THE FUTURE PERFECT	
Future	*Future action:* We *will race* in the main event. *Future condition:* The room *will be* warm soon.
Future Perfect	*Future action completed before another:* I *will have finished* the book by the end of the week. *Future condition completed before another:* My sister *will have been* out of school five years by the time I graduate.

The uses of the two progressive forms that express future time are shown in the following chart.

USES OF PROGRESSIVE TO EXPRESS FUTURE TIME	
Future Progressive	*Continuing future action:* The team *will be practicing* during July and August.
Future Perfect Progressive	*Continuing future action completed before another:* By the time of our first game, I *will have been practicing* for two months.

NOTE ABOUT EXPRESSING FUTURE TIME WITH THE PRESENT TENSE: Sometimes, the present and the present progressive are used to suggest future time.

EXAMPLES: Ted *plays* Romeo in the play tomorrow night.
We *are flying* to Spain next week.

EXERCISE D: Identifying the Uses of Tense in Future Time. Identify the use of each underlined verb, using the labels above and on page 204.

EXAMPLE: Louise will have finished her report before I begin.
future action completed before another

1. Mr. Drake will be visiting our class this afternoon.
2. Clare will tell you her decision tomorrow.
3. I will have been studying for two hours before you arrive.
4. He will have been here a year next June.
5. The company will provide free refreshments at the party.
6. The buses will be late today because of the snow.
7. Ethel will be practicing this afternoon.
8. He will have left by the time we get there.
9. I will have been driving all night when I reach Maine.
10. The fortuneteller will tell you only pleasant things.

EXERCISE E: Using Tense in Future Time. Write the indicated form of each verb in parentheses.

EXAMPLE: Carol (deliver—*future*) her speech tonight.
will deliver

1. The plane (arrive—*future*) in about two hours.
2. By the time I return home in September, I (travel—*future perfect progressive*) for six months.
3. Before school ends, Steven (make—*future perfect*) his career decision.
4. We (visit—*future progressive*) parts of Canada in June.
5. In another ten years, they (open—*future*) the time capsule.
6. The musicians (perform—*future perfect progressive*) for three months by the time they reach Sweden.
7. In May, she (be—*future perfect*) vice-president for a year.
8. They (go—*future progressive*) to the convention in April.
9. Before college, Terry (work—*future*) for a year.
10. By tonight, we (drive—*future perfect*) 400 miles.

Shifts in Tense

In sentences with more than one verb, it is important to keep the time sequence consistent.

When showing a sequence of events, do not shift tenses unnecessarily.

A sentence with a compound verb should generally have both verbs in the same tense.

INCORRECT: Father *turned* (PAST) the key and *starts* (PRESENT) the car.

CORRECT: Father *turned* (PAST) the key and *started* (PAST) the car.

You should also not shift tenses unnecessarily from one sentence to another.

INCORRECT: The actor *collapsed* (PAST) on stage. Then he *sits* (PRESENT) up.

CORRECT: The actor *collapsed* (PAST) on stage. Then he *sat* (PAST) up.

Sometimes, it will be necessary to shift tenses. Only the meaning can tell you for sure when you must shift tenses.

INCORRECT: If we *have* (PRESENT) time, we *visit* (PRESENT) our uncle in Boston.

CORRECT: If we *have* (PRESENT) time, we *will visit* (FUTURE) our uncle in Boston.

EXERCISE F: Avoiding Unnecessary Shifts in Tense. Rewrite each sentence, correcting tense problems by changing the second verb.

EXAMPLE: When I finished my work, Jim comes in.
When I finished my work, Jim came in.

1. My father growled at the salesman and tells him to leave.
2. I landed in Stockholm and arrive an hour later at my hotel.
3. Beethoven conducted the first performance of his Ninth Symphony when he is already deaf.
4. It has been several years since I last see my grandfather.
5. I walked into the room and find no one there.
6. As soon as the operation was over, I visit him.
7. He exercises in the health spa before he left for work.
8. The visitor stayed two hours and then leaves abruptly.
9. The first story Hemingway wrote was "Up in Michigan," and the last is "Old Man at the Bridge."
10. The referee asked a question or two and stops the fight.
11. The car has front-wheel drive and came with power brakes and power steering.
12. If Susan wins first prize, she will have been getting many offers to perform.
13. They were sailing to Bermuda when you are on your trip.
14. My family had dinner at a Japanese restaurant, and then they go to the movies.
15. When she completed the assignment, she achieves a first for an American architect.
16. When I drive for more than ten hours, I got very tired.
17. This museum is open seven days a week, but the art gallery was not.
18. Dad walked into the factory and sees an unbelievable sight.
19. When I reached him, he has already contacted his sister.
20. The receptionist sat at his desk and ignores my question.

EXERCISE G: Correcting Errors in Tense. Rewrite the following paragraph, correcting unnecessary shifts in tense.

(1) Bucharest, the capital of Romania, has a charm that was unique in Eastern Europe. (2) There have been still many old, elaborately decorated Baroque buildings that survive the bombings of World War II. (3) The National Gallery of Art, open

daily except on Mondays, featured the work of Constantin Brancusi. (4) It is a short distance to the Presidential Palace from the museum. (5) Both were close to the colorful Cismigiu Gardens. (6) If your legs hold out, it will be only a short walk to the National Opera House. (7) Most of the time you will probably used the excellent public transportation to get around the city. (8) Fare on the trolleys and trams was only seven cents. (9) Most of the time, you will want to walk since the downtown area was only two miles across. (10) For a side excursion, you may want to visit the Black Sea coast, only two hundred miles to the east.

Modifiers That Help Clarify Tense

Sometimes, you can make the time something took place clearer by adding a modifier. Useful modifiers include adverbs such as *always* and *occasionally* and phrases such as *at times* and *yesterday night*.

Use modifiers when they can help clarify tense.

EXAMPLES: Grandmother walks *occasionally* in the park.

In the evening he walked along the beach.

Now and then, I try to bake fresh bread.

EXERCISE H: Using Modifiers to Improve Meaning. Complete each sentence with a modifier of your choice that helps to clarify the meaning.

EXAMPLE: I ______ brush my teeth in the morning.

always

1. ______ Sandy walks to the bus terminal.
2. Mom and Dad expect to visit me ______ at college.
3. Our principal ______ visits conventions in other states.
4. ______ I will speak to the manager about a raise.
5. She developed ______ into a fine artist.
6. The agent said the flight will arrive ______ .
7. ______ I enjoy driving alone into the country.
8. I wrote to the hotel for directions ______.
9. The missing child appeared ______, terribly confused.
10. ______ my father worked as a leather craftsman.

DEVELOPING WRITING SKILLS: Using the Correct Tense in Your Writing. Begin or complete each sentence with words of your own choice.

EXAMPLE: We waited patiently until ______.

We waited patiently until the rescue team arrived.

1. We are going to the movies after ______.
2. The committee reached a decision and ______.
3. ______ as soon as she can.
4. If he is disappointed, ______.
5. By the time the game ends, ______.
6. ______ and finished before the deadline.
7. When I phoned the office later, ______.
8. I really do intend to go if ______.
9. He had been working on his stamp collection when ______.
10. The jury agreed that ______.
11. ______ since she really wants to drive.
12. Jasper answered the bell, opened the door, and ______.
13. I had hoped that ______.
14. The driver reached the crossroads and ______.
15. ______ and then she saw the bridge.
16. ______ and with great joy hugged his dad.
17. My sister did expect an offer, but ______.
18. Our old roof often leaks when ______.
19. He will have earned half a million dollars before ______.
20. Before we leave California, ______.

Active and Passive Voice 10.3

In addition to showing time by their tense, most verbs can show whether the subject is performing the action or having the action performed on it. This quality of a verb is called *voice*.

Voice is the form of a verb that shows whether the subject is performing the action.

There are two voices in English: *active* and *passive*. Only action verbs show voice; linking verbs do not.

Differences Between Active and Passive Voice

Any action verb, with or without a direct object, can be in the active voice.

A verb is active if its subject performs the action.

Notice in the examples below that the subjects are performing the action. In the first example, the subject, *Ken,* performs the action, and the direct object, *typewriter,* receives the action. In the second example, the subject, *sister,* performs the action, but there is no receiver of the action.

ACTIVE VOICE: Ken *bought* a new typewriter.
My sister *drives* carefully.

Most action verbs can also be used in the passive voice.

A verb is passive if its action is performed upon the subject.

Notice in the examples below that the performer of an action may or may not be named. In the first sentence, the word *Ken* is no longer the subject; it is the object of the preposition *by.* In the second sentence, the driver is not named.

PASSIVE VOICE: A new typewriter *was bought* by Ken.
My sister *was driven* to school.

EXERCISE A: Distinguishing Between the Active and Passive Voice. Identify each verb as *active* or *passive.*

EXAMPLE: The movie was seen by our whole family.
passive

1. The letter was obviously signed by a stranger.
2. The gates in front of the embassy were closed each night.
3. Several business people raced through the airport to catch their flights.
4. I try to watch as little television as possible.
5. Most of the books have been chosen by the librarians.
6. All four of these symphonies were composed by Brahms.

7. The next morning we began our long trek through the steaming jungle.
8. The air conditioner was delivered later in the day.
9. The mayor asked for volunteers to serve on the new committee for planning the city's holiday festival.
10. A decaying tooth was extracted by my dentist.
11. The patient was being taken by ambulance to the plane.
12. With wild abandon the players charged across the field.
13. My mother saves manufacturers' discount coupons.
14. On a trip across country, the car will have been driven by several people.
15. The guest speaker explained his theory to a rather uninterested audience.
16. The judge suddenly called the lawyers into her chamber.
17. A strange creature has been spotted for some time now in the mountains.
18. Gordon Grant painted pictures of magnificent sailing ships on the high seas.
19. The crates were received months late on the wharf.
20. The celebrity waved to his loyal fans.

The Forms of Passive Verbs

Changing from the active to the passive voice alters the form of the verb. Passive verbs always have two parts.

A passive verb is made from a form of *be* plus the past participle of a transitive verb.

A transitive verb, as you may recall, is one that can have a direct object.

The tense of a passive verb is determined by the form of the verb *be*. In the passive verb *was bought*, for example, the helping verb *was* makes the verb phrase past tense.

Remember that all forms of a verb in the passive voice require the past participle, regardless of the tense. It is only the helping verb that changes and thus determines the tense.

The chart on the next page gives a short conjugation in the passive voice of the verb *drive* with the pronoun *he*. Notice that there are only two progressive forms and no emphatic forms.

THE VERB *DRIVE* IN THE PASSIVE VOICE	
Present	he is driven
Past	he was driven
Future	he will be driven
Present Perfect	he has been driven
Past Perfect	he had been driven
Future Perfect	he will have been driven
Present Progressive	he is being driven
Past Progressive	he was being driven

EXERCISE B: Forming the Tenses of Passive Verbs. Conjugate each verb in the passive voice, using the chart above as your model.

1. give (with *we*)
2. tell (with *they*)
3. call (with *you*)
4. send (with *she*)

Using Voice Correctly

Once you have learned how to form verbs in the active and passive voice, you need to know when to use which voice. There are no firm rules, but good writers follow certain conventions with regard to voice.

Use the active voice whenever possible.

The active voice is generally preferred because fewer words are required. The passive voice requires a form of the helping verb *be* and often a prepositional phrase beginning with *by*. Compare the following two sentences. Notice that the sentence with the passive verb is longer and less direct.

ACTIVE VOICE: Billy *delivered* the clarinet.

PASSIVE VOICE: The clarinet *was delivered* by Billy.

There are, of course, times when it is more appropriate to use the passive voice.

Use the passive voice to emphasize the receiver of an action rather than the performer of an action.

Placing a word at or near the beginning of a sentence helps emphasize its importance. When you want to stress the importance of the receiver of an action, then it is proper to use the passive voice.

PASSIVE VOICE: Mr. Stevens *was given* the award yesterday by a city official.

The passive voice is also effective when the performer of the action is unknown or unimportant.

Use the passive voice to point out the receiver of an action whenever the performer is not important or not easily identified.

EXAMPLES: The nuclear material *was removed* to a safe location.

The unsigned letter *was left* under the door.

EXERCISE C: Using the Active Voice. Rewrite each of the ten sentences in Exercise A that have verbs in the passive voice. Change or add words as necessary in order to put each verb into the active voice.

EXAMPLE: The movie was seen by our whole family.

Our whole family saw the movie.

EXERCISE D: Correcting Unnecessary Use of the Passive Voice. Rewrite the following paragraph, changing at least five uses of the passive voice to active.

EXAMPLE: The uses of aspirin have been studied by scientists for many years.

Scientists have studied the uses of aspirin for many years.

(1) After eighty years of use, aspirin today is still regarded as a "wonder drug." (2) Aspirin, acetylsalicylic acid, was first developed as a painkiller by Felix Hoffman, a German chemist, in 1893. (3) He had been asked by his father, who was suffering from rheumatism, to develop a pain-reliever that would not irritate the stomach. (4) Though the formula worked, how it worked could not be told by scientists. (5) Since its introduc-

tion, aspirin has been used successfully to reduce fever, pain, and inflammation. (6) Not long ago, a new use for aspirin was uncovered by researchers. (7) The one major drawback of aspirin has always been its tendency to cause intestinal bleeding. (8) This drawback now has been turned into an advantage. (9) It has been discovered that this quality of aspirin may prevent blood clots that often lead to heart attacks and strokes. (10) This is welcome news to the aspirin industry.

DEVELOPING WRITING SKILLS: **Using the Active and Passive Voice in Writing.** Write a short description of something exciting that happened to you recently. Include two appropriate sentences using the passive voice correctly. Make sure all the other sentences use the active voice.

Skills Review and Writing Workshop

Verb Usage

CHECKING YOUR SKILLS

Rewrite the following paragraph, correcting all errors in verb usage. Use the active voice where appropriate.

(1) The oldest bat fossils which have been founded are 50 million years old. (2) The dark world of bats have been hidden for a long time. (3) Recently, however, their nocturnal habits has been studied by scientists. (4) By 1990 Dr. Merlin D. Tuttle will have been studied bats for nearly 30 years. (5) Despite popular opinion, bats have not been attacking humans. (6) People has also thought bats is attracted to women's hair, but that is a myth. (7) More than 130 different kinds of trees and shrubs has been pollinated by bats. (8) Unfortunately, bats are hunted and catched for food by people in undeveloped countries. (9) Laws which have recently been past have hurted bats by closing up their caves. (10) If that happens too often, entire species were eliminated.

USING USAGE SKILLS IN WRITING

Writing the History of a School Chair

The writer who knows how to use verbs is in charge of time. Compare the person who might have sat in your school chair 100 years ago with the person who will sit in it 100 years from now. Follow the steps below to write your comparison.

Prewriting: Imagine a student who lived 100 years ago. What did he or she wear? What and how did he or she study? Ask the same questions about a student who will sit in your chair 100 years from now.

Writing: You may want to write about the past and future classroom as well as the past and future student. Organize your comparison by discussing one subject at a time.

Revising: Check your verbs. Make sure they are correct and that the majority are in the active voice. Use the checklists on Pages 189–192. After you have revised, proofread carefully.

Chapter 11

Pronoun Usage

At one time in the history of the English language, both nouns and pronouns changed their forms to indicate how they were being used in a sentence. Today, nouns change form only to show possession: A noun is made possessive by adding an apostrophe and an *-s* (a *girl's* scarf) or just an apostrophe (the two *boys'* gloves).

Pronouns in modern English, however, still change their form often to show how they are being used in a sentence. This chapter will explain the various forms of pronouns and their uses in sentences.

11.1 The Cases of Pronouns

Case is a term used to describe the different forms of nouns and pronouns.

Case is the form of a noun or a pronoun that indicates its use in a sentence.

In this section you will learn how to recognize the three cases of pronouns and when to use them in sentences.

The Three Cases

Both nouns and pronouns have three cases.

The three cases are the nominative, the objective, and the possessive.

The following chart shows the uses of each of these three cases.

Case	Use in Sentence
Nominative	Subject or Predicative Nominative
Objective	Direct Object, Indirect Object, Object of a Preposition, or Object of a Verbal
Possessive	To Show Ownership

Using the correct case of nouns is seldom a problem because the form changes only in the possessive case.

NOMINATIVE: The *car* would not start.

OBJECTIVE: We could not start the *car*.

POSSESSIVE: The *car's* battery was dead.

In the first sentence, *car* is *nominative* because it is the subject. In the second, *car* is *objective* because it is the direct object. The same form is used for both cases. Only the *possessive* case of nouns requires a change in form, usually by adding an apostrophe and an *-s*.

This section focuses on personal pronouns because they often require a change in form for all three cases. The chart below shows the various forms of the personal pronouns in the three cases.

Nominative	Objective	Possessive
I	me	my, mine
you	you	your, yours
he, she, it	him, her, it	his, her, hers, its
we	us	our, ours
they	them	their, theirs

EXERCISE A: Identifying Case. Write the case of each underlined pronoun. Then write its use.

EXAMPLE: The witness finally told the truth about <u>them</u>.
objective (object of a preposition)

1. Father and he will meet Mother at the station.
2. Please give him the letter now.
3. Our reasons are not really important.
4. The doctor agreed to discuss the symptoms with them.
5. Between you and me, I think Bill is telling the truth.
6. The team captain is she.
7. Our poster is the best so far.
8. In the morning they began to cross the lake.
9. Are you sure that's her work?
10. The principal spoke to us.
11. My friends and I collected funds for cancer research.
12. Your congressional representative just phoned.
13. This unpleasant matter is between him and them.
14. I gave her a number of ideas about the campaign.
15. Bring the reports to us at once.
16. Won't you tell the reporters what really happened?
17. Undoubtedly, those keys belong to them.
18. We want to pay for the gift.
19. A special effort was made by her.
20. I know my records are there.

The Nominative Case

There are two major uses of pronouns in the nominative case.

Use the nominative case for the subject of a verb and for a predicate nominative.

The chart below illustrates these two uses.

NOMINATIVE PRONOUNS	
Use	**Examples**
Subject	*She* is the conductor of the band. *I* will wait only a few minutes. *They* danced while *we* sat.
Predicate Nominative	The conductor is *she*. It is *I*. Our delegates have always been *they*.

As the last three sentences in the chart show, formal usage requires that the nominative case be used after a linking verb. In informal usage, however, it has become customary to use the objective case after linking verbs.

INFORMAL USAGE: The conductor is *her*.
It is *me*.
Our delegates have always been *them*.

Informal usage is appropriate for casual conversations, but you should use the nominative case after linking verbs in formal writing.

Nominative Pronouns in Compounds. Using the nominative case is sometimes a problem when the pronoun is part of a compound subject or a compound predicative nominative. For a compound subject, check yourself by mentally removing the other subject.

COMPOUND SUBJECT: Marie and *I* washed the dishes.
(*I* washed the dishes.)
He and Beth will make the arrangements.
(*He* will make the arrangements.)

When the pronoun is part of a compound predicate nomintive, check yourself by mentally rewording the sentence.

COMPOUND PREDICATE NOMINATIVE: The winners were Tim and *she*.
(Tim and *she* were the winners.)
The candidates are Kay and *I*.
(Kay and *I* are the candidates.)

Nominative Pronouns with Appositives. Appositives sometimes follow a pronoun in order to rename it or identify it. If a pronoun used as a subject or predicate nominative is followed by an appositive, you still use the nominative case.

SUBJECT: *We* cheerleaders attend every home game.

PREDICATE NOMINATIVE: The ones who suffer the most are *we* the students.

EXERCISE B: Identifying Pronouns in the Nominative Case. Choose the pronoun in the nominative case to complete each sentence. Then write the use of the pronoun.

EXAMPLE: Phyllis and (us, we) are giving the party.
we (subject)

1. Terry and (me, I) went to a movie last night.
2. (We, Us) sophomores are planning the activities.
3. (She, Her) and Robert are the only ones absent.
4. The losers were Maureen and (I, me).
5. I can't believe that (her, she) and Greg are in town.
6. Your new teacher is (he, him).
7. Craig and (her, she) cleaned the whole house.
8. The new students are Cynthia and (he, him).
9. Barry and (I, me) solved the problem.
10. The counselor to see about that problem is (her, she).

EXERCISE C: Using Pronouns in the Nominative Case. Write a nominative pronoun to complete each sentence. Then write the use of the pronoun.

EXAMPLE: Alma and ______ will do the shopping.
I (subject)

1. Fred and ______ will finish all the chores.
2. ______ volunteer fire fighters will respond to the call.
3. The leaders of the combat team are ______.
4. Have ______ seriously considered his offer?
5. ______ is snowing more than an inch an hour.
6. ______ has been elected captain of the Boosters.
7. The lieutenant is ______.
8. ______ himself agreed to speak to the captain.
9. Yes, ______ is my favorite grandmother.
10. The bakers are Betty and ______.
11. The real culprits are ______ second-year players.
12. ______ can't be expected to do it all.
13. Mr. Bogan and ______ decided to speak to the principal.
14. Honestly, ______ men will prepare the entire picnic.
15. I believe the winner is ______.
16. My brother and ______ are best friends.
17. The last leader of the Brownies was ______.
18. ______ won't believe my astonishment.
19. Jerry and ______ are going to Washington.
20. It is ______ who revealed the secret.

The Objective Case

The objective case is used with the objects of verbs and prepositions as well as with the objects of verbals.

Use the objective case for the object of any verb, preposition, or verbal.

The chart below provides examples of objective pronouns used as direct objects, indirect objects, objects of prepositions, and objects of participles, gerunds, and infinitives.

OBJECTIVE PRONOUNS	
Use	**Examples**
Direct Object	I baked *them* yesterday. Our teacher praised *her*.
Indirect Object	Give *him* the good news. Alice gave *us* the tickets.
Object of Preposition	Between *us*, there are no secrets. Walk beside *them*.
Object of Participle	Racing *her*, he crashed into a fence. The girl chasing *them* was her sister.
Object of Gerund	Dad likes helping *me* with my homework. Warning *them* was my primary concern.
Object of Infinitive	To tell *her* clearly, he had to shout. He wants to ask *me* about the party.

Objective Pronouns in Compounds. If an objective pronoun is part of a compound, make sure you have selected the correct form by removing the other part of the compound.

EXAMPLES: The manager promoted John and *her*.
(The manager promoted *her*.)

Tom gave my sister and *me* five dollars.
(Tom gave *me* five dollars.)

The newcomers voted for Charles and *her*.
(The newcomers voted for *her*.)

The man helping Louise and *me* was a fire fighter. (The man helping *me* was a fire fighter.)

Catching the twins and *him* was a major problem. (Catching *him* was a major problem.)

Grandmother wanted to invite my cousins and *me*. (Grandmother wanted to invite *me*.)

A special problem with compound objects occurs with the preposition *between*. As with any other preposition, you must use an objective pronoun after this preposition.

INCORRECT: This matter is between you and *I*.

CORRECT: This matter is between you and *me*.

Objective Pronouns with Appositives. If an appositive appears after a pronoun used as an object, make sure you use an objective pronoun.

DIRECT OBJECT: The dean reprimanded *us* girls.

INDIRECT OBJECT: They awarded *us* leaders a service letter.

OBJECT OF PREPOSITION: All of *us* troublemakers were severely punished.

EXERCISE D: Identifying Pronouns in the Objective Case. Choose the pronoun in the objective case to complete each sentence. Then write the use of the pronoun.

EXAMPLE: The principal wants to see (him, he) immediately.
him (object of infinitive)

1. Larry saw (I, me) in town yesterday.
2. Give the apple to (her, she).
3. My uncle sent a letter to (me, I).
4. I had lunch with (they, them) just last week.
5. Carol wants to tell (him, he) about the new program offered by her high school.
6. Just between you and (I, me), I don't think Tim will win.
7. The woman babysitting (they, them) was very responsible.
8. Mary tried to ask (he, him) about the incident.
9. The officer found (her, she) in the playground on the new set of swings.
10. Please stand in front of (me, I).

EXERCISE E: Using Pronouns in the Objective Case. Write an objective pronoun to complete each sentence. Then write the use of the pronoun.

EXAMPLE: My parents gave ______ a watch for my birthday.
me (indirect object)

1. Of all of ______, I like Mary the best.
2. Bruce told ______ his side of the story.
3. The clerk can't imagine how he found ______.
4. I expect the argument will have to be settled between Bob and ______.
5. Your plan pleased Sue and ______.
6. The coach scolded ______ girls.
7. You must give Arthur and ______ the entire report.
8. To you and ______, I must apologize for my rashness.
9. Grandfather always gave ______ good advice.
10. I bought new sweaters for Charles and ______.
11. The teacher handed Mary, Louise, and ______ our passes.
12. Between you and ______, I know that I am right.
13. I gave ______ a chance to try out.
14. From ______, we got much useful information.
15. They lent ______ boys a trailer.
16. I warned Bess about Michael and ______.
17. Give ______ another week to reach a decision.
18. I refused to speak about ______.
19. Monet's work gave ______ new ideas about style.
20. Without Steven and ______, we would have failed.

The Possessive Case

The possessive case of pronouns does not generally cause the same problems as the other two cases. It is used to show possession before nouns and before gerunds. Some possessive pronouns are also used by themselves.

Use the possessive case before nouns to show ownership.

EXAMPLES: *My* shoes do not fit properly.
The principal visited *our* class.
Their engagement came as a surprise.

Use the possessive case before gerunds.

EXAMPLES: *Your* complaining bothers all of us.

We did not like *his* chattering in the theater.

Use certain possessive pronouns by themselves to indicate possession.

EXAMPLES: That book is *hers*, not *his*.

Is this money *yours* or *mine*?

Sometimes, possessive pronouns cause problems because they are incorrectly spelled with an apostrophe. Spellings such as *your's, our's, their's,* and *her's* are incorrect. In addition, do not confuse a possessive pronoun with a contraction.,

POSSESSIVE PRONOUN: The monkey wanted out of *its* cage.

CONTRACTION: *It's* hard to believe that they are not coming.

EXERCISE F: Using Pronouns in the Possessive Case. Choose the correct word in each set of parentheses.

EXAMPLE: The teacher was tired of (his, him) talking in class.

his

1. I think this book is (yours, your's).
2. The door fell off (its, it's) hinges.
3. (Its, It's) a beautiful day today.
4. (Their, They're) answers were unsatisfactory.
5. The angry woman finally told him that (his, him) nagging had to stop.
6. The camera and the manual are (ours, our's).
7. The dog looked for (its, it's) master.
8. I'm quite sure that this pencil is (mine, mine's).
9. Are all of those gowns (hers, her's)?
10. Father wants (their, them) practicing to stop soon.
11. I can't see why you object to (my, me) borrowing your book for the afternoon.
12. He thinks that (you, you're) very well prepared.
13. (They're, Their) scheduled to arrive in an hour.
14. (Our, Us) dancing did not impress the audience.
15. Do you know how many of these magazines are (their's, theirs)?

16. Mother liked (my, me) singing.
17. (Your, You) leaving the committee meeting now is out of the question.
18. The insulted woman demanded (his, his's) apology.
19. (Her, Hers) singing delighted the children.
20. I wonder if (its, it's) raining outside.

EXERCISE G: Using All Three Cases. Choose the correct word in each set of parentheses.

1. The doctor told both William and (she, her) his reasons for prescribing the medicine.
2. (He, Him) and (she, her) make a fine team.
3. (Their, They're) contributions cannot be overestimated.
4. These sketches are definitely (her's, hers).
5. Mozart and the young Beethoven were similar in (their, they're) musical styles.
6. Why can't we reach David and (they, them)?
7. Unquestionably, the outstanding speaker was (she, her).
8. Between (we, us), nobody expected such a victory.
9. Those skates surely are (their's, theirs).
10. The team waited for (him, he) until (he, him) arrived.
11. The company broke (its, it's) promise to (us, we) all.
12. Next to (he, him), our section leader is a saint.
13. Undoubtedly, the two best runners are (they, them).
14. Disraeli and (he, him) were the two best English prime ministers of the nineteenth century.
15. (They're, Their) by far our best musicians.
16. With (your's, your) experience, we should succeed.
17. The Student Council president told (we, us) girls the news.
18. Is (her, she) really serious about going to Europe?
19. In truth, it was (he, him) who left early.
20. Won't you join (us, we) players for a game of bridge?

DEVELOPING WRITING SKILLS: Writing Sentences with Nominative, Objective, and Possessive Pronouns. Use each item in a sentence of your own.

EXAMPLE: my mother and her

I told the news to my mother and her.

1. my staff and he
2. them and Pedro
3. his friends and I
4. our team and they
5. you and me
6. Ricky and him
7. we and the Smiths
8. he and my father
9. she and you
10. Bill, Ellen, and she
11. the coach and I
12. she and they
13. us and them
14. your dog and me
15. you and him
16. her and Ms. Wallenberg
17. us football players
18. we sophomores
19. us cheerleaders
20. she and I

11.2 Special Problems with Pronouns

In this section you will study the proper uses of *who* and *whom* and the related forms *whoever* and *whomever*. You will also study the use of pronouns in clauses where some words are omitted but understood.

Using *Who* and *Whom* Correctly

Choices involving *who* and *whom* and the related forms *whoever* and *whomever* are less confusing when the specific uses of the words are understood.

***Who* and *whoever* are nominative. *Whom* and *whomever* are objective.**

The chart below shows the forms of these pronouns and their uses in sentences.

Case	Pronouns	Use in Sentence
Nominative	who, whoever	Subject or Predicate Nominative
Objective	whom, whomever	Direct Object, Object of a Verbal, or Object of a Preposition
Possessive	whose, whosever	To Show Ownership

The following pages focus on the nominative and objective pronouns since the possessive case rarely causes problems.

NOTE ABOUT *WHOSE:* Do not confuse the contraction *who's*, which means *who is*, with the possessive pronoun *whose*.

POSSESSIVE PRONOUN: *Whose* short story won the contest?

CONTRACTION: *Who's* our first singer tonight?

The Nominative Case: *Who* and *Whoever*. The nominative case is used for subjects and for predicate nominatives.

Use *who* or *whoever* for the subject of a verb.

EXAMPLES: *Who* is the president of France?

I know *who* was the most valuable player last year.

He chose *whoever* volunteered to serve.

In the last two sentences, *who* and *whoever* are the subjects of subordinate clauses. You can be sure you are using the correct case in a subordinate clause by determining the use of the pronoun. Consider the pronoun in the following sentence.

EXAMPLE: I will accept help from *whoever* will offer it.

The first step in checking the case of the pronoun is to isolate the subordinate clause. In this example the subordinate clause is *whoever will offer it*, a noun clause acting as the object of the preposition *from*. The next step is to see how the words in the subordinate clause are used. The verb in the clause is *will offer*; the direct object is *it*. *Whoever* is the correct pronoun because it acts as a subject and, therefore,must be in the nominative case.

The nominative case is also used for predicate nominatives.

Use *who* or *whoever* for a predicate nominative.

EXAMPLE: The victim is *who*?

A problem may arise when the pronoun is the predicate nominative in a subordinate clause.

EXAMPLE: The police do not know *who* the victim is.

To see if the pronoun is correct, first isolate the subordinate clause (*who the victim is*). Next, determine each word's use within the clause. Since this clause is inverted, put it into normal word order: *the victim is who*. You can now see that the subject is *victim*, the verb is *is*, and *who* is the predicate nominative of the linking verb. Since predicate nominatives require the nominative case, *who* is correct.

The Objective Case: *Whom* and *Whomever.* The objective case of these pronouns is used for direct objects of verbs, the objects of a verbal, and for objects of prepositions.

Use *whom* and *whomever* for the direct object of a verb or the object of a verbal.

In the following example, *whom* is the object of the infinitive *to find*. Check the pronoun's case by mentally rewording the sentence.

EXAMPLE: *Whom* did you expect to find?
(You did expect to find *whom*?)

Pronouns in the objective case also occur in the subordinate clauses of complex sentences.

EXAMPLES: She did not know *whom* he chose.

You can select *whomever* you want.

To see if the correct pronouns have been used, first isolate the subordinate clause (*whom he chose, whomever you want*). Next, put the clauses in normal word order: *he chose whom, you want whomever*. It now becomes clear that the subjects are *he* and *you* and that the direct objects are correctly *whom* and *whomever*.

The objective case is also used for the object of a preposition.

Use *whom* and *whomever* for the object of a preposition.

Whom is the object of the preposition in both of the following examples even though it is separated from the preposition in the second example.

EXAMPLES: From *whom* did you receive the message?

Whom did you receive the message from?

If the pronoun is used to connect the clauses of a complex sentence, it is necessary to check the pronoun's case more carefully. Consider the two sentences with adjective clauses at the top of the next page.

EXAMPLES: I spoke to the artist with *whom* we had lunch.

I spoke to the artist *whom we had lunch with.*

In the first sentence, the objective pronoun immediately follows its preposition, *with*. In the second sentence, however, the pronoun and the preposition are separated by many words. To check the case, begin by isolating the subordinate clause: *whom we had lunch with*. Next, put the clause in the normal word order: *we had lunch with whom*. The clause has a subject (*we*), a verb (*had*), and a direct object (*lunch*). It also has a prepositional phrase (*with whom*). *Whom* is the correct pronoun because the objective case is required for the object of a preposition.

Checking Case in Subordinate Clauses with Parenthetical Expressions. Occasionally, parenthetical expressions such as *I think, we suppose,* or *critics believe* are included in subordinate clauses. These expressions do not affect the case of *who* and *whom* in subordinate clauses.

EXAMPLES: Steinbeck was the writer *who*, critics believed, deserved the Nobel Prize.

Steinbeck was the writer to *whom*, the critics predicted, the judges would award the Nobel Prize.

NOTE ABOUT *WHOM* AND *WHOMEVER* IN INFORMAL ENGLISH: *Whom* and *whomever* are used less frequently in informal English. This is especially true when an object of a preposition is separated from its preposition. When the pronoun follows the preposition, however, it is still customary to use the objective case.

INFORMAL: *Who* did you receive a letter from?

FORMAL AND INFORMAL: From *whom* did you receive a letter?

EXERCISE A: Using *Who* and *Whom* Correctly in Questions. Choose the correct pronoun in each sentence.

EXAMPLE: With (who, whom) are you going to the concert?
whom

1. (Who, Whom) is our new foreign language teacher?
2. (Who, Whom) will you choose to represent us?
3. About (who, whom) are you speaking?

4. The principal chose (who, whom)?
5. (Whose, Who's) pen did you borrow?
6. (Who, Whom) has been elected to the council?
7. From (who, whom) did you hear that rumor?
8. (Who, Whom) on our staff can read Spanish?
9. (Whose, Who's) the Speaker of the House?
10. (Who, Whom) did you ask about the football tickets?

EXERCISE B: Using *Who* and *Whom* Correctly in Clauses. Write the subordinate clause in each sentence. Then indicate how the form of *who* or *whom* is used.

EXAMPLE: He will select whoever is available.

whoever is available (subject)

1. Finally, he told us who was in charge.
2. She is the legislator who always researches both sides of an issue.
3. The generals knew whom they needed for the mission.
4. We spoke to whoever answered the phone.
5. I approached the clerk from whom I received the information.
6. Whoever is chosen will have complete authority.
7. Allison wondered whom you agreed to sponsor.
8. Whomever she wants can have the position.
9. The penalty will be given to whoever is responsible.
10. Tell whomever you wish the good news.
11. The singer whom they picked was unattractive.
12. They always agree with whoever speaks the loudest.
13. Would you tell us whom he picked?
14. This is the writer whom I like most.
15. Only those who are in line will be admitted.
16. I bought the camera from a dealer who has a shop in the neighborhood.
17. I cannot understand who would attempt something like that.
18. The committee will accept whomever they nominate.
19. A person who is honest should have nothing to fear.
20. She is a member of the debate team whom we vanquished.

EXERCISE C: Using *Who* and *Whom* in Questions and Clauses. Choose the correct pronoun in each sentence.

EXAMPLE: I wonder (who, whom) won the election today.

who

1. With (who, whom) are you arguing?
2. I wonder (who, whom) will win.
3. (Whose, Who's) the spokesperson for the company?
4. The director (who, whom) was fired left the city.
5. The shortstop is the player (who, whom), experts feel, will achieve stardom.
6. (Whoever, Whomever) they select will represent us in Paris.
7. Dr. Goodman is the only doctor (who, whom) I know in town.
8. Give (whoever, whomever) appears this package.
9. (Who, Whom) has been your delegate to the convention?
10. About (who, whom) were they talking?
11. The lady (who, whom) I usually see is ill.
12. I telephoned the person (who, whom) makes the decisions.
13. (Whose, Who's) car will we take this time?
14. (Who, Whom) is Gustav Mahler?
15. About (who, whom) did Thomas Mann write *Death in Venice*?
16. Margery Smolins is the only jeweler (who, whom) I trust.
17. She is the woman (who, whom), I believe, is a candidate.
18. Is it he (who, whom) was rejected?
19. It is Vince Lombardi (who, whom), I think, the sportswriters named one of the greatest of all football coaches.
20. To (who, whom) can we refer them?

EXERCISE D: More Work with *Who* and *Whom*. Write *who, whoever, whom, whomever, whose, whosever,* or *who's* to complete each sentence.

EXAMPLE: Lee is the one _______ told me to come early.

who

1. She is a teacher _______ we all admire.
2. _______ is your favorite recording star?
3. The policeman asked _______?
4. Tell _______ you want about the discovery.
5. He wonders _______ cheated on the exam.
6. She is the artist _______, I feel, has the least talent.

7. ______ the trainer of the hockey team?
8. A person ______ is persistent has a chance of success.
9. ______ wants tickets should see the manager.
10. ______ do you intend to visit in Chicago?
11. With ______ were you planning to go?
12. Only those ______ arrive early will get seats.
13. Bring the package to ______ you were told.
14. With ______ have you raced?
15. I cannot promise to support ______ will be selected.
16. Is it she to ______ I should report?
17. Those ______ train diligently usually finish the event.
18. ______ dictionary is this?
19. They are actors ______ can play a variety of roles.
20. Under ______ authority was this order issued?

Using Pronouns Correctly in Elliptical Clauses

In an *elliptical clause*, some words are omitted because they are understood. Sentences with elliptical clauses are often used to draw comparisons. Such sentences are usually divided into two parts connected by *than* or *as*: *Fran is smarter than he* or *Tom is as happy as I*. In selecting the case of the pronoun, you must know what the unstated words are.

In elliptical clauses beginning with *than* or *as*, use the form of the pronoun that you would use if the clause were fully stated.

The case of the pronoun depends upon whether the omitted words belong before or after the pronoun. In the examples below, the omitted words are supplied in brackets.

WORDS LEFT OUT AFTER PRONOUN: Jo is as talented as *he*.
Jo is as talented as he [is].

WORDS LEFT OUT BEFORE PRONOUN: We gave Scott the same choices as *her*.
We gave Scott the same choices as [we gave] her.

If the words left out come *after* the pronoun, use a nominative pronoun because it is the subject of the omitted verb. If the words left out come *before* the pronoun, use an objective pronoun because the pronoun will be an object, generally the direct object or indirect object of the omitted verb.

Often the entire meaning of the sentence depends on the case of the pronoun. Compare, for example, the meaning of the following sentences when the nominative pronoun is changed to an objective pronoun.

WITH A NOMINATIVE PRONOUN: Stan taught us more than *she*.

Stan taught us more than she [did].

WITH AN OBJECTIVE PRONOUN: Stan taught us more than *her*.

Stan taught us more than [he taught] her.

Always follow these steps in making your decision.

CHOOSING A PRONOUN IN ELLIPTICAL CLAUSES

1. Consider the choices of pronouns: nominative or objective.
2. Mentally complete the elliptical clause.
3. Base your choice on what you find.

EXERCISE E: Identifying the Correct Pronoun in Elliptical Clauses. Rewrite each sentence, choosing one of the pronouns in parentheses and correctly completing the elliptical clause.

EXAMPLE: She is more beautiful than (I, me).

She is more beautiful than I am.

1. Steven is as dedicated as (she, her).
2. Under the circumstances Lucy is as pleased as (he, him).
3. I think he is more aggressive than (I, me).
4. Shostakovich was at least as successful as (they, them).
5. Without a doubt you are as misguided as (he, him).
6. You can tell her as easily as (I, me).
7. Judy can dance better than (she, her).
8. The real estate investment was more costly to them than (we, us).

9. Greg practices more than (she, her).
10. The trip to Alaska next summer means more to me than (he, him).

EXERCISE F: Using the Correct Pronoun in Elliptical Clauses. Rewrite each sentence, choosing an appropriate pronoun and completing the elliptical clause.

EXAMPLE: Joanne writes more often than ______.

Joanne writes more often than I do.

1. I study more than ______.
2. The lawyer charged him less than ______.
3. Paul is a better actor than ______.
4. He is undoubtedly more arrogant than ______.
5. The storekeeper gave them more than ______.
6. In the second race, she was faster than ______.
7. I admire Picasso as much as ______.
8. The performance is more important to me than ______.
9. Barbara exercises more than ______.
10. Harrison worked longer on the project than ______.

DEVELOPING WRITING SKILLS: Writing Sentences with *Who, Whom,* and Elliptical Clauses. Use each item in a sentence of your own.

EXAMPLE: as strong as I

My brother is as strong as I.

1. taller than she
2. as capable as they
3. less than him
4. whoever is elected
5. more than her
6. wiser than I
7. whomever you like
8. whoever finishes
9. as much as he
10. faster than she
11. who the winner is
12. as much as them
13. as poorly as he
14. whom he promised
15. better than us
16. with whom we traveled
17. more important to her
18. as sympathetic as he
19. more graceful than she
20. as well as them

Skills Review and Writing Workshop

Pronoun Usage

CHECKING YOUR SKILLS

Write the pronoun in each sentence. Then identify its case as nominative, objective, or possessive.

(1) Ben was an apprentice for a newspaper edited by his brother James. (2) James's friends often wrote essays for the paper and signed them with pen names. (3) But Ben knew that the paper would never publish an essay by its young apprentice. (4) So Ben invented a middle-aged widow, Silence Dogood, and signed her name to the essay. (5) As conceived by Ben, she had a good heart and a sharp tongue. (6) When the essay was done, Ben copied it in disguised handwriting. (7) Late at night, he put the essay under the door of the newspaper office. (8) When James read the essay, he was impressed. (9) "I had the pleasure," said Ben Franklin years later, "of hearing guesses about the author, naming men of learning and wit." (10) James and the other writers never suspected the author was Ben, whom the older men thought of as a tongue-tied teenager.

USING USAGE SKILLS IN WRITING

Writing a Feature Article for a Newspaper

Write a feature story about the perfect birthday party. It must be concise, interesting, and grammatically correct. Follow the steps below to write it.

Prewriting: Why was it perfect? Did something special happen? Was it in a special place? Did someone special come?

Writing: You might want to start with a "tease." That is, indicate you have something interesting to reveal, but don't reveal it until you have built some suspense in your story.

Revising: Be sure all the pronouns are grammatically correct, that possessives are accurate, and that there are no other grammatical errors.

Chapter **12**

Agreement

In the English language, some words must *agree* with other words. You might say, for example, *"He walks* faster than *they walk."* By adding the *-s* to *walk* when the subject is *he,* you are making the verb agree with its subject.

Most of the time, you automatically make some words agree with other words. Grammatical agreement, however, is not always obvious. In this chapter you will learn to make a subject and its verb agree as well as a pronoun and its antecedent.

12.1 Subject and Verb Agreement

The basic idea of subject and verb agreement is very simple. You must make sure that both the subject and verb are *singular* or that both are *plural.* In this section you will learn to identify singular and plural subjects. You will also learn to determine if a verb is singular or plural.

Number: Singular and Plural

The grammatical concept of *number* is not difficult.

Number refers to the two forms of a word: singular and plural. Singular words indicate one; plural words indicate more than one.

The only parts of speech that indicate number are nouns, pronouns, and verbs.

12.1 Subject and Verb Agreement

The Number of Nouns. The difference between singular and plural nouns is usually obvious. Compare the singular and plural forms of the nouns in the chart below.

NOUNS			
Singular	**Plural**	**Singular**	**Plural**
record	records	child	children
tax	taxes	goose	geese

As you know, most nouns form their plurals by adding *-s* or *-es* (record*s*, tax*es*). Some nouns, however, form their plurals in special ways (child*ren*, g*ee*se). If you are in doubt about the plural form of a noun, check a dictionary.

The Number of Pronouns. Many pronouns also have different forms to indicate their number. The personal pronouns *I, he, she,* and *it* are singular; *we* and *they* are plural. *You* can be either singular or plural.

PERSONAL PRONOUNS		
Singular	**Plural**	**Singular or Plural**
I	we	you
he, she, it	they	

The Number of Verbs. Many verbs can be either singular or plural. The number of such verbs depends on their subjects.

SINGULAR: I *see*. I *have seen*.

PLURAL: We *see*. They *have seen*.

Sometimes, a verb can only be singular. In the present tense and the present perfect tense, *he, she, it,* and all singular nouns have special forms that are always singular.

ALWAYS SINGULAR: He *sees*. He *has seen*.

The verb *be* also has a few special forms that are only used with certain singular subjects. In the present tense, the pronoun *I* has its own form. *He, she, it,* and singular nouns also have their own singular verb form.

ALWAYS SINGULAR: I *am*. He *is*.

In the past tense, there is one form of *be* that is shared by *I, he, she, it,* and singular nouns.

ALWAYS SINGULAR: I *was*. He *was*.

The chart below shows the verb forms that are always singular as well as those that can be either singular or plural.

VERBS	
Always Singular	**Singular or Plural**
(he, Tina) sees	(I, you, we, they) see
(he, Tina) has seen	(I, you, we, they) have seen
(I) am (he, Tina) is	(you, we, they) are
(I, he, Tina) was	(you, we, they) were

If a verb has had an *-s* or *-es* added to it (sees) or if it includes the words *has, am, is,* or *was,* it will be singular. The number of any other verb depends on its subject.

EXERCISE A: Determining the Number of Nouns, Pronouns, and Verbs. Identify each item as *singular, plural,* or *both*.

EXAMPLE: writes
singular

1. animals
2. we
3. child
4. is
5. candle
6. tempt
7. it
8. they
9. geese
10. gives
11. delivers
12. river
13. have
14. apples
15. were
16. has agreed
17. tulips
18. collapses
19. elephant
20. shatter

Singular and Plural Subjects

The following two rules govern all other rules about subject and verb agreement.

A singular subject must have a singular verb.

A plural subject must have a plural verb.

In the examples at the top of the next page, subjects are underlined once and verbs twice.

SINGULAR SUBJECT AND VERB: Father always drives to work.

She is about to leave for school.

Charlie was reading a book.

PLURAL SUBJECT AND VERB: The Smiths drive to work.

We are about to leave for school.

My brothers were reading books.

Verbs must agree with their subjects even if a phrase or clause comes between them.

A phrase or clause that interrupts a subject and its verb does not affect subject-verb agreement.

In the first example below, the subject and verb are interrupted by a participial phrase. As you can see, the singular subject still requires a singular verb. In the second, the subject and verb are interrupted by an adjective clause. The plural subject nonetheless requires a plural verb.

EXAMPLES: The actor most admired by the students is on stage.

The two raccoons that were being chased by our dog were last seen climbing a tree.

EXERCISE B: Making Subjects Agree with Their Verbs. Choose the verb in parentheses that agrees with the subject of each sentence.

EXAMPLE: The twins (was, were) dressed alike.

were

1. The red and brown boxes (was, were) destroyed in the fire.
2. The concert (begins, begin) at eight.
3. Of all of my subjects, woodworking (is, are) my favorite.
4. Old clocks (has, have) interesting histories.
5. My grandfather often (goes, go) to the adult center.
6. In desperation the heroine (clutches, clutch) for air.
7. Marilyn (has, have) finally finished her work.
8. Yesterday, both dictionaries (was, were) on that desk.
9. I guess this (is, are) the only possible explanation.
10. Lately, our evergeeen plants (has, have) been yellowing.

EXERCISE C: Making Separated Subjects and Verbs Agree. Choose the verb in parentheses that agrees with the subject of each sentence.

1. The old books in the attic (was, were) thrown away.
2. The climates of both countries (is, are) very good.
3. A carton of grapefruits from Florida (was, were) delivered.
4. The vegetables in the stew (is, are) unusually tasty.
5. The men working on the platform (is, are) quitting early.
6. Flights from this airport (leaves, leave) infrequently.
7. Our neighbor, who was abroad, (has, have) returned.
8. The pages of the book (is, are) in poor condition.
9. The bouquet of flowers (has, have) a nice aroma.
10. The speakers in my stereo (is, are) poorly balanced.

Compound Subjects

A compound subject has two or more subjects usually joined by *or* or *and*. Four rules apply to compound subjects.

Singular Subjects Joined by *Or* or *Nor*. If both parts of a compound subject joined by *or* or *nor* are singular, you must use a singular verb.

Two or more singular subjects joined by *or* or *nor* must have a singular verb.

EXAMPLE: A car or bus is the only means of travel upstate.

Plural Subjects Joined by *Or* or *Nor*. If both parts of a compound subject connected by *or* or *nor* are plural, you must use a plural verb.

Two or more plural subjects joined by *or* or *nor* must have a plural verb.

EXAMPLE: Only the fathers or the mothers are to be invited.

Subjects of Mixed Number Joined by *Or* or *Nor*. If one part of a compound subject is singular and other plural, the verb agrees with the subject closer to it.

If one or more singular subjects are joined to one or more plural subjects by *or* or *nor*, the subject closest to the verb determines agreement.

EXAMPLES: Neither David nor my parents are going with us.

Neither my parents nor David is going with us.

Subjects Joined by *And*. Only one rule applies to compound subjects joined by *and*.

A compound subject joined by *and* is generally plural and must have a plural verb.

EXAMPLES: One boy and one girl are the finalists.

Two boys and one girl were chosen.

This rule has two exceptions. If the parts of a compound subject add up to one thing, the compound subject is singular and takes a singular verb. A singular verb is also required if the word *every* or the word *each* precedes the compound subject.

EXAMPLES: Ham and eggs is a hearty breakfast.

Every dog and cat was inoculated.

EXERCISE D: Making Compound Subjects Agree with Their Verbs. Choose the verb in parentheses that agrees with the subject of each sentence.

EXAMPLE: Neither Kay nor Irene (is, are) available to babysit.

is

1. Both my boss and her partner (collects, collect) coins.
2. Trish or Kathy (plans, plan) to represent us.
3. Neither Jack nor Tim (wants, want) to make the delivery.
4. Snow, hail, and sleet (has, have) been forecast for today.
5. Fruits and vegetables (provides, provide) many minerals.
6. Spaghetti and meatballs (is, are) her favorite dish.
7. A train or several buses (is, are) available on Sundays.
8. Both the twins and Greta (is, are) visiting Grandmother.
9. Either my uncle or my aunt (phones, phone) each week.
10. Books and magazines (is, are) appreciated by the patients.
11. Neither the sedan nor the truck (has, have) a spare tire.
12. Three men and a woman (was, were) approaching the door.
13. The two sons and their father (is, are) very close.

14. The lamps or the end tables (is, are) on sale tomorrow.
15. Every apple and pear (was, were) eaten by the guests.
16. Franks and beans (is, are) what I want for dinner.
17. Phil or Mary usually (opens, open) the office each day.
18. Three candles or a flashlight (is, are) needed.
19. Either Jim or John (sing, sings) the anthem.
20. Each boy and girl (receive, receives) a prize.

Confusing Subjects

Some kinds of subjects require special attention.

Hard-to-Find Subjects. Hard-to-find subjects that come after their verbs can sometimes cause problems.

A subject that comes after its verb must still agree with it in number.

Sentences in which the subject comes after the verb are in inverted word order. Check to make sure the verb agrees with the subject by mentally rewording the sentence so that the subject comes first.

EXAMPLE: At the bottom of the hill are two silos.
(Two silos are at the bottom of the hill.)

Some inverted sentences begin with *there* or *here*. In the first sentence below, the plural subject *photos* agrees with the plural verb *are*. In the second sentence, the singular subject *edition* agrees with the singular verb *is*.

EXAMPLES: There are the photos of the castle.
Here is the revised edition of that book.

NOTE ABOUT *THERE'S* AND *HERE'S:* Both of these contractions contain the singular verb *is: there is* and *here is*. They should not be used with plural verbs.

CORRECT: There's only one concert planned for this semester.
There are two concerts planned for next semester.

Subjects of Linking Verbs. A sentence with a linking verb and a predicate nominative sometimes presents an agreement problem.

A linking verb must agree with its subject, regardless of the number of its predicate nominative.

In some sentences the subject and the predicate nominative may not be the same in number. In the first example below, the plural subject *stereos* agrees with the plural verb *are* even though the predicate nominative *reason* is singular. In the second example, the singular subject *reason* takes the singular verb *is* even though the predicate nominative *stereos* is plural.

EXAMPLES: The loud stereos are one reason for his complaints.

One reason for his complaints is the loud stereos.

Collective Nouns. Words such as *audience, class, couple, crowd, family, faculty, group, orchestra, team,* and *United States* are collective nouns and can be either singular or plural depending upon how they are used.

A collective noun takes a singular verb when the group it names acts as a single unit.

A collective noun takes a plural verb when the group it names act as individuals with different points of view.

SINGULAR: The orchestra is playing at Symphony Hall tonight.

The football team has been invited to a bowl game.

PLURAL: The jury have been unable to agree on a verdict.

The faculty have been discussing the new policy.

Plural-Looking Nouns. Other confusing subjects are plural-looking nouns that end in *-s* but are singular in meaning.

Nouns that are plural in form but singular in meaning agree with singular verbs.

Many of these nouns name branches of knowledge: *ethics, mathematics, physics, politics, acoustics, social studies*. Others name a single unit or idea: *spaghetti, measles, news, series*.

SINGULAR: Mathematics is an exciting subject for some.

The news today is good.

Some of these words can be tricky. When words such as *ethics, politics,* and *acoustics* do not name branches of knowledge but rather indicate characteristics, their meanings are plural. Similarly, such words as *eyeglasses, pliers,* and *scissors,* though they name single items, generally take plural verbs.

PLURAL: The acoustics in the auditorium are bad.

The Senator's ethics have been questioned.

The scissors are in the top drawer.

Indefinite Pronouns. Most indefinite pronouns do not cause agreement problems because their number is self-evident. Some are always singular (*anybody, each, everyone,* and so on). Others are always plural (*both, many,* and so on). There are two simple rules for these indefinite pronouns.

Singular indefinite pronouns take singular verbs.

Plural indefinite pronouns take plural verbs.

These rules apply even if there is an interrupting phrase.

ALWAYS SINGULAR: Each of the players was cited for excellence.

Everyone on the team has left for the day.

ALWAYS PLURAL: Both of the students were reprimanded.

Many of the performers were at the party.

The indefinite pronouns that deserve special attention are those that can be either singular or plural.

The pronouns *all, any, more, most, none,* and *some* take a singular verb if the antecedent is singular and a plural verb if it is plural.

In the first example below, the antecedent of *some* is *stew,* a singular noun. In the second example, the antecedent of *some* is *cars,* a plural noun.

SINGULAR: Some of the stew is spoiled.

PLURAL: Some of the cars are expensive.

Titles. The title of a book or other work of art, even if it looks plural, always takes a singular verb.

A title is singular and takes a singular verb.

The plural words *Lives* and *Grapes* in the examples below do not make the titles plural.

EXAMPLES: *Atlantic Brief Lives* is a useful reference.

The Grapes of Wrath is Steinbeck's best novel.

Amounts and Measurements. Although they sometimes appear to be plural, many amounts and measurements express single units.

A noun expressing an amount or measurement is usually singular and requires a singular verb.

In the first three examples below, the subjects take singular verbs. *Seventy-nine cents* is one sum of money; *four feet* is a single measurement; and *three quarters* is one part of a container. In the last example, *half* refers to a number of individual chickens and therefore takes a plural verb.

EXAMPLES: Seventy-nine cents is the price for two.

Four feet was the height of the chain link fence.

Three quarters of the bushel of fruit was wasted.

Half of the chickens were sold.

EXERCISE E: Making Confusing Subjects Agree with Their Verbs. Choose the item in parentheses that agrees with the subject of each sentence.

EXAMPLE: Some of the money (was, were) missing.

was

1. Physics (is, are) my brother's favorite subject.
2. (There's, There are) a raincoat and umbrella in the closet.
3. In the back of the cupboard (is, are) two light bulbs.
4. The United States (is, are) one nation indivisible.
5. Here (is, are) three examples of the Romantic Period.
6. The news (hasn't, haven't) changed for days.
7. Smallpox (was, were) once a serious disease.
8. Storms at sea (is, are) a reason for extreme caution.
9. Social studies (is, are) my best subject.
10. Another cause of accidents (was, were) poor, unlit roads.

11. Someone among them (has, have) to assume leadership.
12. There (has, have) been three attempts on his life.
13. A group of pilgrims (is, are) wending its way toward the shrine.
14. Finally, the jury (has, have) made its decision.
15. Local politics (has, have) caused many problems here.
16. After the long, impressive hallway (is, are) two elevators.
17. All of the soup (was, were) spilled on the new floor.
18. (Here's, Here are) one last question from the director.
19. The acoustics in the studio (was, were) excellent.
20. The committee (has, have) taken their seats.
21. A candidate's ethics (is, are) an important consideration.
22. Near the fence between two tires (lies, lie) the treasure.
23. Fifty cents (is, are) not much of a tip these days.
24. Not one of the tomatoes (has, have) ripened.
25. *Wuthering Heights* (is, are) Emily Brontë's only novel.

EXERCISE F: More Work with Confusing Subjects. Choose the item in parentheses that agrees with the subject of each sentence.

1. There (was, were) several weaknesses in that survey.
2. Most of the reports (was, were) of poor quality.
3. Civics (has, have) always been a favorite subject of mine.
4. At the top of the hill (stands, stand) two majestic oaks.
5. *The Brothers Karamazov* (rank, ranks) as a great novel.
6. The audience (has, have) not given its verdict.
7. Each of the turntables (has, have) a drawback.
8. Dirty streets (is, are) just one of our complaints.
9. The couple always (disagrees, disagree) with each other.
10. Where (is, are) my new pliers?
11. All of the nails (is, are) bent.
12. Others in the council (joins, join) me in criticism.
13. The jury (is, are) arguing over the details of the case.
14. One fifth of our income (goes, go) for taxes.
15. Bartlett's *Familiar Quotations* (is, are) a reference book.
16. In back of the house (is, are) planted beans and cucumbers.
17. Half of the new cars (has, have) significant defects.
18. *The Best of the Beatles* (was, were) bound to be a classic.
19. (There's, There are) only one person I can recommend.
20. Four inches of growth in a year (is, are) outstanding.

EXERCISE G: Using All of the Rules of Subject and Verb Agreement. Choose the verb in parentheses that agrees with the subject of each sentence.

1. My brother or my mother (wants, want) to meet the train.
2. Both sailors (was, were) attempting to grasp the lifeline.
3. Most of the roast (seems, seem) too dry.
4. Fine artists often (work, works) together on a performance.
5. Everyone (knows, know) what to expect from her.
6. Fruits or assorted nuts (is, are) excellent to serve.
7. Either Chris or the twins (is, are) in the backyard.
8. Trips to Europe (has, have) become more expensive.
9. The series of recitals (appears, appear) to be successful.
10. That couple (has, have) left its mark on this group.
11. *The Sense of the 60's* (depicts, depict) a turbulent era.
12. Examples of his poor judgment (has, have) been documented.
13. At the other end of town (is, are) a French restaurant.
14. More of our teammates now (agrees, agree) with me.
15. The Marx Brothers' films (is, are) still popular.
16. Either my cousins or Jim (is, are) planning to visit me.
17. Hockey and football (attract, attracts) many fans.
18. The strings in the orchestra (is, are) outstanding.
19. Either plan (is, are) acceptable to us.
20. Three fifths of the members (supports, support) it.

DEVELOPING WRITING SKILLS: Applying the Rules of Subject and Verb Agreement. Use each item at the beginning of a sentence, followed by the verb *is* or the verb *are*.

EXAMPLE: all of my cousins

All of my cousins are coming to the reunion.

1. everybody
2. the committee
3. all of the players
4. one of our radios
5. two thirds of the cake
6. economics
7. *Great Expectations*
8. neither he nor she
9. the jury
10. tennis and golf
11. a trip to Europe or Asia
12. most of the plants
13. all of the candy
14. several copies of the book
15. sixty-five cents
16. social studies
17. each of the dogs
18. bacon and eggs
19. half of the cheese
20. an umbrella or a raincoat

12.2 Pronoun and Antecedent Agreement

Antecedents are the nouns (or the words that take the place of nouns) for which pronouns stand. Although the word *antecedent* comes from a Latin word meaning "to go before," an antecedent often follows its pronoun. In this section you will learn how to make a pronoun agree with its antecedent.

Agreement Between Personal Pronouns and Antecedents

One general rule of pronoun and antecedent agreement governs all the others.

A personal pronoun must agree with its antecedent in number, person, and gender.

The number of a pronoun indicates whether it is *singular* or *plural*. The person of a pronoun indicates whether the pronoun refers to the *first person* (the one speaking), the *second person* (the one spoken to), or the *third person* (the one spoken about).

Some nouns and pronouns can also indicate *gender*. Nouns referring to males, such as *father* or *nephew*, are *masculine* in gender. Nouns referring to females, such as *mother* or *niece*, are *feminine*. Nouns that refer to neither males nor females, such as *book* or *truth*, are *neuter*.

Only third-person singular pronouns indicate gender. The chart below shows the genders of these personal pronouns.

GENDER OF THIRD-PERSON SINGULAR PRONOUNS		
Masculine	**Feminine**	**Neuter**
he, him, his	she, her, hers	it, its

In the example below, note that the pronoun *(his)* agrees with its antecedent *(Byron)* in number (both are singular), in person (both are third person), and in gender (both are masculine).

EXAMPLE: *Byron* received *his* masters degree from Cambridge.

Agreement in Number. Making personal pronouns agree with their antecedents in number is usually a problem only when the antecedent is a compound.

Use a singular personal pronoun with two or more singular antecedents joined by *or* or *nor*.

EXAMPLE: Neither *Tim* nor *John* likes *his* part in the play.

Use a plural personal pronoun with two or more antecedents joined by *and*.

EXAMPLE: *Darlene* and *Carol* like *their* parts in the play.

Agreement in Person and Gender. A personal pronoun and its antecedent will not agree if there is a shift in either person or gender in the second part of the sentence.

When dealing with pronoun-antecedent agreement, take care not to shift either person or gender.

SHIFT IN PERSON: *Michele* is studying Spanish, a language *you* will need in the Peace Corps.

CORRECT: *Michele* is studying Spanish, a language *she* will need in the Peace Corps.

SHIFT IN GENDER: *Vienna* is noted for *its* musical activities as well as *her* other cultural highlights.

CORRECT: *Vienna* is noted for *its* musical activities as well as *its* other cultural highlights.

Generic Masculine Pronouns. When the gender of an antecedent is not specified as either masculine or feminine, a masculine personal pronoun has traditionally been used. This use of the masculine pronoun is called *generic*, meaning that it covers both masculine and feminine genders. The use of the generic masculine pronoun is still widely accepted, but many writers prefer to rephrase the sentence.

When gender is not specified, use the masculine or rewrite the sentence.

EXAMPLES: A *guest* might thank *his* host with a small gift.

A *guest* might thank the host with a small gift.

Guests might thank *their* host with a small gift.

EXERCISE A: Making Personal Pronouns Agree with Their Antecedents. Write an appropriate personal pronoun to complete each sentence.

EXAMPLE: Neither Kevin nor Bill rode ______ bike to school.
his

1. Aunt Marie sent us ______ best wishes.
2. My brother and sister explained ______ objections.
3. Each boy designed ______ own poster.
4. Lisa briefly told us about ______ experiences in Paris.
5. Neither Bob nor Jerry wanted to drive ______ car to work.
6. I ordered two crates of fruit, but ______ have not arrived.
7. The waiter asked me for ______ choice of salad dressing.
8. The delegates rose and thundered ______ approval.
9. Sam and Jill urged us to use ______ summer cottage.
10. The car has trouble with ______ transmission.

Agreement with Indefinite Pronouns

If you use an indefinite pronoun (such as *each, either, somebody, both, few,* or *all*) in a sentence with a personal pronoun, you must make sure the two pronouns agree. This is rarely a problem when both are plural.

Use a plural personal pronoun when the antecedent is a plural indefinite pronoun.

EXAMPLE: *Both* of the women gave *their* support.

When both pronouns are singular, a similar rule applies.

Use a singular personal pronoun when the antecedent is a singular indefinite pronoun.

EXAMPLE: *Each* of the girls handed in *her* assignment on time.

Notice that when both pronouns are singular, they must also agree in gender. The pronoun *her* is used in the example above because the phrase after *each* specifies *girls*. If no gender is specified, you can use the generic masculine pronoun or you can reword the sentence.

EXAMPLES: *One* of the players forgot *his* racket.
One of the players forgot a racket.

For those indefinite pronouns that can be either singular or plural, agreement depends on the antecedent of the indefinite pronoun. In the first example below, the singular pronoun *its* is used because the antecedent of *some* is the singular noun *paint*. In the second example, the plural pronoun *their* is used because the antecedent of *some* is the plural noun *actors*.

EXAMPLES: *Some* of the paint had lost *its* sheen.

Some of the actors forgot *their* lines.

NOTE ABOUT *EVERYBODY* AND *EVERYONE:* In formal English, *everybody* and *everyone* require singular pronouns. In informal English, it is becoming common to use the plural pronoun *their*.

INFORMAL: *Everyone* wants to express *their* opinions.

EXERCISE B: Making Personal Pronouns Agree with Indefinite Pronouns. Choose the correct pronoun in each sentence.

EXAMPLE: Each of the men signed (his, their) name.

his

1. Both of the trucks had delivered (its, their) shipments.
2. Each of the girls made (her, their) own dress.
3. All of the students completed (his, their) assignments.
4. Several of the dancers promised (her, their) autographs.
5. Neither of the girls offered to lend me (her, their) notes.
6. One of the victims volunteered to tell (his, their) story.
7. All of the members agreed to give (his, their) support.
8. Many of the witnesses offered (his, their) opinions.
9. Few of the reporters have (her, their) credentials on them.
10. Only one of the women explained (her, their) reasons.
11. Each of the musicians has (his, their) music ready.
12. Which one of the women wanted (her, their) coat?
13. Some of the townspeople have voiced (its, their) approval.
14. Neither of my uncles will bring (his, their) car.
15. All of the students have found (his, their) books.
16. Not one of the girls was tired after (her, their) speech.
17. All of the children want to take (his, their) naps.
18. Some of the delegates weren't wearing (his, their) badges.
19. Jim and Scott forgot (his, their) baseball bats.
20. Either Ellen or Mary will recite (her, their) poem next.

Agreement with Reflexive Pronouns

Reflexive pronouns end in *-self* or *-selves* and refer to an antecedent earlier in the sentence, as in "*Marie* told *herself* to remain calm."

A personal pronoun requires an antecedent that is either clearly stated or clearly understood.

Notice that the antecedent of *myself* in the example below does not appear in the sentence. The personal pronoun *me* should be used instead.

POOR: The messenger brought Peter and *myself* the good news.

CORRECT: The messenger brought Peter and *me* the good news.

EXERCISE C: Using Reflexive Pronouns Correctly. Rewrite each sentence, correcting the misused reflexive pronoun.

EXAMPLE: Either Mark or myself will provide the punch.
Either Mark or I will provide the punch.

1. Christine wants Bob and myself to make a presentation.
2. I'm sure that the right actor for this part is yourself.
3. Herself is the person with the best chance for success.
4. The nurse thought he had hurt both himself and myself.
5. Neither Ginger nor myself was willing to go alone.
6. Myself am the only one interested in the new computer.
7. John will help you since herself is not here right now.
8. The one to handle that complaint is himself.
9. Surely, Rita and ourselves can manage the children.
10. She saw herself and myself in the mirror.

Four Special Problems in Pronoun Agreement

One special agreement problem is the use of a personal pronoun that does not have a clearly identified antecedent.

A reflexive pronoun must agree with an antecedent that is clearly stated.

In the example below, the pronoun *they* does not have a clear antecedent. The problem can be corrected by replacing *they* with *it* or by substituting a noun.

POOR: The movie was disappointing because *they* never made the characters seem realistic.

CORRECT: The movie was disappointing because it never made the characters seem realistic.

The movie was disappointing because the director never made the characters seem realistic.

A second special agreement problem involves *ambiguous* pronouns—that is, pronouns that refer to two or more possible antecedents.

A personal pronoun should always refer to a single, obvious antecedent.

In the example below, the pronoun *it* is ambiguous because it can refer to either *letter* or *book*.

POOR: I put the letter in a book, but I've lost *it*.

CORRECT: I put the letter in a book, but I've lost the book.

I can't find the letter that I put in a book.

A third special agreement problem concerns personal pronouns that are not close enough to their antecedents.

A personal pronoun should always be close enough to its antecedent to prevent confusion.

In the example below, the pronoun *he* is too far from its antecedent, *Macbeth*. The passage is much clearer if the word *Macbeth* is repeated. You could also reword the passage to move the pronoun closer to its antecedent.

POOR: At the banquet Macbeth was stunned by Banquo's ghost. Lady Macbeth and the guests showed concern but, shaken by the appearance, *he* paid them no heed.

CORRECT: At the banquet Macbeth was stunned by Banquo's ghost. Lady Macbeth and the guests showed concern but, shaken by the appearance, Macbeth paid them no heed.

The fourth special agreement problem concerns the use of *you* in general statements.

Use the personal pronoun *you* only when the reference is truly to the reader or the listener.

In the example below, the pronouns are imprecise because a reader or listener could not have been in ancient Rome.

POOR: In ancient Rome, the emperors often made *you* offer sacrifices as a sign of *your* loyalty.

CORRECT: In ancient Rome, the emperors often made citizens offer sacrifices as a sign of their loyalty.

EXERCISE D: Correcting Special Problems in Pronoun Agreement. Choose the word or words in parentheses that best complete each sentence.

EXAMPLE: The bulletin says (you, students) must register now.
students

1. Sue gave Kay the present after (she, Kay) arrived.
2. The film was good because (they, it) had a surprise ending.
3. Sam angered Todd, but (he, Todd) didn't say what happened.
4. I hid the key in a jar, but now I can't find (it, the key).
5. Going to camp is good for (you, a youngster).
6. The end of the book was confusing because (they, the author) didn't explain what happened to the hero.
7. We cleaned the whole house for him, but he didn't even thank us for (it, our work).
8. (They, The theater) showed the film out of focus.
9. Ken told Bill that (he, Ken) had been made captain.
10. Deciding on a career is a big step in (your, one's) life.

EXERCISE E: More Work with Special Problems in Pronoun Agreement. Rewrite each sentence, correcting the error in pronoun agreement.

EXAMPLE: I was delayed because they were having a parade.
I was delayed because the city was having a parade.

1. Take the papers from the folders and then file them.

2. At school they expect students to be on time for class.
3. Marge told Gloria about the bazaar and they decided not to go today. She said that perhaps they could go another time.
4. The quarterback faded to pass. The receiver and the defender converged on the ball, and he dropped it.
5. When Mother spoke to Alice, she nodded.
6. Take the breadbox off the table and clean it.
7. The ad says that you should be able to type.
8. My brothers chased the intruders until they fell.
9. Going to college out of town makes you feel lonely.
10. When I visited Athens in 1968, you could still walk inside the Parthenon.
11. A person's integrity should be very important to them.
12. They expect applicants to submit references.
13. Bob told Billy that he is the new monitor.
14. Bring the bushel of apples into the kitchen and sort it.
15. When Sally makes lunch for Mother, she is always sorry.
16. Father put the number in his wallet, but he can't find it.
17. My sister read her story to Fran, but she didn't like it.
18. At my father's college they expected more out of you.
19. If they want the term papers to have a certain format, we should not change it.
20. Kay and Rita were quarreling because she lost the tickets.

DEVELOPING WRITING SKILLS: Making Pronouns and Antecedents Agree. Write a sentence for each item below, using each as the antecedent of a personal pronoun.

EXAMPLE: either

Either of the boys will bring his mitt.

1. most
2. Suzanne
3. neither
4. few
5. both
6. someone
7. several
8. each
9. anyone
10. either candidate
11. John and James
12. all
13. the city officials
14. any
15. everyone
16. some protestors
17. Valerie or Ann
18. some of the coffee
19. one of the boys
20. two of the teachers

Skills Review and Writing Workshop

Agreement

CHECKING YOUR SKILLS

Rewrite the following paragraph correcting all errors in agreement.

(1) Almost everybody in my class play an instrument. (2) George and Carrie are students who plays the piccolo. (3) Beth studies music because you don't have to pay for lessons at school. (4) She told Kate they were buying a new piano. (5) The number of horn players we have are amazing. (6) Our orchestra, consisting of sixteen people, play all over the city. (7) Both of the drummers knows how to drive. (8) Each of the musicians bought their own instruments. (9) Carrie and myself arrange all the music for our orchestra. (10) Rhythm and blues are the music our orchestra plays most.

USING USAGE SKILLS IN WRITING
Writing a Guide

Think back to when you were in the ninth grade and you didn't know your way around school. You may have had some difficult moments that could have been avoided. Follow the steps below to write a guide for new students.

Prewriting: Decide which aspects you are going to discuss: getting a good schedule, selecting the best courses and/or teachers, joining the best extracurricular clubs, getting the best food in the cafeteria or at a nearby hangout.

Writing: Organize your guide into sections so the new student can easily find the information he or she needs. Headings are often helpful.

Revising: You are writing this guide as an authority. If your reader finds a grammatical mistake you will be demoted instantly. Be accurate! After you have revised, proofread carefully.

Chapter 13

Adjective and Adverb Usage

Adjectives and adverbs are important parts of speech because they describe, add color, clarify, and make distinctions. A carefully chosen adjective or adverb often turns an ordinary sentence into a superior one.

These modifiers are also important because they are used to make comparisons. In the first section of this chapter, you will learn how to form the various adjectives and adverbs used in comparisons. In the second section, you will learn how to avoid a number of common usage problems involving comparisons.

Degrees of Comparison 13.1

Most adjectives and adverbs have three forms, called *degrees,* that are used to modify and make comparisons.

Most adjectives and adverbs have different forms to show degrees of comparison.

Recognizing Degrees of Comparison

Each of the three degrees of comparison has a name.

The three degrees of comparison are the positive, the comparative, and the superlative.

Adjectives and adverbs have different ways of forming the *comparative* and *superlative* degrees. Notice, for example, how the forms of the adjectives and adverbs in the following chart change to show the degrees of comparison.

DEGREES OF ADJECTIVES		
Positive	**Comparative**	**Superlative**
simple	simpler	simplest
impressive	more impressive	most impressive
good	better	best

DEGREES OF ADVERBS		
Positive	**Comparative**	**Superlative**
soon	sooner	soonest
impressively	more impressively	most impressively
well	better	best

EXERCISE A: Recognizing Positive, Comparative, and Superlative Degrees. Identify the degree of each underlined modifier.

EXAMPLE: She is the tallest player on the team.
superlative

1. My father is more industrious than I am.
2. Sometimes it is best not to argue.
3. I think she is hungry now.
4. This novel by Charles Dickens is one of the most impressive I've ever read.
5. You will be more agreeable after a nap.
6. I like baseball better than football.
7. Her swollen arm requires treatment.
8. The banker is the richest person in town.
9. This is the most informative article I've read about Laos.
10. He has more money now than when he returned from college.
11. For those who want to work, this course is challenging.
12. Who do you think is prettier?
13. Laura is the happiest person I know.

14. You are better at statistics than he is.
15. Beth is the fussiest person in our family.
16. Unfortunately, he is more talkative than he used to be.
17. Judy apparently is sleepy this morning.
18. In your opinion, which photo is more attractive?
19. Clark was the most qualified candidate in the group.
20. That meal was the most satisfying I've had in a long time.

Regular Forms

Modifiers can be either regular or irregular. There are two rules for forming the comparative and superlative degrees of regular modifiers. The first rule applies to modifiers with one or two syllables.

Use *-er* or *more* to form the comparative degree and *-est* or *most* to form the superlative degree of most one- and two-syllable modifiers.

The more common method for forming the comparative and superlative degrees of one- and two-syllable modifiers is to add *-er* and *-est* to the modifier rather than to use *more* and *most*.

EXAMPLES:	tall	taller	tallest
	nice	nicer	nicest
	shiny	shinier	shiniest

More and *most* are used with one- and two-syllable modifiers when adding *-er* and *-est* would sound awkward.

EXAMPLES:	famous	more famous	most famous
	obese	more obese	most obese
	pungent	more pungent	most pungent

Regardless of the number of syllables, all adverbs with the suffix *-ly* form their comparative and superlative degrees with *more* and *most*.

EXAMPLES:	justly	more justly	most justly
	evenly	more evenly	most evenly

The second rule applies to modifiers with three or more syllables.

Use *more* and *most* to form the comparative and superlative degrees of all modifiers with three or more syllables.

EXAMPLES:	difficult	more difficult	most difficult
	affectionate	more affectionate	most affectionate
	diligent	more diligent	most diligent

NOTE ABOUT COMPARISONS WITH *LESS* AND *LEAST*: *Less* and *least*, the opposite of *more* and *most*, are also used to form the comparative and superlative degrees of most modifiers.

EXAMPLES:	tall	less tall	least tall
	hopeless	less hopeless	least hopeless
	ambitious	less ambitious	least ambitious

EXERCISE B: Forming Regular Comparative and Superlative Degrees. Write the comparative and superlative form of each modifier.

EXAMPLE: small

smaller smallest

1. beautiful	6. exciting	11. informative	16. fattening
2. cold	7. light	12. popular	17. hungry
3. fast	8. likable	13. impressive	18. demanding
4. slowly	9. pretty	14. complex	19. sad
5. fruitful	10. weak	15. quickly	20. safe

Irregular Forms

A few commonly used adjectives and adverbs form their comparative and superlative degrees in unpredictable ways.

The irregular comparative and superlative forms of certain adjectives and adverbs must be memorized.

Notice in the chart at the top of the next page that some irregular modifiers differ only in the positive degree. The modifiers *bad, badly,* and *ill,* for example, all have the same comparative and superlative degrees *(worse, worst)*.

IRREGULAR MODIFIERS		
Positive	**Comparative**	**Superlative**
bad	worse	worst
badly	worse	worst
far (distance)	farther	farthest
far (extent)	further	furthest
good	better	best
ill	worse	worst
late	later	last *or* latest
little (amount)	less	least
many	more	most
much	more	most
well	better	best

NOTE ABOUT *BAD* AND *BADLY:* Because *bad* is an adjective, it cannot be used as an adverb after an action verb. Notice in the second example, however, that it can be used as an adjective after a linking verb.

INCORRECT: Keith plays tennis *bad*.

CORRECT: Keith feels *bad*.

Because *badly* is an adverb, it cannot be used as an adjective after a linking verb. It can, however, be used as an adverb after an action verb.

INCORRECT: Keith feels *badly*.

CORRECT: Keith plays tennis *badly*.

NOTE ABOUT *GOOD* AND *WELL:* Like *bad, good* is an adjective and cannot be used as an adverb after an action verb. It can, however, be used as an adjective after a linking verb.

INCORRECT: Jennifer plays tennis *good*.

CORRECT: Jennifer feels *good*.

Well is generally an adverb. Like *badly,* it can be used after an action verb.

CORRECT: Jennifer plays tennis *well*.

When *well* is used to mean "healthy," it is an adjective. Thus, *well* can also be used after a linking verb.

CORRECT: Jennifer feels *well* now that her fever has broken.

EXERCISE C: Forming Irregular Comparative and Superlative Degrees. Write the appropriate form of the underlined modifier to complete each sentence.

EXAMPLE: I am still ill, but I was ______ yesterday.
worse

1. Cherry pie is good, but pecan pie is even ______.
2. I played better than Sue, but Katy played the ______ of all.
3. There were many flowers in the garden and even ______ in the greenhouse.
4. Mother felt bad last night, but today she feels ______.
5. We were late for dinner, but Rita was even ______.
6. Tucson is farther from here than Denver, but Los Angeles is the ______ of the three.
7. Practice went well today, but it went ______ yesterday.
8. I did *badly* on the test, but Sam did even ______.
9. The school library has more books than the church library, but the public library has the ______ books in town.
10. She has little interest in opera and even ______ in jazz.
11. The lawn needs much care, but the garden needs ______.
12. Sue came later than Tim, and was the ______ to arrive.
13. I had much homework yesterday and even ______ today.
14. We had hiked quite far, but we had much ______ to hike.
15. The first performer was bad, but the second was ______.
16. I had less money than Sam, but Lou had the ______.
17. Jan Peerce was a good tenor, but Caruso was ______.
18. Craig is better than Robert, but Nancy is the ______.
19. Greg did worse than Jim, but Chris did the ______ of all.
20. I have less talent than Jane, but Lou has the ______ talent.

DEVELOPING WRITING SKILLS: Using Adjectives and Adverbs to Make Comparisons. Use each item in a sentence of your own.

EXAMPLE: most ambitious

Clark is the most ambitious person in our class.

1. strongest
2. best
3. friendliest
4. hardest
5. slower
6. good
7. well
8. bad
9. badly
10. better
11. likable
12. worse
13. most unusual
14. kindest
15. latest
16. most impatient
17. least demanding
18. strangest
19. more charming
20. less difficult

Clear Comparisons 13.2

In this section you will learn the correct uses of the comparative and superlative degrees. You will also learn how to change an illogical comparison into a logical comparison.

Using Comparative and Superlative Degrees

There are two simple rules that govern the use of the comparative and superlative degrees.

Use the comparative degrees to compare two people, places, or things.

Use the superlative degree to compare three or more people, places, or things.

Notice in the examples below that specific numbers need not be mentioned. The context of the sentence indicates whether two or more than two things are being compared.

COMPARATIVE: An air conditioner is *more effective* than a fan.

My report is *more detailed* than his.

The hotel is *nearer* than the cottages.

SUPERLATIVE: We went to the *most expensive* restaurant in town.

This hospital has the *largest* staff in the state.

Hercules is probably the *strongest* man in Greek mythology.

NOTE ABOUT DOUBLE COMPARISONS: Do not add both *-er* and *more* or *-est* and *most* to a regular modifier. In addition, do not add any of these endings or words to an irregular modifier.

INCORRECT: That race car is *more faster* than the other.

John's stereo is *more better* than mine.

CORRECT: That race car is *faster* than the other.

John's stereo is *better* than mine.

EXERCISE A: Using the Comparative and Superlative Forms Correctly. Choose the correct comparative or superlative form in each sentence.

EXAMPLE: Of the two, Glenda is the (faster, fastest) swimmer.

faster

1. Boston is the (more, most) historic of all American cities.
2. His condition is (poorer, poorest) this week than last.
3. Which of the triplets is the (prettier, prettiest)?
4. Mr. Willis gave him a (better, best) introduction than her.
5. This is the (less, least) I can do for you.
6. Which of the three cars is the (cheaper, cheapest)?
7. She is (more, most) willing to help than I.
8. Is this the (worse, worst) case you have seen?
9. Of the two brothers, which is the (faster, fastest)?
10. She is the (more, most) able legislator in the Senate.

EXERCISE B: Supplying the Comparative and Superlative Degrees. Write the appropriate comparative or superlative degree of the modifier in parentheses.

EXAMPLE: Alfred is the (young) of all their children.

youngest

1. Marianne is the (old) of the two sisters.
2. He is the (capable) hair stylist I know.
3. Gladys is the (warm) person on the staff.
4. Charles is the (talented) member of the string quartet.
5. This camera is (good) than that one.
6. The temperature today is (low) than it was yesterday.
7. Grandfather is (ill) this morning than he was last night.

8. Harold is the (strong) member of our school's wrestling team.
9. Which of the twins is (tall)?
10. Mr. Adler is the (generous) person in town.
11. Rita is (knowledgeable) about computers than Rick.
12. I think *My Antonia* is the (good) of the two books.
13. Karen speaks Italian (well) than I do.
14. Uncle Sid is my (old) living relative.
15. The Pattersons arrived (late) than the Andersons.
16. Louise is the (shy) person in our class.
17. The cellar is the (cold) room in the house.
18. This coffee is the (good) I've ever tasted.
19. Pat's house is (far) from school than Joe's is.
20. Stewart was the (alert) person in the audience.

Logical Comparisons

In order to write logical comparisons, you must make sure you do not mistakenly compare two unrelated items and that you do not unintentionally compare something with itself.

Balanced Comparisons. Sometimes, when you are in a hurry, you may compare two or more unrelated items. It is then necessary to rephrase the sentence so that the comparison is properly balanced.

Make sure that your sentences compare only items of a similar kind.

Because an unbalanced comparison is illogical, it may be unintentionally humorous. In the first example below, the size of one animal's brain is compared to another entire animal. In the second example, the speed of sound is compared to air.

UNBALANCED: A *dolphin's brain* is bigger than a *shark.*

BALANCED: A *dolphin's brain* is bigger than a *shark's.*

UNBALANCED: The *speed* of sound through dry air is greater than humid *air.*

BALANCED: The *speed* of sound through dry air is greater than the *speed* of sound through humid air.

***Other* and *Else* in Comparisons.** An illogical comparison can also be caused by failing to use the words *other* or *else.*

When comparing one of a group with the rest of the group, make sure that your sentence contains the word *other* or the word *else.*

Adding *other* or *else* in this type of comparison will prevent comparing something with itself. For instance, since the Beatles were one group, they cannot be compared to all groups. They must be compared to all *other* groups.

ILLOGICAL: The Beatles were *greater than any* group.

LOGICAL: The Beatles were *greater than any other* group.

ILLOGICAL: Kay has worked *longer than anyone* in the firm.

LOGICAL: Kay has worked *longer than anyone else* in the firm.

EXERCISE C: Making Balanced Comparisons. Rewrite each sentence, correcting the unbalanced comparison.

EXAMPLE: Ginger's essay was better than Albert.
Ginger's essay was better than Albert's.

1. Aren't my new pants more attractive than Jacqueline?
2. The truck's engine is more powerful than the station wagon.
3. Trish's debating record is better than Mary.
4. My father's coin collection is better than my uncle.
5. At the meeting last night Bruce's presentation was better than John.
6. A larger orchestra is needed to perform Bruckner's symphonies than Haydn.
7. Harry's telescope is stronger than Edward.
8. My jacket is warmer than Steven.
9. Maine's weather is generally colder than Florida.
10. An infection of the liver is as dangerous as the kidneys.
11. Our ideas for the fair are much better than the seniors.
12. My bar graph on population growth is more accurate than the book.
13. Sally's hair is longer than Elinor.
14. My new gloves are smaller than Betty.
15. The efficiency of this computer is greater than yours.
16. Driving in the winter requires more caution than the summer.

17. My grandmother's pecan pie is sweeter than my mother.
18. Gretchen's short story about a tame dolphin was more interesting than Jamie.
19. The football team's record is more impressive than the baseball team.
20. The days in summer are longer than winter.

EXERCISE D: Using *Other* and *Else* in Comparisons. Rewrite each sentence, correcting the illogical comparison.

EXAMPLE: Richard is more talkative than anyone in class.
Richard is more talkative than anyone else in class.

1. Mount Everest is higher than any mountain.
2. My friend William plays baseball with more enthusiasm than anyone I know.
3. Our apartment is longer than any in the building.
4. Your charitable contribution to the emergency fund was more than any we received.
5. My room is colder than any in the house.
6. Eric skated faster than everyone in the competition.
7. I needed more help in spelling than anyone in class.
8. Robert Frost's poetry is more popular than that of any American poet.
9. Mrs. Thalenburg said my term paper was more carefully researched than every student's in the class.
10. This brand of writing paper contains at least as much cotton fiber as any on the market.
11. Bay scallops are usually more costly than any seafood in this part of the country.
12. Jacqueline's new electronic camera is more automatic than any I have seen.
13. My speech was longer than any in the contest.
14. Her new flashlight is better than any on the market.
15. This fantail guppy is more expensive than any tropical fish.
16. This ski slope is steeper than any.
17. Rose spelled more words correctly than anyone in the spelling bee.
18. Jan is taller than anyone in the class.
19. Our oak tree is older than any tree on our farm.
20. This card game is harder than any we have ever played.

DEVELOPING WRITING SKILLS: Writing Effective Comparisons. Use the following instructions to write ten sentences of your own.

EXAMPLE: Compare the weather in two states.

I like California's dry summers more than the humid summers we had in Georgia.

1. Compare the leading characters of two television shows.
2. Compare the work of two authors you admire.
3. Compare the personalities of two pets.
4. Compare the service at three restaurants.
5. Compare one area of your city or town to all the others.
6. Compare two of your favorite teachers.
7. Compare three sports events you have attended.
8. Compare the film version of a novel you have read with the novel.
9. Compare two classes you have especially enjoyed.
10. Compare your home town with another town or city you have visited.

Skills Review and Writing Workshop

Adjective and Adverb Usage

CHECKING YOUR SKILLS

Label the underlined modifier in each sentence as positive, comparative, or superlative. Then write the two other degrees of comparison.

(1) The worst postal service in our history occurred during the Revolution. (2) The war resulted in postal rates four thousand percent higher than those under the British mail system. (3) After the war, however, postage soon became much cheaper. (4) And mail was distributed more widely. (5) However, rates were still exorbitant by today's standards. (6) The shortest letter cost as much to send as a package. (7) Home delivery was rare. (8) The addressee more often than not had to pay the postage. (9) In those days, Americans were reluctant to trust the post office with the delivery of money. (10) The most popular solution was to mail half of a bill and wait until the addressee got it before sending the other half.

USING USAGE SKILLS IN WRITING
Writing a Comparison

Writers often make comparisons in order to draw conclusions. Follow the steps below to write a comparison.

Prewriting: Decide what you want to compare. You might compare the film version of a novel you've read; the personalities of two people you know; your hometown with another town or city you have visited.

Writing: Be sure the aspects you compare are comparable. For example, don't compare the houses in one town with the stores in another. Use a variety of degrees of comparison in the modifiers you use.

Revising: Check your comparisons. Are they balanced? Make any needed improvements in your work. After you have revised, proofread your work carefully.

Chapter **14**

Miscellaneous Problems in Usage

In this chapter you will study those usage problems that have not been presented earlier. In the first section of this chapter, you will learn how to form negative sentences correctly. In the second section, you will study a list of troublesome words and expressions.

14.1 Negative Sentences

At one time, it was correct to use several negative words in one sentence. It was correct, for example, to say, "Father *didn't* tell *nobody nothing.*" Today, however, only one negative word is used to make the entire sentence negative. The above sentence can be restated correctly in one of three ways: "Father *didn't* tell anybody anything," "Father told *nobody* anything," or "Father told *nothing* to anybody."

Recognizing Double Negatives

A *double negative* is the use of two negative words in a sentence when only one is needed.

Do not write sentences with double negatives.

The chart below gives examples of double negatives and the two ways each can be corrected.

CORRECTING DOUBLE NEGATIVES	
Double Negatives	**Corrections**
Bill *hasn't* invited *no one.*	Bill has invited *no one.* Bill *hasn't* invited anyone.
She *couldn't* eat *nothing.*	She could eat *nothing.* She *couldn't* eat anything.
I *can't* see *nothing.*	I can see *nothing.* I *can't* see anything.

EXERCISE A: Avoiding Double Negatives. Choose the word in parentheses that makes each sentence negative without forming a double negative.

EXAMPLE: Ann didn't go (nowhere, anywhere) last night.
anywhere

1. He hasn't eaten (none, any) of his food.
2. That lady hasn't (never, ever) purchased anything here.
3. She couldn't have told them (nothing, anything) important.
4. No one in the office reviewed (any, none) of the reports.
5. Nobody said (anything, nothing) to me about a quiz today.
6. I did (none, any) of the work I was supposed to do.
7. I don't need (no, any) money from you.
8. The Glenns saved (nothing, anything) from the wreckage.
9. Vegetables shouldn't (never, ever) be cooked too long.
10. Our new car (is, isn't) no gas guzzler.

Forming Negative Sentences Correctly

Negative sentences are formed correctly in one of three ways.

Using One Negative Word. The most common way to make a statement negative is with a single negative word, such as *no, not, none, nothing, never, nobody,* or *nowhere,* or with the contraction *-n't* added to a helping verb.

Do not use two negative words in the same clause.

Using two of these negative words in the same clause will create a double negative.

DOUBLE NEGATIVE: He *hasn't never* told us the truth.

CORRECT: He has *never* told us the truth.

He *hasn't* ever told us the truth.

Using *But* in a Negative Sense. When *but* means "only," it usually acts as a negative.

Do not use *but* in its negative sense with another negative.

DOUBLE NEGATIVE: She *didn't* offer *but* one reasonable excuse.

CORRECT: She offered *but* one reasonable excuse.

She offered only one reasonable excuse.

Using *Barely, Hardly,* and *Scarcely.* These words have a negative sense and should not be used with other negative words.

Do not use *barely, hardly,* or *scarcely* with another negative.

DOUBLE NEGATIVE: She *wasn't barely* able to recognize him.

CORRECT: She was *barely* able to recognize him.

DOUBLE NEGATIVE: The driver *couldn't hardly* see the road sign.

CORRECT: The driver could *hardly* see the road sign.

DOUBLE NEGATIVE: The concert *hadn't scarcely* begun.

CORRECT: The concert had *scarcely* begun.

EXERCISE B: Avoiding Problems with Negatives. Choose the word in parentheses that makes each sentence negative without creating a double negative.

EXAMPLE: There (is, isn't) but one possible explanation.

is

1. You (can, can't) hardly mean what you say.
2. I don't owe the bank (nothing, anything).
3. My sister (has, hasn't) reported nobody.

4. Cindy couldn't eat (anything, nothing) for dinner.
5. He shouldn't have told (anyone, no one) about the trip.
6. Don't you want (anything, nothing) from the bazaar?
7. Ann (had, hadn't) revealed the strategy to no one.
8. The counselors did not have (any, no) better suggestions.
9. I (would, wouldn't) never agree to such a plan.
10. We haven't traveled (anywhere, nowhere) in South America.

EXERCISE C: Correcting Double Negatives. Rewrite each sentence, correcting the double negative.

EXAMPLE: We couldn't barely hear the doorbell.
We could barely hear the doorbell.

1. Can't you never do anything right?
2. There hadn't been but two possibilities.
3. This old jalopy isn't never going to run properly.
4. I don't take the bus to school no more.
5. Of course, she doesn't expect nothing.
6. On week nights we never go nowhere.
7. The doctor isn't suggesting but one new treatment for Suzanne's illness.
8. Weren't you never able to contact him?
9. We don't have no plans for this evening.
10. They haven't never attended a concert in the city.
11. We don't know no one in our neighborhood yet.
12. Carol didn't like none of her Christmas presents.
13. We couldn't hardly stand his violin playing.
14. They didn't leave us but one choice.
15. We couldn't see no way out of our dilemma.
16. Brad didn't scarcely recognize his own brother.
17. Jane wasn't going nowhere without Molly.
18. Evans would not agree to sign no petition.
19. They didn't see but one path in the forest.
20. Rhea couldn't hardly understand a word the boy said.

DEVELOPING WRITING SKILLS: Writing Negative Sentences. Use each item in a negative sentence of your own.

EXAMPLE: scarcely arrived
We had scarcely arrived when Paul became ill.

1. was hardly ever
2. hasn't been anywhere
3. shouldn't ever give
4. want never
5. has but one
6. could travel nowhere
7. isn't any
8. had scarcely left
9. is not common
10. offered nothing
11. are hardly accurate
12. can't ever make anything
13. would barely come
14. has not explained
15. never agreed to
16. had brought none of
17. would give no
18. has nothing to do with
19. has visited nowhere
20. has left nothing

14.2 Sixty Common Usage Problems

This section presents an alphabetical list of sixty usage problems that sometimes cause problems in writing and speaking.

Solving Usage Problems

People commonly confuse many of the words in this list because of their similarities. One way to use this glossary is to study all the entries. A second way is to use it to check individual words when you use them in your work.

Study the items in this glossary, paying particular attention to similar meanings and spellings.

You will also find in this glossary a few reminders about words that are nonstandard and should generally be avoided.

(1) a, an The article *a* is used before consonant sounds; *an* is used before vowel sounds. Words beginning with *h, o,* or *u* sometimes have a consonant sound and sometimes a vowel sound.

CONSONANT SOUNDS: A *h*istory book (*h*-sound)
a *o*ne-time opportunity (*w*-sound)
a *u*nanimous decision (*y*-sound)

VOWEL SOUNDS: An *h*onor society (no *h*-sound)
an *o*nly child (*o*-sound)
an *u*gly wound (*u*-sound)

(2) accept, except *Accept* is a verb meaning "to receive." *Except* is a preposition meaning "other than" or "leaving out."

VERB: We *accept* your offer to mediate the dispute.
PREPOSITION: All the singers attended *except* the tenor.

(3) accuse, allege *Accuse* means "to blame" or "to bring a charge against." *Allege* means "to claim something that has not yet been proved."

EXAMPLES: The state has *accused* the man of murder.

The defense will try to prove that the *alleged* crime never actually occurred.

(4) adapt, adopt *Adapt* means "to change." *Adopt* means "to take as one's own."

EXAMPLES: She *adapts* and arranges the music of others.

In the play the actor *adopted* an Irish accent.

(5) advice, advise *Advice* is a noun meaning "an opinion." *Advise* is a verb meaning "to give an opinion to."

NOUN: I will accept your *advice.*

VERB: His doctor *advised* him to lose weight.

(6) affect, effect *Affect,* almost always a verb, means "to influence." *Effect* may be used as a noun or as a verb. As a noun, it means "result." As a verb, it means "to bring about" or "to cause."

VERB: I was deeply *affected* by her tribute.

NOUN: Students are warned about the *effects* of alcohol.

VERB: The managers *effected* important changes in the firm.

(7) ain't *Ain't* was originally a contraction of *am not,* but it is no longer considered standard English.

NONSTANDARD: Your friend *ain't* prepared to speak.

CORRECT: Your friend *isn't* prepared to speak.

(8) allot, a lot, alot *Allot* is a verb meaning "to divide in parts" or "to give out in shares." *A lot* is an informal expression meaning "a great many." It should never be spelled as one word.

VERB: Each of us has been *allotted* ten dollars to spend.

INCORRECT: We visited *alot* of state parks last summer.

CORRECT: We visited *a lot* of state parks last summer.

(9) all ready, already *All ready,* two separate words used as an adjective, is an expression meaning "ready." *Already,* an adverb, means "even now" or "by or before this time."

ADJECTIVE: The team has been *all ready* to leave for the airport for over an hour now.

ADVERB: He has *already* reached Washington.

(10) all right, alright *Alright* is a nonstandard spelling. Make sure you use the two-word form.

NONSTANDARD: Grandfather is feeling *alright* today.

CORRECT: Grandfather is feeling *all right* today.

(11) all together, altogether *All together* means "together as a single group." *Altogether* means "completely" or "in all."

EXAMPLES: Let's sing the school song *all together.*

We were *altogether* disappointed with the play.

(12) among, between Both of these words are prepositions. *Among* always implies three or more. *Between* is generally used with two things only.

EXAMPLES: *Among* my five friends, I divided my time.

The argument is *between* Mary and me.

(13) anxious This adjective implies uneasiness, worry, or fear. Do not use it as a substitute for *eager.*

LESS ACCEPTABLE: I am *anxious* to go to the concert tonight.

PREFERRED: I am *eager* to go to the concert tonight.

I am *anxious* about driving in the snowstorm.

(14) anywhere, everywhere, nowhere, somewhere Never end these adverbs with an *-s.*

NONSTANDARD: The baby is *nowheres* in sight.

CORRECT: The baby is *nowhere* in sight.

(15) as to *As to* is awkward. Replace it with *about.*

NONSTANDARD: He has no idea *as to* how to spend his money.

CORRECT: He has no idea *about* how to spend his money.

(16) at Do not use *at* after *where.* Simply eliminate it.

NONSTANDARD: We're lost and don't know *where* we are *at.*

CORRECT: We're lost and don't know *where* we are.

(17) awhile, a while *Awhile* is an adverb that in itself means "for a while." *A while* is an article and a noun. The expression is usually used after the preposition *for.*

ADVERB: Let's sit *awhile* and talk.

NOUN: Come talk with me for *a while.*

(18) because Do not use *because* after *the reason.* Say, "The reason . . . is that" or reword the sentence.

NONSTANDARD: *The reason* for his happiness is *because* he won.

CORRECT: *The reason* for his happiness is *that* he won.

He is happy *because* he won.

(19) being as, being that Do not use either expression. Use *because* or *since* instead.

NONSTANDARD: *Being as* (or *that*) I wanted a better score, I took the SAT again.

CORRECT: *Because* (or *Since*) I wanted a better score, I took the SAT again.

(20) beside, besides *Beside* means "close to" or "at the side of." *Besides* means "in addition to."

EXAMPLES: The pool is *beside* the house.

Besides my parents, my aunt will also attend.

(21) bring, take *Bring* means "to carry from a distant place to a nearer one." *Take* means the opposite: "to carry from a near place to a more distant one."

EXAMPLES: *Bring* those papers to me.

Take these financial reports with you to the president's office.

(22) burst, bust, busted *Bust* and *busted* are nonstandard. The present, past, and past participle of *burst* are all *burst.*

NONSTANDARD: The doctor will *bust* the blister.
She *busted* the cellophane wrapper.

CORRECT: The doctor will *burst* the blister.
She *burst* the cellophane wrapper.

(23) can't help but This is a nonstandard expression. Use *can't help* plus a gerund instead.

NONSTANDARD: She *can't help but* want another chance.

CORRECT: She *can't help wanting* another chance.

(24) different from, different than *Different from* is preferred.

LESS ACCEPTABLE: His camera is much *different than* Arlene's.

PREFERRED: His camera is much *different from* Arlene's.

(25) doesn't, don't *Doesn't* is the correct verb form for third-person singular subjects. *Don't* is used with all other subjects.

NONSTANDARD: She *don't* intend to go.
It *don't* seem right.
The air conditioner *don't* work.

CORRECT: She *doesn't* intend to go.
It *doesn't* seem right.
The air conditioner *doesn't* work.

(26) done *Done,* the past participle of *do,* should always follow a helping verb.

NONSTANDARD: She *done* what was expected of her.

CORRECT: She *has done* what was expected of her.

(27) due to *Due to* means "caused by" and should be used only when the words *caused by* can logically be substituted.

NONSTANDARD: *Due to* an error, he received two checks.

CORRECT: His receiving two checks was *due to* an error.

(28) due to the fact that Replace this awkward expression with *because* or *since.*

LESS ACCEPTABLE: *Due to the fact that* he was ill, he stayed home.

PREFERRED: *Because* (or *Since*) he was ill, he stayed home.

(29) emigrate, immigrate *Emigrate* means "to move *out of* a country." *Immigrate* means "to move *into* a country."

EXAMPLES: Heidi *emigrated* from Austria to the U.S. in 1934.

In 1970, she *immigrated* to Israel.

(30) enthused, enthusiastic *Enthused* is nonstandard. Replace it with *enthusiastic.*

NONSTANDARD: I am *enthused* about going to Nantucket.

CORRECT: I am *enthusiastic* about going to Nantucket.

(31) farther, further *Farther* refers to distance. *Further* means "to a greater degree or extent" or "additional."

EXAMPLES: The college is *farther* away than I would like.

I want to develop your ideas *further.*

She expects a *further* explanation.

(32) fewer, less *Fewer* is used with objects that can be counted. *Less* is used with qualities or quantities that cannot be counted.

EXAMPLES: *fewer* ships, *fewer* newspapers, *fewer* calories

less excitement, *less* water, *less* supervision

(33) former, latter *Former* refers to the first of two previously mentioned items. *Latter* refers to the second.

EXAMPLE: We visited Mexico City and Acapulco. The *former* is a bustling city; the *latter* is a modern seaside resort.

(34) gone, went *Gone* is the past participle of *go.* It should be used as a verb only with a helping verb. *Went* is the past of *go* and is never used with a helping verb.

NONSTANDARD: My parents *gone* to a restaurant.

We *could have went* to the movies if we had money.

CORRECT: My parents *have gone* to a restaurant.

My parents *went* to a restaurant.

We *could have gone* to the movies if we had money.

(35) healthful, healthy Things are *healthful.* People are *healthy.*

LESS ACCEPTABLE: Too much bread and cake is not *healthy.*

PREFERRED: Too much bread and cake is not *healthful.*

(36) in, into *In* refers to position. *Into* suggests motion.

POSITION: The children stood ankle deep *in* the water.

MOTION: Jennifer ran down to the beach and dived *into* the cold water.

(37) irregardless Putting *ir* on this word makes it a double negative. Use *regardless* instead.

NONSTANDARD: I cannot agree, *irregardless* of her plea.

CORRECT: I cannot agree, *regardless* of her plea.

(38) just When you use *just* as an adverb meaning "no more than," place it right before the word it logically modifies.

LESS ACCEPTABLE: I *just* want two quarters.

PREFERRED: I want *just* two quarters.

(39) kind of, sort of These expressions should not be used to mean "rather" or "somewhat."

NONSTANDARD: I am *kind of* disappointed.

CORRECT: I am *rather* disappointed.

(40) lay, lie *Lay* means "to put or set (something) down." Its principal parts—*lay, laying, laid,* and *laid*—are usually followed by a direct object. *Lie* means "to recline." Its principal parts—*lie, lying, lay,* and *lain*—are never followed by a direct object.

LAY: *Lay* the tools on the bench.

The child is *laying* his blocks on the table.

I don't know where I *laid* my keys.

Have you *laid* the money where Scott will see it?

LIE: I will *lie* down after I finish the work.

Mother is *lying* on the sofa in the living room.

I *lay* down yesterday for a short nap.

I have *lain* here thinking about the party for hours.

(41) learn, teach *Learn* means "to acquire knowledge." *Teach* means "to give knowledge to."

EXAMPLES: I *learned* how to change a flat tire today.

Will you *teach* me how to drive?

(42) leave, let *Leave* means "to allow to remain." *Let* means "to permit."

NONSTANDARD: *Let* him alone in the room.

Leave us try once more.

CORRECT: *Leave* him alone in the room.

Let us try once more.

(43) like *Like* is a preposition and should not be used in place of the conjunction *as.*

NONSTANDARD: This pie doesn't taste *like* it should.

CORRECT: This pie doesn't taste *as* it should.

(44) of Do not use the preposition *of* in place of the verb *have. Of* after *outside, inside, off,* or *atop* is also undesirable in formal writing. Simply eliminate it.

NONSTANDARD: She would *of* wanted that role.

CORRECT: She would *have* wanted that role.

LESS ACCEPTABLE: The clever thief hid the precious jewels *inside of* a toy.

PREFERRED: The clever thief hid the precious jewels *inside* a toy.

(45) only Be sure to place *only* in front of the word you mean to modify.

EXAMPLES: *Only* my sister wanted to go camping. (No one else wanted to go camping.)

My sister *only* wanted to go camping. (She did not want to do anything else.)

(46) raise, rise *Raise* usually takes a direct object. *Rise* never takes a direct object.

EXAMPLES: The Cotters *raise* corn in their back field almost every year.

The sun *rises* in the east every day.

(47) seen *Seen* is a past participle and can be used as a verb only with a helping verb.

NONSTANDARD: Jose *seen* the new movie already.

CORRECT: Jose *has seen* the new movie already.

(48) set, sit *Set* means "to put (something) in a certain place." Its principal parts—*set, setting, set,* and *set*—are usually followed by a direct object. *Sit* means "to be seated." Its principal parts—*sit, sitting, sat,* and *sat*—are never followed by a direct object.

SET: *Set* the basket on the floor.

The children are *setting* the table.

I *set* the wrench on the counter yesterday.

He *set* the vase on the mantel.

SIT: She usually *sits* in the front row.

She is *sitting* in the back row today.

She *sat* in the third row last year.

She has *sat* in the front row most of this year.

(49) so *So* is a coordinating conjunction. It should be avoided when you mean "so that."

LESS ACCEPTABLE: We worked overtime *so* we could finish.

PREFERRED: We worked overtime *so that* we could finish.

(5) than, then Use *than* in comparisons. *Then,* an adverb, usually refers to time.

EXAMPLES: Billy is more dependable *than* Glenn.

We ate lunch and *then* went to a film.

(51) that, which, who Use these relative pronouns correctly. *That* refers to things or people; *which* refers only to things; *who* refers only to people.

EXAMPLES: The paper *that* (or *which*) you lost has been found.
She is the only one *who* (or *that*) was reelected.

(52) that there, this here These nonstandard expressions should never be used. Simply leave out *there* and *here.*

NONSTANDARD: *That there* car is too expensive.

CORRECT: *That* car is too expensive.

(53) their, there, they're *Their,* a possessive pronoun, always modifies a noun. *There* can be used either as an expletive at the beginning of a sentence or as an adverb. *They're* is a contraction for *they are.*

PRONOUN: We lost *their* immigration papers.

EXPLETIVE: *There* are three chickens in the basket.

ADVERB: The monument will be erected *there.*

CONTRACTION: *They're* studying right now.

(54) them Do not use *them* as a substitute for *those.*

NONSTANDARD: Give me *them* pliers.

CORRECT: Give me *those* pliers.

(55) to, too, two *To,* a preposition, begins a phrase or an infinitive. *Too,* an adverb, modifies adjectives and other adverbs. *Two* is a number.

PREPOSITION: *to* the house, *to* them

INFINITIVE: *to* eat, *to* speak

ADVERB: *too* rich, *too* rapidly

NUMBER: *two* apples, *two* ships

(56) unique *Unique* means "one of a kind." It should not be used to mean "odd" or "unusual." It is also illogical to say *very unique, most unique,* or *extremely unique.*

ILLOGICAL: This is a *most unique* ring.

CORRECT: This is a *unique* ring.

(57) ways *Ways* is plural. Do not use it after the article *a.*

NONSTANDARD: The hikers have *a* great *ways* yet to go.

CORRECT: The hikers have *a* great *way* yet to go.

(58) when, where Do not use *when* or *where* directly after a linking verb. Do not use *where* in place of *that.*

NONSTANDARD: A new year is *when* you get to start over.
A discount store is *where* I can get good buys.
Amy read *where* people are smoking less.

CORRECT: A new year will allow you to start over.
I can get good buys at a discount store.
Amy read *that* people are smoking less.

(59) win, beat *Win* means "to achieve victory in." *Beat* means "to overcome (an opponent)."

NONSTANDARD: I *won* him again at table tennis.

CORRECT: I *beat* him again at table tennis.

(60) -wise Do not create new words with this suffix.

LESS ACCEPTABLE: *Schoolwise,* I did well last semester.

PREFERRED: I did well *in school* last semester.

EXERCISE A: Avoiding Usage Problems 1–10. Choose the correct expression to complete each sentence.

EXAMPLE: My teacher gave me very sound (advise, advice).
advice

1. Unfortunately, I cannot (accept, except) your offer.
2. They were (already, all ready) to go when I arrived.
3. I am searching for (a, an) honorable solution.
4. We had (alot, a lot, allot) to eat at the picnic.
5. I hope that your mother will be (all right, alright).
6. The puppy has (already, all ready) ripped up her new toy.
7. Who among them can (adopt, adapt) the play?
8. The stereo components are sold as (a, an) unit.
9. What is the (effect, affect) of the new medicine?
10. Such (advice, advise) is hardly ever helpful.
11. All of us (accept, except) Jon had a good time.
12. There (ain't, isn't) one reason for us to change our minds.
13. The Secretary of State had difficulty in (affecting, effecting) changes in the State Department.
14. An eyewitness (accused, alleged) him of the crime.

15. She (adapted, adopted) a peculiar accent after her trip.
16. Would you (advice, advise) him to see another doctor?
17. Coffee (affects, effects) my nerves.
18. We (accuse, allege) that they stole the typewriter.
19. She is (a, an) outstanding citizen.
20. How should we (a lot, allot, alot) the profits?

EXERCISE B: Avoiding Usage Problems 11–20. Choose the correct expression to complete each sentence.

1. (Nowhere, Nowheres) will you get a better bargain.
2. I am (anxious, eager) to taste the pie you baked.
3. (Being as, Because) I am sick, I can't work today.
4. (Between, Among) the three boys, there is no leader.
5. Do you really know where we (are at, are)?
6. Grandmother sat (besides, beside) us at the concert.
7. My teacher was (all together, altogether) satisfied.
8. We haven't heard (as to, about) her last adventure.
9. My wallet must be here (somewhere, somewheres).
10. The reason he failed is (because, that) he did not study.
11. We swam (a while, awhile) and then cooked a barbecue.
12. There is a parking lot (besides, beside) the restaurant.
13. Working (altogether, all together), we finished in an hour.
14. I found the letter (between, among) two old books.
15. She invited no one from our class (beside, besides) you.
16. We were (anxious, eager) about the weather reports.
17. Rest for (a while, awhile) before you shovel more snow.
18. I stayed home (being that, because) I had no money.
19. Put the packages (beside, besides) the table.
20. Do you know anything (as to, about) his strange behavior?

EXERCISE C: Avoiding Usage Problems 21–30. Choose the correct expression to complete each sentence.

1. Your stereo is much different (from, than) mine.
2. My sister (don't, doesn't) agree with your decision.
3. (Bring, Take) these cards to the receptionist upstairs.
4. (Due to the fact that, Because) he is ill, we had to postpone the meeting.
5. My mother (burst, busted) into the room and smiled.
6. I am (enthused, enthusiastic) about our vacation.

7. His story is very different (from, than) mine.
8. When you come to my house, (bring, take) your new record.
9. My grandfather (immigrated, emigrated) from Poland.
10. I wanted to (bust, burst) out laughing.
11. He (done, has done) as he was told.
12. (Due to, Because of) his absence, he was not paid.
13. I am late (due to the fact that, because) my car failed.
14. I (doesn't, don't) know where she hid the presents.
15. The doctor (has done, done) everything possible.
16. I couldn't help (but cry, crying).
17. My headache is (due to, because of) failing eyesight.
18. My father (immigrated, emigrated) to the U.S. in 1935.
19. I become (enthused, enthusiastic) whenever we rehearse.
20. It (don't, doesn't) seem possible that I could be wrong.

EXERCISE D: Avoiding Usage Problems 31–40. Choose the correct expression to complete each sentence.

1. Jerry (gone, has gone) to Portland for the weekend.
2. How much (farther, further) is the state park?
3. (Irregardless, Regardless) of your excuse, I am angry.
4. Does he have (fewer, less) horses now than last year?
5. I visited both Moscow and Peking. I enjoyed the (former, latter) more because I can speak Chinese.
6. Cindy (just wants, wants just) a small salad.
7. The bus crashed (in, into) a telephone pole.
8. This morning I (lay, laid) in bed until nine o'clock.
9. Wheat germ is considered (healthful, healthy) for you.
10. This milk is (sort of, somewhat) sour.
11. This cereal has (fewer, less) vitamins than the other.
12. Barbara was (kind of, rather) upset by the phone call.
13. Please (lie, lay) the gifts on the table by the door.
14. The Smiths (gone, have gone) shopping in the city.
15. Leave the ice cream (in, into) the freezer.
16. We went to a zoo and a museum. At the (former, latter), we were delighted by the chimpanzees.
17. My grandmother is very (healthy, healthful) for her age.
18. Noreen is (lying, laying) down in the bedroom.
19. She has (fewer, less) free time now that she is working.
20. Distracted by the street singers, I walked (in, into) a brick wall.

EXERCISE E: Avoiding Usage Problems 41–50. Choose the correct expression to complete each sentence.

1. You should (of, have) reported the accident to the police.
2. We have been (sitting, setting) here for over an hour.
3. Carolyn writes (like, as) she speaks.
4. She plans to (rise, raise) at seven.
5. Will you (teach, learn) me how to play the guitar?
6. The child said she (seen, had seen) the movie before.
7. We left very early (so, so that) we would arrive on time.
8. You have been told twice to (leave, let) the dog alone.
9. I did (like, as) I was told.
10. (Only attend, Attend only) the events that interest you.
11. The Pharaoh (than, then) gave in to Moses's demands.
12. They (sat, set) the flowers in the vase.
13. A crow perched (atop, atop of) the tree.
14. Today I (learned, taught) three new words from my teacher.
15. Why won't you (leave, let) me sit here in peace?
16. Bill held two jobs (so, so that) he could buy a car.
17. The old traveler's face looked (like, as) a map of all his journeys.
18. Your impersonation could (of, have) fooled me.
19. I (seen, have seen) three movies this week.
20. My brother is always hungrier (then, than) I am.

EXERCISE F: Avoiding Usage Problems 51–60. Choose the correct expression to complete each sentence.

1. I like (them, those) new shoes you are wearing.
2. The dean found (there, their) explanation hard to believe.
3. There are (to, too, two) ways to get to Reno from here.
4. Students (who, which) buy tickets now get a discount.
5. I am doing well this year (classwise, in class).
6. Spring is (when, the time when) flowers bloom.
7. The oldest stamp in my collection is (unique, most unique).
8. The agent traveled a great (ways, way) to see you.
9. We can (win, beat) them in the second half of the game.
10. I read in this book (where, that) most sharks drown if they stop moving through the water.
11. The groundhog is (there, their, they're), in the garden.
12. (That, That there) restaurant serves excellent steaks.

13. The ducks (that, who) were nesting near the pond didn't fly south last winter.
14. (They're, There) waiting for the bus on that road.
15. Her custom sports car is (unique, more unique than mine).
16. (This here, This) book really is frightening.
17. Would you believe I have (won, beaten) him six times?
18. She thinks she ate (to, too) much for lunch.
19. (Workwise, At work) I have been unusually successful.
20. We walked a long (way, ways) into the woods.

EXERCISE G: Correcting Usage Problems. Rewrite each sentence, correcting the error in usage.

EXAMPLE: The child was anxious to open her Christmas presents.

The child was eager to open her Christmas presents.

1. Yesterday, I wanted too tell him the truth.
2. Due to the fact that it was snowing, we postponed our trip.
3. My grandparents have been healthful for many years.
4. She can't help but want another chance.
5. Next, the villain busted into the room in a rage.
6. The matter was quickly settled among my brother and me.
7. The affect of the medicine was immediate.
8. To attend the inauguration of a President is a honor.
9. Sit the glass to the right of the plate.
10. Being that you asked, I'll tell you my feeling about him.
11. The coach sat besides my brother and me.
12. Their are three boxes in the attic.
13. Partywise, I have had my fill if you really want to know.
14. You will find similar problems anywheres you go.
15. If she were smart, she wouldn't of made up an excuse.
16. Like I have often told you, I prefer chocolate cake.
17. There apparently lost in the wilderness.
18. Everyone accept John passed the exams.
19. My little brother seen our grandfather only once.
20. Sara's costume is much different than Evelyn's.
21. My father gone to the same doctor for years.
22. Irregardless of what you say, I cannot be persuaded.
23. We were very enthused about the wedding announcement.
24. There were less awards given at this year's ceremony.
25. Can you tell me where the train depot is at?

DEVELOPING WRITING SKILLS: Using the Correct Expressions in Your Writing. Use each expression in a sentence of your own.

EXAMPLE: adapt

The composer will adapt a score he wrote last year.

1. all together
2. due to
3. different from
4. further
5. everywhere
6. gone
7. healthful
8. between
9. alleged
10. former
11. unique
12. their
13. all right
14. accept
15. only
16. lie
17. the reason is
18. can't help wanting
19. immigrate
20. affect
21. except
22. sat
23. allot
24. all ready
25. adopt

Skills Review and Writing Workshop

Miscellaneous Problems in Usage

CHECKING YOUR SKILLS

Rewrite the paragraph below, correcting all errors in usage.

(1) When a subway was first proposed in the 1890's, most New Yorkers didn't hardly consider it practical. (2) The reason was because most of Manhattan island is formed from granite. (3) Critics said that the affects of tunneling through this rock would be disastrous. (4) Property owners claimed that there buildings would collapse. (5) Protests came from city water board members, which claimed that construction would destroy underground water pipes. (6) People should not of worried, because the first subway was completed in 1904 without mishap. (7) Three miles of tracks were lain. (8) Today the New York City subway system extends much further—about 230 miles. (9) In 1973 two subway buffs decided to set a record by riding all 230 miles, like a British rider had done in the London underground. (10) The New York riders visited 462 stations all together.

USING USAGE SKILLS IN WRITING

Writing a Story with Dialogue

When you use correct expressions and proper grammar, you announce the kind of person you are. Write a story about two people who have met for the first time and want to impress each other. Follow the steps below to write your story.

Prewriting: Decide who your two people are, how they meet, where they meet, and why they want to impress each other.

Writing: Begin the story with your characters' accidental or arranged meeting. Give us their thoughts so we understand their motivation. Write their conversation.

Revising: Make sure the grammar is *perfect*. Neither of these two people wants to make a mistake! After you have revised, proofread carefully.

UNIT III

Mechanics

Chapter **15**

Capitalization and Abbreviation

The engravings of many ancient civilizations were originally done using all capital letters. Since this form of writing took up so much space, smaller or lower-case letters and a system of abbreviations evolved to save room. Capital letters continued to be used only in certain situations. Though the alphabet has altered over the years, capitalization and abbreviation are still used. Capitals signal important words and abbreviations shorten other words that are often better known today in their abbreviated form.

Today, many rules govern the use of capitalization and abbreviation. Writers must know these to maintain clarity in their work and to communicate efficiently and effectively. This chapter will introduce you to the most widely accepted rules, showing you when and where to capitalize and abbreviate correctly.

15.1 Rules for Capitalization

Capital letters work as a visual clue to the reader by making certain words stand out more prominently on a printed page. This section will focus on the rules used in capitalization.

To capitalize means to begin a word with a capital letter.

Capitals for First Words

Since first words in writing usually signal the beginning of a new idea, writers capitalize them. First words requiring the use of an initial capital letter occur in sentences, as well as in a number of other situations outlined below.

In Sentences. You will always see a capital letter used in the first word of complete sentences.

Capitalize the first word in declarative, interrogative, imperative, and exclamatory sentences.

Note that each of the following sentences is complete. Each contains both a subject and a verb and makes sense by itself.

DECLARATIVE: Raoul sent the letter yesterday.

INTERROGATIVE: Did you mail the monthly bills?

IMPERATIVE: Get a stamp out of the drawer.

EXCLAMATORY: This letter says I've won the contest!

In Interjections and Incomplete Questions. Capitals are also used to begin interjections and incomplete questions.

Capitalize the first word in interjections and incomplete questions.

Exclamatory interjections fall under this rule.

EXAMPLES: Fantastic! Ouch! Darn!

First words of incomplete questions (in which the subject and verb are understood) also require a capital letter. If a question mark follows the question (as in the following examples), you should begin the question with a capital letter.

EXAMPLES: When? For Maria? How much?

In Quotations. There is also a general rule regarding capitalization of quotations.

Capitalize the first word in a quotation if the quotation is a complete sentence.

EXAMPLE: "Man is not made for defeat."—Ernest Hemingway

Even when the quotation appears with a "he said/she said" expression, a capital is still used to begin the quotation.

EXAMPLES: Maya answered, "We bought some stationery."
"Packages are difficult to wrap," the man grumbled.

If a "he said/she said" expression comes in the middle of quoted material that is one continuous sentence, only the first word of the quotation gets a capital letter.

EXAMPLE: "If you go out," Liz said, "please mail this letter."

If a "he said/she said" expression sits between two complete sentences, both sentences receive capital letters.

EXAMPLE: "Mail order catalogs provide hours of fun," Arleen exclaimed. "My family loves to look at them."

When a portion of a quotation that is not a complete sentence is contained within a longer sentence, do not capitalize the first word of the quoted part of the sentence.

EXAMPLE: The early Pony Express riders stated that "neither snow nor rain nor heat" would stop their deliveries.

In the preceding example, no capital is used at the start of the quoted fragment since it is found in the middle of a longer sentence. If the quoted fragment shifts to the beginning of the sentence, however, the first word should then be capitalized.

EXAMPLE: "Neither snow nor rain nor heat" kept the early Pony Express riders from completing their mail deliveries.

After a Colon. Complete sentences may follow colons.

Capitalize the first word after a colon if the word begins a complete sentence.

If a list follows the colon, it is not a complete sentence and, therefore, no capital letter is used.

SENTENCE FOLLOWING COLON: We saw what was in the package: It was my lost wallet.

LIST FOLLOWING COLON: The mail carrier delivered our mail: two letters, a package, and a card.

In Poetry. Generally, the first word in each line of poetry also needs capitalization.

Capitalize the first word in each line of most poetry.

If you examine the following poem, you will notice that a capital letter begins the second line even though the line does not begin a new sentence. Follow this policy for most poems.

EXAMPLE: Were it not better to forget
Than to remember and regret?—Letitia E. Landon

For *I* and *O*. Some words always require capitalization.

Capitalize *I* and *O* throughout a sentence.

EXAMPLES: "I have painted my life—things happening in my life—without knowing."—Georgia O'Keeffe

"Your dreams, O years, how they penetrate through me!—Walt Whitman

Do not confuse *O* with the word *oh. Oh* only receive a capital when it serves as a first word in a sentence.

EXERCISE A: Using Capitalization with First Words. Copy the following items, adding the missing capitals. Some items may require more than one capital.

EXAMPLE: generally, i finish my assignments on time.

Generally, I finish my assignments on time.

1. put the book back on the shelf.
2. where does the Great Wall of China start? and end?
3. good grief, Charlie Brown! you can't do anything right!
4. "o time too swift, o swiftness never ceasing!—George Peele
5. the team was successful: it won the championship.
6. Mary, Mary, quite contrary,
   how does your garden grow?
   with silver bells and cockleshells
   and pretty maids all in a row.—Mother Goose
7. goodness! that truck is traveling too fast.
8. "in some ways," wrote Henry Wallace, "certain books are more powerful by far than any battle."
9. "whoever is happy will make others happy too," wrote Anne Frank. "he who has courage and faith will never perish in misery!"
10. in studying Latin America, you should not overlook these interesting aspects: the dress, the culture, and the food.

Capitals for Proper Nouns

A proper noun is a noun that names a specific person, place, or thing.

Capitalize all proper nouns.

Names. Whenever a person's specific name is given, capital letters should be used.

Capitalize each part of a person's full name.

As the following examples show, the given or first name, the initials standing for a name, and the surname or last name all receive capital letters.

EXAMPLES: Chester Worth, Maria A. Lopez, S. D. Schneider

In some cases, surnames may consist of several parts. If a surname begins with *Mc,* or *O',* or *St.,* the letter immediately following it also gets capitalized.

EXAMPLES: McGregor, O'Callahan, St. John

However, surnames beginning with *de, D', la, le, Mac, van,* or *von* are not so consistent. The capitalization of these surnames will vary.

EXAMPLES: De Mello or de Mello
La Coe or Lacoe
von Hofen or Von Hofen

In these cases, ask for a spelling of the name to insure accuracy.

Capitalize the proper names of animals.

EXAMPLES: Silver, the horse; Miss Piggy, the pig

Geographical and Place Names. When writing, you will often have to refer to specific places. One group of proper nouns that must be capitalized is made up of geographical names.

Capitalize geographical names.

The chart at the top of the next page provides examples of some types of geographical names that must be capitalized.

GEOGRAPHICAL NAMES	
Streets	Stokes Avenue, Fallen Leaf Lane
Towns and Cities	Elk Grove, Salinas, Miami
Counties	Cheyenne County
States and Provinces	Idaho, Utah, Ontario
Nations	China, Nigeria
Continents	Australia, North America
Mountains	the Andes Mountains, Mount Shasta
Valleys and Deserts	Imperial Valley, Mojave Desert
Islands	the Galapagos Islands
Sections of a Country	the Northwest
Scenic Spots	Badlands of South Dakota, the Grand Canyon
Rivers and Falls	Amazon River, Bridalveil Falls
Lakes and Bays	Lake Ontario, Hudson Bay
Oceans and Seas	Indian Ocean, the Red Sea
Celestial Bodies	Pluto, the Milky Way

Two celestial bodies that are not capitalized are the moon and the sun. When you use the word *earth* as one of the planets, you should capitalize it. However, when the word *earth* is preceded by the article *the,* do not capitalize it.

EXAMPLES: The astronauts left Earth and landed on the moon.
The astronauts left the earth far behind.

Compass points also need special attention. When a compass point is used just to show direction, it is not capitalized. A specific location, on the other hand, is capitalized.

EXAMPLES: We headed northwest.
My cousin lives in the Southwest.

Another group of proper nouns that must be capitalized are place names such as the names of monuments, buildings, and meeting rooms.

Capitalize the names of monuments, buildings, and meeting rooms.

The following chart shows examples of monuments, buildings, and meeting rooms.

SPECIFIC PLACES	
Monuments and Memorials	the Washington Monument, the Lincoln Memorial
Buildings	the Smithsonian Institution, the Superdome, the Actor's Conservatory Theater
School and Meeting Rooms	Room 20B, Laboratory C, the Oval Office

Do not capitalize the words *theater, hotel,* and *university* unless they are part of a proper name.

EXAMPLES: The theater is one of the oldest buildings in town.

The Fallon House Theater is in an old ghost town.

The word *room* is capitalized only if it refers to a specific room and is combined with a name, letter, or number.

EXAMPLE: The exam will be given in Room 46.

Other Proper Nouns. References to time and history also follow certain capitalization rules.

Capitalize the names of specific events and periods of time.

The following chart illustrates several categories of specific events and periods of time covered by this rule.

SPECIFIC EVENTS AND TIMES	
Historical Periods	the Stone Age
Historical Events	the War of 1812
Documents and Laws	the Gettysburg Address, the Homestead Act
Days and Months	Monday, April
Holidays and Religious Days	Labor Day, Good Friday
Special Events	the Kentucky Derby

Do not capitalize the seasons.

EXAMPLE: We felt a winter chill in the air.

The names of various groups are also capitalized.

Capitalize the names of various organizations, government bodies, political parties, races, nationalities, and languages.

Study the following chart to see how each of these names is capitalized.

SPECIFIC GROUPS AND LANGUAGES	
Clubs	Rotary Club, Lynbrook Speech Club, Lions Club
Organizations	League of Women Voters, American Cancer Society, United Farm Workers
Institutions	University of Miami, Marymount General Hospital, Ford Foundation
Businesses	International Business Machines, Ford Motor Company
Government Bodies	the Senate of the United States, the Houses of Parliament, Department of Defense
Political Parties	the Republicans, the Communist Party
Races	Caucasian, Mongoloid
Nationalities	American, French, Russian, Mexican
Languages	English, Spanish, French, Yiddish

When using words such as *black* or *white* to refer to race, however, do not use capitals.

Religious references make up another group of proper nouns that requires capitalization.

Capitalize references to religions, deities, and religious scriptures.

Each religion has a set of words referring to the important and sacred beliefs it holds. Although you may not be a believer in that faith, courtesy demands that references to each religion be capitalized. The major religious groups you are likely to refer to in your writing include Christianity, Judaism, Buddhism, Islam, and Hinduism. A partial list of words from these faiths is given below.

CHRISTIANITY: God, the Lord, the Father, the Son, the Holy Spirit, the Bible, the books of the Bible (Exodus, Mark, Romans)

JUDAISM: God, the Lord, the Prophets (Moses, Abraham), the Tora, the Talmud

EASTERN RELIGIONS: Buddhism (Buddha, the Tripitaka); Islam (Allah, the Koran); Hinduism (Brahma, the Vedas)

This list is not complete. Other religious references that you encounter must also be capitalized. These include any pronoun references made to the deity in Christian or Jewish writings.

EXAMPLE: Praise be to the Lord, for He made all things in heaven and on earth.

The only time that religious references are not capitalized occurs when writing about mythological gods and goddesses. Although the proper names of gods and goddesses are capitalized, the words *god* and *goddess* are not.

EXAMPLES: the god Pluto, the goddess Athena

Special awards and presentations are often named after people. Even when they are not, awards and presentations should be capitalized.

Capitalize the names of awards.

Notice in the following examples that the word *the* is not capitalized.

EXAMPLES: the Kevin E. Morris Scholarship; the Nobel Peace Prize; the Academy Awards; the Oscar; Eagle Scout

Another group of names requiring capitalization includes the names of air, sea, space, and land craft.

Capitalize the names of specific types of air, sea, space, and land craft.

When capitalizing the names of air, sea, space, and land craft, do not capitalize the word *the* preceding a name unless the word is part of the official name.

AIR:	Boeing 747	SPACE:	*Sputnik I*
SEA:	*Lusitania*	LAND:	the Model T

As a writer, you will also write the names of products.

Capitalize brand names.

This rule applies both to brand names used as adjectives and to full trademark names. If the full trademark name is used, all the words in the name are considered a proper noun and should be capitalized.

EXAMPLES: a Honda import
the Honda Accord

EXERCISE B: Using Capitals in Sentences with Proper Nouns. Copy the following sentences, adding the missing capitals.

EXAMPLE: We read a poem by edna st. vincent millay.
We read a poem by Edna St. Vincent Millay.

1. After hearing the news, the united nations called a meeting of the security council.
2. Illustrators of children's books all hope to win the coveted caldecott award.
3. Anyone who loves animal stories should read about the horse known as flicka.
4. Most people in india are hindus and worship brahma.
5. One goddess in mythology that you will read about often is the goddess hera.
6. As he made a purchase from the store called stamp house, inc., I noticed that the russian spoke english very well.
7. If you want passport information, you should contact the state department in washington, d.c.
8. My timex is now ten years old but still works.
9. The concorde crosses the atlantic ocean in just a few hours.
10. We inducted sixty new members into the national honor society at our school last week.

EXERCISE C: Adding Capitals for Geographical Places, Specific Events, Periods of Time, and Other Proper Nouns. Copy the following paragraph, adding the missing capitals. Note that some sentences do not need additional capitalization.

(1) The early years of this century brought with them a variety of new names, exciting events, and far-reaching ideas. (2) The century got off to a flying start when Orville and Wilbur Wright took to the air in december 1903. (3) Excitement continued into the next year when the st. louis world's fair began, bringing over 20,000 visitors flocking to the city. (4) Sports lovers also enjoyed the olympic games that were held in conjunction with the fair that year. (5) Formation of the american baseball league in 1901 had also brought the sports fans joy since it introduced a new level of competition to this popular sport. (6) Many people enjoyed activities in their own communities during the 1900's: Parades and picnics held as part of the july celebration of independence day brought pleasure to people of all ages. (7) Of course, all was not fun and games; many important laws were passed during these years. (8) One of the most influential pieces of legislation in the early 1900's was the pure food and drug act passed in the summer of 1906. (9) Advertisements of many "quack" medical cures came to a quick halt. (10) All this began in those first few years of 1900 as america boldly entered a new century—the time period labeled by some as the progressive era.

Capitals for Proper Adjectives

A proper noun used as an adjective or an adjective formed from a proper noun is called a proper adjective.

Capitalize most proper adjectives.

EXAMPLES: Swiss government, American people, Gothic art

Some proper adjectives are no longer capitalized, however, because they have been used for so long.

EXAMPLES: french fries, teddy bear, venetian blinds

In some cases, a brand name is used as a proper adjective and is followed by a common noun. In these situations, the brand name serves as a proper adjective describing the common noun and, thus, the brand name deserves a capital. The common noun following the brand name remains uncapitalized.

Capitalize brand names used as adjectives.

EXAMPLES: Timex watches, Samsonite luggage

Sometimes prefixes precede proper adjectives.

Do not capitalize prefixes attached to proper adjectives unless the prefix refers to a nationality.

EXAMPLES: pre-Mayan architecture, pro-American sentiment

However, if the prefix itself is a nationality, it should be capitalized.

EXAMPLES: Indo-European, Afro-American

You must also watch the other parts of hyphenated proper adjectives.

In a hyphenated adjective, capitalize only the proper adjective.

EXAMPLE: Spanish-speaking Americans

EXERCISE D: Using Capitalization with Proper Adjectives. Copy the sentences that need capitals, adding the missing capitals. If a sentence does not need additional capitals, write *correct.*

EXAMPLE: The swedish student spoke the english language.
The Swedish student spoke the English language.

1. Charles Drew, who developed the use of plasma in emergency transfusions, was of afro-american heritage.
2. The baby sitter hunted for the child's teddy bear.
3. That store sells many bottles of chanel no. 5. perfume.
4. The pro-american speaker at the rally was cheered.
5. Did you use kodak equipment to take this photograph?
6. India's population is 77 percent indo-aryan.
7. I asked for brazilian coffee.

8. Please close the venetian blinds because the sun is in my eyes.
9. The story of St. Joan is one well loved by the french people.
10. We met many italian-speaking tourists in Mexico.

Capitals for Titles

Capitals are used to indicate titles of people and works.

Capitalize titles of people and titles of works.

Titles of People. Titles used before names and in direct address require capitalization.

Capitalize a person's title when it is used with the person's name or when it is used in direct address.

The following chart provides examples of some of these titles and shows when they should and should not be capitalized.

SOCIAL, BUSINESS, RELIGIOUS, AND MILITARY TITLES		
With Proper Names	**In Direct Address**	**In General References**
Social		
Sir Henry Bellamy, Dame Mary Cottrell, Lord and Lady Ansley, Madame Lallemand	May I help you into the car, Sir? Could you tell me, Madame, if this is the main post office?	The duke attended the coronation. A woman who has received an order of knighthood is a dame.
Business		
Professor Scott Casentini, Dr. Pauline Greer, Superintendent B.K. Wallaker, B. Lawley, Ph.D.	Professor, your lecture was very interesting. I feel fine, Doctor.	The doctor set the broken leg. The superintendent spoke at the meeting.

Religious		
Reverend James, Bishop Potter, St. Bernadette, Rabbi Frankel	I received your letter, Rabbi. Are you going to be there, Father?	The father plays the trombone. She is a saint.
Military		
Sergeant Ford, Major D. Moyer, Lieutenant Lowe, Ensign Garcia, General Fratini	Ensign, raise the flag. I'm glad you could be here, Major.	The captain flew helicopters. Tell the sergeant what happened.

The titles of government officials also require capitalization in certain cases.

Capitalize titles of government officials when they are followed by a proper name or when used in direct address.

In the United States, titles such as supervisor, mayor, governor, congressman, congresswoman, senator, judge, and ambassador are used for different government officials. Officials of other countries also have titles. All of these are capitalized when they are used in front of a proper name or in direct address. General references, however, usually omit the capital.

PRECEDING A PROPER NAME: Mayor Martin Hanley will speak.

IN DIRECT ADDRESS: Will you speak tonight, Mayor?

IN A GENERAL REFERENCE: The mayor works on the budget.

If the title is for an extremely high-ranking official (President, Vice President, Chief Justice, Queen of England), the title will always be capitalized.

Capitalize the titles of certain high government officials even when the titles are not followed by a proper name or used in direct address.

EXAMPLES: The President cut short his stay at Camp David.

He will meet with the Queen of England today.

The Supreme Court of the United States has eight justices and a Chief Justice.

Although the references to the government officials in the preceding examples are classified as general references, they still are capitalized to show the respect due the high office.

Other titles are sometimes capitalized to show special respect when referring to a specific person holding the office.

EXAMPLES: The Senator spoke in favor of the legislation.

A senator is elected for a six-year term.

Confusion often results when a title is longer than one word.

Capitalize all important words in compound titles, but do not capitalize prefixes and suffixes added to titles.

EXAMPLES: Lieutenant Governor

Assistant Secretary of the Interior

Commander in Chief

ex-Senator Jorgenson

Governor-elect Richter

Notice, in the preceding examples, that when the prefix *ex-* or the suffix *-elect* is used in connection with a title, the prefix and suffix remain uncapitalized.

In families, titles of relatives are often capitalized.

Capitalize titles showing family relationships when they refer to a specific person, unless they are preceded by a possessive noun or pronoun.

EXAMPLES: Did Uncle John bring the package?

When did this package arrive, Dad?

This package is for Grandmother.

Watch for instances in which these names are used as common nouns, for then the capitals are dropped. It may also help to realize that when these names are preceded by a possessive noun or pronoun such as *my, their,* or *our* they do not require capitalization.

EXAMPLES: Mrs. Jackson is a grandmother.

I wonder if my dad saw the package arrive.

Anne's uncle brought the package.

People may also have abbreviated titles attached to their names to identify their degrees, professions, marital status, and so forth. These titles all need capitalization.

Capitalize abbreviations of titles before and after names.

The most common abbreviations found before and after names include *Mr., Mrs., Jr.,* and *Sr.*

EXAMPLES: Mr. Kevin Peterson, Jr. Mrs. Ann Sikorski

The title *Ms.* is not an abbreviation for another word. It starts with a capital and ends with a period, however, as if it were an abbreviation. You can use *Ms.* before a proper name to refer to either a single or a married woman.

Note that *Miss* should also be capitalized. It is not an abbreviation, so no period is put at the end.

Titles of Things. Writers often make references to the titles of works that must be capitalized.

Capitalize the first word and all other key words in the titles of books, periodicals, poems, stories, plays, paintings, and other works of art.

BOOK: *Heart of Darkness*

PERIODICAL: *Better Homes and Gardens*

POEM: "Flower in the Crannied Wall"

STORY: "Bernice Bobs Her Hair"

PLAY: *How to Succeed in Business Without Really Trying*

PAINTING: *The Artist's Daughter with a Cat*

MUSIC: *The Triumph of Time and Truth*

As you look at the preceding examples, there are a number of things to notice. First, the words *a, an,* and *the* are only capitalized when they are the first word of the title. Second, conjunctions and prepositions shorter than five letters are capitalized only when they are the first word in the title. Third, adjectives, nouns, pronouns, verbs, and adverbs are all considered key words and are always capitalized.

When capitalizing a subtitle, the same rule is used.

EXAMPLE: *Language: A Reflection of People and Culture*

Titles of courses sometimes require capitalization as well.

Capitalize titles of courses when the courses are language courses or when the courses are followed by a number.

Any references to language classes will always receive capital letters since languages are always capitalized. However, other subjects will only be capitalized when the reference is made to a specific course, which will generally be followed by a number or letter identifying the course.

WITH CAPITALS: Latin II, English, California History 1A

WITHOUT CAPITALS: mathematics, history, home economics

EXERCISE E: Using Capitalization with Titles of People. Copy the sentences that need capitals, adding the missing capitals. If a sentence does not need additional capitalization, write *correct.*

EXAMPLE: My aunt introduced me to David Jones, sr.

My aunt introduced me to David Jones, Sr.

1. Do you remember your first day of school, grandma?
2. The well-known reverend John Hall, jr., spoke at the service.
3. With no hesitation, mayor Roberts approached the speaker's platform.
4. The president of the United States held a press conference.
5. Very few officers in the service ever attain the rank of general.
6. May I introduce miss Ann Schmidt and mr. Louis Ward, sr.?
7. Here is aunt Louise, who is a professor at the college.
8. Please give me advice, rabbi.
9. The queen of England will be visiting Australia next week.
10. Do you know senator-elect Garcia personally?

EXERCISE F: Capitalizing Titles of Things. Write the following titles, adding the missing capitals. Underline the titles that are printed in italics.

EXAMPLE: Play: *fiddler on the roof*

Fiddler on the Roof

1. Painting: *at the circus*
2. Poem: "lines composed a few miles above tintern abbey"
3. Short story: "before the wolves come"
4. School courses: german geometry business 312
5. Sculpture: *variation within a sphere*
6. Opera: *the siege of rhodes*
7. Book: *wellington: the years of the sword*
8. Periodical: *national geographic*
9. One-act play: "the wonderful ice cream suit"
10. Song: "by the light of the silvery moon"

Capitals in Letters

Certain words in letters always require capitalization.

Capitalize the first word and all nouns in letter salutations and the first word in letter closings.

SALUTATIONS: Dear Brian, My dear Friend, Ladies:

CLOSINGS: With deepest regards, Sincerely, Yours truly,

EXERCISE G: Using Capitalization in a Letter. If an underlined word in the following letter requires a capital, write *yes* after the corresponding number; if it does not, write *no.*

(1) my (2) dear Friends,

Recently I have discovered a brand new hobby—hot air ballooning! (3) what a thrill it is to drift slowly above the farms and house tops! Last week I saw the most spectacular sight: (4) a slender steeple rose majestically above the fog.

Of course, this new hobby is not cheap. (5) do you have any idea how much a hot air balloon costs? Over $5,000! Just taking a ride costs about $50. I think I will investigate building one. So far, I've learned that the baskets people ride in are usually constructed from one of four materials: (6) rattan, fiberglass, aluminum, or wood. (7) "it's possible to build a basket," a salesman told me. (8) "however, you'll need to purchase the balloon."

Since my pocketbook is empty, I'll have to settle for an occasional flight. I guess I should try to remember the words of

Dorothy in The Wizard of Oz when she said, (9) "there's no place like home."

With fondest (10) regards,

Archie

EXERCISE H: Using Capitals Throughout Writing. Copy the following sentences, adding the missing capitals. Underline any words that appear in italics.

EXAMPLE: on my vacation in new york, i visited the statue of liberty.

On my vacation in New York, I visited the Statue of Liberty.

(1) a mighty statue, a symbol of america's love of freedom, sits on liberty island as a welcome to visitors from europe, asia, latin america, and other parts of the world. (2) known as the statue of liberty, it is slightly over 152 feet tall. (3) the statue was designed by frederic bartholdi, a frenchman. (4) the french government liked the designs and thus formed the franco-american union to raise funds for it. (5) the statue was presented formally to u.s. minister morton. (6) to prepare the foundation for the arriving statue, joseph pulitzer, for whom the pulitzer prize is named, helped solicit donations. (7) mr. pulitzer was the owner of the new york *world*, a newspaper in the city. (8) president grover cleveland dedicated the statue on october 28, 1886. (9) did you know that a poem by emma lazarus entitled "the new colossus" was added to the pedestal in 1903? (10) recently, the american museum of immigration was opened here.

DEVELOPING WRITING SKILLS: Using Capitals Correctly in Your Own Writing. Here is a list of some imaginary titles for the best-sellers of this decade.

A. *Deadly Danger in the Ocean Depths*
B. *A Step Through Space and Time*
C. *Why I Flunked Physical Education 1A*
D. *Twelve Hours to the Big Game*
E. *Me and More Me—My Years as a Hollywood Star*

Choose one of these imaginary titles and write a paragraph summarizing the plot. Include in your paragraph the following information, correctly capitalized.

1. Name of the main character
2. Hometown and state
3. His/her title
4. His/her nationality
5. Business he/she works for
6. Organization or club he/she attended
7. A special event he/she attended
8. The title of a book that influenced the main character
9. The most famous line the main character speaks
10. A trade name for some object the main character uses

Rules for Abbreviation 15.2

Abbreviations were first developed to enable writers to save time and space.

To abbreviate means to shorten an existing word or phrase.

Some abbreviated forms of words have become so popular that people no longer think of them as abbreviations. *Gym, auto, memo,* and *exams* fall into this category. So many abbreviated forms now exist that entire books are needed to catalog them. In order to insure some consistency in these abbreviations, certain rules are followed. This section will show you how and when to abbreviate correctly.

Names and Titles of People

Abbreviations for names and titles of people are governed by a number of rules. One of these concerns given names.

Use a person's full given name in formal writing, unless the person uses initials as part of his or her formal name.

If you consider a person important enough to mention in formal writing, that person deserves to have his or her full name included. In addresses or lists, using initials in place of the given name is considered acceptable.

IN FORMAL WRITING: My friend Steven Pratt (not S. Pratt) had knee surgery recently.

IN AN ADDRESS OR LIST: Steven Pratt or S. Pratt

Unlike names, the titles that precede a person's name are often abbreviated in formal writing.

Abbreviations of social titles before a proper name begin with a capital letter and end with a period.

Consider first the common abbreviated titles in the following examples.

EXAMPLES: Mr., Mrs., Mme. (Madam or Madame)

Messrs. (plural of Mr.), Mmes. (plural of Mrs. or Mme.)

The title *Ms.* is not an abbreviation of another word. It begins with a capital and ends with a period as if it were an abbreviation, however. It may be used before a proper name to refer to either a single or married woman.

You may use these abbreviated titles in formal writing whenever they are followed directly by a proper name. Never use them without a proper name.

INCORRECT: The Mrs. is not at home.

CORRECT: Mrs. Birdsall is not at home.

You should also remember that the social title *Miss* is not an abbreviation. Thus, no period is placed at the end of it.

Formal titles indicating professional, religious, political, and military rank may also be abbreviated before proper names in some cases.

Abbreviations of other titles used before proper names also begin with a capital letter and end with a period.

The chart on the next page provides some of the more common abbreviations of rank and position. Study the examples closely so that you can understand how the abbreviated form is constructed.

ABBREVIATIONS OF COMMON TITLES OF POSITION AND RANK			
Professional		**Religious**	
Dr.	Doctor	Rev.	Reverend
Atty.	Attorney	Fr.	Father
Prof.	Professor	Sr.	Sister
Hon.	Honorable	Br.	Brother
Political		**Military**	
Pres.	President	Sgt.	Sergeant
Supt.	Superintendent	Lt.	Lieutenant
Rep.	Representative	Capt.	Captain
Sen.	Senator	Lt.Col.	Lieutenant Colonel
Gov.	Governor		
Treas.	Treasurer	Col.	Colonel
Sec.	Secretary	Gen.	General
Amb.	Ambassador	Ens.	Ensign
		Adm.	Admiral

Several guidelines will help you use these abbreviations appropriately. First, when only the surname is given, write out the title: Do not use the abbreviated form.

INCORRECT: Amb. Leonard conducted the negotiations.

CORRECT: Ambassador Leonard conducted the negotiations.

The abbreviation *Dr.* is an exception to this guideline. *Dr.* is abbreviated before a proper noun just as *Mr.* and *Mrs.* are.

EXAMPLE: Dr. Tyson gave her patient a tetanus shot.

Second, when the first name or initials are provided, you may use the abbreviated form of the title.

EXAMPLE: Our guest lecturer was Prof. Milton R. Douglas.

Finally, you must remember that certain religious titles *(Reverend, Father, Sister,* and *Brother)* and the professional title *Honorable* are customarily not abbreviated even when a first name or initials are used.

A number of abbreviations also exist for titles that follow immediately after a name.

Abbreviations of titles after a name start with a capital letter and end with a period.

The abbreviations *Jr.* and *Sr.* often appear after names.

EXAMPLE: Roberto Garcia, Jr., looks like his father.

Academic degrees after a name follow this rule as well. The chart below lists common academic abbreviations.

COMMON ACADEMIC ABBREVIATIONS			
B.A. (or A.B.)	Bachelor of Arts	Ph.D.	Doctor of Philosophy
B.S. (or S.B.)	Bachelor of Science	D.D.	Doctor of Divinity
		D.D.S.	Doctor of Dental Surgery
M.A. (or A.M.)	Master of Arts		
M.S. (or S.M.)	Master of Science	M.D.	Doctor of Medicine
M.B.A.	Master of Business Administration	R.N.	Registered Nurse
		Esq.	Esquire (lawyer)
M.F.A.	Master of Fine Arts		

Do not use the abbreviations for Junior and Senior or for academic degrees unless they follow a proper name.

INCORRECT: The M.D. checked the child's pulse.

CORRECT: Craig Fredericks, M.D., checked the child's pulse.

EXERCISE A: Abbreviating Titles of People. Write the abbreviation for each title in the following sentences. Then rewrite the sentences in which the abbreviations can be used appropriately in formal writing, using the abbreviations.

EXAMPLE: Sergeant Alvin York was a hero of World War I.

Sgt. Sgt. Alvin York was a hero of World War I.

1. The will stated that Henry Larson, Junior, should receive half the estate.
2. We will attend the play with Madame Cousteau.
3. The bestseller was written by Anna Moore, Doctor of Philosophy.

4. At graduation, Admiral Hawkes gave the invocation.
5. He wrote on the application Delmar David Benson, Bachelor of Science.
6. The judge finally assigned Attorney Jeffrey Abbott to the case.
7. The news reported that Father Martin Kidd would be traveling to Atlanta.
8. The keynote speaker, Representative Martha Santos, will fly in tonight.
9. Can you tell me, Mister, when the new models will be available?
10. When he finished at the seminary, he had a brass plaque put on his office door that read, Carl Shelby, Doctor of Divinity.

Geographical Terms

Abbreviations for geographical terms are generally used only in addresses, lists, charts, and informal writing.

Abbreviations for geographical terms before or after a proper noun begin with a capital letter and end with a period.

The following chart provides a look at some of the more common geographical abbreviations.

COMMON GEOGRAPHICAL ABBREVIATIONS					
Ave.	Avenue	Dr.	Drive	Prov.	Province
Bldg.	Building	Ft.	Fort	Pt.	Point
Apt.	Apartment	Is.	Island	Rd.	Road
Blk.	Block	Mt.	Mountain, Mount	Rte.	Route
Blvd.	Boulevard			Sq.	Square
Co.	County	Natl.	National	St.	Street
Dist.	District	Pen.	Peninsula	Terr.	Territory
		Pk.	Park, Peak		

Two sets of abbreviations for states exist: one traditional set and one put out more recently by the U.S. Postal Service.

Traditional abbreviations for states begin with a capital and end with a period. The Postal Service abbreviations are all capitals with no periods.

Study the abbreviations for the states, noticing how the two sets of abbreviations differ from one another.

STATE ABBREVIATIONS

State	Traditional	Postal Service	State	Traditional	Postal Service
Alabama	Ala.	AL	Montana	Mont.	MT
Alaska	Alaska	AK	Nebraska	Nebr.	NB
Arizona	Ariz.	AZ	Nevada	Nev.	NV
Arkansas	Ark.	AR	New Hampshire	N.H.	NH
California	Calif.	CA	New Jersey	N.J.	NJ
Colorado	Colo.	CO	New Mexico	N.M.	NM
Delaware	Del.	DE	North Carolina	N.C.	NC
Florida	Fla.	FL	North Dakota	N. Dak.	ND
Georgia	Ga.	GA	Ohio	O.	OH
Hawaii	Hawaii	HI	Oklahoma	Okla.	OK
Idaho	Ida.	ID	Oregon	Ore.	OR
Illinois	Ill.	IL	Pennsylvania	Pa.	PA
Indiana	Ind.	IN	Rhode Island	R.I.	RI
Iowa	Iowa	IA	South Carolina	S.C.	SC
Kansas	Kans.	KS	South Dakota	S. Dak.	SD
Kentucky	Ky.	KY	Tennessee	Tenn.	TN
Louisiana	La.	LA	Texas	Tex.	TX
Maine	Me.	ME	Utah	Utah	UT
Maryland	Md.	MD	Vermont	Vt.	VT
Massachusetts	Mass.	MA	Virginia	Va.	VA
Michigan	Mich.	MI	Washington	Wash.	WA
Minnesota	Minn.	MN	West Virginia	W. Va.	WV
Mississippi	Miss.	MS	Wisconsin	Wis.	WI
Missouri	Mo.	MO	Wyoming	Wyo.	WY

NOTE ABOUT *D.C.*: The traditional abbreviation for the District of Columbia is *D.C.*; the Postal Service abbreviation is *DC.* Use the traditional abbreviation in formal writing whenever it follows the word *Washington.*

EXAMPLE: The meeting was held in Washington, D.C., three weeks ago this Friday.

You should generally use the abbreviations for states only in lists, addresses, and informal writing. The Postal Service prefers that you use its method of abbreviating the states on envelopes or packages to be mailed.

In formal writing, avoid abbreviations for streets, cities, counties, states, and countries. One exception to this rule does exist, however. When you refer to the U.S.S.R. or the U.S. (especially when they are used as adjectives), abbreviations are acceptable even in formal writing.

EXAMPLE: The U.S.S.R. (or Union of Soviet Socialist Republics) bought some U.S. (or United States) grain.

EXERCISE B: Abbreviating Locations. If an underlined abbreviation is used correctly in the following letter, write *correct.* If it is not, write the correct form.

1721 Lafayette (1) Dr.
Buffalo, (2) WY 82834
July 10, 1985

Mr. Ray Byrne
326 Payne (3) Ave.
San Carlos, (4) NM 43180

Dear Mr. Byrne:

I wanted to thank you personally for that intriguing article on travel; your suggestions for unique vacations have my family extremely excited. Right now, we are considering a backpack trip to the Yukon (5) Terr., a trip to the Flower Festival in British Columbia, or an excursion to see our web-footed friends of the Galapagos (6) Is. We were at least able to eliminate the bus tour of (7) Mt. Rushmore and Yellowstone (8) Natl. Park since we've already taken that fantastic tour. One suggestion: If you decide to take that bicycle trip through Milpitas, (9) CA, be sure to see the Court House (10) Bldg. No visitor should miss it!

Sincerely,

Arden DeMoss

Time, Measurements, and Numbers

In your writing, you will often need to include references to time, measurements, and numbers. The use of abbreviations in these situations is governed by a number of rules.

Time References. Time references fall into three major categories: time spans, A.M. and P.M., and B.C. and A.D. First, consider the rule governing the abbreviation of time spans.

Abbreviations for clocked time begin with a small letter, but those for days of the week and months begin with a capital. All three end with a period.

Some abbreviations used for various time spans follow.

TIME ABBREVIATIONS					
Clocked Time					
sec.	second(s)	min.	minute(s)	hr.	hour(s)
Days of the Week					
Mon.	Monday	Thurs.	Thursday	Sat.	Saturday
Tues.	Tuesday	Fri.	Friday	Sun.	Sunday
Wed.	Wednesday				
Months of the Year					
Jan.	January	May	May	Sept.	September
Feb.	February	June	June	Oct.	October
Mar.	March	July	July	Nov.	November
Apr.	April	Aug.	August	Dec.	December

Although the abbreviations in the chart are used only in informal writing, the abbreviations *A.M.* and *P.M.* are permitted in both formal and informal writing.

Abbreviations of time before and after noon are formed with either capital letters followed by periods or small letters followed by periods.

In any one piece of writing, be sure to use either all capitals or all small letters. Do not mix the two styles.

ABBREVIATIONS: A.M. or a.m. (ante meridiem, before noon)
P.M. or p.m. (post meridiem, after noon)

Use these abbreviations only when referring to the time of day in numerals; otherwise, write the words out.

EXAMPLES: We had a fire drill at 11:05 a.m. today.
I have to get my haircut sometime before noon tomorrow.

The abbreviations *B.C.* and *A.D.* may also be used in both formal and informal writing.

Abbreviations for historical dates before and after the birth of Christ require capital letters followed by periods.

EXAMPLES: B.C. (before Christ)
A.D. (*anno Domini,* the year of the Lord)

These two time references are usually used with numerals. Place the *B.C.* after the number it refers to.

EXAMPLE: Beginning with the Eastern Cho dynasty in 770 B.C., Chinese culture started to spread to the rest of the world.

A.D. may come before or after the number. If you wish to use *A.D.* in a sentence that refers to a century, *A.D.* must go after the word *century.*

EXAMPLES: The Reformation began about A.D. 1500.
The Reformation began about 1500 A.D.
The sixteenth century A.D. has been labeled the beginning of the Reformation.

Measurements. Generally, abbreviations for traditional and metric measurements follow the next rule.

For the abbreviations of traditional measurements use small letters and periods. For metric measurements use small letters and no periods.

Some measurement abbreviations follow.

ABBREVIATIONS OF MEASUREMENT

Type of Measurement	Traditional		Metric	
Linear	inch (es)	in.	millimeter(s)	mm
	foot (feet)	ft.	centimeters(s)	cm
	yard(s)	yd.	meter(s)	m
	mile(s)	mi.	kilometer(s)	km
Volume	teaspoon(s)	tsp.	milliliter(s)	mL
	tablespoon(s)	tbsp.	centiliter(s)	cL
	pint(s)	pt.	liter(s)	L
	quart(s)	qt.	kiloliter(s)	kL
	gallon(s)	gal.		
Temperature	Fahrenheit	F.	Celsius	C

Notice the exception in the volume measurements for the metric abbreviations: A capital letter is used for *liter*. Capital letters are also used for both *Fahrenheit* and *Celsius*.

For a more complete listing of measurements and their abbreviated forms, refer to a dictionary or almanac. There you are also likely to find a conversion chart that will help you change traditional measurements to metric ones.

The abbreviations for temperature are used in all kinds of writing. The other abbreviations may be used in technical writing and informal writing. If you spell out the number, however, spell out the measurements as well.

IN INFORMAL WRITING: The piano weighed 750 lb.

IN FORMAL WRITING: The piano weighed 750 pounds.

IN ALL TYPES OF WRITING: The baby weighed seven pounds.

Numbers. Several rules govern the abbreviation of numbers (the use of numerals rather than words).

In formal writing, spell out numbers or amounts of less than one hundred and any other numbers that can be written in one or two words.

EXAMPLES: At least seven children broke out with chicken pox.

The senator took in ten thousand dollars at the fund raiser.

The senior class has 623 members.

Sometimes, numbers will occur at the beginning of the sentence. If possible, relocate the number to another place in the sentence. If this cannot be done, use this rule.

Spell out all numbers found at the beginning of sentences.

EXAMPLES: Four hundred and seventy-three homing pigeons were released during the half-time show.

During the half-time show, 473 homing pigeons were released.

Certain special types of numbers are almost always abbreviated.

Use numerals when referring to fractions, decimals, and percentages.

Remember to place the numerals within, not at the beginning of the sentence.

EXAMPLES: The boy stood 49½ inches tall.

The correct answer was 61.9.

The results of the election revealed that he had captured 57 percent of the vote.

Another frequent use of numerals is in addresses. These references should always be abbreviated.

Use numerals when writing addresses.

EXAMPLE: Donald Marshall
882 Teneda Dr.
Englewood, Cliffs, NJ 07631

A final frequent use of numerals is in dates.

Use numerals when referring to a date.

EXAMPLE: The man predicted the world would end January 27, 1979, but he was mistaken.

When you write these abbreviations or others, situations will occur when you will not be completely sure whether you may use an abbreviation or not. In these cases, follow this advice: "When in doubt, spell it out."

EXERCISE C: Abbreviating References to Time, Measurements, and Numbers. Write the choice in parentheses that is more appropriate in formal writing. Remember that some abbreviations are a standard part of formal writing.

EXAMPLE: On (Mon., Monday) I auditioned for a part in the class play.

Monday

1. (435, Four hundred and thirty-five) students attended the rally.
2. At 2:00 (A.M., before noon) our cat delivered her first litter of kittens.
3. Porky Pig
   (21, Twenty-one) Trough Dr.
   Gorge, PA 52154
4. The company wanted to borrow ($1,000,000.00, one million) dollars.
5. Figures showed that company profits had increased (28, twenty-eight) percent last year.
6. A recent book discusses the Bronze Age, which began around 2500 (B.C., before Christ).
7. He had that surgery on June (27, twenty-seven) of this year.
8. This (Feb., February) I plan to visit my grandparents.
9. The Muslim religion started in the (A.D. seventh century, seventh century A.D.) when Muhammad began preaching.
10. The recipe calls for six (tbsp., tablespoons) of flour and three (tbsp., tablespoons) of sugar.
11. My brother can run the mile in (five min. and ten sec., five minutes and ten seconds).

12. We purchased two (lb., pounds) of food for my guinea pig.
13. I put six (L, liters) of gas in the car.
14. My birthday falls on (Dec., December) 18.
15. As we waited for the doctor to arrive, the (hr., hour) ticked slowly by.
16. The table stood (18½, eighteen and one-half) inches tall.
17. Many interesting events happened in (B.C., the years before Christ).
18. In 1215 (A.D., the year of our Lord), the Magna Carta was signed.
19. Should the drawing be held (a.m., before noon)?
20. The twins were born on February (2, second), 1981.

Latin Expressions

You may also need to use abbreviations for Latin phrases.

Use small letters and periods for most abbreviations of Latin expressions.

The following common Latin abbreviations have become a part of the English language. They usually are used only in bibliographies, footnotes, and lists. In formal writing, use the English equivalent instead of the Latin abbreviation.

EXAMPLES:	c., ca., circ.	about (used to show approximate dates)
	f.	and the following (page or line)
	ff.	and the following (pages or lines)
	e.g.	for example
	et al.	and others
	etc.	and so forth
	i.e.	that is

EXERCISE D: Abbreviating Latin Phrases. Write the English words for the abbreviations of the Latin expressions in the following sentences.

EXAMPLE: For information about that subject, check page 63 ff.
and the following pages

1. The antique dealer told us the chair was made c. 1820.
2. Swimming, hiking, sailing, etc., kept us busy at camp.
3. Alicia Mendes et al. wrote the textbook.
4. Vaccines can prevent some diseases, e.g., polio.
5. My vacation, i.e., a ski trip, was spoiled by the weather.
6. Your assignment is Chapter 9 on page 352 ff.
7. The Apache Indian chief Geronimo was born circ. 1829.
8. Line 121 f. of "The Ancient Mariner" are well known.
9. Many animals, e.g., hamsters, guinea pigs, and parakeets, are suitable for apartment living.
10. The cookies were made with raisins, nuts, dates, etc.

Other Abbreviations

A variety of methods exist for abbreviating names of businesses, organizations, government agencies, and other groups. Not all of these abbreviations, however, are considered appropriate in formal writing.

The first type of abbreviation occurs when one word in the name (usually the last) is shortened. The names of business firms often contain this type of abbreviation.

An abbreviated word in a business name begins with a capital letter and ends with a period.

Some of these business abbreviations follow.

EXAMPLES:	Bros.	(Brothers)	Ltd.	(Limited)
	Co.	(Company)	Mfg.	(Manufacturing)
	Corp.	(Corporation)	&	(and) This symbol for the word *and* is called an ampersand.
	Inc.	(Incorporated)		

In formal writing, write out the full name of most businesses. Limit your use of abbreviations to *Inc.* and *Ltd.*

EXAMPLES: The Ford Motor Company produces the Mustang.

My mother reads *Better Homes and Gardens*.

The magazine *Field and Stream* provides fishing tips.

In the last example, you could use the ampersand in a list or address since it is part of the magazine's official name.

Occasionally, names are shortened so that only the first letter of each word in the name is used. The word, when pronounced letter by letter, is called an *initial abbreviation.*

Use all capitals and no periods to abbreviate names whose abbreviations are pronounced letter by letter as if they were words.

The following chart demonstrates this method.

INITIAL ABBREVIATIONS		
Organizations	NHS	National Honor Society
	NFL	National Football League
	NEA	National Education Association
Business Firms	TWA	Trans-World Airlines
	CBS	Columbia Broadcasting System
Government Agencies	IRS	Internal Revenue Service
	FDA	Food and Drug Administration
Persons/Places/ Things	VP	Vice President
	YMCA	Young Men's Christian Association
	TV	Television

In these abbreviations, each letter is individually pronounced. In other cases, the initials are blended together and pronounced as a single word called an *acronym.*

Use all capital letters and no periods for acronyms that form names.

EXAMPLES: NASA National Aeronautics and Space Administration

NATO North Atlantic Treaty Organization

BASIC Beginner's All-Purpose Symbolic Instruction Code

Both initial abbreviations and acronyms may be used in formal writing. However, the complete title should be used first.

EXAMPLE: The National Boxing Association is considering new regulations. The NBA indicates that they are needed.

EXERCISE E: Abbreviating Other Names. Write the full name of each of the following ten items. Then identify each abbreviation as one of the following.

A. An abbreviation that cannot be used in formal writing
B. An abbreviation that can be used in formal writing, in some cases, after it has first been written out in full

EXAMPLE: FDA

Food and Drug Administration (B)

1. NFL
2. Racquet Sports Ltd.
3. FBI
4. Roberts & Klein
5. IRS
6. NEA
7. Homac Mfg. Company
8. TV
9. Philips Bros.
10. NASA

DEVELOPING WRITING SKILLS: Using All the Abbreviation Rules. If the underlined items in the following paragraph are used correctly, write *correct.* If not, write the correct form.

EXAMPLE: Most students spend hrs. doing research in libraries.

hours

The oldest known written tablets date back to (1) c. 2000 (2) before Christ. Even in those times, people were recording ideas, facts, procedures, (3) etc. for future generations. One leader, Ptolemy I, saw the need to centralize information. Around (4) B.C. 300, he began to collect what would become a library of over (5) 500,000 scrolls. More and more libraries grew as the (6) yrs. passed. In the (7) U.S., the first library began as a gift from (8) Rev. John Harvard in 1638. Later, (9) B. Franklin founded the Library (10) Co. of Philadelphia, the first subscription library. Today, the (11) N.Y. Public Library alone contains over (12) 7,000,000 volumes. Libraries may now use microfilm—a way of condensing huge amounts of writing into a space smaller than a (13) sq. inch. In the Library of Congress, written and microfilm records are maintained on all important events ((14) e.g., the election of (15) Pres. Reagan, the rulings of the (16) FDA, and progress made by (17) NASA). A student who wants to check the (18) mo. and date of a law and a state (19) sen. who needs information about new legislation can both come to Washington, (20) D.C., to use this library.

Skills Review and Writing Workshop

Capitalization and Abbreviation

CHECKING YOUR SKILLS

Rewrite the following paragraph correcting all capitalization errors. Write out in full those words or phrases that should not be abbreviated in formal writing.

(1) 12 years ago the national aeronautics and space administration sent apollo astronauts to walk on the moon. (2) unfortunately, one important person missed that trip: me. (3) the space-shuttle astronaut, kathryn a. sellic, said, "i would love to be the first woman to walk on the moon." (4) My friend, Ms. Mimi Randolph, ph.d., who works for the u.n. in N. Y. C., has the same desire. (5) So does mrs. maria mcdonald from the imperial valley. (6) I think president Reagan wants to establish a lunar base, lunar trips, etc. (7) Dr. michael h. duke talked last Mon. about bldg. a lunar base. (8) Modules might land in Jan. or Feb. One co., G.E., wants to use the moon commercially. (10) A rep. from nasa said that might be feasible.

USING USAGE SKILLS IN WRITING:
Writing Instructions

When you write notes to yourself, you may not capitalize carefully and you may abbreviate freely. When you write notes for others to read, however, you need to use capitals and abbreviations correctly. Imagine you are the president of a small company and must write instructions for your secretary.

Prewriting: Assign office tasks to your secretary, including writing letters, paying bills, and dealing with various people who may call during your absence. Include instructions about when and how to contact you in an emergency.

Writing: Some abbreviations may be appropriate on a chart. They are not appropriate in the body of an instruction sheet.

Revising: Check your abbreviations, capital letters, and grammar. After you have revised, proofread carefully.

Chapter 16

Punctuation

When Beethoven wrote the *Moonlight Sonata* more than 150 years ago, he included in his music not only the notes he wanted played but also *how* he wanted them played. Through the use of accepted music notation, he left precise instructions on the tempo he wished, the mood he wanted to convey in the passages, the volume, and the rests. By following Beethoven's instructions, today's musicians are able to play that piece almost exactly as Beethoven played it himself.

Just as a composer must do more than set down notes on paper, a writer must do more than set down words on paper. Just as a composer must tell musicians how to play the music, so a writer must tell readers how the words are to be read. To give the reader this information, a writer uses a set of standard marks called punctuation.

Punctuation is a commonly accepted set of symbols used in writing to convey specific directions to the reader.

The most important punctuation marks are the period (.), question mark (?), exclamation mark (!), comma (,), semicolon (;), colon (:), quotation marks (" "), parentheses (( )), dash (—), hyphen (-), and apostrophe (').

By using these marks carefully, writers give readers such information as when to pause for clarity, when to read with a particular emotion, or when to stop completely. The key word here is carefully; you cannot insert punctuation according to your own whims but must carefully follow certain rules. This chapter will focus on the generally accepted rules of punctuation so that you, the writer, can punctuate your own writing more effectively.

End Marks 16.1

Just as every sentence must begin with a capital letter, so every sentence must end with an end mark. The three end marks are the period (.), the question mark (?), and the exclamation mark (!). These marks clearly indicate to a reader that you have arrived at the end of a thought. End marks also indicate the emotion or tone of a sentence so that the reader knows with what kind of expression it should read. End marks can serve other important functions, as well. In this section, you will have the opportunity to review the more common uses of end marks and to study some of their other functions.

Basic Uses of End Marks

The period, the most common end mark, has three basic uses.

Use a period (.) to end a declarative sentence, a mild imperative, and an indirect question.

Declarative sentences include statements of fact and statements of opinion. Both types of statements require a period.

STATEMENT OF FACT: Clothing styles have changed**.**

STATEMENT OF OPINION: The movie was boring**.**

You should also place a period at the end of a mildly worded order called a *mild imperative.* You can recognize these sentences easily since they often begin with a verb and have an "understood you" as their subject.

MILD IMPERATIVE: Change your shoes quickly**.**

Indirect questions also require a period. An indirect question needs no answer; instead, it is a statement that refers to a question that might be or has been asked.

DIRECT QUESTION: Are the pants on sale**?**

INDIRECT QUESTION: I asked whether the pants were on sale**.**

A sentence that asks a direct question, one to which an answer might be made, is an interrogative sentence. The end mark used for interrogative sentences is the question mark.

Use a question mark (?) to end a direct question, an incomplete question, or a statement intended as a question.

A direct question demands an answer; it stands as a direct request. All direct questions must end with a question mark.

DIRECT QUESTIONS: Did you go to the discount clothing store**?**

What color looks best with these pants**?**

A helping verb or the words *how, to what degree, what, when, where, who,* or *why* at the beginning of a sentence often signal direct questions. Noticing these clues will help you put the proper punctuation at the end of the sentence.

In some cases, only a portion of the question is written out and the rest is simply understood. When this occurs, place a question mark at the end of the incomplete question.

INCOMPLETE QUESTIONS: Where**?** What color**?** How much**?**

In formal writing, you should generally avoid writing incomplete questions except when writing conversation.

Sometimes, a question is phrased as if it were a declarative sentence. Use a question mark to show that the sentence is a question.

STATEMENTS INTENDED AS QUESTIONS: You called me**?**

They have four dogs**?**

Since some sentences express a great amount of emotion, another ending mark was developed—the exclamation mark.

Use an exclamation mark (!) to end an exclamatory sentence, a forceful imperative sentence, or an interjection expressing strong emotion.

An exclamatory sentence shows strong emphasis or emotion. It expresses more feeling than other sentences. An exclamation mark is used at the end of an exclamatory sentence to indicate the emphasis or emotion it expresses.

EXCLAMATORY SENTENCES: That evening gown looks stunning**!**

This dress costs $250**!**

A strongly worded imperative that demonstrates forcefulness or strong emotion will also take an exclamation mark.

STRONG IMPERATIVE: Give me back those pearls, thief!

Occasionally (especially in conversations), one or two words are delivered emphatically. These strong interjections should also be followed by an exclamation mark.

STRONG INTERJECTIONS: Breathtaking! Ouch! Oh!

Sometimes a strong interjection may appear before a short exclamatory sentence. If this happens, you may use either a comma or exclamation mark after the interjection.

WITH COMMA: Goodness, that thunder was loud!

WITH EXCLAMATION MARKS: Goodness! That thunder was loud!

NOTE ABOUT EXCLAMATION MARKS: Remember, overdoing the exclamation mark undoes its effectiveness. Use this mark sparingly to achieve the most effective writing.

EXERCISE A: Using the Period and Question Mark. Copy the following items, adding the necessary periods or question marks.

EXAMPLE: I wonder which state was named after a Greek island

I wonder which state was named after a Greek island.

1. Who has more bones—a baby or an adult
2. I have often asked in what country a person can expect to live the longest
3. What was the name of Roy Roger's horse
4. Which state has produced the most Presidents
5. How many Who
6. The scientist questioned how long a queen termite can live
7. Who knows what Lawrence Welk's license plate says
8. Of all the animal personalities, who was first named to the Animal Hall of Fame
9. Where can you find the tallest living thing in the world
10. I wondered where the name Typhoid Mary came from

EXERCISE B: Using the Period and Exclamation Mark. Copy the following items, adding the necessary periods or exclamation marks.

EXAMPLE: Wow That was a spectacular catch

Wow! That was a spectacular catch!

1. Please bring me that pin cushion
2. His voice is fantastic
3. Don't step on the cat
4. Darn
5. A child is caught in that burning building
6. Do it this minute
7. The house looked fresh after its new paint job
8. Well, I have never been so insulted in my entire life
9. Try to finish those essays for tomorrow, class
10. I just won the Boston Marathon

EXERCISE C: Using All of the End Marks. Copy the following paragraph, adding all necessary end marks.

EXAMPLE: Do you enjoy eating popcorn as much as I do

Do you enjoy eating popcorn as much as I do?

(1) Hey Get your fresh, hot, buttered popcorn right here (2) The cry of the vendor selling popcorn has been heard for years at circuses, ball games, and county fairs (3) But some may wonder who first learned about this delicacy (4) Even before Columbus sailed to this continent, the Indians of Central and South America were popping little kernels of corn (5) They ate them, made popcorn soup from them, and wore them during religious ceremonies (6) Today popcorn is one of America's favorite snack foods (7) Just how much popcorn do Americans eat in a year (8) According to statistics, they eat an average of two pounds per person each year (9) For the popcorn industry that figure is larger than it sounds (10) As a group, Americans eat an incredible amount of popcorn—almost half a billion pounds each year

Other Uses of End Marks

Periods and question marks both serve other more specialized functions as well.

The Period. A major use of the period is in abbreviations.

Use a period to end most abbreviations.

Study the following chart; if you want a more complete list of abbreviations requiring periods, see Section 15.2.

SOME COMMON ABBREVIATIONS REQUIRING PERIODS		
Initials	**Titles of People**	**Geographical Locations**
S. K. Biren Matthew J. Kinney	Mr. Jr. Mrs. Sr. Dr. M.D. Rev. Ph.D. Lt. R.N.	47 Mountain Rd. 14 Peach Blossom St. Savannah, Ga. Laramie, Wyo. U.S.A.
Time References	**Numbers**	**Business Terms**
A.M. B.C. Mon. Jan.	$7.21 4.2	Prentice-Hall, Inc. Smith Bros. U.P.S. (United Postal Service)

Remember that *Miss* is not an abbreviation, so do not use a period after it. Some businesses and organizations use letters but have dropped periods after the letters. *NBC* and *FBI* are examples of these. Check a dictionary when you are in doubt.

When an abbreviation requiring a period comes at the end of a sentence, do not add an additional period as an end mark.

INCORRECT: The letter was addressed to K. Hillman, Ph.D..

CORRECT: The letter was addressed to K. Hillman, Ph.D.

If, however, the sentence requires any other punctuation mark besides the period, that punctuation mark should be inserted after the period.

EXAMPLES: Is that letter addressed to K. Hillman, Ph.D.**?**

The letter was addressed to K. Hillman, Ph.D.**,** but Bob opened it anyway.

The period also has a function when you write an outline.

Use a period after numbers and letters in outlines.

EXAMPLE: I. Addressing an envelope
A. The mailing address
1. Location on the envelope
2. Necessary information to include
3. Appropriate abbreviations

The Question Mark. Besides acting as an end mark, the question mark has one additional function.

Use a question mark in parentheses (?) after a fact or statistic to show its uncertainty.

EXAMPLE: The letter arrived on June 14(**?**).

Use caution when employing the question mark to show uncertainty. Its use should be limited to a fact that for some reason you simply cannot verify. Do not insert it just because you do not wish to check the accuracy of a fact.

Furthermore, do not use the question mark in parentheses to indicate humor or irony.

INCORRECT: The intelligent (**?**) mail carrier couldn't read the address.

CORRECT: The supposedly intelligent mail carrier couldn't read the address.

In good writing, the words themselves should convey the humorous or ironic tone you are seeking. You should not have to provide visual clues for your reader.

EXERCISE D: Using End Marks in Other Situations. Copy the following items, adding the necessary punctuation marks. Many items will require more than one mark.

EXAMPLE: 178 Union St
178 Union St.

1. 600 A D
2. Kim Partridge, Ph D
3. 7:24 a m
4. Six dollars and fifteen cents (Use numerals.)
5. Dr and Mrs Iseri
6. Tues, Oct 17
7. II The shark's teeth
   A Many rows of teeth
   B Indestructible
8. Lisa Holmes was born in 1905. (Show doubt about the year.)
9. Morales Enterprises, Inc
10. Austin, Tex

DEVELOPING WRITING SKILLS: Using End Marks. Follow the directions to write ten sentences of your own.

EXAMPLE: Write an indirect question about the weather.
Al asked us if we played the game in the rain.

1. Write a direct question about trucks.
2. Write an exclamatory sentence about barbecues.
3. Write a sentence that contains an abbreviation of a person's title.
4. Write an indirect question about baseball.
5. Write a mild imperative about stereos.
6. Write a declarative statement of fact about roller skates.
7. Write a sentence that includes a price.
8. Write a sentence about food using a question mark in parentheses to show uncertainty.
9. Write a mild imperative about a flower.
10. Write a declarative statement of opinion about a sport.

Commas 16.2

The shape of the comma (,) resembles a fish hook, and just as a fish is caught on a hook, so a reader's voice is caught slightly on the comma. The comma tells the reader to take a short pause before continuing the sentence.

The comma is used more than any other internal punctuation mark. As a result many errors are made in its use. This section presents rules to help you use the comma correctly to separate basic elements and to set off added elements in sentences.

Commas with Compound Sentences

A compound sentence is two or more indepenent clauses joined by one of the following coordinating conjunctions: *and, but, for, nor, or, so,* and *yet.* A comma is needed to separate the independent clauses.

Use a comma before the conjunction to separate two independent clauses in a compound sentence.

Always check to make sure that you have written two complete sentences joined by a coordinating conjunction before you insert a comma.

EXAMPLES: We polished the silver**,** and the boys then used it to set the table.

Neither did the monkeys eat our peanuts**,** nor did the seals devour our gift of fish.

The most common error that writers make with this rule is not making sure that complete sentences sit on both sides of the coordinating conjunction. They see the conjunction and insert a comma automatically. Remember, coordinating conjunctions can also join compound subjects, verbs, prepositional phrases, and clauses. When they are used in one of these ways, no comma is required.

COMPOUND VERB: The old friends chatted and laughed as they ate lunch.

TWO PREPOSITIONAL PHRASES: The next round I hit the golf ball into the water and then into a sand trap.

TWO SUBORDINATE CLAUSES: My brothers enjoy books only if they are relatively short and only if they offer a lot of action.

EXERCISE A: Using Commas in Compound Sentences. If a comma is needed in one of the following sentences, write the word before the comma, the comma, and the conjunction following the comma. If no comma is needed, write *correct.*

EXAMPLE: I practice my typing daily but I still make mistakes.

daily, but

1. The drummers beat out the rhythms and the band marched proudly along the parade route.
2. The photograph clearly showed your feet but somehow your head was cut off.
3. Neither did we visit the aquarium nor did we watch the show at the planetarium.
4. You may have either hot chocolate or coffee to drink.
5. Jack and Wendy will lead the songfest.

6. The hateful mosquito bit me and I have had a huge welt ever since.
7. My mother lost her favorite earrings so I will get her another pair for her birthday.
8. The airplane circled once and then came in for the landing.
9. The student saved time for the last essay question yet he found the time was not sufficient.
10. The TV blared but the child slept on.

Commas with Series and Adjectives

Commas are also used to separate items in a series and certain kinds of adjectives.

Series. Whenever a series of words, phrases, or clauses occurs in a sentence, you will need to insert commas.

Use commas to separate three or more words, phrases, or clauses in a series.

WORDS: I gathered the socks, shirts, and pants for the wash.

PREPOSITIONAL PHRASES: The cat carried her kittens into cupboards, under beds, and into the broom closet.

CLAUSES: The bank filled quickly with people who transferred their accounts, who cashed checks, and who opened their safe deposit boxes.

It may help you to know when you use this rule that the number of commas is one fewer than the number of items in the series. In the examples above, each series consists of three items; therefore, two commas are used in each of the series.

Some writers omit the last comma in a series. This is permissible as long as the writer follows a consistent pattern. In your own work, you will find that the full use of commas generally works better. This is especially true in those cases where the last comma is needed to prevent confusion.

CONFUSING: Endless streams of people, honking geese and police officers were all leaving the fair.

ALWAYS CLEAR: Endless streams of people, honking geese, and police officers were all leaving the fair.

Commas are not needed when all the items in a series have already been separated by conjunctions (usually *and* or *or*).

EXAMPLE: I cut and chopped and diced onions until I cried.

Commas should also be avoided between pairs of items that are used together so frequently that they are thought of as a single item. Notice in the following example that commas separate the pairs but not the items in the pairs.

EXAMPLE: I asked for ham and eggs**,** coffee and cream**,** and bread and butter.

Adjectives. Use commas to divide adjectives of equal rank. Such adjectives are called *coordinate adjectives.*

Use commas to separate adjectives of equal rank.

To determine if adjectives in sentences are of equal rank ask yourself two questions. First, can you put an *and* between the adjectives and still have the sentence retain its exact meaning? Second, can you switch the adjectives and still have a sentence that sounds grammatically correct? If the answer to the two test questions is yes, you have adjectives of equal rank, and a comma should be placed between them.

EXAMPLE: The dog's matted**,** filthy coat needed washing.

In this example, *matted* and *filthy* qualify as coordinate adjectives.

If you have adjectives that must remain in a specific sequence, do not use a comma to separate them. Such adjectives are called *cumulative adjectives.*

Do not use commas to separate adjectives that must stay in a specific order.

EXAMPLE: I watched several lanky boys play basketball.

These adjectives must stay in the order in which they are written. Therefore, no comma is used to separate them.

EXERCISE B: Separating Items in a Series. Copy each sentence that needs commas, adding the necessary commas. For sentences that need no commas, write *correct.*

EXAMPLE: I added oregano parsley and garlic to the spaghetti sauce.

I added oregano, parsley, and garlic to the spaghetti sauce.

1. We plan to sing and dance and act in our summer theater troupe.
2. I carefully watered the philodendrons the ivy and the African violet.
3. The crowd sat on the edge of their seats listened with awe and absorbed the speaker's powerful words.
4. The politician answered with great patience diplomacy and knowledge.
5. I looked under the bed in the closet and through my desk to find my homework.
6. Cloris Leachman Henry Fonda and other well-known stars performed in the play.
7. I described the symptoms to the doctor: a temperature aching bones nausea and a rash on my legs.
8. Send that letter to the President the Secretary of State and the Ambassador of France.
9. We went first to pick up Beth and then to find Barry and finally to get Peter.
10. The sun shone brightly the clouds drifted lazily overhead and we waded in the warm water.

EXERCISE C: Using Commas with Adjectives. For each of the following phrases, write *cumulative* if the adjectives are cumulative and require no comma. If the adjectives are coordinate, write the phrase, inserting the comma.

EXAMPLE: a vivid beautiful scene

a vivid, beautiful scene

1. many delicious jams and jellies
2. ripe juicy oranges
3. dark angry clouds
4. several sharp pencils
5. the dusty yellowed documents
6. bright red dress
7. disorganized crowded cabinet
8. three new books
9. hot greasy french fries
10. a friendly good-natured grin

Commas After Introductory Material

Commas are also used after introductory material.

Use a comma after an introductory word, phrase, or clause.

Following are examples of commas with introductory material.

KINDS OF INTRODUCTORY MATERIAL		
Words	Introductory Words	No**,** I will not drive you to the bowling alley
	Nouns of Direct Address	Cindy**,** could you hold this painting?
	Common Expressions	Of course**,** we can get that printed for you.
	Introductory Adverbs	Obviously**,** the student had tried. Hurriedly**,** she hid the present she had wrapped.
Phrases	Prepositional Phrases (of four or more words)	In the deep recesses of the couch**,** I found the watch I had lost.
	Participial Phrases	Jumping over the fence**,** the horse caught its back hoof.
	Infinitive Phrases	To get to the appointment on time**,** the man left early.
Clauses	Adverb Clauses	When the steaks were medium rare**,** we took them off the grill.

EXERCISE D: Using Commas After Introductory Material. For each of the following sentences, write the introductory material and the comma, if one is needed.

EXAMPLE: My friend do you know how soap was discovered?
My friend,

(1) Though we probably do not think about it often we use soap every day. (2) In fact a person who lives in the United States uses an average of twenty-eight pounds of soap and detergent a year. (3) According to old legends soap was invented over three thousand years ago. (4) On top of Sapo Hill in Rome fat from sacrificed animals soaked through the ashes on the altar and into the soil. (5) Soon after the women of Rome discovered that the soil around the altar produced a soapy clay that helped wash their clothes. (6) Working with caustic soda in the 1700's Nicolas Leblanc discovered that an inexpensive soap could be produced from salt. (7) To have soap in the early days of American history most people had to make their own lye soap. (8) When the 1800's arrived the soap industry began. (9) However it was not until 1916 that Fritz Gunther developed the first synthetic detergent for industrial use. (10) In 1933 Procter and Gamble began to produce the first household detergents for the marketplace.

Commas with Parenthetical and Nonessential Expressions

Commas are often used within a sentence to set off parenthetical and nonessential expressions. First, consider parenthetical expressions.

Parenthetical Expressions. A parenthetical expression is a word or phrase that is unrelated to the rest of the sentence and interrupts the sentence's general flow. Study the following list of common parenthetical expressions.

NOUNS OF DIRECT ADDRESS: Don, Mrs. Burke, my son, sweetheart

CONJUNCTIVE ADVERBS: also, besides, furthermore, however, indeed, instead, moreover, nevertheless, otherwise, therefore, thus

COMMON EXPRESSIONS: by the way, I feel, in my opinion, in the first place, of course, on the other hand, you know

CONTRASTING EXPRESSIONS: not that one, not there, not mine

For any parenthetical expressions, use the following rule.

Use commas to set off parenthetical expressions.

Two commas are used to enclose the entire parenthetical expression when the expression is located in the middle of the sentence.

NOUN OF DIRECT ADDRESS: We will go, Marge, as soon as your father arrives.

CONJUNCTIVE ADVERB: The boys, therefore, decided to call a tow truck.

COMMON EXPRESSION: The flowers, in my opinion, have never looked healthier.

CONTRASTING EXPRESSION: It was here, not there, that we found the answer.

If one of these expressions is used at the end of the sentence, however, only one comma is necessary.

EXAMPLE: We will go as soon as your father arrives, Marge.

Essential and Nonessential Expressions. Since commas are only used with nonessential expressions, writers need to learn to distinguish between essential and nonessential material. (The terms *restrictive* and *nonrestrictive* are sometimes used to refer to the same type of expressions.)

An *essential expression* is a word, phrase, or clause that provides essential information in a sentence: information that cannot be removed without changing the meaning of the sentence. In the following example, the clause following *boy* tells *which* boy the writer means. It, thus, provides essential information in the sentence.

EXAMPLE: The boy who is holding the book won the contest.

Because the clause in the sentence above is an essential expression, it is not set off with commas.

Nonessential expressions provide additional, but not essential, information in a sentence. You can remove nonessential material from a sentence, and the remaining sentence will still contain all the necessary information required by the reader.

EXAMPLE: Joe Warren, who is holding the book, won the contest.

Here the boy is specifically named, and the information contained in the clause only provides an additional fact. Thus, this clause is nonessential.

Once you have decided whether or not an expression is essential, you can apply this rule.

Use commas to set off nonessential expressions.

When applying this rule, be alert for three types of word groups: appositives, participial phrases, and adjective clauses. They often serve as either essential or nonessential expressions. Check them carefully to avoid committing comma errors. Study the following chart until you feel confident that you can tell the difference between essential and nonessential expressions.

ESSENTIAL AND NONESSENTIAL EXPRESSIONS

Appositive	Essential	My sister Joanne went to the University of Indiana.
	Nonessential	Joanne, my sister, went to the University of Indiana.
Participial Phrase	Essential	The teacher wearing a blue dress took the students on the field trip.
	Nonessential	Mrs. Goff, wearing the blue dress, took the students on the field trip.
Adjective Clause	Essential	The hotel that we enjoyed the most had three swimming pools and lighted tennis courts.
	Nonessential	The Royal Tahitian Hotel, which rated as our favorite, had three swimming pools and lighted tennis courts.

The examples in the chart show only expressions that are located in the middle of the sentence; each nonessential expression is set off with two commas. If the expression shifts to the beginning or the end of the sentence, use only one comma.

EXAMPLE: That evening he met Joanne, my sister.

EXERCISE E: Setting Off Parenthetical Expressions. Copy each of the following sentences, inserting any commas necessary to set off parenthetical expressions.

EXAMPLE: The story was considered so important in fact that it was placed on the front page.

The story was considered so important, in fact, that it was placed on the front page.

1. We have enough paper plates left over I think.
2. The suit nevertheless needed drastic alterations before I could wear it.
3. When does your ship sail Mr. Harville?
4. I will type up the letter Kim if you get it written by tomorrow.
5. I therefore went out shopping for a bathing suit.
6. My performance was absolutely perfect of course!
7. We went instead to see the award-winning play.
8. You may ask your question Ed as soon as I finish.
9. The candidate furthermore supports Proposition A.
10. The newspaper on the other hand carries more business news than its competitor.

EXERCISE F: Distinguishing Between Essential and Nonessential Expressions. If one of the following sentences contains an essential expression needing no additional commas, write *essential.* If the sentence contains a nonessential expression, copy the sentence, adding the necessary commas.

EXAMPLE: Those who tried to make their fortunes as pirates sometimes succeeded and sometimes failed.

essential

(1) Pirates those colorful, legendary plunderers of the ocean made many spectacular heists on the high seas. (2) Bartholomew Roberts who allowed no drinking or gambling on board his vessel caught and pirated over four hundred ships. (3) Long Ben Avery beginning his pirating career at age twenty captured two million dollars worth of booty—the largest amount of loot ever stolen. (4) The pirates who possessed a very strong code of honor within their own ranks had strict rules for dealing with problems on board. (5) Pirates stealing from their mates had their ears and noses cut off as punish-

ment. (6) Ships that were attacked by pirates often sank with all the men and treasures still aboard. (7) Experts studying cases of buccaneering believe as much as forty million dollars in gold may rest in watery graves. (8) In 1962, excavators who were digging off the coast of Florida discovered three million dollars in sunken treasure. (9) Excavation for sunken treasure has recently started at the pirate city Port Royal. (10) An earthquake that hit in 1692 killed over 2,000 pirates and sank much of their wealth.

Other Uses of the Comma

Commas are used in several additional situations.

With Locations. Whenever you are citing a specific place, check to see if a comma is required.

When a geographical name is made up of two or more parts, use a comma after each item.

EXAMPLE: I traveled from Taos**,** New Mexico**,** to Oklahoma City**,** Oklahoma.

With Dates. Dates containing numbers require commas.

When a date is made up of two or more parts, use a comma after each item except in the case of a month followed by a day.

EXAMPLES: On Friday**,** April 17**,** we will have a special meeting.

The city's new mass transit system ran its first train on June 11**,** 1974**,** after a dedication ceremony.

You may use or omit the commas if the date contains only the month and the year.

EXAMPLES: February**,** 1980**,** was one of the wettest months on record.

February 1980 was one of the wettest months on record.

If the parts of a date have already been joined by prepositions, no comma is needed.

EXAMPLE: The city's new mass transit system ran its first train on June 11 in 1974.

With Titles. Use a comma with titles that follow a name.

When a name is followed by one or more titles, use a comma after the name and after each title.

EXAMPLE: I noticed that Jeremy McGuire**,** Sr.**,** works here.

A similar rule applies with some business abbreviations.

EXAMPLE: She worked for Heller and Ramirez**,** Inc.**,** for a year.

With Addresses. Addresses consisting of two or more parts need commas to separate the parts.

Use a comma after each item in an address made up of two or more parts.

EXAMPLE: My new address is Katie Wedel**,** 243 Park Street**,**
St. Louis**,** Missouri 63131.

If this address was on an envelope, most of the commas would be omitted. Notice in both cases that extra space, instead of a comma, is left between the state and the ZIP code.

EXAMPLE: Katie Wedel
243 Park Street
St. Louis**,** Missouri 63131

Avoid using commas if prepositions join parts of an address.

EXAMPLE: Katie Wedel lives on Park Street in St. Louis.

With Salutations and Closings. You will need to use commas in the openings and closings of many letters.

Use a comma after the salutation in a personal letter and after the closing in all letters.

SALUTATIONS: Dear Rupert**,** Dear Aunt Lucy**,**

CLOSINGS: Sincerely**,** In appreciation**,**

With Numbers. Certain numbers also need commas.

With numbers of more than three digits, use a comma after every third digit from the right.

EXAMPLES: The projected complex would house 1**,**245 people.
The company has sold 498**,**362**,**719 jelly beans.

There are several exceptions to this rule: ZIP codes, phone numbers, page numbers, serial numbers, years, and house numbers do not have commas.

EXAMPLES: ZIP code 26413

Telephone number (612) 555–3702

Page number 1047

With Omissions. Sometimes, you will purposely omit a word or phrase from a sentence; this is then known as an elliptical sentence. For clarity, you can insert a comma where words have been left out.

Use a comma to indicate the words left out of an elliptical sentence.

In the following example, the omitted word is clearly understood. The comma serves as a visual clue to the reader that an omission exists.

EXAMPLE: The man walked quickly; the woman**,** slowly.

With Quotations. Commas are also used with quotations containing a "he said/she said" phrase.

Use a comma to set off the quoted words in a "he said/she said" quotation.

As the examples below show, the placement of the comma varies with the placement of the "he said/she said" phrase.

EXAMPLES: The guest asked**,** "Do you know of any nearby drug stores that are open all night?"

"If you don't mind a little drive**,**" the host said**,** "you will find one about three miles down the road."

"Oh, that will be perfect**,**" the guest replied.

For a more detailed study of punctuating quotations with commas, see Section 16.4.

For Clarity. You will occasionally run across a sentence structure that may be confusing without a comma. By inserting a comma, you can reduce the confusion and prevent misreading.

Use a comma to prevent a sentence from being misunderstood.

UNCLEAR: She studied French and English literature.

BETTER: She studied French, and English literature.

The first sentence above could easily be misread. The addition of the comma prevents this.

NOTE ABOUT CARELESS USE OF THE COMMA: Generally, you should not use a comma unless you have a rule clearly in mind. Study the following examples of careless overuse of commas, and try to avoid such use in your own writing.

MISUSE WITH ADJECTIVE AND NOUN: The furry, kitten padded across the floor.

CORRECT: The furry kitten padded across the floor.

MISUSE WITH COMPOUND SUBJECTS: We watched as the man, and woman executed some fancy dance steps.

CORRECT: We watched as the man and woman executed some fancy dance steps.

MISUSE WITH COMPOUND VERBS: The dancers leaped, and twirled around the stage.

CORRECT: The dancers leaped and twirled around the stage.

MISUSE WITH PREPOSITIONAL PHRASES: The dancers bowed to the audience, and to the conductor.

CORRECT: The dancers bowed to the audience and to the conductor.

MISUSE WITH SUBORDINATE CLAUSES: I won't forget that you gave me the ticket, or how much I enjoyed the performance.

CORRECT: I won't forget that you gave me the ticket or how much I enjoyed the performance.

EXERCISE G: Using Commas in Other Situations. Copy the following sentences, adding the necessary commas.

EXAMPLE: Number (702) 555–4818 was billed for $2352.

Number (702) 555–4818 was billed for $2,352.

1. The drive from Seattle Washington to Portland Oregon is a pretty one.
2. He was elected on Tuesday November 5 and inaugurated in January of the next year.
3. There were 52500 people watching the parade.
4. "Please move into the left lane" the officer patiently instructed.
5. My brother asked "Have you eaten dinner yet?"
6. Our class will have Martin Deardorf Ph.D. as our guest.
7. I read the address on the business card: R.P. Mendosa 615 Taggert Lane Cupertino California 95014.
8. The irate customer spoke belligerently; the public relations officer gently.
9. "When I reached the age of eight" the woman recalled "I decided to become a dental hygienist."
10. During the afternoon tea and pastries were always served.

EXERCISE H: Correcting Careless Use of Commas. Some of the commas have been used incorrectly in the following sentences. Rewrite each sentence, removing any incorrect commas.

EXAMPLE: I knew that I was right, and that they would agree.
I knew that I was right and that they would agree.

1. During the initial training period, the falcon, sits on a gloved hand with a hood covering its head.
2. Bees have existed for about fifty million years, and live everywhere but the North and South Poles.
3. An interesting fact about the buffalo is, that it is found on a ten dollar bill.
4. Bill, don't forget to clean the garage, and the deck.
5. The cost of World War II, in deaths and suffering, was enormous.
6. She bought shoes, and presents for her grandparents.
7. If eaten, the beautiful, Christmas poinsettia is poisonous.
8. The crayfish is the freshwater counterpart of the lobster, and is found in freshwater springs and lakes.
9. The queen bee, really does not rule the colony but only serves to reproduce the bees.
10. When new seedlings begin to grow, they need water, and sunshine.

DEVELOPING WRITING SKILLS: Using Commas in Your Own Sentences. Write ten sentences of your own, using the following sentence parts.

EXAMPLE: a geographical name made up of two or more parts
My family lived in San Antonio, Texas, when I was born.

1. an introductory phrase
2. two complete sentences joined by a conjunction
3. an essential clause
4. a nonessential modifier
5. a series of items
6. a quotation containing a "he said/she said" phrase
7. a parenthetical expression
8. coordinate adjectives
9. cumulative adjectives
10. an elliptical construction

16.3 Semicolons and Colons

The semicolon (;) is a punctuation mark that serves as the happy medium between the comma and the period. It signals to the reader to pause longer than for a comma but to pause without the finality of a period. The colon (:) is used primarily to point ahead to additional information. It directs the reader to look further.

The first part of this section will cover the rules that govern the use of semicolons. The second part will present the ways in which you can use colons.

Uses of the Semicolon

The semicolon is used to separate independent clauses that have a close relationship to each other. A semicolon is also used to separate independent clauses or items in a series that already contain a number of commas.

With Independent Clauses. Semicolons are most often used between independent clauses.

Use a semicolon to join independent clauses that are not already joined by the conjunction *and, but, for, nor, or, so* or *yet.*

Two sentences joined by a conjunction need a comma before the conjunction.

EXAMPLE: The child rode the merry-go-round**,** but she soon grew dizzy going in constant circles.

Since the semicolon carries more strength than the comma, it replaces both the comma and the conjunction. Notice in the following example that the second independent clause of two joined by a semicolon starts with a small letter. Do not use a capital following a semicolon unless the word following a semicolon would call for a capital in any position.

EXAMPLE: The child rode the merry-go-round**;** she soon grew dizzy going in constant circles.

Do not use a semicolon to join unrelated independent clauses. Use a semicolon to join only those that are closely related. Most often they will be related in meaning. Notice, for instance, the relationship in the second example that follows.

INCORRECT: Ann is a good chess player**;** rain is expected.

CORRECT: The dog patiently sat near the table**;** he hoped some table scraps might come his way.

Sometimes, the independent clauses will share a similar structure as well as a similar meaning.

EXAMPLE: With enthusiasm, he cast his line out into the lake**;** with pleasure, he later cooked his fish.

Notice that both sentences center around a shared subject—fishing. The sentences are also similar to one another in structure. This is a situation in which to use a semicolon.

Occasionally, independent clauses may set up a contrast between one another.

EXAMPLE: My sister excels at art**;** I can barely draw a straight line.

As you can see in this example, the sentences center around a central subject by looking at the two extremes of that subject.

So far, the discussion has concentrated on using a semicolon to join two independent clauses. However, if there are more than two independent clauses, you can still use semicolons.

EXAMPLE: The horse nibbled at the grass**;** the cowboy picked despondently at his food**;** the prairie dog watched the scene from a safe distance.

Independent clauses also need a semicolon when they are joined by either a conjunctive adverb or a transitional expression.

Use a semicolon to join independent clauses separated by either a conjunctive adverb or a transitional expression.

The following list contains common conjunctive adverbs and transitional phrases.

CONJUNCTIVE ADVERBS: also, besides, consequently, furthermore, however, indeed, instead, moreover, nevertheless, otherwise, therefore, thus

TRANSITIONAL EXPRESSIONS: as a result, at this time, first, for instance, in fact, on the other hand, second, that is

Notice in the following examples that the semicolon is placed before the conjunctive adverb or the transitional expression. A comma follows the conjunctive adverb or the transitional expression since it serves as an introductory expression in the second independent clause.

CONJUNCTIVE ADVERB: A cloudless blue sky dawned that morning**;** nevertheless**,** rain was expected.

TRANSITIONAL EXPRESSION: We needed to get to the spare tire in the trunk**;** as a result**,** we had to unload all the trunk's contents.

Since words used as conjunctive adverbs and transitions can also interrupt one continuous sentence, use a semicolon only when there is an independent clause on each side of the conjunctive adverb or transitional expression.

INCORRECT: The team was**;** consequently**,** disqualified.

CORRECT: The team was**,** consequently**,** disqualified.

In these examples, *consequently* interrupts one continuous sentence; therefore, a semicolon would be incorrect.

Using the Semicolon to Avoid Confusion. The semicolon can also be used to avoid confusion in sentences that contain other internal punctuation. Consider, for example, two independent clauses that contain their own internal punctuation.

Consider the use of semicolons to avoid confusion when independent clauses already contain commas.

When a sentence consists of two independent clauses joined by a coordinating conjunction, the tendency is to place a comma before the conjunction. However, when one or both of the sentences also contain commas, a semicolon may be used before the conjunction to prevent confusion.

EXAMPLE: The thieves stole my favorite painting, a scene of a small fishing village**;** but they did not locate my valuable jewelry.

The semicolon also helps avoid confusion in a series of items containing their own internal punctuation.

Use a semicolon between items in a series if the items themselves contain commas.

A series generally has several items separated by commas.

EXAMPLE: We visited the Averills**,** the Wilsons**,** and the Garcias.

Sometimes, the items in the series may contain their own commas; in that case, a semicolon is used to prevent a whole string of commas from confusing the reader. The semicolon helps make clear to the reader where each complete item of the series ends.

EXAMPLE: We visited the Averills, who live in Wisconsin**;** the Wilsons, friends in Michigan**;** and the Garcias, former neighbors now living in North Dakota.

You will use the semicolon in a series most commonly when the items contain either nonessential appositives, participial phrases, or adjective clauses.

APPOSITIVES: I sent notes to Mr. Nielson, my science teacher**;** Mrs. Jensen, my history instructor**;** and Mrs. Seltz, my coach.

PARTICIPIAL PHRASES: I developed a terrible headache from listening to my cat, meowing at the door; my dog, howling at the neighbors; and my sister, babbling on the phone.

ADJECTIVE CLAUSES: The car that I bought has spare tires, which are brand new; a stereo, which has just been installed; and a great engine, which has been newly tuned-up.

Notice that commas are used to separate the nonessential material from the word or words they refer to or modify. The semicolons separate the complete items in the series.

EXERCISE A: Using the Semicolon with Independent Clauses. Decide where a semicolon is needed in each of the following sentences. Write the word that goes before the semicolon, the semicolon, and the word that goes after it.

EXAMPLE: I once had a red yo-yo my sister had a green one.
yo-yo; my

(1) Yo-yos have been enjoyed for years in fact, people in ancient Greece played with toys like yo-yos for entertainment. (2) In France, the popularity of the yo-yo grew quickly for instance, the nobles in seventeenth-century France played with yo-yos in the royal courts. (3) Napoleon's soldiers played with them while waiting to fight France's prisoners supposedly played with them while waiting for the guillotine. (4) Even King George IV is pictured with a yo-yo a cartoonist satirically drew him spinning his top. (5) In Europe they played with yo-yos in the Philippines they used them for more serious purposes. (6) In the sixteenth century, the people of the Philippines hunted with yo-yo-like weapons they sat in trees and sent the yo-yos hurtling down to stun the animals below. (7) History reports that Donald Duncan first promoted the yo-yo in America in 1926 however, recent evidence shows Lothrop Llewellyn selling a metal yo-yo as early as 1906. (8) He sold his yo-yos in Gloucester Llewellyn even took out a patent on his invention. (9) The latest yo-yo craze occurred in the 1960's indeed, Duncan reportedly sold fifteen million in 1961 alone. (10) Today, the most difficult yo-yo trick is the whirlwind it requires performing inside and outside loop-the-loops.

EXERCISE B: Using Semicolons with Internal Punctuation. Copy each sentence, adding semicolons where they are needed to avoid confusion.

EXAMPLE: I baked cookies, made with raisins muffins, made with dates and a cake, made with walnuts.

I baked cookies, made with raisins; muffins, made with dates; and a cake, made with walnuts.

1. When the milk carton fell, it split but I managed to pick it up before all the milk flowed out onto the floor.
2. Joe, Maria, and I drove into the city last night and we went to a delightful concert in the park.
3. As I watched, the tall, thin man reached into the pedestrian's pocket, removing his wallet but before I could even protest, the pickpocket was lost in the crowd.
4. As she tried to lay out the pattern on the material, she finally concluded that she was short of fabric and so she switched to another pattern, one requiring less material.
5. My grandmother knew more about people, places, and life in general than many world travelers yet she never left the state of Nebraska.
6. When the cast was posted, you should have seen the look of joy on Martin's face for to get a lead in the play was his dream.
7. Walking home from the store, I found an injured, frightened cat and I knew, at that moment, he was meant to be mine.
8. I peeked out of my sleeping bag and saw a squirrel, who was busily gathering his winter food a bird, who was welcoming the morning in song and a doe, who was surveying her peaceful domain.
9. During this morning's practice, we have to master the routine or the coach says we will work, work, work all day.
10. Neither did that young gymnast waver on the balance beam, which is only four inches wide nor did she make one error on her floor exercises.

Uses of the Colon

The colon acts mainly as an introductory device. It is also used in several special situations.

Colons as Introductory Devices. To use the colon correctly as an introductory device, you must be familiar with the different things it can introduce. Perhaps most important, the colon can introduce a list.

Use a colon before a list of items following an independent clause.

EXAMPLE: We must bring the following items**:** a flashlight, a thermos, and a blanket.

As shown in this example, the independent clause before a list often ends in a phrase such as *the following* or *the following items.* You should familiarize yourself with these phrases since they often indicate the need for a colon. Of course, you should not depend on these phrases alone to signal the need for a colon. The most important point to consider is whether or not an independent clause precedes the list. If it does, use a colon.

EXAMPLE: I bought several pieces of clothing on sale**:** a blouse, a skirt, and two pairs of pants.

Colons can also be used to introduce certain quotations.

Use a colon to introduce a quotation that is formal or lengthy or a quotation that does not contain a "he said/she said" expression.

Often, a formal quotation requiring a colon will consist of more than one sentence. However, your best guideline for inserting a colon should be the formality of the quotation. The more formal the quotation, the more likely you will need a colon. Do not use a colon to introduce a casual quoted remark or dialogue, even if more than one sentence is used.

COLON: The speaker began with these words**:** "I have never been so honored in all my life."

COMMA: As Ann left the room, she called**,** "I really must hurry. I don't want to be late."

Remember, also, to notice whether or not the quotation contains a "he said/she said" expression. You will want to use a colon to introduce even a casual quotation that does not contain a "he said/she said" expression.

EXAMPLES: He walked stiffly to the door and then turned: "Your accusations are false. You have gone too far this time."

Teresa stood up slowly: "I think I'll go home, It's been a long day."

A colon can also serve as an introductory device for a sentence that either amplifies or summarizes what has preceded it.

Use a colon to introduce a sentence that summarizes or explains the sentence before it.

When a complete sentence follows a colon, use the capitalization rule that appears in Section 15.1. Capitalize the first word after a colon if the word begins a complete sentence.

EXAMPLES: The garage attendant provided me with one piece of advice: He said to check my water level often until I could get my car in for the needed repairs.

His tuna casserole lacked a rather vital ingredient: He forgot the tuna!

In both of these sentences, the colon points to the explanation contained in the next sentence. These sentences, in turn, amplify or summarize the information presented in the preceding independent clause.

Another basic use of the colon is to point to a formal appositive following an independent clause.

Use a colon to introduce a formal appositive that follows an independent clause.

Using a colon, instead of a comma, to introduce an appositive that follows an independent clause gives additional emphasis to the appositive. Thus, using a colon makes the appositive more important than using a comma would.

EXAMPLE: I missed one important paragraph lesson: writing the topic sentence.

In this example, notice that the first clause could stand alone. It contains both a subject and a verb, and it makes sense by itself. When you are using colons in sentences, always check to be sure that an independent clause comes before the colon.

INCORRECT: We decided to: see an old movie.

CORRECT: We decided to see an old movie: *An American in Paris.*

INCORRECT: Our tour took us by: the rose gardens, the Japanese park, and the hanging gardens.

CORRECT: Our tour took us by some beautiful spots: the rose gardens, the Japanese park, and the hanging gardens.

Although an independent clause must precede a colon, it is not necessary that the words following the colon be an independent clause. An appositive composed of a word or short phrase may, for example, follow a colon.

EXAMPLES: From the jeep, I looked out over the dry grass and saw the king of beasts: a lion.

She asked that we all play her favorite game: Boggle.

As you can see, the word *lion* is an appositive for the *king of beasts,* and the word *Boggle* is an appositive for *game.*

You could successfully argue that a comma would also be appropriate where the colon is inserted. However, the colon provides a slightly more dramatic, profound effect than that which would be achieved by the comma. As a writer, you will have the responsibility of deciding whether the comma or the colon more precisely fits the tone you are trying to establish in your writing.

Special Uses of the Colon. The colon has several specialized functions that you will probably encounter in your reading and writing.

Use a colon in a number of special writing situations.

Many special situations require the use of a colon. Among them are references to time, volume and page numbers, chapters and verses in the Bible, book subtitles, business letter salutations, and labels that are used to introduce important ideas. Study the examples that are given in the chart on the next page; it shows how the colon is used in each of these special situations.

SPECIAL SITUATIONS REQUIRING COLONS	
Numerals Giving the Time	5:22 A.M 7:49 P.M.
References to Periodicals (Volume Number: Page Number)	*Forbes* 4:8
Biblical References (Chapter Number: Verse Number)	Genesis 1:5
Subtitles for Books and Magazines	*Fixing Hamburger*: *One Hundred Ways to Prepare Delicious Meals*
Salutations in Business Letters	Dear Mr. Biggs: Ladies: Dear Sir:
Labels Used to Signal Important Ideas	Warning: Cigarette smoking can be hazardous to your health. Note: This letter must be postmarked no later than the tenth of this month.

EXERCISE C: Using Colons as Introductory Devices. Write the following sentences, adding the necessary colons and capitalization. Underline any words that appear in italics.

EXAMPLE You will hear about a man with talent and imagination he is a man whose work you know well.

You will hear about a man with talent and imagination: He is a man whose work you know well.

(1) This man was born December 5, 1901, and until his death in 1966, he carried one of the best known names in the world Walt Disney. (2) Of course, he is best remembered as the creator of some of our most beloved cartoon characters Mickey Mouse, Pluto, and Donald Duck. (3) Walt Disney studied one subject with diligence he concentrated on art. (4) Walt Disney

felt he had to go to the one city where he could possibly become successful he headed to Hollywood. (5) In Hollywood, he made money from his drawings, but he finally hit success with a now-classic Mickey Mouse cartoon short "Steamboat Willie." (6) Disney went on to create many of the following famous films *Snow White and the Seven Dwarfs, Fantasia,* and *Mary Poppins.* (7) In 1955 he started something that was to change family entertainment he opened Disneyland. (8) Parents appreciated Walt Disney "Our children can explore the worlds of Frontierland, Fantasyland, Tomorrowland, and Adventureland in a clean environment." (9) Several years later Disney directed his efforts in a new direction television. (10) Yes, Disney has left us the kind of memorials that will continue to be enjoyed by millions Mickey Mouse, Snow White, Bambi, and the rest of the Disney gang.

EXERCISE D: Using Colons for Special Writing Situations. Copy each of the following items, adding the necessary colons. Underline any words that appear in italics.

EXAMPLE: Our textbook is *Psychology Exploring Behavior.*

Our textbook is <u>Psychology: Exploring Behavior</u>.

1. Warning Pull the plug after you finish using the iron.
2. School ended at 235 p.m., and we were expected to be ready for the presentation at 300 p.m.
3. *The Readers' Guide* listed *Time* 1623, but I could not find that issue.
4. "Dear Mr. Nelson" is the way I started my business letter.
5. The Old Testament reading came from Psalms 1305.
6. I read *Caring for Livestock A Guide for Beginners.*
7. I should be finished with my homework at 1000 p.m.
8. Danger This water is polluted. No swimming is allowed.
9. Note The meeting will begin one hour late.
10. The movie starts at 730 p.m.

DEVELOPING WRITING SKILLS: Writing Sentences Using Semicolons and Colons. Using your imagination, write one or more words for each blank in the following sentences. Then follow the instructions given after each sentence, using the topic you put in the blank.

EXAMPLE: This year, I learned a great deal about ______ .

a. Write a sentence with a semicolon joining two independent clauses with a close relationship.

b. Write a sentence with a colon pointing to a list.

history

a. We studied a number of ancient civilizations; most of them were fascinating.

b. I especially enjoyed the following topics: the Old Kingdom in Egypt, the Trojan War, and Crete.

1. My favorite sport is ______.
   a. Write a sentence using a semicolon to join two independent clauses with a close relationship.
   b. Write a sentence using semicolons to separate a series of items that contain internal punctuation.
2. I have a hard time studying when ______ is on TV.
   a. Write a sentence with a colon pointing to an explanation.
   b. Write a sentence containing a semicolon and conjunctive adverb.
3. My favorite dinner has ______ as its main course.
   a. Write a sentence with a colon pointing to a list.
   b. Write a sentence with a semicolon placed before a transitional expression.
4. If I could see any musician perform, I would see ______.
   a. Write a sentence using volume and page numbers.
   b. Write a sentence with a semicolon joining two contrasting clauses.
5. The most annoying habit I can think of is ______.
   a. Write a sentence joining two independent clauses—each with its own internal punctuation.
   b. Write a sentence with a colon pointing to a formal appositive.

Quotation Marks with Direct Quotations 16.4

Writers try to provide concrete support for their ideas and arguments. Directly quoting an expert can provide support for your statements while making your writing more colorful.

Direct Quotations

This section will take a close look at direct quotations to help clarify any uncertainties you may have regarding the way to punctuate them.

A direct quotation represents a person's exact speech or thoughts and is enclosed in quotation marks (" ").

DIRECT QUOTATION: "No barrier of the senses shuts me out from the sweet gracious discourse of my book friends."—Helen Keller

Do not confuse direct quotations with indirect ones.

An indirect quotation reports only the general meaning of what a person said or thought and does not require quotation marks.

INDIRECT QUOTATION: Helen Keller wrote that being blind and deaf did not prevent her from enjoying reading.

Paraphrasing, like that in this example of an indirect quotation, does not lend itself to dynamic, strong writing the way a direct quote does. Therefore, you should avoid indirect quotations when possible.

All direct quotations in your writing must be indicated by quotation marks. There are various ways a writer may present a direct quotation. One way is to quote an uninterrupted sentence. Another way is to present a quoted phrase within an otherwise complete sentence. Writers may also use an introductory, concluding, or interrupting expression with a quotation.

To enclose a sentence that is an uninterrupted direct quotation, double quotation marks (" ") are placed around the quoted material. Of course, each complete sentence of any quotation begins with a capital letter.

EXAMPLE: "Suspicion always haunts the guilty mind."
—William Shakespeare

Sometimes, you will insert only a quoted phrase into a sentence. You must set this fragment off with quotation marks also. Notice in the following examples that the first word of a phrase or fragment is capitalized only when it falls at the beginning of a sentence or when it would be capitalized regardless of its position in a sentence.

EXAMPLES: In defining bureaucracy, Honore de Balzac called it "a giant mechanism operated by pygmies."

"A giant mechanism operated by pygmies" is the way Honore de Balzac referred to bureaucracy.

Generally, you will wish to add a "he said/she said" expression to a quotation to show who is speaking. Use the following rule for a "he said/she said" expression that comes before the quotation.

Use a comma or colon after an introductory expression.

INTRODUCTORY EXPRESSION: Shakespeare wrote**,** "Suspicion always haunts the guilty mind."

If you do not use a "he said/she said" expression in your introduction to a quotation or if the introductory phrase takes a more formal tone, use a colon instead of a comma before the quotation.

EXAMPLES: The President turned to face the cameras**:** "We are pleased to announce that agreement has finally been reached."

Solemnly, she stated**:** "I will resign as treasurer of this corporation, effective the first of next month."

In the second example, you could argue that a comma before the quotation would also be appropriate. However, the formal tone of the introductory phrase makes a colon a more effective method of punctuation.

On some occasions, a "he said/she said" expression may conclude a quoted sentence.

Use a comma, question mark, or exclamation mark after a quotation followed by a concluding expression.

CONCLUDING EXPRESSION: "Suspicion always haunts the guilty mind**,**" wrote Shakespeare.

When a direct quotation is interrupted by a "he said/she said" expression, quotation marks enclose both parts of the quotation.

Use a comma after part of a quoted sentence followed by an interrupting expression. Use another comma after the expression.

INTERRUPTING EXPRESSION: "Suspicion**,**" wrote Shakespeare**,** "always haunts the guilty mind."

Two quoted sentences may also be interrupted.

Use a comma, question mark, or exclamation mark after a quoted sentence that comes before an interrupting expression. Use a period after the expression.

EXAMPLE: "Should we expect rain through the weekend**?**" the weather forecaster asked**.** "Looking ahead, we can plan on a pleasant, warm weekend."

EXERCISE A: Indicating Direct Quotations. Copy each sentence that needs quotation marks, adding the necessary marks. Quoted phrases are underlined so that you will know where they begin and end. If no quotation marks are needed, write *correct.*

EXAMPLE: Ashley Montagu said The cultured man is a wise man.

Ashley Montagu said, "The cultured man is a wise man."

1. Hain't we got all the fools in town on our side? And ain't that a big enough majority in any town?—Mark Twain
2. Ginny told me she did very well on her science test.
3. Among mortals, Euripides commented, second thoughts are wisest.
4. Her favorite saying was <u>to each his own</u>.
5. James Martineau once said, Religion is no more possible without prayer than poetry without language or music without atmosphere.
6. Wit has truth in it; wisecracking is simply calisthenics with words.—Dorothy Parker

7. My aunt told me I was the only one who remembered her birthday.
8. Longfellow often expressed the philosophy that people should act in the living present.
9. I rode this bicycle, Felipe gasped, at least two miles up the hill.
10. Maybe I can go shopping with you at the mall this afternoon, Carolyn said.

EXERCISE B: Indicating and Capitalizing Quotations. Copy the following sentences, making the necessary corrections in punctuation and capitalization. Quoted phrases are underlined.

EXAMPLE: as for looking back, I do it reluctantly wrote Joyce Maynard sentimentality or bitterness—it breeds one or the other almost inevitably.

"As for looking back, I do it reluctantly," wrote Joyce Maynard. "Sentimentality or bitterness—it breeds one or the other almost inevitably."

1. it is better to wear out than rust out.—Bishop Cumberland
2. Marya Mannes says that in judging a work of art, you must apply standards timeless as the universe itself.
3. tell the truth Sir Henry Wotton advised and so puzzle and confound your adversaries.
4. honest differences of views and honest debate are not disunity. they are the vital process of policy-making among free men wrote Herbert Hoover.
5. in one of her poems, Mary Lamb referred to a child as a young climber-up of knees.
6. sympathy was once described by Charles Parkhurst as two hearts tugging at one load.
7. if you pick up a starving dog and make him prosperous, he will not bite you Mark Twain remarked this is the principal difference between a dog and a man.
8. the greatest powers of the mind are displayed in novels Jane Austen wrote.
9. better late than never has become a favorite proverb for those who never get anything done on time.
10. in 1957, Theodore Reid wrote these words work and love—these are the basics. without them there is neurosis.

Other Punctuation Marks with Quotation Marks

Whether to place punctuation inside or outside the quotation marks presents a problem for some writers. Four basic rules, once learned, will help you avoid most of the confusion.

Always place a comma or a period inside the final quotation marks.

EXAMPLES: "You exhibited greater skill in today's lesson**,**" the driving instructor announced.

"As I passed the coffee house**,**" Margaret explained, "the aroma of fresh coffee lured me inside**.**"

Note in the second example that the quotation is split but that this makes no difference in the placement of the comma. It still goes inside the quotation marks.

The semicolon and colon always go outside the quotation marks.

Always place a semicolon or colon outside the final quotation mark.

EXAMPLES: One repair person said, "I can't do it for less than eighty dollars"**;** another indicated he could fix it for half that price!

She listed the ingredients for "an absolutely heavenly salad"**:** spinach, mushrooms, hard-boiled eggs, and bacon.

Question marks and exclamation marks are slightly more difficult to punctuate.

Place a question mark or exclamation mark inside the final quotation mark if the end mark is part of the quotation.

EXAMPLES: The patient asked, "Is my blood pressure normal**?**"

The TV announcer exclaimed, "You just won the $10,000 jackpot**!**"

On the other hand, if the exclamation mark or question mark refers to the entire sentence, the mark goes outside the quotation marks.

Place a question mark or exclamation mark outside the final quotation mark if the end mark is not part of the quotation.

EXAMPLES: Did you hear that speaker when he said, "We must reduce energy consumption"**?**

I was thrilled when they said, "And for president, Debbie Schmidt"**!**

With question marks and exclamation marks, only one mark is needed. In the following, the quote is a question and the sentence is a statement. No period, however, is needed.

EXAMPLE: My mother asked, "Did you feed the animals**?**"

EXERCISE C: Adding Other Punctuation Marks. Copy the following sentences, adding any needed commas, colons, semicolons, or end marks.

EXAMPLE: The young child shouted gleefully, "Someone just found my lost dog"

The young child shouted gleefully, "Someone just found my lost dog!"

1. The woman asked, "Officer, how much will this ticket cost"
2. My mother remarked, "Today, please clean your room"
3. "The next stop will be Fresno" the bus driver announced.
4. The girl shrieked, "There is a spider on my desk"
5. "But I have already seen that movie" I patiently explained.
6. "What time is your appointment" my mother inquired.
7. She had the nerve to call it "a piece of junk not worth paying to tow away" my beloved Chevy!
8. I let loose a blood-curdling scream when the doctor said, "This won't hurt a bit"
9. My mother usually says, "Harry, you're getting fat around the middle" my father then tells her that she is looking at muscle, not fat.
10. Did you hear the coach say, "Run the track three times"

EXERCISE D: Adding Quotation Marks and Other Punctuation Marks. Copy the following sentences, adding the necessary quotation marks and punctuation.

EXAMPLE: Did you say Let's meet at 4:00 o'clock

Did you say, "Let's meet at 4:00 o'clock"?

1. The car keeps overheating she explained to the mechanic
2. We enjoyed perfect skiing weather my friends told me The sun came out and the wind died down completely
3. We watched the principal on the closed circuit TV I am pleased to announce that one of our own teachers will be on the school board this year
4. Watch that child a driver called out
5. Will you go to the Senior Ball with me asked my friend
6. Ouch Archie yelped I'm having a few problems with this project
7. Doesn't that kite look beautiful floating in the air up there the father asked his young child
8. She explained I got the job at Mervyn's I start working there tomorrow morning
9. I sent the package first class the secretary reported
10. Since the milk has turned sour the clerk apologized let me get you a new quart right away

Quotation Marks in Special Situations

Several special situations may occur when you write direct quotations. These include dialogues, quotations of more than one paragraph, and quotations within other quoted material.

First, consider the use of quotation marks when writing a dialogue—a direct conversation between two or more people. Use quotation marks to enclose the directly quoted conversation and a new paragraph for each change of speaker.

When writing dialogue, begin a new paragraph with each change of speaker.

EXAMPLE: The station attendant shouted from behind the hood, "You're a quart low on oil, Mrs. Lowell. Would you like me to put some in for you?"

"Yes, thank you," she replied.

"What kind of oil do you use in the car?"

She hesitated and then replied, "I believe the car takes multi-grade."

In cases where one quotation consists of several paragraphs of quoted material, remember the following rule.

For quotations longer than a paragraph, put quotation marks at the beginning of each paragraph and at the end of the final paragraph.

EXAMPLE: "Experts are noticing a change in the types of food Americans are buying. More fast foods, such as TV dinners and canned meals, are being purchased by food shoppers.

"Many people who used to spend a great deal of time preparing meals now work outside their homes. Researchers conclude that this is the reason more fast foods are being purchased.

"People need well-balanced meals. They now buy meals that can be prepared quickly. Thus, people today have more time to spend at work and not in the kitchen."

Occasionally, you may need to indicate a quotation contained within another quotation.

Use single quotation marks for a quotation within a quotation.

EXAMPLE: The fund raiser concluded, saying, "As we try to raise money for this worthy cause, let us not forget that old English proverb that says, 'Where there's a a will there's a way.' "

EXERCISE E: Punctuating and Capitalizing in Longer Selections. The following dialogue has no paragraphing, quotation marks, capitalization, or punctuation. Each number indicates a new speaker. Copy the dialogue, indenting paragraphs and adding the necessary quotation marks, capitalization, and punctuation.

(1) today we are lucky to have dr. margaret sherman to discuss the subject of dreams (2) it is a pleasure to be with you today dr. sherman began as i talk please feel free to interrupt and ask questions (3) someone in the audience raised a hand will you cover the interpretation of dreams (4) yes the doctor replied but first let me talk about the importance certain cul-

tures place on dreams for instance the cheyenne indians sent their boys out to dream a vision that would reveal their destinies in the ibans tribe in borneo they believe that a secret helper comes in a dream to provide advice (5) i have heard that people have gotten inspirations and inventions from their dreams can you verify this an individual asked (6) the doctor turned to the questioner mozart reported that he saw whole musical pieces composed in his dreams and friedrich kekulé solved the structure of benzene based on his dream (7) and did einstein discover the theory of relativity through a dream someone in the back of the room challenged (8) as a matter of fact the lecturer explained he had been sick from overwork he worked out his theory while experiencing a feverish dream (9) i find this fascinating a girl in the front row whispered (10) ten minutes later the speaker concluded we should welcome our dreams—not fear them let me leave you with these words from william wordsworth come blessed barrier between day and day

DEVELOPING WRITING SKILLS: Punctuating Quotations in Your Own Writing. Choose one famous figure from List A and one from List B. Write a dialogue between the two. Write at least ten sentences, using paragraphing, quotation marks, capitalization, and punctuation correctly. Vary the location of the "he said/she said" expressions you use.

List A:	List B:
Reggie Jackson	Mary Tyler Moore
Dracula	Abraham Lincoln
Susan B. Anthony	Charlie Brown
Nancy Drew	Wonder Woman
Tom Selleck	Barbra Streisand

16.5 Underlining and Other Uses of Quotation Marks

In printed material, italics and quotation marks are used to set some titles, names, and words apart from the rest of the text. In handwritten or typed material, italics are not available, so underlining is used instead. Quotation marks, on the other hand, are used in both printed and handwritten materials.

16.5 Underlining and Other Uses of Quotation Marks

This section gives rules for using underlining and quotation marks and rules for titles and names that require neither.

Underlining

You should use underlining in your writing or typing to highlight titles of long written works and other major artistic works. You will also need to indicate certain names and foreign expressions by underlining them. Finally, you can use underlining to indicate words you want to emphasize.

The most common use of underlining is with titles of long or complete written works.

Underline the titles of long written works and the titles of publications that are published as a single work.

Following are examples of titles you should underline.

TITLES OF WRITTEN WORKS THAT ARE UNDERLINED	
Titles of Books	Jane Eyre by Charlotte Brontë
Titles of Plays	A Raisin in the Sun by Lorraine Hansberry The Man Who Came to Dinner by Moss Hart
Titles of Periodicals (magazines, journals, pamphlets)	Skiing Magazine Time Journal of American History Five Ways to Keep Heating Costs Down
Titles of Newspapers	The New York Times the Palm Beach Post the Chicago Sun-Times
Titles of Long Poems	Idylls of the King by Alfred Lord Tennyson Beowulf

NOTE ABOUT NEWSPAPER TITLES: The portion of the title that should be underlined will vary from newspaper to newspaper. The New York Times should always be fully capitalized and underlined. Other papers, however, can usually be treated in one of two ways: the Los Angeles Times or the Los Angeles Times. Unless you know the true name of a paper, choose one of these two forms and use it consistently.

Many media presentations and pieces of artwork also require underlining.

Underline the titles of movies, TV and radio series, lengthy works of music, paintings, and sculptures.

The following chart provides a closer look at each category.

OTHER ARTISTIC WORKS THAT ARE UNDERLINED	
Titles of Movies	The Caine Mutiny
Titles of Radio and TV Series	The Shadow Happy Days
Titles of Long Musical Compositions and Record Albums (any musical work made up of several parts, such as operas, musical comedies, symphonies, and ballets)	Bach's Christmas Oratorio the Beatles' Abbey Road Puccini's Tosca Schubert's Surprise Symphony Tchaikovsky's Swan Lake
Titles of Paintings and Sculptures	Dancers at the Bar (Degas) Indian on Horseback (Mestrovic)

Not only titles but also some names need underlining.

Underline the names of individual air, sea, space, and land craft.

AIR: the Spirit of St. Louis

SEA: the S.S. Seagallant

SPACE: Explorer I

LAND: the Best Friend of Charleston

If a *the* precedes the name, do not underline or capitalize it since it is not considered part of the official name. Note also that a specific name given to a group of vehicles (for example, the Explorer spaceships) is capitalized but not underlined.

Occasionally, you will want to use a foreign phrase in your writing.

Underline foreign words not yet accepted into English.

EXAMPLES: It is verboten to leave the building without permission. (German: forbidden)

Everyone said the coq au vin was delicious. (French: chicken cooked in wine)

Since the process of accepting words and phrases into the English language is a continuous one, you cannot always be certain whether a phrase is still considered foreign. Check those doubtful phrases in the dictionary. If the foreign word or phrase is not in the dictionary, you can generally consider it foreign. If it is in the dictionary, it will either be labeled with the name of the foreign language, in which case you should underline it, or it will be given standard treatment as an English word, in which case you should not underline it.

Certain other words need underlining because they are being used in a special way.

Underline numbers, symbols, letters, and words used to name themselves.

NUMBERS: When I say the number three, you start running.

SYMBOLS: Is that an ! at the end of that sentence?

LETTERS: Is that first letter a G or an S?

WORDS: She wrote the word fluid, but she meant fluent.

Finally, underlining can be used for emphasis.

Underline words that you wish to stress.

EXAMPLE: We will need a minimum of six dollars for the trip.

Although the underlining of the word in this example clarifies the meaning of the sentence, do not overdo underlining for emphasis. In most cases, you should rely on precise word selection to convey your meaning and emphasis.

EXERCISE A: Underlining Titles, Names, and Words. Write and underline titles, names, or words that require underlining. If a sentence needs no correction, write *correct.*

EXAMPLE: She graduated magna cum laude.

magna cum laude

1. The movie Star Wars made a profit of millions of dollars.
2. Many books such as Gone with the Wind have been made into movies.
3. Margot Fonteyn, a famous ballerina, appeared in the production Marguerite and Armand.
4. My favorite record album is We Are the World.
5. Renoir depicts a summer outing in his painting Luncheon of the Boating Party.
6. The word nice is too often used in place of a more descriptive word.
7. She reads The New York Times every day.
8. Many important historical events occurred in and around Boston's Faneuil Hall.
9. In 1830, the people held a race between a horse and a train, the Tom Thumb; the horse won.
10. I thought I heard the clerk say the number fifteen, but she apparently called out the number fifty.

Quotation Marks

Section 16.4 discussed the use of quotation marks (" ") with spoken words. Quotation marks also set off certain titles.

Use quotation marks around the titles of short written works.

Short works include short stories, chapters from books, one-act plays, short poems, and essays and articles.

SHORT STORY: "The Jockey" by Carson McCullers

CHAPTER FROM A BOOK: "Mental Development"

ONE-ACT PLAY: "Trifles" by Susan Glaspell

SHORT POEM: "Boy Breaking Glass" by Gwendolyn Brooks

ESSAY TITLES: "Self-Reliance" by Ralph Waldo Emerson

ARTICLE TITLE: "How to Organize Your Life"

Certain other short works also need quotation marks.

Use quotation marks around the titles of episodes in a series, songs, and parts of a long musical composition.

EPISODE: "The Iran File" from 60 Minutes

SONG TITLE: "Swing Low, Sweet Chariot"

PART OF A LONG
MUSICAL COMPOSITION: "Spring" from The Four Seasons

Occasionally, you may refer to a title of one long work contained in a larger work. Singly, each title would require underlining; when used together, another rule applies.

Use quotation marks around the title of a work that is mentioned as part of a collection.

EXAMPLE: "Plato" from Great Books of the Western World

EXERCISE B: Using Quotation Marks with Titles. From each of the following sentences, copy the title and enclose it in quotation marks.

EXAMPLE: The story Rear Window is a classic tale of suspense.
"Rear Window"

1. I read the assigned chapter: Building the Affirmative Case.
2. Our foreign visitor had learned The Star-Spangled Banner.
3. The short poem Ozymandias by Shelley conveys the theme that no one can achieve immortality.
4. Woody Guthrie wrote the famous song This Land Is Your Land.
5. I tried out for a part in the one-act play called The Veldt.
6. Road to the Isles is my favorite Jessamyn West story.
7. A Modest Proposal is a satirical essay written by Jonathan Swift in 1729.
8. This month's issue had an interesting article about elephants called What Do You Do with a 300-Pound Nose?
9. Henry David Thoreau's famous essay Civil Disobedience was first published in 1849.
10. The Open Window, a short story by H. H. Munro, has a surprise ending.

Titles Without Underlining or Quotation Marks

Some titles require neither underlining nor quotation marks. The first such classification consists of various religious works.

Do not underline or place in quotation marks the name of the Bible, its books, divisions, or versions or other holy scriptures, such as the Koran.

EXAMPLE: He received a Bible on the day of his confirmation.

Similarly, you should not underline or enclose in quotation marks certain government documents.

Do not underline or place in quotation marks the titles of government charters, alliances, treaties, acts, statutes, or reports.

EXAMPLES: Declaration of Independence
Civil Rights Act

EXERCISE C: Punctuating Different Types of Titles. Copy the titles, enclosing them in quotation marks or underlining them. If neither quotation marks nor underlining is needed, write *correct.*

EXAMPLE: The Bill of Rights protects the rights of individuals.
correct

1. I just finished the chapter called Life with Max in the book Agatha Christie: An Autobiography.
2. The magazine Short Story International published Before the Wolves Come by Hugh Munro.
3. I would much rather read short poems like Poe's Dream Within a Dream than long ones like Lord Byron's The Prisoner of Chillon.
4. Waltz of the Flowers is often a featured excerpt from The Nutcracker Suite.
5. The Treaty of Versailles officially ended World War I in 1919.
6. The episode Still Waters from the weekly show Nova looked at the constantly changing life of a pond.

7. Genesis is the first book in the Bible.
8. I love the song Climb Every Mountain from the musical The Sound of Music.
9. Just reading the poem The Eve of St. Agnes took forever.
10. In the symphony Indian by Edward MacDowell, one piece called In War Time consists of an arrangement of a popular song of the Atlantic coast Indians.

DEVELOPING WRITING SKILLS: Writing Titles Correctly. Write four sentences containing titles that require underlining. Write three sentences containing titles that require quotation marks. Write two sentences containing titles that do not need underlining or quotation marks.

Dashes and Parentheses 16.6

Commas, dashes, and parentheses all perform a similar function—that of separating certain words, phrases, and clauses from the rest of the sentence. To use these marks effectively, a writer must become thoroughly acquainted with the different qualities of the three marks. The comma is the most common mark and, therefore, draws the least attention to itself. The dash sets off material more dramatically. This flamboyant mark often encloses editorial remarks from the writer. Parentheses, on the other hand, are a more reserved, intellectual mark, setting off technical or explanatory material quietly, but clearly, from the rest of the sentence.

Which marks you, as a writer, choose will largely depend on your purpose in writing. This section will focus on the uses of the dash and the parentheses, giving you rules to follow in using them.

Dashes

The dash, a long horizontal mark made above the writing line (—), functions to set off material in three basic ways.

Use dashes to indicate an abrupt change of thought, a dramatic interrupting idea, or a summary statement.

In the following chart, examples illustrate the three basic uses of the dash.

USES OF THE DASH	
To indicate an abrupt change of thought	I cannot believe what the barber did to my beautiful hair—oh, I don't even want to think about it!
To set off interrupting ideas dramatically	Oatmeal—which tastes delicious with honey and raisins—makes a nutritious breakfast when served with milk. Next Saturday—do you have to work that day?—we want you to go fishing with us.
To set off a summary statement	Vanilla, rocky road, strawberry, blackberry, and butter brickel—deciding which of these flavors to get took me a full five minutes. To see my name in lights—this was my greatest dream.

It may help to know that words such as *all, these, this,* and *that* frequently begin a summary sentence preceded by a dash.

In certain circumstances, nonessential appositives and modifiers are also set off with dashes. Although nonessential appositives and modifiers—those not necessary to the meaning of a sentence—are usually set off with commas, dashes are sometimes used in the case mentioned in the following rule.

Use dashes to set off a nonessential appositive or modifier when it is long, when it is already punctuated, or when you want to be dramatic.

An appositive or a modifier must follow the rule to need a dash. Notice how the examples in the charts on the next page each meet at least one of the three criteria in the rule.

USING DASHES WITH NONESSENTIAL APPOSITIVES	
Reasons for Use	**Examples**
Length	The chairperson—a socialite more concerned with her stomach than the empty stomachs of the world's hungry millions—will hold a fund-raising dinner.
Internal Punctuation	Some of the stores in the mall—for example, The Bathing Beauties Bath Shop—never have any customers.
Strong Emphasis	The movies—three box-office blockbusters—were not among our favorites.

Nonessential modifiers are generally set off only when they have internal punctuation or when strong emphasis is desired.

USING DASHES WITH NONESSENTIAL MODIFIERS	
Internal Punctuation	The mongrel—who, for some reason known only to himself, decided to follow me home—has no identifying tags.
Strong Emphasis	The dog's hopeful expression—which he has mastered so well that even Lassie could take lessons from him—is slowly winning me over.

And now, take a moment to consider a final kind of sentence interrupter—a parenthetical expression. You may recall that a parenthetical expression consists of words or phrases that are inserted into a sentence but have no essential grammatical relationship to it. Parenthetical expressions are often enclosed by dashes.

Use dashes to set off a parenthetical expression when it is long, already punctuated, or especially dramatic.

Of course, not every parenthetical expression will take a dash. Short expressions hardly need dashes.

EXAMPLES: I will, I think, go.

Give it to me, Susan.

However, as with nonessential appositives, if the parenthetical expression is long or contains its own punctuation, you will often want to set it off with dashes.

EXAMPLE: This continual downpour—we had two inches Monday, one inch yesterday, and an inch already today—will certainly replenish our water supplies.

The use of dashes is especially likely if the parenthetical expression is a question or an exclamation.

EXAMPLE: After Mr. Mathers was caught stealing—did you have any idea?—he was taken to the police station and booked.

You can also enclose a parenthetical expression in dashes if you want the expression to stand out dramatically from the rest of the sentence.

EXAMPLE: At her birthday party—she actually tried to tell me that she was celebrating her twenty-ninth—she had assembled more than forty guests.

Although the dash has many uses, be careful not to overuse it. Using an occasional dash adds sentence variety and interest; putting dashes in too often will make your thoughts seem confused and disjointed. Therefore, always follow one of the rules when you use dashes. In all other situations, insert commas or in some cases parentheses for maximum effectiveness.

EXERCISE A: Using the Dash. Copy the following sentences, adding one or two dashes in each.

EXAMPLE: I take care of our family pet that is, sometimes.

I take care of our family pet—that is, sometimes.

1. The marching band which has been, I might point out, practicing for weeks won a blue ribbon at the competition.
2. Our new gardener she is a genius with all plants! pruned the roses recently.
3. The scenery long, sandy beaches, desolate lava beds, and fiery sunsets brings many tourists to Hawaii.
4. Cats are lovable and hey, stop eating my plant, you bad cat!
5. To be able to see exotic fish in their natural habitat that provides one of the greatest joys of snorkeling.
6. That runner what was his name? looked tired after his race.
7. We ordered Valentine arrangements carnations, daisies, and roses to be sent to our relatives.
8. The family bookkeeping system which just looks like a jumble of numbers to me is designed to keep me on a budget.
9. Some ski resorts for example, Lake Placid in New York provide for a variety of skiing activities.
10. Baseball, soccer, football, and tennis these probably represent America's favorite sports.

Parentheses

Parentheses set off supplementary material not essential to the understanding of the sentence. Though not as dramatic as the dash, parentheses are the strongest separator you can use.

Rules for Using Parentheses. The following rules will help you determine when using parentheses is appropriate.

Use parentheses to set off asides and explanations only when the material is not essential or when it consists of one or more sentences.

Note that you can take out all the material in parentheses in the following examples without altering the meaning.

EXAMPLES: The committee looks at each student's entrance file **(**transcript, application, recommendations, SAT scores**)** when deciding which students to admit.

The bill passed **(**only after two days of heated debate**)** and will now be sent to the Senate.

We will pick up the stereo tomorrow. **(**The manager promised that she would have it ready this time.**)** By 5:00 p.m., I should be listening to my records.

Supplementary numbers may also be enclosed in parentheses.

Use parentheses to set off numerical explanations such as dates of a person's birth and death and around numbers and letters marking a series.

EXAMPLES: We established a memorial fund for Mary Tsai **(**1965–1981**)**, which will be used to buy books.

One half of the club's members **(**37**)** attended the potluck dinner.

You need to put a minimum of twenty thousand dollars **(**$20,000**)** down on the house.

Pick up these items: **(**1**)** milk; **(**2**)** eggs; **(**3**)** margarine; and **(**4**)** unsweetened chocolate.

Who signed the Declaration of Independence first? **(**a**)** Ben Franklin **(**b**)** Paul Revere **(**c**)** John Hancock

In following these rules, be careful not to overuse parentheses. As with the dash, overuse can lead to choppy, unclear prose—something every good writer wants to avoid.

Capitalizing and Punctuating with Parentheses. Several guidelines will help you punctuate and capitalize the material in parentheses.

Consider a phrase or declarative sentence placed in parentheses.

When a phrase or declarative sentence interrupts another sentence, do not use an initial capital or end mark inside the parentheses.

EXAMPLE: Lentil soup (my family tasted it for the first time in Germany) provides a delicious, filling meal.

However, if the sentence is exclamatory or interrogative, the rule changes.

When a question or exclamation interrupts another sentence, use both an initial capital and an end mark inside the parentheses.

EXAMPLE: CBS's *60 Minutes* (**T**hat show has done some outstanding investigative reporting**!**) reaches millions of viewers every week.

There is another rule for sentences between sentences.

With any sentence that falls between two complete sentences, use both an initial capital and an end mark inside the parentheses.

EXAMPLE: We drove to the Ashland Shakespeare Festival. (It took over fifteen hours**.**) The quality of the performances there surpassed even our high expectations.

Be aware of punctuation that falls after a parenthetical phrase.

In a sentence with a set-off phrase, place any punctuation belonging to the main sentence after the parentheses.

Apply this rule for commas, semicolons, colons, and end marks.

EXAMPLES: The ocean water felt icy cold (about 45°)**!**

I own a Ford (a Mustang, to be exact)**,** and I like it.

EXERCISE B: Using Parentheses. Copy the following sentences, adding the necessary parentheses.

EXAMPLE: Toni Morrison Have you read any of her books? creates fascinating characters.

Toni Morrison (Have you read any of her books?) creates fascinating characters.

1. We watched the second one-act play "The Devil and Daniel Webster," but then we had to leave.
2. The skater looked confident perhaps more confident than the judges liked as he left the ice.
3. Our new exchange student German speaks English well.
4. Mopeds motorized bicycles first became popular in Europe.
5. Check the boat for the following safety supplies: a extra gas; b life preservers; c flares.
6. Claude Engles 1911–1983 was a wonderful neighbor to us for many years.
7. I must remember to do my homework in these classes 1 algebra; 2 speech; and 3 history.
8. This painting by Picasso see the picture on page 75 is considered one of his best.

9. My report card came today. I've been checking the mail every day for a week. The grades will please my parents.
10. While the lion was completely out the effects of the tranquilizer, the vet entered the cage confidently.

EXERCISE C: Using Capitals and Punctuation with Parentheses. Copy each sentence that needs capitalization or punctuation, making the necessary changes. If no corrections are needed, write *correct.*

EXAMPLE: When I finished the assignment (what a tough one it was) I took a nap.

When I finished the assignment (What a tough one it was!), I took a nap.

1. Helmers Electronic firm (did they open up in 1974) showed a 25-percent increase in profits.
2. The sale went well (over one thousand dollars profit) and we now have room for the new merchandise.
3. After the fashion show (held at 11:00 a.m.) a lunch was served.
4. My antique music box (it was constructed in 1880 in Düsseldorf) operates with a hand wheel.
5. The cowboy hat (i planned to wear it skiing) fit perfectly.
6. The coral reefs (what a beautiful underwater sight they make) have meant destruction for many unknowing ships.
7. I watered the plant (which has a water indicator that shows when it needs moisture) Then, I added some fertilizer to the soil.
8. The new tires (guaranteed for a minimum of forty thousand miles) already show signs of wear.
9. My alarm watch stopped (could the battery be dead already) and made me late for school.
10. I purchased a new umbrella (the kind that folds up); it worked well in this heavy rainfall.

DEVELOPING WRITING SKILLS: Using Dashes and Parentheses in Sentences. Write six sentences to illustrate six different ways dashes may be used. Then write four sentences to illustrate four different ways parentheses may be used.

EXAMPLE: I am enjoying this picnic—oh, no, is that thunder?

Hyphens 16.7

As a writer, you should appreciate the versatility of the hyphen, for this punctuation mark makes it possible not only to join but also to divide certain words. Unfortunately, the hyphen is often mistaken for its cousin, the dash, since the two share a similar appearance. However, you should note that the hyphen is distinctly shorter than the dash; in fact, in typing the hyphen takes one mark (-) while the dash takes two (--). In books and other printed material, the hyphen is only about half as long as the dash.

The primary uses of the hyphen are to divide certain numbers and parts of words, to join some compound words, and to divide words at the ends of lines. This section will focus on the rules governing the appropriate use of the hyphen in these cases.

Using Hyphens

Hyphens are used with certain numbers, word parts, and words. First, look at the use of hyphens with numbers.

With Numbers. When you write out numbers in words, some of them require hyphens.

Use a hyphen when writing out the numbers *twenty-one through* ninety-nine.

EXAMPLE: Someone stole from her wallet a sum of *twenty-seven* dollars!

Some fractions also require a hyphen.

Use a hyphen with fractions used as adjectives.

EXAMPLES: A *three-fourths* majority passed the controversial bill.

The recipe calls for *one-half* cup of mushrooms.

In the preceding examples, the fractions function as adjectives. If they were used as nouns, the hyphen would then be omitted.

EXAMPLE: *Three fourths* of the junior class came to the meeting.

With Word Parts. Some word parts require the use of a hyphen.

Use a hyphen after a prefix that is followed by a proper noun or adjective.

EXAMPLES: The vacation trip that we took through Canada started in *mid-August.*

The population of the thirteen colonies grew during the *pre-Revolutionary* period to over two million people.

Certain prefixes and suffixes demand the use of hyphens even when no proper noun or adjective is involved.

Use a hyphen in words with the prefixes *all-*, *ex-*, and *self-* and in words with the suffix *-elect.*

EXAMPLES: all-powerful   self-addressed
ex-teacher   senator-elect

Always check to make sure that a complete word joins the prefix or suffix. When these prefixes and suffixes combine with only part of a word, no hyphen is needed.

INCORRECT: ex-ecutive

CORRECT: executive

With Compound Words. You must also use hyphens with some compound words.

Use a hyphen to connect two or more words that are used as one word, unless the dictionary gives a contrary spelling.

The use of hyphens in compound words is a matter of changing style. The dictionary should always be your authority on this matter. Three examples, hyphenated in most dictionaries, follow.

EXAMPLES: merry-go-round   crow's-feet   spin-off

You will also need to use a hyphen with certain compound modifiers.

Use a hyphen to connect a compound modifier that comes before a noun.

EXAMPLES: The dark clouds cast a *grayish-blue* tint on the water.

The *well-groomed* lawn added to the value of the house.

With great reluctance, the child took the *cod-liver* oil.

If a compound modifier comes after the noun, however, the hyphen is dropped.

BEFORE: We got the prescription from an *all-night* druggist.

AFTER: A druggist open *all night* filled the prescription.

The only exception to this rule is when the dictionary shows the compound modifier with a hyphen. In this case, the word remains hyphenated regardless of its sentence position.

EXAMPLES: We water skiied behind a *jet-propelled* boat.

Our ski boat was *jet-propelled.*

Hyphens should also be avoided with adverbs ending in *-ly,* in compound proper adjectives, and in compound proper nouns acting as adjectives.

Do not use hyphens with compound modifiers that include words ending in *-ly* or with compound proper adjectives or compound proper nouns acting as adjectives.

INCORRECT: The *badly-damaged* car sat in the body shop.

CORRECT: The *badly damaged* car sat in the body shop.

INCORRECT: The *North-American* continent has some large oil supplies.

CORRECT: The *North American* continent has some large oil supplies.

For Clarity. Certain letter combinations may cause a reader to misread a passage. Inserting a hyphen can prevent this.

Use a hyphen within a word when a combination of letters might otherwise be confusing.

EXAMPLES: *co-op* versus *coop*

re-lay versus *relay*

Unusual combinations of words can also be made clearer with hyphens.

Use a hyphen between words to keep the reader from combining them erroneously.

EXAMPLES: *a new home-owner* versus *a new-home owner*
three-point makers versus *three point-makers*

EXERCISE A: Using Hyphens in Numbers, Word Parts, and Words. Rewrite the sentences that need hyphens, adding the necessary hyphens. Use a dictionary when in doubt. If no hyphen is needed, write *correct.*

EXAMPLE: The politician congratulated the Senator elect.
The politician congratulated the Senator-elect.

1. My mother's yoga class is part of her self improvement plan.
2. We had forty three senior citizens on the bus trip.
3. When I was three fourths of the way to Dan's house, I realized I had left behind the folder he wanted.
4. The happy go lucky child played contentedly.
5. The miniature elephant measured only one quarter inch.
6. Each year many people celebrate the Chinese New Year.
7. A United Nations committee will study the proposals.
8. The all important decision will be handed down tomorrow.
9. With my last arrow, I made a bull's eye.
10. During the post World War II days, the United States experienced a baby boom.

EXERCISE B: Using Hyphens to Avoid Ambiguity. Copy the sentences, adding hyphens to make each sentence clear.

EXAMPLE: We had to relay the bricks in the garden wall.
We had to re-lay the bricks in the garden wall.

1. The clay head that I had modeled needed to be reformed.
2. Eager for the game to start again, he watched the half time clock.
3. The walk up to the walk up I saw in the ad was tiring.
4. The six foot soldiers walked across the bridge; one fell off and then there were five.

5. The dress my mother made was a recreation of an older one.
6. She gave him the five dollar bills to pay for the notebook.
7. They had barely enough money to decorate their new coop.
8. Liking food well done, he refused the half baked potato.
9. Recoiling the hose took more time than they had expected.
10. We were told to wait for the express mail clerk.

Using Hyphens at the Ends of Lines

"To divide or not to divide?" This question comes up again and again when a writer reaches the end of a line of writing. In such a situation, you must decide whether to put one last word on the line, drop the word down to the next line, or divide it. The decision should be based on certain rules. The most important rule is the one regarding syllables.

If a word must be divided, always divide it between syllables.

If you are in doubt about how to divide a word into syllables, check a dictionary. It will show, for example, that the word *intricately* has four syllables, *in tri cate ly,* and can be divided as in the following example.

EXAMPLE: The museum tapestry was a masterpiece of intricately woven threads.

Always place the hyphen at the end of the first line—never at the start of the next line.

INCORRECT: We cannot continue to sup
-port this candidate.

CORRECT: We cannot continue to support this candidate.

Prefixes and suffixes provide a natural place for division.

If a word contains word parts, it can almost always be divided between the prefix and the root or the root and the suffix.

PREFIX:	ex-tend	out-side	mis-fortune
SUFFIX:	hope-less	four-some	fif-teen

If the suffix is composed of only two letters, however, do not divide the word between the root and suffix.

INCORRECT:	walk-ed
CORRECT:	walked

In addition to avoiding a two-letter suffix, there are a number of other words that should not be divided. Be on the lookout for one-syllable words that sound like two-syllable words or look as if they are long enough to be two syllables. Do not divide them.

INCORRECT:	lod-ge	clo-thes	thro-ugh
CORRECT:	lodge	clothes	through

Each of these examples consists of only one syllable; therefore, dividing them is inappropriate.

You will also need to watch divisions that result in a single letter standing alone.

Do not divide a word so that a single letter stands alone.

INCORRECT:	stead-y	a-ble	e-vict
CORRECT:	steady	able	evict

Another problem occurs with proper nouns and proper adjectives.

Do not divide proper nouns and adjectives.

The following divisions have traditionally been considered undesirable or even incorrect.

INCORRECT: We recently hired Sylvia Rodri-
guez.

INCORRECT: I just finished eating a Chiqui-
ta banana.

You may occasionally need to divide a word that already contains a hyphen.

Divide a hyphenated word only after the hyphen.

If you use the word *apple-pie* as an adjective, you would hyphenate it. When dividing the word at the end of a line, divide it only at the hyphen.

INCORRECT: Everything appeared to be in apple-pie order.

CORRECT: Everything appeared to be in apple-
pie order.

Remember the next rule when you end a page.

Do not divide a word so that part of the word is on one page and the remainder is on the next page.

Often chopping up a word in this manner will confuse your readers or cause them to lose their train of thought.

EXERCISE C: Using Hyphens to Divide Words. If a word has been divided correctly, write *correct.* If not, divide the word correctly or write it as one word if it cannot be divided.

EXAMPLE: Have you given much thought to this problem?
Have you given much
thought to this problem?

1. My father is self-em
ployed.
2. Beth injured the liga-
ments in her knee.
3. Jane pruned the hed-
ge for us.
4. The instructor can-
celed the music lesson.
5. At dinner, I had Roque-
fort dressing.
6. The new house has e-
lectric appliances.
7. I measured both the length and width of the box.
8. The weary campers headed back to their trailer.
9. Be sure to clip that cou-
pon for a free dinner.
10. The mannequin looked life-
like to me.

DEVELOPING WRITING SKILLS: Examining the Use of Hyphens. Choose a short magazine or newspaper article and circle all the hyphens. Write the rule that applies to each hyphen used. Note for discussion any hyphens that do not follow the rules.

16.8 Apostrophes

Though the apostrophe (') is classified as a punctuation mark and not as a letter, its misuse can result in the misspelling of many words. The apostrophe serves two purposes: to show possession and to indicate missing letters. In most cases, you must place the apostrophe between the letters of the word, not before or after it. Thus, misplacement of the apostrophe leads to spelling errors. This section will provide you with rules so that you can use the apostrophe correctly.

Apostrophes with Possessive Nouns

An apostrophe must be used to indicate possession or ownership with nouns.

With Singular Nouns. First, consider possessives formed from singular nouns.

Add an apostrophe and -s to show the possessive case of most singular nouns.

As shown in the following examples, this rule applies to most singular nouns.

EXAMPLES: The toy of the *child* becomes the *child's* toy.

The desires of the *customer* becomes the *customer's* desires.

The frosting of the *cake* becomes the *cake's* frosting.

The success of *Roy* becomes *Roy's* success.

The sleeve of the *dress* becomes the *dress's* sleeve.

When a singular noun ends in *-s,* as in the last example, you can still follow this style in most cases. The only exception is when the additional *-s* makes the word difficult to pronounce.

AWKWARD: I like Burns's poetry.

BETTER: I like Burns' poetry.

With Plural Nouns. Showing possession with plural nouns ending in *-s* or *-es* calls for a different rule.

Add an apostrophe to show the possessive case of plural nouns ending in -s or -es.

EXAMPLES: The dishes of the *dogs* becomes the *dogs'* dishes.

The words of the *girls* becomes the *girls'* words.

The growth of the *cities* becomes the *cities'* growth.

Not all plural nouns end in *-s* or *-es,* however. Another rule will help you form the possessive case of these nouns.

Add an apostrophe and -s to show the possessive case of plural nouns that do not end in -s or -es.

EXAMPLES: The books of the *men* becomes the *men's* books.

The songs of the *people* becomes the *people's* songs.

With Compound Nouns. Sometimes, you will find that a noun showing ownership consists of several words.

Add an apostrophe and -s (or just an apostrophe if the word is a plural ending in -s) to the last word of a compound noun to form the possessive.

This rule refers to names of businesses and organizations, names with titles, and hyphenated compound nouns.

APOSTROPHES WITH COMPOUND NOUNS	
Businesses and Organizations	the Good Earth's menu the Lions Clubs' motto
Names with Titles	the Secretary of Defense's visit Edward VIII's abdication
Hyphenated Compound Nouns Used to Describe People	my father-in-law's glasses the secretary-treasurer's pen

With Expressions Involving Time, Amounts, and the Word *Sake*. If you use possessive expressions involving time, amounts, or the word *sake*, you will need to use an apostrophe.

To form possessives involving time, amounts, or the word *sake*, use an apostrophe and -*s* or just an apostrophe if the possessive is plural.

TIME:	a day's journey	six years' time
AMOUNT:	one quarter's worth	fifty cents' worth
SAKE:	for Pete's sake	for the Andersons' sake

With the word *sake* and a singular noun, the final -*s* is often dropped, as in *for convenience' sake*.

To Show Joint and Individual Ownership. When two nouns are involved, take care to show ownership accurately.

To show joint ownership, make the final noun possessive.

EXAMPLES: Roger and Jeremy's pet dachshund
(They share the same pet.)

the husband and wife's car
(They share one car.)

With individual ownership, use the next rule.

To show individual ownership, make each noun possessive.

EXAMPLES: Roger's and Jeremy's pet dachshunds
(They each have their own pets.)

the husband's and wife's cars
(Each owns a separate car.)

Checking Your Use of the Rules. Often confusion results over the application of the various rules because writers forget to ask themselves if they are writing about a singular noun or a plural noun. First, you should determine whether the owner is singular or plural. Then you should consider the word before the apostrophe you are going to add. If you place the apostrophe correctly, the letters to the left of the apostrophe should spell out the owner's complete name. Look at the checking technique in the chart at the top of the next page.

CHECKING THE USE OF APOSTROPHES		
Incorrect	**Explanation**	**Correction**
Jame's car	the owner is not *Jame,* but *James.*	James's
one boys' book	The owner is not *boys,* but *boy.*	boy's
two girl's lunches	The owner is not *girl,* but *girls.*	girls'

EXERCISE A: Using Apostrophes with Single-Word Possessive Nouns. Copy the underlined nouns, which may be singular or plural, putting them into the possessive form when necessary. For sentences that do not require possessive forms, just write the underlined word.

EXAMPLE: We will have to borrow Jeff book.
Jeff's

1. The kittens string was tangled after they finished playing.
2. The lass blond curls framed her cherubic face.
3. The skater sloppy leaps cost him the competition.
4. The bright canary yellow of the taxis provided a splash of color against the gray of the city buildings.
5. The town main offices were located off First Street.
6. Mavis eyes certainly were her nicest feature.
7. We listened to the waves as they rolled into shore.
8. The babies cries filled the tiny nursery.
9. Next the tourists visited Charles Dickens home.
10. The people reactions to the announcement varied.

EXERCISE B: Using Apostrophes with Compound Nouns. Copy the underlined nouns, putting them into the possessive form.

EXAMPLE: He always enjoys his mother-in-law cooking.
mother-in-law's

1. The Sierra Club actions pleased environmentalists.
2. My great-uncle farm produces many fat Thanksgiving birds.

3. The National Honor Society colors are blue and gold.
4. Jack-in-the-Box drive-up windows make buying food easy.
5. The Director of Transportation recommendations would mean an increase in mass transit fares.
6. The secretary-elect first responsibility was to go over the minutes with the current officer.
7. Hershey Food Corporation headquarters is located in Hershey, Pennsylvania.
8. This home-owner policy gives needed protection against fire and theft.
9. Queen Elizabeth II reign of twenty-five years was celebrated in 1977 with a Silver Jubilee celebration.
10. The editor-in-chief office was filled with new manuscripts.

EXERCISE C: Using Apostrophes to Show Joint and Individual Ownership. From each of the following sentences, copy the underlined words, changing them to show joint or individual ownership as the instructions indicate.

EXAMPLE: Bob and Ann aunt invited them to visit her. (joint)
Bob and Ann's

1. The formal style of Rhonda and Emily dresses did not blend with the informal attire of the rest of the guests. (individual)
2. The sororities and fraternities Greek heritage sets them apart from other clubs. (joint)
3. Fred and Marilyn joint tax return is being audited by the IRS. (joint)
4. Since Laura and Marcello papers were identical, the teacher accused them of cheating. (individual)
5. Doug and Hy desks were covered with graffiti. (individual)
6. The faculty and administrators complaints have been formally lodged with the mediator. (individual)
7. We celebrated Mike and Kristin tenth anniversary with a party. (joint)
8. Richard and Karen oldest boys have graduated from college already. (joint)
9. The boys and girls teams from our school all won ribbons at the track meet. (individual)
10. Phil and Ruth property taxes increased last year. (joint)

Apostrophes with Pronouns

Some pronouns showing ownership require an apostrophe.

Use an apostrophe and -s with indefinite pronouns to show possession.

EXAMPLES: another's nobody's one's
anyone's someone's everybody's

If you form a two-word indefinite pronoun, add the apostrophe and the *-s* to the last word only.

EXAMPLES: nobody else's one another's

Possessive personal pronouns do not need an apostrophe.

Do not use an apostrophe with the possessive forms of personal pronouns.

With the words *yours, his, hers, theirs, its, ours,* and *whose,* no apostrophe is necessary. These already show ownership.

EXAMPLES: Looking at the competition, I decided *yours* far outdistanced the other entries.

Its delicious aroma drew everyone inside for dinner.

Pay special attention to the possessive forms *whose* and *its* since they are easily confused with the contractions *who's* and *it's.* Just remember, *whose* and *its* show possession.

PRONOUNS: *Whose* wallet is this?

Its chimes rang out clearly.

Who's and *it's,* on the other hand, are contractions from the words *who is* and *it is.* They both require apostrophes to indicate the missing letters.

CONTRACTIONS: *Who's* doing telephoning for the meeting?

It's the responsibility of the Chairman.

EXERCISE D: Using Apostrophes with Pronouns. Rewrite any sentences in which pronouns are used incorrectly, making the necessary changes. If a sentence is already correct, write *correct.*

EXAMPLE: That sweater is her's.
That sweater is hers.

1. Do you think that clearing the table is nobody's job?
2. Someone's else's letter came to our address.
3. She gave the minutes to the one who's in charge.
4. The child gave his' address to the police officer.
5. We must not be jealous of one anothers' good fortune.
6. Your's was the most beautiful quilt on display at the fair.
7. As I looked at the rose, I was awed by its simple beauty.
8. Is this anybody's necklace—its' clasp is broken.
9. I asked whose pen it was.
10. People have told me that it's a fantastic play.

Apostrophes with Contractions

The meaning of a contraction is implied by its name. It is a word contracted in size by the removal of some letter or letters and the insertion of an apostrophe to indicate the missing letters. This leads to the following basic rule for contractions.

Use an apostrophe in a contraction to indicate the position of the missing letter or letters.

Contractions with Verbs. Verbs often come in contracted form. Look at the following chart, taking a moment to notice how often these verb contractions are used in common speech patterns.

COMMON CONTRACTIONS WITH VERBS		
Verbs with *not*	are not = aren't do not = don't	was not = wasn't were not = weren't
Pronouns with *will*	I will = I'll you will = you'll	she will = she'll they will = they'll
Pronouns and Nouns with the Verb *be*	I am = I'm you are = you're	who is = who's Mark is = Mark's
Pronouns with *would*	I would = I'd he would = he'd	we would = we'd they would = they'd

One special contraction changes letters as well as drops them: *Will not* becomes *won't* in contracted form.

Try to avoid most verb contractions in formal writing. They tend to make your style more informal than you may wish.

INFORMAL: He's promised that he'll postpone the test if we're still confused about the procedure.

FORMAL: He has promised that he will postpone the test if we are still confused about the procedure.

Contractions with Years. In writing about years, insert an apostrophe in places where a number is left out.

EXAMPLE: Decathlon Champion of '75

Contractions with *o', d',* and *l'.* These letters followed by the apostrophe make up the abbreviated form of the words *of the* or *the* as spelled in several different languages.

EXAMPLES: o'clock d'Carlo
O'Sullivan l'Abbé

As you can see, these letters and apostrophes are combined most often with surnames.

Contractions with Dialogues. When writing dialogue, you will usually want to keep the flavor of the speaker's individual speaking style. Therefore, you should use any contractions the speaker might use. You may also want to include a regional dialect or a foreign accent. Since this often includes pronunciations with omitted letters, you should insert apostrophes to show those changes.

EXAMPLES: C'mon—aren't you comin' fishin'?
'Tis a fine spring morn we're havin'.
That li'l horse is afeelin' his oats!

As with most punctuation, overuse reduces the effectiveness and impact, so watch the overuse of the apostrophe with contractions—even in dialogues.

EXERCISE E: Using Apostrophes with Contractions. If a contraction is underlined in the following paragraph, write the two words that make it up. If two words are underlined, write the contraction they would form.

EXAMPLE: Aren't people who regard graphology seriously thought to be silly?

Are not

Graphology, the study of handwriting, (1) is not a new science. Though we (2) don't know with complete certainty, (3) it is believed that it began as far back as 1000 B.C. in China and Japan. Many historical figures (4) did not discount graphology as a "false science." In fact, Shakespeare wrote, "Give me the handwriting of a woman, and I will tell you her character." Other figures who (5) did not regard graphology as silly included Sir Walter Scott, Edgar Allan Poe, Goethe, and both of the Brownings. To prove it (6) was not false, a scientist by the name of Binet tested seven graphologists in the 1800's. He showed them the handwriting of different people and asked, "Who would you pick as intelligent, average, or dull based on their handwriting?" All the graphologists did better than mere chance would have allowed. Today, there are still people (7) who will call it a false science, but (8) that's becoming less frequent. Even the American Medical Association (9) will not call it that. (10) They have written, "There are definite organic diseases that grapho-diagnostics can help diagnose. . . ." In the business world, many people consult graphologists before they hire new employees. And so graphology, once nothing more than a silly parlor game, has grown in respectability, and it shows every sign of continung to do this in the future.

Special Uses of the Apostrophe

One final method for employing the apostrophe exists—using it to show the plural of numbers, symbols, letters, and words used to name themselves.

Use an apostrophe and -s to write the plurals of numbers, symbols, letters, and words used to name themselves.

EXAMPLES: There are two *8*'s in that number.

You need two more *?*'s.

Her *b*'s and *d*'s all look the same.

A's and *an*'s cause confusion.

EXERCISE F: Using the Apostrophe in Special Cases. Copy the following sentences, adding an apostrophe and an *-s* to numbers, symbols, letters, and words whenever necessary. Underline all items in italics.

EXAMPLE: On my last report card I got all *A* and *B*.

On my last report card I got all A's and B's.

1. Hearing all those *Merry Christmas* from people has put me in a holiday mood.
2. I think you are leaving the *s* and *ed* off the ends of your words.
3. We sing eight *do-da* in a row before we get to any lyrics in the song.
4. Ten , in one sentence make the sentence too choppy and confusing.
5. Europeans put an extra line in their *7* to show they are different from the *1*.
6. We both had *H* for our first and last initials.
7. The girl said twenty *however* during the course of her short speech.
8. I always get carried away writing *!* in my letters.
9. He always forgets the *r* in those words.
10. The Emporium stores use *E* in various sizes as a symbol of their name.

DEVELOPING WRITING SKILLS: Using Apostrophes in Your Own Writing. Use your imagination to write a short passage of your own. Include at least one of each of the following uses of an apostrophe.

EXAMPLE: an apostrophe with a compound noun

They will celebrate their great-grandmother's eightieth birthday on Saturday.

1. an apostrophe with a possessive noun
2. an apostrophe with a pronoun
3. an apostrophe in a contraction
4. a special use of an apostrophe with a number, symbol, letter, or word used to name itself
5. an apostrophe used to show ownership of something by at least two people

Skills Review and Writing Workshop

Punctuation

CHECKING YOUR SKILLS

Rewrite the paragraph correcting all errors in punctuation.

(1) I remember the old expression Feed a cold starve a fever that my mother used to say said the lecturer (2) He continued Many people starve a fever because they dont feel like eating when they are sick (3) Later he explained that one should drink fluids even when not eating Drinking fluids prevents dehydration (4) Fasting that is going without eating for more than twenty four hours may not be a good idea however (5) The nutrients carbohydrates fats and proteins from each meal are absorbed in order to maintain the body and provide energy (6) The reserve supply of carbohydrates which is stored in the body as glycogen is used up in about twelve hours (7) When the glycogen has been used up stored fat provides the energy needed to keep the body functioning (8) Reserves of essential vitamins and minerals however also disappear (9) Eventually the body is forced to use up the protein of its own tissues (10) This starvation can cause serious illness and even death

USING USAGE SKILLS IN WRITING: Writing a Recipe

Some cookbooks include experiences the writer had while cooking, eating, or discovering a dish. Follow the steps below to write an entry for a cookbook in a paragraph form.

Prewriting: Pick a dish you know how to prepare. Invent an occasion on which the food was prepared and eaten.

Writing: Tell how to prepare the dish and where you ate it. Be sure the cooking instructions and circumstances during which you ate the dish are blended.

Revising. Be sure you have used a variety of punctuation marks correctly. After you have revised, proofread carefully.

UNIT **IV**

Composition

The Writer's Techniques

Chapter 17

The Writing Process

The gymnast who achieves a perfect "10" first goes through a long process of preparation. The final result may look effortless—and, after a time, even become so—but it would have been impossible without following the training process. To write an effective paper you must go through certain steps as well. To achieve excellence, the writer needs to follow the three stages of the writing process. These are prewriting, writing the first draft, and revising.

17.1 Prewriting

The first step in the writing process is the prewriting or planning stage. It includes exploring ideas, choosing a topic, determining audience and purpose, deciding on a main idea, and developing and organizing supporting ideas effectively.

Exploring Ideas

There is no shortage of topics to write about. Magazines, newspapers, books, TV, and other people can suggest ideas that arouse your curiosity and make you want to find out more about them or that remind you of experiences or thoughts you have had. You, yourself, are the best source of writing topics. The things that intrigue or annoy you, your hobbies, your positive and negative experiences—all provide a fruitful source for writing. Remember, it is easier to interest your reader if the topic you are writing about interests you.

To explore ideas for writing topics, take inventory of your interests, experiences, and ideas.

Although many of the topics for school compositions will be assigned by your teachers, you will increasingly be asked to come up with your own topics or to choose one from within a broad subject area. Even for those papers where the topic has been assigned, knowing how to work out what aspects of the assigned topic interest you will help you write them. Here are some techniques for exploring your own interests and generating ideas for potential writing topics.

Interview Yourself. Pretend that an interviewer is trying to learn of your interests by asking you the questions in the chart below.

QUESTIONS FOR INTERVIEWING YOURSELF
1. What activities do you enjoy?
2. What events have happened to you in the past that made you frightened, glad, or wiser?
3. What events would you like to have happen to you in the future?
4. What books, articles, or movies have made an impression on you, and why?
5. What people do you know whose lives and/or stories interest you?
6. What ideas or actions have made you angry? What ideas or actions do you approve of?
7. Do you have any "pet peeves"?

Free Writing. Set aside several pages and write without stopping until you have filled them. Write as quickly as you can and don't worry about repeating yourself or not making sense. Set the completed pages aside and read them later for possible topics or ideas to write about. Free writing allows you to let your imagination run free without censoring your thoughts.

Journal Writing. Write *something* in your journal every day. As with any skill, daily practice increases confidence and diminishes fear of not performing well. Write character sketches of the people you meet; interesting phrases used by friends and classmates or overheard on the radio or TV; names of birds, animals, and cars. Try to use concrete details for sights, sounds, and smells. At the end of each week, read the journal to see what kinds of things have caught your attention. Can these be used for possible writing topics?

Reading and Saving. Read as often and as variously as you can: books, magazines, newspapers, encyclopedias, and so forth. Write down topics that you would like to learn more about. Make a fair copy of particularly apt and expressive ways of saying something. Cut out magazine and newspaper articles and make subject files of potential writing topics.

Clustering. Clustering is a technique that is used to narrow a broad topic into one appropriate for a short paper. Pick a topic (music, for instance) and write it in the center of a piece of paper. Think of all the words that you associate with that word (drummer, clarinet, rock-and-roll) and write them around the word in the center, the nucleus word. Continue this process until you have a topic narrow enough for a short paper. See page 408 for an example of clustering.

Brainstorming. This is a way of exploring as many ideas as possible relating to a central subject. To brainstorm on your own, write down ideas as quickly as you can. Do not stop to evaluate or question them, but let your thoughts flow freely. Brainstorming in a group is another way of exploring ideas. Appoint one member of the group to record the suggestions.

Cueing. Cueing devices are a useful way of narrowing a topic and generating ideas about it. Journalists often use the 5 W's—Who? What? Where? When? Why? (or How?)—when writing a news story.

Topic:	Driving
Who:	Me
What:	Learning to drive safely
Where:	At school (simulated), on quiet roads
When:	School, on weekends
Why:	An essential skill, to gain mobility

Alphabet cueing is another way of coming up with ideas for your topic. Write down an idea relating to your topic for each letter of the alphabet. For example, you might write *aircraft* and *altitude* for the letter *A* under the topic of flying.

Using the five senses of touch, taste, sight, sound, and smell is a useful way of cueing, particularly for descriptive essays. Describe your topic purely in visual terms, then by sound, smell, and so forth.

In all these methods of exploring ideas, it is important not to limit your thinking. Do not be critical too early. Freewriting is the time to let your subconscious imagination run free.

EXERCISE A: Interviewing Yourself. Write down your answers to the questions under the heading "Interview Yourself" on page 405.

EXERCISE B: Free Writing. Free write for ten minutes, nonstop, on any of the following topics. Then, read over what you have written. Do you detect a direction for your ideas?

a conflict	censorship
a quiet moment	music
your childhood home	the "generation gap"
your worst day ever	the opposite sex

EXERCISE C: Brainstorming. Work in a group of four or five. Create a new species of animal, such as a hamster that flies and sings like a bird. Try to come up with as many possibilities as you can. Then choose one and, working on your own, write about the advantages and problems of having such a pet.

EXERCISE D: Cueing. Imagine that you are a historical character (Christopher Columbus, for example) who has just discovered a new country. Using the cueing method of your choice—5W's, alphabet, or five senses—write down words or sentences to describe this place.

Choosing and Narrowing a Topic

Not all the ideas that you have come up with in your prewriting can be adequately covered in a short paper. If you try to write about a topic that is too broad, you will most likely overgeneralize and lose your way.

Choose a topic that can be effectively covered in the allotted amount of space.

You may be assigned a broad topic, such as driving, for a short paper, or you may choose that topic yourself. In either case, the topic of driving is too broad to cover satisfactorily, even in a longer paper. One way to narrow such a topic is to use the clustering method described earlier. The diagram below shows how the clustering method could be used to narrow the topic of driving:

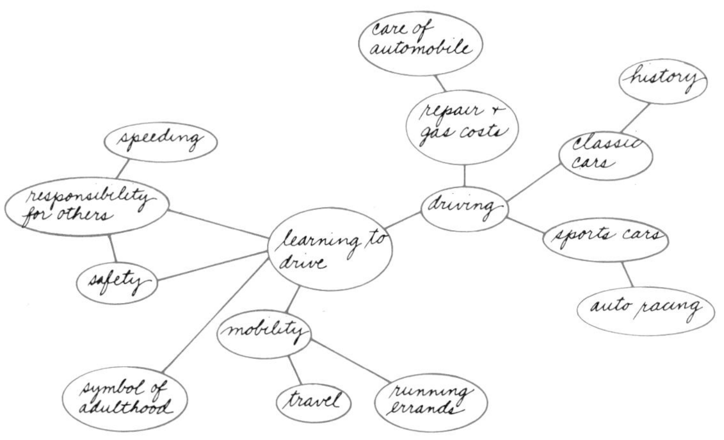

EXERCISE E: Narrowing a Topic. Select one of the five broad topics below and use the clustering technique to narrow it enough to be covered in a short paper.

nature health fashion hobbies travel

Determining Audience and Purpose

Everything you write is directed at an audience, and the style and content of your writing should depend, to a great extent, on the audience for whom it is intended and on your purpose for writing.

Determine your audience and purpose before you begin writing.

Your audience, or potential readers, might be your teacher, your classmates, a friend, or an imaginary audience of scientists of the future, for example. Your purpose might be to inform, to persuade, or to entertain.

The following chart shows possible audiences and purposes for three topics that have been narrowed from the large topic of driving.

Topic	Audience	Purpose
Against drinking and driving	High school students	To persuade
Classic cars	Readers of school newspaper	To inform
My favorite "lemon"	Classmates	To entertain

By identifying an audience and purpose for your writing, you know what kinds of details to include, as well as the appropriate language to use.

EXERCISE F: Determining Audiences and Purposes. Use the narrow topic you developed for Exercise E. Choose two possible purposes for a paper that could be written about that topic. Then, identify a potential audience for each of the purposes that you have chosen.

Developing a Main Idea and Support

Once you have chosen a topic, a purpose, and an audience, state your main idea and gather supporting details.

State a main idea. Then gather and organize supporting information to develop the main idea effectively.

Your main idea is the most important thought, the principal idea, you want your readers to remember from your writing. You should be able to state it in one sentence, which need not necessarily appear in the final paper.

MAIN IDEA: I have learned that driving is a responsibility as well as a privilege.

Once you have decided upon your main idea or thesis statement, you will find that it is easier for you to develop support for that idea. Use the techniques that were described under Exploring Ideas (pages 404–407) to find support for your main idea or thesis statement.

When you have gathered all your supporting material, you are ready to decide on the best method of organization. To do this, you must consider your purpose and the most effective way of ordering your material to achieve this purpose. The following chart shows the principal means of organizing information.

ORGANIZATION OF SUPPORTING INFORMATION	
Chronological order	Information arranged in time sequence
Spatial order	Information arranged according to space relationships
Order of importance	Information arranged from the least to the most important piece of information or vice versa
Comparison and contrast	Information arranged according to similarities and differences between items
Developmental	Information arranged so that one point leads logically to the next point

A list of supporting information for a short paper that gives the writer's thoughts about learning to drive appears below. Notice that the supporting information is listed in chronological order.

1. before ever driving: joyful anticipation of increased mobility and independence
2. first time at the wheel: nervousness
3. after having driven for several months: an understanding of a driver's responsibility, combined with more confidence

EXERCISE G: Developing a Topic. Select one of the topics, one of the purposes, and one of the audiences listed below. Write a main idea about the topic. Then jot down supporting ideas for developing the topic. Finally, choose a method of organization and write that down.

Topics: an unforgettable experience, how to start a stamp club or some other type of school club, the ideal place to live
Purposes: to inform, to entertain, to persuade
Audiences: your classmates, young people aged 8–10, readers of a school newspaper

EXERCISE H: Prewriting. Put the ideas from this section into practice by going through the prewriting stage of the writing process. Choose a general topic that interests you, then narrow it down by any of the techniques mentioned. Next, jot down notes on the topic and number them according to the best method of organization for your audience and purpose. Save your work for use later in the chapter.

DEVELOPING WRITING SKILLS: Prewriting. Choose another general topic and follow all the steps of the prewriting stage to create an outline for a short paper.

Writing 17.2

After you have chosen a topic, a purpose, and an audience and you have a well-organized set of notes, you are ready to begin writing.

Writing a First Draft

A first draft is a rough stage. The main goal is to get your ideas into sentences and paragraphs.

Translate your prewriting notes into sentences and paragraphs, without worrying about punctuation, spelling, grammar, or perfect sentences.

The first draft is the time to experiment with new ideas. The act of writing sentences and paragraphs often helps suggest points you may have overlooked or a more effective focus for your paper. Do not be afraid to change your approach or even your entire topic at this stage.

Here is a first draft of the *final* paragraph from a paper on driving.

> I've been driving for several months now. I feel more confident handling a car than I did that first day. I have learned that driving is a responsibility as well as a privilege. I still want to make that trip to the mountains with Pete, but I want first to make sure I really know how to handle a car in traffic. I want to get there and back safely.

Notice that the writer has saved the main idea from page 409 for the last paragraph. Placing the main idea at the end leaves the reader with this idea as a conclusion and also keeps the progression of ideas consistent with the choice of chronological order.

A rough draft is an essential stage in the writing process because it gives writers something concrete on which to make improvements. When writers create a rough draft, they often discover for themselves the meaning of what they are writing. The next stage, revising, must not be skipped. The revising stage is the time writers reorganize ideas and change word choice to communicate most effectively their meaning to readers.

EXERCISE A: Writing a First Draft. Write a first draft of a short paper based on your notes from Exercise G on page 411. Do not worry about grammar, spelling, or punctuation. Just get your thoughts down on paper.

Overcoming Writer's Block

Perhaps the only thing that can go wrong with writing the first draft is writer's block. Writer's block is a panic reaction to the thought of putting down words on paper. One's mind "just goes blank" or is filled with a thousand jumbled thoughts. Do not worry if this happens to you. Writer's block afflicts just about everybody at one time or another. It is, however, easily overcome. Just write anything, no matter what, and keep on writing. Your ideas will again start to flow smoothly as the words on the paper suggest further thoughts and ideas.

If you feel incapable of writing, write anything. Remember, you can always change it later.

Keeping a daily journal is a good way to avoid writer's block, since you will get used to the act of writing as a natural, everyday activity. The prewriting techniques at the beginning of this chapter help to overcome a block: free write, talk to people about your ideas, read a magazine or a book.

EXERCISE B: Overcoming Writer's Block. The following paragraph is incomplete because the writer encountered a "block." Decide what suggestions you would give the writer to overcome the block. Write three specific activities that the writer could perform to complete the paragraph.

> Everyone should be prepared in at least four ways for power failures caused by storms or earthquakes. First, candles, matches, and flashlights should be readily available in case all electricity is cut off. A transistor radio should be handy so that people without electrical power can learn the extent of the damage and can estimate the time needed for repairs.

DEVELOPING WRITING SKILLS: Writing a First Draft. Write a first draft based on your notes from Developing Writing Skills on page 411.

Revising 17.3

Revision is as essential to the writing process as is prewriting and composing a first draft. This is the time to put your internal editor to work and to evaluate critically what you have written. In the process of moving from the prewriting stage to the first draft, you naturally will make some revisions. For a polished and perfected final product, you now need to approach revising in a thorough and carefully thought-out manner.

Revising for Sense

The first stage in the revision process involves reading your paper critically to make sure that it makes sense.

Make sure that all of the ideas in a paper support your purpose and that they are presented in a logical way with clearly perceivable connections between them.

When you read your paper for sense, try to imagine that you are someone else seeing this paper for the first time. Ask yourself the questions that appear in the following chart.

REVISING FOR SENSE

1. Have I clearly stated my topic?
2. Will the main idea be clear to my readers?
3. Is there enough relevant supporting information?
4. Are the ideas presented in a logical order?
5. Are the connections between ideas expressed clearly and logically?
6. Are there any facts or ideas that are unrelated to the main idea?

EXERCISE A: **Revising for Sense.** Using the checklist on this page, revise the following paragraph so that it makes sense to you.

There are many things to see in tidepools. Sometimes I take my younger brothers to the tidepools. They like them. There are many kinds of animals in tidepools. Some of these are sea urchins, sea anemones, hermit crabs, and fish like blennies and rockfish. I like the birds' names. Egrets, turnstones, plovers, terns, and sandpipers are some of the birds you can see around tidepools. The best time to go to tidepools is at low tide. Check the weather section in the newspaper for the times of the lowest tides. The lowest tides of the year are usually in the spring. Or get a tide calendar from the fishmarket or a bookstore. It is fun. Everyone should have a hobby.

Editing for Word Choice and Sentences

The second stage in the revision process involves reading your work critically for your word choices and for variety in your sentences. This stage of the revision process is often called *editing*.

Read your paper several times, making sure that every word is the best possible one to express your thoughts and that your sentences are clear and varied.

Read your paper aloud or have someone else read it to you. Any breaths taken in the wrong place or words stumbled over may indicate a need for a different sentence structure or word choice.

When you edit for word choice and sentences, ask yourself the questions in the following chart.

EDITING WORDS AND SENTENCES
1. Does each word mean exactly what I want to say?
2. Is the language appropriate for the intended audience?
3. Is the meaning of each sentence clear?
4. Have I used a variety of sentence lengths and structures?

Here is the rough draft of the paper on driving. It has been revised for sense and edited for word choice and sentences.

How many times ~~have~~ I wished I knew how to drive? If I could drive, I could go to ~~that~~ ballgame on Saturday when Mom and Dad ~~are~~ busy around the house. I could go camping with my friend Pete, and best of all I wouldn't have to bother Mom every time I wanted to go ~~some place~~.

I used to dream about speeding along in a car ~~usually in the country.~~ I didn't know what I was getting into until the first time I sat behind the wheel. One fine Saturday morning, my dad drove me out into the country*,* ~~. He~~ stopped the car, and ~~we~~ changed places *with me*. I started the engine, which I knew how to do, released the emergency brake, and *inched slowly* ~~went~~ into the road. ~~Slowly.~~ Then *awareness* ~~it~~ hit me! I was in charge of this huge machine: two tons of metal that seemed to have a mind of its own. I panicked and hit the brake hard, *jolting* ~~jerking~~ us to a stop. "Take it easy," my dad said, when he got his breath back.

The thought of being responsible for an automobile scared me *then*. ~~It~~ still scare~~s~~ me. ~~because of~~ the dangers involved. I could kill someone by *my carelessness,* ~~driving,~~ or I could ~~hurt and~~ injure myself. ~~You often read things in the~~ *N*ewspapers *often contain stories* about ~~young~~ people *my age* getting into accidents. ~~People my age.~~ My brother's best friend is lucky to be *still* alive *after* ~~because~~ a drunk hit his car.

I've been driving for several months now*, and* I feel *much* more confident handling a car than I did that first day. *Most important,* I have learned that driving is a responsibility as well as a privilege. I still want to make that trip to the mountain with Pete, but *I* want to *first* make sure I *can drive well in* ~~really know how to handle a car and to understand~~ traffic. I want to get *us* there and back safely.

EXERCISE B: Editing for Word Choice and Sentences. Using the checklist on page 415, edit the following paragraph for word choice and variety in sentence structure.

Are you afraid of talking to a live audience? I used to be. I would get tongue-tied when I had to talk to a live audience. I could not think of anything to say. This was true even if I knew a whole lot about the subject. You can get rid of this fear. It is called a phobia. There are a bunch of different phobias. Some people are afraid of heights. Some people are afraid of getting shut up in an elevator. Or crowds. One way to get rid of this fear is to say what you are going to say into a tape recorder. Do this the night before. Or make your speech to your family. Another way is to choose one person in the audience. Look at him directly. Pretend you are having a conversation, like with a friend or something. Or imagine in your head that you are giving the speech and you've done it fine. Phobias are a drag, but you can get rid of them. I got these suggestions from a book. There are lots of books that help get rid of phobias.

EXERCISE C: Revising and Editing Your Paper. Use the checklists on pages 414 and 415 to revise and edit the paper that you wrote for Exercise A on page 412.

Proofreading and Publishing

Proofreading is the final stage in the writing process. It is your chance to make sure that your paper makes the best possible impression on your audience.

Proofreading involves making final corrections in spelling, capitalization, punctuation, and grammar.

You have worked hard on your paper and it would be unfortunate to spoil the final effect with misspelled words, misplaced punctuation, and incorrect grammar. If possible, set your paper aside for a time so you can approach it afresh. Read the paper carefully, line by line, word by word. Use a dictionary to check the spelling of any words you are unsure of. Read it aloud for a final time.

If you needed to make numerous corrections, retype or recopy your paper. Presenting your final product in the best possible condition is important. It tells your reader that you care about what you have written.

Now that you have the final version of your paper, you are ready to publish it. Publishing may mean printing your paper in a school newspaper or magazine, or it may mean simply giving it to your teacher or presenting it to your class. In any event, you are now ready to get feedback and evaluation from your audience.

EXERCISE D: Proofreading a Paragraph. Proofread the following paragraph. Correct any errors in grammar, spelling, punctuation, and capitalization.

(1) I dicided i was going write a Novel gooder than the one I read by ernest hemingway. (2) I buyed the paper from a Bookstore to blocks from my house I also buy a book their call how to write a Novel. (3) I decide riting will make me tyred so I sleep all the next Morningg and i woke up with an headick. (4) I new I needed exacise so I went runing. (5) Then i sit down to rite but I ain't got no pensills so I wented to the shop on mulberry street and bought alot of sharp pensills now I am reddy to wright my Noval.

EXERCISE E: Proofreading Your Paper. Proofread the paper you revised for Exercise B on page 416. Recopy your work neatly, if necessary. Then think of how you want to present your work to your audience.

DEVELOPING WRITING SKILLS: Revising, Proofreading, and Publishing Your Writing. Revise the rough draft you wrote for Developing Writing Skills on page 413, proofread the revision, and present the final copy to an audience of your classmates or submit it to the school newspaper.

Writing Workshop: The Writing Process

ASSIGNMENT 1

Topic Our Legal System

Form and Purpose A research paper that informs and persuades readers of your viewpoint

Audience People attending a seminar on our legal system

Length Five to seven paragraphs

Focus Your thesis statement should present a main idea about a specific topic related to our legal system. Develop your thesis with supporting facts, details, examples, and reasons. Conclude with a summary statement and a quote.

Sources Books, magazines, newspapers

Prewriting Narrow your topic. Then research it, taking notes on bibliography cards. Then prepare an outline.

Writing Use your outline to write a first draft, including footnotes and a bibliography.

Revising Use the checklists on pages 413 and 414 to revise, edit, and proofread your paper.

Chapter **18**

The Use of Words

In good writing, each word serves an exact purpose; the writing is *precise*. In addition, all the words should work together to create a unified *tone*, or impression, suited to a particular audience. Finally, good writers avoid using too many words; good writing is *concise*.

18.1 Choosing Precise Words

You can learn to take advantage of the many word choices available in the English language to make your writing more precise. Learn to use action words and specific words, create lively expressions, and explore a variety of words.

Using Action Words

Weak verbs include unnecessary linking verbs and verbs unnecessarily in the passive voice.

Use action verbs and verbs in the active voice to make your writing more precise.

Learning to use action verbs in the active voice can make your writing clearer and more interesting.

Action Verbs. Some linking verbs are necessary, but others sap the action and energy from your sentences. Frequently, you can replace a linking verb and a noun with a specific action verb related in meaning to the noun.

LINKING VERB: His comment *was* an insult to my aunt.

ACTION VERB: His comment *insulted* my aunt.

LINKING VERB: Many settlers *were* the victims of pirates.

ACTION VERB: Pirates *victimized* many settlers.

Active Voice. Verbs in the passive voice increase the number of words in a sentence. They also move the doer of the action from the beginning of the sentence to the middle or end. By lengthening and inverting a sentence, verbs in the passive voice can confuse a reader and weaken your writing. Notice how the following verbs sound more definite and direct in the active voice than in the passive.

PASSIVE VOICE: A dress code *was established* by the school.

ACTIVE VOICE: The school *established* a dress code.

PASSIVE VOICE: The mistakes *had been made* by the computer.

ACTIVE VOICE: The computer *made* the mistakes.

EXERCISE A: Using Action Verbs in the Active Voice. Rewrite each of the following sentences, changing the linking verbs to action verbs and the passive voice to the active voice.

EXAMPLE: Report cards were mailed out by the school.
The school mailed out report cards.

1. Ten new courses will be offered by the college next fall.
2. Fund raising and the election of officers are included in this week's agenda.
3. The movie was an insult to our intelligence.
4. Everyone will be required to write a library paper for Ms. Sanchez.
5. An address was delivered to the union leaders by their president.
6. This jacket is a match for my new slacks.
7. The storm was a threat to shorefront properties in Maine.
8. Three new members have been admitted to the club.
9. A buffet dinner will be served by the staff at midnight.
10. That book is a summary of the Battle of Britain.

Using Specific Words

Specific words have much more impact on a reader than general words do because specific words help a reader to visualize what you are describing.

Specific Versus General Meaning. Learn how to replace weak, general verbs, nouns, and adjectives with precise ones.

Use specific verbs, nouns, and adjectives, not general ones, to make your meaning precise.

Like action verbs and verbs in the active voice, specific, colorful verbs give the reader sharp pictures and vivid impressions. Specific verbs, such as *assert, whisper, proclaim,* and *shout,* help a reader in a way that the general verb *say* does not. Notice that the specific verbs in the following sentences spark a reader's interest more than the general verbs do.

GENERAL: She *ran* from the starting line as the gun *went* off.

SPECIFIC: She *dashed* from the starting line as the gun *exploded.*

GENERAL: He watched her *walk* down the hall.

SPECIFIC: He watched her *stroll* down the hall.

You can also gain greater accuracy by using more specific nouns. For example, instead of saying you watched a *television show,* you can indicate what kind of show you watched with the same number of words by saying *situation comedy, game show,* or *crime drama.* In the following, notice that the specific nouns improve the clarity of the sentences.

GENERAL: Dr. West had practiced his theory at several *educational institutions.*

SPECIFIC: Dr. West had practiced his theory at several *colleges* and *universities.*

GENERAL: Most students claimed to have gained *something* from the dance class.

SPECIFIC: Most students claimed to have gained *firm muscles and endurance* from the dance class.

Specific adjectives can further sharpen your meaning. The words in the following chart are vague adjectives that should be avoided. You should use vague adjectives only when you intend to explain your idea further with specifics and details.

VAGUE ADJECTIVES				
awful	excellent	great	nice	terrific
beautiful	exciting	interesting	tasty	typical
cute	fantastic	lovely	terrible	wonderful

Vague adjectives such as *exciting* can express your general feeling, but to communicate with someone else precisely you must use more specific words. Notice how the following sentences are improved by using more specific adjectives or by giving details that add specific meaning.

VAGUE: The movie was *exciting*.

SPECIFIC: The movie was *fast-paced, with hair-raising chase scenes and impressive special effects*.

VAGUE: It was a *beautiful* day.

SPECIFIC: It was a *cloudless* day, *warm enough for swimsuits and straw hats*.

Denotation Versus Connotation. The *denotation* of a word is its literal definition. For example, the denotation of the word *doctor* is "physician or surgeon; a person licensed to practice any of the healing arts." The *connotation* of a word is a broader area of meaning, which includes the suggested meanings and associations that the word has. To many people the word *doctor* might also carry associations of a prestigious, successful member of society or a hard-working professional. Your general knowledge of words, a thesaurus, a dictionary of synonyms, or the synonyms listed after many definitions in the dictionary can help you find the exact words you want.

Choose words with the best connotations for your meaning.

To choose the best word for a sentence, consider whether the word has positive, neutral, or negative associations. Then decide which association fits the meaning you are trying to achieve. In the following sentences, the adjectives in italics change the description from neutral to negative.

NEUTRAL CONNOTATION: The cashier was *forgetful,* sometimes adding the sales tax twice. (*Forgetful* suggests that a person has a poor memory and can not be blamed entirely for mistakes.)

NEGATIVE CONNOTATION: The cashier was *inattentive,* sometimes adding the sales tax twice. (*Inattentive* suggests that a person has the ability to do things correctly but lacks discipline.)

STRONGER NEGATIVE CONNOTATION: The cashier was *negligent,* sometimes adding the sales tax twice. (*Negligent* suggests that a person does not try and does not care. It is the most negative of the three words.)

EXERCISE B: Replacing General Words with Specific Words. Rewrite the following sentences, replacing the underlined words with more specific words.

EXAMPLE: My parents insisted that I pick up my stuff from the floor.

My parents insisted that I pick up my school books and dirty clothes from the floor.

1. He hit the door with his fists over and over again.
2. Hundreds of people will attend a medical convention at the Civic Center.
3. Something was bothering me, but I didn't want to talk about it.
4. She told us over and over again please not to tell Mother.
5. News magazines give us the information we need to keep abreast of things.
6. My little sister's singing was terrible.
7. The look on his face told us he did not understand English.
8. Dr. Wilson put her notebook on the table with an awful thud and looked at me.
9. Her parents give her a wonderful birthday party.
10. We found the food tasty.

EXERCISE C: Choosing Connotations. Choose the word in parentheses that has the best connotation for each sentence.

EXAMPLE: The nurse (raced, hurried) to the auditorium.
hurried

1. The doctor's positive report (consoled, reassured) us.
2. The baby (moaned, wailed) until she was fed.
3. The President (proclaimed, called) Martin Luther King Day.
4. Webster High (defeated, trounced) our hockey team, 6 to 1.
5. The army inducted thousands of (citizens, civilians).
6. His faint (grin, smile) told us he had guessed the secret.
7. Meg (teased, harassed) Allan about his haircut.
8. (Crumbling, Degenerating) wood surrounded the nest.
9. During the power failure, Grover (lit, ignited) a candle.
10. John had a (habit, custom) of being late for math class.

Using Vivid Words

Besides using specific words that communicate accurately, you will often want to use colorful, vivid expressions. One problem you may encounter, however, is that many phrases that come to mind easily are clichés.

Avoiding Clichés. *Clichés* are worn-out expressions that have lost their descriptive power. Phrases such as *last but not least, at this point in time,* and *when the chips are down* take away from, rather than add to, the clarity of your ideas.

Replace clichés with specific words that more clearly express your meaning.

In order to remove clichés from your writing, you should first become aware of some of these familiar sayings.

RECOGNIZING CLICHÉS		
apple of someone's eye	big as life	memory of an elephant
at a loss for words	goes without saying	priming the pump
at this point in time	heart of the matter	pull the rug out from under
benefit of the doubt	in the doghouse	slow as molasses

You can remove clichés from your sentences by reexamining the idea you want to communicate and by expressing it more specifically and directly. Notice that the revised sentences that follow the chichés sound more precise.

CLICHÉ: His brother advised him not to *cry over spilled milk.*

REVISED: His brother advised him not to mope about losing the tennis match.

CLICHÉ: The radio club is growing *by leaps and bounds.*

REVISED: The radio club is adding more new members each week.

Creating Fresh Similes and Metaphors. Although you should avoid clichés, you can make your writing more vivid by creating fresh comparisons that help a reader grasp your idea. Two useful kinds of comparisons are *similes* and *metaphors*.

Write your own similes and metaphors to sharpen your ideas and impressions.

A *simile* uses the words *like* or *as* to draw a direct comparison between two basically dissimilar things. The following examples show how similes can create mental pictures and enhance understanding.

SIMILES: Between Harriet and Mr. Pomfret there occurred one of those silences into which the first word spoken falls like the stroke of a gong.—Dorothy Sayers

Grandfather stood on the wide front porch like a captain surveying the vast unmotioned calms.—Ray Bradbury

Like a simile, a *metaphor* is a comparison between two dissimilar things, but a metaphor goes a little further. Instead of saying something is *like* another thing, a metaphor imaginatively says that something *is* the other thing. The following examples show how metaphors create images and add meaning.

METAPHORS: I would I were alive again to kiss the fingers of the rain.—Edna St. Vincent Millay

Linda Frantianne was a dancing flame in red as she whirled toward figure-skating glory, only to flicker out just short of the gold.—Peter Axhelm

Sometimes you can make a comparison a little less obvious by using a *submerged metaphor*. In the following example notice that there is a subtle comparison between a boat and a bird.

SUBMERGED METAPHOR: Slowly the white wings of the boat moved against the blue cool limit of the sky.—F. Scott Fitzgerald

NOTE ABOUT DEAD SIMILES AND METAPHORS: When you write similes and metaphors, avoid comparisons that are overused and too familiar. Such direct and implied comparisons as *easy as falling off a log* and *food for thought* are actually dead similes and metaphors, a subcategory of clichés. These expressions are dead because they no longer evoke visual images.

EXERCISE D: Avoiding Clichés. Rewrite each of the following sentences, replacing the clichés with clearer, more specific words.

EXAMPLE: Bob thought his job was a rat race.

Bob thought his job involved too much pressure.

1. For me, good grades in chemistry and math are a matter of life or death.
2. She became all hot and bothered because I would not agree to hold the party at my house.
3. Please touch base with me before the end of school tomorrow so that I can borrow your geometry book.
4. My aunt puts everything but the kitchen sink in her homemade soup.
5. When he had only a pair of three's in his hand, he threw in the towel and decided not to play poker again.
6. Poor Dexter has a spare tire that he is trying to lose by exercising.
7. The fog was as thick as pea soup and made navigation along the coast impossible.
8. Losing the class election by such a wide margin took the wind out of Bob's sails.
9. By hook or by crook Jane was determined to get that job.
10. Motorists flew through our town like blazes before the twenty-five-miles-per-hour speed limit was imposed.

EXERCISE E: Writing Your Own Similes and Metaphors. Complete each of the following similes and metaphors with a vivid, imaginative image. Identify each completed sentence as a *simile* or a *metaphor*.

EXAMPLE: Sparrows sat on the fence like

Sparrows sat on the fence like clothespins on on a line. (simile)

1. His hands and wrists stuck out of his sleeves like
2. The thruway, clogged with traffic, was
3. Fog enveloped the city like
4. The pet shop was as noisy as
5. Betsy cut the engine, and quiet covered them like
6. The maple tree was a
7. The power shovel perched at the edge of the pit like
8. The bobbing needle on the sewing machine was
9. The cluttered drugstore was
10. The dense ivy on the trunks and walls was

Using Varied Words

In addition to using specific words and vivid comparisons, you can make sentences more precise by choosing varied words.

Avoiding Overuse of the Same Word. If you use the same word or form of it several times in a sentence, your sentence can sound tedious and awkward. You must learn to distinguish between useful repetition and careless repetition.

Avoid careless overuse of the same word.

The following two sentences show the difference between useful and careless repetition. In the first sentence, the word *played* is used logically to create a contrast. In the second sentence, the word *picture* is overused and weakens the writing.

USEFUL REPETITION: The members of the team *played* brilliantly in the first half, but they *played* like beginners in the second.

CARELESS REPETITION: Thomas painted a *picture* of the old barn, and in the *picture* he *pictured* the barn as mysterious and deserted.

The following examples show various ways of improving sentences with overused words.

OVERUSED WORD: In a makeshift shed the construction company *housed* equipment for building *houses*.

VARIED WORDS: In a makeshift shed the construction company *stored* equipment for building houses.

OVERUSED WORD: We *noticed* Ricardo's bright purple shirt, which was extremely *noticeable* among the faded brown uniforms of the band.

VARIED WORDS: We easily *spotted* Ricardo's bright purple shirt among the faded brown uniforms of the band.

Avoiding Obvious Modifiers. An obvious modifier is an adjective that has been linked so often with a noun that it has lost its meaning. Phrases such as *unforgettable experience, blushing bride,* and *high mountain* add little to your sentences.

Replace obvious and unnecessary modifiers with modifiers that are more precise and vivid or with specific details.

If a modifier does sound obvious or unnecessary in a particular sentence, you can either (1) delete it and let the noun stand by itself or (2) substitute a more striking and more precise modifier, possibly by rewriting the sentences. The following sentences show different ways to make sentences more precise.

OBVIOUS MODIFIER: The *loud* siren under her window shattered her dreams.

REVISED: The screaming siren under her window shattered her dreams.

OBVIOUS MODIFIER: They stretched out on the park benches and gazed at the *fluffy* clouds.

REVISED: They stretched out on the park benches and gazed at the shapes appearing and dissolving in the clouds.

EXERCISE F: Replacing Overused Words and Obvious Modifiers. Rewrite each sentence, replacing overused words and obvious modifiers.

EXAMPLE: In the distance we could see high mountains.

In the distance we could see snow-covered mountains.

1. The painter painted the subject's dog in the foreground of the painting.
2. The yellow lemons and green parsley were an attractive garnish.
3. The staff at the special emergency number respond quickly to all emergencies.
4. That barking dog kept me awake all night with its barking.
5. A ringing bell will signal the end of the exam.
6. All competitors will compete in the final competition.
7. In overcoming a fear of heights, Sandy overcame a major obstacle to a career of skydiving.
8. We rode through the deserted streets of the ghost town.
9. Neither suspect recently brought in by the police had any police record with the local police.
10. The cold, wet waves turned our legs blue.

DEVELOPING WRITING SKILLS: Choosing the Most Precise Words. Rewrite the following short composition, eliminating or replacing linking verbs and verbs in the passive voice, weak, general words, worn-out expressions, overused words, and obvious modifiers.

(1) The dark moonless night gradually gave way to a dull glow. (2) A bearded man in brown clothes was motionless in the low undergrowth. (3) A rifle and some other things lay by his side. (4) Although a dull ache passed through his body, the man dared not move.

(5) Again, the burning sensation in his foot brought back memories of the last battle. (6) It had been so awful that it brought tears to his eyes. (7) His regiment had been attacked by the attacking guerrillas. (8) Only he had survived. (9) And the bullet in his knee kept him from flight. (10) He was a sitting duck for the enemy.

(11) The man sat himself into a sitting position. (12) Again the terrible pain went through his foot and ankle. (13) He was made alert by the snap of a twig. (14) In that moment he resolved to push aside other thoughts and concentrate on survival.

Maintaining an Appropriate Tone 18.2

Tone is the impression that a passage makes on the reader. A writer's attitude toward the audience and the subject reflected by the words he or she uses creates the tone of a passage. This section will explain how an awareness of audience and tone can help you choose precise, appropriate words.

Understanding the Ingredients of Tone

Whenever you write, you are usually writing to communicate with someone. The readers to whom you are speaking in your writing are your *audience*. The topic about which you are writing is your *subject*, and your reason for writing is your *purpose*. In any piece of writing, your attitude—thoughts and feelings—toward your audience, subject, and purpose create the tone of your writing.

Consider your audience, subject, and purpose to determine the tone for a piece of writing.

Before you begin to write, try to determine some basic information about the people who will make up your audience.

INFORMATION YOU NEED ABOUT YOUR AUDIENCE	
General age level	Interest in subject
Educational background	Relationship to you
Jobs or professions	Any other special characteristics (prejudices, nationalities, physical limitations, special or shared knowledge)
Geographic location	
Knowledge of subject	
Feelings about subject	

Not all of these points will be important for everything you write, and information on these points will not always be available to you. No matter how much or how little you know, you should decide on an attitude toward your audience that will allow you to choose the best words to communicate with them.

Also important in determining the tone you want to use is your attitude toward the subject matter. Decide whether your attitude should be objective or involved, humorous or serious. Also determine your purpose in writing. Do you want to inform, persuade, or entertain? Notice that the writer's awareness of the audience and purpose helps to create the tone in the following passages.

In the first passage, from *Soul,* a newsmagazine, the tone is light, chatty, and breezy. The short sentences, exclamation marks, and words such as *jazz lovers, odd,* and *get a good grip on yourself* create a casual, enthusiastic tone. They work together to show the writer's direct, familiar attitude toward the audience.

Casual, conversational tone

Jazz lives! And jazz lovers live too! They live everywhere from the lower east side to the upper west side. They are students, custodians, and stock brokers. They ride in subways, buses, Cadillacs, and jets. And if you think these combinations are odd, then get a good grip on yourself because the greatest oddity is yet to come. Many jazz lovers don't even know that's what they are!—R. A. Wilson

In contrast, the following passage from a medical magazine establishes a serious, objective tone, which appeals to a specially trained and concerned audience. It suggests by the use of medical terms, explanations in parentheses, and the words *you* and *ask yourself* that the writer's purpose is to explain and teach.

Serious, objective tone

Your first glance at the patient may give you the feeling that a cardiac problem exists, though it takes a systematic examination to pinpoint all the clues. As you come into the room, ask yourself if the patient appears to be in distress. Note his general appearance and apparent state of health. Does he appear older (as a result of chronic heart disease) or younger (due to suppressed growth from congenital heart disease) than his chronological age?—Christine Cannon

Some of the many possible tones a passage can have are described by the adjectives in the following chart.

POSSIBLE TONES WRITING CAN HAVE			
aloof	confidential	indifferent	playful
angry	conversational	informal	pretentious
calm	emotional	ironic	scholarly
casual	familiar	light	sentimental
chatty	formal	matter-of-fact	serious
coaxing	humorous	nostalgic	solemn
condescending	impersonal	objective	somber

EXERCISE A: Identifying Tone. Read the following two passages taken from books. Decide what word or words best describe the tone of each passage. Then, list specific words and phrases in each passage that contribute to the tone. Finally, state who you think is the intended audience of each passage.

(1) Sometimes it's hard to believe that English is the official language in Sydney, Australia; so many people speak, from habit or choice, a delightful, distorted form of English called Strine. It comes out as a colorful combination of British cockney and pure Australian. Words may emerge in a rush, or be shortened beyond recognition. Thus "How much is it?" sounds like someone named Emma Chizzit, and to "do a uey in a ute at the uni" really means making a U-turn in a utility truck at the university.—Adapted from Ethel A. Starbird

(2) Do you know why twelve inches is called a foot? Long, long ago, a foot was the distance from a man's heel to his toe. On every man it was different. Sometimes a foot was ten inches, and sometimes more. On a very large man, a foot might even be nineteen inches. Then some wise men, in the days of King Edward II of England, in the year 1324, decided that thereafter a foot would be twelve inches.—Adapted from Hester and Shane

EXERCISE B: Examining Tone in Your Own Writing. Bring to class a short letter or a composition you have written recently. Briefly describe your intended audience, your attitude toward that audience, your subject matter, and your purpose in writing. Then sum up the tone of the writing in one or two words.

Avoiding Inappropriate Words

Once you have chosen a tone, you should strive to keep it consistent. One way to maintain a consistent tone is to avoid words that may destroy the tone you have chosen.

Slang. *Slang* consists of popular words and phrases used by people of a certain age or region. Most slang expressions are current for a short time and then disappear. Slang words also tend to be vague and imprecise, mainly depending upon a speaker's intonation and expression to make sense. If you use slang in writing, therefore, you not only risk a distortion of tone but you also risk being misunderstood by your audience.

Replace slang words with words that are suitable for your established tone.

In the following examples, notice that the revised sentences are more consistent in tone and clearer than the sentences with slang.

SLANG: Our basketball players will have to *get their act together* if they want support from the student body next year.

REVISED: Our basketball players will have to start practicing seriously if they want support from the student body next year.

SLANG: We hope that you and other members of the community will not be *hung up* on the cost of the new Fine Arts Program at Butler High. Instead, we hope that you will be *keyed up* for our performances and that you will promote them by advertising and attending them.

REVISED: We hope that you and other members of the community will not be disturbed by the cost of the new Fine Arts Program at Butler High. Instead, we hope that you will be enthusiastic about our performances and that you will promote them by advertising and attending them.

Jargon. *Jargon* is specialized vocabulary consisting of technical terms from a profession or hobby. It may have its place when you are writing to an audience that shares your knowledge of a particular field. Used with the wrong audience, however, jargon may be confusing and even irritating.

Replace jargon with words that are appropriate for your specific audience.

You can maintain a consistent tone by explaining difficult terms and by replacing jargon with simpler language.

JARGON: When the truck hit my uncle's car, he suffered injuries to his head and chest and developed an *aortic aneurism*.

REVISED: When the truck hit my uncle's car, he suffered injuries to his head and chest and developed a heart problem, a weakening of the main artery carrying blood from his heart to the rest of his body.

JARGON: From the ski lodge, we watched Heidi flying down the slope, doing *wedel turns* and then relaxed *parallel christies*.

REVISED: From the ski lodge, we watched Heidi flying down the slope doing short, snaky turns and then relaxed, wider turns.

Self-Important Language. *Self-important language* includes words that sound impressive but are actually long-winded, vague, or weighty. It may be flowery, with too many adjectives and adverbs creating useless decoration. Or it may be falsely formal with vague, general nouns and long verbs ending in *-ate* or *-ize*.

Replace self-important language with simpler, more direct words.

The following sentences illustrate the differences between self-important language and language that is useful and clear.

SELF-IMPORTANT LANGUAGE: If you *utilize* the *assorted educational opportunities* provided by the *community college system*, you can *maximize* your *learning situations*.

REVISED: If you take advantage of the classes, lectures, and free movies offered by the local community colleges, you can learn about many subjects.

SELF-IMPORTANT LANGUAGE: A *familiarity* with the subway system will *facilitate* a tourist's *movement* about the city.

REVISED: Understanding the subway system helps a tourist travel in the city.

Euphemisms. *Euphemisms* are words or phrases that are used to soften or sugarcoat a truth or fact that someone might not want to face or that might embarrass someone. Euphemisms, such as *released from employment* for *fired,* are sometimes useful to avoid hurting someone's feelings. Used carelessly or frequently, however, euphemisms can give writing an insincere tone.

Avoid an insincere tone in your writing by removing euphemisms from your sentences.

In the following sentences, clearer and more direct words and phrases replace euphemisms and make the tone of the sentences unified.

EUPHEMISM: Three *peace officers* inspected the house after the burglary and concluded that the burglars had entered through the kitchen window.

REVISED: Three detectives inspected the house after the burglary and concluded that the burglars had entered through the kitchen window.

EUPHEMISM: After they were arrested, both of the suspects said that they regretted their *mistake*.

REVISED: After they were arrested, both of the suspects said that they regretted their part in the burglary.

Emotional Language. *Emotional language* includes words with strong negative connotations and words that express strong and often unsupported opinions. Emotional language yells at the audience and sours your tone by making it offensive and insulting. Words such as *cheap, neurotic, bigoted, low class, freeloader,* and *babyish* should generally be avoided.

Replace overly emotional language with reasonable words that are more neutral.

In the following sentences, emotional language has been replaced with more neutral words.

EMOTIONAL LANGUAGE: Cars manufactured by that company are *rattletraps*.

REVISED: Cars manufactured by that company have a record of breaking down after a few years.

EMOTIONAL LANGUAGE: My parents will not vote for that candidate because they say he is a *pig-headed fool* who *sponges off* the community.

REVISED: My parents will not vote for that candidate because they say he is stubborn when he makes mistakes and indifferent to the needs of the community.

EXERCISE C: Avoiding Inappropriate Words. Identify the underlined words in each sentence as *slang, jargon, self-important language, euphemisms,* or *emotional language*. Then rewrite each sentence using more appropriate words. Look up any words that you do not understand.

EXAMPLE: Older people are becoming cognizant of the new philosophy that says life begins at sixty.

(self-important language) Older people are recognizing the new philosophy that says life begins at sixty.

1. A group of leather-jacketed dudes on motorcycles raced through the town.
2. Governor Williamson sought to prioritize impending legislation.
3. The defeated army quickly made a strategic withdrawal.
4. Ralph said his job interview was a bummer.
5. The doctor suggested the possibility of hypoglycemia.
6. The owners of the prosperous eating establishment decided to initiate a new enterprise and open a second coffee shop.
7. Mary couldn't help thinking that the persistent salesman was a jerk.
8. At the end of the movie, several characters passed to their final reward.
9. Manuel's new car is out of sight.
10. The marching soldiers came to parade rest.

DEVELOPING WRITING SKILLS: Maintaining an Appropriate Tone. Follow these directions to examine the tone of writing.

1. Choose a special field of knowledge with which you are familiar, such as a sport, a hobby, a craft, or a parent's job. List five technical terms used by people who are familiar with the field, and use each term in a sentence for other experts. Then rewrite the sentences for an audience of ordinary readers, translating the jargon into understandable words.
2. Choose some issue in which you are emotionally involved. Write a short paragraph explaining your views but using calm, reasonable language.

18.3 Using Words Concisely

When you write, you should take care to use only the words that you truly need in order to communicate your ideas. Extra words can get in the way of clear communication. Thus, you should learn to make your sentences as *concise* as possible by identifying and eliminating unnecessary words.

Eliminating Deadwood

Unnecessary words that take up space without furthering your meaning are called *deadwood.* There are two different kinds of deadwood that you should watch out for: empty words that add nothing to your ideas and hedging words, made up of unnecessary qualifying expressions.

Eliminate empty words and hedging words from your sentences.

A sentence with empty words contains phrases that contribute nothing to the ideas you want to present. A sentence with hedging words makes a statement and then backs away from it, watering down the idea by adding an unnecessary qualifying word or phrase.

Empty words and hedging words are not difficult to identify. The following chart gives examples that can help you recognize both kinds of deadwood.

RECOGNIZING DEADWOOD		
Empty Words	**More Empty Words**	**Hedging Words**
as I said before	needless to say	almost
by way of	to the extent that	it seems
despite the fact that	there are	kind of
given the fact that	the reason was that	quite
in my opinion	there is	rather
it is a fact that	the thing is	somewhat
it is also true that	the type of	sort of
it is my opinion that	what I mean is	tends

The following examples show how to eliminate deadwood from your sentences.

WITH DEADWOOD: *What I want* for my birthday, *I think,* is a typewriter *for the reason that* I *tend to* type faster than I write.

CONCISE: For my birthday, I want a typewriter because I type faster than I write.

EXERCISE A: Eliminating Deadwood. Rewrite each of the following sentences, eliminating the empty words and hedging words.

EXAMPLE: I became somewhat frightened to the extent that I shook and stuttered.

I became so frightened that I shook and stuttered.

1. There were three reasons the man gave for his decision.
2. It is a fact that to buy a new stereo, Sara saved half of her allowance.
3. On account of the fact that they can eat wooden beams and supports, the termites in our house must be exterminated.
4. It seems that the early pioneers came to America with high hopes of being free.
5. Most computers, I think, can calculate and print figures to the extent that they are faster than any human abilities.
6. The convict escaped by way of following a somewhat lonely country road.

7. When a rather large ship enters the harbor, tugboats kind of crowd around it.
8. There is nothing more disappointing than friends who tend to make excuses for not doing their fair share.
9. The reason we stayed home was because the rainstorm spoiled the plans for a camp-out.
10. As I said before, the thing is the coach should not allow tardiness.

Avoiding Redundancy

Redundancy is the unnecessary repetition of an idea. Like deadwood, it can weaken the expression of your ideas.

Eliminate redundant words, phrases, and clauses from your sentences.

Redundant Words. Redundant words repeat the meaning of other words in the sentence. Adjectives that repeat the meaning of nouns and adverbs that repeat the meaning of verbs should be eliminated.

In the following examples redundant adjectives and adverbs are eliminated.

REDUNDANT ADJECTIVE: He studied *past* history extensively.

CONCISE: He studied history extensively.

REDUNDANT ADVERB: The boys advanced *forward* and shook their fists.

CONCISE: The boys advanced and shook their fists.

Redundant Phrases. Redundant prepositional phrases can clutter your sentences with ideas that have already been expressed by other words in the sentences. You should examine your sentences for these repetitious phrases and remove them.

REDUNDANT: Pat's face turned red *in color,* and he ran from the room.

CONCISE: Pat's face turned red, and he ran from the room.

Redundant Clauses. Redundant clauses can make sentences illogical or even pointless. Delete redundant clauses either by letting the main clause stand alone or by adding a meaningful subordinate clause. The following examples show both ways to correct redundant clauses.

REDUNDANT: The child asked unanswerable questions *that no one could answer.*

CONCISE: The child asked unanswerable questions.

CONCISE WITH TWO IDEAS: The child asked unanswerable questions that vexed his parents.

EXERCISE B: Avoiding Redundancy. Rewrite each sentence, eliminating redundant words, phrases, and clauses.

EXAMPLE: She had an idea in her head that would solve the problem.

She had an idea that would solve the problem.

1. The car was so dark in color that it was hard to see when parked at night.
2. After sitting in silence for most of the school year, Jeff finally spoke out loud to the whole class.
3. We like the incumbent candidate who is now in office.
4. When he was finally alone by himself, Jeb took out a book.
5. On their way home, the girls stamped noisily by our room.
6. He was a negligent driver because he was careless.
7. We were assigned a biography about the life of John Keats.
8. To find my keys, I retraced my steps back to my front door.
9. The river caused a flood that overflowed the town.
10. He was fired for an excess of too many absences.

Avoiding Wordiness

Often you can make your sentences more concise by looking for simpler ways to express your ideas. You can turn many phrases into single-word modifiers and many clauses into phrases.

Reduce a wordy phrase or clause to a single word or a shorter structure.

Prepositional phrases and adjective clauses can often be replaced with words that provide the same details more effectively.

Wordy Phrases. Sometimes you can replace a prepositional phrase with a single-word modifier, a noun, or a pronoun to create a shorter, clearer sentence.

WORDY: Detectives discovered that the name *of the suspect* was Smith.

CONCISE: Detectives discovered that the *suspect's* name was Smith. (reduced to an adjective)

WORDY: Aunt Bess moves *in a slow manner.*

CONCISE: Aunt Bess moves *slowly.* (reduced to an adverb)

WORDY: He sent letters *to her* and hoped she would visit.

CONCISE: He sent *her* letters and hoped she would visit. (reduced to a pronoun)

WORDY: Volunteers brought books and magazines *for patients* to read.

CONCISE: Volunteers brought *patients* books and magazines to read. (reduced to a noun)

Wordy Clauses. Adjective clauses add words that are not always needed to a sentence. Words such as *who is* or *which are,* the subject and verb beginning many adjective clauses, make a sentence sound drawn out. In some sentences you can simplify adjective clauses by omitting the subject and verb.

EXAMPLE: The young man *who was wrestling with the grocery cart* looked confused. (Omit the subject and verb of the clause to reduce the clause to a participial phrase.)

The young man *wrestling with the grocery cart* looked confused.

Below, wordy adjective clauses are followed by shortened versions. Notice that adjective clauses can be reduced to participial phrases, prepositional phrases, appositive phrases, part of a compound verb or complement, or a single-word modifier.

WORDY: Explorers discovered a passage *that went through the mountains.*

CONCISE: Explorers discovered a passage *through the mountains.*
(prepositional phrase)

WORDY: Brasilia, *which is the capital of Brazil,* lies many miles inland.

CONCISE: Brasilia, *the capital of Brazil,* lies many miles inland. (appositive phrase)

WORDY: My grandmother, *who gave me a novel by Charles Dickens,* also told me the story.

CONCISE: My grandmother *gave me a novel by Charles Dickens* and told me the story. (part of a compound verb)

WORDY: The teacher *who was a coach on an Olympic team* was also a player on an Olympic team.

CONCISE: The teacher was *a coach* and a player on an Olympic team. (part of a compound complement)

WORDY: We lifted the chest, *which was heavy.*

CONCISE: We lifted the *heavy* chest. (single-word modifier)

Verb/Noun Constructions. Phrases using verbs such as *have, give,* and *hold* followed by nouns sound heavy-handed. The idea can usually be expressed more clearly with only a verb. Notice the difference in sound and length in the following pairs of sentences.

WORDY: She *will give help to* you if you ask her.

CONCISE: She *will help* you if you ask her.

WORDY: The club plans to *hold discussions on* the new rules.

CONCISE: The club plans to *discuss* the new rules.

EXERCISE C: Reducing Wordiness. Rewrite each of the following sentences, eliminating the underlined wordy phrases, wordy clauses, and verb/noun constructions.

EXAMPLE: Vandals threw paint onto a car which was parked.

Vandals threw paint onto a parked car.

1. The new counselor intends to provide assistance to unemployed students.
2. Almost half of the money which was in their savings account was paid in taxes.
3. Some of the fur on our dog has fallen out in clumps.

4. The nurse will carry out inquiries about the nature of the illness.
5. Grandpa's favorite movie, which is an old silent comedy, will be shown this week on television.
6. A truck stopped and offered a ride to us into town.
7. The speaker agreed to give answers to questions from the audience.
8. The exhibition of dinosaur bones in the museum attracted people of all ages.
9. Dr. Harris, who buys hand-carved statuettes, sells them to his friends.
10. That species of flower that was endangered is now thriving in the wild.

DEVELOPING WRITING SKILLS: Writing Concise Sentences. Rewrite the following composition, eliminating deadwood, redundancy, wordy phrases, wordy clauses, and verb/noun constructions.

(1) During the time that he walked down the long, dark corridor, Ted thought that he heard a noise that was like the sound of a window opening. (2) He was of the opinion that there was someone else besides himself in the empty building.

(3) There was another noise that sounded sharply. (4) A moment later the sound of a window opening repeated again. (5) This was the time that Ted was sure of it. (6) Someone was trying to gain entrance by breaking into the building.

(7) Ted had to reach a decision about the idea of what to do. (8) He knew that there was no one else who was in the building so no one could be called to help him. (9) In addition, if he made any audible noises that the intruder could hear, he might cause a confrontation to happen.

(10) The action was chosen that Ted thought was sort of safest. (11) He tiptoed as noiselessly as he could walk, and he reached a door that was an exit without being seen or heard. (12) Opening the door carefully, Ted stepped outside and broke into a fast run. (13) Within seconds, he found a telephone and dialed the number for police emergencies.

Skills Review and Writing Workshop

The Use of Words

CHECKING YOUR SKILLS

Rewrite the following paragraph to make it more precise, concise, vivid, and consistent in tone.

(1) Jack and Noreen had a pretty interesting adventure when they went for a walk in the country. (2) There, big as life, was this big animal. (3) The animal growled a loud noise. (4) Jack suggested to Noreen that they get a move on. (5) Noreen was cool, but she wasn't feeling exactly wonderful. (6) Anyhow she and Jack started to run like the wind. (7) That big thing followed, but luckily it fell down. (8) Noreen and Jack walked into the cabin which looked like heaven. (9) They thought about maximizing this experience to the utmost. (10) So they wrote about it in the best way they could.

USING COMPOSITION SKILLS

Writing a "True" Adventure

When you write about an experience, you want to keep your audience's attention. Vivid, strong words help you accomplish this. Think of an an adventure you'd like to write about. It can be something that actually happened or something you invent. Follow the steps below to write about the adventure.

Prewriting: List all of the events that make up the incident. Next to each event, describe your feelings at the time, the setting, and any other characters in the story. Number the events in the order in which they happened.

Writing: Describe the main events in chronological order. Focus on giving a full picture of the events, but at this point don't think too much about each individual word.

Revising: When revising change words that could be more precise, vivid, or original. Check the list of vague adjectives on page 423 and the list of clichés on page 425 and eliminate them from your story. Then proofread carefully.

Chapter 19

Sentence Style

One important step toward improving your writing style is learning how to write more effective sentences. This chapter will show you several ways to improve your sentences. You will learn how to combine sentences, write varied sentences, and connect your sentences logically.

19.1 Sentence Combining

Inexperienced writers often write very short, undeveloped sentences. Short sentences can sometimes be useful, but too many short sentences can make your writing choppy. One way to overcome excessive use of short sentences is to combine some of them to make longer sentences.

Combining Ideas

If your sentences are short and choppy, you can group your ideas into longer, smoother sentences.

Join two or more short sentences by using compound subjects or verbs, by using phrases, or by writing compound, complex, or compound-complex sentences.

You can combine simple sentences in many ways. Notice in the following charts how sentence structures are changed to form longer, more interesting sentences.

Some simple sentences can be joined by using a compound subject or verb.

USING COMPOUND SUBJECTS OR VERBS
Forming Compound Subjects
Juan Tores is running for class president. So is Jennifer Wise. *Juan Tores* and *Jennifer Wise* are running for class president.
Forming Compound Verbs
Sandra heard the late bell. She ran to her next class. Sandra *heard* the late bell and *ran* to her next class.

Other sentences can be joined by changing one of them into a phrase modifier or an appositive phrase.

MAKING A SENTENCE INTO A PHRASE
Making a Sentence a Prepositional Phrase
The husky puppy whined for attention. It was in the cramped cage in the corner. The husky puppy *in the cramped cage in the corner* whined for attention.
Making a Sentence an Appositive Phrase
Dr. Maguire joined the staff in 1983. He is our new superintendent of schools. Dr. Maguire, *our new superintendent of schools,* joined the staff in 1983.
Making a Sentence a Participial Phrase
She heard a police siren. She pulled to the side of the road. *Hearing a police siren,* she pulled to the side of the road.
Making a Sentence an Infinitive Phrase
Here is a screwdriver. It can put these shelves together. Here is a screwdriver *to put these shelves together.*

Sometimes you can join short sentences by forming a compound, complex, or compound-complex sentence. The chart on the next page gives examples.

CHANGING SENTENCE STRUCTURES
Making a Compound Sentence
The moon disappeared behind a cloud. A wind stirred. The moon disappeared behind a cloud, *and* a wind stirred.
Making a Complex Sentence
Strong gusts blew leaves and branches. Drops of rain began to fall. Strong gusts blew leaves and branches, *as* drops of rain began to fall.
Making a Compound-Complex Sentence
We tried to change her mind. She insisted. We were to take her to the scene of the accident. We tried to change her mind, *but* she insisted *that* we take her to the scene of the accident.

EXERCISE A: Combining Sentences. Rewrite each of the following items, combining sentences.

EXAMPLE: A tan car sped along the highway. It attempted to turn sharply. It nearly flipped.

Speeding along the highway, a tan car attempted to turn sharply and nearly flipped.

1. Snow fell steadily upon the Acadian Forest. It fell for seven days.
2. Jason lost his grip on the rope tow. He slid all the way to the bottom of the hill.
3. Eating balanced meals is essential for good health. Exercising regularly is necessary too.
4. Thomas Jefferson was the third President of the United States. He helped to write the Declaration of Independence.
5. Horses communicate with each other. They snort and make sounds of different pitch.
6. Reading magazines is a good way to stay informed. They usually give several different viewpoints on a subject.
7. A walrus looks clumsy. It appears sluggish. It is quite agile when it swims.

8. The temperature rose. The snowbanks glistened in the sun. Tiny beads of water trickled down the hill.
9. We were miles away. We could hear Alan. He was practicing his trumpet.
10. The Tower of London was built almost nine hundred years ago. It was originally a prison. Today it houses the crown jewels.

DEVELOPING WRITING SKILLS: Further Practice in Combining Sentences. Rewrite each of the following items, combining sentences.

EXAMPLE: Martha and Lois paid twenty dollars for their tickets. Their seats were far from the stage. The actors looked like ants.

Although Martha and Lois paid twenty dollars for their tickets, their seats were so far from the stage that the actors looked like ants.

1. Writers often supplement their incomes with part-time jobs. The same is true of construction workers.
2. They stood tightly packed against one another. There was no place to sit.
3. Electric automobiles may someday provide more economical transportation. They may significantly reduce air pollution.
4. The horn finally blew. Our basketball team walked off the court triumphant.
5. Hurricane damage forced many shorefront residents to make major repairs. Others had to abandon their property altogether.
6. The moon is full. Coyotes will howl.
7. The experiment found that nonsmokers who did not live in a smoky environment had normal lung function. Those who were regularly exposed to smoke had a significant degree of respiratory impairment.
8. The audience erupted into applause. The candidate reached the podium.
9. Penny couldn't go on the retreat. Tony couldn't go on the retreat.
10. An unsigned article appeared in the last issue of our school newspaper. It caused a big debate in class.

19.2 Varying Your Sentences

If all your sentences are alike, your readers will quickly lose interest. Varying the lengths and structures of your sentences will help you to hold your readers' attention.

Expanding Short Sentences

Excessive use of short, choppy sentences can often be overcome by combining sentences. But some sentences are so plain that the reader would still receive only minimal information even if they were combined. In that case, you should lengthen sentences by including more details.

Expand short sentences by adding details.

The following chart shows how to add details with single-word modifiers, prepositional phrases, verbal phrases, and appositives.

EXPANDING SHORT SENTENCES
Short Sentence
The cyclist passed the van.
Expanded with Adjectives and Adverbs
The *leading* cyclist *quickly* and *unexpectedly* passed the *delivery* van.
Expanded with Prepositional Phrases
The cyclist *in the lead* passed the van *near the finish line.*
Expanded with Verbal Phrases
The cyclist *wearing number eight* passed the van *to avoid the vehicle's exhaust.*
Expanded with Appositives
The cyclist, *Byron Connors, an expert racer,* passed the van.

EXERCISE A: Adding Details. Rewrite each short simple sentence by adding the item or items in parentheses.

EXAMPLE: Science boasts a staggering amount of published information. (Appositive phrase)

Science, the last and probably endless frontier, boasts a staggering amount of published information.

1. Some of the local residents use the service road. (Prepositional phrase)
2. The president addressed the board of trustees. (Prepositional phrase)
3. A coat of paint brightened my room. (Two adjectives)
4. Mrs. Hamilton did her best to influence the town council. (Appositive phrase)
5. The mechanic pried the flat tire from the wheel rim. (Verbal phrase)
6. My opponent easily won the game. (Prepositional phrase)
7. Our coach led a triumphant team. (Appositive phrase)
8. The house aroused people's curiosity. (Two adjectives and an adverb)
9. The racehorse broke stride. (Verbal phrase)
10. The legislature passed a controversial bill. (Two adverbs)

Shortening Long Sentences

A well-written long sentence can strengthen a passage. But packing too much information into rambling compound sentences or awkward compound-complex sentences will make your ideas difficult to follow.

Break up lengthy, overly complicated sentences into simpler, shorter sentences.

If you find you have written a long, overloaded sentence or too many long sentences in a row, separate your ideas into shorter, more concise sentences.

One long rambling sentence

Old houses may look attractive and unusual, but buyers should not be swayed by their quaintness because old houses often require much renovation and many repairs since plumbing and electrical fixtures can be outdated and worn, or roofing and siding material can be weathered and leaky, and even supporting walls and beams can be rotten or decaying.

Several shorter, clearer sentences

Old houses may look attractive and unusual, but buyers should not be swayed by their quaintness. Old houses often require much renovation and many repairs. Plumbing and electrical fixtures can be outdated and worn. Roofing and siding material can be weathered and leaky, and even supporting walls and beams can be rotten or decaying.

EXERCISE B: Shortening Long Sentences. Divide each long sentence into shorter, clearer sentences.

EXAMPLE: Denver, which is the capital of Colorado and sits on the Great Plains of America, began as a mining camp in 1858 and quickly became a boomtown.

Denver, the capital of Colorado, sits on the Great Plains of America. The city began as a mining camp in 1858 and quickly became a boomtown.

1. Many people laughed at Adam when he first set out to find an old Spanish galleon that had sunk in 1622, but within a year he had converted many a disbeliever, because in that short time he had found millions of dollars of submerged treasure.
2. The art of wood carving was perfected so early in history that few records have been preserved, except relics, such as a recently excavated set of wood carver's tools, which prove that even before metal was used, people cut and decorated wood with tools of shell, bone, and flint.
3. I finally saw the movie, and I am glad that I read the book first because important plot details and even some characters that made the story understandable were left out of the movie version.
4. She clutched the letter tightly, refusing to talk about it and refusing to show it to us, yet tears streamed down her face and small sobs shook her, and we did want to help her, but she was unreachable.
5. In the first few hours of torrential rain, flood waters began to rise, and many people left their homes in search of higher ground, but most of these people got stuck in traffic jams and had to wait out the crisis in their stalled automobiles.

Using Different Sentence Openers and Structures

Besides varying the length of your sentences you can achieve variety by concentrating on using different beginnings and different structures.

Use a variety of sentence openers and structures in a passage.

The most common way to begin sentences is with a subject followed by a verb. You should certainly begin many of your sentences in this way. By varying the beginnings of some of your sentences, however, you can add life to your writing style.

The following chart gives examples of different ways to begin sentences. Notice how many alternatives there are to choose from. Each can help you to avoid excessive reliance on the basic subject-verb sentence opening.

VARYING SENTENCE OPENERS
Subject first: *We* took skiing lessons in the Italian Alps for several weeks.
Adjective first: *Amused,* we allowed her to finish her wildly exaggerated tale.
Adverb first: *Frantically,* hundreds of ants scurried in all directions trying to escape.
Participial phrase first: *Hearing strange noises,* we crept downstairs to investigate.
Infinitive phrase first: *To prepare for a short-answer vocabulary test,* Ellen makes flash cards and quizzes herself daily.
Adverb clause first: *Because the train was traveling so fast,* it vanished in seconds.
Several adverbs first: *Quickly* and *smoothly,* the swimmers dived into the pool.
Transition first: *Nevertheless,* you are still required to complete four years of English.
Inverted with phrase first: *Out of the sky* came a mystery.

All of the sentences in the following passage begin with subjects followed by verbs. If you read the passage aloud you will see that repeating the subject-verb opener in all the sentences contributes to the dull rhythm.

Monotonous passage with sentences all beginning with subjects and verbs

(1) I'll always remember my trip to White Horse Inn. (2) I met my best friend Karen there. (3) She was on holiday with her parents. (4) I was traveling with my parents. (5) I was pleased to meet another person my age. (6) I soon discovered that we shared many interests. (7) We became constant companions before long. (8) We hiked, swam, played gin rummy when it rained. (9) We sampled all the activities offered by the inn. (10) We eventually shared a common secret. (11) We both felt awkward with groups of people our age. (12) That similarity especially helped to make us close friends.

When you rewrite a passage to vary your sentence openers, you will often want to use different sentence structures as well. Read the following revision of the same passage. A number of different openers are used. In addition, some of the original sentences have been combined to create a variety of lengths and structures. The variety clarifies the ideas, increases the readability, and improves the rhythm of the sentences.

Revised passage with varied sentence openers and structures

(1, 2) I'll always remember my trip to White Horse Inn because there I met my best friend Karen. (3) She was on holiday with her parents. (4, 5, 6) Since I was traveling with my parents, I was pleased to meet another person my age with many of my interests. (7, 8, 9) Before long, we became constant companions, hiking, swimming, playing gin rummy when it rained, and sampling the other activities offered by the inn. (10, 11) Eventually, we shared a common secret; we both felt awkward with groups of people our age. (12) That similarity especially helped to make us close friends.

EXERCISE C: Using Different Sentence Openers. Rewrite each of the following sentences, rearranging the words to make the sentence begin differently.

EXAMPLE: I tossed and turned constantly during the night.
During the night I tossed and turned constantly.

1. Oceanographers have worked endlessly to study the habits of undersea animals.
2. I lost my concentration when the phone began to ring.
3. The confused tourists stared at the timetable in the train station.
4. Lucky contestants have won hundreds of thousands of dollars on television game shows.
5. Burning coals and boiling lava erupted from the mouth of Mount Etna.
6. Clarissa, running to answer the phone, slipped on a magazine and twisted her ankle.
7. You must fulfill basic requirements to be a good student and earn high grades.
8. The mountain, jagged and menacing, loomed above us.
9. A building can be condemned if it does not meet safety standards.
10. My uncle, however, would not play golf again.

EXERCISE D: Varying Sentence Structure. Rewrite the following passage using a variety of sentence structures.

(1) Aunt Helen's heirs were an eager group. (2) Eight men and nine women sat around the giant parlor table. (3) They waited anxiously for the lawyer's arrival. (4) Enthusiastically, they exchanged talk of "our dear, departed Helen." (5) Most of the heirs had never met before this evening. (6) Each pair of eyes glanced regularly toward the parlor doorway. (7) The attorney finally appeared. (8) He was carrying an impressive-looking document. (9) Suddenly, the heirs fell silent. (10) The atmosphere became tense.

Using Special Sentence Patterns

Special patterns within sentences and within groups of sentences can be used to emphasize certain ideas.

Using Parallelism. The use of similar patterns within your sentences is called *parallelism*.

Use parallelism to underscore ideas.

Parallelism is the use of similar grammatical structures in a series, that is, the use of single words together, phrases together, and clauses together. The following sentences illustrate the differences between sentences without parallelism and sentences with parallelism. Notice the greater strength of those with parallelism.

WITHOUT PARALLELISM: She was lazy, proud, and a fool. (adjective/adjective/noun)

WITH PARALLELISM: She was lazy, proud, and foolish. (parallel adjectives)

WITHOUT PARALLELISM: The boy ran angrily and in fear from the accident. (adverb/prepositional phrase)

WITH PARALLELISM: The boy ran in anger and in fear from the accident. (parallel prepositional phrases)

You can use parallelism to draw attention to ideas. Parallelism can also help you show contrast.

PARALLELISM FOR EMPHASIS: In a dead city, in a musty warehouse in a dilapidated laboratory, the scientist studied his beakers and vials.

PARALLELISM TO SHOW CONTRAST: She wanted publicity and power; he wanted privacy and peace.

Breaking a Pattern. Another way to emphasize one or more ideas is to establish a pattern with a series of sentences and then to write a sentence with a totally different structure to break the pattern.

Use a new structure after a series of similar structures to underscore an idea.

In the following example, the writer sets up a pattern with a series of questions and then expresses the main idea by breaking the pattern with a declarative sentence.

BREAKING A PATTERN: Can Robert "Bud" Gibson provide the leadership we need? Can he halt the trend of rising taxes? Can he lower the city's crime rate? You bet he can.

EXERCISE E: Using Patterns for Emphasis. Tell whether the strength of each of the following passages is achieved purely through *parallelism* or through *breaking a pattern*.

EXAMPLE: Spittle physically nauseated Dickens; slavery morally sickened him.—Jeanne and Norman MacKenzie

parallelism

1. Education makes a people easy to lead, but difficult to drive; easy to govern, but impossible to enslave.—Lord Brougham
2. The past is only the present become invisible and mute; and because it is invisible and mute, its memorized glance and its murmurs are infinitely precious. We are tomorrow's past.—Mary Webb
3. Feast, and your halls are crowded; fast, and the world goes by.—Ella Wilcox
4. The country needs, and unless I mistake its temper, the country demands bold, persistent experimentation. It is common sense to take a method and try it: If it fails, admit it frankly and try another. But above all, try something.—Franklin Delano Roosevelt
5. Better by far you should forget and smile than that you should remember and be sad.—Christina Rossetti

DEVELOPING WRITING SKILLS: Writing Varied Sentences. Rewrite the following composition, varying the lengths, beginning, structures, and possibly the patterns of the sentences.

(1) Millions of people are injured yearly in their own homes. (2) Every area of your home can possess a safety hazard. (3) No one can afford to overlook possible hazards. (4) You should inspect all rooms of your house. (5) You should then eliminate all of the dangers you recognize.

(6) Too many home accidents happen in kitchens so you must take special care to ensure safety by making sure that electrical appliances are away from the sink and by preventing their cords from slipping into the water, and you should keep a fire extinguisher in the kitchen because fires can occur all too quickly and they can spread rapidly.

(7) You can also help prevent accidents in bath-

rooms. (8) Inspect them for potential hazards, keep pills and medicines out of the reach of children, and label all medicines to avoid dangerous mix-ups, and cover a slippery floor with a carpet or bath rug that can not slip, and never place a telephone near the tub or sink. (9) The phone cord can become wet. (10) It can cause an electrical shock.

19.3 Making Clear Connections

As you concentrate on making your sentences varied in length and structure, you should also think about their clarity and smoothness. Using transitions, coordination, subordination, and logical order, you can connect your ideas smoothly and improve the reader's understanding.

Using Transitions

Transitions are words and phrases that act as bridges to link your ideas from sentence to sentence and often as guideposts to indicate the direction of your thoughts. Transitions enable your ideas to flow together smoothly.

Use transitions logically to clarify the relationship between ideas in different sentences.

Different transitions establish different relationships between ideas. The following chart lists some commonly used transitions and shows the relationships they establish.

SOME USEFUL TRANSITIONS			
To Show a Time Sequence			
after	during	first, second, third	meanwhile
at the same time	earlier	in a few minutes	next
before then	finally	later	then
To Compare or Contrast			
conversely	indeed	likewise	on the other hand
however	in like manner	nevertheless	similarly
in contrast	instead	on the contrary	unlike

To Show a Cause or Effect			
as a result	consequently	then	
because of	on account of	therefore	
To Add More Information			
also	besides	furthermore	moreover
as well	first, second, third	in addition	too
To Emphasize a Point			
indeed	in other words		
in fact	most important		
To Introduce Examples or Explanations			
also	for example	in particular	that is
as an illustration	for instance	namely	

Notice that the following sentences without transitions are isolated and sometimes confusing. When the same sentences are rewritten to include transitions, the logical relationship between the ideas becomes clearer. Also notice that the transition does not always have to be placed at the beginning of the second sentence.

UNCONNECTED: George and Al disappeared into another room. They emerged wearing clown costumes.

WITH TRANSITION: George and Al disappeared into another room. *In a few minutes,* they emerged wearing clown costumes.

UNCONNECTED: North Americans often serve hot chocolate with whipped cream. South Americans often add cinnamon and sometimes orange rind.

WITH TRANSITION: North Americans often serve hot chocolate with whipped cream. South Americans, *on the other hand,* often add cinnamon and sometimes orange rind.

EXERCISE A: Using Transitions. Rewrite each pair of sentences, using transitions to show the most logical relationship between the two ideas.

EXAMPLE: We waited endlessly for a package from home. One arrived on the day we least expected it.

We waited endlessly for a package from home. Finally, one arrived on the day we least expected it.

1. Not everyone did poorly on the exam. Janet scored over 90 percent.
2. My mother does not approve of dates on school nights. I will not be able to go to the hockey game with you next Wednesday.
3. The sunlight disappeared and the sky darkened. Large hailstones began to fall.
4. Ingrid Plotkin has been named vice president in charge of advertising for the Bradley Corporation. She was a copywriter and account executive.
5. You can plan to arrive early. I will be behind schedule if you don't.
6. Maryanne has built several pieces of summer furniture. She built an awning for the outdoor deck.
7. Nesting birds use their body heat to keep their eggs warm. Other animals, such as kangaroos, use their bodies to incubate their young.
8. Beyond a doubt, the security guard was frightened. He shook and trembled and could not lift his arm.
9. There are many ways to save money. You can enroll in a payroll deduction plan where you work.
10. I will not allow you to take this test over. You may write a separate report for extra credit.

Using Coordination and Subordination

While transitions show the relationship between ideas in separate sentences, coordination and subordination connect ideas in the same sentence.

Using Coordination. By using coordination to join words, phrases, and clauses, you can indicate to the reader that these items or ideas are related and equally important.

Use coordination logically to join equal and related words, phrases, and clauses in a sentence.

You can join ideas of equal importance using four main methods noted in the chart below.

METHODS OF COORDINATION		
Method	**What to Join**	**Use**
Coordinating conjunctions: and, but, for, nor, or, so, yet	words phrases clauses	Choose a coordinating conjunction to suit the meaning you intend.
Correlative conjunctions: but . . . and either . . . or neither . . . nor not only . . . but also	words phrases clauses	Choose a correlative conjunction to suit the meaning you intend.
Conjunctive adverbs: ;consequently, ;furthermore, ;however, ;indeed, ;otherwise, ;therefore,	independent clauses	Choose a conjunctive adverb to indicate time, contrast, result, addition, or emphasis.
Semicolon alone: ;	independent clauses	Use a semicolon alone for a close relationship needing no other words.

The following examples show these four methods.

UNCONNECTED: Don Whillans repeatedly tried to reach the summit of Mount Masherbrum. He failed.

WITH COORDINATION: Don Whillans repeatedly tried *and* failed to reach the summit of Mount Masherbrum.

UNCONNECTED: I suggest you subscribe to a morning newspaper. An evening newspaper is also acceptable.

WITH COORDINATION: I suggest you subscribe to *either* a morning *or* an evening newspaper.

UNCONNECTED: Factory workers had to be promised a pay raise last month. They would have gone on strike.

WITH COORDINATION: Factory workers had to be promised a pay raise last month; *otherwise,* they would have gone on strike.

UNCONNECTED: The people of Athens studied and valued the arts. Those of Sparta practiced the techniques of war.

WITH COORDINATION: The people of Athens studied and valued the arts; those of Sparta practiced the techniques of war.

There are three major problems with coordination that you should try to avoid: (1)excessive coordination; (2)coordination that connects unrelated ideas; and (3)unclear coordination.

Excessive coordination occurs when you try to connect too many ideas in a compound sentence. To correct excessive coordination, break some ideas into separate sentences.

EXCESSIVE COORDINATION: I had planned to arrive at your party early to help you get ready, but my car broke down, and I had to walk the last three miles, and I was wearing these new shoes.

APPROPRIATE COORDINATION: I had planned to arrive at your party early to help you get ready, but my car broke down. I had to walk the last three miles in these new shoes.

A second common error is trying to connect unrelated ideas. If you do find unrelated ideas in a sentence, separate the ideas into different sentences. If necessary, change or add words in order to make two or more complete sentences.

UNRELATED IDEAS CONNECTED: The old Williams mansion burned down last night, and we once played in that deserted house.

UNRELATED IDEAS SEPARATED: The old Williams mansion burned down last night. I remember when we played in that deserted house.

A third major problem with coordination is unclear coordination caused by using a conjunction that does not fit. To clarify vague connections, replace the wrong conjunction with one that shows a logical relationship between the ideas.

UNCLEAR COORDINATION: The soccer field is under an inch of rain water; *furthermore,* the opening game will have to be postponed.

CLEAR COORDINATION: The soccer field is under an inch of rain water; *consequently,* the opening game will have to be postponed.

Using Subordination. Another way to connect ideas within a sentence is to use subordination. By making one clause subordinate to another, you can make that clause describe or modify another in a complex sentence.

Use subordination logically to connect related but unequal ideas in a single sentence.

When you use subordination, you indicate to the reader that one idea is less important and therefore subordinate to another idea. The subordinate idea limits, describes, or explains the main idea. By making unequal but related ideas into complex sentences, you can indicate relationships of time, result, comparison, contrast, or condition, or you can simply add information. The subordinate clauses begin with words such as *while, because, as if,* and *which* and contain the supporting ideas.

The following examples show the logical relationships that can be indicated by the use of subordinate clauses.

TIME: *While* Carlotta swept the garage, I mowed the lawn.

RESULT: Alex always looks unkempt *because* he refuses to have his hair cut.

COMPARISON: The little boy walked with jerky steps and made humming noises *as if* he were a robot.

CONDITION: The new restaurant, *which* has a colonial decor, has received much publicity lately.

There are three major subordination problems that you should avoid in your writing: (1)excessive subordination; (2)illogical subordination; and (3)weak coordination used instead of subordination. Any of these problems can cloud the relationship between ideas in your sentences.

Excessive subordination occurs when too many subordinate clauses are joined in one sentence, often obscuring your meaning. To correct excessive subordination, make one or more of the subordinate clauses into separate sentences.

EXCESSIVE SUBORDINATION: While trying to write a composition, Len was watching a wrestling match on television, which was distracting him because he was thinking about the Regional Tournament when he would be wrestling on Monday and when he would try to do his best to please his coach.

IMPROVED SUBORDINATION: While trying to write a composition, Len was watching a wrestling match on television. It was distracting him because he was thinking about the Regional Tournament on Monday. He would be wrestling then and trying to do his best to please his coach.

Illogical subordination is another problem to avoid. As you combine two ideas to form a complex sentence, you should be careful to establish a logical relationship between the main idea and the subordinate idea. If you choose the wrong clause to subordinate, the connection between your ideas may not make sense. To correct illogical subordination, make the main idea into the main clause.

ILLOGICAL SUBORDINATION: Before you brush your teeth, go to bed.

LOGICAL SUBORDINATION: Before you go to bed, brush your teeth.

A third problem is using coordination where subordination would be stronger. Using coordination to join certain ideas may create a weak connection between those ideas. Using subordination instead can tighten and sharpen the relationship.

WEAK COORDINATION: My grades started to drop, *and* I realized I needed to spend more time on my homework.

STRENGTHENED BY SUBORDINATION: *When* my grades started to drop, I realized I needed to spend more time on my homework.

EXERCISE B: Correcting Problems in Coordination. Rewrite each of the following sentences, correcting the problem in coordination.

EXAMPLE: We had planned to arrive at the airport before noon; otherwise, the trip took us longer than we had expected.

We had planned to arrive at the airport before noon; however, the trip took us longer than we had expected.

1. My grandfather enjoys working in his garden, and he spends much of his free time making furniture.
2. The car is an antique Model T Ford; therefore, it is still in good running condition.
3. We had planned a trip to the beach, but it rained on Saturday, so we stayed in the house and played a long game of Monopoly, and we watched a movie, and later in the afternoon, the sun came out and we played croquet.
4. David planned to repay the loan quickly, or he also wanted to buy a new bowling ball.
5. My grandmother recently dislocated her hip, and she likes game shows and crossword puzzles.
6. To reach the senator for his comment, I telephoned his office; however, I also called his home.
7. No one thinks of swimming in the frozen Yukon, for warm mineral springs make swimming possible.
8. You can pay the fine to the clerk, and you can instead serve thirty days in jail.
9. We changed the oil in our car, but my brother forgot to screw the oil plug in, and the new oil passed through the car engine and spilled over the driveway.
10. There are rats living in our attic; moreover, I will move out.

EXERCISE C: Correcting Problems in Subordination. Rewrite each sentence, correcting the problem in subordination.

EXAMPLE: Bats frighten many people; the creatures are harmless.

Although bats frighten many people, the creatures are harmless.

1. She was hungry and tired because she decided to go home.
2. Because tornadoes are powerful enough to destroy the sturdiest of buildings, many homeowners in the Midwest have built underground shelters, which will provide them with the necessary protection when a "twister" comes into their area, which usually happens several times a year.
3. Neil loved the fields and woods around his new home, and he felt uncomfortable in the house.
4. Whenever the dog howled to drown the music, my mother sang and played the piano.
5. Although I had read everything written by this author, I had no idea what she would be like in person before I had the pleasure of meeting her at the airport when we were boarding the same plane, which was departing for Rome.
6. My uncle had a stroke; he could not use his left arm.
7. During the war years, this was a very popular recipe, and it doesn't call for expensive milk, eggs, or butter.
8. We have a case, and we can prove that the suspect was in town on the day of the crime.
9. After he prepared supper, he assembled all the ingredients.
10. Because the animal was safe, it scurried into its den.

Using Logical Order

Another method of making your sentences clear and smooth involves arranging ideas within your sentences and within groups of sentences according to logical plans. Some commonly used plans are chronological order, spatial order, order of importance, and comparison and contrast order.

Order your ideas logically and consistently within sentences and groups of sentences.

Related ideas within a sentence should be arranged in a logical order. As you read the following examples, notice that a sentence with ideas in an illogical order forces the reader to jump back and forth between unconnected ideas.

ILLOGICAL ORDER: I dressed in my best clothes, took a shower, and left for the reception.

LOGICAL ORDER: I took a shower, dressed in my best clothes, and left for the reception.

ILLOGICAL ORDER: The tour guide showed us the dungeon deep underground, the estate around the castle, and the interior of the castle.

LOGICAL ORDER: The tour guide showed us the estate around the castle, the interior of the castle, and the dungeon deep underground.

An illogical order in a series of sentences is even more confusing to a reader than illogic within a single sentence. The following examples show you how the smoothness and the clarity of a passage improve when the sentences are rewritten in a logical order.

ILLOGICAL ORDER: Mix the melted butter and the brown sugar. Fold in the flour, salt, and spices. Sift the flour, salt, and spices. Add the oatmeal, nuts, and raisins to the mixture. Make sure the nuts and raisins are finely chopped.

LOGICAL ORDER: Mix the melted butter and brown sugar. Sift the flour, salt, and spices. Fold in the flour, salt, and spices. Make sure the nuts and raisins are finely chopped. Then add the oatmeal, nuts, and raisins to the mixture.

ILLOGICAL ORDER: Like tennis, racquetball is a game of strategy. But unlike tennis, it must be played indoors. Like tennis, racquetball requires good eye-hand coordination.

LOGICAL ORDER: Like tennis, racquetball is a game of strategy that requires good eye-hand coordination. Unlike tennis, racquetball must be played indoors.

EXERCISE D: Using Logical Order. If an item is written in logical order, write *logical* on your paper. If an item is in illogical order, rewrite it to follow logical order.

EXAMPLE: We loaded the car, packed our suitcases, and left for California.

We packed our suitcases, loaded the car, and left for California.

1. The designated hitter watched the pitcher wind up, walked up to the plate, and then swung with all his might.
2. Write your composition about the story. Read the story. Then revise your composition.
3. The annual scholarship dinner was topped off with strawberry shortcake. The main course was roast beef. Shrimp cocktails were served for an appetizer.
4. This radio station broadcasts state, national, local, and international news.
5. The grand prize in the drawing is a weekend in a resort hotel for the winner's whole family. The prize for runners-up is a fifty-dollar bill. The second prize is a set of golf clubs.
6. The car chugged and jerked down the road. Gradually the grating and roaring of the engine increased. Then the engine screeched and died.
7. Both snow skiing and water skiing use muscles in the legs. In contrast to snow skiing, water skiing also strains muscles in the back.
8. Intelligence sources report that the army could not control the problem. They said total anarchy was imminent. They announced that citizens were rioting.
9. The diver plunged into the pool, stepped to the end of the board, and stood motionless for a moment.
10. Rene passed the final exam, studied hard all semester, and got an A in the course.

DEVELOPING WRITING SKILLS: Making Clear Connections. Rewrite the following passage using transitions, coordination, subordination, and logical order to create smooth, clear relationships between the ideas.

(1) Cross-country skiing offers several advantages that downhill skiing does not. (2) Downhill skiing mainly involves executing turns down wide, steep slopes. (3) Cross-country skiing can be done on flat land, on hills, or on narrow trails. (4) Downhill skiers must pay to use lifts and tows to carry them to the top of slopes. (5) Cross-country skiers can ski through parks or woods for free. (6) The boots used for cross-country skiing are flexible and comfortable. (7) They are like

soccer shoes. (8) The skis are light. (9) Downhill equipment anchors the skiers' feet and ankles to the solid skis with heavy, inflexible boots.

(10) Cross-country skiing is an excellent way to enjoy exercising in the winter, and it is like hiking in the snow. (11) The basic stride is a gliding shuffle, a combination of walking and skating. (12) Maintaining the stride uses shoulder, arm, and leg muscles, but it stimulates the circulation system. (13) Skiing along park trails or golf course, skiers breathe fresh air. (14) They can see deer tracks and may hear a brook trickling beneath its layer of ice. (15) Skiers become hot from the exercise. (16) A cooling mist may blow down from the snow-covered trees.

Skills Review and Writing Workshop

Sentences

CHECKING YOUR SKILLS

Rewrite the following paragraph to improve the style of the sentences.

(1) The High Sierras are above Yosemite National Park. (2) There are five High Sierra trail camps. (3) You can get to them by foot. (4) You can get to them by saddle animal. (5) The main attractions at the camps are the trails which wind through valleys that are thick with firs which are centuries old and over mountain passes that have been scraped and polished by glaciers and which allow you to see a glacial lake at one moment and a startled deer at another. (6) On our first night at a trail camp, we were awakened by a scratching noise. (7) Because we jumped out of our sleeping bags, we were afraid. (8) We lit a candle and did not see the bear we expected. (9) We fell asleep. (10) We found a chipmunk trapped in the wastebasket.

USING COMPOSITION SKILLS
Writing a News Item

Newspaper reporters often keep their readers' interest by varying their sentence openers and structures. Write a short news item about some recent event in your school or community by following the steps below.

Prewriting: Free write for five to ten minutes to help you choose an event. Then list all of the information about this event and number your list in a logical order.

Writing: Write a first draft of your news item. Include all of the information readers would need to understand what happened and why it was newsworthy.

Revising: When revising, make sure that you have used a variety of sentence openers and structures, and make sure that events are described in a logical order and that there are logical transitions between ideas. Then proofread carefully.

UNIT **V**

Composition

Forms and Process of Writing

Chapter **20**

Paragraphs

A *paragraph* is a group of related sentences that represent a unit of thought. It is generally marked by the indentation of the first word of the first sentence.

Understanding Paragraphs 20.1

A good paragraph is a unit of thought in which all the sentences work together to present and develop one main idea. The main idea is usually found in one sentence called the *topic sentence*. The other sentences support the main idea with examples, details, facts, reasons, or incidents.

Topic Sentences

The topic sentence in a paragraph indicates what the paragraph is about and often suggests the purpose of the paragraph—to explain, to persuade, to describe, and so on.

The topic sentence expresses the main idea of a paragraph.

Many paragraphs begin with the topic sentence. Other paragraphs have the topic sentence in the middle. Still other paragraphs end with a topic sentence that summarizes in one final statement the specific information that came before.

To find the topic sentence in a paragraph, look for the sentence that acts as an umbrella for all the ideas in the other sentences. In the following paragraph, notice that the first sentence expresses the main idea of the paragraph.

TOPIC SENTENCE

Supporting information

Cyrus West Field envisioned and brought about the first transatlantic telegraph cable. He thought up the cable and interested others in the idea. Field also helped form the Atlantic Telegraph Company, which financed the laying of the cable, and he found talented people to work on the project. Most important, Cyrus West Field made sure that the cable was completed, even after repeated disasters had injured or discouraged others.

In the next paragraph, the first two sentences introduce the topic sentence, which is the third sentence. The topic sentence is followed by supporting information.

Introductory sentences

TOPIC SENTENCE

Supporting information

There are few places that can boast an act of creation every day. A newspaper is one of them. *Out of the daily newsroom whirl emerges a remarkable product.* In a matter of hours, thousands of words and pictures are put together in a cohesive pattern designed to inform, enlighten, and entertain the reader. To a casual observer, the men and women working in the newsroom may appear to be running about aimlessly amid the clatter of typewriters and the continually ringing telephones. Actually, the scurrying around, the occasional shouting, the general air of excitement are all part of a controlled procedure. Each editor, reporter, and copyboy has a designated job, the end result of which is the newspaper that rolls off the press on time.—M.L. Stein

The final paragraph shows how a topic sentence at the end of the paragraph can act as a summary to state the point behind all the specific supporting information.

Supporting information

TOPIC SENTENCE

Quarterbacks must have skill in the art of throwing a pass, and they must think quickly because football is a fast-moving, complex sport. Running backs must also be fast on their feet and quick to move away from tacklers. Linemen, on the other hand, must be good at blocking the running advances of the other team, and they must develop strength and determination. *Each position in football requires special skills.*

EXERCISE A: Identifying Topic Sentences. Write down the topic sentence of each of the following paragraphs. Two of them fall at the beginning; two of them fall at the end.

(1) Curiously, Venetian blinds neither originated nor gained fame in Venice. A type of Venetian blind seems to have existed in Nero's Rome, and archaeologists note that Egyptian tomb walls depict a primitive prototype of blinds—an artifact made of reeds, over which slaves poured water to cool the passing air. No one is sure how or when Venetian blinds came to the Western world. Some historians believe that Marco Polo brought them to Italy early in the fourteenth century; others assert that a liberated Persian slave took them to France in order to create a livelihood for himself. Venetian traders introduced the blinds to Great Britain, which probably accounts for our name for them.—Teresa Byrne-Dodge

(2) Wall paintings of many ancient Egyptian tombs picture the deceased playing a board game called *Senet*. Other *Senet* diagrams, scratched onto the walls of ancient temples and other buildings, indicate that the game was popular among watchmen, priests, and building workers. Peasants played it in the sand, with stones or ceramic pieces. But the pharaohs played it on magnificent boards of rare woods, ivory, and faience. Archaeological evidence clearly reveals that *Senet* was played by people at all levels of ancient Egyptian society. —Adapted from an article in *Games of the World*

(3) Dr. Sidney A. Gauthreaux, Jr., a professor at Clemson University, will never forget September 28, 1977. That night he surveyed migrating birds with radar and telescope at South Carolina's Greenville-Spartanburg Airport. Dr. Gauthreaux scanned a front, or line, across the path of migration and computed the number of birds that passed through it in a six-hour period. He got a peak count of 218,700 in one hour and more than a million in six hours. From his data, he decided it was possible that fifty million birds were flying through the area over a front extending fifty miles.—Allan C. Fisher, Jr.

(4) Only about 30 percent of humanity lives in industrial areas, such as Europe and North America, but these people consume about 60 percent of the world's food supply. Such percentages indicate that the world faces an ongoing problem. The majority of the world's people, constituting about 70 per-

cent of the population, must attempt to live on only about 40 percent of the world's food supply. As a result, millions of people throughout the world live near starvation every day of their lives, while others in more industrialized nations have adequate or even abundant supplies of food.

Support

While the topic sentence presents the main idea, the supporting sentences in a paragraph help the reader understand that main idea.

Examples, details, facts, reasons, and incidents support the topic sentence.

Support can be of several kinds. *Examples* are typical instances or samples of ideas or principles. *Details* are small parts or specific items that make up something larger. *Facts* are statements or observations that can be verified. *Reasons* are explanations, justifications, or causes. *Incidents* are minor events or happenings.

Sometimes the main idea in a paragraph has only one kind of support. Frequently, however, paragraphs contain support of several kinds, called *mixed support*. As you examine the paragraphs that follow, notice the kinds and amounts of support used to develop the topic sentences.

In the following paragraph, the support for the main idea consists of three examples, each of which is explained further with facts and details.

TOPIC SENTENCE

Examples with facts and details

Railroads have a great variety of cars in which to transport different kinds of goods. Perhaps the most familiar is the boxcar, which is completely enclosed with sides and a roof. It carries products that must be protected from the weather or from theft. A stockcar is a boxcar with slatted sides, to allow air for the animals inside. Less familiar, but equally important, is the refrigerator car, a boxcar chilled by means of ice or a machine. The refrigerator car is used to preserve perishable items. These different cars are specialized to suit the many different kinds of cargo that are sent along the rails.—*The New Book of Popular Science*

A topic sentence can also be developed with an incident. In the following paragraph, the topic sentence at the end draws a conclusion from the incident. Notice the use of facts and details to make the incident authentic and interesting and to make the topic sentence convincing.

Incident with facts and details	In April 1912, the RMS *Titanic* left Southampton, England, on her maiden voyage. Less than a week out of port, the *Titanic* was sailing through a dense evening fog when the officers on the bridge sighted an iceberg approaching on the starboard side. Veering to port, the great ship could not clear the submerged arms of the iceberg, and she sideswiped the ice below her water line. Shutting down the engines, the crew immediately closed the watertight doors between the ship's compartments and began pumping out the sea water that had flooded the forward compartments. In less than one hour, the ship had taken in enough water to submerge her bow dangerously and list to starboard. Because of the shortage of lifeboats and jackets, as well as the speed with which the ship sank, 1,517 passengers and crew—more than half of the *Titanic*'s population—perished in the frigid waters of the North Atlantic.
TOPIC SENTENCE	*The sinking of the RMS* Titanic *was one of the worst naval disasters in modern history.*

The final paragraph in this section is also about the sinking of the *Titanic*. It has a topic sentence similar to the one in the preceding paragraph. But unlike the preceding paragraph, which presents an incident, this paragraph simply presents reasons and facts to support the main idea. The paragraph offers three reasons—the loss of lives, the insufficient rescue operations, and poor preparations for emergencies—to explain why this was one of the worst naval disasters in modern history. Notice that facts are used to back up the reasons.

TOPIC SENTENCE	*One of the worst naval disasters in modern history was the sinking of the RMS* Titanic *in the North Atlantic on April 15, 1912.*
Reasons with facts	This event was disastrous because the loss of lives was staggering. Of the 2,224 persons on board, 1,517 perished. Insufficient rescue operations contributed to the disaster. One nearby

understood or overlooked the *Titanic*'s distress signals, and another ship, the *Carpathia*, was several miles' distance away. Perhaps the main reason the collison with the iceberg became a calamity was the lack of preparation for just such an emergency. The ship had lifeboat space for less than half of the ship's passengers and crew and had too few life jackets for all the people aboard.

EXERCISE B: Identifying Support. Reexamine the paragraphs in Exercise A. Then tell which one is developed with (a) examples, (b) facts, (c) reasons, and (d) a full incident.

Unity

A paragraph is unified if all the specific information belongs together and supports one main idea. Any information outside the range of the topic sentence destroys the unity of a paragraph.

A paragraph is unified if all of its sentences illustrate and develop the topic sentence.

If you examine a paragraph without unity, you will see how confusing and unsatisfactory such a paragraph can be. In the following paragraph, the unrelated ideas are italicized.

TOPIC SENTENCE

The basic pattern of penguins, dark above and white below, has survival advantages. In the southern oceans, dense with plankton, the water is murky, and a penguin's dark back viewed from above as it slips through the depths is hard to see. Viewed from below, its white front all but disappears against the silvery light that filters down from the sky. *Penguins look like proud little men in tuxedos. Their flippers, which look like short, stiff arms, have prompted some scientists to argue that penguins never flew. Other scientists, however, maintain that the ancestors of penguins lost their ability to fly and developed their flippers as they adopted other methods of locomotion, such as swimming, sliding on their chests, and running.*

Supporting information without unity

In contrast to the preceding paragraph, the paragraph that follows, taken in its entirety from a magazine, does have unity. It begins with a discussion of the protective coloring of penguins and sticks with this idea throughout instead of changing to a discussion of the appearance of penguins and the development of their flippers.

TOPIC SENTENCE

Supporting information with unity

The basic pattern of penguins, dark above and white below, has survival advantages. In the southern oceans, dense with plankton, the water is murky, and a penguin's dark back viewed from above as it slips through the depths is hard to see. Viewed from below, its white underparts all but disappear against the silvery light that filters down from the sky. This natural camouflage, known as "countershading," serves the penguin well when eluding the leopard seal and the sharks. It matters little that this same bicolored pattern is blatantly conspicuous on the shore; land-based predators are not usually found on the islands where penguins consort for breeding.—Roger Tory Peterson

To maintain the unity of a paragraph, you should examine your supporting information before, during, and after writing the paragraph and ask yourself what each piece of support contributes to the reader's understanding of the main idea. Remove any sentence that does not fit in with the sentences that come before and after it as well as with the paragraph's topic sentence.

EXERCISE C: Recognizing Unity. Read each of the following three paragraphs. If a paragraph is unified, write *unity* on your paper. If a paragraph lacks unity, write down the sentences that stray from the main idea.

(1) A hurricane begins as a small, seemingly insignificant tropical storm and grows into a spinning, rampaging killer. A hurricane first appears as a tropical disturbance caused by a drop in barometric pressure. Tornadoes also result partly from changes in pressure but do not always develop from tropical storms. As the drop in pressure attracts heat, wind activity builds, and the storm begins to move. As it moves, the storm then joins other warm, moisture-laden air and converts to high

winds and rain. Precipitation is not usually a characteristic of tornadoes. Finally, the storm reaches hurricane intensity, spinning counter-clockwise. Few other forces in nature are as unpredictable—and as deadly—as a hurricane.

(2) Cartoons, whether short features or full-length movies, are the product of real team effort. First, artist-writers prepare storyboards, which serve as the cartoon's script. Working with the storyboards, a composer and actors step in to handle the recording of dialogue and music. Then, background artists and animators prepare drawings so that another group of artists can create color cels, transparent celluloid sheets painted in color on their reverse sides that give both color and depth to the final footage. Finally, photographers take frame-by-frame shots of each drawing, the sound track is added, prints are made, and the cartoon is released.

(3) The plot of *Love Story* centers on two characters. Oliver Barrett IV, a boy from a wealthy New England family, is an undergraduate at Harvard University. There, he meets a girl named Jennifer Cavilleri. Though Jennifer is poor, her liveliness and wit attract Oliver, who soon falls in love with her. The story is about the problems involved in their love and marriage. Another character, Mr. Barrett, Oliver's father, disapproves of Oliver and Jennifer's relationship. Still another character, Mr. Cavilleri, Jennifer's father, supports their relationship. The story is also about religious and social differences and prejudices.

Coherence

In addition to being unified, a paragraph should be coherent.

A paragraph is coherent if all of the sentences are ordered logically and connected clearly.

In a coherent paragraph, the writer may guide the reader by using transitions and by repeating main words or finding synonyms for them. Clear pronouns, parallel structures, or a concluding sentence can also help.

Orders for Supporting Information. The following chart shows one of the most common orders used in paragraphs.

ORDERING SUPPORTING INFORMATION	
Order	**How It Works**
Chronological	Major pieces of supporting information or steps are arranged in a time sequence according to when they happened or should happen.
Spatial	Major details and other supporting information are arranged by position—near to far, far to near, top to bottom, and so on.
Order of Importance	Major pieces of supporting information are arranged from least important to most important or vice versa.
Comparison and Contrast	All the supporting information for one item is presented, and then all the supporting information for the other is presented (AAA-BBB) or supporting information for both is compared and contrasted point by point (AB-AB-AB).
Developmental	When none of the other orders fits, support is arranged in the most logical fashion; for instance, several related and equally important items could be mentioned in the topic sentence and then be discussed in that order.

The paragraphs and explanations that follow show how each of the orders in the chart can be used effectively.

Chronological order arranges support in a time sequence, for example, from first to last, from past to present, or from the present to the future. Historical topics, procedures, and processes often follow a time order. In the following paragraph, the words *first, once, then,* and *finally* help the reader see immediately that the support is organized by time.

TOPIC SENTENCE

Students who wish to become doctors must plan on many years of demanding study and strenuous work beyond high school. *First,* they must complete four years of liberal arts studies including certain pre-

Support organized in chronological order

med courses. *Once* they have finished college, premed students must attend medical school, usually for an additional four years of intensive study in medicine. *Then,* following medical school, doctors must complete internship and residency requirements at a hospital or other medical facility for at least another one to two years. *Finally,* when reviewed by supervisors and other doctors, the new doctors are ready to practice their profession.

Spatial order, which organizes ideas over space rather than over time, is most useful for descriptions. It tells a reader the position of each object.

The following paragraph uses spatial order. The words in italics show the placement of each detail, from right to left.

TOPIC SENTENCE

Support organized spatial order

We didn't know where to begin hunting for the baseball glove in the incredibly messy room. *To our right* were shelves littered with broken transistor radios, bowling trophies, erasers, bubble gum, chess pieces, and a plastic tarantula. *In the center* of the room, the sheets and blankets of the bed were barely visible beneath record albums, gym clothes, muddy jeans, and stacks of socks. *The wall on the left* displayed a bicycle rack and an old ten-speed.

Order of importance is particularly useful in paragraphs that persuade as well as in many paragraphs that explain. By building from least important to most important, a writer can gradually gain the audience's understanding or agreement and then conclude forcefully. In the following paragraph, the words *more significant* and *greatest* indicate that the order of the pieces of support is from least important to most important.

TOPIC SENTENCE

Support organized in order of importance

Certain advantages helped the American colonists win their war for independence. The Americans had the initial advantage of fighting on their own soil, whereas English troops had to travel 3,000 miles. A *more significant* advantage was the experience of the Americans; unlike the English, the colonists were already seasoned wilderness fighters, having previously battled to win upstate New York and the Northwest Territory. The *greatest* advantage, however, for the

Americans was the strength, courage, and dedication of such leaders as George Washington, General Nathanael Greene, and John Paul Jones.

Comparison and contrast can be regarded as a purpose as well as a method of organizing ideas. As an order, comparison and contrast has two main variations. You can present all of the supporting information for one item and then compare and contrast the second item with the first: AAA-BBB. Or you can present the similarities or differences between items point by point: AB-AB-AB.

The following paragraph shows the AAA-BBB method of comparison and contrast. Notice the words in italics that guide the reader in understanding the similarities and differences.

TOPIC SENTENCE

Support organized in comparison-and-contrast order (AAA-BBB)

There is a definite distinction between science and engineering. The scientist is usually interested only in extending knowledge of some aspect of the natural world. Scientists want to know why things happen, but are not necessarily interested in useful applications of their discoveries. They usually do not create a product such as a steam-turbine electric generating unit. Their ideas and concepts are their products. Scientists isolate new chemical elements, explore the atom, and make discoveries in fields such as dietetics and thermodynamics. They seek answers to questions concerning space, sound, and nuclear physics. Engineers, *on the other hand,* are concerned with the intelligent application of scientific knowledge to the solution of technical problems. They want to know not only why and how things work, but how they can be made to work better and more economically. Engineers must be cost-conscious, because projects are considered practical only if each dollar invested yields a satisfactory return. Furthermore, the engineer has a definite responsibility for public safety.
—Charles N. Gaylord

The same paragraph could also be written using a point-by-point method of comparison and contrast, as shown in the next paragraph. Notice the words in italics that guide the reader in understanding the similarities and differences.

TOPIC SENTENCE

Support organized in comparison-and-contrast order (AB-AB-AB)

There is a definite distinction between science and engineering. The scientist is usually interested mainly in extending knowledge of some aspect of the natural world. Engineers, *on the other hand,* are concerned with the intelligent application of scientific knowledge to the solution of technical problems. *While* scientists want to know why things happen, they are not necessarily interested in useful applications of their discoveries. Engineers also want to know why and how things work, *but in addition,* they want to discover how things can be made to work better and more economically. Scientists usually do not create a product such as a steam-turbine electric generating unit. *Instead,* their ideas and concepts are their products. Scientists isolate new chemical elements, explore the atom, and make discoveries in such fields as dietetics and thermodynamics. They ask questions concerning space, sound, and nuclear physics. Engineers, *however,* must be cost-conscious, because their projects are considered practical only if each dollar invested yields a satisfactory return. *Furthermore,* the engineer has a definite responsibility for public safety.

Many paragraphs, such as the next one, are in *developmental order*. The sentences work together logically to develop the topic sentence.

TOPIC SENTENCE

Support organized in developmental order

The high point of our seven-park pilgrimage came at Corcovado when we stepped out of the plane into the deep, cool shade of the tropical forest. Huge trees, some more than 200 feet high and six feet in diameter, towered over a rich tangle of smaller trees and vegetation. *Here and there* we heard a sound like the patter of rain and discovered it was thousands of tiny pink and yellow blossoms floating down from tall trees. Hummingbirds hovered *above* the fallen blossoms, whose fragrance mingled with the earthy odor of the damp, decomposing leaves underfoot. *Now and then* there was a loud chattering as parrots flashed by.—Robert and Patricia Cahn

Transitions. Transitions are words and phrases that connect one idea to another. The words italicized in the preceding paragraphs are transitions. By highlighting the logical order of supporting ideas and relating one idea to another, they make paragraphs flow smoothly.

Many words can function as transitions. The following chart presents some examples of transitions grouped according to the orders they usually clarify.

SOME WORDS THAT CAN BE TRANSITIONS			
For Chronological Order		**For Order of Importance**	
after	formerly	also	least
at last	later	another	less
at present	meanwhile	even greater	moreover
before	next	finally	most
during	now	first	next
finally	soon	foremost	one reason
first	then	greatest	primarily
For Spatial Order		**For Comparison and Contrast**	
above	closer	and	like
ahead	in front	although	on the contrary
around	inside	besides	similarly
behind	near	both	than
beneath	outside	however	whereas
beyond	overhead	in addition	while
For Developmental Order			
along with	for example	in fact	other
also	for instance	moreover	therefore
as a result	furthermore	namely	thus
consequently	in addition	next	yet

Other Helpful Words. Repeated main words and well-chosen synonyms and pronouns also help to connect ideas.

The following paragraph uses repetition of main words, synonyms, and a number of clear pronouns. The words in italics form one connecting thread of ideas, and the words in bold letters form another. Notice how these threads contribute to the clarity of the ideas.

TOPIC SENTENCE Support connected by main words, synonyms, and pronouns	For years now on the mud flats on the east side of the San Francisco Bay, *artists* and *ordinary people* have been creating **imaginative sculptures** by nailing together driftwood and debris. *These sculptors* build **trains** and **ballerinas, chickens** and **totem poles, whales** and **airplanes** with wood, hubcaps, old tires, rusty cans, and whatever washes ashore. **Some of the pieces** are skillfully done; **others** are quite crude. **Some** manage to remain standing for a year or two; **others** last only a few days before succumbing to the winds or the tides or the hands of *another artist* who needs the materials for **another work**. Almost **all** are done anonymously, all for the sheer fun of it. The result is an outdoor gallery of **pop art**. The thousands of motorists who daily drive the nearby freeway provide the audience.—Adapted from J. Fritz Lanham

In the preceding paragraph, one thread is formed by the words *artists* and *ordinary people, these sculptors,* and *another artist*. The main thread is the idea *imaginative sculptures,* created with the following words and synonyms: *trains, ballerinas, chickens, totem poles, whales, airplanes, some of the pieces, others, some, others, another work, all,* and *pop art*.

Parallelism and Concluding Sentences. The structure and placement of sentences can also link ideas within paragraphs. *Parallelism* is the use of similar grammatical structures in a series; single words go together, phrases go together, and clauses go together. By writing sentences with parallel clauses, for example, you can indicate to the reader that two ideas are equal in importance.

In the following paragraph, the repetition of the subject-verb pattern and the verb *must be* link the support.

TOPIC SENTENCE Support in parallel sentences	The basic ingredients of an isolated air-mass thunderstorm are fairly simple. The moisture in the air must be plentiful, up to a level of 10,000 feet or higher. The surface of the ground and the air just above it must be heated by the sun. And the atmosphere must be unstable, which means that the air at higher levels must be a great deal cooler than the air at lower levels. —Adapted from Henry Lansford

A *concluding sentence* can sometimes be used to strengthen the coherence of a paragraph. A concluding sentence can summarize the supporting ideas in a paragraph, restate the topic sentence in different words, or function as a punch-line by expressing a final point forcefully. This last kind of concluding sentence is often called a *clincher*.

In the following paragraph, Virginia Woolf's description of the wax statue of Queen Elizabeth I in the Abbey Waxworks ends with a concluding sentence that echoes the topic sentence and captures the mood of the paragraph.

TOPIC SENTENCE

The Queen dominates the room as she once dominated England. Leaning a little forward so that she seems to beckon you to come to her, she stands, holding her sceptre in one hand, her orb in the other. It is a drawn, anguished figure, with the pursed look of someone who goes in perpetual dread of poison or a trap; yet forever braces herself to meet the terror unflinchingly. Her eyes are wide and vigilant; her nose thin as the beak of a hawk; her lips shut tight; her eyebrows arched; only the jowl gives the fine drawn face its massiveness. The orb and the sceptre are held in the long thin hands of an artist, as if the fingers thrilled at the touch of them. She is immensely intellectual, suffering, and tyrannical. *She will not allow one to look elsewhere.*—Virginia Woolf

Concluding sentence

EXERCISE D: Recognizing Orders of Supporting Information. Identify the kind of order used in each paragraph.

(1) The surface of a mountain may appear placid, quiet, and covered with snow. Yet beneath the surface, the weight of the snow compresses itself at the lower levels. Deeper down, the weight of the snow displaces air and forms layers of ice. One layer of ice slides along another. From thousands of feet beneath the surface, a glacier "walks."

(2) Buster Keaton produced one kind of comedy, Charlie Chaplin quite another. And Keaton's was the purer use of the form. Keaton was cool, detached, and very strictly funny, never suggesting for a moment that we need worry ourselves about what might happen to him. If a building fell on him during a

cyclone, we were not to be apprehensive: When the dust cleared, he would be standing in the small space made safe for him by an open second-story window. Keaton himself never displayed emotion. Chaplin's comedy, by comparison, was blurred. Chaplin would be in love with a girl until she snatched a bit of his food. Then he hit her. But there would be none of Keaton's detachment or objectivity in the quick slap. Chaplin would be momentarily asserting his self-interest. And yet a moment later he would sigh and share everything he had with the girl. As comedy, Chaplin's work is hopelessly impure. Yet no one has ever questioned Chaplin's superiority to Keaton. The impure comedian is greater than the pure comedian: He shows us *more;* he shows us who he is and how he got that way. —Walter Kerr

(3) The presence of scientists is no accident, for Costa Rica is a kind of Mecca for tropical research. It has sweltering lowland rain forests along both Caribbean and southern Pacific coasts; dry, thorny forests along the northern Pacific Coast; and cool, lush cloud forests in the central mountains. As part of a narrow land bridge joining two continents, it has an exceptional variety of fauna and flora. At Corcovado, American scientist Gary Hartshorn once identified 111 different species of trees on a two-acre plot. Costa Rica has close to 800 species of birds, over 100 more than can be found in all of North America above Mexico.—Robert and Patricia Cahn

(4) In colonial America a family's place on the social scale might vary considerably through the course of two or three generations. Several factors account for this relatively high degree of social mobility. For one, America had no titled aristocracy, no dukes and duchesses, lords and ladies, monopolizing positions of political and economic power. For another, labor was constantly in great demand, and a man willing to work hard could move up the social scale. Still more significant was the cheap land available in the unsettled interior of the country. People discontented with their life in established communities could move in search of new opportunities.—Adapted from the *Encyclopedia Americana*

EXERCISE E: Recognizing the Devices That Add Coherence. For each paragraph in Exercise D, make a list of (a) transitions and (b) one set of main words, synonyms, and pronouns. Then write down (c) any parallel sentences and (d) the concluding sentence of the one paragraph that does have a strong concluding sentence.

EXERCISE F: Improving Coherence. Rewrite the following paragraph to improve its coherence. Use transitions and a concluding sentence to help clarify the topic sentence. Also make use of any other devices you think will help.

(1) In the movie *Breaking Away,* the title has a number of meanings. (2) The movie features a bicycle race. (3) When a rider "breaks away," takes the lead, and charges ahead of the rest of the pack, the audience feels like cheering. (4) Four friends in the movie spend the year after their high school graduation drifting with little to do and no goals for their lives. (5) Dave Stoller's obsession with bicycles helps him to escape from the discontent and aimlessness of Mike, Cyril, and Moocher. (6) The setting is the university town of Bloomington, Indiana. (7) The young residents of the town, called "cutters" because the townspeople once engaged in marble cutting, resent the university students and feel inferior to them. (8) Dave leaves the "cutters" to enroll in the university.

Special Kinds of Paragraphs

A standard paragraph includes a topic sentence and logically presented support. Occasionally, you will encounter paragraphs by professional writers which differ from the standard in some way. Such paragraphs may have an implied rather than a stated topic sentence, or they may consist of only one or two sentences.

Special paragraphs differ from the standard paragraph but remain unified and logical.

These special kinds of paragraphs differ from the standard because they have special purposes. They usually work with standard paragraphs in a longer piece of writing, sometimes serving as an introduction, a conclusion, or a transition or connection between standard paragraphs.

In the following passage, even though the second and third paragraphs are not standard, each nonetheless has a clear purpose, as well as unity and coherence. The second paragraph contains no clear topic sentence. Instead, its purpose is to present details that support the first paragraph. Notice that the second paragraph sticks to the topic. Furthermore, transitions such as *nearby* give the information a clear spatial order. The third paragraph is also nonstandard, since it consists of a single sentence. Its purpose is to act as a clincher for the preceding two paragraphs.

Standard (main idea and support)	After decades of neglect, the industrial area at the edge of town showed signs of irreversible decay. Once it had been the home of several prosperous manufacturing concerns, but that had all changed long ago. Few businesses, and even fewer residents, remained. Those that did faced a bleak prospect.
Not standard (support arranged spatially to develop paragraph 1)	Hills of garbage, sprinkled with paper and tin, and swamps, with half-submerged machinery rusting, bordered the highway. Nearby, thick smoke billowed from industrial pipes like evil vapors from a witch's cauldron. Fumes reeking of gasoline, roach and mosquito spray, burning rubber, and stewing garbage seeped through the airvents and cracks of passing cars.
Not standard	It was a wasted land.

If you want to use nonstandard paragraphs in your own writing, you must first be able to identify them as having one of several legitimate purposes. Learn to identify nonstandard paragraphs as either introductory, concluding, or transitional and make sure that the paragraph sticks to that purpose.

EXERCISE G: Understanding Special Kinds of Paragraphs. Identify the two nonstandard paragraphs in the following passage. Then label them as *introductory, concluding,* or *transitional.*

(1) Some department stores exhibit a new attitude toward shoppers: Confuse and conquer. They cleverly manipulate shoppers into buying.

(2) With attractive displays of elegantly furnished rooms, of towels, sheets, and quilts in designer prints and flashy colors, and of jaunty mannequins in the latest suits and sportswear, the stores overwhelm the shopper. Unintentionally the shopper flits from rack to rack like a butterfly, forgetting what he or she intended to get and finding additional things to buy. The hanging mirrors and glittering mirror walls multiply the dazzle, increasing the shopper's disorientation even more.

(3) In addition, department stores often have puzzling organizations. One item, such as blouses or shoes, may be scattered throughout the store in four or five little sections like boutiques. The shopper cannot easily get an overview of the entire selection and then choose one item. Consequently, the shopper may wander from section to section and end up buying two blouses or two sports shirts instead of one. Or on some floors, one department may spill over into the next, again exposing the shopper to the appeal of more merchandise.

(4) Artistically stocked with everything from tie tacks to silk flowers and from swim suits to Persian rugs, some department stores have become powerful persuaders, tempting the shopper to make unnecessary purchases.

DEVELOPING WRITING SKILLS: Recognizing the Ingredients of a Paragraph. Write down the following information about the paragraph below: (a) the topic sentence; (b) the order of the supporting information; (c) any transitions; (d) one set of repeated main words, synonyms, and pronouns; and (e) any use of parallelism.

(1) In recent years, a new method of using the computer called "time-sharing" has become popular. (2) It makes the computer more convenient for many people to use. (3) Time-sharing computer systems still have all the usual pieces of equipment but, in addition, they have input/output devices called terminals which can be located in the next room, the next block, the next town, or thousands of miles away. (4) The terminals can be connected to the central computer by ordinary telephone lines. (5) With time-sharing, users can input their data and immediately receive the output right in their offices, at a department store check-out counter, in the warehouse, the classroom, or even in their homes.—Judith B. Edwards

20.2 Planning Your Paragraph

Although the writing process can differ somewhat from person to person, following certain basic planning, writing, and revising steps can help you prepare your paragraphs.

PREWRITING: Exploring Topics

As you begin preparing a paragraph, you must first generate ideas for topics.

Generating Ideas. To generate possible ideas for topics, think of your interests and experiences. You can also use techniques such as interviewing yourself, free writing, journal writing, reading and saving, clustering, cueing, and brainstorming to find ideas for topics. (These techniques are presented in Section 17.1.)

Choosing and Narrowing a Topic. A suitable paragraph topic is one that you can comfortably develop in a single paragraph. In order to do this, you should make sure that the topic you choose is not too big or too general.

Narrow a general topic into a smaller topic that can be managed in a single paragraph.

You may have decided to write a paragraph about, for example, water-skiing. But you could never say all there is to say about water-skiing in one paragraph, so you would have to find a narrower, more focused topic. The following chart shows the general topic divided into smaller ones.

Any one of the narrowed topics would be suitable for a para-

NARROWING A PARAGRAPH TOPIC	
Broad Topic	**Narrowed Paragraph Topics**
water-skiing	equipment needed for water-skiing
	resorts featuring water-skiing
	water-skiing versus snow skiing
	safety on water skis
	water-skiing for the first time

graph. You would choose your final topic by deciding which one interested you the most or seemed likely to have the fullest supporting information.

Focusing on a Main Idea. To decide what you want to say in your topic sentence, you will have to probe your thoughts and the paragraph topic further. Thinking about your audience will help you select and focus on a main idea. Often you can find a main idea about a topic if you first determine the interests, background, and knowledge of your audience. Ask yourself questions about your topic that you think your audience might like to have answered. You should learn to think of questions that can stimulate your own thinking as well: Why are *you* interested in the topic?

Another decision involves your purpose. Will you be explaining, persuading, describing, or telling a story? You must make these decisions before you will be ready to write your topic sentence.

Think about your audience to focus on a main idea for your paragraph. Consider your purpose as well.

The following chart shows some questions you might ask yourself to generate ideas about one of the paragraph topics on water-skiing.

QUESTIONS LEADING TO POSSIBLE MAIN IDEAS	
Paragraph Topic: Water-skiing for the first time	
Questions	**Main Ideas**
Why am I interested in the topic?	Last summer I learned how to water-ski.
What is a major idea about this topic?	The first time on water skis can be difficult.
What would my audience want to know about this topic?	Water-skiing can be a memorable experience, especially the first time.

When you have examined several different main ideas, you should select one to write about. Make sure that the main idea you select suits your audience and your purpose. Notice that in the first idea in the preceding chart, your purpose would probably be to tell a story, in the second idea your purpose would be to explain, and in the third idea, your purpose would be to describe.

Writing Your Topic Sentence. With the answers to your questions about the main idea, you are now ready to write your topic sentence.

State your main idea in a topic sentence that is appropriate to your audience and purpose.

You should actually write at least two versions of your topic sentence. Try different words, maybe different lengths, as you attempt to express the main idea clearly and concisely.

If you were using the third of the main ideas listed in the chart, you might write these versions of your topic sentence.

POSSIBLE TOPIC SENTENCES

1. Water-skiing for the first time is a memorable experience.
2. Your first time on water skis may be nerve-wracking.
3. The first-time water skier is liable to be nervous.
4. The first time on water skis can be a strain on both nerves and muscles.

Although you could use any of these four topic sentences, some of them are more focused than others. For example, the first topic sentence is the most open-ended of the four because it tells the reader the least about the paragraph that will follow. The other three experiment with slightly different wordings. You might choose the fourth version to be your topic sentence because it gives the most information to the reader and the clearest guidelines to you.

EXERCISE A: Narrowing Topics for Paragraphs. From the list of general topics at the top of the next page, choose the five that appeal to you most and write them on your paper. Beneath each, write two smaller topics that might be suitable for a paragraph. Then circle the one smaller topic that you would most like to write about.

Home Movies	Travel	Professional sports
Boats	Safety hazards	Classical music
Weather	Camping	Biographies
Astronomy	Crafts	Car engines
Conservation	Deserts	Favorite movies
Being a good sport	Friendship	Unusual jobs
Gardening	Archaeology	Car safety
Hobbies	School spirit	High-tech careers

EXERCISE B: Preparing Topic Sentences. Using the paragraph topic that you chose in Exercise A, follow these steps.

1. Write the paragraph topic on your paper.
2. Decide on your audience and briefly describe it (for example, people unfamiliar with the topic, experts, strangers, friends, and so on).
3. Find possible main ideas about your paragraph topic by asking yourself at least three questions. Write the questions and your answers on your paper.
4. Identify the probable purpose of each idea: to inform or explain, to persuade, to describe, or to entertain.
5. Choose the main idea that best suits your audience and the purpose you have in mind.
6. Write three versions of your topic sentence.
7. Finally, choose the topic sentence that most clearly expresses your main idea and that has the greatest appeal to you. Circle it.

PREWRITING: Brainstorming for Support

Once you have a topic sentence, your second major step is to gather the supporting information that will explain and develop your main idea.

Gathering Supporting Information. The main idea in your topic sentence, even the words you have chosen to express that idea, can help you come up with supporting information.

Brainstorm for examples, details, facts, reasons, and incidents that explain the main idea in your topic sentence.

Your goal is to produce a list of strong, relevant supporting information that will fulfill the expectations set up by your topic sentence. Two possible methods you can use to achieve this goal are (1) using questions to determine the information your audience might want to know about your main idea and (2) free-associating with your topic sentence to find related ideas.

Using the questioning method, you should put yourself in the reader's place and try to see your topic sentence as your reader would see it. Ask yourself questions that you would want answered if you were part of your audience. Then answer the questions with information about the main idea. The following chart shows a list of possible questions and answers for the topic sentence on water-skiing.

QUESTIONING TO FIND SUPPORT FOR A TOPIC SENTENCE

Topic Sentence: The first time on water skis can be a strain on both nerves and muscles.

How is it a strain on nerves?	
—clumsy skis are hard to manage, making the skier nervous —many different things have to be done at once in order to stay afloat	—people in the boat are watching the novice skier —experienced skiers are all around
How is it a strain on muscles?	
—constant shifts of weight to maintain balance —choppy waves put a strain on leg muscles —holding the towline uses arm, shoulder, and back muscles	—the beginner will probably be stiff and sore the next day

While you are writing down answers that occur to you, you should put down all the different examples, details, facts, reasons, and incidents that answer the questions. Later you can sort out and discard unimportant answers.

The second method, free-associating with your topic sentence, can also produce many possible pieces of supporting information. To free-associate, write your topic sentence at the top of your paper. Read it carefully several times. As you concentrate on your topic sentence, write down all the ideas that occur to you until you have a list of possible support. If you used the free-associating method with the topic sentence on water-skiing, you might jot down a list like the following.

FREE-ASSOCIATING TO FIND SUPPORT FOR A TOPIC SENTENCE

Topic Sentence: The first time on water skis can be a strain on both nerves and muscles.

—people in the boat are watching the novice skier
—experienced skiers are all around
—the novice skier can become confused and embarrassed by an unwelcome audience
—clumsy skis are hard to manage, making the skier nervous
—choppy waves put a strain on leg muscles
—beginner may be worried about the possibility of injury from possible collision or from tumbling into the water at fairly high speed
—holding on to the towline uses arm, shoulder, and back muscles
—constant shifts of weight to maintain balance put a strain on leg muscles
—the beginner will probably be stiff and sore the next day

You may sometimes find it useful to revise your topic sentence to fit the support you have actually gathered.

Checking for Unity. With either the questioning method or the free-associating method of finding support information, you will probably gather much more information than you can actually use in one paragraph. Therefore, you should evaluate your list and remove any information that does not directly bear on your main idea.

Eliminate unrelated information and fill in any gaps you notice in your list of support.

As you read each item on your list, ask yourself, "Does this piece of information help to explain or illustrate my main idea? Is this piece of information necessary to explain another piece of information?" Any item that does not meet one of these requirements should be crossed out.

In the list of support about water-skiing, you would probably want to delete the information about experienced water-skiers and people in the boat watching the novice skier, since it does not directly relate to the experience of water-skiing. You might also want to add further information about the sequence of events in getting up on skis, to reinforce the main idea of what the experience was actually like. Your revised list of support would then look like the following.

EVALUATING A LIST OF SUPPORTING INFORMATION

Topic Sentence: The first time on water skis can be a strain on both nerves and muscles.

How is it a strain on nerves?

—clumsy skis are hard to manage, making the skier nervous

—many different things have to be done at once in order to stay afloat

—people in the boat are watching the novice skier

—experienced skiers are all around

How is it a strain on muscles?

—constant shifts of weight to maintain balance

—choppy waves put a strain on leg muscles

—holding the towline uses arm, shoulder, and back muscles

—the beginner will probably be stiff and sore the next day

—learning how to get on and off the skis

EXERCISE C: Brainstorming for Support. Use your topic sentence from Exercise B in the following prewriting steps.

1. Write your topic sentence on your paper.
2. Use either the questioning method or the free-associating method to find supporting information for your main idea. Revise your topic sentence if that seems necessary to make it fit your supporting information.
3. Check your list of support for unity and thoroughness. Using another color, cross out the pieces of information that do not directly contribute to your main idea. Add any other pieces of information that will help develop the main idea.

PREWRITING: Organizing Your Support

Before you actually write out your paragraph in complete sentences, you should carefully organize your supporting information. First, choose a logical order for the paragraph. Examine the information to see if a particular kind of logical order naturally suggests itself or seems especially appropriate. Then you should prepare a modified outline to guide you as you write.

Organize your supporting information logically and prepare an outline.

If you were organizing the support gathered for the topic sentence on water-skiing, you might decide that chronological order would most logically fit the main idea and supporting information. After reexamining the topic sentence, you might decide to organize the paragraph around three steps in the process of getting on and off the skis. You would then list the other information logically under each of these steps and write down the topic sentence. You might also add a possible concluding sentence. Your outline might then look like this:

<u>Topic Sentence</u>
The first time on water skis can be a strain on both nerves and muscles.

<u>Starting on skis</u>
1. Handling awkward, buoyant skis
2. Getting into position to begin
3. Taking the towline
4. Starting the boat and launching

<u>Staying afloat</u>
1. Weighting both skis equally to maintain balance
2. Trying not to cross the boat's wake

<u>Stopping</u>
1. The boat slowing down
2. Letting go of the towline and skiing toward shore
3. Gradually sinking into the water

<u>Concluding Sentence</u>
If the beginner succeeds in staying on top of the water for long, his or her shoulders, arms, back, and thighs will probably feel sore and stiff the next day.

EXERCISE D: Organizing Supporting Information. Use the supporting information that you gathered in Exercise C in the following steps.

1. Examine your list of supporting information to see which order fits your topic the best and which most clearly develops your main idea for your audience. Then choose an order (chronological order, spatial order, order of importance, comparison-and-contrast order, or developmental order) and write your choice on your paper.
2. Put your supporting information in an outline according to the order you have chosen. Write your complete topic sentence and your complete concluding sentence, if you can think of an appropriate one, at the beginning and end of your outline.

DEVELOPING WRITING SKILLS: Planning Paragraphs. Select a general topic of your own. Divide the topic into three narrowed topics suitable for paragraphs. Write a different topic sentence for each narrowed topic, gather different supporting information for each, and organize the supporting information for each topic in a different way.

20.3 Drafting Your Paragraph

By this point in the writing process, you have put a good deal of time and effort into preparing a thorough and logical paragraph. Once you have an outline, you should be able to draft the paragraph rapidly.

WRITING: Creating a First Draft

With your outline before you, begin writing your paragraph by putting your ideas in complete sentences. Use transitions and other linking devices to make the relationship between your ideas logical and clear to the reader.

Use transitions, repetitions of main words, synonyms, pronouns, and, possibly, parallelism to write a first draft based on your outline.

If you were to write a draft from the outline in the last section, your paragraph would probably resemble the following paragraph. Notice the transitions, in italic, and the repeated main words and synonyms. Also notice that some of the ideas in the outline have been worded slightly differently in the complete draft.

TOPIC SENTENCE — The first time on water skis can be a strain on both nerves and muscles. The beginner usually wades out waist deep in the water and tries to put on the awkward, buoyant skis. *Then* the nervous skier crouches with the tips of the skis sticking out of the water. *Soon* the people in the boat throw the skier the towline. The skier tells the driver to "Hit it," and the boat leaps ahead, the line tightens, and the skier is yanked out of the water. If the beginner does not weight both skis equally and pull against the tug of the boat, he or she will fall over. *After* getting up on skis, the skier must face the boat's bumpy, frothy wake by skiing in it or outside it. The choppy little waves can upset the skiers balance. When the beginner's muscles have fought the steady pull for a while, someone in the boat usually motions to the skier asking him or her for instructions to slow down, speed up, or head for shore. *To stop,* the skier lets go of the towline and skis off toward the shore, gradually sinking into the water. If the beginner has succeeded in staying on top of the water for long, his or her shoulders, arms, back, and thighs will probably feel sore and stiff *the next day*.

Support organized chronologically

Concluding sentence

EXERCISE: Writing a First Draft. Before you begin to write your paragraph from your outline in Exercise C on page 498, list some of the transitions and some of the main words and synonyms you will use in the paragraph. Then with your outline in front of you, draft your paragraph. Put all the ideas in the outline in complete sentences. Try to include transitions as you move from thought to thought and sentence to sentence. When you have completed your first draft, underline the transitions and add others if you need them to make the paragraph more coherent. Label your topic sentence and your concluding sentence, if you have one.

DEVELOPING WRITING SKILLS: Writing a Paragraph. Think of a general topic of your own and follow these instructions.

1. Narrow the general topic to one suitable for a paragraph.
2. Choose your audience and think about your purpose.
3. Ask yourself questions to find a main idea about your paragraph topic and write a topic sentence.
4. Use either the questioning or the free-associating method to brainstorm for supporting examples, details, facts, reasons, or incidents. Revise your topic sentence, if necessary, to fit your supporting information.
5. Study your list of support and eliminate unrelated information. Add information to give complete support.
6. Choose an order for the supporting information in your paragraph and outline the paragraph.
7. Draft the paragraph from the outline. Concentrate on connecting your ideas logically with transitions, main words, synonyms, and pronouns.
8. Exchange paragraphs with someone in your class and write down two strengths and two weaknesses of the other student's paragraph.
9. Reread your own paragraph and the other person's comments. Make any necessary changes to improve clarity and smoothness.
10. Recopy your paragraph.

20.4 Polishing Your Paragraph

Once you have completed your first draft, you have accomplished a big task. However, your writing should not stop here. Now you should reexamine your paragraph to make sure that all the parts work together to communicate your ideas. This final step is called revision.

REVISING: Using a Checklist

Whenever you complete a first draft, evaluate your paragraph by asking yourself questions about it.

Use a checklist to evaluate the first draft of a paragraph.

The following questions are a tool for revising. They will help you analyze your paragraph objectively.

CHECKLIST FOR REVISING
1. Does the topic sentence clearly focus and express the main idea of the paragraph?
2. Does the paragraph contain enough examples, details, facts, reasons, or incidents to develop the topic sentence?
3. Is all of the supporting information appropriate? Is any of the supporting information weak, vague, or repetitive?
4. Does the paragraph stick to the main idea?
5. Is the supporting information presented in the most logical order?
6. Are there enough transitions, repetitions of main words, synonyms, and pronouns to connect the ideas?
7. Is a concluding sentence needed to wrap up the ideas of the paragraph?
8. Does the paragraph as a whole achieve its purpose? Will the audience find the paragraph interesting?
9. Are there choppy, awkward, or confusing passages?
10. Are there any mistakes in grammar, mechanics, or spelling?

Using this checklist will help you to discover problems that should be corrected in your paragraphs.

EXERCISE A: Evaluating a Paragraph. Use the checklist on this page to examine a paragraph you have recently written. Write down an answer for each question about your paragraph. Then write a few sentences evaluating the overall strengths and weaknesses of your paragraph.

REVISING: Improving Your Topic Sentence

You should always make sure that your topic sentence does not set up false expectations. A topic sentence that does not fit in with the rest of the paragraph will confuse a reader.

Revise a topic sentence that is too general or too specific for your paragraph's support.

In the following paragraph, the broad topic sentence at the end does not accurately sum up the preceding details.

Overly general topic sentence

Lines now etched his forehead and circled his eyes. He had developed an uncontrollable quiver about the hands, and his eyelids seemed to blink more rapidly than normal. When he walked, his strides were short and unsure, and his shoulders had acquired a droop. As each month of worry, unsolved problems, and new conflicts passed, his body resisted more feebly. *Many people in his position have suffered similarly.*

The writer could improve this paragraph with a topic sentence that gives a reason for the man's appearance: *His short term as President had aged him immensely.*

In the following paragraph, the overly narrow topic sentence prepares the reader for only one of several supporting ideas.

Overly narrow topic sentence

Thomas Edison invented the incandescent light bulb. Trying to create small light bulbs that could be used indoors, he sensed that the key to making them work was to find the right material for the filament (the wire that actually "lights" the bulb). When he accomplished this by using carbonized thread, Edison earned the title "The Wizard of Menlo Park." This title was well deserved because he had already invented the stock ticker, a machine that was used from its invention until recently, when Wall Street changed to computers. He also invented motion pictures and the mimeograph machine, and he improved the typewriter and the telephone. Edison's personal favorite among his inventions was the phonograph, claimed to be among the most novel ideas ever conceived.

In addition to the light bulb, the supporting information in the preceding paragraph mentions other Edison inventions: the stock ticker, motion pictures, the mimeograph machine, and the phonograph. It also mentions improvements in the typewriter and the telephone. A better topic sentence would be *Thomas Edison was involved in many conveniences we take for granted.*

EXERCISE B: Revising Topic Sentences. Identify the topic sentences in the following paragraphs as *too general* or *too narrow*. Then rewrite each topic sentence to suit its paragraph.

(1) Shakespeare's plays are noted for happy endings. Among his comedies, *Measure for Measure* and *The Tempest* are mostly serious, dramatic pieces, but they end satisfactorily for the principal characters. Other comedies, such as *The Taming of the Shrew* and *A Midsummer Night's Dream,* are boisterously funny and, again, end happily. But among Shakespeare's many tragedies, happy endings are not on the program. At the ends of plays such as *Hamlet, Macbeth,* and *Othello,* the principal characters die tragically or suffer terrible emotional pain.

(2) Insomnia is one of many health problems experienced by Americans. One cause, some claim, is poor eating habits. Drinking coffee or tea late at night may result in wakefulness. Overeating, particularly on a regular basis, can result in a continual state of indigestion, robbing the overeater of normal patterns and routines. Most experts, however, believe that nervous conditions—worry and deeper forms of anxiety—are the chief villains. And although doctors will often explore an insomniac's eating habits, treatment for insomnia usually depends on curing or easing nervous conditions.

(3) The Colosseum of ancient Rome stood imposingly at the center of the great city. An enormous circular amphitheater, it was more than six hundred feet in diameter. Over four stories high, it seated at least fifty thousand spectators in long, semicircular tiers. The condition of the structure today, however, will disappoint the sightseer who does not expect the ravages of centuries. The Colosseum now stands partly, or largely, in ruins. The central tiers have long since fallen, and the vast arena and subterranean passages are buried. The grand outer walls, including two layers of proud arches, have partially crumbled. Yet by inspecting the ruins and using imagination, the visitor can still piece together the splendor that once was Rome.

(4) Greenfield Village, near Detroit, is just one of the many interesting tourist attractions in Michigan. The village, created by Henry Ford, contains a fascinating group of special exhibits. One building brings together thousands of watches from the

medieval period to the present. The Wright brothers' bicycle repair shop, bodily transported from its original site, is next door. Thomas Edison's workshop is perhaps even more striking. In homage to Edison, Ford had the workshop transported from its original location in Menlo Park, New Jersey. Ford had workers sift through all the dirt around the Menlo Park site for relics of Edison's genius. Consequently, bits of paper, pieces of trash, and fossilized lumps of chewing gum have all been placed on display along with more important objects for posterity to wonder at.

REVISING: Improving Your Support

Besides reexamining your topic sentence, you should look again at the extent and quality of your support.

Revise weak support by adding or replacing examples, details, facts, reasons, and incidents.

When you revise your paragraphs, you may discover that you did not include enough specific information or that you left out information as you drafted your paragraph.

The following paragraph illustrates the problem of inadequate support. The topic sentence suggests that many examples will follow, but the writer has mentioned only a few.

Paragraph with inadequate supporting information

Washington, D.C., can occupy a visitor for days merely with trips to museums. A visitor can study the replicas of Colonial American homes and the displays that document the history of our government in the National Museum of History and Technology. The National Museum of Natural History houses some of the world's largest diamonds, rubies, and emeralds.

By giving more thought to the paragraph, the writer could revise it to include enough examples to fulfill the promise of the topic sentence.

Paragraph with thorough supporting information

Washington, D.C., can occupy a visitor for days merely with trips to museums. A visitor can study replicas of Colonial American homes and displays that document the history of our government in the National Museum of History and Technology. The National Museum of Natural History houses some of the world's largest diamonds, rubies, and emeralds, as well as meteorites, mummies, dinosaur skeletons, reptiles, birds, and mammals. Yet another museum, the National Air and Space Museum, chronicles the history of flight from balloons and Lindbergh's *Spirit of St. Louis* to today's rockets and missiles.

A paragraph can also fail if it does not have the right kind of supporting information. Check to make sure that your support is not repetitious, general, or full of opinions.

The following paragraph contains repetitious sentences, generalized statements, and unsupported opinions. Notice that the paragraph is vague and unconvincing.

Repetitions, generalized statements, and unsupported opinions

Recently a number of near accidents involving taxis on Pelham Road have caused concern among residents. Taxis collecting and discharging commuters and travelers at the train station are entirely to blame. Taxis should not be allowed in the town. All the taxi drivers exceed the speed limit and drive recklessly. Every day residents see taxis jumping the traffic lights, careening around corners, and barely missing children on bicycles and elderly residents with their shopping carts. The taxis are completely at fault for these near collisions. Taxis are a menace to life and limb.

When specific support replaces the repetitions, generalizations, and opinions, the paragraph gains strength and credibility.

Specific supporting information

Recently a number of near accidents involving taxis on Pelham Road have caused concern among residents. Taxis collecting and discharging commuters and travelers at the train station have been involved in most of the close calls. Four residents have filed complaints with the town police, reporting that taxis have exceeded the speed limit. Last month our neighbor observed a taxi jumping the light and careening around a corner, barely missing two children on bicycles and an elderly woman with a shopping cart. Last week another taxi sideswiped a parked car on

Pelham Road. As a result of these dangerous incidents, the town police and officials have promised to investigate the driving practices and safety records of local taxi drivers.

EXERCISE C: Revising Support. Revise each paragraph using specific examples, details, facts, reasons, or incidents.

(1) By the end of the nineteenth century, immigrants from Europe had good reason to come to America. They saw America as a land of opportunity, where steady work was available and where farming land could be purchased cheaply. Immigrants looked to America for acceptance and equality.

(2) People who smoke have neither respect for their own bodies nor concern for the health and comfort of those around them. People are foolish to continue this dreadful habit despite the warnings of the Surgeon General. Smoking is not a healthy habit, and it is unclean besides. Smoking is an irritating habit that infringes on the rights of others.

(3) Many television commercials insult the audience in a variety of ways. Some commercials for detergent, for example, make the people in them appear stupid. Other commercials make idle boasts about the superiority of one product over another. Viewers can sense that the comparison is unfair and that the results are fabricated.

(4) The first landing on the moon was an exciting historic event. What a thrill it was to see people actually walking on the moon. Nothing people have ever done, or ever will do, can rival the accomplishment of the first landing on the moon. It was a truly earth-shaking occurrence. Everyone was proud.

REVISING: Checking for Unity

Another weakness that may sometimes need correcting during revision is lack of unity. You can improve sentences that lack unity by removing sentences and ideas that do not relate to the topic sentence. You may also need to rewrite some of the other sentences in your paragraph to make your words read smoothly.

Restore unity by eliminating unrelated or insignificant ideas.

In the following paragraph, the unrelated sentences which would confuse a reader are in italics.

Paragraph with unrelated ideas

Canada's geographical dimensions are impressive. Canada covers the continent of North America from the Atlantic to the Pacific. *It is a growing nation producing nuclear power as well as other industrial commodities. And it is a nation of fishermen. Canadians export tons of cod and lobsters annually.* Canada's northern boundary stretches toward the North Pole and includes the frozen Arctic region. On its southern boundary, it borders the entire United States from the state of Washington to the state of Maine, a distance of 4,000 miles. As a result, Canada covers an area of 3.8 million square miles, second in size only to the Soviet Union.

In this case, the writer can improve the paragraph by simply removing the unrelated ideas and thus shortening the paragraph. If you read the paragraph leaving out the unrelated sentences, you will notice how much clearer the paragraph is. In some cases it might be necessary to rewrite some sentences for smoothness after the unrelated information has been removed.

EXERCISE D: Revising for Unity. Rewrite the following paragraph, removing unrelated information and making any other necessary changes for smoothness.

(1) Twenty years ago roller-skating was almost the exclusive activity of children after school and on Sunday afternoons. (2) But more recently the sport was taken up by a much wider age group. (3) Skating became both a method of transportation that was faster than walking and an opportunity for a new form of dancing, which brought discos out onto the sidewalks. (4) Disco music was a phenomenon of the 1970's much the same as rock music was a creation of the 1950's. (5) People used to sit around and simply listen to rock music, but people danced to disco music. (6) Rock music fans looked unfavorably on disco in the same way that waltzers found rock and roll offensive.

REVISING: Improving Coherence

The coherence of your paragraphs requires special attention during the revising stage. During the writing stage, you are likely to have focused mainly on expressing your ideas in complete sentences and on following your outline. The revising stage enables you to reexamine your writing for logical order, clear relationships between ideas, and the flow of your words.

Improve coherence by clarifying logical order, adding transitions, and repeating main words, synonyms, and pronouns.

You can often clarify the logical order of a paragraph by choosing your transitions more carefully. Transitions act as signals to tell the reader what kind of logical order is being used. In addition, transitions can make your important pieces of supporting information stand out for the reader. They can improve the meaning as well as the flow of ideas.

Repeating certain words and using synonyms and pronouns for those words can also help you connect the ideas in a paragraph. As you revise, determine if you have used main words clearly and if you have employed useful synonyms and consistent pronouns.

The following paragraph does not achieve coherence. Its logical order is not made clear to the reader. Nor are there enough transitions and repeated main words.

Paragraph lacking coherence

Students interested in geology must understand the term "mineral." Minerals are chemical elements or compounds of different chemicals. These solid substances can be identified by their physical and chemical properties. A characteristic of many minerals is color. Jadeite is often bright green, although it sometimes appears brown or yellow. Spodumene appears pink or opaque. Minerals can be identified by their relative hardness. Some minerals can be scratched with a fingernail. Others can only be scratched by a harder substance, such as a knife. Many minerals, particularly crystals, can be split and examined for shape. When the mineral obsidian is fractured, it splits in a clearly circular pattern.

When transitions are added to identify examples and connect ideas, the paragraph gains smoothness and sharpness. The logical order has been clarified and reinforced; key words have been repeated to link ideas further.

Coherent paragraph with logical order, transitions, and repetitions

Students interested in geology must understand the term "mineral." Minerals are chemical elements or compounds of different chemicals. These solid substances can be identified by their physical and chemical properties. *The most noticeable characteristic* of many minerals is color. Jadeite, *for example,* is often bright green, although it sometimes appears brown or yellow. *Another mineral,* spodumene, appears pink or opaque. Minerals can *also* be identified by their relative hardness. Some minerals, *for instance,* can be scratched with a fingernail. Others can only be scratched by a harder substance, such as a knife. *Finally,* many minerals, particularly crystals, can be split and examined for shape. When the mineral obsidian is fractured, it splits in a clearly circular pattern.

EXERCISE E: Improving Coherence. Rewrite the following paragraph to improve coherence. Reorganize supporting information to clarify the logical order, add transitions, and repeat some main words, synonyms, and pronouns.

(1) A new driver in a standard shift car may think that tollbooths were invented for an octopus: Eight arms or legs *might* be enough to perform the many simultaneous actions required. (2) While the car immediately ahead goes through the tollbooth, the new driver must find a quarter in a pocket or wallet. (3) Downshifting, the driver must choose a toll gate and head for it, all the while watching for other cars which may try to scoot in ahead. (4) The driver must steer the car to no more than an arm's length from the metal mesh basket. (5) As the tollbooth comes in sight, the driver must brake gently and cruise to a crawl. (6) Then with the left arm, the driver must toss the quarter into the basket. (7) The driver must then accelerate away from the tollbooth, shift, and roll up the window. (8) If the coin drops into the basket or rebounds off the side, a green sign flashes "Thank you," and the driver may pass

through. (9) If the coin misses the basket, a buzzer sounds alerting an attendant who appears to retrieve the lost coin. (10) Then finally the embarrassed new driver may accelerate, shift, roll up the window. (11) The driver can try to hide his or her shame by disappearing amid the stream of cars.

REVISING: Improving Style

Revising your paragraph also gives you an opportunity to improve style. Examine each sentence in the paragraph to see whether its structure and phrasing can be improved.

Improve the style of your paragraph by refining sentence structure and wording.

Begin by checking your choice of words. Make sure that you have not repeated any one main word too often. If you have, try instead to use a variety of appropriate synonyms. In addition, sentences can often be made livelier and clearer. Try to create a variety of sentence lengths, structures, and openers to maintain the reader's interest. Use a mixture of simple, compound, complex, and compound-complex sentences. You should also review the rhythm created by the sequence of your sentences. Better transitions can improve the overall rhythm of your writing.

The following paragraph shows several of these problems, especially poor word choices and choppy, disconnected sentences.

Paragraph with weak word choices and choppy sentences

Picnickers probably wouldn't admit it, but ants are more than pests. Ants prevent other insects from becoming too plentiful by feeding on them. Many other animals, including birds, frogs, and lizards, eat ants. Ants dig through the earth. They break it up, they loosen it, and they mix it. Air pockets form in the soil, so water can run through easily. This is how ants can be a help to farmers. Some kinds of ants tunnel through the wooden beams in houses. Some get into houses, restaurants, hospitals, and other buildings and eat whatever food they find there. It's hard to know whether ants are good or bad.

When the paragraph is revised, combining some sentences and changing the wording of others, the style is greatly improved.

Revised paragraph with improved word choices and smoother sentences

Picnickers probably wouldn't admit it, but ants do more than pester people. Because they feed on other insects, ants prevent them from becoming too plentiful. Then, from the opposite perspective, ants are an important food source for many animals, including birds, frogs, and lizards. Ants also tunnel through the earth, breaking it up, loosening it, and mixing it. Air pockets form in the soil, allowing water to run freely through it. Thus, ants can be helpful to farmers. On the other hand, some kinds of ants tunnel through wooden beams, damaging houses. Others infest houses, restaurants, hospitals, and the like raiding the food stored there. You decide: Are ants our friend . . . or foe?

EXERCISE F: Improving Style. Rewrite the following paragraph to improve its style. Consider word use, sentence structure, and overall rhythm.

(1) Visitors who come to the Grand Canyon for the first time are often surprised. (2) They are surprised at the sheer length of this awesome gorge. (3) They expect this awesome natural wonder to be deep. (4) Photographs never prepare them for the miles of twists and turns along the canyon's upper rim and don't give them an accurate idea of the shape and dimensions of this tremendous sight. (5) No one vantage point lets one see all of this national treasure. (6) You must board an airplane. (7) From thousands of feet in the air, you can get a better idea of this natural wonder.

REVISING: Proofreading Your Paragraph

The last stage in revising a paragraph is proofreading. After you have made all necessary improvements in the topic sentence, supporting information, unity, coherence, and style of the paragraph, you should check for errors in grammar, mechanics, and spelling.

The following checklist shows some of the mistakes you should look for in proofreading a paragraph.

CHECKLIST FOR PROOFREADING A PARAGRAPH

1. Does your paragraph contain any sentence fragments, run-ons, problem modifiers, or any other sentence errors?
2. Have you used verbs and pronouns correctly throughout?
3. Have you used correct capitalization?
4. Have you used the right kinds and the right amount of punctuation?
5. Have you checked the spelling of any unfamiliar words or any other words that you are unsure of?

Most smaller errors, such as misspelling, can be corrected right on your final copy. If you find larger mistakes that require rewriting sentences, however, you will have to make a fresh copy of the paragraph and proofread it again.

EXERCISE G: Proofreading a Paragraph. Using the checklist on this page, proofread a paragraph you have recently written. If you find many errors, recopy your paragraph and proofread it again.

DEVELOPING WRITING SKILLS: Revising a Paragraph. Evaluate a paragraph you have recently written, using the checklist on page 503. Answer each question on the checklist. Then follow the steps for revising presented in this section to overcome any weaknesses you discover in your paragraph. Finally, make a clean copy of your revised paragraph and proofread it. Submit both the original and revised versions to your teacher.

Topics for Writing: Paragraphs

Topic An Unexplained, Mysterious Event

Form and Purpose A paragraph that informs

Audience Publisher of a book entitled *Strange Events*

Length One paragraph

Focus In a topic sentence identify the event and indicate why it was mysterious. In your supporting sentences give specific details of the event in the order they happened.

Sources Books, magazine articles, and newspaper stories about mysterious events of the past

Prewriting If necessary, research the event, take notes, and outline your notes with a topic sentence and support.

Writing Use your outline to write a first draft.

Revising Check your paragraph's unity and coherence. Then revise your paragraph using the checklist on page 503.

ASSIGNMENT 2

Topic An Important Natural Resource of the United States

Form and Purpose A paragraph that informs

Audience Readers of a magazine for young people ages 8–12

Length One paragraph

Focus Your topic sentence should identify the resource. Your support should include specific facts and examples.

Sources Books, encyclopedias, magazine and newspaper articles

Prewriting Write a topic sentence that clearly states why the resource is important. Then brainstorm for supporting information. Outline your information in order of importance.

Writing Use your outline to write a first draft.

Revising To help you make changes, use the checklist on page 514. Then prepare a final draft.

"Have you given any thought to what you'll do with your Saturdays when the world's fossil fuels are used up?"

Koren, © 1973, *The New Yorker* Magazine, Inc.

Topics for Writing: Paragraphs

The Beatles

The photo above may suggest a topic for a paragraph. If so, narrow your topic so that it can be developed in a single paragraph. If you wish, write a paragraph about one of the following topics.

1. The Power of Music
2. What Music Means to Me
3. What Is Special About a Particular Singer or Band?
4. A Review of a Concert I Attended
5. The Worst Song of the Year
6. How Does Clothing Style Reflect a Singer's Image or Personality?
7. A Career in the Music Industry
8. Money in the Music Business
9. A Common Theme in Songs
10. The Censorship Issue in Music

Chapter 21

Kinds of Writing

There are four basic kinds of writing: *expository,* which informs, explains, or instructs; *persuasive,* which attempts to convince others to agree or act; *descriptive,* which paints pictures of people, places, or things; and *narrative,* which relates sequences of events. This chapter uses paragraphs as models to discuss these basic kinds of writing because paragraphs are concise units in longer works.

21.1 Expository and Persuasive Writing

Expository writing sets forth information with the purpose of explaining it to the reader. Persuasive writing attempts to convince others or move others to take action.

Expository Writing

Because so much writing is informative, you probably have already done much expository writing. This section will sharpen your understanding of writing meant to inform, explain, or instruct and help you to become even better at such writing.

Understanding Expository Writing. In expository papers, the writer must explain an idea. All aspects of the paper, then, should reflect and serve this explanatory purpose.

The purpose of expository writing is to explain by setting forth information.

Expository writing should consist of factual statements. It does not present an opinion. Notice the difference between the following two types of statements.

STATEMENT OF FACT: The Space Shuttle program has cost billions of dollars.

STATEMENT OF OPINION: The Space Shuttle program is much too expensive and should be cut back.

Supporting information in expository writing should include objective examples, details, facts, and possibly reasons and incidents. Supporting information should be complete and logically arranged to serve the explanatory purpose.

The language of expository writing should also reflect the explanatory purpose. The writer should present ideas in the clearest, most direct and unbiased manner, choosing words that the reader is likely to understand. The writer should consider the reader's background and knowledge of the topic so that the explanation can be offered in terms that are neither too easy nor too difficult.

In the following paragraph, notice how the clear topic sentence, the detailed supporting information, and the simple, direct language work together to create a precise explanation.

TOPIC SENTENCE (factual statement)

Explanation with instructions and details

To do the snowplow, simply push out the tails of your skis, keeping the tips together. This should be done with a gentle brushing motion. Avoid jerkiness, keep your knees well flexed, and hold your body erect. Except for angling the skis inward, the snowplow stance is essentially the same as for straight running. The skis will ride slightly on their inside edges, the knees being closer together than the feet, and this, combining with the V angle of the skis, produces the plow effect. Be careful not to overdo the edging by pressing the knees together as this will lock you into a cramped position. To increase the braking power, simply push the tails out farther and flex more in the knees and ankles.—*The Skier's Handbook*

Prewriting, Writing, and Revising. When writing an expository paper, you will follow the usual writing steps. Throughout each of these steps, however, you should specifically concentrate on fulfilling your explanatory purpose.

In expository writing, concentrate on explaining your main idea logically and fully.

In planning your paper, let your explanatory purpose guide you in finding a suitable topic, main idea, and support. Select an aspect of the topic that can be treated in a factual manner; focus on facts and ideas, not opinions. Once you have gathered enough support to explain your main idea, organize your information in a logical order and prepare an outline.

As you write a first draft, put yourself in your reader's place. Try to avoid technical terms beyond the general reader's knowledge; if such terms are essential, define them. Use transitions and other linking devices to make the logical order of your paragraph clear to your reader.

When revising, consult the checklist for revision on page 503. You may also find the following suggestions useful for checking the clarity and completeness of an expository paper.

SUGGESTIONS FOR EVALUATING AN EXPOSITORY PAPER

1. Read your paper to someone unfamiliar with the topic. Ask that person to tell you what your paper has explained.
2. Have someone else read your paper and list any questions your paper should answer but does not.
3. If your paper explains a process, try to do the steps or have someone else try using your explanation. See if you have omitted any important steps or details.

EXERCISE A: Identifying an Expository Paragraph. Identify which of the following two paragraphs has an explanatory purpose. Give two reasons why you think the writer's purpose is to explain. Then tell what you think the writer's purpose is in the other paragraph and explain why you think so.

(1) The rocks found on the earth and the moon are composed of the same minerals and elements. Both contain minerals such as pyroxene, ilmenite, and olivine, and both contain elements such as titanium and nitrogen. But while the same minerals and elements are found in both places, they exist in very different amounts. An element such as titanium is much more abundant on the moon, whereas oxygen is very scarce. In addition, enormous amounts of glass exist on the moon.

(2) Consider spending your vacation with us, the Explorer Line, on a seven-day, fourteen-day, or eighty-day cruise. We can take you to all those places you have always wanted to visit: the Caribbean, the Mexican Riviera, South America, the Pacific Islands, the Far East, and Africa. With us, you will cross the oceans and seas Columbus and Magellan once traveled but in comfort undreamed of by those explorers.

EXERCISE B: Identifying Problems in an Expository Paragraph. Find three terms or statements in the following paragraph that the writer should have defined or explained for the general reader. Then write three questions that you wish the writer had answered about these terms or points.

(1) Surprisingly enough, playing a harpsichord requires an entirely different technique from playing a piano. (2) For one thing, the harpsichord player must employ a quicker finger action, almost a plucking motion, whereas a pianist will apply weight through the fingers to depress keys. (3) This is partly because key movements on a harpsichord are stiffer than on a piano. (4) In addition, a harpsichord does not have dampers, as does a piano. (5) So the harpsichord player will not use a pedal to hold notes and chords, as a pianist will.

EXERCISE C: Writing an Expository Paragraph. Follow these instructions to write an expository paragraph. Choose one of the topics listed after the instructions.

1. Narrow the topic and think about your explanatory purpose as you write a topic sentence.
2. Gather supporting information and decide on a logical order for your support.

3. Prepare an outline for your paragraph.
4. Write a first draft based on your outline using transitions to connect your ideas.
5. Evaluate and revise your paragraph using the checklist on page 503 and the chart on page 520.

A landmark
Icebergs
Rugby and American football
Unusual pets
Space travel
Musical instruments
Junior and senior high school
Styles of dancing
A school sport
A detective story

Persuasive Writing

The writer of a persuasive paper must concentrate on presenting and defending an opinion or on urging readers to take a particular course of action. The writer's goal is to convince the reader to agree with an opinion or at least to seriously consider the writer's viewpoint.

Understanding Persuasive Writing. The persuasive purpose should be apparent in all main ideas and supporting information.

The purpose of persuasive writing is to obtain the reader's agreement on a matter of opinion.

The main ideas in persuasive writings should be statements of opinion. To be suitable, opinions should be controversial; that is, they should be statements with which some people might disagree, not factual statements.

CONTROVERSIAL STATEMENT: Tests for new drivers should be longer and more difficult.

FACTUAL STATEMENT: Most tests for a driver's license involve a written test and a driving test.

The opinion should also be significant, of interest to others, rather than trivial or highly personal.

SIGNIFICANT OPINION: Bull mastiffs make reliable, companionable watchdogs for families.

INSIGNIFICANT OPINION: I like bull mastiffs.

In addition, the opinion should be supportable with evidence, rather than a personal opinion that cannot be so defended.

SUPPORTABLE OPINION: Classical musicians must have more technical skill than rock musicians.

UNSUPPORTABLE OPINION: Michelangelo would like the paintings of Picasso.

The support in persuasive papers often consists primarily of reasons, which are then explained with facts, details, and examples. Support is frequently organized in order of importance in persuasive writing, but other orders can also be effective, depending on the topic.

Fair, reasonable language helps create a persuasive tone. Emotional or strongly negative words can offend your audience and interfere with the persuasive purpose.

Notice that the following paragraph presents a significant opinion, supported by reasons, facts, examples, and details. The tone of the paragraph is insistent but fair.

TOPIC SENTENCE (statement of opinion)	The task of maintaining an adequate water supply for a violently expanding population accustomed to heavy use of water presents an urgent and immediate problem. The water needs of the average American citizen have doubled in this century, partly because
Reasons and examples presented with reasonable language	of the demand for showers, flush toilets, air conditioners, dishwashers, lawn sprinklers, and swimming pools. The really heavy users of water, *however,* are industry and farmers. It ordinarily takes 60,000 gallons of water to make a ton of paper or steel. Farmers use quantities of water for irrigation. Because of the increase in use, water tables are falling. In some communities water is being withdrawn twenty times as fast as it is being replaced. And in some areas of North Dakota and Long Island, underground water levels have fallen so low that further "mining" of the water is curbed by regulation.—Adapted from Vance Packard

Prewriting, Writing, and Revising. As you plan, write, and revise a persuasive paper, always concentrate on your persuasive purpose.

Concentrate on influencing your audience in persuasive writing.

Concentrating on your persuasive purpose will help you find an appropriate controversial topic and to develop an opinion. State your opinion in one, clear sentence. Then test your sentence by thinking of an opinion opposite to yours. As you gather supporting information, focus on defending your opinion with convincing reasons, facts, and examples.

One method of gathering support is to list the evidence for and against your opinion. Listing the arguments against your opinion can help you think of stronger evidence for your own view. It can also help you fill the gaps in your defense. The following chart shows an example of building a defense.

BUILDING YOUR DEFENSE	
Main Idea: Residents of apartments should not be allowed to have cats or dogs.	
Evidence For	**Evidence Against**
—Cats and dogs are noisy, meowing and barking at all hours —Cats and dogs can bring odors and fleas —Cats and dogs damage rugs, floors, woodwork, drapes —Cats and dogs have no place to exercise in apartments	—Owners can train pets to be obedient and housebroken —Dogs, especially, can provide protection —Tenant's deposit covers cost of pets' damage —Cats and dogs give joy to their owners

Considering evidence of the opposite side can also help you plan the persuasive approach you will take. As you outline your paper, you may decide to admit that although your points are stronger, the other side does have one or two good points. This practice is called *conceding a point*. It can show the reader how reasonable you are.

You can organize support in many ways, but you may find order of importance particularly useful as you prepare your outline. Building up to your strongest reason can help you maintain the reader's interest and end forcefully. A concluding sentence that contains a summary, warning, personal appeal, or call to action can also strengthen persuasive writing.

While drafting your paper, focus on connecting your evidence to make your arguments easy for the reader to follow. Avoid words or phrases that could offend or confuse the reader.

To revise a persuasive paper, use a checklist such as the one on page 503. Also, consider the following suggestions as a means of testing the effect of your paper on a reader and of improving the persuasiveness of your work.

SUGGESTIONS FOR EVALUATING A PERSUASIVE PAPER

1. Have someone who *disagrees* with your opinion read your paper. Ask that person if your paper is reasonable and convincing.
2. Have someone who *agrees* with your opinion read your paper. Ask that person what other reasons or evidence would strengthen your defense.

EXERCISE D: Identifying a Persuasive Paragraph. Identify which of the following two paragraphs has a persuasive purpose. Describe two characteristics of the paragraph that indicate its persuasive purpose. Then identify the purpose of the other paragraph and tell why you think that is its purpose.

(1) The ancient Egyptians sought eternal life above all else. If they could but placate the hundreds of deities who regulated every event; if they could save prized possessions for perpetual use; if they could preserve their bodies as permanent shelters for their souls; then, surely, they would live forever, free from illness and harm, continuing the colorful existence they enjoyed along the fertile banks of the Nile.—Alice J. Hall

(2) The concerned citizens in this school district urge that the members of the school board repair the unsafe stairway leading to the elementary school playground. Children use this stairway all day long, running to and from recess and other activities. Many wooden steps are cracked and several wooden supports are splintered and shaky. If the steps or supports should collapse, serious injury could result. Let's think ahead and prevent a playground tragedy.

EXERCISE E: Improving Tone in a Persuasive Paragraph. List examples of emotionally loaded words, vague, general words, and unexplained terms in the following paragraph. Look up the unexplained terms in the dictionary, then rewrite the paragraph to create a reasonable, persuasive tone. You can add or rearrange supporting information to make the paragraph more persuasive.

(1) All students should be required to take a speech course in high school. (2) Most students cannot get up in front of the class without making total fools of themselves. (3) They tend to be mumbling, rambling idiots. (4) They are terribly boring to listen to. (5) A speech course could correct these problems, however, by teaching students to project their voices and to think out and practice their speeches. (6) A speech class would also help them with enunciation and effective eye contact. (7) All jocks, super brains, and conceited student officers could use public speaking in their classes and later in job and college interviews and in their careers. (8) Students could benefit from learning how to give informative speeches, sales talks, dramatic interpretations, and impromptu and extemporaneous speeches. (9) Finally, a speech course could give mousy students confidence. (10) And it could help loudmouths have something meaningful to say.

EXERCISE F: Writing a Persuasive Paragraph. Follow these instructions to write a persuasive paragraph. Choose one of the topics listed at the top of the next page.

1. State your opinion about the topic in a clear, supportable topic sentence.
2. Write an opinion opposite to yours and brainstorm for supporting information for both your side and the opposite side.
3. Outline your paragraph using order of importance or another order.
4. Write a first draft based on your outline, being careful to use fair, reasonable language and to connect your arguments logically.
5. Evaluate and revise your paragraph by using the checklist on page 503 and the suggestions in the chart on page 525.

The best place for a vacation
The highest quality television show
The most important subject in school
The animal that makes the best pet
A book that everyone should read
The most effective diet plan
The most exciting spectator sport
The most talented athlete, singer, or dancer

DEVELOPING WRITING SKILLS: **Writing Expository and Persuasive Paragraphs.** Select a topic of your own and follow the steps in this section to write an expository paragraph. Then using the same topic, plan, write, and revise a persuasive paragraph. Make a list of the differences between your two paragraphs.

Descriptive and Narrative Writing 21.2

Descriptive writing paints pictures with words or re–creates a scene or experience for the reader. *Narrative writing,* relates a series of events—either real or imaginary—in chronological order and from a particular point of view.

Descriptive Writing

A description must appeal to the reader's senses and imagination. The writer's goal is to make the reader see, hear, smell, or experience what is described.

Understanding Descriptive Writing. In descriptive writing, all parts of the paper work together to present a particular person, place, or thing.

Descriptive writing conveys a dominant impression through specific details, sensory impressions, and figures of speech.

The topic sentence in a descriptive paragraph usually focuses on a central *dominant impression*. Placed at the beginning of the paragraph, the topic sentence can set the scene, give the reader a preview, and arouse the reader's curiosity. A topic sentence in the middle can focus the reader's attention on the most important impression to be made. A topic sentence at the end of the paragraph can show how all the specific details in the paragraph fit together and add up to one dominant impression.

The support in a descriptive paragraph makes the person, place, object, or experience real to the reader. It usually includes *sensory impressions*—sights, sounds, smells, textures, feelings—that the writer has experienced or imagined. Most of all, support in a descriptive paragraph should consist of specific details that give the reader a complete impression of someone or something.

In addition to using complete, specific details, the writer should organize the details so that the reader can visualize them easily. Often a description can be organized in spatial or chronological order.

The following paragraph develops the dominant impression of wonder at the perfection of an object. Notice the specific details of the trees, fruit, birds, and animals. Also notice that the presentation of these details follows spatial order. (The transitions are in italics.)

TOPIC SENTENCE (dominant impression)	The king's greatest treasure was a wondrous invention: a mechanized miniature forest perfect in every detail.
Specific details in spatial order	Encased in a carved box, approximately two feet square, the little forest shone deep green in the sunlight. Dense sugar pines, elms, and walnut, apple, and pear trees clustered *around the inner walls of the box*. The little trees had real, scratchy bark and bristled with leaves and needles. Some of the branches held tiny pine cones, walnuts, apples, and pears. *Toward the inner part of the forest,* the trees thinned. *On the ground,* amidst the scrubby brush, twigs, and fallen leaves, tiny animals romped. A squirrel dug among the leaves for nuts, and a deer grazed. A rabbit sniffed the wind not far from a bushy red fox hiding behind a log. When the king turned a switch, the fox lunged and the rabbit hopped into the thicker trees.

Besides focusing on a dominant impression and developing it with specific details, a writer can fulfill a descriptive purpose by making good use of descriptive language. Descriptive language, with its sensory impressions and figures of speech, appeals to the reader's senses, imagination, and emotions.

Sensory impressions are a kind of specific detail. The writer can convey these impressions to the reader by using sharp, precise verbs and vivid nouns and adjectives. The following chart gives examples of sensory impressions, many of them by professional writers. Notice that the sensory impressions for sounds actually use words that imitate the sounds.

SENSORY IMPRESSIONS

Sights	**Sounds**	**Smells**
The shadows of the trees were long and twisted—Madeleine L'Engle Eyes lined with tiny red veins	A woodpecker went into a wild ratatattat—Madeleine L'Engle A sudden hiss of arrows—Lloyd Alexander	The smell of starch in her crisp, white apron—Catherine Marshall The night air was scented with burning pine chips and resin—Sid Fleischman
Tastes	**Feelings (touch)**	**Sensations**
The gluey licorice of cough syrup Hot chili, peppery and spicy	The cool, rounded smoothness of marble polished by many feet	Her legs and arms were tingling faintly, as though they had been asleep—Madeleine L'Engle

Figures of speech can also appeal to a reader's imagination and understanding. Figures of speech are often imaginative comparisons formed by seeing similarities between essentially unlike things. By describing one thing as like another, the writer helps the reader see the thing described in a new light. Some examples of figures of speech are similes, metaphors, and personifications. (See Section 18.1 for more details about similes and metaphors.)

The following chart explains these figures of speech and gives several examples of each.

FIGURES OF SPEECH	
Figures of Speech	**Examples**
Simile: a comparison of two unlike things introduced by *like* or *as*	The furnace purred like a great, sleepy animal.—Madeleine L'Engle He was swift and light on his feet as a ball bouncing away ahead of me.—Sid Fleischman
Metaphor: a comparison of two unlike things by complete identification (X is Y; the comparison may be implied, not written out, in a *submerged metaphor*)	The lake of melted butter in the steaming mound of hominy grits—Catherine Marshall The sky had begun to unravel in scarlet threads.—Lloyd Alexander
Personification: describing objects or ideas as if they were human	Unmasked now, the ship went swaggering before the wind as if with a knife clasped between her teeth—Sid Fleischman There was a faint gust of wind and the leaves shivered in it. —Madeleine L'Engle

NOTE ABOUT PERSONIFICATION: Personification should not be overused; too much personification can make a description seem artificial and forced.

Prewriting, Writing, and Revising. Throughout the planning, writing, and revising steps, you should assume that the reader is not familiar with the subject you are describing. Consequently, you must concentrate on your descriptive purpose and descriptive language to appeal to the reader's senses, imagination, and understanding.

In descriptive writing, focus on helping the reader to see or know your topic.

Sometimes preliminary observation or thinking will be necessary for you to arrive at a dominant impression or mood. Once you have reached a dominant impression or mood, state it clearly.

You can gather support for descriptive writing in a number of ways: through direct observation, through memory, or through imaginative thinking. With all three ways, however, you should look for features that identify and distinguish your subject. List your observations carefully as specific details, sensory impressions, and even figures of speech, if any occur to you. Try to take a mental photograph and reproduce it with your words.

In order to make someone or something seem real, interesting, and memorable to the reader, you must gather exact, specific information. The following chart suggests some kinds of details you should gather.

DETAILS TO GATHER

Topics	What to Describe
A person	height, weight, mannerisms, facial expressions, features, gestures, voice, walk, clothing, mood
A place or an experience	dimensions, weather or season, time of day, number of people, activity of people, atmosphere, surroundings, sounds, smells, sensations
An object	size, shape, texture, use, color, condition, location, any motion, noise, speed, smells, taste

As you select and organize your details, concentrate on making them clear to the reader. Whether you order details by time, by location, or by some other order, keep the relationship of one detail to another clear for the reader.

In the drafting step, try to use strong action verbs, specific nouns, and exact, vivid adjectives. Use specific details that include the reader. Think of any figures of speech that could make your description more exact, vivid, and imaginative.

As you revise, you should use the checklist on page 503. Also consider the suggestions for evaluating descriptive writing in the following chart.

SUGGESTIONS FOR EVALUATING A DESCRIPTIVE PAPER

1. Ask someone *unfamiliar* with what you are describing to read your paper and react by saying what the description made him or her see, feel, sense, and so on.
2. Ask someone *familiar* with what you are describing to read your paper and comment on its accuracy and the completeness of its details.
3. Put your paper aside for a while and then reread it. Look for too little detail, too much detail, or fuzzy details.
4. If possible, return to observe your person, place, or object again. Check the accuracy, vividness, and completeness of your description against the original.

EXERCISE A: Recognizing Descriptive Language. List at least five specific details that contribute to the descriptiveness of the following paragraph.

(1) Then the sun was sinking and every prismatic color was reflecting back from this ice-encased world. (2) The valley had become like Ali Baba's Treasure Cave that I had read about as a child. (3) I found my eyes and throat aching with the beauty that blazed outside the train windows. (4) Jewels seemed to glitter from every bush, every withered blade of grass, every twig: sapphires and turquoise, emeralds and amethysts, rubies crystals, diamonds.—Catherine Marshall

EXERCISE B: Using Sensory Impressions. For each of the following items, write a sensory impression that appeals to the sense in parentheses.

EXAMPLE: a dandelion (touch)
the soft, whispering feel of the downy petals

1. a parade (sound)
2. a restaurant (smell)
3. a bridge (sight)
4. a train (sound)
5. a Ferris wheel (sensation)
6. an old apple (taste)
7. a baby's hair (touch)
8. a rainstorm (sensation)
9. a parking garage (smell)
10. corn on the cob (taste)

EXERCISE C: Using Figures of Speech. Follow the instructions to write similes, metaphors, and examples of personification.

1. After observing an animal, write a simile.
2. After observing a child, write a metaphor.
3. After observing a machine in motion, write an example of personification.
4. After observing a person in motion, write a simile.
5. After observing traffic, write a metaphor.
6. After observing a pet, write an example of personification.
7. After observing clouds, write a simile.
8. After observing a sunset, write a metaphor.
9. After observing a sleeping person, write a simile.
10. After observing a crowd, write a metaphor.

EXERCISE D: Writing a Descriptive Paragraph. Choose one of the general items listed below and follow these directions.

1. Observe the topic of your description to determine a dominant impression, and then write a topic sentence.
2. Jot down details and sensory impressions that develop your dominant impression.
3. Organize your support in an outline.
4. Write a first draft of the paragraph.
5. Use the checklist on page 503 and the chart on page 532 to revise your paragraph. Make a final copy of the paragraph.

A certain beach
A new car
Your room
A pet or other animal
A hospital at night
A piece of machinery
A building people say is haunted
A favorite article of clothing
A person you'll never forget
A piece of machinery

Narrative Writing

Narrataive writing tells a story. It relates a series of events, which may be either true or imaginary.

Understanding Narrative Writing. Narrative writing is often used to tell a complete story. Everything is told from a single point of view.

Narrative writing relates a chronological series of events from a single point of view.

The main idea is usually stated at the beginning of a narrative paper, leading the reader to expect a story of some kind, setting the scene, and providing necessary background information. If the narrative is meant to illustrate some lesson or truth, the main idea, which will generally explain the lesson or truth, may be found at the end instead.

The main-idea statement usually establishes the *point of view* or *narrator*. The following chart explains the different kinds of narrators that can be used.

DIFFERENT POINTS OF VIEW (OR NARRATORS)	
Point of View or Narrator	**Definition**
First person	The narrator, using the word "I," tells the story as he or she saw it and participates in the action. The "I" may be either the actual writer or a character in the story.
Limited third person	The narrator, who is not in the story, tells the story using the pronouns "she" or "he." The narrator makes only factual observations and does not see into the characters' minds.
Omniscient third person	The narrator, who is not in the story, tells the story using the pronouns "she" or "he." The narrator can see into the minds of the characters and tell their thoughts.

The point of view helps determine the kind of supporting information used to develop the story. An experience related through the eyes of a first-person participant would be quite different from one related by a limited third-person observer who can report only physical appearances and action.

The supporting information is usually arranged in straight chronological order. Occasionally, however, a writer may vary this order by establishing the endpoint, or result of the experience, and then narrating the events that led up to it.

The word choices should be vivid, as with descriptive writing. But narrative writing must also *move*; it must create the flow of events through time. Precise and active verbs are essential to this sense of movement. Transitions and other connecting words can also help to make the sentences flow.

In the following paragraph, the first-person point of view, vivid word choices, and many linking words work together to create a strong narrative. The transitions and other linking words are in italics.

TOPIC SENTENCE (sets the scene and establishes first-person narrator)

Developed with active verbs and specific, lively language

A silence fell as I picked up the wreath and walked slowly up to the statue. It was *then* that I realized, and with a stab to the heart, why I had been chosen May Queen. I had been chosen because I was the tallest girl in the school. *It was equally clear,* as I peered at the massive stone figure looming four or five feet above me, that, tall as I was, I wasn't tall enough. Was it possible, I wondered, that we would all have to stand here until I grew another six inches! *Then* I remembered Mother Claire's oft-repeated adage, "Desperate diseases require desperate remedies." I took the wreath firmly in my two hands, grasping it like a basketball, and hurled it up onto the head of the statue. *For a brief moment* it looked as though I had succeeded, for the wreath seemed to be resting firmly on the prongs of the stone crown. *But then,* slowly and majestically, it slid down until it settled rakishly over one large stone eye. The effect was decidedly disreputable, and there was a hiss of horror from the nuns as well as a gasp from the girls that quickly degenerated into muffled laughter. The *first* to be affected were the flautists, who, in an effort to suppress their giggles, had blown spit into their flutes and rendered them useless. The singers, without a flute to guide them, fell silent. The little girl who had borne the wreath burst into tears and a first grade flower girl was heard to inquire loudly, "Is it over?"—Jean Kerr

Prewriting, Writing, and Revising. In planning, writing, and revising narratives, focus on the order of events.

In narrative writing, concentrate on presenting a clear sequence of events.

When you have decided on a basic story, select a point of view. A first-person narrator, for example, might be best for a story about a personal experience, but you might give yourself more freedom if you talked about yourself in the third person.

Write a main idea that either sets the scene or focuses on some general truth or principle. Then decide which specific events and details should be included. Remember that the kind of narrator will determine the support you can use. Arrange your supporting information in chronological order.

When you draft your narrative, concentrate on making the story seem real to the reader. Link your sentences with transitions and other devices to connect the events in the story. Keep your language as specific as possible, using strong verbs, precise nouns, and lively adjectives.

As you revise, you should use the checklist on page 503. Also consider the suggestions in the following chart.

SUGGESTIONS FOR EVALUATING A NARRATIVE PAPER

1. Ask someone unfamiliar with the experience you are relating to read your narrative and tell you what he or she saw, felt, or thought as it unfolded. Ask also if your reader has noticed any skips or breaks in the narrative and whether or not the reader thinks the ending is satisfactory.
2. Reread the story yourself, trying to approach it as if you were an outsider coming across the paragraph in a magazine or book. Ask yourself if the story arouses your interest, if it makes sense, and if it has a satisfactory ending.
3. Look closely at the language in the story: How graphic is the language? Can it be made more lively, more real, more specific? Do your sentences seem connected to one another?

EXERCISE E: Identifying the Features of Narrative Paragraphs. Identify the point of view used in the following paragraph. Then list at least three examples of transitions and other connecting devices used in the paragraph. Finally, list at least five examples of vivid, graphic nouns, verbs, and modifiers.

(1) A short distance away a young eagle dragged a partially eaten salmon carcass out of the water. (2) Gripping the nearly frozen fish awkwardly, the bird tore off pieces of meat with a force that threw it back several feet in the snow each time. (3) Composing itself, the bird cautiously eyed the other eagles, then lifted its head up and finished the meat. (4) A magpie and gull landed on the dead fish and began eating. (5) As the eagle waddled back for more food, the two stepped gingerly aside, stopping just two feet away. (6) Again the eagle fell back with a huge piece, and again the two smaller birds returned to the carcass. (7) This dance for dinner was repeated until the eagle was so gorged that despite labored beats of its four-foot wings, it couldn't take off.—Vic Banks

EXERCISE F: Writing a Narrative Paragraph. Choose one of the general experiences listed below, or think of a topic of your own, and follow these instructions to write a narrative paragraph.

1. Think through the experience, decide on a point of view that you want to use, and write a topic sentence.
2. List the major events, actions, and thoughts that your narrator will relate.
3. Check that the events follow a chronological order.
4. Write a first draft of your paragraph, using graphic language and clear transitions.
5. Use the checklist on page 503 and the chart on page 536 to evaluate and revise your paragraph.

A familiar legend or myth told from a fresh perspective
An interview, audition, or other challenging experience
A day without food or a day of silence
The longest moment in someone's life
A funny or painful lesson

DEVELOPING WRITING SKILLS: Writing Descriptive and Narrative Paragraphs. Select a place that you can actually observe and follow the steps presented in this section to plan, write, and revise a descriptive paragraph about it. Revise the paragraph using the chart on page 514. Then use the scene you described as the setting for a narrative paragraph.

Writing Workshop: Kinds of Writing

Dinosaurs

ASSIGNMENT 1

Topic An Extinct or Nearly Extinct Animal

Form and Purpose An expository paragraph that explains how a particular species became or nearly became extinct

Audience Visitors to an exhibit on animal extinction

Length One paragraph

Focus Introduce your subject and main idea in a topic sentence. Then provide specific facts, details, and examples to develop your topic sentence.

Sources Natural history and science books, nature and wildlife magazines, interviews with wildlife conservationists

Prewriting Research your subject and take notes. Organize your information in a logical manner.

Writing Using your notes, write a first draft.

Revising Revise your paper following the suggestions on page 520.

ASSIGNMENT 2

Topic Description of a Painting or a Sculpture

Form and Purpose A paragraph that describes a painting or a sculpture

Audience Someone who has not seen the painting or sculpture

Length One paragraph

Focus In your topic sentence, state your dominant impression of the painting or sculpture. Then, use descriptive language to tell about the specific details.

Sources Art books, museums, posters, prints

Prewriting Write your dominant impression of the painting or sculpture. Then list descriptive details that support that impression. Organize the details in a spatial order.

Writing Use your notes to write a first draft. Use figures of speech and sensory language to create vivid details.

Revising Revise your paper using the suggestions on page 532.

J. Espejo, *Les Patineurs*

Topics for Writing: Kinds of Writing

The poster above may suggest a writing topic to you. If so, narrow that topic so that it can be adequately covered in a paragraph. Decide on a purpose and an audience. Then write an expository, persuasive, descriptive, or narrative paragraph about your topic. If you prefer, write about one of the following topics.

1. The American Dream: A New Automobile
2. More Bikes; Less Pollution
3. Where Do All of the Old Cars Go?
4. How Important Is Image and Style in the Purchase of an Automobile?
5. A Bike-Touring Trip
6. BMX Racing: The New National Sport
7. BMX Racing: Big Business Today
8. Have Cars Changed Our Lives?
9. Does Our Town or City Need Bike Paths?
10. The Automobile of the Future

Chapter 22

Essays

Once you are familiar with analyzing and writing paragraphs, you are ready to study essays. An essay is a longer composition that focuses on one main point. In this chapter you will examine the structure and content of essays in detail, and you will learn some practical steps to follow in writing essays. When you can write essays, you will be prepared to handle many of the writing assignments and situations you will meet in and out of school.

Understanding Essays 22.1

An essay is a longer composition written to communicate a main point to a particular audience for a specific purpose. It is a shaped and structured piece of writing with a series of well-connected paragraphs.

The Parts of an Essay

The parts of an essay generally follow a basic pattern. The title usually indicates the topic of the essay and can hint at the writer's main point. The introductory paragraph presents background material on the topic and then zeroes in on a main point in one sentence, called a *thesis statement*. Each paragraph in the body of the essay develops and explains the thesis statement. Finally, a concluding paragraph reminds the reader of the thesis statement and pulls together all the ideas in the essay. The following diagram illustrates this pattern.

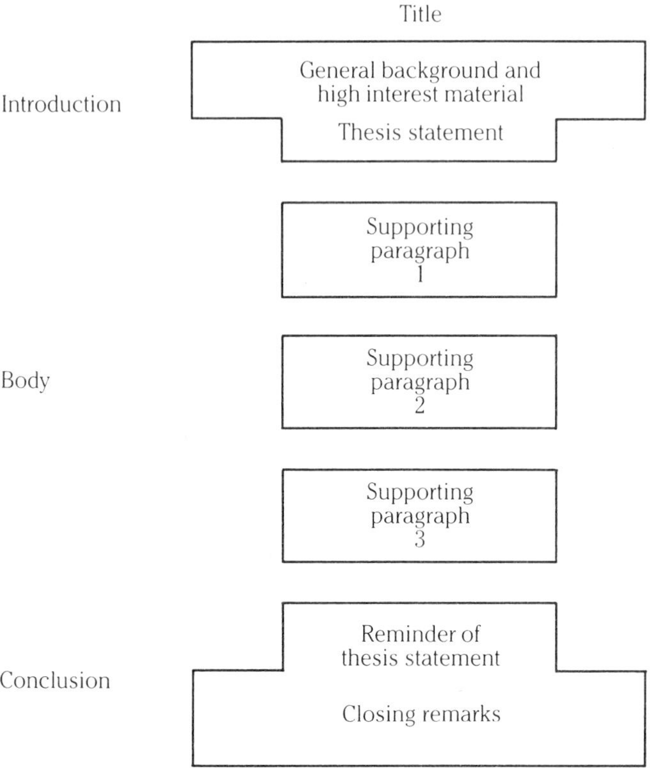

The following pages explain in greater detail each of these parts and features of an essay.

The Title. The title is the first part of the essay that a reader notices. It functions as a preview of the thesis statement and an advertisement for the essay.

The title attracts the reader's attention and previews the essay's main point and tone.

A well-written, appropriate title will help make the reader want to read the essay. A title should provide clues to the topic of the essay and the writer's focus on that topic. Usually, a title is original, short, and direct. It can also be clever and catchy, but it should never be cute or misleading. For example, a humorous title should prepare a reader for a humorous essay.

The following chart gives some sample topics and titles.

SAMPLE TOPICS WITH TITLES	
Topics	**Titles**
Misunderstandings about wolves	The Most Slandered Animal: The Wolf
The development of early airplanes	Airborne at Last
Walking as better exercise than jogging	Walk, Don't Run

Notice that the titles give some indication of the writer's idea about the topic and of the essay's tone.

The Introduction. The introduction is the first major part of the essay. It is usually the first paragraph, although it can be longer than one paragraph. Its purposes are (1) to clarify the topic of the essay in a way that will spark the reader's interest, (2) to establish the tone of the essay, and (3) to zero in on the thesis statement, which gives the essay's main point.

The introduction defines the topic, sets the tone, and presents the main point in a thesis statement.

An introduction will usually begin with general remarks about a topic that provide necessary background information or raise questions that will be answered in the essay. The words and flavor of the introduction will also set the tone for the entire essay by creating certain expectations in the reader. From the introduction, the reader will expect the tone of the essay to be, for example, scholarly, casual, objective, formal, or familiar.

Like a funnel narrowing to its smallest end, the introduction will usually begin with general remarks and end with a focused thesis statement. In this key position at the end of the introduction, the thesis statement signals the reader that this idea is the main point that the rest of the essay will develop.

An introduction can begin with a thought-provoking question, an incident, startling facts, a historical account, or concise, lively statements about the topic. Notice how some of these methods are used in the following introduction. Also notice that the introduction paves the way for the thesis statement, which is the last sentence.

Background information

Why do people dress up in masks and costumes on Halloween and imagine ghosts and goblins behind gravestones and dark trees? Halloween gets its name from "All Hallows' Eve," the night before All Saints' Day. Actually, in establishing All Saints' Day, the Catholic Church adopted an older celebration. The customs and beliefs behind the ghosts and ghouls go back much further in history. *Halloween appears to trace its origin to two ancient festivals: the Celtic festival of the New Year and the Roman tribute to the dead.*

Thesis statement

A thesis statement always narrows and focuses the topic of the essay to one main point. In addition, it indicates to the reader the writer's purpose, such as to explain or to persuade. Finally, some thesis statements contain stated *subtopics*. These subtopics order the essay by identifying parts of the main point that will be examined in the body.

The following chart gives sample thesis statements. Notice that two have stated subtopics while one does not. Notice also that the writer's purpose is usually clearly presented in the thesis statement.

SAMPLE THESIS STATEMENTS

Thesis Statements	Purposes	Stated Subtopics
Doctors and scientists think diabetes may be caused by viruses, a body's abnormal immune response, and overeating.	to explain	(1) viruses (2) a body's abnormal immune response (3) overeating
Hitting a golf ball involves choosing a club, assuming the correct position, and swinging properly.	to explain	(1) choosing a club (2) assuming the correct position (3) swinging properly
Our town should vote money for a para-medic service.	to persuade	none

Placed at the end of the introduction, the thesis statement prepares the reader for the information to be presented in the body of the essay.

The Body. The body of an essay consists of two or more paragraphs in the middle of the essay. The body contains the supporting information for the thesis statement. The number of paragraphs and the amount of information in each paragraph will vary according to the thesis statement. However, to be complete and well developed, the body must have enough support to explain or defend the thesis statement thoroughly and adequately, meeting all of the expectations set up by the thesis statement.

The body supports the thesis statement with examples, details, facts, reasons, or incidents.

The paragraphs in the body of an essay develop the subtopics, either stated or unstated, of the thesis statement. Often, a writer will choose to devote one or more paragraphs to each subtopic. The topic sentences of the body paragraphs often restate the subtopics, which become the main ideas of the individual paragraphs.

The Conclusion. The conclusion is usually one final short paragraph that completes the essay. The conclusion generally includes a reminder of the thesis statement. It also suggests to the reader that the main point has been covered thoroughly and that the essay has achieved its purpose.

The conclusion reminds the reader of the thesis statement and smoothly brings the essay to a close.

Often the conclusion begins specifically with a different version of the thesis statement and then ends generally, with closing remarks on the topic. In a long essay, the conclusion may be used to summarize the ideas presented in the essay, although it should not simply repeat in a tedious fashion the information from the body. Nor should it bring in a group of totally new ideas that are not related to the thesis statement in any way. The final sentence in a conclusion may be a forceful, witty, or memorable statement, called a *clincher*.

Notice that the following conclusion begins specifically with a reminder of the thesis statement. The paragraph moves from the past to the present, ending with a statement about modern-day activities. Notice that this conclusion returns to the starting point of the introduction on page 544.

Reminder of thesis statement

The ancient Celts, dancing in animal masks and skins, and the ancient Romans, honoring their dead, have influenced the way Halloween is celebrated today. Over the past 2,000 years these ancient festivals joined with those of other cultures and gradually became our Halloween. Today, people shrieking in a deserted house and haunting the streets in the likenesses of ghosts and other creatures are following traditions that have ancient roots.

Putting the Parts Together. The following essay by a student shows the parts and structure of the basic essay. Notice that it is aimed at the general reader, that the purpose is to explain a process, and that the tone is casual and informative. The comments in the margins identify the main features of the essay.

Wrap That Parcel Right

Introduction

Have you ever received a package with the box mangled and the contents damaged? Or have you mailed one that never arrived? Damage and disappearance can happen when packages are not properly wrapped and labeled. To give items a better chance of reaching their destinations in good shape, follow this easy process: Secure outside containers, protect the inside with padding, close and seal the parcel properly, and label it correctly.

Thesis statement with four subtopics

Body paragraph 1 (develops subtopic 1)

Always begin with strong, secure outside containers. The United States Postal Service allows self-supporting paperboard boxes or padded draft paper bags for most clothing and noncrushable items up to ten pounds. The United Parcel Service recommends that a corrugated carton be used. Although you will probably have to pay for a box of this type at a department store, they are yours for the asking at any supermarket. When choosing a carton, check the bottom for the pounds-per-square inch figure. Also check to see that the flaps are intact and that the box is in no way broken.

Body paragraph 2 (develops subtopic 2)

Secondly, provide protection inside the carton with padding. A parcel that gets dropped from a high platform or is hit by some object can suffer heavy damage. To make the package shockproof, put several inches of cushioning on the bottom, along the sides, and on the top. Crumpled grocery bags, newspapers, foamed plastic shells, and air-pocket padding are all good choices. When mailing more than one item in the same carton, wrap each item separately, and then package all the items with padding around them. Never package fragile and heavy items in the same carton.

Body paragraph 3 (develops subtopic 3)

Another step involves closing and sealing the body parcel properly. Use sealing tape, not string or twine, because string can become tangled in the postal sorting machines. Nylon and glass reinforced tape are the best. You must use water to activate the gummed surface and apply the tape immediately. Close the flaps, tape them together securely, and then band the box with two tapes around the length and two around the girth. You may want to tape the midsection for added strength. The Postal Service frowns on outer wrapping paper. If you use it, it should be at least the weight of a standard grocery bag.

Body paragraph 4 (develops subtopic 4)

As the final step, you should label the package properly. Remove all other labels from the parcel you have prepared. In the lower right-hand corner of the top side of the box, print with indelible ink the name and address of the recipient, including the zip code. In the upper left-hand corner, mark "From:" with your complete name and address. If you use a gummed label, type or print your name and address clearly, and make sure it is attached securely.

Conclusion with reminder of thesis statement

Following these easy steps will help you and the post office work together to ensure that your package reaches its destination safely. You can save yourself the frustration of sending someone a package that looks as if it has been in a tug-of-war or has been stepped on by an elephant. And your friend will not be angry at you for supposedly forgetting his birthday.

—James Dattilo

EXERCISE A: Identifying the Parts of an Essay. Read the following essay. Then answer the questions that follow.

Those Mystifying Allergies

For some people the little green tassels dropping from the trees and the fluffy pink, white, and yellow blossoms announce the arrival of allergy season. For others a big, furry dog or a soft feather pillow brings on the sneezes or itchy eyes. Still others are in trouble if they accidentally eat honey, chocolate, or water chestnuts. Although millions of Americans have allergies, no one knows definitely how allergies develop or why some people have them and others do not. Doctors have made some progress in diagnosis. Yet allergies remain a mystery that is only partially understood and only partially treatable.

Doctors do understand that allergies are abnormal reactions of the body to ordinary harmless substances, but why these abnormal reactions occur is unknown. Despite this common root cause, the symptoms of allergies vary greatly. Most allergic people only suffer for a week or two each year. For example, as the ragweed or grass pollen blows in the wind, these people become rapid-fire sneezers or develop red eyes, stuffy heads, or runny noses, but in a few weeks they return to normal. Slightly more serious allergic reactions can occur throughout the year, either during several seasons or whenever a person comes in contact with certain foods, materials, or drugs. Varied substances such as penicillin, soap, flowers, duck meat, wool, cigarette smoke, and sunshine may cause symptoms ranging from severe asthma to hives to serious sinus congestion. And a small percentage of allergy victims suffer near-crippling migraine headaches and even nausea that can leave them bedridden.

Given these diverse allergic reactions, doctors, not surprisingly, are only moderately successful in understanding the specific causes of allergies. Some allergies are easy to figure out. A person whose tongue swells after eating strawberries is clearly allergic to strawberries. Other times, diagnosis proves more complicated, such as when symptoms do not appear immediately after contact. Some food allergies, for example, are characterized by delayed reactions. Pollen and ordinary house dust are other common causes of allergic reactions, but identifying the exact cause from among the grasses, trees, and flowers and their seeds and pollen and from among fibers, lint, mold, food particles, and pet hair can be difficult.

Treatments for these numerous and confusing allergic reactions vary in effectiveness. Most treatments, though, can boast only temporary success. For many allergies the best treatment is to stay away from the apparent cause by avoiding certain animals, foods, and drugs. But what about such substances as cigarette smoke, pollen, and dust, which are in the air and consequently unavoidable? Partial treatment for allergies to these substances may involve staying away from all fields and gardens, sleeping in an air-conditioned room, and not having indoor pets. Over-the-counter prescription decongestants, antihistamines, and other medicines can provide some relief. In even more severe cases, the person can undergo allergy tests in a hospital. During one such test, a grid is drawn on the person's back, and a small pronged instrument is used to scratch each square of skin and inject a different substance under the skin. If a swelling like a mosquito bite and itching occur in a square, the person is allergic to that substance. The doctor can then prepare allergy shots to be given over many months in order to increase the persons tolerance to that substance.

Despite relief from planned avoidance, from medicine, and from shots, the cause and treatment of some allergies puzzle doctors, and the cures still elude them. Some people outgrow allergies while others develop them. Each year victims wheeze with asthma, itch with rashes, and suffer from nosebleeds. Even worse, about fifty people die every year from violent allergic reactions to bee and other insect stings. Undoubtedly, allergies remain a mysterious menance.

1. What is the title of the essay? Is it a good title for the essay? Why or why not?
2. How long is the introduction?
3. What is the thesis statement? Does it have stated subtopics? If so, what are they?
4. How does the writer try to spark the reader's interest in the introduction?
5. From the introduction and the thesis statement, what would you say is the intended purpose of the essay? What audience did the writer have in mind? What tone does the writer establish?
6. How many body paragraphs does the essay have?

7. What are the topic sentences in the body paragraphs?
8. What are three pieces of specific supporting information in each body paragraph?
9. How long is the conclusion? What sentence in the conclusion reminds the reader of the thesis statement?
10. Is the conclusion effective? Why or why not?

Unity and Coherence in Essays

Unity and coherence are characteristics of good paragraphs (as explained in Chapter 20). They are also characteristics of good essays. Unity and coherence should appear in an essay on two levels: within each paragraph and within the essay as a whole. For more information on unity and coherence within individual paragraphs, see Section 20.1. The following pages focus on unity and coherence in the essay as a whole.

Overall Unity. In a unified essay, the reader senses that all the information in the paragraphs and all the paragraphs themselves belong in this piece of writing. The introduction and thesis statement, the body, and the conclusion stick to one main point and, together, cover that main point completely.

As essay is unified if each paragraph has unity and helps develop the thesis statement.

A clear, concise thesis statement can contribute greatly to the unity of an essay. By clearly focusing on only one main point to be developed, the thesis statement helps the writer weed out vague or unrelated supporting information.

Carefully thought-out subtopics can also contribute to overall unity. If there is a close relationship between every subtopic and the thesis statement and between all the subtopics, an essay will have unity.

The introduction and conclusion can function as another aid to overall unity. The introduction directs the reader's attention to the main point, and the conclusion brings the reader's attention back to it. Furthermore, the conclusion can reinforce the tone established in the introduction and carried through in the body, strengthening the sense of unity.

Overall Coherence. Besides exploring only one main point in depth, a good essay reads smoothly and carries the reader along from idea to idea. If the order of ideas is logical and consistent and if appropriate connections are used, the essay will hold together.

An essay has coherence if the ideas within each paragraph and within the whole essay are logically ordered and smoothly connected.

Like a paragraph, an essay should have a logical, consistent overall order. The subtopics in the body of the essay should be arranged according to a logical order, the same order in which the subtopics are stated in the thesis statement. (See Section 20.1 for a detailed explanation of orders and coherence.)

The following chart suggests orders that might be suitable for subtopics both in the thesis statement and in the body of the essay.

POSSIBLE ORDERS FOR SUBTOPICS

Subtopics	Possible Orders
Stages of my first experience in mountain climbing Steps in building the Golden Gate Bridge	Chronological Order
Four important sights along the Mississippi The design of the Wright brothers' famous airplane	Spatial Order
Four reasons to vote for a new community center Some causes of chemical fires	Order of Importance
The difference between gasohol and gasoline Lake fishing and stream fishing	Comparison-and-Contrast Order
The best way to insulate a home Four kinds of skiers	Developmental Order

Like a coherent paragraph, a coherent essay links ideas with transitions and repetitions of main words, synonyms, and pronouns. Transitions often come in the first and last sentences of body paragraphs to indicate the movement to a new subtopic, while repetitions of main words and synonyms can keep the thesis statement in the forefront of the reader's mind.

The following student essay shows both unity and coherence. The essay sticks to the thesis statement and the subtopics that naturally grow out of it. The writer also creates coherence by using a logical order and some important linking devices. The subtopics follow a developmental order both in the thesis statement and in the body of the essay. The three subtopics—loyalty, naiveté, and simplicity—are main words that the writer repeats. These words and a few other main words are boxed. They connect each paragraph to the thesis statement and often to the preceding paragraph. The words in bold type are transitions that also help connect the paragraphs.

Title	Melanie: The Silent Pillar
Introduction Thesis statement: subtopics— (1) loyalty (2) naiveté (3) simplicity	*Gone with the Wind* is not just Scarlett O'Hara's story; it is also the story of another remarkable woman, Melanie Wilkes. The author describes Melanie as having "the face of a sheltered child who had never known anything but simplicity and kindness, truth and love, a child who had never looked upon harshness or evil, and would not have recognized them if she saw them" (page 155). *Strangely enough, the qualities that weakened Melanie in Scarlett's eyes—loyalty, naiveté, and simplicity—actually proved to make Melanie a strong person.*
Subtopic 1A: loyalty to a way of life	Melanie Wilkes was a truly loyal person. Many times during the reconstruction of the South, life would have been easier for Melanie if she had chosen to join the Yankees. Yet she remained loyal to the only way of life she really knew or understood. Because of this loyalty, her friends, family, and even strangers "clung to her skirts" (page 1000). She was an oasis in a desert of people who were suspended between a way of life which was no more and a new way of life which was utterly confusing.
Subtopic 1B: loyalty to loved ones	Melanie was **also** loyal to her loved ones, especially to Scarlett O'Hara. Although Scarlett intensely disliked Melanie, Scarlett could not make Melanie dis-

loyal to her. Melanie once said, "Now dear, I love you and you know I love you, and nothing you could do would make me change" (page 863). Scarlett did not even attempt to disguise her dislike for Melanie, just as Rhett Butler (another recipient of Melanie's loyal love) did not try to disguise his dealings with the "Watling woman" and the scalawags. But Melanie defended them both vehemently and protectively as a mother would her children. Her loyalty to these two in particular occasionally put her in situations where she had to fight "Yankees, fire, hunger, poverty, public opinion, and even her beloved blood kin" (page 1000). Though the public might ridicule her, she remained loyal. It takes a strong person openly to defend people and causes which others openly shun.

Subtopic 2A: naiveté with a focus on good

To many, Melanie's loyalty to certain people seemed unwarranted, and yet if they had seen the world through Melanie's naive eyes, they would have understood her. Her naiveté led her to overlook the ugly qualities and to concentrate on the redeeming qualities in a person. She saw the good before the bad, and when she finally did see the bad, she chose not to accept it. Because of this vision of people "that comes sincerely and spontaneously from a generous heart, everyone flocked to her, for who can resist the charm of one who discovers in others admirable qualities undreamed of even by himself" (page 156).

Subtopic 2B: naiveté and reliability

Those that "flocked" to Melanie did so for **other reasons as well**. Her naiveté made her reliable. She lacked the desire to put up a facade. Because of her naiveté she had a serene innocence, not like that of a child, but rather like that of a placid soul, untouched by irrational prejudice. And just as her naiveté kept her from seeing the bad qualities in others, it also kept her from realizing the strong characteristics in herself. Her naiveté strengthened her by preventing her from discovering that so many people depended on her.

Subtopic 3: simplicity

The bad qualities in others that Melanie could not overlook by her naiveté could be condoned by her simplicity. Her emotions were not complex. Melanie did not allow new, unpleasant facts to complicate her feelings about people. For example, at one point in the novel, Melanie found out that Scarlett had entertained scalawags. Even though the thought was horrid to Melanie, she said to Scarlett, "Darling, what you do, you always do for a good reason. Everybody thinks differently and everybody's got a right to their own opinion" (page 863). Melanie's simplicity also made her refuse to listen to talk of Rhett Butler's bad qualities. Another example is Melanie's relationship with her husband, Ashley Wilkes. She knew all along that he was a dreamer, that he wasn't practical, but she loved him anyway. Being able to accept others as they were strengthened Melanie more than anything else. Her simplicity enabled her to realize that a person cannot expect to make changes in other people.

Reminder of thesis statement

Loyal, naive, simple Melanie was the underlying strength of so many people. Even Scarlett finally had to admit that Melanie was the one upon whom "she had relied unknowingly for so many years" (page 1000). She eventually realized that Melanie had been her "sword and her shield, her comfort and her strength" (page 997). Melanie may not have tackled the job of building a new world, but she was the essential link which kept others in touch as they daringly forged ahead. People like Melanie are the maintainers of sanity, the stabilizing influences. Only at her death did her friends fully appreciate the "terrible strength of the weak, the gentle, the tender-hearted" (page 1001).—Tracy Martin

Clincher

EXERCISE B: Recognizing Overall Unity and Coherence. Reread the essay in Exercise A. Then answer these questions.

1. What is the single, clear point the writer makes in the thesis statement?
2. In what order has the writer arranged the subtopics?
3. Why is this order of subtopics appropriate?
4. Which subtopic is covered in each body paragraph?
5. What small-scale order does each body paragraph follow?
6. Why is this order appropriate?
7. What words or phrases function as transitions in the essay?

8. What repetitions of main words and synonyms connect the ideas in the essay?
9. How does the conclusion echo the introduction? How does it maintain a consistent tone with the introduction and body?
10. How would you rate the overall unity of this essay?

DEVELOPING WRITING SKILLS: Understanding an Essay. Find an essay or article of about five hundred words in a book or magazine. After you have read the article, answer the following questions about it.

1. What is the title? Does the title fit the essay?
2. What is the main point of the thesis statement? Where is it located in the essay?
3. Does the essay have an introduction, body, and conclusion?
4. How does the introduction attempt to interest the reader?
5. What are the subtopics developed in the body of the essay?
6. What supporting information is given under each subtopic?
7. In what order has the writer arranged the subtopics?
8. Does the conclusion include a reminder of the thesis statement? Does it refer to the introduction in any other way? Does it have a clincher?
9. What transitions connect the ideas in the essay?
10. What repetitions of main words, synonyms, and pronouns make the essay coherent?

Writing an Essay 22.2

Writing an essay involves thinking, shaping, and developing your ideas and making a series of decisions. This section offers suggestions that can help you make the best decisions in the planning, writing, and revising steps of preparing an essay.

PREWRITING: Planning Your Essay

As the first step in writing an essay, you must be prepared to do some detailed planning. Spending time choosing an essay topic, writing a thesis statement, and organizing supporting information will make the rest of the writing go more smoothly.

Generating Ideas and Choosing a Topic. Sometimes, essay topics may be assigned to you. At other times, however, you may need to choose your own topic. To find possible topics for an essay, use your imagination and explore your interests and experiences. Using techniques such as interviewing yourself, free writing, journal writing, reading and saving, clustering, cueing, or brainstorming can help you generate ideas. (See Section 17.1 for a discussion of these various techniques.)

Once you have a list of topics, you will usually need to reduce them to smaller, narrower essay topics. A suitable essay topic is one that you can develop thoroughly in approximately four to six paragraphs. To find a suitable essay topic, make a list of possible topics you could write about. Then examine those topics, select one that particularly interests you, and narrow it down if it is too big for an essay.

Generate ideas for topics, divide a general topic into smaller ones, and select a manageable essay topic.

Using the brainstorming method to generate ideas, you might make a list of topics similar to the following. Notice that a few of the topics would make suitable essay topics, whereas others have been broken down further.

BRAINSTORMING FOR AN ESSAY TOPIC

Dorothy Sayers' mystery *Strong Poison*
—the character of Lord Peter Wimsey
—the character of Katherine Climpson

The tests a seeing-eye dog must pass

Golf
—basic equipment
—different swings and grips
—the first golf course in St. Andrews, Scotland
—the beginner's view of golf
—famous golf tournaments

Tips on moving without a moving van

The Hawaiian Islands
—how they were formed
—Hawaiian kings and queens
—characteristics of the Hawaiian language
—modern industries
—Hawaiian volcanoes

The training of a circus clown

Playing the guitar
—playing an electric guitar
—playing flamenco guitar
—teaching yourself to play

After examining your list, you might decide that the beginner's view of golf would make a suitable essay topic.

Writing a Thesis Statement. To arrive at a main point or thesis statement for your essay, you should carefully examine your essay topic and your thoughts about it. Decide what audience you are writing for: Will they be people learning about your topic for the first time, or will they already have an opinion on the matter? Also decide on the purpose of your essay: Do you want to inform or do you want to persuade?

Think about your audience and purpose as you write a thesis statement that presents your main idea.

An essay topic must be shaped and refined to one main point to become a thesis statement. You can begin focusing an essay topic by asking the questions in the chart below.

QUESTIONS LEADING TO POSSIBLE MAIN POINTS	
Essay Topic: The beginner's view of golf	
Questions	**Main Points**
How can I define the beginner's view of golf?	Golf is an easy game to lose and a difficult game to win.
What one idea would I like to tell others about it?	Golf will tease and frustrate a new golfer in many ways.
What is the most important idea the audience should know about it?	Only people with patience and determination should take up golf.
What are some things that a beginner has to learn?	To learn golf, one must learn to concentrate on stance, grip, and swing, all at once.

Once you have a number of main points, choose one to write about. Consider each main point in light of your audience and purpose. Each of the main points in the chart speaks to an audience of nonplayers. The first three main points express opinions and could be used in essays that would try to persuade. The fourth main point would suit an explanatory purpose.

When you have selected a main point that suits your audience and purpose, you are ready to write your thesis statement. Begin by experimenting with different ways to express your main point in a sentence.

The following chart gives sample thesis statements you might write if you chose the second of the possible main points listed in the preceding chart.

POSSIBLE THESIS STATEMENTS
1. Golf will tease and frustrate a new golfer in a great number of ways.
2. For new players, golf can be extremely frustrating.
3. Golf will challenge but frustrate new players in a number of ways.
4. The three main frustrations of the beginning golfer are the hazards of the course, other players, and inconsistent shots.
5. For new players, golf can be extremely frustrating, a constant conflict between the way they try to play and the way they do play.
6. For beginners, golf is a fascinating frustration because fun and success are often just out of reach.

When you have at least three possible thesis statements, you should select the one you will use in your essay. Notice that the six versions of the thesis statement in the chart each give a slightly different emphasis and focus to the main point. Notice also that the first three thesis statements are less specific and give less information than do the last three. The fourth thesis statement includes stated subtopics while the others do not. After reading each of your thesis statements, you might decide to use the sixth version because you like the twist that the word "fascinating" gives to the main point.

Brainstorming for Support. Once you have a thesis statement, you can begin gathering the supporting information that will become the body of your essay.

Brainstorm for facts, details, examples, reasons, and incidents that support your thesis statement.

The goal of the brainstorming stage is to produce a long list of supporting information from which you can choose the strongest, clearest pieces of support for the body of your essay. To reach this goal, professional writers use a number of methods. Among them are the question-and-answer method and the free-association method. To use the free-association method, read your thesis statement over several times and write down any and all thoughts that come to mind. To use the questioning method, put yourself in the reader's place and ask yourself questions about the thesis statement. Think particularly about ideas that may need expanding. Then answer these questions with specific information. Write down all of the examples, details, facts, reasons, and incidents that come to mind.

If you were to use the questioning method for the thesis statement on golf, you might write a list of questions and answers like the following.

QUESTIONING TO FIND SUPPORT FOR A THESIS STATEMENT

Thesis Statement: For beginners, golf is a fascinating frustration because fun and success are often just out of reach.

Why is golf fascinating? (Why do people want to play?)

—the golf course is a world of lawns, hills, greenness, lakes, ponds, trees
—players are outdoors for hours in the fresh air
—players can take up golf at almost any age
—a person gets away from everyday concerns on a golf course
—courses are often scenic, overlooking oceans, lakes, mountains, hills
—a person can play alone or against others
—chance to meet friendly golfers
—golf challenges a player to be accurate, precise, to keep on trying to improve
—a person can hope to do better on each hole
—a person gets away from crowds of people
—the joy when the player really connects with the ball
—the joy when drives, fairway shots, and putts go well
—the joy when a player gets a low score near par (considered the best reasonable score for that hole)

Why is golf frustrating? (Why are fun and success out of reach for beginners?)

—new players hit some good shots and some bad ones
—on some holes players have a strong start and a bad finish
—on other holes players have a bad start and a strong finish—can't do all things well
—new players get angry at themselves
—there are many ways to make bad shots
  —miss completely
  —top the ball
  —hit behind the ball
  —slice
  —hook
—courses require accuracy and control that beginners don't have
—often other players try to give beginners advice
  —new players lose self-confidence, become flustered
—other players want to play faster, get irritated with new players hunting for lost golf balls or making many short shots
—bad shots lose the ball
—courses are too long for beginners
—bad shots are embarrassing
—tall grass and shrubbery at the sides of course swallow up golf balls
—trees on sides of course obstruct shots and hide or cause balls to bounce
—players lose balls in water hazards: ponds, creeks, nearby ocean
  —difficult for beginner to avoid water hazards
  —must hit just the right direction and distance
—where backyards border golf courses, players can't hunt for their golf balls in people's yards
—other players watch beginners making mistakes
—other players criticize and make fun of new players so that new players get discouraged
—other players on other holes lose golf balls, take the new players' by mistake
—beginners are not sure of grip and stance, varying from swing to swing

Organizing Your Essay. Once you have a list of supporting information, you will have the raw materials for your essay. To organize the information so that it will clearly develop the thesis statement, you should group your support into subtopics and then outline your essay.

Choose appropriate subtopics, put them in a logical order, and then outline your essay.

If you have stated your subtopics in your thesis statement, you may have already grouped your supporting information into subtopics. But if your thesis statement does not provide subtopics, you must examine your list of support to determine natural subtopics of your main point. Check to see if your subtopics fit with the thesis statement and with each other.

Next, decide which logical order is the best way to arrange the subtopics. If your subtopics are locations, you will probably choose spatial order. Other types of subtopics could be arranged in chronological order, in order of importance, in comparison-and-contrast order, or in developmental order.

In the list of supporting information on the frustrations of golfing, you might observe that the material seems to divide naturally into three different kinds of frustration: frustration caused by the golf course, frustration caused by other players, and frustration caused by inconsistency. These three categories could become your subtopics. Then you might decide that they actually follow an order of importance, from least frustrating to most frustrating.

The following chart shows a plan for organizing the essay this way, devoting one paragraph of the body to each subtopic.

PLAN FOR AN ESSAY

Logical Order: Order of Importance

First paragraph	=	Introduction	
Second paragraph	=	Subtopic 1:	Frustration caused by golf course
Third paragraph	=	Subtopic 2:	Frustration caused by other golfers
Fourth paragraph	=	Subtopic 3:	Frustration caused by beginners' own inconsistency
Fifth paragraph	=	Conclusion	

When you have decided on the subtopics and the rough plan of your essay, group your support under each subtopic, eliminating those pieces of support that are unnecessary or irrelevant. Add further information if any of your subtopics are not covered thoroughly. You may also need to revise your thesis statement at this point so that it will fit your subtopics and your final list of supporting information.

Writing an outline for the body of your essay can speed up the drafting of the essay. You can use a modified outline or a formal topic outline. Include your thesis statement at the beginning of your outline. You may also include possible concluding sentences for some or all of the individual subtopics.

You might write a topic outline like the following for the body of the essay on golfing.

Thesis Statement: For beginners, golf is a fascinating frustration because fun and success are often just out of reach.

I. The new player's first frustration: the course itself
    A. Long, winding, hilly course
        1. Need for accuracy
        2. Beginners take many strokes to reach green
    B. Rough on the sides of course
        1. Tall grasses and shrubbery hide golf balls
        2. New players often lose one to several balls in a game
    C. Trees on sides of fairways
        1. Golf balls disappear in and under trees
        2. Golf balls bounce off trees and disappear
    D. Water hazards
        1. Players lose balls—hit right distance but wrong directions
        2. Players lose balls—hit right direction but wrong distance
II. Second frustration: other players
    A. Need to team up with other players
        1. Experienced golfers try to give advice—fluster new golfers
        2. Experienced or other golfers criticize new golfers—discourage and annoy new golfers
    B. Relaxing, uncrowded course becomes crowded when players behind want to go faster
        1. Players behind interrupt the new golfers' game
        2. Cause new players to hurry and play more poorly

III. Greatest frustration: unfulfilled expectations of doing well caused by new golfers' inconsistency
   A. New players lack control and aim so make many mistakes
      1. Swing and miss
      2. Top the ball
      3. Hit behind ball
      4. Slice
      5. Hook
   B. New players' anger at alternating good and bad shots
      1. At ruining a good score with bad putts
      2. At not beginning as well as they ended

Once you have completed your outline, jot down any ideas you have for your title, introduction, and conclusion.

EXERCISE A: Planning an Essay. Choose one of the general topics listed below and follow these directions to plan an essay.

1. Narrow the general topic by dividing it into three or four smaller topics suitable for an essay.
2. Develop a main idea about your topic by considering your audience and purpose. Express your main idea in at least three verions of a thesis statement.
3. Brainstorm for supporting information using either the questioning method or the free-association method.
4. Decide on an overall plan for your essay by finding subtopics, putting them in a logical order, and grouping your support under each subtopic. Eliminate irrelevant support and add further support if necessary.
5. Prepare a modified outline or a topic outline for the body of your essay. Put your thesis statement at the top and include any tentative ideas you have for closing sentences for individual subtopics.
6. Jot down any ideas you have for your title, introduction, and conclusion.

Your town or city	Part-time jobs	Architecture
Advantages and disadvantages of a small family	Bowling	A national park
	Reading mysteries	Painting
		After school sports

WRITING: Creating a First Draft

With a thorough outline and ideas for your title, introduction, and conclusion, you are ready to put all the parts of your essay together.

Write a first draft by connecting the ideas in your outline with transitions and other linking devices.

As you draft your essay, use transitions within paragraphs and between paragraphs to indicate a new subtopic or further development of the preceding subtopic. Also, try to repeat the main words in your thesis statement and in your subtopics and to use synonyms for these main words. You may also find consistent pronouns, parallel structure, and concluding sentences—at the end of subtopics—useful for guiding the reader.

The following essay was based on the outline about golfing. The marginal notes point out the essay's structure. The words in italics are transitions. Also notice the repetition of main words and synonyms: *frustration, aggravation,* and *problems* and *new golfers, new players,* and *beginners*.

Title — The Most Frustrating Game

Introduction — Tan, trimly muscular, Nancy Lopez and Lee Trevino walk on the golf course, address the ball with confidence, swing with powerful control, and watch the ball drop neatly on the green near the hole. Their appearance and actions have summed up the glamor, challenge, and rewards of golf. No doubt golf does have much to offer. Players can leave the strains of everyday life behind as they enter a world of grassy slopes and rugged cliffs, sparkling ponds, manicured greens, and swaying trees. Players can walk for exercise or ride in golf carts for comfort. Players can smile with satisfaction as they beat their last week's score by ten strokes. *Furthermore,* golf is a sport players can take up at almost any age and play long into their retirement years. For beginning golfers, *however,* the problems and aggravations equal the benefits and rewards. Golf will tax new golfers' patience and test

Thesis statement

their determination. For beginners, golf is a fascinating frustration because fun and success are often just out of reach.

Topic sentence for subtopic 1

The *first* frustration new players must contend with is the scenic, appealing course itself. Every feature that contributes to the peaceful charm makes the course more impossible for beginners. The area, called the hole, between the teeing ground, where players begin to play each hole, and the putting green, where players end each hole by putting the ball into a small hole, can be as long as 550 yards. On many holes, golfers will not be able to see the putting green from the teeing ground because the course is so long, or because it ends, drops down a cliff, or climbs a hill. To hit from the teeing ground to the putting green in the fewest possible strokes requires accuracy and control that most players lack. While professionals might take two strokes, beginners might need as many as seven to reach the green. The unmowed or scrubby territory on the sides of the course, called the rough, can also pose definite problems for beginners. The tall grass and shrubbery can seem to swallow golf balls, and new players can plan to lose one or more golf balls a game. Trees in the rough and between the holes can obstruct beginners' shots, causing the ball to lodge in some dense thicket or ricochet out of sight. The refreshing ponds, creeks, and lakes bordering holes, called water hazards, are guaranteed to frustrate beginning golfers. A shot can go the right distance but curve and land in the pond to sink in the mud, where only the ducks or fish could find it. And a ball hit in the right direction, but hit too soft or too hard, can have exactly the same miserable fate.

Transitional sentence

Topic sentence for subtopic 2

Most new players accept the hazards of the course as a challenge and reconcile themselves to losing some golf balls. Few new golfers, *however,* realize that other friendly golfers and seemingly uncrowded conditions can easily become frustrations. Usually golfers must play in groups of three or four. *Thus,* two new golfers could be teamed up with one or more other players, usually strangers, who are likely to be better golfers. When these experienced players see any new players struggling, they often begin giving advice: "You moved your head again. You've got to watch the ball." This analysis of their mistakes easily unhinges new golfers. Since golf is largely a game of attitude and concentration, the more flustered new golfers become, the worse they play. *Besides* The Friendly Advisors, the Wise-Guy Commentators can annoy and discourage new players: "Well, you'll never find that ball. It's a goner for sure. In the creek." *Perhaps the most frustrating players* are those speedy threesomes who turn an uncrowded course and a relaxing game into just the opposite when they play behind beginners. No sooner do new golfers begin to look for one lost ball or have one bad short shot, than the impatient players behind yell, "Can we play through?" *Then* the new players have to step aside and wait while the golfers behind play the hole and go on ahead. *Meanwhile* the new golfers have lost time and become even slower. *Soon* other players behind want to play through too. *Now* feeling guilty about taking more time, the new players rush their strokes and play even worse.

Topic sentence for subtopic 3

But of all the frustrations encountered by new golfers, inconsistency will tease and frustrate them the most, giving them that "if only . . ." feeling. New players lack the control and aim needed to hit the ball the right distance in the right direction every time. In golf, there are many ways to make mistakes, and new players usually find them all. Drawing back from the ball can cause new players to swing and miss. Poor form can cause players to top the ball, making it hop or roll only a short distance. *Or* players can swing awkwardly and gouge the ground, sending a huge piece of dirt flying instead of the ball. If players do swing into the ball, it can arc off to the right in a slice or curve away to the left in a hook, out of bounds either way. Hitting bad shots like these can make new players feel ineffective, unskilled, and foolish. Hitting some good shots and some bad shots, *however,* can be *even more frustrating*. When new players hit a long, straight drive and then hit three poor shots and take four putts to sink the ball, they become furious with themselves for throwing away the chance for a good score. On the other hand, a poor beginning with a strong finish on a hole can lead new players to ask themselves, "Now why couldn't I do that before?" And nothing is quite so embarrassing and aggravating as, after one good hole, teeing off in front of other players, only to watch the ball bound off the tee and land five yards away in a hedge.

Conclusion with reminder of thesis statement

One golfer confided to to his friend, "Golf's got to be the most frustrating game in the world. Those good times and good shots every now and then won't let me give up, but golf makes me so mad sometimes." Many new golfers would probably agree. Those cartoons of golfers with broken clubs attacking their golf carts or their partners must have captured some truth. But just when new golfers have vowed to forget golf and stick to tennis, they swing and hear a solid "thwak," as the ball soars two hundred yards onto the green. Suddenly the fascination of the game returns. After all, the new players think, I have thirty years to learn this sport. Again, golf demonstrates its true nature; it is not just a frustration, but a lure and a challenge as well: a fascinating frustration.

Clincher

EXERCISE B: Writing a First Draft. Using your outline and list of support from Exercise A, write a complete first draft of your essay.

REVISING: Polishing Your Essay

The revising step allows you to correct, improve, and polish your essay. Try to evaluate the essay objectively and read it as an outside reader would.

Use a checklist to evaluate your essay and then revise it for sense and for correctness.

Use the following checklist to evaluate your essay. Check each item from the list as you evaluate your essay for that point. Then make final changes and corrections in structure, content, grammar, mechanics, and spelling.

CHECKLIST FOR REVISING

1. Does the title attract attention, suit the essay, and give clues to the main point of the essay?
2. Does the introduction capture the reader's interest, provide any necessary background information, establish the tone, and lead smoothly into the thesis statement?
3. Does the thesis statement present a clearly focused main point?
4. Does each body paragraph develop a subtopic of the thesis statement or part of a subtopic with enough specific facts, details, examples, reasons, and incidents?
5. Are the subtopics all closely related to the thesis statement and to each other? Are they in the most logical order?
6. Does each paragraph in the body of the essay have a clear topic sentence?
7. Does the supporting information in each body paragraph follow a logical order clarified by transitions?
8. Have you guided the reader from paragraph to paragraph with appropriate transitions and repetitions of main words, synonyms, and pronouns?
9. Does the conclusion include a reminder of the thesis statement, echo the introduction, and bring the essay to a satisfactory end?
10. Are there any sentences that should be rewritten for clarity, conciseness, or for correctness of grammar, mechanics, or spelling?

After you have marked your first draft with any necessary changes and corrections and perhaps rewritten sections of your essay, you are ready to recopy it in final, neat form. Be sure to proofread your final copy. Make any final corrections that still may be needed.

EXERCISE C: Revising an Essay. Use the checklist on the previous page to evaluate the first draft you wrote in Exercise B. Make additions, corrections, and improvements on your draft, recopy your essay in final form, proofread it, and make final corrections if need be.

DEVELOPING WRITING SKILLS: Planning, Writing, and Revising an Essay. Before you begin to write your next essay, read an essay published as a short article in a magazine. Evaluate the essay's thesis statement, supporting information, and overall unity and coherence. List two good points or features that you would like to include in the next essay you write. Then follow the steps you have learned in this section to plan, write, and revise an essay on a topic of your choice, incorporating the two good points or features that you listed.

Writing Different Kinds of Essays 22.3

Essays are often categorized by purpose. The *expository essay* attempts to explain an idea, process, or event with factual information. The *persuasive essay* attempts to convince the reader of an opinion with reasonable arguments and evidence. In this section, you will study the special features of each of these two kinds of essays.

Writing Expository Essays

Before you can begin to write effective expository essays, you should clearly understand the special purpose and characteristics of this kind of writing.

Understanding Expository Essays. The expository essay explains a factual main point to the reader. All the material in the essay, from the beginning of the introduction to the end of the conclusion, should work together to achieve this purpose.

The purpose of an expository essay is to present information.

The thesis statement of an expository essay is a statement of fact that the rest of the essay will explain. It does not offer an opinion that requires defense.

Notice the difference between the statement of fact and the statement of opinion in the following examples. The statement of fact could be checked, since it is a matter of public record. The statement of opinion, however, could be questioned by someone having a contrary view and is open to debate.

STATEMENT OF FACT: Most Presidents of the United States retire from public office when they leave the White House.

STATEMENT OF OPINION: Most Presidents of the United States make no significant contributions after they leave the White House.

The following chart gives other examples of thesis statements that are appropriate for expository essays. Notice that all present factual main points that can be developed with objective information. Notice also that the first thesis statement includes stated subtopics.

SAMPLE THESIS STATEMENTS FOR EXPOSITORY ESSAYS

Thesis Statements	Stated Subtopics
While *The Magic Three of Solatia* by Jane Yolen and *Greenwitch* by Susan Cooper both incorporate myth and fairy tale, they differ in length, intended readers, and use of myths and fairy tales.	(1) length (2) intended readers (3) use of myths and fairy tales
You can learn to take excellent photographs of your tropical fish with a close-up camera.	none stated
Benjamin Disraeli played an important role in British government and politics in the mid-nineteenth century.	none stated

The body of an expository essay develops the main point with a complete explanation. The supporting information presented in the body may come from personal knowledge or from research. The body includes enough examples, details, and facts to fulfill the reader's sense that the topic has been covered thoroughly.

An expository essay should also have an *informative tone,* presenting information in an unbiased, explanatory way that is appropriate to both the topic and the readers. All difficult or specialized terms are defined and examples are used to illustrate concepts.

Prewriting, Writing, and Revising. When writing expository essays, you should follow the usual planning, writing, and revising steps. In addition, you should use your explanatory purpose as a guide throughout the steps.

Concentrate on explaining your main point to a particular audience in preparing an expository essay.

As you begin planning, be sure to select a topic that lends itself to factual explanation and does not involve matters of opinion. Find a main point about your topic that can be illustrated and developed objectively and factually. Then gather supporting information by asking yourself which aspects of the topic the reader will want to have explained and which terms, if any, need to be defined. A logically organized outline can also help you prepare comprehensible explanations.

While you draft, you should think about writing clear, thorough explanations. Draft an introduction that will interest the reader as well as provide enough background information to pave the way for your thesis statement. As you write the body paragraphs, concentrate on explaining your main points in language your readers can understand. Connect your ideas smoothly with transitions and repetitions of main words and synonyms. Think of a fitting reminder of your thesis statement for your conclusion and try to end the essay with a final remark that states your main idea in a nutshell.

When you have completed your first draft, revise your essay for clarity and correctness. Use the checklist for revising on page 568. Also consider the following specific suggestions for revising an expository essay.

SUGGESTIONS FOR REVISING AN EXPOSITORY ESSAY

1. Check for clarity by having someone unfamiliar with your topic read and summarize the information you present.
2. Check for clarity by having someone unfamiliar with your topic read your essay and point out any passages that are confusing or any special terms that are not defined.
3. Check for completeness by having someone familiar with your topic read your essay and point out any significant ideas of relevant information that you did not include.
4. Check for completeness by having someone unfamiliar with your topic read your essay and write down any important questions that your essay leaves unanswered.
5. Ask a reader to identify any places where the tone is not objective and informative.
6. If your essay explains a process, ask someone to follow the steps as you have presented them.

After revising your essay, make a clean final copy. Be sure to check the final copy for typographical errors.

EXERCISE A: Analyzing an Expository Essay. Read the following expository essay. Then answer the questions that follow the essay.

Ozzie Goes to the Office

Throughout the decades of commercial television in the United States, the situation comedy—or "sitcom"—has remained one of the most popular and successful forms of television entertainment. Certain basic aspects of the sitcom have persisted unchanged since the early 1950's. Sitcoms have always been geared to entertaining a mass audience for half-hour chunks of time during the prime viewing period between 7:30 p.m. and 10:00 p.m. Also, they have always involved a small core of regular characters who are very different from one another and who behave in a consistent and predictable manner. An interesting change, however, took place in the 1970's when situation comedies moved out of the house and into the office:

The settings changed drastically, but many of the roles remained very much the same.

The "real" family situation comedies of the 1950's focused almost entirely upon the home and relations among parents and children. *Ozzie and Harriet, The Donna Reed Show, Father Knows Best,* and *Leave It to Beaver*—to name a few—took place almost without exception in a single-family house located in a small town or suburb. The family usually consisted of a mother, father, and two or three children of varying ages. The mother was usually a housewife. The father was always employed outside the home, but his job, if discussed at all, rarely entered the family drama. (One exception, *Make Room for Daddy,* with Danny Thomas, involved a father with a colorful show business career.) Because the setting was confined to the home, the personal and professional difficulties of the adult characters received very little attention. As a result, these series tended to center on the problems and accomplishments of the children. The parents acted chiefly as counselors and benevolent authorities, guiding the children through the process of growing up.

In the 1970's, however, a number of situation comedies moved out of the home into the workplace with a new core of characters, called the "office family." The "office family" series were populated almost entirely by adults thrown together because of their occupations. While the "real family" situation comedies were set in small towns and suburbs, the office family sitcoms took place principally in large cities: *The Mary Tyler Moore Show* in Minneapolis, *The Bob Newhart Show* in Chicago, *WKRP in Cincinnati* in Cincinnati. The absence of children in the office usually carried over into the personal lives of the characters as well. Nearly all of them were childless, and a large percentage were single. The office family series focused, therefore, entirely upon the problems of adults—on their professional, personal, and romantic triumphs and tribulations. Still, some of the old family relationships remained. Members of the office family got to know each other well from working closely together. Like the real family, the office family had a clear structure of authority. The bosses in the office family even had some of the wisdom and authority that the home family granted to parents. Sometimes members of the office family took on the role of children. Occasionally, these adults acted "childishly" as other members of the family offered more mature "parental" counsel.

Thus, despite differences in setting and characters, the "real family" comedies of the 1950's and the "office comedies" of the 1970's shared many parallel features and relationships. In a sense, the "office family" carried the structure of the "real family" into a new setting. One might even say that the Ozzies and Harriets of the old family sitcoms had not entirely departed from America's living rooms. They had simply left their kitchens and backyards for the office cubicles and coffee machines of the 1970's.

1. What does the title add to the essay? Can you think up alternative titles?
2. How does the introduction prepare the reader for the rest of the essay?
3. What is the thesis statement?
4. What are two pieces of supporting information given in each body paragraph?
5. In what basic order have the two body paragraphs been presented? What other order might have been used?
6. What terms does the writer explain? Do any of these terms require more explanation than the writer has given? Are any other terms confusing?
7. What transitions link ideas between paragraphs?
8. How is the concluding paragraph related to the thesis statement? What words and ideas link the introduction and the conclusion?
9. What does the last sentence add to the essay? Write a final sentence of your own to substitute for it. What have you added or taken away from the essay?
10. To what extent does the essay fulfill its explanatory purpose? To what extent does the essay maintain an informative tone?

EXERCISE B: Writing an Expository Essay. Choose one of the topics listed on the next page and follow these instructions to write an expository essay.

1. Narrow your topic, decide on a main point, and write a thesis statement.

2. Brainstorm for supporting information, and then group your support into subtopcis.
3. Outline the body of your essay. Then sketch out a rough introduction and try to write down several ideas for your conclusion and two or three possible titles for the essay.
4. Write a complete first draft of the essay.
5. Use the checklist for revising on page 568 to evaluate your essay. Also use one of the suggestions in the chart on page 572. Then revise your essay and recopy it.

Planning a garden (tool shed, playroom,or display cabinet)
The design changes in this year's new automobiles
Preparing for a final exam
The causes of the Great Depression
The steps involved in repairing an automatic dishwasher (radio, television, or other appliance)
The accomplishments of a famous person (for example, Henry Ford, Thomas Edison, Marie Curie, or Carrie Nation)
Designing a stage set
The earliest forms of written communication
Planning fire escape routes from a house
Solar energy
Protecting an endangered species

Writing Persuasive Essays

Knowing how to write effective persuasive essays can be useful to you in schoool, in future jobs, and in your personal writing. This section will point out the special features of persuasive essays and will help you incorporate them into your own writing.

Understanding Persuasive Essays. A persuasive essay defends an opinion or takes a stand on an issue in order to convince others. It may seek to change people's minds or it may attempt to move them to action.

The purpose of a persuasive essay is to convince the reader to accept an idea or to act.

The introduction establishes the persuasive purpose. It often begins by presenting background information, followed by the writer's opinion in the thesis statement. The thesis statement must be controversial, open to disagreement, not a fact. The thesis statement must also take a position that is significant and defensible. It should seem worthwhile and not trivial to the reader and be supportable with evidence that the reader will find convincing.

Notice the difference between the following statements of opinion. One is genuinely controversial and could be debated. The other is merely a personal opinion that could not be proven one way or the other; it is, therefore, not suited to a persuasive essay.

CONTROVERSIAL OPINION: Smoking should be banned in all public places.

TRIVIAL OPINION: Smoking is a disgusting habit.

The following chart provides further examples of significant, defensible thesis stastements that are suitable for persuasive essays. Notice that the thesis statements take opposing positions on two issues. Also notice that the last two thesis statements include stated subtopics.

SAMPLE THESIS STATEMENTS FOR PERSUASIVE ESSAYS	
Thesis Statements	**Stated Subtopics**
The rights of farm and other domesticated animals deserve more attention.	none stated
Farm and other domesticated animals exist purely to serve human needs.	none stated
In *Romeo and Juliet,* the young couple's impatience and Romeo's hot temper bring about their tragic end.	(1) young couple's impatience (2) Romeo's hot temper
In *Romeo and Juliet,* both families' foolish feuding and the Capulets' insensitivity to Juliet bring about the young couple's tragic end.	(1) both families' foolish feuding (2) the Capulets' insensitivity to Juliet

To carry through the persuasive purpose, the body of a persuasive essay presents supporting information that defends the thesis statement. Sometimes the support also includes answers to specific arguments that might be raised by the opposing side in a controversy. In many cases, the support will be organized in order of importance, so that the reader is led slowly up to the final and most convincing argment.

The conclusion of a persuasive essay draws all the arguments together in order to make the final attempt to convince the reader. Often, the conclusion will summarize the main arguments and most effective items of evidence from the body of the essay. It frequently contains a clincher—a strong closing comment that attempts to win the reader over.

The entire essay should also have a reasonable, *persuasive tone*. The wording of the thesis statement and the choice and arrangement of the support should contribute to the persuasiveness of the tone. The choice of language can help convince the reader that the opinions expressed are worth thinking about seriously. Name-calling, words with inappropriate shades of meaning, and other emotional language can destroy a reasonable tone and alienate readers. Because persuading involves informing too, specific and clear language helps readers understand the arguments presented.

Prewriting, Writing, and Revising. All of the planning, writing, and revising steps that go into creating a persuasive essay should be directed toward your persuasive purpose. Imagine that your audience disagrees with you or simply does not care. Keeping the opposition in mind will help you sharpen your own reasoning and be more convincing.

Concentrate on persuading an unsympathetic reader to accept your viewpoint in a persuasive essay.

Select a topic that you know well and consider important for others to care about. Make sure that the thesis statement you draft is indeed an opinion and not a fact by drafting a sentence that presents an opposing position. Be sure that the controversial main point you choose and your wording of it are defensible with factual evidence and reasonable arguments.

When gathering supporting information, your goal should be to build a strong defense. To do this you will need to anticipate the arguments of readers who disagree with you. Remember that your support should answer the opposing arguments. Try to make two lists of support, one for your side and one for the opposing side. Then create a third list, giving further support for your side by directly answering the specific arguments of the other side. Such a process of answering arguments with counter-arguments will help you not only to meet the opposition arguments but also to find and correct weaknesses in your own case. In fact, you may find it helpful to include in your essay a few of the arguments for the other side. Mentioning those arguments will enable you to answer objections to your opinion which may come up in your reader's mind and will often add to the persuasiveness of your essay. As you organize your arguments, arrange them so that you build up to the strongest and most convincing argument.

In drafting your essay, bear in mind the effect you want to have on the reader. As you write your introduction, try to capture the reader's attention, lead up to the thesis statement gradually, and then express the main point clearly and strongly. Maintain a consistent, reasonable tone in your draft of the whole essay. Restate the controversial main point in your conclusion and try for a forceful ending—a warning, a call to action, or a statement relating the issue to the reader's life.

Use the checklist on page 568 to evaluate and revise your essay. You might also use the following suggestions to make your essay more persuasive.

SUGGESTIONS FOR EVALUATING A PERSUASIVE ESSAY

1. Have someone with a neutral viewpoint read your essay. Ask that person to evaluate how interesting and convincing your essay is. Then make any necessary improvements in the essay.
2. Have someone who disagrees with you read your essay and ask that person to comment on the strength, development, and order of your arguments. Make any necessary improvements to strengthen your essay.

EXERCISE C: Analyzing a Persuasive Essay. Read the following persuasive essay. Then answer the questions that follow the essay.

Why Fly?

Not everyone flies. In fact, some people go to a good deal of trouble to avoid taking airplanes altogether. This attitude may be difficult to understand, particularly for veteran air travelers, who appreciate the benefits of airplane travel and could not accomplish half of what they do if they did not fly. Confirmed nonfliers, however, mention problems of air travel, and those most hostile to flying cite the dates and locations of airplane disasters. Yet in spite of complaints and some travelers' deep-seated fears of flying, air transport continues to offer a combination of convenience, speed, and safety unmatched by any other means of transportation.

Opponents of flying point out that air travel can be inconvenient. They maintain, for example, that passengers on closely connecting flights may have to wait several hours at their destinations before their luggage appears. Actually, though, airlines provide conveniences unparalleled anywhere else in the travel industry. Luggage is almost never lost or mishandled, and if it should be delayed, the airlines always arrange to deliver the luggage to the passenger. Statistics vary among airlines, but most confirm that only one passenger in ten thousand will suffer a loss or delay with baggage. Unlike train and bus stations, most airports also have set aside long-term parking areas where passengers can safely leave their cars for extended periods of time. In addition, most have rapid transfer systems, such as buses and carts, which conduct passengers and their luggage from the parking areas to the terminal. The airlines also relieve their customers of the burden of hauling their luggage with curbside check-in service.

Some people may say that flights are often delayed or cancelled, but such problems are really infrequent and do not lessen the overall speed of air travel. Even with an occasional few hours' delay, travel time by air is well ahead of travel by car, bus, or train. No one can deny that airplanes cut to a fraction the traveling time between two points. And for great distances, anything but air transport is inconceivable. Imagine spending three and one-half days of a short vacation or of a work week sitting on a bus between Washington, D.C., and San Francisco, when an airplane could have flown you from coast to coast in about five hours.

Despite the speed and convenience of air travel, however, many people are troubled by an overwhelming fear of flying, based quite understandably on the attention given to airplane crashes. But these events are truly rare, almost freakish occurrences. In fact, it is their rarity that makes them newsworthy. The chances of being involved in an airplane accident are minuscule for any air traveler. Those who ride in automobiles are one hundred times more likely to suffer injury than are air passengers, yet people ride in and drive automobiles every day. Most people do not realize that airplanes actually enjoy the best safety record of all the modes of travel, given the huge numbers of people they carry and the millions of miles they cover every year.

Clearly, flying makes traveling easier, faster, and safer than other methods of transportation. While those who shun airplanes constitute only a small percentage of travelers, they might be fewer still if they examined the facts and statistics. And if these people could conquer their fears enough to give flying a chance, they might make some pleasant discoveries. With veteran travelers, they might come to enjoy the automatic ramps that whiz passengers from one end of a terminal to another, the thrill of takeoffs, and the view of clean clouds, rainbow sunsets, and the earth curving thousands of feet below. These people would then know why they fly.

1. Do you consider the title of this essay appropriate or inappropriate?
2. How does the introduction prepare the reader for a persuasive essay?
3. At what point did you first realize what the writer's position was?
4. What is the thesis statement? What, if any, are the subtopics?
5. What are the major arguments offered in support of the thesis statement? What supporting information is provided for each of these arguments?
6. Where does the writer mention opposing arguments? Which points, if any, are actually conceded?
7. What additional arguments for or against the controversial main point can you think of?
8. What is the arrangement of subtopics in the body?

9. What transitions and repetitions of main words and synonyms do you find in the essay?
10. What are some examples of the writer's reasonable, persuasive tone?

EXERCISE D: Writing a Persuasive Essay. Choose one of the topics listed below and follow these directions to write a persuasive essay.

1. Determine your stand on the topic, sharpen your main point, and write a thesis statement.
2. Brainstorm for supporting information by listing arguments for and against your position. Develop counter-arguments to meet the opposing position.
3. Group your evidence into subtopics, and then organize your material using order of importance or some other logical order. Outline the body of your essay.
4. Write a complete first draft, based on your outline.
5. Use the checklist on page 568 and one of the suggestions in the chart on page 578 to evaluate and revise your essay. Make a clean copy of the final essay.

The need for improvements in the school cafeteria (or classrooms or gym)
The importance of voting (in school elections or national elections)
The usefulness of the the Electoral College
The quality of movie sequels as compared to the original films
The value of athletic scholarships
The need for synthetic fuels
The most talented popular musician
The inventor (politician, artist, and so on) who has made the biggest contribution to society
The quality of television commercials

DEVELOPING WRITING SKILLS: Writing Different Kinds of Essays. Select a topic of your own to use as the basis of two separate essays. First, write down a statement of fact about the topic. Then write down a statement of opinion about the same topic. Develop the first statement into an expository essay and the second statement into a persuasive essay.

Writing Workshop: Essays

ASSIGNMENT 1

Topic The Professional Athlete: A Select Few

Form and Purpose An expository essay that informs readers about the process of becoming a professional athlete in one sport

Audience Students interested in an athletic career

Length Five to seven paragraphs

Focus Develop a thesis statement that includes a quotation from a professional athlete. Then support that thesis with facts, details, and examples.

Sources Books, magazine and newspaper articles

Prewriting Choose a sport. List questions about the process of becoming a professional athlete in that sport. Research answers to those questions. Use your notes to develop a thesis statement and an outline of subtopics.

Writing Follow your outline when writing a first draft. In your concluding paragraph, use a clincher sentence.

Revising Use the checklists on pages 568 and 572 to help you make changes. Then write a final draft of your essay.

ASSIGNMENT 2

Topic What "Democracy" Means to Me

Form and Purpose A persuasive essay that attempts to convince your readers of your viewpoints about democracy

Audience The editors of a newspaper in a country that does not have a democratic form of government

Length Five to seven paragraphs

Focus In your opening statements, cite a main idea about what democracy means to you. Develop your thesis by providing supporting facts, examples, and reasons.

Sources Books, films, magazines, newspapers, news programs, and personal experiences and observations

Prewriting Write a thesis statement that clearly reflects your opinion. List supporting facts, examples, and reasons. Organize them into an outline of related subtopics.

Writing Using your outline, write a first draft of your essay. End with a clincher statement.

Revising Use the checklists on pages 568 and 578 to revise your paper.

Statue of Liberty

Democratic National Convention, 1972

Topics for Writing: Essays

© 1968, United Feature Syndicate, Inc.

If the cartoon above suggests a topic for an expository or a persuasive essay, write a five- to seven-paragraph essay about it. Other possible related topics are listed below. If you wish, choose one and plan, write, and revise an essay on it.

1. The Construction of a Pyramid—An Amazing Accomplishment
2. A Human Rights Leader of the Past
3. An Important Writer, Artist, or Musician from the Past
4. A College Education—Is It Really Necessary?
5. Are We a Literate Society Today?
6. The Computer As an Educational Tool
7. Why Television Shows Are Mediocre and All Alike
8. A Future Solution to an Important World Problem
9. A New Sport for the Year 2050
10. Communication in the Year 2050

Chapter 23

Research Papers

In school and later on in your work, you will often need to prepare papers based on research about particular topics. In most cases, you will find the information you need in a library. This chapter focuses on the special characteristics of a research paper and shows you how to prepare and write one.

Understanding Research Papers 23.1

A research paper, like an essay, must be focused on a particular point: the thesis statement. Unlike many essays, however, these papers must always be based on information that is gathered through research. The paper may begin with your own ideas, but it must be developed through outside sources that provide new information.

Sources of Information

A research paper is the product of investigation. You will generally begin with a number of ideas about a topic and then explore the topic further by consulting a variety of sources in the library. You will need to check the card catalog, *The Readers' Guide to Periodical Literature,* and the vertical file for potential references to your subject. Then you will have to follow up your leads by reading books, newspapers, magazines, and such specialized reference works as encyclopedias, almanacs, atlases, and biographical dictionaries. (See Chapter 34 for a detailed guide to the use of the library.)

Citing Sources of Information. Sources of information should be cited throughout your paper, both to show that you have used sources and to give your reader information about the sources you have used.

A research paper should give credit to its sources in footnotes at the bottom of the page or at the end of the paper.

To use footnotes, place a small number above the line just after the quotation, fact, or idea that you are taking from your source. Then place the same number at the bottom of the page or at the end of the paper, followed by information that identifies the source. The numbers should be consecutive whether you place them at the bottom of the pages or at the end of the paper.

The following passage shows footnotes for two different kinds of sources. The first one is for a magazine. The second one is for a book.

Use of footnotes

Pablo Picasso, one of the greatest artists of the twentieth century, was also one of the most productive painters of all time. In his ninety-one years, he created over six thousand paintings, and when he died, his estate was valued at $1.1 billion.[1] Picasso's great and varied output had a tremendous influence over the artists of his time. In fact, the entire abstract movement in twentieth-century painting owes its origin largely to the ground-breaking work of Picasso.[2]

---

[1]Peter Hamill, "Picasso the Man," New York, May 12, 1980, p. 35.

[2]H.W. Janson, History of Art (Englewood Cliffs, N.J.: Prentice-Hall, 1962), p. 521.

The chart that begins on the next page shows how to cite a number of different kinds of sources. Note that any time your source does not have an author, you can use exactly the same form, starting with the name of the book or article, instead of with the name of the author. For example, for a magazine article without an author you would cite the article title, the magazine, the date, and the page number.

FORMS FOR THE CITING SOURCES	
Kinds of Sources	**Footnotes**
Book	[1]Jean Lipman and Alice Winchester, The Flowering of American Folk Art (New York: Viking Press, 1974), p. 86.
Magazine Article	[2]Andrew Porter, "Musical Events," The New Yorker, July 30, 1984, p. 56.
Encyclopedia Article	[3]Donald and Monique King, "Embroidery," The Encyclopedia Americana, 1980 ed.
Newspaper Article	[4]Jennifer Dunning, "Two Premieres at American Ballet Theatre," The New York Times, June 13, 1984, p. C13.
Collection	[5]William Shakespeare, The Complete Plays and Poems of William Shakespeare, ed. by William Allan Neilson and Charles Jarvis Hill (Cambridge, Mass.: Riverside Press, 1942), p. 7.
Translation	[6]Fyodor Dostoyevsky, The Idiot, trans. by Constance Garnett (New York: Dell Publishing Co., 1959), p. 210.
Work in Several Volumes	[7]Elting E. Morison, ed., The Letters of Theodore Roosevelt, vol. 3 (Cambridge, Mass.: Harvard University Press, 1951), p. 425.

NOTE ABOUT THE MODERN LANGUAGE ASSOCIATION (MLA) SYSTEM FOR CITING SOURCES: The MLA has recently endorsed a system that is becoming more and more popular, especially in colleges and universities. It calls for in-text citations rather than footnotes. Each of the citations gives only a very limited amount of information, listed in parentheses right after the quotation, fact, or idea that is being cited at that point in the report.

The chart on the next page shows the information that would be given for each of the items shown in the chart above. The reason so little information is given is that all research papers, including those with footnotes, must also have a bibliography at the very end which lists details about all sources.

Thus, the reader interested in more information can check the bibliography.

MLA CITATIONS	
Kinds of Sources	**Citations**
Book	(Lipman and Winchester 86)
Magazine Article	(Porter 56)
Encyclopedia Article	(King and King)
Newspaper Article	(Dunning C13)
Collection	(Shakespeare 7)
Translation	(Dostoyevsky 210)
Work in Several Volumes	(Morison 425)

If a book or an article does not have an author, the MLA system would list just the title and the page number.

When to Cite Outside Sources. Besides knowing *how* to acknowledge your sources of information, you need to know *when* to indicate that you have incorporated outside information into your paper. If you do not cite the use of outside sources, you will be guilty of *plagiarism,* the act of presenting someone else's work as your own.

Research papers cite all sources from which words, little-known facts, or ideas have been taken.

Three kinds of information always require citation.

First, whenever you repeat a source's exact words, the statement must be placed in quotation marks and the source must be acknowledged. This is true no matter how short the quote and no matter whether it was written or spoken.

Second, whenever you refer to a fact that is not widely known, you will need to give an ackowledgement. You would not, for example, need to credit the commonplace fact that the Industrial Revolution changed world history. But you would need to cite a source for a less common fact about the early factories of the Industrial Revolution.

Third, whenever you summarize or reword the ideas in a single source, you must acknowledge the source of the ideas.

Imagine that you are doing research on the subject of endangered species. You might come across the following passage in a magazine article that is closely related to the topic you are working on.

Passage from a magazine

The chief reasons for the decreases in wild animals and plants fall into understandable categories. Exploitation of the wild resources for useful products heads the list. Second, and increasing rapidly, is destruction of the natural environment in which animals and plants live. Third is competition from introduced species, whether livestock or pests (such as rats and plant diseases) or kinds of life from which some good was anticipated (such as starlings or mongooses). Today the most dreadful threat is the unselective poisoning of the environment by chemical compounds that have been added either in attempts to minimize losses from pests or merely as industrial wastes.—Lorus and Margery Milne

The following passage from a paper shows the incorrect use of this research material. Both the words and ideas of the magazine article have been used without acknowledgment. The italicized words and phrases are lifted directly from the article and indicate that the writer of this report would be guilty of plagiarism.

Unacceptable passage with plagiarism

There are many reasons why wild animals and plants are decreasing. One major reason is that the wilderness areas are constantly shrinking, causing the *destruction of the natural environment in which animals and plants live.* In addition, *competition from introduced species, whether livestock or pests,* also takes a toll. But the greatest danger *is the unselective poisoning of the environment by chemical compounds.*

In contrast, the following passage is also based on the article, but with a difference. The passage combines information from the source with the writer's own ideas. Furthermore, all the ideas except those in quotations are expressed in the writer's own language. Finally, the writer is careful to give credit where credit is due.

Acceptable passage with source cited

There are many reasons why wild animals and plants are decreasing. For example, the wilderness areas in which wild animals and plants live are constantly shrinking; there is less and less land available to provide the appropriate habitats for survival. In addition, rival species have sometimes been introduced which successfully compete with the native populations, primarily for food. But the greatest danger, it has been pointed out, is "the unselective poisoning of the environment by chemical compounds that have been added either in attempts to minimize losses from pests or merely as industrial wastes."[1]

---

[1]Drs. Lorus J. and Margery Milne, "Will the Environment Defeat Mankind?" The Saturday Evening Post, September 1979, p. 103.

Writing a Bibliography. *All* of the sources that you consult in your research—both those cited in the body of the paper and those that you have read but not specifically cited—must be presented at the end of the paper in a complete bibliography.

A research paper must include a bibliography listing all of the sources that have been consulted in preparing the paper.

The bibliography is usually a separate page at the end of the paper. Each entry in the bibliography gives complete information about every book, magazine, encyclopedia, or newspaper that you have consulted in your research. In your bibliography, you should list each author's name, last name first, followed by all the information found in a footnote. The one exception is for page numbers. You do not need to list the page numbers of books in bibliographic entries since you are simply identifying the work as a source that you have consulted. You should, however, give the pages on which an article in a periodical can be found. The entries in your bibliography should be listed in alphabetical order by the authors' last names or by the titles of the articles or books if the authors are not given. Ignore *The, An,* and *A* when alphabetizing.

The following chart includes the basic forms for the bibliographic entries of a number of different types of sources. Here they are listed by categories, but in a true bibliography they would appear in alphabetical order, beginning in this case with Dostoyevsky.

FORMS FOR BIBLIOGRAPHY ENTRIES

Kinds of Sources	Bibliography Entries
Books	Janson, H.W. History of Art. Englewood Cliffs, N.J.: Prentice-Hall, 1962.
	Lipman, Jean, and Alice Winchester. The Flowering of American Folk Art. New York: Viking Press, 1974.
Magazine Articles	Porter, Andrew. "Musical Events." The New Yorker, July 30, 1984, pp. 56–59.
	"Talk of the Town." The New Yorker. July 30, 1984, pp. 21–25.
Encyclopedia Article	King, Donald, and Monique. "Embroidery." The Encyclopedia Americana, 1980 ed.
Newspaper Article	Dunning, Jennifer. "Two Premieres at American Ballet Theatre." The New York Times, June 13, 1984, p. C13.
Collection	Shakespeare, William. The Complete Plays and Poems of William Shakespeare. Edited by William Allan Neilson and Charles Jarvis Hill. Cambridge, Mass.: Riverside Press, 1942.
Translation	Dostoyevsky, Fyodor. The Idiot. Translated by Constance Garnett. New York: Dell Publishing Co., 1959.
Work in Several Volumes	Morison, Elting E., ed. The Letters of Theodore Roosevelt, vol. 3. Cambridge, Mass.: Harvard University Press, 1951.

EXERCISE A: Practicing the Citation of Sources. Look in your library for sources on *one* of the following topics. Use the card catalog, *The Readers' Guide to Periodical Literature,* and any other means you can to find sources on your topic.

Choose at least *five* sources, including at least one book and one magazine article. For each source, write down the information that would be included in a footnote within the text of the paper. If you cannot find at least five sources on your topic, choose another one.

Solar power
A famous movie star
Scuba diving
The San Francisco earthquake
Modern American painters
Medieval armor and weapons
A tourist attraction
Extrasensory perception (ESP)
Dinosaurs
The space shuttle
Sports medicine

EXERCISE B: Practicing Bibliographic Entries. Take the sources that you found for Exercise A and write bibliographic entries for them. List them together in the order that they would follow in a complete bibliography.

Structure and Features

A research paper is organized much like an essay. However, it also includes references to sources of information and a bibliography of sources consulted.

Research papers include a title, introduction with a thesis statement, body, conclusion, citation of sources throughout, and bibliography.

The *title* and *introduction* prepare the reader for the information that will be presented. The introduction should also offer a *thesis statement,* the main point of the paper. This statement will keep the paper focused on a topic that can be covered reasonably. Even more important, this statement explains the purpose of the paper.

The *body* of the paper develops the thesis statement, usually through subtopics. It presents information gathered through research and arranged in a logical sequence to support the point made in the introduction.

The *conclusion* ties together the thesis statement and the evidence presented in the body. It should do this in a way that puts the "finishing touch" on arguments or ideas.

Research papers also include the systematic and consistent citation of sources throughout, generally in footnotes, and a bibliography at the end listing all of the sources consulted.

The following paper incorporates all of these special features. Notice how the footnotes are given in full for the first citation of a work but later abbreviated.

The Boy Genius

The Austrian composer Wolfgang Amadeus Mozart achieved great fame during his short but brilliant life two centuries ago. He composed an amazing number of highly original, imaginative works and contributed many new ideas to the classical music of his time. His mature works are still played by orchestras around the world and cherished by music lovers everywhere. These works are, however, only a part of his musical career. Mozart wrote his first symphony—a complex musical composition consisting of a number of separate sections or movements—at the age of nine.[1] Such talent amazed the people of his own time and has contributed greatly to the lasting fame he achieved. In fact, Mozart is perhaps best remembered as a boy wonder; a child prodigy who showed an incredible aptitude for music at a very young age.

Born in January of 1756 in Salzburg, Austria, Wolfgang Amadeus Mozart was the last child of Anna Maria and Leopold Mozart, a musician. As an infant in a musical household, young Wolfgang showed a profound interest in music. When he was only four years old, he began to listen to his sister's music lessons. He was soon able to copy her music, having learned notation partly from his father and partly on his own. At the age of five, he composed his first original piece of music, a piano concerto.[2] Moved by his son's accomplishment, Leopold decided that this child was sent from God, and that it was his special duty to train the boy.[3]

Leopold Mozart believed that his son's talents as a composer as well as his skills as a pianist should receive recognition. Embarking with his son and daughter on a tour of Europe, Leopold first presented his children in a concert in Vienna, Austria, where they received overwhelming ovations and became an instant success. They were invited to perform at the homes of wealthy Austrian aristocrats and they even played for the Emperor and Empress. Soon the children became the "darlings of Vienna" and were showered with gifts.[4]

One of Mozart's most remarkable youthful achievements took place in Rome during Holy Week, when he heard a choir sing Allegri's Miserere. This was a sacred piece of church music which singers were not allowed to copy under the threat of excommunication. After hearing it only once, Wolfgang wrote down the entire work from memory—note by precise note. Scholars have compared Mozart's version with the original and have found it flawless.[5]

Leopold Mozart continued to present his brilliant son to the public, developing but also exploiting his talent. For example, he advertised his son's concert in Frankfurt in 1763 like a barker at a carnival: "He will play a concerto for the violin, and will accompany symphonies on the harpsichord, the manual or keyboard being covered with cloth, with as much facility as if he could see the keys; he will instantly name all the notes played at a distance, whether singly or in chords on the harpsichord or any other instrument, bell, glass, or clock. He will finally improvise as long as may be desired, and in any key, on the harpsichord and organ."[6] These exhibitions earned young Mozart considerable praise and some important appointments as a church and court musician. It was not until Mozart was in his early twenties that he escaped the domination of his father and sought important and lucrative appointments, which, unfortunately, never came to him.

Mozart lived only thirty-six years but produced highly original works that often departed from the traditional music of his time. While his career was characterized by frequent disappointments and financial problems—he failed to receive coveted court appointments, and he made several important enemies in the Church—his life was distinguished by an outstanding talent. Mozart's experience as a child prodigy led to a highly productive mature career and helped to establish him as a legend in his own brief lifetime.

---

[1]Alfred Einstein, Mozart—His Character, His Work, trans. by Arthur Mendel and Nathan Broden (New York: Oxford University Press, 1945), p. 215.

[2]Charlotte Haldane, Mozart (London: Oxford University Press, 1960), p. 7.

[3]Erich Valentin, Mozart—A Pictoral Biography (New York: Viking Press, 1959), p. 153.

[4]J.E. Talbot, Mozart (London: Duckworth, 1934), p. 25.

[5]Talbot, Mozart, pp. 60–61.

[6]Milton Cross and David Ewen, New Encyclopedia of the Great Composers and Their Music (Garden City, N.Y.: Doubleday and Co., 1963), pp. 641–42.

BIBLIOGRAPHY

Cross, Milton and Ewen, David. New Encyclopedia of the Great Composers and Their Music. Garden City, N.Y.: Doubleday and Co., 1953.

Davenport, Marcia. Mozart. New York: Charles Scribner's Sons, 1956.

Einstein, Alfred. Mozart—His Character, His Work. Translated by Arthur Mendel and Nathan Broden. New York: Oxford University Press, 1945.

Haldane, Charlotte. Mozart. London: Oxford University Press, 1960.

Kolb, Annette. Mozart. Westport, Conn.: Greenwood Press, 1975.

"Mozart, Wolfgang Amadeus." The Encyclopaedia Britannica, 14th ed.

Talbot, J.E. Mozart. London: Duckworth, 1934.

Valentin, Erich. Mozart—A Pictoral Biography. New York: Viking Press, 1959.

NOTE ABOUT OTHER FEATURES: In most cases, your paper should also have a special, separate title page, which includes the title, your name, the class, the date, and any other information that your teacher may require. You might also be asked to provide a separate formal outline of your paper.

EXERCISE C: Analyzing a Report. Answer the following questions about the research paper about Mozart.

1. How does the title capture the reader's interest?
2. What does the reader learn in the paper's introduction?
3. What is the thesis statement of the paper?
4. How has the writer organized the supporting information in the body of the paper?

5. How does the conclusion refer to the thesis statement?
6. How many footnotes are included?
7. How many different sources does the writer cite in the footnotes?
8. How many footnotes include quotations?
9. What *types* of sources were consulted: books, magazines, and so on?
10. What other types of sources of information might have been consulted?

DEVELOPING WRITING SKILLS: Practicing with Thesis Statements and Titles. Using the topic you chose in Exercise A and the bibliographic sources you collected, write out several possible thesis statements that could be supported by your sources. Then choose one thesis statement and write out several possible titles that would prepare the reader for the thesis statement.

23.2 Writing a Research Paper

Your paper will be both better and easier to do if you approach the assignment as a series of planning, writing, and revising steps. This section describes ways to plan and carry out your research, organize your paper, write a first draft, and revise your work.

PREWRITING: Planning Your Paper

You should plan your research paper with great care, taking into account the assignment, your own interests, and the amount and kinds of information you are likely to find.

Choosing and Narrowing a Topic. To make sure you have a workable topic, you should spend a fair amount of time choosing and narrowing your topic. Make sure that it meets several specific criteria.

Choose a topic that is interesting, that can be supported with research, and that can reasonably be covered in one paper.

You might give yourself three or four general ideas to choose from and then visit the library to see the amount and kind of research material available on each topic. After checking the card catalog and *The Readers' Guide to Periodical Literature,* you may find that one of your topics simply does not lead you to enough sources. The information on another topic may be so abundant that you would not know where to begin. Avoid these topics and select one that is more manageable.

Your review of sources can also help you decide on a specific topic that can be handled in a short paper. Suppose, for example, that you have chosen the general topic of taking care of your health in the summertime. The general topic could lead to a number of smaller, more manageable topics, some of which are shown in the following chart.

NARROWING A GENERAL TOPIC

General Topic	More Specific Topics
Safeguarding health in the summertime	Red Cross programs for teaching swimming and safety in boating
	Immunization and other health requirements for travel to foreign countries
	Special nutrition needs, such as salt, in hot weather
	Hazards and precautions in suntanning
	Camping safety and first aid

Note that this is only a preliminary narrowing. You may need to limit the specific topic you choose even further, once you have begun to collect information.

Planning Your Research. Once you have a topic, make up about five questions that you would like to pursue in your research and state your thesis statement in preliminary form.

Always direct your research with several key questions and a draft of your thesis statement.

If your topic were hazards and precautions in suntanning, you might ask yourself questions such as the following.

SAMPLE QUESTIONS TO DIRECT RESEARCH

1. Why do people spend so much time and effort to get a suntan?
2. What are the hazards of excessive exposure to the sun?
3. How can people protect themselves from the dangerous effects of suntanning?
4. Do suntan lotions and sunscreens actually help protect people in the sun? How do they work?
5. What is the best way get a tan safely?

These questions will help you to formulate a one sentence main point for your paper, which will serve as a preliminary or rough version of your thesis statement. You will need this preliminary focus to pull your thoughts together and guide you through the quantities of information that you are likely to scan in doing your research. For the topic about hazards and precautions in suntanning, you might begin with the following rough thesis statement.

PRELIMINARY THESIS STATEMENT:	People should take precautions to avoid the hazards of excessive suntanning.

Making Bibliography Cards. Even at this early stage of preparation, you should begin to keep track of the sources you plan to consult. Once you have decided on a topic and have prepared your questions and preliminary thesis statement, you should begin making bibliography cards.

Record all information necessary for citations and bibliographic entries for each source.

The number of sources that you will need will depend on your topic and your teacher's requirements. You should definitely plan to use at least four sources. Since all sources may not be useful, it may be helpful to have a few more than you need listed on your bibliography cards so you will not have to go back to the catalog later.

Make a separate card for each source. On each card, list the library location symbol, or call number, and the appropriate data about the author, title, and publication of the work. Follow suggestions in the chart at the top of the next page.

PREPARING BIBLIOGRAPHY CARDS

1. Use one card for each source.
2. At the top of each card, list all the information you will need to prepare a bibliography entry. See the chart on page 591 for details.
3. Include the location symbol or call number when available, since you may need to consult the book or periodical again later on.
4. Note any mention of illustrations, maps, charts, or tables that you may want to use.

Taking Notes. With your questions and preliminary thesis statement to guide you, you should scan the sources you have chosen, read the relevant sections, and take notes to answer your questions and develop your main point. Keep these notes as neat and organized as possible.

Take accurate notes, recording page numbers and direct quotations exactly, to develop your thesis statement.

The following chart offers a number of suggestions for orderly note-taking.

TAKING NOTES

1. Keep your notes from each individual source on a separate card.
2. In the upper left-hand corner of each card, record all of the information necessary for citing the source in the paper.
3. In the top right-hand corner of each note card, set up a subject heading to include what the card covers. You are likely to have several cards for each source, each card referring to a particular subject within your topic. Later you can sort the cards by subject.
4. Remember to include the page numbers for each quotation, fact, or idea you note.

For some sources, you will want to record exact quotations that are particularly appropriate. These quotations should be clearly marked and listed separately from the other notes on the card. Outlining or summarizing can be used for other types of information you find in your sources, depending on the nature and quantity of the information involved. No matter how you take your notes, you *must* include the page numbers for every item of information you record. The following card demonstrates these methods of note-taking.

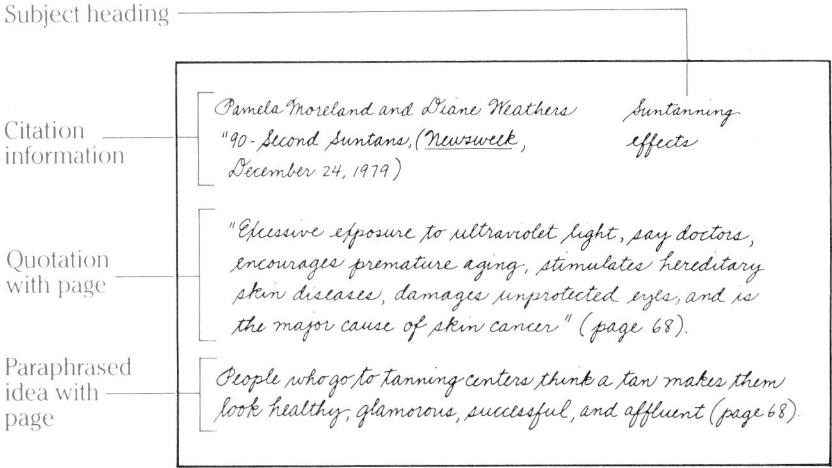

Writing a Precise Thesis Statement. The information you gather in answer to your key questions will prepare you to write a more precise thesis statement.

Write a more precise thesis statement that reflects your research.

Your thesis statement should cover all the information that you plan to use and should tell your audience what you want them to learn from your paper. For the research paper on hazards and precautions in suntanning, a revised thesis statement might resemble the following.

REVISED THESIS STATEMENT: People who enjoy suntanning should be aware of the hazards involved, the value of sunscreens, and the need for sensible tanning procedures.

Preparing an Outline. With your thesis statement and supporting information in mind, plan your paper so that it presents your knowledge of your topic clearly and logically.

Organize your information in a logical outline based on your notes and thesis statement.

Begin ordering your ideas and your research information by performing the steps in the following chart.

ORGANIZING A REPORT
1. Determine the subtopics you want to develop in order to explain your thesis statement.
2. Group the note cards containing information on each of these subtopics together.
3. Decide on an order for effectively presenting your supporting information in the body of your paper. Support can, for example, be organized in chronological order, in spatial order, in order of importance, or in developmental order.

You should then write an outline for the body of your paper showing the order you have chosen. (See Section 31.2 for more information on outlines.)

The following topic outline for the paper on suntanning will give you an idea of the kind of outline you should prepare for your own report.

Thesis Statement: People who enjoy suntanning should be aware of the hazards involved, the value of sunscreens, and the need for sensible tanning procedures.

Subtopic 1

I. Hazards involved in suntanning
  A. Damage to skin
    1. Possibility of damage to deeper tissues
    2. Can trigger hereditary skin disease
    3. Can cause skin cancer
    4. Rashes
    5. Aging and wrinkling of skin

B. Various other dangers
  1. Shock
  2. Headaches
  3. Eye problems
  4. Sunstroke

Subtopic 2 — II. Sunscreens
  A. Benefits of sunscreens
    1. Protect skin from damage, especially sunburn
    2. Still allow skin to tan
  B. Different kinds of sunscreens
    1. Zinc oxide
    2. "Paba"

Subtopic 3 — III. Taking an intelligent approach to suntanning
  A. Extra care before and after
  B. Limiting time of exposure
  C. Using moisturizers

When you have completed your outline, examine it to decide if you need to add anything or change the order in which your ideas are presented. If you prepare your outline carefully and critically, you will find that it will be easier to write your paper and that it will be much more logical.

At this point you should also jot down any ideas you have for your title, introduction, and conclusion.

EXERCISE A: Choosing and Narrowing a Topic. Choose one of the following topics or use one of your own. Consult the card catalog and *The Readers' Guide to Periodical Literature* in the library to see how much material is available on the topic. Then break the topic down into five more specific topics, and choose one that you would like to research and write about. Finally, prepare several questions and a rough thesis statement.

Dolphins
Earthquakes
Changes in clothing styles
The Ice Age
Stonehenge
The discovery of oil
Presidential campaigns
American generals
Space stations
Volcanoes

EXERCISE B: Researching Your Topic. Use the topic you narrowed down in Exercise A, and follow these instructions.

1. Prepare bibliography cards for the sources you expect to use.
2. Scan the sources for those that contain the information that is the most relevant to your thesis statement and questions.
3. Read these sources carefully and take notes. Include several direct quotations in your notes. Remember to record the appropriate information on each card.

EXERCISE C: Organizing Your Research Paper. Use the information you gathered from sources in Exercise B to develop a precise thesis statement. Then follow the steps presented in this section for organizing your information and preparing an outline. Finally, list any ideas you have for your title, introduction, and conclusion.

WRITING: Creating a First Draft

With a detailed outline of the body of your paper and ideas for your title, introduction, and conclusion, you should be ready to write your first draft.

Use your outline and notes to write a first draft of your research paper.

Begin your first draft by writing an introduction that leads up to your thesis statement. Follow your outline and groups of note cards in presenting your supporting information. Remember to cite the source for every quotation, fact, and borrowed idea that you include in your paper. You should also make certain that every paragraph has a clear topic sentence and that your ideas are linked by transitions within and between paragraphs. Your conclusion should remind your audience of your thesis statement, should refer to the important points in your paper, and should bring the paper to a definite and satisfying end.

At this point you should also decide on the title of your paper, if you have not already done so. The title should go on a separate page at the beginning of the paper. The title should be centered on the page, followed by your name, the title of the course for which the paper was written, and the date the paper was turned in. Be aware that your teacher may request a special format for this material or may ask for additional information.

You can generally follow the format of this sample unless your teacher asks for further information.

Suntanning: Problems and Precautions

by

Roberta Ellison

English 10
February 1, 1986

The following is a draft of the paper on suntanning. Notice that it follows the organization shown in the outline. Also notice the footnotes grouped at the end of the paper, followed by the bibliography.

Tanning: Problems and Precautions

Introduction

Tanning has become an obsession for many people. If they cannot go to the beach, they pursue tanning by other methods, such as indoor tanning with ultraviolet lamps. According to an article in Newsweek, many people think that a tan makes them look healthy, glamorous, successful, and even affluent.[1] Many people, however, are unaware of the problems that can result from tanning. People who enjoy suntanning should be aware of the hazards involved, the value of sunscreens, and the need for sensible tanning procedures.

Thesis statement

Subtopic 1

Suntanning can damage the skin and cause other problems. Tanning is "nothing more than a pigmentary response to light; but if it is allowed to become a deep burn, serious injury can be done to the deeper tissues."[2] Doctors say that too much sun can also trigger hereditary skin diseases and cause skin cancer.[3] Not only can suntanning damage skin, but it can also cause the body to go into shock. Overexposure to the sun may result in rashes, headaches, eye problems, and even sunstroke. Furthermore, excessive suntanning contributes greatly to the aging and wrinkling of the skin.[4]

Subtopic 2

The hazards of suntanning can be minimized, however, with sunscreens, which decrease the likelihood of sunburn. There are many products on the market that contain sunscreens. A zinc oxide ointment will block out all or most of the sun's rays. Some people will put a thin film of this white ointment on tender areas such as the nose. A white nose is not particularly attractive, however, so many people prefer to use a sunscreen which will only partly block the burning rays of the sun. According to Foreman and Zizmor, "the miracle ingredient to look for in any sunscreen product is paraaminobenzoic acid, or more simply, paba."[5] Lotions containing paba allow skin to tan while protecting it from the more harmful rays. The amount of time the skin is protected by a product with paba depends on the concentration of the paba.

Subtopic 3

An intelligent approach to suntanning is important. The skin needs extra care before and after sunning. A sunscreen should be applied about thirty minutes before a person goes out into the sun. After exposure to the sun, moisturizing cream should be applied to the skin. Almost any moisturizer can be used to help the skin retain moisture. Particular attention should be paid to the tender areas around the eyes, mouth, and forehead. Another precaution that should be taken is limiting time in the sun to ten minutes the first day and increasing the time spent in the sun gradually. "The secret of avoiding sunburn is to get exposure gradually. If you do this, your skin will become accustomed to the effect of the sun's rays."[6]

Reminder of thesis statement

Sunburn and excessive tanning can cause serious health problems, but proper care of the skin can reduce the dangers involved and safeguard physical appearance. A tanning regimen that includes screening lotions will help prevent wrinkles and skin damage. In addition, a tan acquired slowly and carefully lasts longer. Sun-worshiping will probably continue despite the hazards, but devotees should be aware of the power of ultraviolet rays and bask with caution. Skin is too precious to sacrifice.

---

[1]Pamela Moreland and Diane Weathers, "90-Second Suntans," Newsweek, December 24, 1979, p. 68.

[2]Edward Darling and Ashley Montague, The Prevalence of Nonsense (New York: Harper and Row, 1967), p. 78.

[3]Moreland and Weathers, Newsweek, p. 68.

[4]Darling and Montague, The Prevalence of Nonsense, p. 78.

[5]John Foreman and Jonathan Zizmor, Super Skin (New York: Thomas Y. Crowell Company, 1976), p. 76

[6]Norman R. Goldsmith, You and Your Skin (Springfield, Ill.: Charles C. Thomas, Publisher, 1953), p. 20.

BIBLIOGRAPHY

Darling, Edward and Montague, Ashley. The Prevalence of Nonsense. New York: Harper and Row, 1967.

Foreman, John and Zizmor, Jonathan. Super Skin. New York: Thomas Y. Crowell Company, 1976.

Goldsmith, Norman R. You and Your Skin. Springfield, Ill.: Charles C. Thomas, Publisher, 1953.

Moreland, Pamela and Weathers, Diane. "90-Second Suntans." Newsweek, December 24, 1979, p. 68.

EXERCISE D: Writing a First Draft. Using the outline and notes from Exercises B and C, draft your paper. Cite your sources in footnotes and add a bibliography and title page.

REVISING: Polishing Your Paper

To revise your draft, you should read it with a critical eye, noting any gaps in logic, weak spots, and confusing statements, as well as any errors in grammar, mechanics, and spelling.

Check your first draft for weaknesses in both form and content.

You should evaluate your first draft using questions such as those in the following checklist and revise it accordingly. Then make a final, clean copy and proofread it.

CHECKLIST FOR REVISING

1. Does the introduction provide necessary background information? Does it include a thesis statement?
2. Is the thesis statement clearly presented?
3. Is the thesis statement intelligently developed in the body of the paper by means of subtopics?
4. Does each paragraph contain a topic sentence?
5. Do transitions link the ideas within each paragraph and between paragraphs?
6. Does the conclusion refer to the thesis statement and summarize the content of the paper without being repetitious?
7. Are all sources used in the paper cited throughout and listed in the bibliography?
8. Does the writing follow the rules of grammar, mechanics, and spelling?

EXERCISE E: Revising Your Research Paper. You should remember to revise and proofread your paper following the checklist on this page.

DEVELOPING WRITING SKILLS: Planning, Writing, and Revising a Research Paper. Follow the steps discussed in this chapter to plan, write, and revise a paper on a subject interesting to you.

Writing Workshop: Research Paper

ASSIGNMENT 1

Topic An Important Entertainer or Political Leader

Form and Purpose A research paper informing readers about the successes of an entertainer or political leader

Audience Readers of a book entitled *Biographical Profiles*

Length Five to seven paragraphs

Focus Choose an entertainer or political leader. In your paper identify that person, provide a brief biographical sketch, and discuss that person's accomplishments.

Sources Books, biographies, encyclopedias, magazines

Prewriting Research your topic, taking notes on bibliography cards. Write a precise thesis statement, and organize your notes into an outline.

Writing Write a first draft, including footnotes and a bibliography.

Revising Use the checklist on page 607 to revise your paper.

Meryl Streep

John F. Kennedy

Salmon migrating

ASSIGNMENT 2

Topic Animals on the March—The Mysterious Migration

Form and Purpose A research paper that informs readers on the topic of animal migration

Audience Readers of a natural science museum's information booklet about animal migration

Length Five to seven paragraphs

Focus Begin your paper with a thesis statement about what animal migration is and why it is an important and mysterious process. Develop your thesis by describing the migration of several different species. Conclude with a summary statement and a quotation from an expert.

Sources Books, nature films, natural science magazines, encyclopedias, interviews

Prewriting As you research your topic, take notes on bibliography cards. Organize your notes into outline form.

Writing Write a first draft, including footnotes and a bibliography.

Revising Use the checklist on page 607 to revise your paper.

Topics for Writing: Research Paper

Mary Lou Retton

Carrying the Olympic torch

The above scenes from Olympic events may suggest a topic for a research paper. Either research, plan, and write a paper about that topic or about one of the following topics.

1. The Olympic Spirit
2. The Origin of the Olympics
3. Politics and the Olympics
4. How a Small Town Prepares to Host the Winter Olympics
5. Professional Athletes and the Olympic Games
6. The High Cost of Modern Olympics
7. An Unusual Event in the Winter Olympics
8. A Magnificent Olympic Performance
9. The Process of Becoming an Olympic Competitor
10. Ancient vs. Modern Olympics

Chapter 24

Writing About Literature

You may often be asked to interpret a work of literature you have read and to give your opinion of it. In school, your response to a work of literature such as a short story, novel, poem, or play will frequently take the form of either a *book report* or a *literary analysis paper.* This chapter discusses the format of both the book report and the literary analysis paper and offers suggestions for writing them.

Book Reports 24.1

A book report gives an overview of a work of fiction or nonfiction and presents a brief commentary on it. Although the structure of a book report can vary depending on the work read, there are several features basic to almost every report.

Understanding Book Reports

Most often, book reports are written to inform those who have not read the book being discussed. A book report tells the reader about the contents of the book and expresses an opinion about whether or not the book would be worth reading.

A book report presents information about a work and makes a recommendation.

The following chart shows a basic format for book reports.

THE PARTS OF A BOOK REPORT	
Introduction	Identifies the book by title and author and offers a brief summary of the contents
Body	Focuses on one or two elements in the book, such as theme, character, or setting
Conclusion	Presents an overall opinion of the book and makes a recommendation to the reader

Because the audience is usually unfamiliar with the work being reviewed, the report begins by clearly identifying the book by title and author and then gives a brief overview of the book's contents. The body of the report can then focus on one or two specific elements of the book, supported by evidence from the book itself. Finally, the conclusion makes an overall evaluation of the book and a recommendation.

The basic elements of a work of literature that a book report will generally focus on are shown in the following chart.

BASIC ELEMENTS OF A WORK OF LITERATURE	
Elements	**Definitions**
Theme	The message or general idea that the author is trying to convey, sometimes about particular people and situations, sometimes about life in general. Although the theme is the main idea that holds the book together, it is often not stated directly.
Characters	The people who participate in the story being told. Characters are presented to the reader in several ways: by what they say and do, by what other characters say about them, and by direct comments on them by the narrator.
Dialogue	What the characters say. A play, of course, is made up of conversation, but dialogue helps to develop character and theme in novels and short stories as well.

Conflict	The tension or struggle between opposing forces or people. Sometimes the conflict is external, involving one character versus another, a character versus society, or a character versus nature. Sometimes, however, the conflict is internal, taking place entirely within one person who must, for example, make a difficult choice or decision.
Plot	The sequence of events that develops a story. The plot usually builds to a *climax,* in which the story's conflict is resolved.
Setting	Where and when a story takes place. The time can be the past, present, or future; the location can be either real or imaginary.
Point of View	The person telling the story is called the *narrator.* A first-person narrator takes part in the action and uses the first-person pronoun "I" to recount events as he or she experiences them. A third-person narrator tells a story about other people and reports events more objectively, using the pronouns "he", "she," and "they." An omniscient third-person narrator can see into the mind of the characters.

The following report on Willa Cather's *My Antonia* uses the basic book report format to describe two elements of the novel. Notice that when direct quotations from the book are given, the page number of the quotation follows in parentheses.

Report on My Antonia

Introduction with brief overview

In her novel My Antonia, Willa Cather accurately portrays the joys and hardships of settling a new land and growing up in Nebraska in the 1880's. Although the novel chronicles the lives of several early settlers, its focus is on two main characters: the narrator, Jim Burden, and his childhood friend, Antonia Shimerda. Jim, a ten-year-old orphan from Virginia, goes to Black Hawk, Nebraska, to live on a farm with his paternal grandparents. Antonia and her family, immigrants from Bohemia in central Europe, arrive in Black Hawk on the same train as Jim. The novel follows Jim and Antonia from their first brief meeting on the train station platform to their reunion over twenty years later.

Body paragraph 1 (discusses first element)

One way Cather makes her story realistic is by using dialogue that reflects the way the early settlers actually talked. The characters use language consistent with their varying backgrounds. The country farmers, the townspeople, and the recent immigrants all speak in slightly different ways. Antonia is a case in point. The first in her family to learn English, she speaks in the halting, somewhat awkward and ungrammatical way that might be expected from someone still unsure of a strange, new language. In the beginning of the story, for example, she translates her father's comments for Jim: "My 'tatinek' say when you are big boy, he give you his gun. Very fine, from Bohemia. It was belong to a great man, very rich, like what you not got here . . ." (page 42). Cather also captures the colorful, unvarnished speech of the country farmers. One of the Burdens' hired hands describes their new neighbors, the Shimerdas, this way: "They ain't got but one overcoat among 'em over there, and they take turns wearing it. They seem awful scared of cold, and stay in that hole in the bank like badgers" (page 70).

Body paragraph 2 (discusses second element)

Willa Cather's detailed description of the setting of My Antonia also helps make the story realistic. Through the eyes of the characters, the reader sees Nebraska the way the early settlers saw it. As Jim narrates his first impressions of the prairie, the reader sees the expanse of the land: "The road from the post-office came directly by our front door, crossed the farmyard, and curved round the little pond, beyond which it began to climb the unbroken swell of the prairie to the west. . . . Everywhere, as far as the eye could reach, there was nothing but rough, shaggy, red grass, most of it as tall as I" (page 14). Descriptions such as this give the reader a sense of sharing the characters' experiences.

Conclusion with overall evaluation and recommendation

In My Antonia, Willa Cather carefully depicts the early Nebraska homesteaders and the land they settled. Through her detailed, vivid descriptions, the author presents a realistic view of what it must have been like for settlers in the American West of the late 1880's. The convincing dialogue makes you feel as if you know these characters personally, and it is well worth making their acquaintance.

EXERCISE A: Understanding a Book Report. Answer each question about the book report on *My Antonia.*

1. What information in the introduction gives an overview of the book's contents?
2. What other information does the introduction include?
3. What element of the novel is discussed in the first body paragraph?
4. What type of supporting information is given in the first body paragraph? How many examples are given?
5. What element is discussed in the second body paragraph?
6. What type of supporting information is given in the second body paragraph?
7. Why do you think the writer used only one example in the second body paragraph?
8. Does the report give you a clear idea what the book is about? What further information could have been added?
9. What is the writer's overall opinion of the novel? Where is this opinion stated?
10. Based on this book report, would you like to read the book? Why or why not?

PREWRITING, WRITING, AND REVISING: Preparing a Book Report

In writing a book report, you should follow the same basic steps as you would for planning, writing, and revising any composition.

Prewriting. To begin planning a book report, you must first select which element or elements of the book you want to focus on. Next, review the book to find supporting information.

Decide which elements to discuss, and then gather and organize specific support from the book.

The following list was made for a book report on John Steinbeck's *The Pearl.* The writer decided to discuss the theme and the main character and then went through the novel, collecting useful information.

LIST OF SUPPORTING INFORMATION FOR A BOOK REPORT	
Book: The Pearl by John Steinbeck	
Theme: Good and evil	
—Kino, innocent and good, wants to better himself and his family —after he finds the pearl, many around Kino seem evil: "He became curiously every man's enemy. The news stirred up something . . . evil in town" (page 30) —even apparently good characters, such as the doctor and the priest, change —Doctor makes Kino's son ill so that he can charge a fee for curing the baby	—Priest will now marry Kino and Juana if they can pay; he hears the news and it "put a thoughtful look in his eyes and a memory of certain repairs necessary to the church. He wondered how much the pearl will be worth" (page 28) —People try to steal the pearl —Pearl buyers try to cheat him —Assassins try to kill Kino and his family
Character: Kino	
—basic goodness of Kino —simple man of simple wants —Kino's dream: "We will be married—in a church . . . We will have new clothes . . . Perhaps a rifle . . . My son will go to school" (pages 31–33)	—not a man well equipped to confront evil forces —his anger and frustration —he can't win with pearl buyers —he can't stop assassins —shows dignity in the end by throwing pearl back

When you have a list of supporting information for the body of your book report, you should then decide on the order of the body paragraphs. Consider which element of the novel it would be best to discuss first. You should also decide at this point what you will say in your introduction and conclusion.

You will find it helpful to make an outline of your report. The following outline shapes the material gathered from *The Pearl* into a complete, well-organized report.

I. Introduction
  A. Title—The Pearl
  B. Author—John Steinbeck
  C. Overview—Story of Kino, a young Mexican-Indian, and his family
    1. Kino tries to better himself and his family
    2. He finds the "Pearl of the World"
    3. The pearl brings loss and sorrow
II. First element—Theme: Good and evil
  A. Kino is innocent and good
  B. The pearl brings out the evil in everyone else
  C. When Kino finds the pearl, good confronts evil
III. Second element—Character: Kino
  A. A man with simple wants
  B. Has dignity even though he is humble
  C. His character is seen in his dreams for his family
  D. Finding the pearl leads to anger and frustration
  E. Retains his personal dignity even in despair
IV. Conclusion
  A. The novel vividly conveys Kino's character and his family's plight
  B. The struggle against evil makes the story both suspenseful and emotional
  C. A book worth reading

Writing. As with any composition, when writing a book report you should prepare a first draft. Your first draft should follow the organization of your outline and incorporate all the relevant items from your list of support.

Write a first draft of your book report based on your outline and list of supporting information.

As you write a draft, use your list of support to fill out your ideas. Focus on connecting your ideas with transitions and with other linking devices, such as repeating main words.

View your first draft as a practice copy of your book report; you will revise it later. The main purpose of this draft is to put together information you want to present in your book report.

The following is a first draft of a book report on *The Pearl,* based on the preceding outline and list of support.

Report on The Pearl

Introduction with brief overview

The Pearl, a short novel by John Steinbeck, tells of the hardships a young Mexican-Indian family faces as they try to gain a better life for themselves. Kino, the father, is a poor pearl diver who believes that finding the "Pearl of the World" will bring his family happiness and comfort. But when Kino does find the pearl, it brings only sorrow.

Body paragraph 1 (discusses first element—theme)

In Kino's quest for the "Pearl of the World," he loses his innocent view of life and realizes that there is much evil in the world. The great pearl brings out the greed of those around him, and "he became curiously every man's enemy. The news stirred up something . . . evil in town. . . ." (page 30). The doctor, who pretended not to be at home when Kino sought his help before, now seeks Kino out to help his son. When the priest heard of Kino's pearl, the news "put a thoughtful look in his eyes and a memory of certain repairs necessary to the church. He wondered how much the pearl will be worth" (page 28). Even the town doctor and priest, two people who would seem dedicated and compassionate, have their greedy side revealed when Kino finds the "Pearl of the World." By contrasting the initial innocence of Kino and his family with the evil that they come to see surrounding them, Steinbeck reminds the reader that good and evil coexist everywhere—that no person can hope to remain unaffected.

Body paragraph 2 (discusses second element—character)

Not only in his confrontation with evil, but in the way he leads his everyday life, Kino wins our respect. Kino shows himself as a decent, honest man whose main concern is his family's well-being. When asked what he will do with his money, Kino's dreams are for simple things to help his family: "We will be married—in a church," he says. "We will have new clothes . . . Perhaps a rifle . . . My son will go to school" (pages 31–33). Unfortunately, the world will not leave Kino and his family alone. The pearl buyers who try to cheat him, the people who try to steal his pearl, and the assassins who kill his son bring about a change in Kino. He becomes angry and fights back. But in the end, Kino regains his dignity and throws the pearl back into the sea.

Conclusion with overall evaluation and recommendation

In The Pearl, John Steinbeck vividly captures the struggle of a poor family searching for a better life. His careful depiction of Kino and those around him holds the reader's interest. It is a suspenseful and emotional story well worth reading.

Revising. After you have written a complete first draft, carefully evaluate and revise your book report.

Use a checklist to revise your book report.

The following suggestions should help you to know what to look for in revising a book report.

CHECKLIST FOR REVISING A BOOK REPORT

1. Is the book clearly identified by title and author in the introduction?
2. Does the introduction give an overview of the book?
3. Do the elements discussed represent the book accurately?
4. Have you given enough supporting information to make your ideas clear to the reader?
5. Is better support available in the book?
6. Is there any irrelevant information that you should remove?
7. Have you used quotation marks correctly and given page numbers following any direct quotations from the book?
8. Does your conclusion make a definite recommendation to the reader?
9. Would adding transitions or rewriting some sentences help your ideas flow more smoothly?
10. Are there any mistakes in grammar, mechanics, or spelling?

When you have made any necessary changes in your report, recopy the paper in final form. Be sure to proofread your final copy for typographical errors before submitting it to your teacher.

EXERCISE B: Planning a Book Report. Choose a book you have read recently and select two elements of the book to discuss in a report. Make a list of supporting information from the book and prepare an outline of your paper.

EXERCISE C: Writing a Book Report. Use the outline and list of support you prepared in Exercise B to write a first draft of your book report.

EXERCISE D: Revising a Book Report. Evaluate the book report you drafted in Exercise C by answering the questions in the checklist on page 619. Make any necessary changes and then prepare and proofread a final, clean copy of your book report.

DEVELOPING WRITING SKILLS: Planning, Writing, and Revising a Book Report. Follow these instructions to prepare a second book report.

1. Choose a work of literature to write about. Following the steps presented in this chapter, plan a book report and write a first draft.
2. Exchange first drafts with another student in your class.
3. Evaluate the other student's paper by answering each of the questions in the checklist on page 619. Also write a few sentences giving your overall evaluation of the paper and making specific suggestions for improvements. Then return the paper to the other student.
4. After your own paper has been returned, revise it by responding to the comments and suggestions made by the other student. Then make a final, clean copy of your report and proofread it.
5. When you turn in your report to your teacher, submit both the first draft, with the other student's comments, and the clean, final copy.

Papers Analyzing Literature 24.2

A literary analysis paper explains and interprets a work of literature—a short story, a novel, a poem, a play, or a piece of nonfiction, such as a biography or autobiography.

Understanding Literary Analysis Papers

Although a literary analysis paper and a book report both focus on the basic elements of a work of literature, they are written for different audiences. While a book report usually introduces a work to an audience that has not yet read it, the literary analysis paper aims at readers who are already familiar with the work. The literary analysis paper goes beyond reporting and describing; it interprets and analyzes.

A literary analysis paper helps interpret a work for readers.

Like an essay, a literary analysis paper focuses on a main point, supported by evidence taken from the work.

The following chart presents a basic format for literary analysis papers.

PARTS OF A LITERARY ANALYSIS PAPER
Title
Can suggest the main point of the paper in addition to naming the literary work to be analyzed
Introduction
Fully identifies the work and its author; presents any needed background information on when and where the author lived
Tells what specific sort of work is to be analyzed, such as a Greek tragedy, a modern short story, or a sonnet
States the main point that will be made in the paper; the main point is generally based on an analysis of one or more elements of the work

Body
Explores subtopics of the main point, often using one paragraph for each subtopic
Presents supporting information in a logical order, such as chronological, spatial, order of importance, comparison and contrast, or developmental
Explains and supports the main point using quotations, examples, details, or incidents taken from the work
Presents enough information to convince a reader that the main point has been covered thoroughly
Conclusion
Reminds the reader of the main point stated in the introduction
Shows how the main point can help explain the work as a whole
Pulls the whole paper together with closing remarks

The title of a literary analysis paper can reflect the topic of the paper and the main point that the writer will make. After fully identifying the work and author, the introduction states the main point that interprets one or more elements of the work for the reader. In the body, supporting information develops the main point, usually within subtopics. The paper's conclusion reminds the reader of the main point and uses it to explain the work as a whole.

The following paper on Carson McCullers's *The Member of the Wedding* illustrates the format of a literary analysis paper.

Frankie Addams: Portrait of an Adolescent

Introduction with statement of main point	Frankie Addams, the twelve-year-old main character in Carson McCullers's short novel <u>The Member of the Wedding</u>, is a lonely, rebellious adolescent living in the South in the 1940's. Searching for where she fits into the world, she finds herself caught between being a child and being an adult.
Body paragraph 1 (discusses first subtopic)	Frankie feels lonely and unhappy because she does not seem to fit in with those around her. When her six-year-old cousin, John Henry, suggests that they go outside to play with the neighborhood children, Frankie refuses and refers to them as "Just a lot of ugly

silly children. Running and hollering and running and hollering. Nothing to it" (page 9). Yet she does not fit in with the older girls (thirteen to fifteen) she knows either. Once when these girls, who do not invite her to join their club, had a party, Frankie "stood in the alley and watched and listened" (page 10); and when John Henry suggests that she might be interested in their club, Frankie tells him, "Don't mention those crooks to me" (page 11). Frankie Addams has outgrown the younger children, yet she is not quite ready to join the older girls. She is not a member of either group.

Body paragraph 2 (discusses second subtopic)

Feeling cut off from the rest of the world, Frankie Addams begins to lose any clear idea of who she is. She has stopped being the old Frankie she knew before, but she has not yet become a new, complete person. For now, she is unpredictable and rebellious. She had begun to change in the spring, stealing a three-way knife from a local store. "This began to change Frankie and she did not understand the change" (page 19). And as the summer wore on she became more and more discontented: "This was the summer when Frankie was sick and tired of being Frankie. She hated herself, and had become a loafer and a no-good who hung around the summer kitchen: dirty and greedy and mean and sad" (page 18). As Frankie became more confused about herself, she often didn't know how to act. She "would do anything that occurred to her" (page 21) without thinking of the consequences. She took her father's pistol in addition to stealing the pocketknife and smoked cigarettes whenever she could snatch them from Berenice, their housekeeper.

Body paragraph 3 (discusses third subtopic)

Her older brother's approaching wedding gives Frankie something, finally, that she wants to be a part of. She fantasizes about it constantly and decides she will leave with her brother and his bride after the wedding. She talks of nothing but the wedding and how the three of them will go away together. Berenice claims that Frankie has fallen "in love with the wedding" (page 68). Frankie even goes so far as calling herself F. Jasmine Addams so that her name, like her brother's and his bride's, will begin with the letters J and A. When the wedding finally takes place, Frankie insists on staying with the newlyweds. As the couple is about to leave for their honeymoon, Frankie makes a terrible scene, desperately clinging to the steering wheel of their car until her father and others have to drag her away.

Body paragraph 4 (discusses fourth subtopic)

Back from the wedding, in a final act of rebellion Frankie tries to run away from home. She is caught by the police and returned to her father. But after that incident, Frankie changes again. It is as if she finally crosses the line and becomes a new kind of person. Returning to school in the fall, Frankie has a new best friend and new interests. She now talks about travel and about art; as she tells Berenice, "I am just mad about Michelangelo" (page 130). Frankie's attitude toward Berenice, her former confidante, has also changed. The way she talks to Berenice shows that she has become cooler and more self-confident. In fact, she becomes almost arrogant when she tells Berenice, "There's no use our discussing a certain party. You could not possibly understand her. It's just not in you" (page 130).

Conclusion with reminder of main point and closing remarks

Frankie Addams goes through a difficult time in The Member of the Wedding, a time when she seems to have no place in the world, seems to be a member of no group. But it turns out also to be a time of great change, a necessary transition from one stage of life to another. She comes out of her rebelliousness and confusion changed, transformed from an insecure, lonely child into a self-assured young woman.

EXERCISE A: Understanding a Literary Analysis Paper. Answer the following questions about the literary analysis paper on *The Member of the Wedding*.

1. What main point about the work is presented in the introduction?
2. How does the title contribute to the reader's understanding of the main point?
3. Besides the main point, what other information is given in

the introduction?

4. What subtopics of the main point are discussed in the body paragraphs?
5. How are the subtopics related to the main point?
6. Give two examples of the supporting information presented for each subtopic.
7. What is the order of the subtopics?
8. Which sentence in the conclusion acts as a reminder of the statement of the main point in the introduction?
9. What does the conclusion add to your understanding of the main point?
10. How do the closing remarks in the conclusion pull the whole paper together?

PREWRITING, WRITING, AND REVISING: Preparing a Literary Analysis Paper

To prepare a literary analysis paper, you can adapt the basic planning, writing, and revising steps that you use to prepare an essay.

Prewriting. A literary analysis paper shows your understanding of a work of literature. Therefore, you should begin planning your paper by carefully analyzing the work and deciding on the main point your paper will make. Focus on one or more of the elements shown in the chart on pages 612 and 613.

Analyze one or more elements of the work to decide on a main point, and then organize support under subtopics of the main point.

The questions in the following chart will help you to analyze the elements of a work of literature and to decide on a main point to pursue in your paper.

QUESTIONS FOR ANALYZING A WORK OF LITERATURE
Theme
1. Does one general idea seem to tie the whole work together?
2. Did the work make you see something in a different way?

Character

1. Which are your favorite and least favorite characters? Why?
2. Which character do you understand most thoroughly? How does the work help you learn about this character?
3. Does the main character undergo any change during the story?

Dialogue

1. Does the way a character speaks help you to understand how that character thinks and feels? If so, how?
2. Does a character's way of speaking change in different situations or with different people? If so, how and why?

Conflict

1. Is the conflict within one character or between a character and some outside force, such as nature, society, or another character?
2. What happens in the story to bring this conflict to a head?
3. Is the conflict resolved at the end of the story? If so, how is it resolved? If not, why do you think the author left it hanging?

Plot

1. What is the high point of the story? Why is this incident more important than the others?
2. What does the author do to keep you interested in the story until the end of the work?
3. Does the end of the story seem to follow naturally from what has come before? Why or why not?

Setting

1. Where and when does the story take place? How would the story be different if it took place in a different setting?
2. Does the setting change significantly?

Point of View

1. Who is telling the story?
2. How would the story be different if it were told from a different point of view?

When you have answered the questions in the chart, read over your responses and select one or two elements to focus on. After you have selected an element or elements to write about, you can use the questions again to help brainstorm for more complete supporting information.

If you were to answer the questions on dialogue in order to write a paper on Shakespeare's *Julius Caesar,* you might produce a list of supporting information like the following.

SUPPORTING INFORMATION FOR A LITERARY ANALYSIS PAPER
Play: Julius Caesar by William Shakespeare **Element to examine: Dialogue**
Does the way a character speaks help you to understand how that character thinks and feels? If so, how? —some speeches are in poetry, others are in prose —often, characters use prose when they are not good public speakers or are not very clever —Casca, for example, recounts events in prose and doesn't catch on to jokes —prose makes him seem dull —Casca turns to violence later in the play —first one to strike Caesar —says "Speak, hands, for me!" when he stabs Caesar —his actions speak more effectively than his words
Does a character's way of speaking change in different situations or with different people? If so, how and why? —difference between Brutus's public and private speeches —in conversation, he can be eloquent and persuasive —but in public speeches, as at Caesar's funeral, he is colorless —Brutus's speech is honest but a little tedious and touches no one deeply —completely the opposite of Mark Antony's speech —Antony wins over the crowd with polished, moving speech in eloquent poetry —difference between their speeches changes course of the action

After you have collected supporting information, you should examine it carefully and decide what your main point will be. Put your main point into a single sentence. Then create subtopics of your main point. If you were writing about *Julius Caesar,* your main point about dialogue might focus on the difference between characters who speak eloquently and those who do not. Then you might decide to treat three characters, Casca, Brutus, and Marc Antony, as subtopics of that main idea.

When you have a statement of your main idea and a group of subtopics, try to make a general plan of your paper. The following plan would suit the material on *Julius Caesar.*

PLAN FOR A LITERARY ANALYSIS PAPER		
First paragraph	=	Introduction Main point to be discussed: How the eloquence of characters' speeches plays an important role in the action
Second paragraph	=	Subtopic 1: Casca's speeches
Third paragraph	=	Subtopic 2: Brutus's speeches
Fourth paragraph	=	Subtopic 3: Marc Antony's funeral oration
Fifth paragraph	=	Conclusion

With a list of supporting information and an overall plan, you will be ready to prepare a complete outline of your paper. An outline will help you organize your ideas and information into an introduction, body, and conclusion.

The following outline was based on the plan and the list of supporting information on *Julius Caesar.*

I. Introduction
   A. Type of work—Elizabethan play
   B. Title—Julius Caesar
   C. Author—William Shakespeare
   D. Element to examine—Dialogue
   E. Main point of paper—How the eloquence of characters' speeches plays a role in the action
II. Body
   A. Casca's speeches
      1. Early speeches report events in prose
      2. Appears dull
      3. Turns to violence later on

B. Brutus's speeches
1. Can be eloquent in private conversation
2. Not a polished public speaker
3. Speech at Caesar's funeral simple and straightforward, not eloquent

C. Marc Antony's funeral oration
1. Immediately follows Brutus's plain speech
2. Is eloquent and very moving
3. Contrast wins over the Romans; starts Brutus's fall and Antony's rise

III. Conclusion
A. Eloquent speeches not only reveal characters but can affect the course of events
B. What characters say can sometimes be less important than how they say it

Writing. The next step in preparing your paper is writing a first draft based on your outline. Concentrate on connecting your ideas and support with transitions. You should also try to use other linking devices, such as occasionally repeating a main word or using pronouns.

Write a first draft based on your outline.

The following literary analysis paper was written using the outline just shown. Notice that it gives in parentheses the act, scene, and line number for all direct quotations from the play. This is the usual way to give citations to a Shakespearean play. In novels and other kinds of literature, however, you will more often simply give the page number of quotations.

Your first draft may not look quite as polished as this one, but you will have a chance to improve it during revision.

The Role of Eloquence in <u>Julius Caesar</u>

Introduction with statement of main point

Probably two kinds of people need eloquence most—politicians and poets. Shakespeare's <u>Julius Caesar</u> has both: It is a play about politics written in dramatic verse. Since the politicians in the play are so attuned to eloquence and prize it so greatly as a political tool, it comes to play an important role in the action. The failure to achieve eloquence can seriously damage the fortunes of a character.

Subtopic 1: Casca's speeches

We see the importance of eloquence right at the beginning of the play when Casca, a minor character, reports to Brutus and Cassius what he observed during the Feast of Lupercal. Because Casca speaks in bare prose while the characters around him are speaking in verse, he seems inarticulate by comparison. His insensitivity to language also makes him misunderstand Cassius. When Cassius makes a pun about Caesar having the "falling" sickness, Casca dimly replies, "I know not what you mean by that, but I saw Caesar fall down" (I, ii, 250). Later in the same scene, Casca is unable to relate what he heard because, as he explains, "Those that understood him smiled at one another and shook their head—but for mine own part, it was Greek to me" (I, ii, 296–271). Casca is not capable of, does not understand, clever speech, and from the beginning the audience sees this as a political liability. Later on, his action in Act III comes as a consequence of this weakness. Casca is the first to strike Caesar, saying, "Speak, hands, for me!" (III, i, 76). The audience already knows that Casca fumbles with words; now we see that his hands have to "talk" for him. Unable to achieve his goals through speech, he turns instead to violence.

Subtopic 2: Brutus's speeches

Eloquence plays an even greater role in the lives of the major characters, such as Brutus. Although Brutus can speak quite well, he is at his best only in private conversations. A public occasion, his important speech at Caesar's funeral, therefore finds him at a serious disadvantage. No polished public speaker, Brutus merely asks for the citizens' consent, saying, "Believe me for mine honour, and have respect to mine honour, that you may believe" (III, ii, 14–16). He does not know how to persuade the crowd with exciting language, naively expecting simple honesty to carry the day.

Subtopic 3: Marc Antony's funeral oration

Marc Antony's famous funeral oration, which immediately follows, stands in direct contrast. Antony's eloquent, emotional language wins the people's hearts: "If you have tears, prepare to shed them now" (III, ii, 169). The people are his. In this crucial scene, eloquence—and the failure to achieve it—changes the course of the action. Brutus gives a colorless speech and from this point on, his fortunes decline, while Marc Antony's rise.

Conclusion with reminder of main point

In Julius Caesar, eloquence plays a major role: Beyond revealing the characters, it affects the outcome of events. Much can be learned, therefore, by examining not only what the characters say but how, and how well, they say it.

Revising. During revision, change both the style and content of your first draft. You may want to tie your conclusion more closely to what you said in your introduction to tighten the organization. Or rewrite some sentences for smoothness or add further transitions within or between paragraphs.

Use a checklist to revise your paper.

The questions in the following chart will help you to evaluate and revise your first draft.

CHECKLIST FOR REVISING A LITERARY ANALYSIS PAPER

1. Does the title of the paper reflect your main point?
2. Is a clear main point stated in the introduction?
3. Does the body of the paper develop the main point with supporting information organized in subtopics?
4. Is there enough support to develop the main point fully?
5. Is there any irrelevant information that should be removed?
6. Are any direct quotations from the work complete and accurate? Are page numbers (or line numbers) given?
7. Does the conclusion recall the main point made in the introduction?
8. Are all paragraphs and subtopics clearly connected by transitions and occasionally repeated main words?
9. Should any sentences be reworded for smoothness or clarity?
10. Are there any mistakes in grammar, mechanics, or spelling?

After you have revised the paper, prepare a neat final copy. Proofread your final copy for typographical errors.

EXERCISE B: Planning a Literary Analysis Paper. Select a work of literature that you have read recently or read one for this assignment. Review the work and choose one element to discuss in a paper. Then gather information on this element, decide on a main point, and express your idea in a sentence. Organize your material into a complete outline of your paper.

EXERCISE C: Writing a Literary Analysis Paper. Use the outline and the list of supporting information you prepared in Exercise B to write a first draft of your paper. Be sure to clearly connect your ideas with transitions and the other linking devices.

EXERCISE D: Revising a Literary Analysis Paper. Use the chart on page 631 to evaluate the paper you wrote in Exercise C. Make any necessary changes and then recopy your paper in final form. Proofread the final copy for typographical errors.

DEVELOPING WRITING SKILLS: Planning, Writing, and Revising a Literary Analysis Paper. Write a second literary analysis paper following these prewriting, writing, and revising steps.

1. Choose a work to write about that is of a different kind from the work you used before. That is, if you wrote about a play before, this time write about a novel, a short story, or a poem. Follow the steps in this section to plan your paper and write a first draft.
2. Exchange first drafts with another student.
3. Using the checklist on page 631 as a guide, write several paragraphs evaluating the other student's paper. Also mark specific suggestions for improvements on the paper itself, using a different color ink.
4. After your own paper is returned, revise it by taking into account the other student's comments and suggestions. Make a final, clean copy of your paper.
5. Submit the rough draft marked by the other student, the other student's paragraphs of comments, and your final, revised version of the paper to your teacher.

Writing Workshop: Writing About Literature

ASSIGNMENT

Topic A Comparison of a Novel and a Film Based on That Novel

Form and Purpose A literary analysis paper that compares a novel to a film version of that novel

Audience Readers of a book-and-film review column

Length Five to seven paragraphs

Focus Develop the differences and similarities between the novel and the film. Concentrate on two or three major elements. Conclude with an evaluation of the two art forms.

Sources Novels, film libraries, video rental stores, television reruns of movies, movie theaters

Prewriting Read the novel and view the film, and take notes. Answer questions like those on pages 625 and 626. Decide on a main idea, and prepare an outline.

Writing Use your outline to write a first draft of your paper.

Revising Use the checklist on page 631 to revise your paper.

Chapter 25

Personal Writing

People often write about their own personal experiences in a variety of composition forms. The journal, the first-person narrative, and the autobiography are among the most popular forms of personal writing.

25.1 Journals

A *journal* is a record of personal interests, insights, and feelings as well as a record of events in a person's life. Sometimes a journal is strictly a private record. In this section, however, you will learn about journals intended for others to read and appreciate.

Understanding Journals

A journal reflects the person who writes it. The individual writer generally decides what to write about and how often to make entries in the journal.

A journal is a personal record of events, feelings, observations, or special interests.

Kinds of Journals. Journal writing fills various needs. The person who keeps a daily diary of events may be seeking a regular outlet for self-expression or a regular means of developing writing skills. The person who keeps a journal for special occasions may have a special hobby or interest that is enhanced by writing.

The following chart lists four different kinds of journals. Notice that the frequency of writing entries may vary depending on the kind of journal. A journal meant to keep track of everyday events would probably be written every day while entries in a special-interest journal would probably be written less frequently.

KINDS OF JOURNALS

Purposes of Journals	Probable Writing Time
To keep track of everyday events	Daily
To express candid feelings and insights	Daily or several times a week
To record key events or moments in life	Weekly
To record experiences in an area of special interest	As each occasion arises

Journal Entries. A journal is a collection of separate, individual entries. An entry can be almost any length, one paragraph or many paragraphs, depending on the amount of ideas and details that the writer wishes to cover. Most often, the journal entry will contain details about people, places, and events and the writer's personal impressions and feelings. A journal writer's selection of vivid details is the mark of a lively, interesting entry.

The following are entries from the journal of the Reverend Walter Colton. They relate events and offer details about a gold rush in California in 1848.

Setting

Monday, May 29, 1848: Our town was startled out of its quiet dreams today by the announcement that gold had been discovered on the American Fork. The men wondered and talked, and the women too; but neither believed. . . .

Descriptive details

Personal observations

Tuesday, June 20: My messenger sent to the mines has returned with specimens of the gold. As he drew forth the yellow lumps from his pockets, and passed them around among the eager crowd, the doubts, which had lingered till now, fled. . . . The excitement produced was intense; and many were soon busy in their hasty preparations for a departure to the mines. The family who had kept house for me caught the moving infection. Husband and wife were both packing up; the blacksmith dropped his hammer, the carpenter his plane, the mason his trowel, the farmer his sickle, the baker his loaf. . . . All were off for the mines, some on horses, some on carts, and some on crutches, and one went in a litter. An American woman, who had recently established a boarding-house here, pulled up stakes, and was off before her lodgers had even time to pay their bills. Debtors ran, of course. I have only a community of women left, and a gang of prisoners, with here and there a soldier, who will give his captain the slip at the first chance. I don't blame the fellow a whit; seven dollars a month, while others are making two or three hundred a day! That is too much for human nature to stand.—Walter Colton

EXERCISE A: Understanding a Journal. Reread the preceding journal excerpt and then answer these questions.

1. What kind of journal does the writer seem to be keeping? How can you tell?
2. How frequently do you think the writer made entries? Give a reason for your answer.
3. How much time do these entries cover? How do you know?
4. What descriptive details are used? List at least three.
5. What personal insights or feelings does the writer share?

EXERCISE B: Looking at Different Journal Entries. Locate three or four published journals and read several entries in different journals that interest you. Then answer the questions in Exercise A for one of the entries.

Keeping a Journal

A journal is a place to keep track of special interests as well as important events in your life and your personal insights and feelings.

Use vivid, significant details as you record events and thoughts in chronological order.

Even though it may seem like a spontaneous kind of writing, a journal will greatly benefit from a little advance planning. Organizing the vivid details that you want to remember into a clear chronological account can produce entries you will enjoy returning to and reading again later.

Planning a Journal. To plan your journal you must first decide what kind of journal to keep—what its purpose will be and how often you will probably need to make entries. Then you can begin planning an individual entry.

The following suggestions should help you to plan a journal.

PLANNING A JOURNAL

1. Reexamine the list of the purposes of various journals on page 635 in order to decide which kind you want to keep.
2. When you have identified the purpose of your journal, decide how frequently you should make entries.
3. Begin planning your first entry by taking notes on happenings or ideas that are related to your journal's purpose. For example, if you want to record a special interest, you might begin taking notes on the books that you read.
4. Find specific information by answering basic questions such as "When?" "Where?" "Who?" "What?" and "Why?" Brainstorm for vivid descriptive details as well.

After these planning steps, you should have a clear idea of why you are keeping a journal as well as the raw materials with which to write a good first entry.

The chart at the top of page 638 shows the material a student gathered for an entry in a special-interest journal on sports. It answers four basic questions and offers a number of useful details.

PREPARING TO WRITE A JOURNAL ENTRY	
When?	First cross-country track meet of the season
Where?	A course I had never run before, at Riverside High
Who?	Me, other members of my team, Coach Evans, and runners from Riverside
What?	The three-mile race —my fast start —slowing down after the first mile —being passed by out-of-shape runners —finally jogging and walking to the finish line —Coach Evans tells me to work out more regularly

Writing a Journal Entry. With a list of ideas, events, and details, you are ready to write your journal entry. Concentrate on connecting details and observations with transitions, following an overall chronological order. Write so that someone else reading your journal would be able to follow it easily.

In the following journal entry, notice that many vivid details are presented within a clear chronological arrangement.

Saturday, March 10

Subject of entry

Today was a milestone: my first cross-country track meet. I had never run the Riverside High course before, and I wasn't too sure how well I would do, especially because I am more of a sprinter than a long-distance runner, but I was in the three-mile race.

Chronological order

I started much too fast. I was the lead runner at the beginning, but I began slowing after the first mile. As I approached a steep hill that led into a wood, other runners started passing me—only good runners at first, but then runners who looked out of shape were huffing and puffing past me.

Descriptive details

My feet started dragging in the third mile; soon I was walking. By the time I got to the finish line, after alternating between erratic jogging and fitful walking the last half mile, the only people around were Coach Evans and a few grinning teammates. Coach said I was going to have to work out much more regularly. I couldn't argue.

EXERCISE C: Planning Your Journal. Reexamine the chart on page 635 and select which kind of journal to write. Use your journal's purpose to decide how frequently you will write entries. Then begin taking notes for a journal entry.

EXERCISE D: Writing a Journal Entry. Write the first entry of the journal that you planned in Exercise C.

DEVELOPING WRITING SKILLS: Keeping a Journal. Regularly make further entries in the journal that you began writing in Exercise D. After you have been keeping your journal for several weeks, decide if you want to change or revise the journal's purpose. For example, if you have been keeping track of everyday events, you might want to become more selective, focusing on a special interest.

Writing from Personal Experience 25.2

When you write a journal, you will be writing primarily for your own enjoyment. In writing from personal experience, however, you will be writing primarily for others. You can often describe or explain your experiences to others by writing either a *first-person narrative* or an *autobiography.*

Writing a First-Person Narrative

When you write a first-person narrative, you relate a personal experience. The experience is part of your memory, though, so you draw on the emotional associations you have attached to the experience to give it meaning.

Understanding First-Person Narratives. A narrative is, by definition, a story. In a first-person narrative, however, point of view becomes crucial.

A first-person narrative relates one or more actual events from a deliberately personal point of view.

The primary focus of a first-person narrative is on an event *outside* the narrator, but the perceptions and feelings *inside* the narrator are included, as well.

The topic of a first-person narrative can be almost anything: a character sketch of someone from your past, an incident involving your family or friends, or some other noteworthy occasion that readers will find interesting.

First-person narratives can be of different lengths. Shorter ones may be essay length and focus on just one observation or incident. A longer first-person narrative may relate a series of incidents and describe several people or places.

First-person narratives frequently convey feelings associated with memories: *humor* resulting from a serious situation that turned out well, for example, or the *security* of being cared for when you were sick.

The following first-person narrative focuses on an automobile accident in which the author's son was injured. Notice how the narrative presents the events from the author's own perspective.

Opening incident

Descriptive details

Two days before his eighth birthday, Laurie rode his bike around a bend, directly into the path of a car. I can remember with extraordinary clarity that one of the people in the crowd that gathered handed me a lighted cigarette, I can remember saying reasonably that we all ought not to be standing in the middle of the road like this, I can remember the high step up into the ambulance. When they told us at the hospital, late that night, that everything was going to be all right, we came home and I finished drying the breakfast dishes. Laurie woke up in the hospital the next morning, with no memory of anything that had happened since breakfast two days before, and he was so upset by the thought that he had ridden in an ambulance and not known about it that the ambulance had to be engaged again to bring him home two weeks later, with the sirens screaming and an extremely proud Jannie sitting beside him and traffic separating on either side.

Second incident

We put him, of course, into our bedroom; my mother always used to put sick children into the "big" bed, and I have still that half-remembered feeling that it is one of the signs of being *really* sick, sick enough to stay home from school. My mother, however, never had to cope with anything more complex than my brother's broken arm: I had under my wavering care this active patient with concussion, a broken hand, and various patched-up cuts and bruises; who was not, under doctor's orders, to excite himself, to move his arm; who was not, most particularly, to raise his head or try to turn over; and who was not, it was clearly evident, going to pay any attention to anything the doctor said.

Dialogue

"Now I'm home I can have whatever I want," Laurie announced immediately after I arrived in the room with the tray of orange juice, plain toast, and chicken soup which my mother before me believed was the proper basic treatment for an invalid; he cast a disapproving eye at the tray, and said, "Doc said I could have *real* food."

"The most important thing," I told him, "is for you to keep yourself quiet, and warm, and not excited. That dog, for instance."

Toby buried his huge head under the pillow and tried to pretend that he was invisible. "What dog?" said Laurie.

"And," I went on with great firmness, patting Toby absently on the shoulder, "you are absolutely not to . . . move without help and if you do—"

"I got to go back to the hospital," Laurie said. He wiggled comfortably into the hollow under Toby's chin. "It wasn't so bad there," he said. "*Food* was good, anyway."—Shirley Jackson

Prewriting, Writing, and Revising. Although your first-person narrative will eventually include descriptive details, one or more incidents, perhaps even several characters and their dialogue, start planning with a specific topic for your writing.

Choose a specific topic and then relate your observations in clear chronological order.

Begin by identifying a specific person, place, or thing to write about. As you focus in on your topic, consider the length of your narrative: One incident involving one person might require only a few paragraphs; an elaborate series of incidents involving several characters might approach the length of a short story.

With a specific topic in mind, ask yourself key questions such as "When?" "Where?" "Who?" "What?" and "Why?" to brainstorm for information. If your narrative will trace several incidents, you might make a preliminary list of the incidents on paper to give yourself practice with the chronology.

Using your prewriting ideas and any notes, draft your narrative. As you write, keep in mind the key features of a first-person narrative and concentrate on maintaining a clear chronological presentation. Try to think of descriptive details that will enliven the composition for your readers.

Look for ways to improve your completed first draft. The following questions can help you strengthen your narrative.

CHECKLIST FOR REVISING A FIRST-PERSON NARRATIVE

1. Does your narrative stick to its subject without straying onto tangents?
2. Are events presented in clear chronological order, with a logical beginning and end?
3. Have you included enough descriptive details to keep the reader interested?
4. Have you included personal observations that will help the reader understand your feelings about the subject?
5. Is a first-person point of view maintained throughout?

EXERCISE A: Understanding a First-Person Narrative. Answer the following questions about the first-person narrative on pages 640–641.

1. What specific descriptive details does the author include in her account of the accident?
2. What personal observations does the author make about her son?
3. How is the treatment of the second incident different from her treatment of the first incident? When do you begin to notice the difference?

4. How does the use of dialogue enhance the narrative?
5. Which person seems more important in the narrative, Laurie or the author? Give a reason for your answer.

EXERCISE B: Writing a First-Person Narrative. Follow these steps to plan, write, and revise a first-person narrative.

1. Select a suitable topic from your personal experience.
2. Answer key questions about the topic and then brainstorm for further details.
3. If you are covering several incidents, list the incidents that will occur in your narrative in chronological order.
4. Use your material from brainstorming and your list of events to write a first draft of your narrative.
5. Evaluate your draft by answering the questions in the checklist on page 642 and make any necessary improvements. Then make a clean, final copy.

Writing an Autobiography

When you write an autobiography, you tell others about your own life. Unlike a first-person narrative in which the focus is primarily on the incident, here the spotlight is primarily on you. A book-length autobiography would probably cover your entire life, whereas a shorter autobiography would focus on one or more incidents during a special time in your life.

Understanding Autobiographies. In reading and writing autobiographies, you will always be seeing things from a first-person point of view. The events follow chronological order and present characters who are part of the author's life.

Your autobiography tells a true story about your life.

Following is part of the autobiography of Helen Keller. After an illness in infancy left her without either sight or hearing, Helen Keller began to overcome her handicaps with the help of an extraordinary teacher, Anne Sullivan.

Incident — The most important day I remember in my life is the one on which my teacher, Anne Mansfield Sullivan, came to me. I am filled with wonder when I consider the immeasurable contrasts between the two lives which it connects. It was the third of March, 1887, three months before I was seven years old.

Author focuses on her own personal feelings

On the afternoon of that eventful day, I stood on the porch, dumb, expectant. I guessed vaguely from my mother's signs and from the hurrying to and fro in the house that something unusual was about to happen, so I went to the door and waited on the steps. The afternoon sun penetrated the mass of honeysuckle that covered the porch, and fell on my upturned face. My fingers lingered almost unconsciously on the familiar leaves and blossoms which had just come forth to greet the sweet southern spring. I did not know what the future held . . . for me. Anger and bitterness had preyed upon me continually for weeks and a deep languor had succeeded this passionate struggle.

Descriptive details

Use of similes to convey feelings

Have you ever been at sea in a dense fog, when it seemed as if a tangible white darkness shut you in, and the great ship, tense and anxious, groped her way toward the shore with plummet and sounding-line, and you waited with beating heart for something to happen? I was like that ship before my education began, only I was without compass or sounding-line, and had no way of knowing how near the harbour was. "Light! give me light!" was the wordless cry of my soul, and the light of love shone on me in that very hour.

I felt approaching footsteps. I stretched out my hand as I supposed to my mother. Some one took it, and I was caught up and held close in the arms of her who had come to reveal all things to me, and, more than all things else, to love me.—Helen Keller

Prewriting, Writing, and Revising. Your first step is to choose an appropriate time span.

Choose a time span, and then present your memories of that period in clear chronological order.

Once you have a time span in mind, you can begin taking notes. Think about the setting. Determine one or more key incidents on which you will focus. Think also of the people involved, trying to list as many interesting details as you can.

If you are covering a series of incidents, you might also want to make a list of them to guide you when you write.

As you write, concentrate on presenting the events and details from a consistent first-person point of view to give the reader a clear idea of what was happening and how you felt about it. Also use descriptive details to make the setting vivid and try to include dialogue to make all of the characters come to life.

As you revise the first draft of your autobiography, look for ways to make it livelier for the reader. The following suggestions should help.

CHECKLIST FOR REVISING AN AUTOBIOGRAPHY

1. Have you consistently presented your material from a first-person point of view?
2. Are the time span of the autobiography and its setting quickly identified for the reader?
3. Have you followed clear chronological order?
4. Have you included enough vivid details and dialogue to make people and places come alive for the reader?
5. Have you included your personal feelings and insights about the incidents you present?

EXERCISE C: Understanding an Autobiography. Reread the excerpt from Helen Keller's autobiography on pages 643–644. Then answer the following questions.

1. What is the main incident recounted in this excerpt?
2. List at least three descriptive details that are included.
3. Why do you think that this incident is recounted in such detail? Could the incident have been effectively told with fewer details?
4. Who is the main focus of the excerpt, Helen Keller or Anne Sullivan? Give a reason for your answer.
5. What personal observations does the author make?

EXERCISE D: Writing an Autobiography. Follow these steps to plan, write, and revise a brief autobiography.

1. Choose a time span that you would like to write about.
2. Take notes on the setting, the incident or incidents you wish to focus on, and the other people involved.
3. If you are covering a series of incidents, list the incidents in chronological order.
4. Follow your notes to write a first draft of your autobiography.
5. Evaluate your autobiography using the checklist on page 645 and make any necessary changes. Then, recopy it in final form and proofread it.

DEVELOPING WRITING SKILLS: Writing from Personal Experience. Allow yourself time to think about your life from your earliest recollections to the present. Let your thoughts and feelings reawaken some event or period of time in your life. As you plan to write, decide if you will write about those events as an autobiography, focusing on your own thoughts and feelings, or as a first-person narrative, focusing on someone or something you observed. Identify the kind of composition you will use. Then follow the planning, writing, and revising steps presented in this section.

Writing Workshop: Personal Writing

ASSIGNMENT 1

Topic What Would Life Be Like Without ____________?

Form and Purpose Journal entries; possible later use of ideas as writing topics

Audience Yourself

Length At least one journal entry on the topic each day over a two-week period; entries will vary in length

Focus Each day complete the above topic question with a simple or complex item; for example, *buttons, electric lights, creativity*. Allow your imagination to take over and record what the world would be like without that item.

Sources Personal experiences and observations

Prewriting Ask and answer who, what, where, when, and why questions about your topic.

Writing Use your notes and ideas to write a journal entry.

Revising Review your entries with this question in mind: Can I clearly see the world I described?

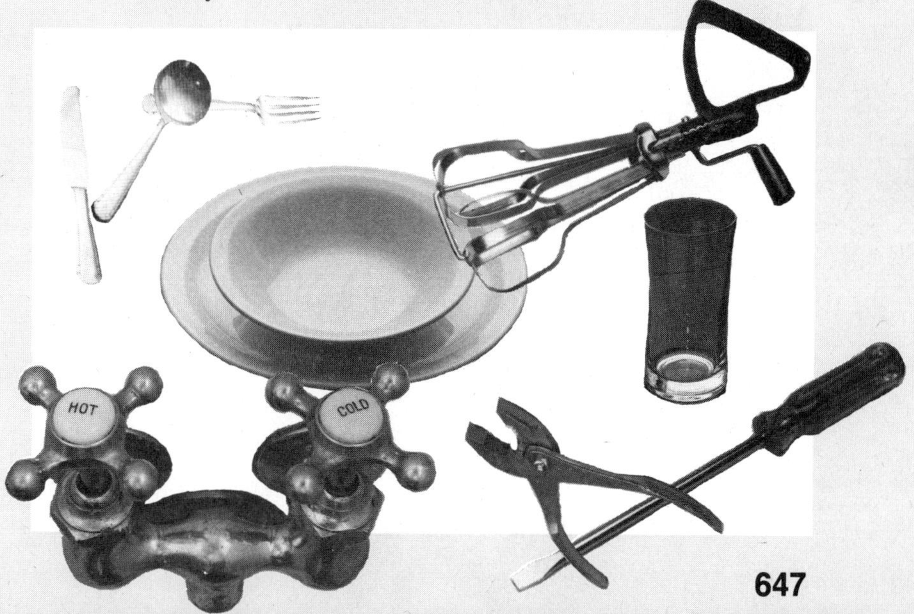

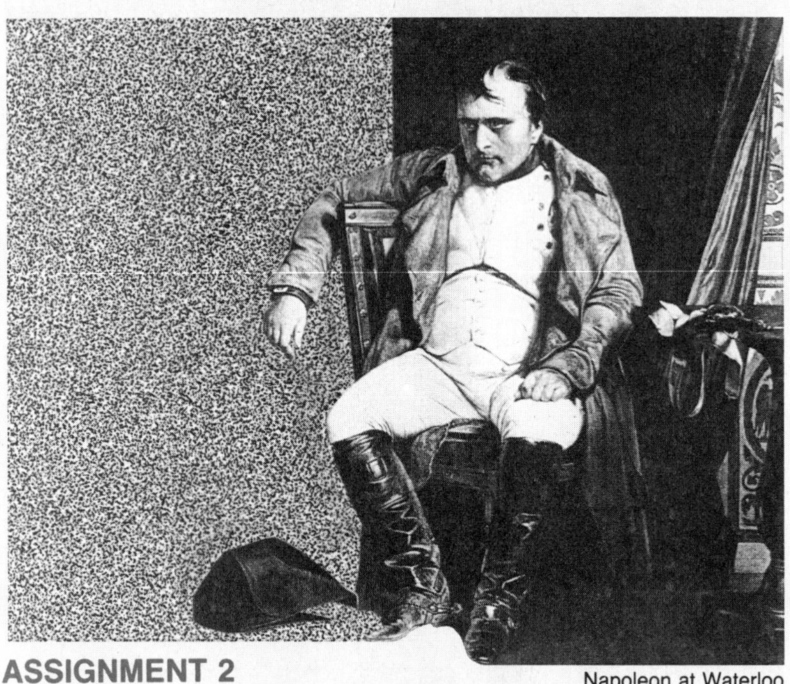

Napoleon at Waterloo

ASSIGNMENT 2

Topic A First-Person Narrative by a Famous Person

Form and Purpose A first-person narrative that informs readers about a significant event in a famous person's life

Audience Members of a story-telling club

Length Four to six narrative paragraphs and dialogue

Focus Write about an important event in the life of a famous person. Use a first-person point of view to convey that person's feelings about the event.

Sources Biography reference books, encyclopedia articles, *Book of Lists,* and *People's Almanac*

Prewriting Choose a famous person and, if necessary, research her or his life. Select an important event and take notes about it. Arrange the notes in chronological order.

Writing Adopt a first-person point of view and narrate the event outlined.

Revising Use the checklist on page 642 when revising. Write a complete, final draft.

Topics for Writing: Personal Writing

© 1963, United Feature Syndicate, Inc.

If the cartoon above suggests a personal experience, then write about it in a journal entry, first-person narrative, or autobiographical sketch. If you prefer, do some personal writing about one of the topics below.

1. Peer Pressure
2. Parent Pressure
3. What Does Education Mean to Me?
4. A Week of Events in My Favorite Class (Journal)
5. A Week of Events in My Least Favorite Class (Journal)
6. Communication: A Family's Lifeline
7. What I Need from My Parents
8. What My Parents Need from Me
9. What Control(s) Would I Like to Have Over My Life?
10. Perfection

Chapter 26

Short Stories

When you relate events, you are creating a narrative, telling a story. A story is a sequence of events that is told from a particular point of view. This chapter will help you to understand how short stories are put together and show you how to write one of your own.

26.1 Understanding Short Stories

A *short story* is a fictional narrative weaving together a number of different elements. In this section you will focus on the elements of character, plot, point of view, and dialogue.

Character and Plot

The people in a short story are called the *characters*. The events that occur in their lives make up the *plot*. The characters and the plot are inseparable; through the characters' speeches, thoughts, and actions the plot unfolds.

Character. In a novel or even in a full-length play, the author has plenty of time to create a character. The reader or the audience can watch the personality of the character being built up, bit by bit, to create a complex portrait. A short story, however, is by definition much briefer. There is no time for leisurely character development. Instead, the author of a short story must focus on quickly creating one *dominant impression* of the character.

A character in a short story creates one dominant impression.

The central impression created by a character will often help you identify the main or central character and let you see how each character will fit into the plot.

Plot. When the main character becomes involved with a *conflict,* the plot of a short story begins to move.

The plot of a short story is a series of events growing out of a conflict.

The conflict will be either external or internal. An external conflict means that the main character is opposed by some outside force, whether that force is nature, society, or some other individual. An internal conflict, on the other hand, shows an opposition within the main character's own personality. The main character may, for example, have to make a difficult decision or choice.

The plot of a short story generally leads up to one crucial event or one main insight. Unlike a novel, which can develop several different plots at great length, a short story is very economical, focusing on one plot and one climax.

The plot generally develops through several stages. These stages and what occurs in each of them are shown in the following chart.

PLOT OF A SHORT STORY

Stages	Functions
Exposition	Introduces the characters and places them in a particular setting Establishes the narrator's point of view Fills in any background information that the reader may need
Opening incident	Creates a conflict Gets the plot going
Rising action	Presents further incidents or insights that intensify the conflict

Climax	Raises the conflict to its greatest intensity Changes the course of events or the way that the reader understands the story
Falling action (not always used)	Relaxes the conflict to prepare readers for the conclusion
Conclusion	Resolves the conflict and brings the plot to a satisfying end Often interprets the story for readers or presents a final insight

EXERCISE A: Understanding Character and Plot. Review a short story you have read recently, and then answer the following questions.

1. Who is the main character in the story?
2. What dominant impression does this character create?
3. Is the character involved with an internal conflict or with an external conflict? Explain your answer.
4. How are other characters in the story involved in the conflict?
5. What information is given in the exposition?
6. What opening incident sets the plot in motion?
7. How does the conflict intensify during the rising action?
8. Identify the climax of the story. Is the climax an event or an insight?
9. Does the story include falling action? If so, how does the falling action prepare the reader for the conclusion?
10. How does the conclusion resolve the conflict? How does the conclusion help you to understand the story as a whole?

Point of View

The perspective from which a story is told is its *point of view*. Everything in the story is related to the reader from a particular vantage point.

A story is narrated from a single, consistent point of view.

Most short stories are told from one of three basic points of view: first person, limited third person, or omniscient third person. These three points of view, also called *narrators,* are explained in the following chart.

KINDS OF NARRATORS	
Narrators	**Functions**
First person	The narrator, using the first-person pronouns "I" and "me," tells the story as he or she saw it and usually participates in the action. The "I" can be either the author or a character created by the author.
Limited third person	The narrator, who is not in the story, uses "he" and "she" to tell the story. The narrator cannot see into the minds of the characters.
Omniscient third person	The narrator uses "he" and "she" to tell the story and is not a part of it. The narrator knows the thoughts of the characters.

Following are three versions of the same story. Each is told from a different point of view. Notice the differences between what each narrator sees and understands.

In the first example, a first-person narrator tells her own story.

First-person narrator

It was ten years since I had left Fairhaven, yet as soon as I stepped off the train, I was struck by how little the town had changed. Across the street, Mr. Walker was leaning against his storefront, watching the passengers arrive, just the way he had watched us depart on the day I left. A fresh crop of children started to play hide and seek in front of his general store, but Mr. Walker shooed them away with a broom as he had scattered my friends, years ago. I caught his eye for a moment; he looked as unfriendly as ever.

The same story could also be told by a limited third-person narrator who would see the events somewhat more objectively.

Limited third-person narrator

Margaret Donaldson had not been to Fairhaven, her home town, in ten years. As she stepped off the train, she paused for a moment, surveying the scene before her. Main Street was quiet, as it always was on a weekday morning. Across the street, business was so slow at Gerald Walker's general store that he was standing out front, watching the passengers getting off the 3:45. As Margaret gazed at the small children playing games in front of the store, she seemed lost in thought; but Mr. Walker suddenly shooed the children away, and the spell was broken.

The last version tells the story from an omniscient third-person point of view. The narrator recounts the events from the outside yet also knows Margaret's thoughts, as well as the thoughts of other characters.

Omniscient third-person narrator

As she stepped off the train in Fairhaven, Margaret Donaldson noticed that little had changed since she had left her home town, ten years before. Seeing the children playing in front of Mr. Walker's general store, across the street, she remembered playing there with her friends as a child. As he shooed them off the porch she thought how frightened she had been when Mr. Walker chased her friends away with a broom.

Her eyes met Mr. Walker's for a moment. She quickly looked away, but he'd already recognized her. Even when they'd grown up and moved away, he didn't often forget the neighborhood children. He never liked having to chase the children away from his store, but their noisy games drove customers to the rival store down the street, and his business wasn't very prosperous. Mr. Walker searched his memory. Why had Steve Donaldson's daughter left town in the first place?

EXERCISE B: Understanding Point of View. Using the story you examined in Exercise A, answer these questions.

1. Who is the narrator of the story?
2. Which of the three basic points of view does this narrator represent?

3. How do you know that the story is being told from that point of view?
4. How would the story be changed if it were told from another point of view?
5. Why do you think the author chose this point of view?

Dialogue

Dialogue is the conversation of two or more people in a short story. It should always represent the way these characters would actually speak and be consistent with their personalities and backgrounds.

Dialogue helps to create believable characters and to develop the plot.

Dialogue advances the plot when characters comment on what they have seen or what they are going to do. In addition, dialogue helps characterize the speakers. The way characters talk reveals much about their personal feelings, sometimes without the characters' realizing it. What is said can be less important than the way it is said or whom a character says it to. In the dialogue of a story, the reader can look for insights into characters' feelings. By letting the characters speak for themselves, dialogue can make the whole story come alive.

In the following example, notice how even a few lines of dialogue help characterize the speakers and advance the plot.

Passage with dialogue

Crossing the street to Gerald Walker's store, Margaret felt her childhood fear of him returning. But she was determined to act like an adult. Boldly she strode to the store, ready to introduce herself.

"Mr. Walker?" she said. "I don't think you'll remember me, but I'm—"

"Margaret Donaldson," he interrupted. "Sure I remember you. Steve Donaldson's little girl." He smiled. "You and Tommy used to live down at the end of Oak Street."

She had never seen him smile before. As a child, it had never occurred to her that he *could* smile. It was just a little thing, but suddenly her home town didn't seem quite the way she had remembered it.

EXERCISE C: Understanding Dialogue. Use the short story you examined in Exercises A and B to answer these questions.

1. How much dialogue does the story contain? How many of the characters speak?
2. How does the dialogue help characterize the speakers?
3. Is each character's dialogue appropriate? Why or why not?
4. How does the dialogue help to advance the plot?
5. How would the story be different without dialogue?

DEVELOPING WRITING SKILLS: Rewriting a Short Story. Reread the beginning and ending of the short story that you examined in Exercises A through C or some other story that you have read recently. Then follow these instructions.

1. Using a different point of view from the one used by the author, rewrite the beginning paragraphs of the story. For example, if the author used a first-person narrator, try rewriting from a limited third-person point of view.
2. Find a passage in the story in which the characters could speak to each other but do not. Rewrite the passage to include a substantial amount of dialogue.
3. Rewrite the concluding paragraphs of the story to make the ending the opposite of the author's original ending.

26.2 Writing a Short Story

When writing a short story, you should follow most of the same basic steps you use for other kinds of writing. This section presents specific suggestions that will help you to plan, write, and revise a short story.

PREWRITING: Planning Your Short Story

When planning a short story you must consider the elements discussed in the first section of this chapter.

Assemble details about characters, conflict, and setting, and organize them within a general plot outline to plan your short story.

One way to begin is with a character that interests you. Ask yourself a series of questions about the character to generate raw material during prewriting. The following list may help you to develop your ideas.

QUESTIONS FOR DEVELOPING A CHARACTER

1. What is the identity of the character (name, age, sex, nationality, era, and so on)?
2. What are the character's principal personality traits? What are the character's main strengths and weaknesses?
3. How does the character speak? What does the character look like?
4. What dominant impression do you want the character to make on readers?
5. What are the character's friends and family like? Should they be brought into the story?

After you have answered these questions, you will have a more complete picture of your character. Although you may not use all the information you gather, it will help you to think through and decide, for example, what kind of conflict the character will become involved in. The following questions can help you further develop the conflict in your story.

QUESTIONS FOR DEVELOPING CONFLICT

1. Will the conflict be internal or external?
2. If the conflict is internal, should it primarily involve the main character's feelings or ideas or both?
3. If the conflict is external, does it bring other characters into opposition with the main character or does it involve more general forces, such as nature or society?
4. Would the conflict, especially its climax, be more effectively presented in events or in dialogue?
5. Should the reader always have a clear sense of who is right and who is wrong? Should that sense change during the course of the story?

After you have answered these questions, try to state your story's conflict in a single sentence.

When you have decided on your main character and conflict, you can sketch a plot that develops around them. Keep in mind that a short story should lead up to a single main event or one moment of insight. Use that central moment, the climax of your story, as your guide in selecting details from the information you have gathered on character and conflict. Also try out dialogue for some of the major characters and scenes. Finally, give your story a specific setting; decide on a time and a place for the action.

Focus on your story's structure as you organize the material you have gathered into a plot outline. Use the chart on pages 651 and 652 to help you present events in an orderly way.

With a plot outline and the other material you have prepared, you can decide what kind of narrator might be most effective. Consider how telling the story from each of the three different points of view would affect, for example, the conflict. An external conflict might best be presented from a limited third-person point of view, in which the narrator could handle the conflict objectively. An internal conflict, however, might require an omniscient third-person narrator who could see and understand the character's feelings.

EXERCISE A: Planning a Short Story. Use the two charts on page 657 to develop a main character and a conflict that interest you. Then organize your material into a plot outline. Read over your material and decide where dialogue could enhance the story. Finally, decide on an appropriate point of view.

WRITING: Creating a First Draft

The first draft of your short story should follow your plot outline. When writing your first draft try to get the story down in order; do not worry about the fine points at this time. Think of your first draft as a practice copy. You will have an opportunity to refine it and change it during revision.

Follow your plot outline to write a first draft maintaining a consistent point of view.

Concentrate on connecting the events with each other by means of transitions and perhaps a few repeated main words. Include dialogue that will fit your characters and situations. Also make sure that your narrator's words and information are appropriate.

When you have a completed first draft, decide on a title.

The following story is in final form. The notes in the margin show the basic structure of the story, based on the chart on pages 651 and 652, as well as other significant points about how the story is told.

The Homecoming

EXPOSITION

On the long train ride up from Boston, Margaret thought about her home town almost for the first time since leaving it, ten years before. In all that time, she had never returned. Not that she was trying to escape from anything in particular; she even remembered Fairhaven with some fondness. But leaving it to go to college had been a definite break with the past, a new kind of life. Leaving Fairhaven had been like leaving her own adolescence behind. She had stopped calling herself Maggie when she left; she had been Margaret now for ten years.

To her friends in Boston, she always described Fairhaven as something in an old movie: an idyllic little New England town where everyone knew everyone else all their lives, where it always snowed on Christmas Eve, where the high point of the social season was the 4th of July picnic. She joked about it with the people at work, about its old fashionedness, even about its name. " 'Fair . . . haven,' get it?" she'd say to her friends.

Before now, she'd had no special reason to return. Family reunions were always held at Tom's place—Tom, her oldest brother, who had a comfortable house just outside Boston, close to most of the other children. Mom and Dad would come down from Fairhaven, and the four brothers and sisters would all converge on Tom's.

OPENING INCIDENT

But now Mom and Dad had both retired; it was about time they sold the large, empty house which had become a burden. For a while, Dad had talked about moving to a warmer climate, where he wouldn't have to shovel snow. But in the end they'd decided to stay close to the children. With Tom's help, they'd found a sunny, but not very large, apartment in Milford. They would have to get rid of most of the furniture, especially from the children's old rooms.

Character's thoughts

Margaret had come to help with packing, to help sort out a lifetime of accumulated bric-a-brac. But she also wanted to see her home town once more while it still *was* her home town—while her mother and father still lived in the house where she had grown up. She wanted a last look before putting her memories away.

RISING ACTION

As she stepped off the train at Fairhaven station, the town looked almost unchanged. A sign atop the station house still proudly proclaimed this was the "Home of the Fairhaven Cougars," the local semi-pro baseball team. Main Street was still, miraculously, free of fast-food restaurants. And the general store across the street from the station had not yet been replaced by a franchised convenience store. Seeing the children playing in front of Mr. Walker's general store, she remembered playing there with her friends as a child. As he shooed them off the porch she thought how frightened her friends had been when Mr. Walker chased them away with a broom.

Description

Walking down Oak Street, retracing her old route home from school, she walked back into her past. A few houses looked different, some had been painted, others had new shrubs, but it was still the street as she remembered it. It was beginning to get dark; a TV set flickered on at one window. As she approached her house, her father was coming from the opposite direction with a bag of groceries.

"Maggie! You made it! Well, what do you think of the old place?" he said as they went inside. Her mother and father had always been fastidious about the house, keeping it tidy and organized. But now, in the middle of packing, chaos was everywhere.

Piles of clothing, stacks of books tied with string, and miscellaneous furniture covered with sheets blocked them at every turn. It made Margaret suddenly feel sad; the whole town was just as she remembered it, but their house, the only part she truly cared about, was a little disaster area, hardly recognizable as the place where her family lived. It was as if she'd come too late; the house was already gone.

Description

In the living room, her mother was carefully packing some large books in a carton. When she kissed her mother, Margaret could see that she'd been crying. All around them, family albums and framed photographs covered the floor. Margaret could scarcely believe there were so many. Tommy, Margaret, Ben, all of them, even the long-deceased German shepherd, Fritz, could be seen in every stage of their lives. There were endless baby photos, graduation pictures, snapshots of birthday parties, and wedding portraits, some in black and white, some in color. It was a vast family chronicle, begun long before she was born and still growing. And in the background of most of the photographs was the house. In the early pictures, it was painted white; later on, the shingles turned blue and an added room became visible at the side. In the last pictures, new siding and a hedge could be seen. The house had changed with the family.

CLIMAX

"I'm going to miss this old house," her mother said when they were alone, "and the town, too. You were all raised here. I feel like I'm leaving my whole life behind. I wish I could make your father understand that. But I guess he's right, at least about the expense, now that we don't use the upstairs anymore. We just can't afford to stay."

"But you'll like it in Milford, Mom. It's nearer Tommy and Nan, too."

"I know I'll like it once we're settled in. But when you've lived somewhere as long as I have, maybe you'll feel the same way I do. It's a funny thing, leaving. Part of you always stays behind."

Beyond the kaleidoscope of photographs, the living room was piled high with cartons of every size, only about half of them full. There was still a lot of packing to do.

Dialogue

"We haven't gotten to your room yet, or Tommy's," Mom said. "Thought you'd want to do those yourselves. Tommy's bringing the pick-up truck tomorrow, if you want any furniture. Oh, and I found this in the attic." It was Margaret's yearbook from Fairhaven High.

CONCLUSION

After dinner, they took a break from packing to look at Margaret's yearbook—first the group pictures of her clubs and activities, full of smiling, forgotten friends. And then her portrait. To her, it was a photograph of someone else, a person who had lived in this house long ago: an adolescent named Maggie. It had nothing to do with her. The outdated clothes, the funny hairdo, even the stiff pose the photographer had insisted on made the picture seem like an artifact for archaeologists to study, a relic of a vanished age. But unmistakably the features in the picture were hers.

"Want to take it back to Boston with you?" her mother asked. Margaret could see that the yearbook meant more to her mother than to herself.

She said, "I'd like you to hold on to it. Okay? Keep it with the rest of the family archives."

Then they all went back to packing.

EXERCISE B: Drafting a Short Story. Using the plot outline you prepared in Exercise A, write a first draft of your short story maintaining a clear point of view. Concentrate on connecting events with transitions and on presenting characters with appropriate dialogue. When you have a complete first draft, add a suitable title.

REVISING: Polishing Your Short Story

During revision you should decide what to add, delete, or change in order to make your story more effective. When you are revising your story, you can experiment with different beginnings and endings, rewriting them until you are satisfied. Or you can reconsider the characters' dialogue, perhaps making their words more appropriate or more closely related to the plot.

Use a checklist to revise your short story.

The following suggestions can help you to revise your story.

CHECKLIST FOR REVISING A SHORT STORY

1. Is the point of view clear and consistent?
2. Does the plot develop in a logical way, with an exposition, rising action, climax, and conclusion?
3. Is the conflict, whether internal or external, made clear to the reader?
4. Does the dialogue accurately reflect the way people in such a position would actually talk?
5. Should any passages be rewritten for clarity or for correctness of grammar, mechanics, and spelling?

EXERCISE C: Revising a Short Story. Use the checklist on this page to revise the short story that you drafted in Exercise B. If you make many changes in your story, prepare a clean, final copy and proofread it.

DEVELOPING WRITING SKILLS: Writing from a Different Point of View. Using the short story you wrote in Exercises A through C, follow these instructions.

1. Use the chart on page 653 to reconsider the point of view in your story. If your original story is told in the first person, think about how the story would be different if told by either a limited or an omniscient third-person narrator.
2. Rewrite the story from the new point of view. Be sure to make whatever adjustments are necessary to the dialogue.
3. Submit both the original and rewritten stories to your teacher.

Writing Workshop: Short Stories

ASSIGNMENT 1

Topic A Short Story Based on a News Event

Form and Purpose A short story that blends fantasy with reality to entertain readers

Audience Your English or literature class

Length Three to five pages

Focus Elaborate on a news event by inventing characters, plot, and conflict based on the original event.

Sources Newspapers, weekly news magazines, television and radio news programs

Prewriting After selecting a news event ask yourself questions like those on pages 652 and 657. Develop a plot outline, and write down character details.

Writing Follow your outline when writing a first draft. Use a single, consistent point of view and include dialogue.

Revising Use the checklist on page 663 to make changes in your short story.

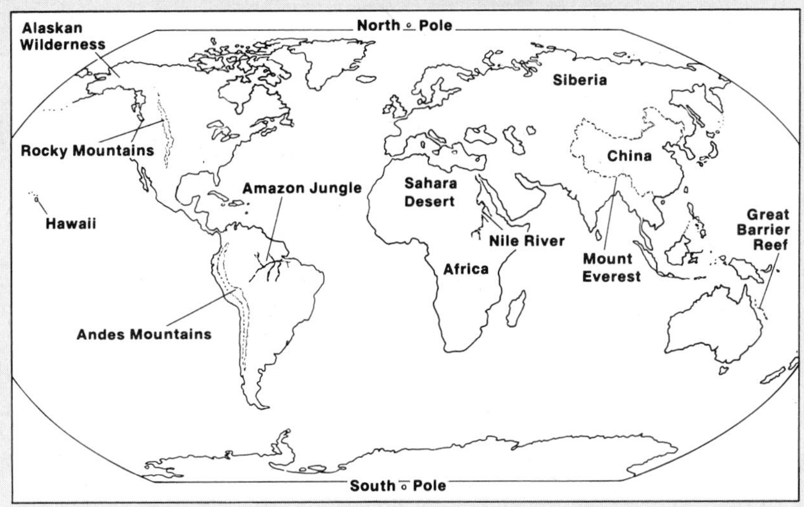

ASSIGNMENT 2

Topic Team Adventure Story with Exotic Setting

Form and Purpose A short story with an exotic setting and with elements of adventure and an external conflict to entertain readers

Audience Readers of a magazine entitled *Adventure*

Length Three to five pages

Focus With two classmates choose a setting that you are unfamiliar with. Then research that location. Together, plan and write an adventure story set in that location. Your characters should be involved in an external struggle.

Sources Atlas, almanac, encyclopedia, geography texts, magazines such as *National Geographic*

Prewriting After researching your setting, write notes about your characters, the conflict, and the plot. Use the questions on pages 652 and 657. Outline your story.

Writing Together, discuss and write a first draft following your outline.

Revising Use the checklist on page 663 during revision. Prepare a final draft, and read it to other story teams.

Topics for Writing: Short Stories

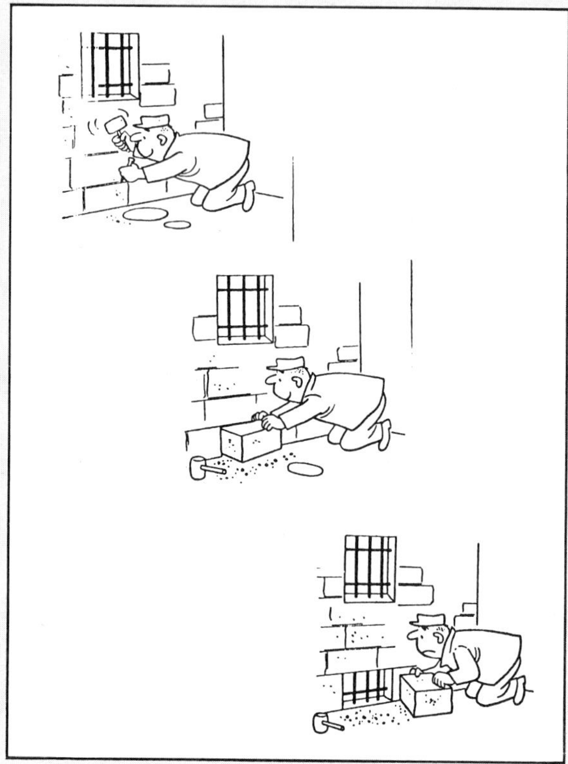

The cartoon may suggest to you another story idea with a twist or an unexpected ending. Plan and write a short story about that idea or use one of the topics below to develop and write a short story.

1. Marooned on an Island
2. A Humorous Incident with a Pet
3. The Discovery of a Sunken Treasure
4. Overcoming a Handicap
5. Fishing in Shark-Infested Water
6. A Malicious Rumor
7. Discovering in Yourself an Unexpected Strength
8. The Courage to Be Different
9. Learning to Trust and Depend Upon Friends
10. Admitting That You Were Wrong

Chapter 27

Letters

Letters serve a number of different needs. They can be a means of transmitting personal information, for formal and informal social reasons. Or, as a means of conducting business, letters can act as concrete records of dates, meetings, applications, orders, and other important business information.

Looking at Letters 27.1

Writing good letters involves putting your ideas into a certain form, a structural and stylistic arrangement for your letter. In this section, you will look at the forms for writing friendly letters, social notes, and business letters.

Friendly Letters and Social Notes

Friendly letters transmit personal information. Social notes are written for formal or informal social reasons.

The Parts of the Friendly Letter and Social Note. Most friendly letters and social notes contain five basic parts, which follow an expected order.

The five basic parts of a friendly letter and social note are the heading, the salutation, the body, the closing, and the signature.

The *heading* should be placed in the upper right-hand portion of your letter. It includes your street address in the first line and your town or city, state, and ZIP code in the second.

(It also includes the name of your country if you are sending the letter to another country.) This information serves a very important purpose. It ensures that the person who receives the letter can easily write back. In the last line of the heading, the date is included.

The *salutation,* or greeting, is placed below the heading at the left of the letter. In most friendly letters, the salutation begins somewhat formally with "Dear" followed by the name of the person who will receive the letter. A comma then follows the salutation.

FORMAL:	Dear Aunt Millie,	Dear Mrs. Donovan,
	Dear Dr. Larkin,	Dear Ms. Rivera,

To greet close friends and family members, however, you might use less formal salutations.

INFORMAL:	Hi, Jim,	Greetings, Tom and Pat,
	My good Friend,	Hello, Pal,

The *body* of a friendly letter begins two or three lines below the salutation. This section can include as many paragraphs as needed to communicate ideas, feelings, and other personal information.

The *closing* is written in the lower right-hand portion of the letter. The first word is capitalized but not the following words and a comma is placed at the end. The closing word or phrase should suit the tone of the letter.

FORMAL:	Sincerely yours,	Very truly yours,
INFORMAL:	Regards,	Love,

The *signature* is placed directly beneath the closing word or phrase. If you do not know the person to whom you are writing very well or if there is a large age difference between you, sign your full name. Otherwise, use your first name or a nickname. A signature is written by hand, even if the rest of the letter is typed.

If your letter is an invitation, you may also want to add an *R.S.V.P.* This abbreviation tells the person who receives the invitation to respond, stating whether he or she will accept or decline the invitation. An R.S.V.P. is usually placed in the lower left-hand corner of the invitation.

Different Styles for Friendly Letters and Social Notes. While the five basic parts of the friendly letter and social note must appear in designated places on the paper, the style that you use for arranging the lines is a matter of choice.

Use either an indented or semiblock style for friendly letters and social notes.

The *indented* style calls for indented lines in the heading and in the closing and signature. In the *semiblock* style, on the other hand, the heading, closing, and signature all begin at the same point.

Indented Style | **Semiblock Style**

Heading

Salutation

Body

Closing

Signature

When you write your envelope remember to use the same style, indented or semiblock, that you used to write the letter. Your envelope should look like one of the following models.

Indented Style | **Semiblock Style**

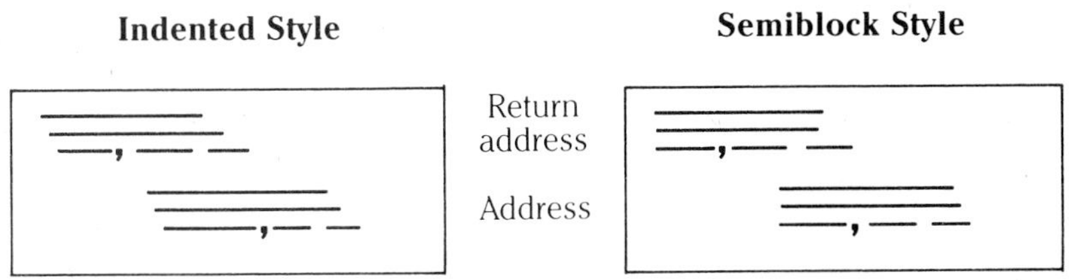

In addition, the following guidelines may be useful in addressing an envelope.

WRITING YOUR ENVELOPE

1. Prepare the envelope in the same manner that you wrote the letter: typed or handwritten.
2. Do not use titles such as Mr., Miss, Mrs., or Ms. in your own name.
3. Include all necessary mailing information in the address of the person who is to receive the letter: apartment number or route number if there is one and the ZIP code.
4. Avoid any abbreviations in addresses that will not be immediately clear to everyone who reads the envelope.
5. On small envelopes, write your name and address on the back instead of in the upper left-hand corner. (With a very small envelope, you may need to check with your post office to make sure it is large enough to meet postal regulations.)

The way in which you fold your letter depends on the size of your stationery and envelope. For a small sheet of paper, you may only need to fold the paper in half. A larger piece of paper, however, must be folded into thirds, as shown in the following diagram.

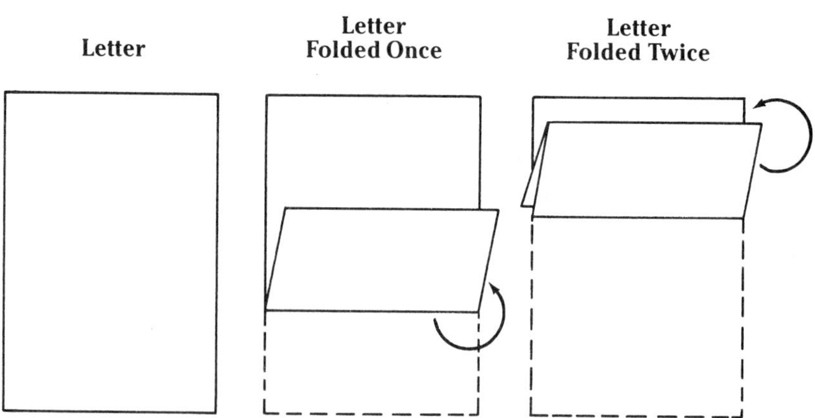

EXERCISE A: Practicing with the Parts of Friendly Letters and Social Notes. Prepare two skeleton letters, with lines instead of words in the body. For one letter, use the indented style. For the other, use the semiblock. Fill in the five parts of each letter by using your own address for the heading and someone else's name for the salutation. Include all five parts of the friendly letter and social note.

EXERCISE B: Mailing Friendly Letters and Social Notes. Prepare envelopes for your skeleton letters from Exercise A. Make sure that each envelope matches the style of its letter. Then fold each letter properly and slip it into its envelope.

Business Letters

The parts of the business letter are similar but not identical to those of the friendly letter. There are also a number of special rules of form to follow when writing a business letter.

The Parts of the Business Letter. Usually written on plain white paper that measures $8\frac{1}{2} \times 11$ inches, a business letter contains a minimum of six parts, in an expected order.

A business letter contains a heading, an inside address, a salutation, a body, a closing, and a signature.

The *heading* of a business letter presents your complete address as well as the date on which you wrote the letter. Place the heading at least one inch below the top of the paper.

The *inside address* states the name and address of the person or persons to whom you are writing. You should place it on the left two to four spaces lower than the heading.

EXAMPLES:	Ajax Rug Cleaning, Inc. 140 Merrick Avenue Merrick, New York 11566	Dr. Bartram Baker Director of Admissions Atlas Community College St. Paul, Minnesota 56556

The *salutation,* placed two spaces beneath the inside address, greets the person to whom you are writing. For business letters, a salutation should be formal. It is always followed by a colon.

EXAMPLE:	Dear Sir:	Gentlemen:
	Dear Sir or Madam:	Dear Mrs. Appleby:

The *body* of a business letter, which begins two spaces below the salutation, can be any length, but short and direct statements are generally appreciated in business.

The *closing* follows two or three spaces beneath the body. The closing begins with a capital letter and ends with a comma. In business letters, closings are usually formal.

EXAMPLE: Respectfully, Sincerely, Yours truly,

The *signature* appears in full beneath the closing. If the letter is typed, you should handwrite your signature and then type your name below it. Women sometimes indicate how they prefer to be addressed (Miss, Mrs., Ms.) by placing the abbreviation in parentheses before the typed name.

Different Styles for Business Letters. The parts of a business letter can be arranged in at least three different ways.

Use either block style, modified block style, or semiblock style in a business letter.

In *block style,* all parts of the letter begin on the left side of the paper, as in the following example.

Block Style

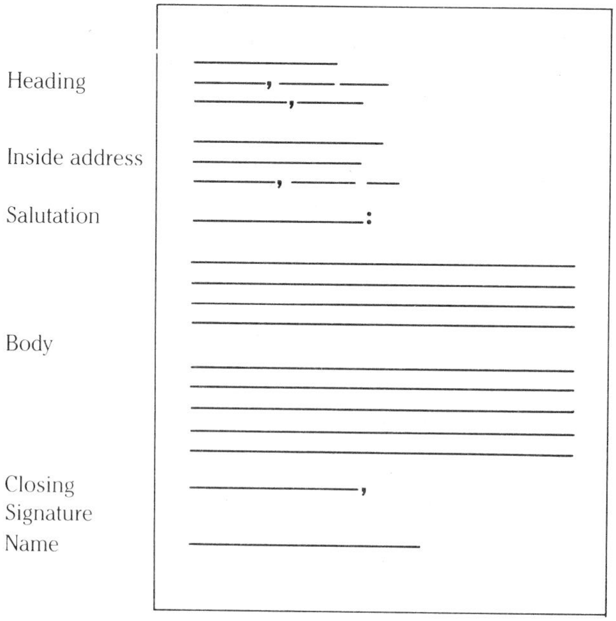

Heading

Inside address

Salutation

Body

Closing

Signature

Name

Notice in block style that no lines are indented, not even the first line of a paragraph. Space is left between paragraphs, however, to show where one ends and the next begins. Block style is a very common choice.

In *modified block style* and *semiblock style,* the heading is placed in the upper right-hand portion of the letter and the closing and signature in the lower right-hand portion. The other parts of the letter—the inside address, the salutation, and the body paragraphs—begin on the left. Again, each new paragraph begins on the left and a space is left between paragraphs. The only difference between the two styles is that in semiblock style, the first line of each paragraph is indented.

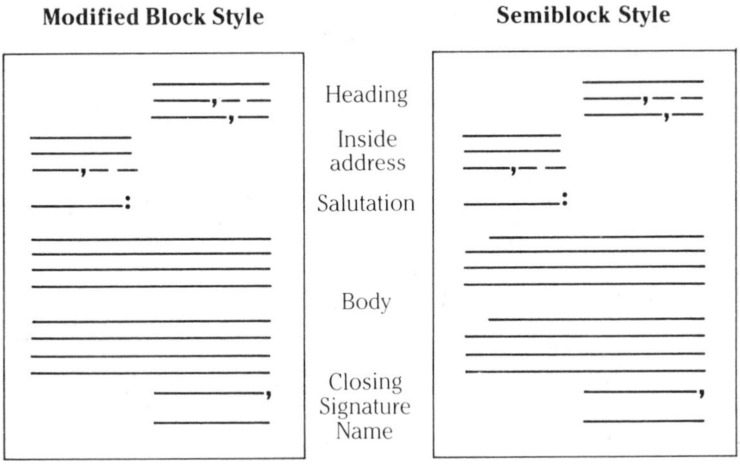

Modified Block Style **Semiblock Style**

Heading
Inside address
Salutation
Body
Closing
Signature
Name

The following rules should help you prepare business letters that will be well received in the business world.

SPECIAL RULES FOR BUSINESS LETTERS

1. Write on unlined, 8½ × 11 inch white paper with a matching envelope.
2. Type your business letter, if possible.
3. Double space between paragraphs and between other parts of the letter.
4. Leave a margin of one inch on all sides of the paper.

The second page of a business letter, if one is necessary, should follow the same style as the first. For the purposes of identification, you should begin the second page with a short heading listing the name of the recipient, the page number, and the date.

The envelope you use for a business letter should be the standard-sized white envelope that matches your stationery. The following example shows the style your envelope would follow regardless of the style followed in the letter itself.

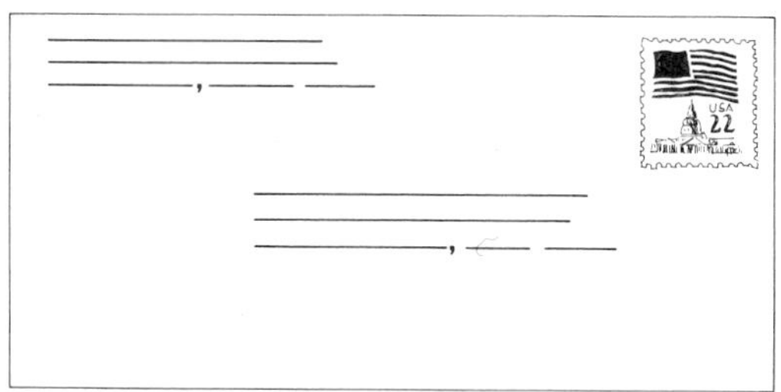

To place your letter inside the envelope, fold the letter in thirds, as shown in the illustration on page 670.

EXERCISE C: Practicing with the Parts of a Business Letter. Use three pieces of paper to set up three skeleton business letters, with lines instead of words in the body. Write one in block style, one in modified block style, and one in semiblock style. Use your name and address, and the following inside address: Complaint Department, Minimart Department Store, 500 S.W. Fifth Avenue, Cooper City, Florida 33328.

EXERCISE D: Addressing Business Envelopes. Prepare an envelope for one of the skeleton letters you wrote in Exercise A. Then fold the letter properly and put it in the envelope.

DEVELOPING WRITING SKILLS: Practicing with Different Kinds of Letters. Using one of the skeleton friendly letters you prepared in Exercise A and one of the skeleton business letters you prepared in Exercise C, state a specific reason you would have for writing each letter, and then write the letters.

Writing Letters 27.2

With a clear understanding of the different kinds of letters and the parts that go into them, you are ready to consider ways of writing letters.

Writing Friendly Letters and Social Notes

Different types of letters suit different personal needs. A long letter to a friend, for example, would differ in many ways from a letter of invitation.

Friendly Letters. A friendly letter, like many more formal pieces of writing, should contain an interesting opening, a body of well-organized information, and a suitable conclusion.

Include well-organized statements of personal information when you write friendly letters.

The following suggestions should help you gather ideas and express them well.

SUGGESTIONS FOR WRITING FRIENDLY LETTERS
1. Think about any questions the person may have asked in his or her last letter. Be sure to answer these questions.
2. Think about previous contacts with the person, through letters, visits, or phone calls. Consider mentioning any thoughts you have had about these occasions.
3. Provide facts and details about people, places, or events that the person will understand and find interesting.
4. Be careful not to concentrate solely on your own experiences. Share information about yourself, but mention the recipient's interests as well and ask questions that he or she will enjoy responding to.
5. Proofread your letter for mechanical errors and for clarity of ideas. Will the person understand the ideas you are presenting? Is more information needed?
6. Rewrite the letter, if necessary, to make any corrections or additions.

Social Notes. Social notes tend to be shorter and slightly more formal than friendly letters. Social notes are written with a specific purpose in mind. In writing a social note, keep that purpose in focus.

Focus on your specific purpose when you write a social note.

An *invitation,* for example, includes all the parts of a friendly letter: heading, salutation, body, closing, and signature. But in addition, there are a number of other specific details that must be included in order to get the response that you desire. The steps in the following chart give you the essentials.

WRITING A LETTER OF INVITATION
1. Give specific details about the time, date, and place of the occasion as well as what kind of event it will be.
2. Mention what to wear and bring, if necessary.
3. Give the people you are inviting time to respond.
4. Include an R.S.V.P.

Whenever you receive a written invitation, you should reply promptly with a *letter of acceptance* or a *letter of regret* unless a phone number is given with the R.S.V.P. Again you must include a heading, a salutation, body, closing, and signature as well as certain special details.

WRITING A LETTER OF ACCEPTANCE OR REGRET
1. If you accept, repeat the time, date, and place to avoid any misunderstanding.
2. If you must refuse, offer a reason for being unable to attend.
3. Always express your appreciation for the invitation.

Notice that the following letter of invitation and letter of acceptance contain all of the basic parts of a social note. They also include the special details needed in each specific kind of letter.

1030 Franklin St.
Delmar, Iowa 52037
November 12, 1986

Dear Bill,

I am planning a surprise birthday party for my sister Eileen. Knowing that you and my sister have been friends for several years, I sincerely hope that you can attend.

The party will begin at 4:00 p.m. on Sunday, November 30. It will be held at our house and will include an informal dinner.

I certainly hope that you can attend.

Sincerely,
Eleanor Donovan

R.S.V.P.

220 Pierce St.
Delmar, Iowa 52037
November 14, 1986

Dear Eleanor,

I will be pleased to attend your party for Eileen. I am glad that you thought of me, and I will look forward to the occasion.

I plan to arrive at your house promptly at 4:00 p.m. on the 30th, with a very special present for Eileen.

Sincerely,
Bill Derby

Whenever you receive a gift, you should reply promptly with a *thank-you note or letter,* mentioning the gift by name. If you are thanking someone for acting as your host, you should again be prompt and specific. Promptness is also important when you send a *letter of congratulation* or a *letter of condolence.* The most important thing in these last two types of notes, however, is a sincere tone, either of joy or sorrow.

EXERCISE A: Getting Ideas for a Friendly Letter. Choose someone to whom you might write a friendly letter. This person can be real or imaginary. Jot down ideas that you might want to include in a letter to this person, using the suggestions in the chart on page 675. Draw up an organized list of these ideas and, next to each idea, tell why you think it would be interesting to the person whom you have chosen.

EXERCISE B: Writing Invitations and Letters of Acceptance or Regret. Think of a real or imaginary social event that you could plan and organize. Then write a letter of invitation to someone whom you would like to attend. Exchange your letter of invitation with someone else in your class. Read his or her letter and write a letter of acceptance or regret.

EXERCISE C: Writing Other Kinds of Social Notes. Write a note or letter responding to a gift or hospitality or to an event in someone else's life. Use one of the following suggestions.

1. A thank-you note for a birthday gift that you received
2. A thank-you note after a weekend at a friend's ski lodge
3. A note to a friend at a private school who has won an award
4. A note to a distant cousin who has broken a leg

Writing Business Letters

Because different needs and situations require that you write different types of business letters, you should become familiar with how to write a number of the most common types of these letters. But whatever kind of business letter you write, your approach should always be clear and direct.

Write business letters that are clear and direct.

In school or later in your career, you may often need to request information from a business or a government agency. A well-written *letter of request* will help you obtain what you want. You may also need to send for merchandise by mail using an *order letter.* Request or order letters must contain the basic parts of any business letter. But the body of such a letter should also contain a number of special details. The following chart should help you cover all the essentials.

WRITING REQUEST AND ORDER LETTERS
1. State your specific request, for information or merchandise, in the first or second sentence.
2. If you require information, give the reason for the request.
3. Make all requests or orders brief and to the point, specifying precisely the items required.
4. If payments are essential, state the total amount and mention the method of payment you are using, such as check, money order, or C.O.D.
5. Offer any other details that will clarify your needs and help the recipient respond.

Notice that the following order letter contains all the essential parts of a business letter. It also covers all necessary details briefly in a clear fashion.

1160 Beaufort Drive
Stockton, Arkansas 72031
March 15, 1986

Supply Department
Crosby's Department Store
1200 Highway 101
Riverside, California 92501

Dear Sir:

Please send me the following items, which were listed in your 1986 Supply Catalog:

1. Canton 3-setting Blow Dryer
   Order number: 006 — $24.95

2. Python Styling Brushes
   Order number: 107 — 14.95

Total $39.90

Enclosed you will find a money order for $39.90. I understand that postage and insurance costs are included in the sales price.

Sincerely,

Jane Hathaway

Jane Hathaway

When you seek employment, you may find it very useful to send *letters of application.* Begin by identifying the position you are applying for. Then summarize the main points of your résumé, if you are including one, or briefly itemize your experience. Be sure to include your address and phone number.

In the following letter of application, notice that the writer relates her experience directly to a possible job opening.

118 Garden Street
Hoboken, New Jersey 07030
April 3, 1986

The Clam Broth House Restaurant
102 First Street
Hoboken, New Jersey 07030

Dear Sir or Madam:

I am seeking summer employment as a waitress or counterperson, and I would like to be considered for any openings that you have.

I am seventeen years old and a senior at Hoboken High School. Last summer I worked for two months as a counterperson at the Royal Seafood Manor in Tenafly, New Jersey. My supervisor in that job is willing to provide a reference:

Ian Roberts, Manager
Royal Seafood Manor
220 Eastern Parkway
Tenafly, New Jersey 07630

I can be reached at my home if an opening becomes available. My telephone number is (201) 420-7777.

Sincerely,

Renata Ciardi

Renata Ciardi

Other situations might lead you to write other kinds of business letters. A *letter of complaint* is often the speediest way to achieve a solution to a business problem. Be sure to include enough specific details to allow the problem to be identified quickly. Always include any order number you may have and, if possible, a copy of any relevant documents.

If you want to express your views to the editor of a newspaper or the head of a television station, you may find that a *letter of opinion* works best. State your views clearly and politely and offer support for your position.

EXERCISE D: Writing a Request or Order Letter. Write a letter requesting information or ordering merchandise using one of the following suggestions.

1. Write an automobile company for details about a car.
2. Write to an embassy or tourist office for travel information about a foreign country.
3. Write to a store in another city to order some item that you cannot find locally.
4. Write to a major department store chain to order an item you found in their catalog.

EXERCISE E: Writing a Letter of Complaint, Application, or Opinion. Write a letter of complaint, application, or opinion using one of the following suggestions.

1. Write to a store complaining about broken merchandise or any item that you ordered but have failed to receive. (Address your letter to the company's complaint department.)
2. Write to a business, government agency, or some other place (park service, hotel, restaurant) where you might find a summer job.
3. Write to a television station to criticize or praise a show that you recently watched. (Address your letter to the general manager of the station.)
4. Write to your local newspaper to express your views on some public issue, such as trash removal or bus service. (Address your letter to the editor of the paper.)

DEVELOPING WRITING SKILLS: Writing a Letter. Think of a social note or a business letter that you want to actually send. Then follow the steps presented in this chapter to write the letter. Proofread your letter and prepare an envelope for it.

Writing Workshop: Letters

ASSIGNMENT 1

Topic Invitation to an Event in the Year 2050

Form and Purpose A formal invitation to an event that takes place in future time; you decide its purpose

Audience Your choice

Length One to two brief paragraphs

Focus Identify the event and its purpose. Provide information about the time, date, and place. You may also wish to mention what to wear or bring. Include an R.S.V.P.

Sources Books and magazine articles that predict the future

Prewriting Write notes about the event and the person or persons you will invite.

Writing Include all the parts of an invitation in their proper positions. Use your notes to compose a first draft.

Revising Use the checklist on page 676 to review the body of your invitation. Then write a final copy.

ASSIGNMENT 2

Topic Taking a Stand on a Political, Social, or Economic Issue

Form and Purpose A formal business letter that either supports or differs with the viewpoint of a state or national political representative

Audience An elected official who represents your area in either the state or federal government

Length Two to three paragraphs

Focus Introduce the issue and state your opinion. Give reasons, facts, and examples that support your opinion. Conclude with a clincher that restates your opinion.

Sources Newspapers, television news programs or news specials and documentaries

Prewriting Identify a political, social, or economic issue. Determine your elected representative's stand on the issue. Write your opinion and support it with details.

Writing Use your notes to write the first draft of a formal, polite business letter.

Revising Check to be sure that your opinion is clearly stated and soundly supported. Write a final draft.

Topics for Writing: Letters

The above illustration may suggest a purpose, audience, and content for a personal or business letter. Plan and write that letter, or choose one of the letter purposes below. Determine an audience and specific letter contents.

1. Requesting Information About a Law
2. Asking to Interview a Famous Person
3. A Complaint About a Product You Purchased
4. A Thank-You Note to a Friend
5. An Invitation to a Skiing or Camping Trip
6. Accepting the Most Distinguished Poet Award
7. Applying for Enrollment in a School or Special Course
8. Ordering Some Equipment for a Science Fair Project
9. Describing a Recent Trip to a Relative
10. Conveying Your Opinion of a Newspaper Editorial or Movie Review

Chapter **28**

Essay Exams

Essay examinations are likely to be part of your school life and professional life for many years to come. When a question requires an answer longer than a sentence, you must plan and organize a written response. But with a knowledge of paragraphs and essays, you already have many of the skills needed.

Preparing Answers to Essay Exams 28.1

In this section, you will look at time considerations and ways of interpreting exam questions. You will also practice writing both paragraph-length and essay-length answers to questions on essay exams.

Budgeting Your Time

Spend a few minutes at the beginning of any test previewing the questions and planning how much time to spend on each.

Plan your time before you begin an essay exam and check to make sure you remain on schedule.

If you have an hour to answer two equally difficult questions, spend about two minutes previewing the entire test and about twenty-nine minutes on each question. Use about half your time on each question in planning and about half in writing. But be sure to save a little time for proofreading.

EXERCISE A: Planning Ahead. Explain how you would divide your time in each of the following situations.

EXAMPLE: Forty-five minutes for two essays

three minutes previewing and twenty-one minutes for planning, writing, and proofreading each essay

1. Fifty minutes for three equally difficult essays
2. Forty minutes for ten true/false questions and two essays
3. Twenty minutes for one essay
4. Forty minutes for twenty true/false questions and one essay
5. One hour for twenty multiple-choice questions and two essays
6. Thirty minutes for one essay
7. Forty minutes for ten one-sentence answers and one essay
8. Thirty minutes for one difficult essay and one easier essay
9. Twenty-five minutes for two essays
10. Thirty minutes for ten true/false questions and one essay

Interpreting the Question

There are generally key words in an essay question that tell you what kind of information is expected.

Look for key words and other indications that show what kind of information to supply.

The following chart can help you identify the key words.

KEY WORDS IN ESSAY EXAM QUESTIONS		
Kinds of Questions	**Key Words**	**What You Should Do**
Comparison	*compare, similarities, resemblances, likenesses*	Look for similarities. If the key word is just *compare,* note any major differences as well.
Contrast	*contrast, differ, differences*	Look for and stress differences.

Definition	*define, explain*	Tell what something means or is. Give examples.
Description	*describe*	Give the main features with specific examples.
Diagram	*diagram, draw, chart*	Give a drawing or chart. Label and explain it.
Discussion	*discuss, explain*	Make a general statement and support it.
Explanation	*explain, why, what, how*	Give information that tells why, what, or how.
Illustration	*illustrate, show*	Give concrete examples and explain them.
Interpretation	*interpret, significance*	Explain certain statements or events.
Opinion	*in your opinion, what do you think*	Support your position with facts and reasons.
Prediction	*If . . . then, What . . . if*	Cite facts and give reasons for what you think would happen.

EXERCISE B: Interpreting Essay Exam Questions. Identify the key words and explain what you must do to answer each question.

EXAMPLE: What is a bicameral legislature?

what Give information that fully defines the term.

1. How do archaeologists determine the age of an artifact?
2. What is the historical significance of the Magna Carta?
3. Compare the nesting practices of two different birds.
4. What do you think was the emperor's reason for killing the flier in "The Flying Machine"?
5. Describe the effects of continental drift.
6. In your opinion, was Charlie, in *Flowers for Algernon,* happier with an I.Q. of 60 or with an I.Q. of 160+?
7. What would happen if the amount of carbon dioxide in the earth's atmosphere increased by 1 percent?
8. Define and illustrate the term *constant of variation.*
9. What were three major causes of the French Revolution?
10. Draw and label the major parts of the cell.

Planning and Writing Your Answer

After you have interpreted the question, you must plan your support, arrange it in a logical order, and write your answer.

Organize supporting information in a modified outline and then write your answer.

List as many examples, details, facts, and reasons as you can to answer the question precisely. Write a modified outline. Begin with a sentence that states the main idea, a topic sentence for a paragraph or a thesis statement for an essay. Choose a logical order for your support and add your support to the outline. Consider adding one or more concluding ideas.

The two outlines below could be used to answer a question about the ways in which space travel affects the human body.

Outline for Paragraph-Length Answer

Topic Sentence: The traveler in space will suffer a loss of fluid, periods of "lightheadedness," and occasional blackouts.

—Weightlessness causes kidneys to speed up, producing loss of fluids
—More blood reaches the upper body, causing lightheadedness
—Confinement, lack of exercise, and perhaps stress cause occasional blackouts

Concluding Idea: Happily, scientists find that the effects of space can be combated.

Outline for Essay-Length Answer

Thesis Statement: By studying the effects of space travel on astronauts, scientists have discovered that the traveler in space will suffer a loss of fluid, periods of "lightheadedness," and occasional blackouts.

—Loss of fluids
  —Weightlessness
  —Kidneys work faster
—Lightheadedness
  —Lack of gravity causes more blood to reach upper body
  —Head becomes "flooded"
—Blackouts
  —Pressures of confinement, lack of exercise, stress
  —Equilibrium is affected

Concluding Ideas:
—Scientists find that effects are not serious
—Effects can be combated

The following essay is an answer to the question about space travel. Notice that the main point of the answer is presented in the introductory paragraph. Three body paragraphs then develop the subtopics of the answer. Finally, a brief conclusion ends the essay with a restatement of the main point and related optimistic findings.

Essay-length answer

Before human beings were actually sent into space, scientists feared that weightlessness and other factors in outer space would undermine an astronaut's ability to function. But by studying the effects of space travel on American and Soviet astronauts, scientists have discovered that the human body suffers only minimal discomforts: loss of fluid, periods of "lightheadedness," and occasional blackouts.

Every astronaut loses fluid in outer space. Because weightlessness allows blood to circulate more readily through the upper body, the kidneys work faster. As a result, the kidneys process and eliminate fluids at an increased rate. The astronaut loses fluids, as well as weight, more rapidly than if he or she were on earth.

In addition to more blood circulating in the midbody region, blood will flow more freely to the head during weightlessness. Most astronauts feel lightheaded, as a result, especially during the early stages of a mission in space.

Even worse, some astronauts have experienced blackouts, either during a mission or when returning to earth. Scientists believe that confinement, lack of exercise, and perhaps stress during the mission cause problems with equilibrium and, so, cause blackouts.

Happily, scientists find that effects of outer space on travelers are not serious. These effects can be combated. Exercise routines in particular will help astronauts combat fatigue and lightheadedness. And special fluid diets can keep fluid loss to a minimum.

EXERCISE C: Planning Your Answer. Select one of the questions from Exercise B or another from your class work. Gather and organize support to answer the question. Write a modified outline for a paragraph-length or essay-length answer.

EXERCISE D: Writing Your Answer. Following your outline from Exercise C, write a paragraph- or essay-length answer.

Checking Your Answer

Before turning in your answer, proofread it to be sure it is clear, complete, correct, and free of mechanical errors.

Proofread your answer for clarity and correctness.

The following checklist shows the kinds of questions you should ask yourself.

CHECKING YOUR ANSWER

1. Does at least one sentence present the main answer to the question?
2. Does the answer directly answer the question that was asked?
3. Is the topic sentence or thesis statement clear?
4. Is all of the supporting information clearly related to the main point of the answer?

5. Is there supporting information to fully answer the question?
6. Is the supporting information well organized?
7. Do transitions connect the ideas?
8. Does the answer end persuasively with a concluding idea?
9. Are all the words, including any corrections, readable?
10. Are there any grammatical, mechanical, or spelling errors?

EXERCISE E: Checking Your Answer. Use the checklist on this page to check the answer you wrote in Exercise D. Then make corrections and revisions to improve the answer.

DEVELOPING WRITING SKILLS: Preparing Answers to Essay Exams. Choose three questions that you have recently received on tests or as homework in any of your classes. Each question should be suitable for a paragraph-length or essay-length answer. Then complete the following steps.

1. Choose the question that you prefer to answer.
2. Decide how much time it will take to prepare your answer. If you wrote a paragraph-length answer in Exercise D, now plan to write an essay-length answer and vice versa.
3. Interpret the question. Gain a clear idea of the types of information that you must offer.
4. Write a sentence that presents the main idea needed to answer the question.
5. List supporting information and then outline your answer.
6. From the outline, write your answer.
7. Use the checklist on pages 690 and 691 to check your answer.

Writing Workshop: Essay Exam

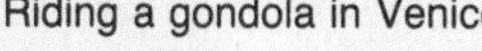
Riding a gondola in Venice

Commuting by bicycle in Saigon

ASSIGNMENT

Topic Contrast One Aspect of Life in Two Different Countries

Form and Purpose Essay-exam answer that compares and contrasts the two subjects

Audience A social studies teacher

Length Three to five paragraphs

Focus Introduce your topic and the two countries and state a main idea that tells how the two countries differ in relation to the topic. Develop your main idea with facts, details, and examples. Conclude with a summary statement.

Sources Books, magazines, encyclopedia articles, films

Prewriting Narrow your topic to one aspect of life in the two countries. If necessary, research and make notes about the differences. Prepare a thesis statement and an outline.

Writing Use your outline to write a first-draft essay answer.

Revising Revise your answer using the checklist on page 690.

UNIT **VI**

Vocabulary and Spelling

Chapter 29

Vocabulary Building

Learning different ways to expand your vocabulary is one of the most useful skills you can acquire. No matter how large your vocabulary is, you can always increase your knowledge of the meanings of words. This chapter will show you how to approach unfamiliar words and make them part of your vocabulary.

29.1 Increasing Your Vocabulary

You encounter new words in many ways. You read new words in your textbooks and your leisure reading. You hear new words in conversations, in class lectures, on the radio, and on television. The best way to build your vocabulary is to work every day on remembering and using new words you have encountered. In this section are a variety of study and review techniques for making new words a part of your own vocabulary.

Making Good Use of Resource Material

A dictionary and a thesaurus are resources that can help you increase your vocabulary. A dictionary is most helpful when you are reading; a thesaurus is most useful when you are writing.

Using a Dictionary. It's a good idea to keep a dictionary in the place where you study and to carry a pocket dictionary with you in school and anyplace else where you might be reading. Whenever you read a word that is unfamiliar to you, look it up in the dictionary. Even if you can guess at the meaning of the word, the dictionary will give you other information that will help you add the word to your working vocabulary.

Use a dictionary to find the meaning, spelling, and proper pronunciation of words.

When you look up a new word in the dictionary, notice the following things about it:

First, the pronunciation is found in parentheses after the word. If you pronounce the word out loud, you are more likely to add it to your vocabulary.

Next, a word's part of speech is usually given as an abbreviation (*n.,v.,adj.*). Many words can be used as different parts of speech. For example, if you look up *meet*, you'll find that it has different meanings as a noun, a verb, and an adjective. Noticing the part of speech of the word you are looking up will help you get just the right meaning for it.

Information about the origin of the word usually appears in brackets. Noticing the origin of a word may help you remember it better.

Sometimes, the dictionary will give a phrase to illustrate a less common use of word. For example, the verb *mark* has several different definitions. One of them is "to show plainly." In one dictionary this definition is followed by brackets containing the phrase "A smile *marking* happiness." The phrase shows how *mark* is used when it means "to show plainly."

An idiom is a phrase that has a meaning different from the literal meanings of the words in the phrase. The dictionary gives meanings for common idioms. Thus, under the word *mark*, you will find the phrase "Make one's mark" with the definition "to achieve success or fame."

Using a Thesaurus. *Thesaurus* comes from a Greek word meaning treasure. A thesaurus gives a list of words similar in meaning to the word you look up.

Use a thesaurus to find a list of words similar in meaning.

The words in the list may have very different shades of meaning. They may also be appropriate for different levels of usage. For example, if you look up *give* in one thesaurus, you will find, among others, the following words: bestow, grant, contribute, tip, fork over, dish out, remit. Notice that some of the words are formal, and some are informal. Some are used in specific situations; others are more general. If your thesaurus does not indicate shades of meaning, use a dictionary to pinpoint the exact meaning of each word.

A thesaurus is most helpful in extending your vocabulary when you are writing. Suppose, for example, that you have written a paragraph and have used the word *exciting* three times. You could look up *exciting* in a thesaurus. There you would find these other words that you could use: stimulating, provocative, stirring, inspiring, impressive, thrilling, breathtaking, and many more.

EXERCISE A: Using the Dictionary to Increase Your Vocabulary. Look up each word in your dictionary and write the definition for the part of speech indicated in parentheses.

EXAMPLE: malcontent (noun)

a discontented, dissatisfied, or rebellious person

1. ruminate (verb)
2. pauperize (verb)
3. hauteur (noun)
4. torpid (adjective)
5. censure (verb)
6. tantamount (adjective)
7. sycophant (noun)
8. wheedle (verb)
9. oration (noun)
10. minatory (adjective)

EXERCISE B: Using the Thesaurus to Increase Your Vocabulary. Find a word similar in meaning to each of the following words. Use each word you find in a sentence.

EXAMPLE: nice

amiable

Because Carla is so amiable, she agreed to do the hardest part of the job.

1. home
2. poor
3. grow
4. interested
5. job
6. false
7. write
8. energetic
9. famous
10. discussion

Recognizing Related Words

Another way of building your vocabulary is to study words that are related to a new word. For example, a new word may have one or more synonyms, antonyms, or homonyms.

Synonyms. Learn a synonym to remember a new word.

Synonyms are words that are similar in meaning.

A thesaurus is made up of lists of synonyms. Often, too, the dictionary gives one or more synonyms for a word. Remembering a one-word synonym may be easier than remembering a long definition. For example, it may be easier to remember the meaning of *attain* if you think of its synonym, *achieve*.

Antonyms. Antonyms help in remembering meanings.

Antonyms are words that are opposite in meaning.

If, for example, you want to remember that the word *inconstant* means "not remaining firm in mind or purpose," you might note that its antonym is *reliable*.

Homonyms. Recognizing that some words are homonyms will help insure that your expanding vocabulary is accurate.

Homonyms are words that sound alike but have different meanings and spellings.

It is important, for example, to know the difference between *stationary* (meaning "not moving") and *stationery* (meaning "writing materials"). Although the two words are pronounced the same, they have different meanings and spellings.

EXERCISE C: Recognizing Synonyms, Antonyms, and Homonyms. Identify each pair of words as *synonyms, antonyms,* or *homonyms*.

EXAMPLE: dulcet/harsh
antonyms

1. lead/led
2. raze/raise
3. irk/annoy
4. defer/delay
5. ample/plentiful
6. rustic/refined
7. whether/weather
8. insurrection/revolt
9. random/deliberate
10. vertical/horizontal

Remembering Vocabulary Words

To make a word part of your vocabulary, you should study its definition, use it in your writing and speaking, and review it from time to time until you are completely sure of it.

Use one or more review techniques to remember the meanings of new words.

Using a Vocabulary Notebook. For each subject you are studying, keep a vocabulary section in your notebook. Here is an example of a vocabulary section from a science notebook.

Vocabulary	Notebook	Science
Words	Bridge Words	Definitions
ornithology	oriole	the study of birds
carnivorous	cannibal	flesh eating
oscillate	pendulum	swing back and forth
effervescent	champagne	bubbling
forceps	the dentist	small tongs for grasping

To make a vocabulary section, follow these steps:

1. Divide each page into three columns.
2. Label the first column "Words," and use this column to write new words. Include pronunciations when necessary.
3. Label the second column "Bridge Words," and use this column to write words that will help you remember the meaning of each new word. For *oscillate,* for example, you might write the word *pendulum* as a reminder that *oscillate* means "to swing back and forth."
4. Label the third column "Definitions," and use this column to write one or more definitions for each new word.

When you have free time at school or at home or when you are preparing for a test, use the vocabulary section of your notebook to help you study. The following chart describes a method of studying with your vocabulary notebook.

USING THE VOCABULARY SECTION OF YOUR NOTEBOOK
Step 1: Study the words by looking at the three columns that give you the word, a bridge word, and the definition.
Step 2: Take a piece of paper and cover the definition column. Using the bridge words, say or write each definition.
Step 3: Then cover both the bridge-word and the definition columns and define each word orally or in writing.
Step 4: Put a check by each word that you miss and study the three columns again.
Step 5: Finally, cover the word and the bridge-word columns and try to say or write the word to match each definition.

Using Flashcards or a Tape Recorder. On one- by three-inch (2.5 by 7.5 cm) cards, list vocabulary words on one side and the definitions on the other. Carry them with you, and when you have spare time—waiting for a bus or in a study hall—flip through the cards to see how many words you can define. As you begin to remember certain definitions, remove these cards and add cards for new words from your classes and your reading.

If hearing something helps you learn and remember it, you might try using a tape recorder to study vocabulary words. Speaking, repeating, and hearing new words and their definitions will reinforce your learning. The following chart explains how to use a tape recorder to study new words.

USING A TAPE RECORDER
Step 1: Read the vocabulary word into the tape recorder.
Step 2: Leave a ten-second blank space on the tape. Then state the definition and give a short sentence using the word in context.
Step 3: Continue with the remainder of the vocabulary words.
Step 4: Replay the tape, and try to give a definition and a sentence during each ten-second pause. As the tape continues, you will see if you are correct. When you have gone through your list once, start over, giving definitions and sentences for only those words you missed. Continue until you have learned all the words.

Listening to your tape several times a week will help you make new words a permanent part of your vocabulary.

Working with a Partner. Working on vocabulary drill with another person gives you an opportunity to practice the pronunciations of new words as well as learn their meanings.

When working with a partner, use flashcards, pages from the vocabulary sections of your notebook, or any other list of new words you have developed for yourself.

One person will read the words and one will define the words in the first round. If the definer does not give a definition quickly, the reader should supply the bridge word. When the definer has given all the definitions correctly, the reader should give each definition while the definer supplies the word that matches it. Another way of doing this is to have the definer give the word and then use it in a sentence.

When one partner has defined all words and then supplied the words for all the definitions, the partners switch roles.

EXERCISE D: Deciding on a Study Method. Decide which of the study methods will work best for you. Then choose a second method you can use occasionally to add variety to your study. Explain your reasons for both choices.

DEVELOPING WRITING SKILLS: Choose the ten most difficult words you currently need to learn at school. Make each of these part of your working vocabulary by using each word in a sentence that clearly shows the meaning of the word.

29.2 Using Context

A word's *context* is made up of the other words in the sentence or passage in which the word is found. You can use these surrounding words, or context clues, to make an educated guess about a word's meaning.

Recognizing Context Clues

By learning to recognize context clues, you often can figure out the meaning of an unfamiliar word as you read.

Use context clues to determine the meanings of unfamiliar words.

There are several types of context clues. A knowledge of the different types of clues can help you use context clues more effectively. The following chart shows three common types. Notice how the italicized clues help you figure out the meanings of the underlined words.

TYPES OF CONTEXT CLUES	
Clue	**Example**
Key words in the sentence that point to the word's meaning.	Climbing *mountains*, being in *tall* buildings, and crossing *high* bridges *frighten* me because I have acrophobia. (Italicized words suggest height and fear. Acrophobia means fear of high places.)
Sentences that set up comparisons or contrasts between several words and suggest that a word means the same as or the opposite of another word.	One of our cats is very *courageous* and *loves adventure*: the other is very timorous. (The sentence leads you to think that timorous is the opposite of courageous. Timorous means fearful.)
Words or phrases that follow another word closely and seem to rename or define it.	Bonsai, *the art of growing trees in small pots*, is well-known in Japan. (The phrase after bonsai renames and defines it. Bonsai means the art of growing trees in small pots.)

To use these types of context clues, follow a few simple steps. You can quickly perform all of the steps mentally, except for the last one.

USING CONTEXT CLUES

Step 1: Read the sentence through carefully, first with, then without, the unfamiliar word.

Step 2: Identify surrounding words that give clues and note which type of clue the sentence provides.

Step 3: Try to guess the meaning of the unfamiliar word, using the context clues.

Step 4: Read the sentence substituting your guess for the unfamiliar word.

Step 5: Check your guess in the dictionary and record the word and its definition in your vocabulary notebook.

The following example shows how these five steps can be used to determine the meaning of the word *ameliorate*.

EXAMPLE: Step 1: In spite of attempts to *ameliorate* the situation, it got worse and worse.

In spite of attempts to ______ the situation, it got worse and worse.

Step 2: *Clues:* "In spite of attempts" "worse and worse"

Type of clue: contrast

Step 3: Guess: *ameliorate* means "improve"

Step 4: In spite of attempts to improve the situation, it got worse and worse.

Step 5: According to the dictionary, *ameliorate* means "to make or become better; improve."

EXERCISE A: Recognizing Context Clues. Using the example above, guess the meaning of the underlined word in each sentence. Then check your guess in the dictionary.

1. Gloria's <u>animosity</u> could be seen in her unfriendly expression and hostile tone of voice.
2. After an eight-mile run, Mel's appetite was <u>voracious</u>, and he consumed everything in the refrigerator.
3. The newcomer appeared <u>morose</u>, but it soon became apparent that, to the contrary, she was in high spirits.

4. Lethargy, extreme sluggishness, overtook him whenever he had nothing pressing to do.
5. The actor remained completely inert for several minutes; he did not so much as blink an eye.
6. We watched the sunset from the hummock, that small hill directly behind the house.
7. The cessation of the loud noise was a welcome relief.
8. Although the message was cryptic, Darcy was clever enough to figure it out.
9. Bad weather did not deter her, and she went ahead with her original plans for the car trip.
10. Louisa had a premonition that it would rain, and it did.

Using Context Clues in Daily Reading

Many people read newspapers and magazines daily. These periodicals are sources of current information and interesting ideas on a variety of topics. Build your vocabulary by adding new words that you come across in your daily reading.

Use context clues to determine the meanings of unfamiliar words in your daily reading.

The paragraph below is similar to the kind of humorous article you might find in a newspaper or magazine. Try to determine the meaning of each underlined word by its context. On a piece of paper, jot down what you think each word means.

EXAMPLE: If a want ad for a rock star existed, it might look like this. Wanted: Young man or woman willing to forgo a serene life for the prospect of incessant rehearsals, months of grueling one-night concerts, and the probability that this life-style is temporary. Applicants for the position must bedeck themselves in flamboyant outfits guaranteed to bedazzle fans. A repertoire of songs that will totally wreck the composure of an audience is also a requirement. A group of staunch followers who will support the singer at all times is the final prerequisite. Anyone who aspires to such a position must possess all these qualifications.

EXERCISE B: Using Context Clues in Daily Reading. For each word choose the definition that most closely matches the meaning of the word as it was used in the paragraph that you have just read.

1. forgo — (a)do without; (b)precede; (c)agree; (d)assert
2. serene — (a)dead; (b)peaceful (c)excited; (d)bored
3. incessant — (a)tiresome; (b)uncomfortable; (c)constant; (d)secretive
4. grueling — (a)exhausting; (b)soupy; (c)fighting; (d)racing
5. bedeck — (a)bend; (b)lure; (c)wear; (d)adorn
6. flamboyant — (a)trivial; (b)overly showy; (c)informal; (d)rare
7. bedazzle — (a)blind, figuratively; (b)adapt; (c)change for the worse; (d)affect
8. staunch — (a)tired; (b)young; (c)strange; (d)loyal
9. prerequisite — (a)list; (b)trifle; (c)basis; (d)precondition
10. aspire — (a)breathe; (b)earnestly desire; (c)influence; (d)die

Using Context Clues in Textbook Reading

A good general vocabulary can improve your reading comprehension of textbook material. In your textbooks you will also find technical words from specific subject areas to add to your vocabulary.

Use context clues to determine the meaning of unfamiliar words in your textbook reading.

The following passage is similar to material you might find in a health or science textbook. As you read the passage, try to determine the meaning of each underlined word by its context. Write down what you think each word means.

EXAMPLE: The field of medicine has greatly advanced from primitive attempts to help the injured and sick. The lifesaving techniques that were used then were based on <u>rudimentary</u> knowledge of the body. Much of this basic knowledge was derived from observation of animals. From various herbs and plants came salves to soothe and <u>anodynes</u> to relieve pain. Interestingly enough, the popularity of many folk remedies is enjoying a <u>resurgence</u> today.

As knowledge about cures of diseases has increased, so too has the <u>range</u> of knowledge about the diseases themselves. Sophisticated procedures and equipment have enabled scientists to determine that there are many different viruses as well as many kinds of <u>virulent</u> bacteria. Success with curing bodily illnesses has made the search for more <u>efficacious</u> methods of treating mental illnesses even more <u>intensive</u>. <u>Prodigious</u> amounts, however, remain to be learned about the human body and brain. No one would make the <u>assertion</u> that <u>pathologists</u> have all the answers.

EXERCISE C: Using Context Clues in Textbook Reading. For each of the following words, choose the definition that most closely matches the meaning of the word as it was used in the passage about the field of medicine that you have just read.

1. rudimentary — (a) elementary; (b) unpolished; (c) incurable; (d) bright
2. anodyne — (a) energetic; (b) stimulant; (c) alcohol; (d) pain reliever
3. resurgence — (a) development; (b) birth; (c) rising again; (d) surgery
4. range — (a) scope; (b) stove; (c) wander about; (d) open land
5. virulent — (a) masculine; (b) cruel; (c) stingy; (d) extremely harmful
6. efficacious — (a) educated; (b) friendly; (c) effective; (d) effortless
7. intensive — (a) very hot; (b) meant; (c) thorough; (d) well-planned
8. prodigious — (a) strong; (b) very smart; (c) very proud; (d) huge

9. assertion (a) desertion; (b) declaration; (c) rejection; (d) aggression
10. pathologist (a) trailblazer; (b) disease; (c) linguist; (d) scientist

Using Context Clues in Other Kinds of Reading

In addition to leisure reading and textbook reading, you are sometimes called upon to read informative or analytical material for research papers. In this kind of reading, you may often come across unfamiliar words.

Use context clues to determine the meanings of unfamiliar words in your reading for research.

The following passage contains the kind of material you might find in a book or in a magazine article about popular culture. If you were doing research for a social studies paper, you might include such an article in your bibliography. Read the passage and try to determine the meaning of each underlined word by its context in the passage. Then jot down what you think each word means.

EXAMPLE: The durability of Superman as a symbol of American popular culture is incontestable. There is no questioning that his popularity has lasted since the 1930's when he was first created. A native of Krypton, Superman comes to earth and makes his home in Metropolis. Always on the side of justice, he battles the perversity of countless villains. Although he has superhuman strength, Superman disguises himself as the meek and impassive Clark Kent, a newspaper reporter. No one would suspect that Kent, whose cowardice is equaled by his extreme torpor, can also operate as the dynamic Superman. Lois Lane, another reporter on the *Daily Planet*, openly admits her preference for Superman with his insatiable appetite for taking on any adversary.

With the advent of television, it seemed that comic-book heroes would cease to enthrall adventure-loving fans. Many heroes did sink into the abyss of neglect and oblivion. Superman, however, has fought his way to stardom, not only in television but in the movies. American culture is ever-changing, but the indomitable Superman lives on.

EXERCISE D: Using Context Clues in Research Reading. For each word choose the definition that most closely matches the meaning of the word as it was used in the passage.

1. durability — (a) capability; (b) hard; (c) doubtfulness; (d) lastingness
2. incontestable — (a) answerable; (b) unquestionable; (c) competitive; (d) arguable
3. perversity — (a) strangeness; (b) wickedness; (c) violence; (d) overwhelming odds
4. impassive — (a) calm; (b) difficult; (c) impressive (d) imposing
5. torpor — (a) antipathy; (b) vibration; (c) sluggishness; (d) stupidity
6. dynamic — (a) engine; (b) forceful; (c) dangerous; (d) dignified
7. insatiable — (a) greedy; (b) unsatisfactory; (c) encouraging; (d) hopeless
8. adversary — (a) celebration; (b) opponent; (c) acquaintance; (d) finance
9. oblivion — (a) a kind of angle; (b) promise; (c) state of being forgotten; (d) geometric shape
10. indomitable — (a) unconquerable; (b) domineering; (c) impossible; (d) unquestionable

DEVELOPING WRITING SKILLS: Using Context Clues to Complete Sentences. Write the word from the following list that best completes each of the following sentences.

anodyne	efficacious	staunch
oblivion	torpor	indomitable
aspires	incessant	virulent
rudimentary		

1. She is a ______ supporter of her favorite basketball team, the New York Knicks.

2. In any field, hard work is necessary if one ______ to greatness.
3. The ______ questioning finally caused the prisoner to break down.
4. Since the ______ was not long-lasting, the pain returned in an hour.
5. Plant cuttings will quickly develop a ______ root system in water.
6. The most ______ way to diet is to forgo desserts.
7. The spider's bite was so ______ they feared for the victim's life.
8. Because of his ______ will to live, he regained his health.
9. Her ______ was a result of illness, not of boredom.
10. The sensational book sold well at first but soon fell into ______.

29.3 Using Structure

A word's structure, or parts, can often give clues to its meaning. There are three kinds of word parts: prefixes, roots, and suffixes.

A prefix is one or more syllables that can be added at the beginning of a word or part of a word to form a new word. In the word *unhappy*, for example, the prefix *un-* has been added to the word *happy* to form a new word.

A root is a word or the base of a word to which prefixes and suffixes may be added. The root *-ject-* may have the prefix *pro-* added to it to form the word *project*. The root *joy* may have the suffix *-ful* added to it to form the new word *joyful*. While many roots can stand alone, some roots, such as *-ject-*, act only as a base to which prefixes or suffixes are added.

A suffix is one or more syllables that can be added at the end of a root to form a new word. In the word *childlike*, the suffix *-like* has been added to the root *child*.

Some words, such as *prove, tense,* and *think*, consist of roots only. Some words, such as *improve,* and *intense*, are made up of a prefix and a root. Other words consist of roots and suffixes: *tensely,* and *thinkable*, for example. Still other words have all three parts: *improvement, intensity,* and *unthinkable*.

Many prefixes, roots, and suffixes come from Greek, Latin, and Old English. Knowing the meanings of certain prefixes, roots, and suffixes should enable you to make reasonable guesses about the meanings of words that contain these parts.

Using Prefixes

Learning the meanings of some common prefixes is one way to work on building your vocabulary. If, for example, you know that the prefix *-af* means "to" or "toward," you can probably guess that the word *affix* means to "fasten" or "attach."

Use the meanings of prefixes to determine the meanings of unfamiliar words.

The following chart contains only twenty of the many prefixes that occur in English words. Learn the meaning of each prefix and the alternate spellings given in parentheses. Then try adding them to different roots or words to see how many new words you can form. (The abbreviations *L.* and *O.E.* stand for Latin and Old English, the origins of the prefixes.)

TWENTY COMMON PREFIXES

Prefix	Meaning	Examples
ab- (a-, abs-) [L.]	away, from	abolish, avert, abstract
ad- (ac-, af-, al-, ap-, as-, at-) [L.]	to, toward	adjoin, acknowledge, affix, allure, appoint, assure, attribute
circum- [L.]	around, about, surrounding, on all sides	circumstance
com- (co-, col- con-, cor-) [L.]	with, together	compress, cooperate, collaborate, contribute, correspond
de- [L.]	away from, off, down	decontrol, debase

dis- (di-, dif-) [L.]	away, apart, cause to be opposite of	disbelief, disconnect divert, diffuse
ex- (e-, ec-, ef-) [L.]	forth, from, out	express, emigrate, eccentric, effluent
in- (il-, im-, ir-) [L.]	not, "un"	inhuman, illegal, impossible, irregular
in- (il-, im-, ir-) [L.]	in, into, within, on, toward	indent, illuminate, immigrate, irrigate
inter- [L.]	between	international
mis- [O.E.]	wrong	misplace
non- [L.]	not	nonsense
post- [L.]	after	postgraduate
pre- [L.]	before	prefix
pro- [L.]	forward, forth, favoring, in place of	produce, protract
re- [L.]	back, again	renew
semi- [L.]	half, partly	semicircle
sub- (suc-, suf-, sup-) [L.]	beneath, under, below	submarine, succumb, sufficient, suppress
trans- [L.]	across	transport
un- [O.E.]	not	unknown

The more prefixes you become familiar with, the more rapidly your vocabulary and your comprehension of new words will grow.

EXERCISE A: Using Prefixes to Build New Words. Add one of the prefixes from the chart beginning on page 709 to each of the words in the first column to form a word that matches the definition in the second column. Write each new word on your paper. Notice that you may have to use one of the prefixes in the parentheses for some of the words. Use a dictionary, if necessary.

EXAMPLE: ______ + join   to join together
conjoin

1. ______ + navigate   to sail around
2. ______ + compress   to free from pressure
3. ______ + standard   not up to standard
4. ______ + mature   happening before the usual time
5. ______ + submit   to submit again
6. ______ + appear   to go away
7. ______ + formal   not very formal
8. ______ + change   to hand over or transfer
9. ______ + moral   not moral
10. ______ + quit   to clear a person of a charge

Using Roots

Of all three word parts, the root is the most important in determining the meaning of a word. For example, any time that you see the root *-scrib-* (or *-script-*), you can guess that the word has something to do with writing.

Use roots to determine the meanings of unfamiliar words.

Roots have come into the English language from many sources. The following chart lists twenty common roots that come from Latin and Greek. Like many roots borrowed from other languages, none of the roots in this chart can stand alone. The chart gives the alternate spellings and the meanings of each root as well as examples of words containing the roots.

TWENTY COMMON ROOTS

Root	Meaning	Examples
-cap- (-capt-, -cept-) [L.]	to take, seize	capable, captivate, accept
-ced- (-ceed-, -cess-) [L.]	to go, yield	procedure, proceed, success
-dic- (-dict-) [L.]	to say, point out in words	indicate, edict
-duc- (-duct-) [L.]	to lead	produce, conduct

-fac-)-fact-, -fec-, -fect-, -fic-) [L.]	to do, make	facsimile, manufacture, infection, defect, fiction
-graph- [Gr.]	to write	autograph
-ject- [L.]	to throw	reject
-mit- (-mis-) [L.]	to send	admit, transmission
-mov- (-mot-) [L.]	to move	movement, motion
-plic- [L.]	to fold	duplicate
-pon- (-pos-) [L.]	to put, place	postpone, depose
-puls- (-pel-) [L.]	to drive	pulsate, propel
-quir- (ques-, -quis-) [L.]	to ask, say	inquire, question, inquisitive
-scrib- (-script-)[L.]	to write	describe, prescription
-spec- (-spect-) [L.]	to see	specimen, inspect
-ten- (-tain-, -tin-) [L.]	to hold, contain	tenure, detain, continent
-tend- (-tens-, -tent-) [L.]	to stretch	distend, extension, extent
-ven- (-vent-) [L.]	to come	convene, inventor
-vert- (-vers-) [L.]	to turn	divert, subversive
-vid- (-vis-) [L.]	to see	evident, vision

EXERCISE B: Using Roots to Define Words. For each word in the first column, write the letter of the meaning in the second column. Refer to a dictionary if necessary.

1. predict	a. to send across
2. transcribe	b. a proclamation
3. recede	c. a legal questioning of a matter
4. exceed	d. to write down in a different form
5. inquest	e. to stretch beyond
6. transmit	f. to hold back
7. intervene	g. to foretell
8. edict	h. to go beyond
9. detain	i. to come between
10. extend	j. to go back

Using Suffixes

Some word endings are used to indicate the plural of a noun or the tense of a verb. For example, to form the plural of *book*, you add the ending *-s*. To form the past tense of *laugh*, you add the ending *-ed*. Other suffixes, however, when added to a base word, form totally new words. In forming new words, suffixes also change the part of speech of the words. The suffix *-ment*, for example, changes the verb *improve* to the noun *improvement*.

Use suffixes to determine the meanings and parts of speech of unfamiliar words.

The following chart shows fifteen suffixes, along with their meanings and parts of speech. Even this short list of suffixes, combined with words you already know, will give you the ability to build a large number of words.

FIFTEEN COMMON SUFFIXES

Suffix	Meaning	Examples	Part of Speech
-able (-ible) [L.]	capable of being; tending to	reliable, edible	adjective
-ance (-ence) [L.]	the act of; the quality or state of being	clearance, confidence	noun
-ate [L.]	make, apply, operate on	decorate, activate	verb
-ful [O.E.]	full of; characterized by; having the ability or tendency to	scornful	noun or adjective
-fy [L.]	to make; to cause to become; to cause to have	clarify	verb
-ist [Gr.]	a person who does or makes; a person skilled in; a believer in	violinist	noun

-ity [L.]	state of being; character; condition of	intensity	noun
-ize (-ise) [Gr.]	to make	idolize, improvise	verb
-less [O.E.]	without; lacking	careless, ageless	adjective
-ly [O.E.]	in a certain way; at a certain time or place	harshly, hourly	adverb or adjective
-ment [L.]	result or product of	improvement, amazement	noun
-ness [O.E.]	state of being; quality	laziness	noun
-or [L.]	a person or thing that; a quality or condition that	spectator error	noun
-ous (-ious) [L.]	marked by; given to	pompous, mysterious	adjective
-tion (-ion, -sion, -ation, -ition) [L.]	the action of; the state of being	action, mission, aviation, position	noun

EXERCISE C: Using Suffixes to Form Words. Use the underlined word in each of the following sentences plus an appropriate suffix to form a word to fill each blank correctly. Write each new word and its part of speech.

EXAMPLE: The state of being <u>industrious</u> is called ______.
industriousness noun

1. A person who <u>conforms</u> to what is expected is a ______.
2. To be unable to <u>help</u> oneself is to be ______.
3. To cause something to become <u>active</u> is to ______ it.
4. When something is marked by <u>dangers</u> it is ______.
5. The quality of being <u>generous</u> is called ______.
6. To cause to become <u>legal</u> is to ______.
7. The act of <u>assisting</u> another is called ______.

8. A person who is characterized by hope is ______.
9. To give glory to is to ______.
10. One who mediates an argument between persons or groups is a ______.

DEVELOPING WRITING SKILLS: Using Word Parts to Form New Words. Choose three prefixes, four roots, and three suffixes from the charts in this section. Add other word parts to make ten complete words. Then use each new word in a sentence.

EXAMPLE: -ize

rationalize

The villain tried to rationalize his inexcusable behavior.

Exploring Etymologies 29.4

Etymology is the study of a word's history from its earliest recorded use to its current use. Knowing the origin and development of a word's meaning can often help you remember its present meaning. For example, knowing that *ambulatory* comes from the Latin word *ambulare*, meaning "to walk," may help you to remember that *ambulatory* means "able to walk."

You can often find a word's etymology in a dictionary. Look for the information in brackets after the word's pronunciation and part of speech. If you are not sure of the meaning of a symbol or abbreviation, check the key at the front of the dictionary. Section 34.3 of this book will give you more information about using the dictionary to find etymologies.

In this section you will learn about words that have been borrowed from other languages, words that have changed their meanings over the years, and words that have been created to meet specific needs.

Borrowed Words

About a thousand years ago, the language that was the forerunner of modern English contained between fifty and one hundred thousand words. Today modern English contains over one million words. Of course, many of these words are technical and scientific terms used by only small groups of people. Nonetheless, in less than a thousand years, the English language has increased by a thousand percent. Many of the new words have been borrowed from other languages.

Loanwords are words in the English language that have been borrowed from other languages.

Most of the loanwords in English come from Greek, Latin, and French. This is because in 1066 A.D. the Normans of France invaded England and conquered the Anglo-Saxons. To England, the Normans brought their own language, which was strongly influenced by classical Greek and Latin. For a long time after the invasion, French was the language of the rulers and the upper classes. Thus, many of the English words borrowed from French are government words (*state, court, parliament, mayor*); legal words (*prison, arrest, pardon, fraud, justice*); military words (*army, navy, peace, enemy*); words for leisure and the arts (*amusement, leisure, sculpture, poetry*); and words for food (*venison, beef, biscuit, fruit*).

Besides the Latin and Greek words that came into English through French, in more recent times scientists have gone to Latin and Greek to name new discoveries, like *protein, allergy, nova,* and *nebula*. In addition, as you may recall from your study of word structure, Greek and Latin have provided many prefixes, suffixes, and roots from which speakers of English have constructed new words.

To a lesser extent, English has borrowed words from other languages of the world. Thus, from Italian we have *tempo, cello, vista, studio*, and many others. Many Spanish words came into English through Spanish settlements in the Americas. For example, we have *canyon, adobe, patio*.

Native American languages have added to English words for things that did not exist in England, like *moccasin, opossum,* and *skunk*, as well as place names like *Mississippi, Oklahoma,* and *Mackinac*.

When we say that a word comes to English from another language, it's important to remember that the word's history may be somewhat more complicated than that. For example, many words that come to English from French came into French from Latin and Greek and may go back even further to a very old and now extinct language called Indo-European. When you check the dictionary for a word's history, you will probably want to remember the source that is closest in meaning to the modern definition. That will be the first language given in the dictionary entry.

EXERCISE A: Discovering the Sources of Loanwords. In a dictionary that provides etymologies, look up each of the following words and write the language of origin. When more than one origin is given, use the first.

EXAMPLE: militia

Latin

1. thug
2. calorie
3. potato
4. kangaroo
5. bonus
6. rhythm
7. toboggan
8. deck
9. egg
10. tong
11. dentist
12. robot
13. dessert
14. prairie
15. delta
16. broccoli
17. kindergarten
18. algebra
19. creature
20. tulip

EXERCISE B: Using Etymology to Improve Vocabulary. In a dictionary that gives etymologies, look up the following words. Write the definition of each word. Then trace the history of each word and write the complete etymology of each of the words.

EXAMPLE: tycoon

a wealthy and powerful industrialist or financier

Japanese *taikun* from Chinese *ta* (great) + *kium* (prince)

1. potpourri
2. leviathan
3. unctuous
4. Mayday
5. tundra
6. crimson
7. pundit
8. ersatz
9. potlatch
10. bonanza

Words with New Meanings

The English language is constantly growing, not only by borrowing words from other languages but also by giving new meanings to words already in the language.

The English language grows by giving new meanings to old words.

To have a good reading vocabulary, it is important to know both the old and new meanings of words. For example, years ago, a common meaning of the word *dear* was "costly" or "expensive." That meaning is rarely used now, but if you found the word in a story written long ago, you would want to know the old meaning.

Some English words changed by becoming more specific in meaning. In Shakespeare's day, for example, the adjective *admirable* was used to describe anything that caused astonishment, whether positive or negative. Now the word has only the positive meaning.

Some words change by retaining their original meaning and also taking on new meanings. For example, *run* still means to "move fast" but has also taken on other meanings. To "run a red light," means to "go through without stopping."

When two words are joined together to form a compound, they often take on new meaning. *Count* and *down*, for example, have a different meaning when joined in the compound word *countdown*.

One common way for a word to change its meaning is for a word used as one part of speech to be used as a different part of speech. For example, the word *eye* as a noun refers to the part of the body used for seeing. Eventually, *eye* came to be used as a verb meaning to "look at," as in "He *eyed* the pie."

In your reading watch for new meanings of familiar words.

EXERCISE C: Discovering New Meanings of Words. Write a definition for each word used as the part of speech indicated in parentheses. Then write a sentence using the word.

EXAMPLE: idle (verb)

to operate without transmitting power

Let the motor idle a while before shifting into gear.

1. elbow (verb)
2. betters (noun)
3. stomach (verb)
4. find (noun)
5. cavalier (adjective)
6. contact (verb)
7. hit (noun)
8. police (verb)
9. pink (noun)
10. mystery (adjective)

Coined Words

The creation of new words is another way in which the English language grows.

The English language grows through the addition of newly coined words.

People invent new words to name new things or activities, like *paperback books* and *skydiving*. People also invent words simply for the pleasure of being creative with language. Invented words are known as *coinages*.

Words from Proper Nouns. The names of people and places are the basis of many new words. Some mythological creatures and characters from literature have given their names to the language. For example, the word *herculean*, meaning "having great size, strength, or courage," comes from the classical hero Hercules. The names of certain historical figures have also become part of the language. The cardigan sweater is named for the seventh Earl of Cardigan, who led the famous Charge of the Light Brigade during the Crimean War. Scientific discoveries have often taken the name of their inventors or discoverers. Thus, the *ohm*, a measurement of electrical resistance, was named for the physicist Georg Simon Ohm.

Portmanteau Words. A portmanteau is a kind of suitcase. A portmanteau word is one that carries the meanings of two other words within it. *Smog*, a combination of *smoke* and *fog*, is a portmanteau word, as is *twirl* (*twist* and *whirl*).

Clipped Words. Some words are shortened versions of longer, older words. Today we say *flu* rather than *influenza* and *cab* instead of *cabriolet*. Other clipped words are informal while the longer version is still used in formal situations. Thus, *condo* has become the informal variation of *condominium*.

Coined Expressions. People often create two-word and three-word expressions whose meanings differ from the meanings of the individual components. For example, the term *white elephant* does not refer to an animal but to a useless object.

EXERCISE D: Finding the Origins of Words from Proper Nouns and Portmanteau Words. In a dictionary that provides etymologies, look up each of the following words and write a definition that includes the origin of the word.

EXAMPLE: martial

of or suitable for war, from the Roman god of war, Mars

1. silhouette
2. mesmerize
3. modem
4. sideburns
5. splurge
6. Lilliputian
7. mausoleum
8. diesel
9. psyche
10. brunch

EXERCISE E: Finding the Origins of Clipped Words and Coined Expressions. In a dictionary that provides etymologies, look up each of the following words and write a definition that includes the origin of the word or expression.

EXAMPLE: pin money

a small sum of money as for incidental expenses, from the time when English husbands gave their wives money on New Year's Day for buying a yearly supply of pins

1. free lance
2. pup
3. space shuttle
4. joy stick
5. ammo
6. job action
7. paper tiger
8. props
9. state of the art
10. flying colors

DEVELOPING WRITING SKILLS: Determining Origins of Words. In a dictionary that provides etymologies, look up each of the following words or expressions and write a sentence explaining the meaning and etymology of the word.

EXAMPLE: niche

Niche, which means a place or position particularly suitable to the person or thing in it, comes from a French word meaning "nest."

1. atlas
2. lunatic
3. buccaneers
4. anchorman
5. derrick
6. shuttle diplomacy
7. confetti
8. eureka
9. muslin
10. calliope

Skills Review and Writing Workshop

Vocabulary Building

CHECKING YOUR SKILLS

In the following paragraph, write a definition for each underlined word by using the context clues.

(1) What impels people to write? (2) Surely it cannot be the desire for affluence, since most writers are poorly paid. (3) Writing is also a solitary profession, so people who need the company of others should not consider it. (4) A writer possesses the desire—some would call it a compulsion—to communicate. (5) Sometimes the message is commonplace; sometimes it is profound. (6) To communicate a message, a writer can choose from a myriad of styles and approaches. (7) These can range from rhythmic poetry to serious prose. (8) How do writers hone their talents to master their craft with precision? (9) First, writers should be readers, immersing themselves in the great literature of the past. (10) They should also garner as much life experience as possible, to be stored away and drawn upon when creating their own work.

USING VOCABULARY SKILLS IN WRITING

Writing a Music Review

A rich vocabulary can make your writing much more effective. Write a review of an album by your favorite recording artist. Follow these steps.

Prewriting: Select an album that has been recently released. Do the songs have a common theme? Are they original? Note how well the music is played and how well the artist interprets the songs.

Writing: Begin with your overall rating of the album. Support your rating by describing various elements of the music and the artist's rendition.

Revising: Look over your words and replace those that could be clearer or more descriptive. After you have revised, proofread carefully.

Chapter 30

Spelling Improvement

Many years ago, few people learned how to read and write at all. Those people who could write in the English language were not overly concerned with spelling words uniformly. William Shakespeare, for example, was very casual about spelling. However, as time passed, the spelling of individual words became more consistent. When Thomas Jefferson wrote to his daughter about her education, he included the following advice: "Take care that you never spell a word wrong. Always, before you write a word, consider how it is spelled, and if you do not remember, turn to a dictionary."

Thomas Jefferson's advice is still valuable, for correct spelling is just as important today as it was 200 years ago. Careless spelling indicates either that you do not know how to spell or that you are a careless writer. In either case, someone reading your work may be unfavorably impressed, and the value of whatever you were trying to communicate may thus be diminished.

Your major goal in studying this chapter should be to learn to spell words that you will use again and again in your daily writing, both in and out of school. In order to spell correctly and easily, you should have an overall strategy for spelling improvement. The first section of this chapter will help you plan your strategy. The second section will present specific spelling rules that will make it easier for you to spell many words accurately.

Improving Your Spelling 30.1

There are a number of ways you can work systematically on improving your spelling skills. First, you must identify words that give you trouble. Then you can use a notebook to list your own problem words, to record memory aids for those words, and to keep track of your personal spelling study schedule.

Proofreading Carefully

Often spelling errors are merely the result of writing quickly to get your thoughts down on paper. Get into the habit of proofreading everything you write. This will eliminate the errors that come from hasty writing and will also help you identify words that repeatedly give you trouble.

Proofread everything you write for spelling errors.

Rereading what you have written for the sake of proofreading is a specialized skill. It is different from rereading for the sake of revising your thoughts. When you proofread for spelling, pay attention only to the spelling of the words, not to the content of what you have written. It is easy to get caught up in your ideas and pay less attention to each word, so it is important to focus on the spelling of each word.

When you proofread for spelling errors, pay special attention to double letters, to common endings like *-ance* and *-ence*, to vowels that frequently appear together like *ea* and *ie*, to letters that can sound alike like *c* and *k* and *z* and *s*, and to homonyms like *to, too, two*.

Whenever you proofread, keep a dictionary close by. If you think a word might be misspelled, check it in the dictionary. Also, check carefully any proper names in your writing. Such words are used less frequently and thus may be less familiar to you. Also many proper names have different spellings. For example, the last name *Johnson* might also be spelled *Jonson*.

EXERCISE A: Proofreading Carefully. Each sentence in this exercise contains one incorrectly spelled word. Write the correct spelling of each misspelled word, using a dictionary when necessary.

EXAMPLE: They announced the new law to the general publick.
public

1. He is quite cheerfull about that unpleasant task.
2. We need your assistence for several moments.
3. The contestants were farely certain of the outcome.
4. She has the abilety to do many things equally well.
5. A peice of pie would taste delicious right now.
6. The exhausted speaker aksed for a glass of water.
7. The monkys ran around the cage and begged for bananas.
8. Our friends incisted that we stay for dinner.
9. The unusual package arrived on Wensday.
10. Penguins exhist only in Antarctica.

EXERCISE B: More Work with Proofreading. Each sentence in the paragraph contains one or more misspelled words. Write the correct spelling for each misspelled word.

(1) Skiing, a populer winter sport, began thousands of years ago in Northern Europe and Asia. (2) The first skis were probaly made from the bones of large animels. (3) No one knows exsactly when wooden skis were first used. (4) However, a musium in Sweeden has some wooden skis that are thought to be around five thousand years old. (5) Early skis could be used onley on flat ground. (6) They were unsuitible for downhill sking because they were held on the foot by loose toe straps. (7) In 1721, skiers in the Norwegian army interduced a method of binding heals as well as toes, making possible downhill skiing. (8) In the mid-1800's Norweegian imigrants brought skiing to the United Sates. (9) By the early 1900's, downhill skiing had become a popular competative sport. (10) Today the oldest form of skiing, cross-country, is having a resurgence of popularety.

Studying Spelling Demons

Spelling demons are words that many people have difficulty spelling correctly.

Review a list of spelling demons to identify words that you may have trouble spelling correctly.

Some words in the chart are spelled according to basic rules. Others are not. Look for words that might give you problems.

200 COMMON SPELLING DEMONS			
abbreviate	capital	despair	interfere
absence	capitol	desperate	knowledge
accidentally	captain	dessert	laboratory
accumulate	career	development	lawyer
achieve	category	dining	library
acquaintance	cemetery	disappear	license
admittance	changeable	disappoint	lieutenant
advertisement	chauffeur	disastrous	lightning
aerial	clothes	dissatisfied	loneliness
aggressive	colonel	distinction	maintenance
aisle	column	distinguish	mathematics
allowance	committee	doubt	meanness
all right	competitor	efficient	mediocre
amateur	concede	eighth	mileage
analysis	condemn	eligible	millionaire
analyze	conscience	embarrass	misspell
anecdote	conscientious	emergency	naturally
anniversary	conscious	envelope	necessary
anonymous	contemporary	environment	neighbor
anxiety	continuous	equipped	ninety
appearance	convenience	exaggerate	nuisance
argument	coolly	exceed	occasion
athletic	cordially	exercise	occasionally
attendance	correspondence	existence	occur
awkward	counterfeit	explanation	occurred
banquet	courageous	extraordinary	omitted
barrel	courtesy	familiar	opinion
behavior	criticism	February	pamphlet
believe	criticize	foreign	parallel
benefit	curiosity	grammar	paralyze
bicycle	curious	guarantee	particularly
bookkeeper	deceive	handkerchief	permanent
bulletin	defendant	hygiene	permissible
bureau	deficient	immigrant	personally
business	delinquent	independence	perspiration
calendar	desert	inflammable	physician

possess	receipt	sophomore	temporary
possession	recommen	souvenir	thorough
prairie	reference	spaghetti	tomatoes
precede	rehearse	straight	tomorrow
preferable	repetition	substitute	tragedy
preparation	restaurant	succeed	truly
privilege	rhythm	superintendent	unforgettable
probably	ridiculous	supersede	unnecessary
procedure	scissors	surprise	vacuum
proceed	secretary	suspicious	vegetable
pronunciation	separate	syllable	villain
psychology	sergeant	technique	Wednesday
really	similar	temperament	weird
recede	sincerely	temperature	whether

EXERCISE C: Working with Spelling Demons. Write the following spelling demons on your paper, filling in the missing letters.

EXAMPLE: so __ __ omore
sophomore

1. effic __ __ __ t
2. chang __ __ ble
3. permiss __ ble
4. contempor __ ry
5. We __ __ __ __ day
6. ath __ __ __ ic
7. develop __ __ nt
8. distin __ tion
9. Feb __ __ __ ry
10. allow __ nce
11. counterf __ __ t
12. vac __ um
13. correspond __ nce
14. gramm __ r
15. analy __ e
16. par __ llel
17. el __ gible
18. anx __ __ ty
19. rid __ c __ lous
20. amat __ __ r
21. independ __ nce
22. p __ __ chology
23. nece __ __ ary
24. vill __ __ n
25. serg __ __ nt

EXERCISE D: More Work with Spelling Demons. Each sentence below contains an incorrect spelling of one of the spelling demons from the chart beginning on page 725. Write the correct spelling for each misspelled word.

EXAMPLE: Louisa took five books out of the local libery.
library

1. We must preserve and protect our natural enviornment.
2. Unexcused absenses will not be tolerated.

3. The guard felt personaly responsible for the theft.
4. Sal's possesions have taken over the attic, the basement, and the garage.
5. "Buisness is great," the shopkeeper replied.
6. As the car was not equiped for snow, the trip became hazardous.
7. Ed brought souveneers of his trip for the whole class.
8. The arguement was brief, but bitter words were exchanged.
9. The weather forecaster predicted rain for tommorrow.
10. Occasionaly, a stray cat takes up residence in our barn.

Keeping a Spelling Notebook

Your spelling errors can be reduced if you keep track of and study words that are especially difficult for you. The best place to do this is in a special section of your notebook.

Make a personal spelling list of difficult words, enter it in your notebook, and keep it up to date.

You can begin your personal list of difficult words with the spelling demons that you have identified as problem words for you. In addition, collect a reasonable sample of papers and tests that you have written over the last few months. Note spelling errors marked by your teachers and then work with a partner to identify any other misspelled words.

In the special section of your notebook, make four columns across the page, as in the sample on page 728. In the first column, headed "Misspelled Words," record each such word exactly as you wrote it on your paper or test. Knowing how you misspelled the word will help you locate and remedy your errors. Put an *X* through the entire column so you will not learn these spellings by mistake.

In the second column, "Correct Spelling," record the correct spelling of each word as it is given in a dictionary.

In the third column, "Practice Sessions," leave enough space to record your progress, following the suggestions you will find on pages 728–729.

In the fourth column, "Memory Aids," leave more space so that you can use the suggestions described on pages 730–731.

Personal Spelling List

Misspelled Words	Correct Spelling	Practice Sessions	Memory Aids
1. artic	arctic	✓✓	There is no art in arctic.
2. seperate	separate	✓	Separate and apart both have 2 a's.
3. alot	allot		a lot (2 words) means "many"; allot (1 word) means "to apportion."

EXERCISE E: Selecting Words for a Personal Spelling List. Look over all the writing you have done in the last month, including personal writing and school assignments. Following the preceding explanation and sample, record any misspelled words in a personal spelling list.

Studying Problem Words

Some of the words on your personal spelling list may be words you seldom use and have misspelled because of lack of practice. Others may be words that you repeatedly misspell. Both kinds of problems can be attacked through the use of a systematic study plan.

Study the words in your personal spelling list using the steps in the chart below.

Once you have completed the first two columns in your personal spelling list, you can use the following steps in a series of practice sessions to master the correct spelling of the words.

STEPS FOR STUDYING PROBLEM WORDS

1. *Look* at each word carefully. Observe the arrangement and pattern of the letters in the word. Consider, for example, the word *moccasin*. Notice that there are two *c*'s and only one *s* in the word. Try to see the word in your mind.

2. *Pronounce* the word accurately. For example, pronounce *athletic*. Notice that there are only three syllables: *ath let ic*.
3. *Write* the word on a piece of paper. As you write the word, pronounce it carefully.
4. *Check* to make sure the spelling is correct. If it is correct, enter a check in the third column of your notebook. If you have made a mistake, take note of the part of the word you misspelled. Then start over again with the first step.
5. *Review* your list of problem words at least once a week. Enter a check in the third column only when you have spelled the word correctly in the first round of a practice session. Consider a word mastered when you have three checks.

EXERCISE F: Working with Problem Words. Write each word in parentheses that is correctly spelled. Then look up your answers in a dictionary. Finally, enter all words you misspelled in your spelling notebook and conduct an initial practice session.

EXAMPLE: The child could not hide her (dissappointment, disappointment).

disappointment

1. The (pronounciation, pronunciation) of some words is difficult.
2. The thunder and (lightening, lightning) terrified us.
3. Their (personnel, personal) office will have information about possible jobs.
4. I hate to fill out (questionairres, questionnaires).
5. Who is (responsable, responsible) for this messy room?
6. The (defendant, defendent) is always presumed innocent until proven guilty.
7. Can you draw (parallel, paralel) lines without a ruler?
8. What kind of (milage, mileage) does your car get?
9. Your (appearance, appearence) should be very neat when you apply for a job.
10. The hotel can (accommodate, accomodate) 250 guests.
11. The whole class is (familiar, familier) with that poem.
12. A late arrival is (preferable, preferrable) to none at all.
13. Sew on that (lose, loose) button, or it may fall off.
14. I love (strawberries, strawberies) and cream for dessert.

15. Always begin a sentence with a (capital, capitol) letter.
16. The jury was instructed to take an (unbiassed, unbiased) look at the facts.
17. Multiply the (lenth, length) by the width to calculate the area.
18. The (advertisements, advertizements) for that car are very imaginative.
19. The shortstop (through, threw) the ball to first base.
20. The coach says that it's a (privilege, privilige) to work with such a dedicated team.

Developing Memory Aids

Some words in the English language are especially difficult to learn, often because they do not follow any set spelling rules. Many of these words can be mastered by using memory aids.

Use memory aids to remember the spelling of words that you find especially difficult to spell.

There are a number of methods that you can use to remember the spelling of problem words. One way is to look for a familiar word whose spelling you already know within the hard word.

EXAMPLES:	bulletin	Watch for the *bullet* in *bullet*in.
	friend	You will be my fri*end* to the *end*.
	principal	Our princi*pal* is like a *pal* to us.
	vegetables	Did you *get* the ve*get*ables from the market?

Another way to memorize the spelling of problem words is to associate a part of a word with the same letters in a related word. You should create your own, but a few suggestions follow.

EXAMPLES:	cellar	A cell*ar* is usually d*ar*k. Both words contain *ar*.
	clientele	Clien*tele* means a group of customers. Customers often order what they want on the *tele*phone.

Once you have decided you need a memory aid to remember a difficult word, develop an aid using one of the ideas given or some more personal clue to the word's spelling. Then enter the memory aid in the fourth column of your notebook.

EXERCISE G: Developing Memory Aids. Choose five particularly difficult words from your personal spelling list. Develop a memory aid for each and enter it in your notebook.

EXAMPLE: *Emma* was in a dil*emma*.

DEVELOPING WRITING SKILLS: Using Problem Words in Sentences. Study the following words, using the steps on pages 728–729. Then use each of the words in a sentence of your own.

EXAMPLE: mediocre

Because he was not feeling well, his performance was mediocre.

1. accumulate
2. knowledge
3. balance
4. develop
5. maintenance
6. process
7. noticeable
8. strenuous
9. presence
10. recognizable

Following Spelling Rules 30.2

Although the list of spelling demons on pages 725–726 includes a number of words for which there are no set spelling rules, it also includes many words that you can easily master if you become familiar with the rules listed in this section. For example, learning how to form plurals, how to add prefixes and suffixes, and when to use *ei* and *ie* will improve your ability to spell a great number of words without having to memorize each one individually.

Plurals

The plural form of a noun is the form that carries the meaning "more than one." The plural forms of nouns are either regular or irregular.

Regular Plurals. Most of the nouns in the English language have regular plural forms that end in *-s* or *-es*.

The plural of most nouns is formed by adding -s or -es to the singular.

In general, you can add *-s* to form the plural of regular nouns. However, there are certain cases where you need to think about whether an *-es* is needed. The following chart gives rules for these special cases.

FORMING REGULAR PLURALS			
Noun Ending	**Rule**	**Examples**	**Exceptions**
-s, -x, -z, -sh, -ch	Add *-es*	masses, foxes fizzes, wishes, benches	
-o preceded by a consonant	Add *-es*	torpedoes tomatoes	Musical terms: altos, pianos
-o preceded by a vowel	Add *-s*	radios cameos	
-y preceded by a consonant	Change *y* to *i* and add *-es*	babies flies	
-y preceded by a vowel	Add *-s*	monkeys delays	

Nouns that end in *-f* or *-fe* are not so simple to classify. Some have plurals formed simply by adding *-s (chiefs, roofs)*. For others, the *f* or *fe* must be changed to *v* before *-es* is added (*calves, knives*). Still others have two acceptable plural forms (*hooves, hoofs*). If you are unsure of how a plural is formed, check a dictionary. If there is any spelling change from the singular form, the plural form or forms will be given. If two plural forms are given, the one listed first is preferred.

Irregular Plurals. A few English nouns have totally irregular plural forms. Nouns such as *child, mouse, basis,* and *datum* form their plurals in ways that generally have to be memorized (*children, mice, bases, data*). A few nouns have the same form for both singular and plural, such as *sheep, trout,* and *moose*. If you are not sure, consult a dictionary.

NOTE ABOUT OTHER SPECIAL PLURALS: To form the plurals of compound nouns that are written as separate or hyphenated words, find the word that is being modified and make it plural.

EXAMPLES:	rule of order	mother-in-law	morning glory
	rules of order	mothers-in-law	morning glories

To form the plurals of letters, numbers, symbols, or words used as words, you must add an apostrophe and an *-s* as explained in Section 16.8.

EXERCISE A: Spelling Plurals. Write the plural for each of the following nouns. Consult a dictionary when necessary.

EXAMPLE: bench
benches

1. ox	6. deer	11. sheaf	16. belief	21. soprano
2. elf	7. alley	12. goose	17. brush	22. memorandum
3. tax	8. stew	13. crisis	18. potato	23. phenomenon
4. half	9. class	14. block	19. volcano	24. passer-by
5. cry	10. jelly	15. finch	20. heart	25. aquarium

Prefixes and Suffixes

Adding a prefix or a suffix to a word may sometimes raise questions about the spelling of the new word. There are some general rules that can be followed.

Prefixes. A prefix is one or more syllables added at the beginning of a word or root to which it is attached.

When a prefix is added to a word, the spelling of the root word remains the same.

Following this rule will help you spell words with double letters that may look rather strange but are actually correct.

EXAMPLES: co- + ordinate = coordinate
dis- + satisfaction = dissatisfaction

Keep in mind, however, that the spelling of certain prefixes may change before certain roots to make pronunciation easier. The following example shows this kind of spelling change.

EXAMPLE: ad- + locate = allocate

Suffixes. A suffix is one or more syllables added to the end of a word. You have studied the rules for adding word endings to form plurals of nouns. Other suffixes change a word's part of speech. The rules for adding endings that change a word's part of speech are similar to those for forming plurals.

Be aware of spelling changes needed in some words or roots when you are adding suffixes.

There are three basic situations in which a root may change its spelling before a suffix: (1) when the word or root ends with *y*; (2) when the word or root ends with *e*; and (3) when the word or root ends with a single consonant after a single vowel.

SPELLING CHANGES BEFORE SUFFIXES

Word Ending	Suffix Added	Rule/ Examples	Exceptions
consonant + *y* (rely, friendly)	most suffixes (-able, -ness)	Change *y* to *i* (reliable, friendliness)	Most suffixes beginning with *i*: *rely* becomes *relying; hobby* becomes *hobbyist*
vowel + *y* (employ, joy)	most suffixes (-ment, -ous)	Make no change (employment, joyous)	A few short words: *day* becomes *daily; gay* becomes *gaily*
any word ending in *e* (desire, separate)	suffix beginning with a vowel (-able, -ed)	Drop the final *e* (desirable, separated)	1. words ending in *ce* or *ge* with suffixes beginning in *a* or *o*: *trace* becomes *traceable; courage* becomes *courageous* 2. words ending in *ee* or *oe: agree* becomes *agreeing; toe* becomes *toeing* 3. a few special words: *dye* becomes *dyeing; be* becomes *being*

any word ending in *e* (nice, separate)	suffix beginning with a consonant (-ness, -ly)	Make no change (niceness, separately)	a few special words: *true* becomes *truly; awe* becomes *awful; argue* becomes *argument; judge* becomes *judgment; acknowledge* becomes *acknowledgment*
consonant + vowel + consonant in a stressed syllable (wrap′, remit′)	suffix beginning with a vowel (-er, -ance)	Double the final consonant (wrap′per, remit′tance)	1. words ending in *w* or *x: row* becomes *rowing; mix* becomes *mixing* 2. words in which the stress changes after the suffix is added: *refer* + *-ing* becomes *referring;* BUT refer′ + -ence becomes *ref′erence*.
consonant + vowel + consonant in unstressed syllable (sig′-nal, ri′val)	suffix beginning with a vowel (-ing, -ed)	Make no change (sig′naling, ri′valed)	no major exceptions

EXERCISE B: Spelling Words with Prefixes. Write the new words formed by combining each of the following prefixes and roots.

EXAMPLE: circum + navigate
circumnavigate

1. ad- + portion
2. de- + activate
3. com + respond
4. in + migrate

5. ex- + fervescent
6. pre- + eminent
7. co- + operate
8. mis- + speak
9. ad- + fluent
10. un- + necessary
11. ad- + knowledge
12. dis- + solve
13. dis + fuse
14. inter + racial
15. semi + annual
16. con + pound
17. re + active
18. ab + base
19. pre + arrange
20. sub + press

EXERCISE C: Spelling Words with Suffixes. Write the new words formed by combining each of the following words and suffixes.

EXAMPLE: happy + ly
happily

1. fascinate + -ion
2. lucky + -ly
3. lobby + -ist
4. swim + -er
5. cease + -less
6. control + -able
7. confer + -ence
8. manage + -able
9. alphabet + -ic
10. apply + -ance
11. extreme + -ity
12. occur + -ence
13. portray + -al
14. benefit + -ed
15. fit + -ness
16. emerge + -ence
17. refer + -ence
18. annoy + -ance
19. imagine + -ary
20. final + -ist

ie and *ei* Words

Probably at some time in grade school you heard or learned the following basic rule for *ie* and *ei* words: "Write *i* before *e*, except after *c*, or when sounded like *a*, as in *neighbor* or *weigh*." This rule can help you spell a number of common words such as *chief, ceiling,* and *freight*. However, like most rules, this one has its exceptions.

Use the traditional rule for *ie* and *ei* words after you have learned the exceptions.

The most common exception to the rule involves words where *c* has the *sh* sound. In these words, the spelling is *ie*, as in *ancient* and *conscience*. In addition, the following common words, grouped by sound for easy association, are exceptions.

EXCEPTIONS:	either	foreign	heir	height	seize
	neither	forfeit	their		

EXERCISE D: Spelling *ie* and *ei* Words. Write each of the following incomplete words, filling in either *ei* or *ie*.

1. ach __ __ ve
2. bel __ __ f
3. dec __ __ ve
4. sl __ __ gh
5. s __ __ zure
6. rec __ __ pt
7. effic __ __ nt
8. h __ __ ress
9. r __ __ gn
10. rel __ __ ve

Words Ending in *-cede*, *-ceed*, and *-sede*

A small group of words that end in *-cede, -ceed,* and *-sede* may cause spelling problems unless the correct spellings are memorized.

Memorize the spellings of words that end in *-cede, -ceed,* and *-sede.*

The task is simpler than it may at first seem. Only one word ends in *-sede*. Only three words end in *-ceed*. The rest end in *-cede*. The following chart summarizes this information.

Words Ending in *-cede*		Words Ending in *-ceed*	Words Ending in *-sede*
accede	precede	exceed	supersede
concede	recede	proceed	
intercede	secede	succeed	

EXERCISE E: Spelling Words Ending in *-cede, -ceed,* and *-sede.* Write the incomplete word for each sentence, filling in the blanks with *-cede, -ceed, -sede.*

EXAMPLE: If you ex __ __ __ __ the speed limit, be prepared to face the consequences.

exceed

1. No repairs can be done until the flood waters re __ __ __ __.
2. To reach the drive-in, pro __ __ __ __ down Elm Avenue for three blocks.
3. The senator will not con __ __ __ __ defeat until the last vote is counted.

4. We would like to ac _ _ _ _ to your request, but circumstances prevent our agreeing to it.
5. These new regulations super _ _ _ _ the old ones.
6. A neutral person should inter _ _ _ _ between the two warring parties.
7. That small island wants to se _ _ _ _ from the country.
8. To suc _ _ _ _ at a sport takes hard work and determination.
9. The speakers must not ex _ _ _ _ the time limit on the debate.
10. Who will pre _ _ _ _ me on the program?

Other Confusing Endings

Word endings that sound similar may be difficult to spell. Among these confusing endings are *-ance (-ant)*, and *-ence (-ent), -ary* and *-ery, -ify* and *-efy*, and *-cy* and *-sy*.

Learn to distinguish between similar word endings that may cause spelling errors.

Both rules and exceptions are presented to help you choose the correct word ending from a confusing pair.

-ance (-ant)* and *-ence (-ent). These suffixes travel in pairs. If a noun has the *a* spelling *(elegance)*, probably the corresponding adjective will also *(elegant)*. The same applies for words with the *e* spelling *(adherence* and *adherent)*.

A helpful thing to remember is that words containing a "hard" *c* or *g* sound usually end with the *a* spelling: *arrogance, litigant*. Those with a "soft" *c* or *g* sound will usually have the *e* spelling: *emergence, deficient*. To learn the spelling of some words that do not contain soft or hard *c* or *g* sounds, study the following lists.

Common words Ending in *-ance*		**Common Words Ending in *-ence***	
abundance	importance	absence	independence
acquaintance	radiance	convenience	patience
appearance	resonance	correspondence	presence
brilliance	romance	difference	reference
defiance	tolerance	excellence	violence

***-ary* and *-ery*.** There is no rule about which of these to choose, but most words end with *-ary*. For adjectives *(honorary, imaginary,* or *voluntary)*, *-ary* is the correct choice.

A few nouns, most of which refer to places, end with *-ery*.

COMMON WORDS ENDING IN *-ery*		
bakery	millinery	stationery
cemetery	monastery	winery

***-ify* and *-efy*.** The ending *-ify* is much more common than *-efy*. In fact, *-efy* is rarely used except for the four words below.

COMMON WORDS ENDING IN *-efy*			
liquefy	putrefy	rarefy	stupefy

***-cy* and *-sy*.** Only a few English words end with *-sy*. Learn those in the chart, and you can be reasonably safe in using *-cy* for the others. When in doubt, however, consult a dictionary.

COMMON WORDS ENDING IN *-sy*			
autopsy	curtsy	epilepsy	hypocrisy
biopsy	ecstasy	fantasy	idiosyncrasy
courtesy	embassy	heresy	pleurisy

EXERCISE F: Writing Words with Confusing Endings. Write each word, supplying the correct letter in the blank.

1. bak __ ry
2. fanta __ y
3. liqu __ fy
4. viol __ nt
5. brilli __ nce
6. auxili __ ry
7. delica __ y
8. fort __ fy
9. idiosyncra __ y
10. millin __ ry
11. nurs __ ry
12. terr __ fy
13. tenden __ y
14. radi __ nt
15. agen __ y
16. element __ ry
17. correspond __ nce
18. biop __ y
19. intellig __ nce
20. milit __ ry

DEVELOPING WRITING SKILLS: Spelling Words in Sentences. Write ten sentences using at least one plural noun and one word with a prefix and/or a suffix in each sentence.

Skills Review and Writing Workshop

Spelling Improvement

CHECKING YOUR SKILLS

Find all the misspelled words in the following paragraph and write them correctly.

(1) The ancient Romans beleived that an effective road system was necessary for their empire. (2) Roman roads were not temperary structures. (3) They were cunstructed out of mortar and flagstones and made to last. (4) These roads were built for the conveneince of Roman merchants and traders. (5) They also made it possible for armies to move eficiently throughout the empire. (6) Historians estimate that the Roman road system exceded fifty thousand miles in length. (7) One of the most famous roads built by Roman tecknology was the Appian Way. (8) This road streches from Rome to Brindisi, on the coast. (9) Part of this extrordinary structure can still be seen today. (10) The Romans were, indeed, incredable engineers.

USING SPELLING SKILLS IN WRITING

Writing a Fund-Raising Letter

Misspelled words reduce the impact of your writing. Imagine you are a fund-raiser for a charitable organization and compose a letter to a select group of philanthropists, requesting contributions.

Prewriting: Decide on the charity you will represent. List some good reasons why people should contribute to your cause.

Writing: Make your arguments strong and persuasive. Major contributors need good reasons to justify donating large sums of money.

Revising: Look over your work and correct any misspelled words. Change any sentences that could be more convincing. After you have revised, proofread carefully.

UNIT **VII**

Study and Research Skills

Chapter 31

Basic Study Skills

Good study skills can be the key to success in school. The more skillful you become at studying, the more you can concentrate your efforts to do your best work. As a result, you will need to study less, your grades should improve, and your attitude toward school should be more positive. In this chapter you will practice skills to help you improve your study habits and your methods of taking notes.

31.1 Good Study Habits

When you have good study habits, you know how to approach assignments and how to prepare for your classes. The first step in improving your study habits is to identify the skills you have already mastered and to identify the ones you still need to improve. In this section you will practice developing a study plan and setting goals for skills improvement.

Developing a Study Plan

Because efficient management of time is essential to your success in school, you should develop a study plan to use time to your best advantage.

Develop a study plan in order to manage your time most efficiently.

Your study plan should include setting up a study area, establishing a study schedule, and using an assignment book.

Study Area. Having an area that you associate only with studying will enable you to concentrate on the work you are doing so that you can do that work better. Set up a study area that is free of distractions, quiet, well lighted, and contains all the materials you need to work.

Study Schedule. Establishing a study schedule will help you fit in all of the assignments and the activities you have to do and want to do. The chart below suggests ways to make a study schedule that will fit your own personal needs.

MAKING A STUDY SCHEDULE

1. Block out areas of time in which you have activities such as the regular school day, after-school clubs, dinner, etc.
2. Block out study periods of no longer than forty-five minutes each. Take a ten-minute break between each period.
3. Schedule study periods for time when you are most alert.
4. Arrange to study your most difficult subject first.
5. Make use of study hall and free time at school to get some assignments completed.

Assignment Book. Keeping track of your assignments by using an assignment book will enable you to plan your time so that you can complete both short-term and long-term assignments efficiently. A long-term assignment such as a research paper can be divided into short-term goals that you must meet in order to complete the assignment.

An easy way to set up your assignment book is to divide the page into four columns. Use one column for the subject, one for an exact description of the assignment, one for the due date, and one for a check when the assignment is completed.

EXERCISE A: Evaluating Your Study Plan. Identify which one of the three study skills you need to improve most: setting up a study area, making a study schedule, or keeping an assignment book. Work to improve that skill for one week and then evaluate your progress.

Setting Goals

In order to improve your study habits, you need to establish reasonable goals that you can achieve without becoming discouraged. You know that your long-term goal is to acquire study habits that work best for you. The best way to achieve any long-term goal is to set short-term goals that will in time lead to your long-term goal.

Set long- and short-term goals to improve your general study habits.

These goals and the timetable for achieving them should be recorded in writing. For example, to improve your ability to take notes, you might prepare a chart like the one below.

SETTING LONG- AND SHORT-TERM GOALS		
Long-term Goal: To take better notes in class		
Short-term Goals	**Timetable**	**Comments**
Practice writing the date and topic on all notes	1 week (by Nov. 8)	Successfully completed
Practice writing all notes in ink	2 weeks (by Nov. 15)	Successfully completed
Take complete notes, using headings and organized lists	1 month (by Dec. 1)	More practice needed; work on skill through Dec. 1

EXERCISE B: Setting Goals for Study Skills. Select one general study skill that you want to master. Divide that long-term goal into short-term goals. Then make a chart, using the one above as a model.

DEVELOPING WRITING SKILLS: Evaluating Your Study Habits. Write a brief evaluation of your study habits. Include comments on the quality of your study schedule, the usefulness of your assignment book, and the appropriateness of any long-term goals you have set. Identify the areas you need to work on and list one way you can improve in each area.

Methods of Taking Notes 31.2

Before you study the various methods for improving your note-taking skills in this section, you should make sure that you have an organized notebook binder. Notes for each subject should be behind a labeled divider. Notes should be neatly written with the date and topic at the top of each page.

Taking notes is an active way to organize and condense material you need to learn. In this section you will practice two methods for taking notes: *outlines* and *summaries.*

Making Outlines

An *outline* is a method for taking notes that shows the relationship between main ideas and other ideas that support the main ideas. There are two basic kinds of outlines: *modified outlines* and *formal outlines.*

Modified Outlines. A modified outline is a skeleton of a subject. In a modified outline, main ideas are written as headings and are usually underlined. The major details relating to each main idea are listed under the main idea using numbers, letters, indentation, or simply dashes.

A modified outline allows you to organize information quickly. It is useful for recording information from lectures, films, discussions, and books. It is also useful in organizing ideas for answering questions on an essay test.

Use a modified outline to take notes while listening or reading.

As you read the following passage about Susan B. Anthony, try to identify the main ideas and the supporting details. Then compare yours with those in the model outline on the next page.

PASSAGE:

Do you know why Susan B. Anthony's image appears on a recent coin? To honor her fight for women's right to vote, her profile was stamped on a 1979 one-dollar coin that is smaller than a fifty-cent piece and is made of copper and nickel.

Susan B. Anthony was born in 1820 in Massachusetts. She inherited the love of freedom from her grandfather, who fought in the Revolutionary War. Early in life, Ms. Anthony became a school teacher and a reform leader. She fought against slavery and the use of alcohol. Her biggest fight was for women's rights, particularly for women's suffrage or the right to vote.

For over thirty years, Ms. Anthony traveled throughout the country speaking out for women's rights. Finally, in 1870 Wyoming granted women the right to vote, but the other states did not follow Wyoming's lead. In 1872, Ms. Anthony voted in a presidential election in Rochester, New York, and she was arrested for voting illegally. She was fined one hundred dollars but not jailed as she had hoped to be.

In 1920 the Nineteenth Amendment, granting women the right to vote, was ratified. Unfortunately, Susan B. Anthony had died fourteen years earlier. For her lifelong work, many people today think she deserved to be the first American woman honored on a coin.—Adapted from *Current Events*

In the modified outline below, main ideas are underlined and supporting details are numbered. Notice the short phrases and occasional abbreviations.

MODIFIED OUTLINE:

<u>Susan B. Anthony on Coin</u>
1. Honored for fight for women's rights
2. 1979, $1.00 coin
3. Smaller than 50¢ piece
4. Made of copper and nickel

<u>S.A.'s Early Background</u>
1. Born 1820, Massachusetts
2. Grandfather fought in American Revolution
3. School teacher and reform leader

<u>Her Causes as Reform Leader</u>
1. Fought against slavery
2. Fought against use of alcohol
3. Fought to gain voting rights for women

<u>Action Taken</u>
1. Spoke for 30 yrs. on women's rights
2. Saw women get vote in Wyoming, 1870
3. Voted illegally in presidential election, 1872
4. Died 14 yrs. before women got the right to vote

Formal Outlines. A formal outline provides more exact and complete information and relationships among ideas than any other form of notes. In addition to listing major details under main ideas, a formal outline also lists minor details under major details. A formal outline is useful when you need to take detailed notes to prepare a speech or write a composition.

Use a formal outline to arrange ideas when preparing major written and oral assignments.

The chart below lists the rules for making a formal outline.

RULES TO FOLLOW FOR FORMAL OUTLINES
1. Use roman numerals for main ideas. Use capital letters for major details. Use arabic numerals for minor details. Use small letters for items under minor details.
2. Place a period after each numeral or letter.
3. Capitalize the first word in each line.
4. Use indentation to indicate importance. Main ideas begin at the left. Items begin farther to the right as they become less important.
5. Do not place a single item under any head. Always place two or more items or no items.

Formal outlines can be either *topic* outlines or *sentence* outlines. In a topic outline, you write information in words and phrases. In a sentence outline, you write information in complete sentences. Notice that the following topic outline on modern magic uses phrases to list ideas.

TOPIC OUTLINE:

I. Development of modern magic
  A. Robert-Houdin in 1880's
    1. French mechanic and watchmaker
    2. Father of modern magic
      a. Developed rules for conjuring
      b. Developed many new tricks
  B. Modern magicians
    1. Better equipment
    2. Greater knowledge of psychology

II. Tools of modern magicians
  A. Skill with hands
  B. Secret devices
  C. Audience psychology
    1. Misdirect people's attention
    2. Encourage false conclusions

A sentence outline provides even more information than a topic outline. Sentence outlines can be used to take notes from textbooks, but you will probably find them most helpful when you are organizing your thoughts for speeches or compositions.

The following example shows the beginning of a sentence outline for a composition about avoiding stage fright.

SENTENCE OUTLINE:

I. How can you face all those people out there in the auditorium when you feel so frightened?
  A. Terror makes you feel and act foolish.
    1. Your hands and legs are shaking.
    2. Your throat is dry and scratchy.
    3. You are afraid you will forget everything.
  B. You can overcome these signs of nervousness, however, with practice and self-confidence.

II. You can lessen your nervousness by selecting a good topic.
  A. Choose a topic you will be comfortable speaking about.
  B. Know your topic well.
    1. Find information in books and from people.
    2. Find material that will be easy to remember.

EXERCISE A: Making a Modified Outline. Listen to a television newscast and take notes in modified outline form, using your own words. After the newscast, read your notes and fill in any information that is needed to make them clear.

EXERCISE B: Making a Formal Topic Outline. Rewrite the sentence outline example above as a topic outline.

EXERCISE C: Making a Formal Sentence Outline. Outline a composition you might write on how to overcome a problem such as fear of a new situation or learning a new skill.

Writing Summaries

Another useful way to record information is to write a *summary* of it. In a summary you state the main ideas of a lecture or printed material in your own words in a few complete sentences. You may take notes in a modified outline and then summarize your notes, or you may take notes in summary form directly from listening or reading.

Use a summary to take notes when you need to remember only the main ideas.

The chart below offers suggestion for summarizing.

WRITING SUMMARIES
1. Carefully listen or read for main ideas.
2. Write down the main ideas using your own words.
3. Shape these main ideas into sentences that express the purpose and point of view of the speaker or writer.
4. Write the summary in paragraph form. The final material should be no more than one third of its original length.

The following summary is developed from the passage about Susan B. Anthony on pages 745 and 746. More than 75 percent of the information from the lecture has been eliminated.

SUMMARY: Susan B. Anthony is the first woman to be honored on an American coin. She was a reform leader who spent over thirty years campaigning for women's right to vote. Fourteen years after her death, the Nineteenth Amendment was passed, and her goal was achieved.

EXERCISE D: Writing a Summary. Write a summary of the notes you took for your modified outline in Exercise A.

DEVELOPING WRITING SKILLS: Evaluating Your Note-Taking Skills. Write an evaluation of your note-taking skills, indicating which methods work best for you and which methods you need to work on further.

Skills Review and Writing Workshop

Basic Study Skills

CHECKING YOUR SKILLS

Take notes on the following paragraph using a modified outline.

John James Audubon, the famous painter and ornithologist, was born in Haiti in 1785. While still a child, his father took him to France where Audubon lived until he was eighteen. Audubon then moved to America and entered the dry-goods business where he was moderately successful. This business came to an end, however, during the Panic of 1819; and Audubon began devoting himself to painting birds. During the next few years he traveled the Mississippi Valley and other parts of America. Audubon developed quite a collection of bird sketches. He wanted to publish them, but he could not find a publisher in the United States. Eventually, Audubon sailed for England where he was widely acclaimed for his talents. Gradually the American painter succeeded in raising the money to pay for having his paintings printed. These were published in a beautiful book titled *The Birds of America.*

USING STUDY SKILLS IN WRITING:
Writing a Summary of a TV Documentary

Summaries are effective tools that help you organize what you read or hear. You can use summaries to remember the main ideas from a reading assignment, lecture, or other types of presentations. Write a summary of a TV documentary by following these steps.

Prewriting: Try to listen carefully for the main ideas presented in the documentary. What is the documentary designed to accomplish? Take notes as you listen.

Writing: State the main ideas in a few sentences.

Revising: Read over the summary and add any important ideas that you may have omitted. After you have revised, proofread carefully.

Chapter 32

Critical-Thinking Skills

The process of analyzing, evaluating, and applying the information that you receive from reading and listening is known as critical thinking. In this chapter you will learn skills to help you think clearly and effectively when you read, listen, speak, and write.

Forms of Reasoning 32.1

An important aspect of critical thinking is analyzing information to determine how *reliable* it is. Another aspect of critical thinking is distinguishing between *valid* and *invalid* forms of reasoning.

Using Fact and Opinion

The first step in critical thinking is analyzing your material to find out whether it is reliable.

Analyze material first to decide whether it is reliable.

In order to determine whether the material is reliable, you must be able to distinguish between fact and opinion.

Fact. A statement of fact is one that can be verified, or proved true by objective means. A fact is objective and can be verified by observation or experimentation.

FACT: To put a satellite in space, a rocket must travel fast enough to escape the earth's gravity.

FACT: On July 20, 1969, Neil Armstrong was the first human being to set foot on the moon.

The first example above could be verified by experimentation, but a simpler method would be to consult a written authority such as a reference book. The second example could be verified by checking a reference book or a human authority such as an eyewitness to the event.

Opinion. A statement of opinion is one that cannot be verified, or proved true by objective means. An opinion is subjective and must be properly supported with facts before it can be accepted as valid. An opinion may express a person's feelings about something, state a judgment based on facts, or make a prediction based on facts. It is important to remember that an opinion may be based on facts, but an opinion is *not* a fact.

FEELING: Space travel is too dangerous.

JUDGMENT: A mechanical flaw in a spacecraft could threaten an astronaut's life.

PREDICTION: NASA says that the next space shuttle mission will be the most ambitious one ever.

The first example above is a purely personal statement, unsupported by facts, and cannot be considered a valid opinion. The second example expresses a judgment based on facts and is a valid opinion. The third example is a prediction and can be proved true only when the event actually happens. This prediction is based on facts so it is a valid opinion.

EXERCISE A: Analyzing Fact and Opinion Statements. First, identify each of the following statements as *fact* or *opinion*. Then, analyze whether each fact statement is *true* or *false* and analyze whether each opinion statement is *valid* or *invalid*.

1. Abraham Lincoln was the greatest President the United States has ever had.
2. Our team is sure to win the baseball game next week.
3. The blue whale is the largest animal that has ever inhabited the earth.

4. Tennis is a more exciting sport than golf.
5. President Lincoln signed the Emancipation Proclamation on November 4, 1860.
6. We will have snow tomorrow because a cold front is approaching.
7. Koalas eat nothing but eucalyptus leaves.
8. Our solar system is part of the Andromeda galaxy.
9. The Supreme Court has eleven members.
10. Marta is an excellent skater who has won several medals.

EXERCISE B: Analyzing Fact and Opinion in Writing. Read the following paragraph and list the fact and opinion statements it contains. Determine whether each fact statement is true or false and whether each opinion is valid or invalid.

The United Nations has not fulfilled its initial promise. When the world organization was created in 1945, just after the end of World War II, its purpose was to further understanding and peace among all nations. It was to function as a world government that would settle international disputes. Instead, the UN has become a forum for airing partisan grievances and intensifying nationalistic strife. Granted, the UN does have some accomplishments to its credit. Its humanitarian programs have saved many lives. But it has not solved the problem of how to achieve world peace.

Using Valid Reasoning

A second step in thinking critically is to think logically, or reasonably, about your material.

Think logically to draw valid conclusions.

Four forms of reasoning— *inference, generalization, analogy,* and *cause and effect*—are discussed in this section.

Inference. Inference is the drawing of a new conclusion from information that is already known. Inference can also be used to predict reasonably or logically what will happen in the future.

A *valid inference* is a reasonable interpretation of the information that is given. An *invalid inference* is an interpretation that is not consistent with the information that is given.

VALID INFERENCE: My sister is excellent at surfing, so she should be good at skateboarding.

INVALID INFERENCE: My sister can ski and skate well, so she should be good at gymnastics.

The first inference is valid because it is logical to conclude that similar skills are required in both sports. The second is invalid because there is not necessarily any connection between the skills required in skiing, skating, and gymnastics.

The following chart lists questions you should ask yourself when you analyze inferences.

VALID/INVALID INFERENCES

1. What details do you observe as clues to the main idea?
2. What main ideas do you conclude from these details?
3. Does your conclusion follow logically from the inferences you have made?
4. Is there any other interpretation of the details that might lead to a different conclusion?

Generalization. A generalization is a conclusion based on a number of particular facts or cases. A valid generalization is a statement that holds true in a large number of cases or is supported by evidence. It takes into account any exceptions or qualifying factors. A hasty generalization is a statement that is made about a large number of cases or a whole group on the basis of only a few examples and without taking into account exceptions or qualifying factors.

VALID: Every homeroom in our school has more girls than boys, so there are more girls than boys in our school.

HASTY: There are 15 girls and 10 boys in my homeroom, so there must be more girls than boys in our school.

The second example is a hasty generalization because a statement about a whole group is based on only a small part of that group.

The chart on the following page lists questions you should ask yourself to help you distinguish between valid and hasty generalizations.

VALID/HASTY GENERALIZATIONS
1. What facts are presented as evidence to support the general statement?
2. Are there any exceptions to the generalization or any qualifying factors you need to take into account?
3. Are enough cases or examples presented to make a valid generalization, or do you need more?

Analogy. An analogy is a comparison between two things that are similar in some ways but are essentially unlike. A complete analogy is one that compares two different objects that are similar in some important way. The two things are compared to describe the nature of one of them by showing its similarity to something more familiar. An incomplete analogy is one that overlooks essential dissimilarities between the two things that are being compared.

COMPLETE: The cell is like a factory—it processes raw materials, produces energy, and discharges wastes.

INCOMPLETE: The human body is like a machine.

The first analogy is complete because it compares particular functions that actually are similar. The second is incomplete because it fails to acknowledge ways in which the body is *not* like a machine.

The following chart lists questions to ask yourself when analyzing analogies.

COMPLETE/INCOMPLETE ANALOGIES
1. How are the two things being compared essentially unlike?
2. How are the two things alike? Is the comparison logical?
3. What statement does the comparison make about one of the objects?

Cause and Effect. When one event happens immediately after another, people sometimes conclude that the first event caused the second event. A *cause and effect sequence* is one in which something is caused by one or more events that occurred before it. An *unrelated sequence* is one in which the first event did not cause the second event. In many cases, events can occur one after the other without signifying a cause and effect relationship.

CAUSE AND EFFECT: When a warm air mass meets a cool air mass, it rains.

UNRELATED: Whenever I wash the car, it rains.

The following chart lists questions to ask yourself when you analyze cause and effect relationships.

CAUSE AND EFFECT RELATIONSHIPS
1. What evidence is there that the first event could have caused the second?
2. What other events could have caused the second event?
3. Could the second event have occurred without the first?

EXERCISE C: Analyzing Forms of Reasoning. First, identify the form of reasoning (inference, generalization, analogy, or cause and effect) used in each of the following statements. Then tell whether each conclusion is valid or invalid.

1. If you leave the lights of a car turned on, the battery will run down.
2. The atom is like a miniature solar system.
3. The two meals I got on the plane were not good, so all airline food must be terrible.
4. Luis has been elected student council president for ninth, tenth, and eleventh grades, so he must be a real leader.
5. As soon as I get into the shower, the telephone always rings.
6. When the available supply of a product increases, the price usually goes down.
7. All our tomato plants died, so the soil in our yard must be lacking in minerals.
8. Most of my class failed the biology test; obviously, the students in our school know nothing about biology.
9. The President of the United States is like a shepherd.
10. Jason enjoys playing baseball, so he must like to play basketball, too.

EXERCISE D: Correcting Invalid Reasoning. Using clear, logical thinking, rewrite each sentence in Exercise C that contains invalid reasoning.

DEVELOPING WRITING SKILLS. Analyzing Writing. Carefully read the following paragraph. Analyze each statement and decide whether the information is reliable and the author's reasoning is valid.

(1) The cause of the American Revolution was a series of repressive British taxes and other regulations. (2) Some Americans objected to "taxation without representation." (3) All the colonists must have resented being controlled by a Parliament thousands of miles away. (4) The hostilities began when British troops killed American civilians in the Boston Massacre. (5) Later, the Boston Tea Party signaled America's intention to govern itself independently. (6) General George Washington led the Continental Army in a series of battles at Lexington, Ticonderoga, Charleston, Long Island, Trenton, Princeton, and Saratoga. (7) Lord Cornwallis, who surrendered at Yorktown, Virginia, in 1781, lost the war for the British.

Language and Thinking 32.2

Human beings think largely by means of language. Language is the tool that we use to make sense out of the world. With language, we express our thoughts and feelings. Critical thinking can be used to analyze how a writer or speaker uses language and to evaluate the writer's or speaker's purpose.

Uses of Language

Language can be used in various ways. It is important to learn how to recognize when language is being used to communicate honestly and when it is being used to distort information and manipulate people into thinking a certain way.

Learn to identify different uses of language.

Discussed on the following pages are some of the ways a writer or speaker can use language to change the meaning of a fact, an event, or an idea.

Word Meanings. The denotation of a word is its literal, or exact, meaning and has a neutral tone. The connotation of a word is its suggested or implied meaning and has a positive or negative tone. Words acquire connotative meanings from the ways they have been used by people over the years. Certain connotations are emotionally loaded and may be used to distort meanings. Connotations can affect a person emotionally, and cause a particular response to the material. The following three statements are similar, yet each gives a different impression of the event described.

DENOTATION: The speaker walked quickly up to the lectern.

CONNOTATION: The speaker strode confidently up to the lectern.

CONNOTATION: The speaker stumbled hastily up to the lectern.

Note that the first statement has a neutral tone, the second a positive tone, and the third a negative tone.

Self-Important Language. Scholarly, technical, or scientific words and overly long phrases are characteristic of self-important language. Such language is sometimes used to impress the listener or reader. Sometimes it is used to conceal rather than reveal the meaning. *Jargon* is the specialized vocabulary used by people in a particular field. Jargon appears to be scientific and precise but actually may obscure ideas that could readily be understood if they were stated more clearly.

SELF-IMPORTANT LANGUAGE: The students took part in an activity-oriented learning experience in the laboratory facility.

DIRECT LANGUAGE: The students performed a science experiment.

JARGON: A navigational misdirection caused friendly fire to be directed at the hamlet.

DIRECT LANGUAGE: The military shelled the village by mistake.

The purpose of the first example may simply be to impress. The purpose of the second example may be to conceal an unpleasant fact and avoid taking responsibility.

Slanting. Writing a passage so that it leans toward one point of view is known as slanting. Because all writers select and arrange words to communicate meaning, some slanting may be unavoidable, even when the author tries to describe something fairly and objectively. However, slanting can be used dishonestly. Dishonest slanting occurs when a writer uses words with positive or negative connotations to distort the truth in order to support an opinion. Dishonest slanting can also occur when the writer presents only the facts that support the writer's point of view and leaves out other significant facts.

SLANTED STATEMENT: More people are out of work this year; the unemployment rate is ten percent in Pittsburgh and fifteen percent in Detroit.

MORE BALANCED STATEMENT: Although certain areas have been hit harder than others, the national unemployment rate is seven percent, the same as last year's.

The facts mentioned in the first statement are true, but they do not tell the whole story. By leaving out necessary information, the writer has created a false impression that the unemployment rate is higher this year than it was last year.

EXERCISE: Analyzing and Evaluating Uses of Language. Carefully read the following passage. Analyze all the uses of connotation, inflated language, and slanting. Then evaluate whether the author's purpose is to communicate ideas clearly and honestly. If not, explain what the purpose might be.

(1) Our space program is one of the most meaningful endeavors ever undertaken in the history of our country. (2) From beginning to end, the United States has always been the leader in space. (3) The first people to walk on the moon were Americans. (4) We have shown the rest of the world what American technology can do. (5) Because of the Apollo Project, navigation, communication, and scientific satellites now circle the earth. (6) Various space probes have photographed the solar system and recorded other data about the universe. (7) The manufacture of useful products in space is facilitated by the presence of microgravity. (8) The space shuttle missions have proved that a permanent space station is a possible future eventuality.

DEVELOPING WRITING SKILLS: Using Critical Thinking in Writing. Using the critical-thinking skills you have learned in this chapter, rewrite the paragraph in the exercise above so that it communicates clearly, logically, and honestly.

Skills Review and Writing Workshop

Critical-Thinking Skills

CHECKING YOUR SKILLS

Rewrite the following paragraph, correcting unreliable information, invalid reasoning, and misuse of language.

The dangers of "acid rain" have been greatly exaggerated. The term refers to atmospheric precipitation that is characterized by containing quantities of sulfuric acid and nitric acid. According to environmental alarmists, these acids are formed when sulfur dioxide and nitrogen oxides react with moisture in the air. Some so-called experts say that such compounds come from industrial factories that burn coal. But there is no proof that this is true. Volcanoes and forest fires also give off sulfur compounds. And automobile exhausts may play a role. Until there is more evidence, it is unfair to penalize American industries that provide many jobs for our workers by compelling them to use more expensive fuels, which would increase costs and cause workers to be laid off.

USING CRITICAL-THINKING SKILLS IN WRITING

Writing an Editorial

Follow the steps below to write an editorial.

Prewriting: Choose an issue about which you have an opinion. First, make a list of the facts involved. Take notes on how they support your opinion. Also, make a list of opposing opinions, taking notes on how the facts support them.

Writing. Write an introductory paragraph that states your thesis and summarizes the facts. Then discuss the arguments for your point of view. Include an honest evaluation of the opposing viewpoints. Write a concluding paragraph that sums up your argument.

Revising. Reread your editorial. Make sure that you have distinguished between fact and opinion and that you have not used slanting. Be sure that you have presented all the facts, not just those that support your point of view.

Chapter **33**

Reading and Test-Taking Skills

Success in school depends on acquiring and using many skills. Two of the most important of these skills are reading and test-taking. In this chapter you will practice various reading skills in order to learn more efficiently from your textbooks. You will also practice skills that will help you take different kinds of objective tests and standardized tests more effectively and more confidently.

Reading Skills 33.1

With each year in school, reading material increases in quantity and difficulty. You are expected to gather and understand information through reading in school and on your own. Improving your reading skills can improve your performance in your school as well as your test grades.

Reading Textbooks

At least 80 percent of the reading you do in school involves textbooks. Although you can simply read a textbook from beginning to end, you can save time and energy by using certain reading and study skills to understand and remember more information with less effort.

Use textbook reading and study aids to help understand what you are reading and to remember it better later.

Reading Aids. The material in a textbook is structured so that you can read and learn it easily. Unlike most other books, a textbook includes a variety of special sections designed to act as reading aids to help you make the best use of the textbook.

The following chart lists the reading aids most often found in textbooks and the type of information that each provides. Not all of your textbooks will have all of the special sections listed here, nor will you need to use all of them regularly. However, knowing which special features your textbooks have and how to use them can save you time and effort when you do need them.

TEXTBOOK READING AIDS	
Table of Contents	Located at the beginning of a book. Shows how the book is organized by listing units and chapters with their page numbers. Offers a quick overview of the book.
Preface or Introduction	Located at the beginning of a book before or after the table of contents. States the author's purpose in writing the book and may give suggestions for using the book.
Index	Located at the back of a book. Lists alphabetically all topics covered in the book and the pages on which they can be found. Makes it possible to locate any information quickly.
Glossary	Located at the back of a book. Gives an alphabetical list of all the specialized words and terms used in the book and defines them clearly. Can be used at any time for quick definitions.

Appendix	Located at the back of a book. Includes such things as charts, lists, documents, or other material related to the subject of the book. Acts as an immediate reference source.
Bibliography	Located at the back of a book. Includes lists of books and articles that the author has used or referred to in writing the book. Many of the entries may be useful in follow-up study or for research projects.

Study Aids. You can also use the organization of a textbook to help you as you study particular assignments. One very useful method for using your text's organization as you study is the SQ4R method. The initials stand for the following six steps: *S*urvey, *Q*uestion, *R*ead, *R*ecord, *R*ecite, and *R*eview.

The chart below explains how to use the SQ4R method.

USING THE SQ4R METHOD	
Survey	Preview the material you are going to read. Notice these features: chapter title, headings, subheadings, introduction, summary, and questions or exercises.
Question	Turn each heading into a question to help you think about what will be covered under that heading. Ask who, what, when, where, and why about it.
Read	Search for the answers to the questions that have been posed in the step above.
Recite	Orally or mentally recall the questions and their related answers.
Record	Take notes to further reinforce information. List the main ideas and the major details.
Review	Review the material on a regular basis, using some or all of the steps above.

EXERCISE A: Examining a Textbook. Choose one of your textbooks and use it to answer the following questions.

1. According to the table of contents, how many units does the text have? In what way are the units organized (by theme, chronologically, or by some other method)?
2. If there is a preface, does it explain the author's purpose in writing the book? If so, what is the purpose? Does it give any suggestions for using the book? If so, what are they?
3. What are two specific terms found in the index?
4. If there is a glossary, what are the definitions of the two terms you found in the index?
5. If there is an appendix, what kind of information does it contain?

EXERCISE B: Using the SQ4R Method. Use the SQ4R method to study an assigned chapter or section of a textbook. Then write a brief review of the ways in which using SQ4R helped.

Varying Your Reading Style

You should vary your reading style according to the material you are studying. For example, if your purpose is to review a particular chapter in your history textbook for important dates, you can afford to skim over portions of the chapter that don't relate to dates. On the other hand, if you are reading and being tested on a particular textbook chapter, there is nothing that you can afford to eliminate.

Change your reading style whenever your purpose in reading changes.

In order to adjust your reading style, you must know how to use each of the following three reading styles: *phrase reading* to understand groups of words, *skimming* to get an overview, and *scanning* to locate specific information. Each of these styles is used for a different purpose. Each follows a different eye pattern. And each requires a different reading rate and comprehension level. These variables are explained in the chart on the following page.

TYPES OF READING STYLES			
Style	**Definition**	**Use**	**Comprehension**
Phrase Reading	Reading groups of words in order to understand all the material	For studying, solving problems, and following directions	Lowest acceptable rate: 70–80%
Skimming	Skipping words in order to read rapidly and get a quick overview	For previewing, reviewing, and locating information	Lowest acceptable rate: 40–50%
Scanning	Reading in order to locate a particular piece of information	For research, reviewing, and finding information	Lowest acceptable rate: 100% (for item found)

Once you learn how to use the various reading styles, you can readily put them to use. For example, your phrase reading skills can be used for memorization, lab work, study, poetry reading, and editing. Skimming can be used for book selection, most newspaper reading, previewing, parts of pleasure reading, and gathering research information. Scanning can be used for reading phone books, indexes, worksheets, matching tests, and charts and graphs.

You should also learn how to change styles rapidly and efficiently. You will need to be able to go with ease from careful phrase reading to skimming and scanning and back, depending on your changing purpose in reading.

EXERCISE C: Varying Your Reading Style. Read the following passage, first by skimming and then by phrase reading. After skimming it for highlights, sum up your findings. After reading it carefully, correct your first findings, if necessary, and add to them.

The largest and most beneficial plant family on earth is undoubtedly the grass family. In one way or another most of our foodstuff originates with grass. We not only eat the seeds from cereal grasses such as rice, corn, and wheat, but the animals from which we get our meat are nourished with these same grasses and grass seeds. Because the grass family is so widespread, at least one member of it grows in every sort of climate. To date more than four thousand different varieties of grass have been classified. This includes the bamboo, which grows as tall as a ten-story building, and the sugarcane, which grows taller than a man.

Reading Critically

The first step in reading is to read for comprehension so that you understand main ideas and major details. The second step is to read critically. After you have grasped the author's main ideas and major details, you must ask yourself questions to analyze the author's ideas. When you have the answers to these questions, you can begin to evaluate how well the author's purpose is accomplished.

Read critically in order to question, analyze, and evaluate what you read.

To read critically, you must read with an open mind and not assume that you know what an author is going to say before you have read the material. You use critical-thinking skills to think logically about the material. A full discussion of critical-thinking skills appears in Chapter 32. The following chart lists the skills you need to be a critical reader.

CRITICAL-READING SKILLS
1. The ability to distinguish between fact and opinion
2. The ability to identify the author's purpose
3. The ability to make inferences
4. The ability to recognize the author's tone
5. The ability to recognize persuasive techniques

Fact and Opinion. In order to determine how reliable your reading material is, you must be able to distinguish between statements of fact and statements of opinion. Otherwise, you may be misled by what you read. A statement of fact is one that can be verified, or proved true, by experimentation, records, or personal observation. A statement of opinion is one that cannot be proved true. It must be validated, or supported, with valid authority or facts before it can be accepted. The following chart lists examples of fact and opinion statements and sources that might be used to verify or validate them.

FACT AND OPINION STATEMENTS	
Fact Statements	**Sources to Verify**
The UN Security Council has five permanent members. (True)	Encyclopedia, almanac, social studies textbook
Water freezes at 10°C. (False)	Experimentation, encyclopedia, science textbook
Romeo and Juliet was written by William Shakespeare. (True)	Library, biographical dictionary
Opinion Statements	**Sources to Validate**
Boxing is a dangerous sport that should be outlawed. (Invalid)	Not supported by any fact or authority
Because many doctors say that repeated blows to the head cause permanent damage to brain tissue, boxers should wear helmets. (Valid)	Supported by testimony of medical authorities

Author's Purpose. To read critically, you must also determine why the material was written. Is the author trying to inform you, persuade you, or simply entertain you? The following chart lists some purposes and clues to identify them.

IDENTIFYING AUTHOR'S PURPOSE IN WRITING	
Purpose	**Informational Clues**
To inform	Series of factual statements that are verified by experimentation, records, or personal observation
To instruct	Sequential development of an idea or process

To offer an opinion	Discussion of an issue with a point of view supported by valid authority
To sell	Persuasive techniques including facts and propaganda designed to sell an idea or product
To entertain	Narration of an event, sometimes in a humorous manner; often used to lighten a serious topic.

Inference. To identify the main idea and the author's purpose, you may have to make inferences about the material. An inference is a logical conclusion drawn from information that is already known. A valid inference is a conclusion that is justified, based on the information that is given. An invalid inference is one that is not justified by the information given.

INVALID INFERENCE: Smoking doesn't cause cancer; my grandfather, a heavy smoker, lived to be ninety-three.

VALID INFERENCE: There are storm clouds in the sky, so it will probably rain soon.

The first statement is an invalid inference because it is not logical to base such a broad generalization on one example. The second inference, however, is valid.

Tone. To read truly critically, you must be sensitive to the tone of the material. Tone shows the author's attitude toward the topic. It can be expressed through the use of words with *connotative,* or implied, meanings that differ from the *denotative,* or literal, meanings. An author chooses words according to his or her attitude toward the topic and how the author expects the reader to respond to the material.

The following statements might have been written by different authors with different attitudes toward their topic.

NEUTRAL TONE: The House of Representatives is considering a new tax proposal.

NEGATIVE TONE: The House of Representatives is frittering away its time on discussion of a hopelessly impractical tax bill.

In the first statement, most of the words are used in their denotative meanings. In the second, words with connotative meanings have deliberately been chosen to give an unfavorable impression of the event.

Persuasive Techniques. Because word connotations can be so emotionally loaded, you must be aware of persuasive techniques that may be used to color the presentation of facts. In addition to manipulating connotations, authors sometimes use *jargon* and *slanting* to influence the reader's attitude toward a subject.

Jargon is the specialized vocabulary used by people in a particular field. In its place, it is useful, but jargon is often misused to impress the reader or to conceal meaning. Then the purpose of jargon is not to inform but to obscure.

JARGON: The village was subjected to pacification.

DIRECT LANGUAGE: The villagers were killed.

Slanting is the writing of a passage so that it leans toward one point of view. Choosing words with either positive or negative connotations is one type of slanting. Another type of slanting is presenting only one side of an issue by leaving out important facts that would support a different point of view.

SLANTED STATEMENT: Management offered the union a salary increase of only seven percent.

MORE BALANCED STATEMENT: Management offered a seven-percent salary increase plus an expanded benefits package including profit sharing.

EXERCISE D: Applying Critical-Reading Skills. Read the following passage and analyze it for statements of fact and opinion, author's purpose, tone, and persuasive techniques. Use the skills you have studied in this section to develop your analysis.

Nowadays it is impossible to drive down any street for more than a few minutes without passing at least one jogger, clad in colorful shorts and expensive running shoes, and usually panting or even gasping for air. The death from a heart attack of Jim Fixx, a fellow slave to the exercise mania, seems not to have deterred these fanatical amateur athletes. Millions of dollars are spent each year in fashionable exercise salons run by sharp entrepreneurs. If you could manage to stop one of the victims long enough to ask why he is putting himself through such torture, he would probably mumble something about the heart being a muscle that needs exercise. There is no medical evidence for this. It is true that exercise is a good thing, but overexercising is too much of a good thing. In fact, victims of the physical fitness craze may actually be harming themselves. Doctors report seeing many more injuries to joints, muscles, and tendons. And, of course, there is always the risk of a heart attack during violent exercise.

DEVELOPING WRITING SKILLS: Evaluating Your Reading Skills. After a week of practice, write a paragraph about your reading skills. Include answers to these questions.

1. Which of the basic textbook reading aids do you find the most helpful and why?
2. Which steps of the SQ4R method have you found most helpful?
3. How long does it now take you to preview a chapter from your science or social studies textbook?
4. Which reading styles have you used and in which situations have you used each?
5. What materials have you read recently where critical reading was necessary? What critical–reading questions did you ask yourself to help you analyze the material?

33.2 Test-Taking Skills

Doing well on tests involves more than studying assigned material and the notes you have taken. You also need to develop a general strategy for taking tests and you need to know how to take different kinds of tests. The following section will help you develop a general strategy for taking objective tests. (Essay exams are covered in Chapter 28). It will also give you a chance to practice with different kinds of objective test questions found in classroom tests and in standardized tests.

Objective tests usually call for short answers to questions about specific, factual information. Having an overall strategy for taking objective tests can help you more effectively recall the information that you have studied for the test. First you must preview the test, then you must answer the questions, and finally you must proofread your answers to make sure you have not made any careless mistakes. Allow enough time for each of these steps in the test period.

Budget your time among previewing the test, answering the questions, and proofreading.

Arrive at the test on time and come prepared with all the necessary materials, such as pens, pencils, erasers, a watch, and any books you have been told to bring. When the test has been handed out and you have been told to begin, you are ready to follow the steps listed in the chart below.

OBJECTIVE TEST-TAKING STRATEGIES	
Preview the Test	1. Write your name on each sheet of paper you will hand in. 2. Skim through the test and figure out how much time you can give to each set of questions. Questions worth more points or that are more difficult require more time.
Answer the Questions	1. If you are allowed to use scratch paper, jot down information you want to remember. 2. Unless you are penalized for guessing, answer all questions on the test. 3. Answer the easy questions first. *Lightly* mark any questions you have difficulty with and come back to them later. 4. Unless specifically directed, give only one answer to each question. Choose the *best* answer of those given. 5. Go with your first response to a question unless you have a good reason to change it.
Proofread Your Answers	1. Check to see that you have followed the directions completely. 2. Reread questions and answers. Make sure that you have answered all the questions.

EXERCISE A: Answering Objective Questions. Write one word to fill each blank.

1. Read each question _______ before answering it.
2. Complete the questions you know best _______.
3. When you insert an answer of any type, _______ it to see if it sounds correct.
4. Set yourself specific _______ limits for each section of the test.
5. Answer _______ test questions, unless incorrect answers are to be counted against you.
6. Most objective test questions will have only _______ correct answer.
7. At the end of a test, you should _______ your answers.
8. If you are undecided about a particular answer, go with your _______ response.
9. When you are having trouble deciding on an answer, _____ answers that can't be correct and concentrate on the remaining answers.
10. _______ difficult questions that you want to return to. You don't want to forget to do these questions.

Mastering Different Kinds of Objective Questions

Besides knowing how to use general strategies for taking objective tests, you also need to know specific strategies to use for different kinds of questions.

Learn specific strategies for handling objective questions to achieve higher test scores.

Predicting Questions. As soon as you are told about an upcoming test that contains objective questions, ask your teacher what *kinds* of questions will be on the test. The main kinds of objective questions are *multiple-choice, matching, true/false,* and *fill-in* questions. Once you know the kinds of questions to expect, you should review your notes and textbook by turning the material into the kinds of questions the test will contain. With continued practice you can learn to predict 60 to 70 percent of the information you will need to know.

Following are suggested strategies to use with different kinds of questions when you are studying for a test and when you are taking the test.

Multiple-Choice Questions. The most commonly used format for testing vocabulary, as well as general comprehension, is the multiple-choice test. It usually provides three to five possible answers to a question. In most cases only two of these answers will come close to being the correct answer. The chart below provides hints for answering multiple-choice questions.

ANSWERING MULTIPLE-CHOICE QUESTIONS
1. Read the question and try to answer it *before* you look at possible answers.
2. Give yourself a reason for not selecting an answer: not logical, too specific, too general, too obvious, and so on.
3. Even if you think a certain answer is correct, read all of the other choices.
4. Turn the question into a statement and insert your answer to see if it makes sense.

EXAMPLE: In the following sentence, circle the letter of the underlined word that is incorrectly used.

1. Tom and <u>me</u> <u>are</u> going to see the movie with <u>her</u>.
   a. me b. are c. her

Answer: a.

Matching Questions. Matching questions require that you connect items in one column with items in a second column. The two columns may or may not have an equal number of items. The chart below offers hints for answering matching questions.

ANSWERING MATCHING QUESTIONS
1. Determine immediately if there are an equal number of items in each column and whether the items in the second column may be used more than once.
2. Read all the items in both columns before you try to match.
3. Match easy items first. *Lightly* cross out each used answer.

EXAMPLE: Match the words on the left with the definitions on the right by writing the letter of the definition in the blank before the word.

_____ 1. erosion	a. limestone rock structure built by living organisms
_____ 2. glacier	b. large body of moving ice and snow
_____ 3. iceberg	c. removal of rock and oil on the earth's surface
_____ 4. windbreak	d. barrier that causes wind speed to decrease
_____ 5. coral reef	e. ridge deposited by a glacier
	f. large chunk of glacial ice that breaks off and drifts into the sea

Answers: 1. c; 2. b; 3. f; 4. d; 5. a

True/False Questions. True/false questions can be difficult to answer because just one word can change a true statement into a false one. The chart below lists rules to follow when answering true/false questions.

ANSWERING TRUE/FALSE QUESTIONS

1. Make certain the *entire* statement is true. A partially true statement is marked false.
2. Look out for absolute words such as *all, always, never, no, none,* and *only.* They can make a statement false.
3. Look out for qualifying words such as *generally, little, most, much, often, some, sometimes,* and *usually.* They can make a statement true.

EXAMPLE: Identify the following statements as true or false by writing *T* or *F* in the blank before each statement.

_____ 1. Teachers often give clues about what will be on a test.
_____ 2. The best way to study for a test is to cram.
_____ 3. Always answer the hardest test questions first.
_____ 4. Most objective test questions have only one correct answer.

Answers: 1. T; 2. F; 3. F; 4. T

Fill-in Questions. Fill-in questions, or short-answer questions, give you more freedom. There is usually more than one way to word a particular answer. However, in this type of test, there are no answers to choose from, just recall of the information. The chart below provides suggestions for answering fill-in questions.

ANSWERING FILL-IN QUESTIONS
1. Use specific information rather than general statements.
2. Make sure that the filled-in words answer the question.

EXAMPLE: List two ways in which good roads were important to western settlers.

a. ______________________

b. ______________________

Answers: a. to send their farm products to the East
b. to bring manufactured goods to the West

EXERCISE B: Predicting Test Questions. Find the date of the next major objective test that you will take. Turn assigned material into the kinds of questions you may get on the test. After you have taken the classroom test, identify how many test questions you were able to predict correctly.

Taking Standardized Tests

A standardized test is a multiple choice objective test given to a large group of people. Its purpose is to give schools or possible employers information about how a person ranks in comparison with other people taking the same test.

Standardized tests differ from classroom tests in two major ways. First, you cannot study specific information to prepare for them. Second, there is no passing or failing grade.

Among the best ways to prepare for standardized tests are to complete all your class assignments carefully and to read as much and widely as you can. The skills you have been developing in reading, writing, listening, and studying are also valuable preparation for taking standardized tests.

Prepare for standardized tests by studying consistently and reading widely.

In October of your junior year in high school you may take a standardized test that will guide you as you start thinking about what college you might attend. The test is called the Preliminary Scholastic Aptitude Test, or PSAT. The verbal section of the PSAT contains four types of questions discussed below. Learning about the kinds of questions and the strategies for answering them can be helpful.

Scoring. On the verbal section of the PSAT, every correct answer is worth one point. An answer left blank receives no point. Each incorrect answer loses one fourth of a point. The penalty for incorrect answers is designed to discourage you from guessing randomly. Make only educated guesses.

Antonym Questions. An antonym is a word with a meaning opposite to that of a given word. Antonym questions test your knowledge of word meanings. You are asked to choose a word or phrase that is most opposite in meaning to that of a given word. The chart below gives suggested strategies to use when you answer antonym questions.

ANSWERING ANTONYM QUESTIONS

1. If you know the meaning of the given word, think of a word that is opposite in meaning *before* you look at the choices.
2. Look for a word among the answer choices that is as opposite as possible and matches the word you have in mind.
3. Look for a word that is the same part of speech as the given word.
4. Give a different antonym for each possible choice if you are having difficulty eliminating choices.

EXAMPLE: Select the word that is most opposite each capitalized word.

1. FORMAL: (A) shapeless (B) spoken (C) elective (D) casual (E) seamless

Answer: (D) casual

Analogy Questions. A verbal analogy is an expression of a relation between two words. Analogy questions test your ability to see the relationship between two given words and to find two other words that are related in the same way. The chart below lists strategies to use with analogy questions.

ANSWERING ANALOGY QUESTIONS

1. Define both words in the initial pair. If you cannot define both words, skip the question and go on to the next one.
2. Define how the initial pair of words are related to each other. See the chart below and on the following page for a description of analogy patterns.
3. Make certain that you keep each pair of words in the order given. If you reverse the order you will come up with an incorrect answer.
4. Make certain that the relationship of the parts of speech are the same for the pair you choose as they are in the initial pair.

EXAMPLE: Choose the pair of words whose relationship is most similar to that expressed by the capitalized pair.

1. LETTER : WORD : :
   (A) club : people (B) homework : school
   (C) page : book (D) product : factory
   (E) picture : crayon

Answer: (C) page : book

Identifying the relationship between the given pair of words is the most important part of solving analogy problems. There are many different types of relationships, but the most common ones are summarized in the following chart. The first one can be translated to read *in is to entrance as out is to exit.*

COMMON ANALOGY PATTERNS

Relationship	Examples
Synonyms	in : entrance : : out : exit
Antonyms	in : out : : entrance : exit

Similar categories	oak : maple : rose : tulip
Main and subcategories	tree : oak : : flower : rose
Sub- and main categories	oak : tree : : rose : flower
Whole to part	fork : tine : : belt : buckle
Part to whole	tine : fork : : buckle : belt
Product and substance	omelet : eggs : : pottery : clay
Vocations or jobs	coal : miner : : crop : farmer

Sentence Completion Questions. Sentence completion questions test your vocabulary and your reading comprehension. One or more words in a statement are left blank and you are asked to fill in the word or words that best completes the statement. The chart below provides strategies you can use for sentence completion questions.

ANSWERING SENTENCE COMPLETION QUESTIONS

1. Read the sentence and try to fill in the blank(s) before you look at the choices.
2. Make use of signal words such as *however, also, because, as a result, instead, before* to predict the correct answer.
3. Make certain that each word or pair of words you choose follows the part of speech required in the statement.
4. Watch for "a" or "an" before a blank to give you a clue whether or not to look for a word beginning with a vowel.
5. Read all possible answers in the sentence blank(s) to see if they make sense.

EXAMPLE: Choose the word or pair of words that best completes the meaning of each sentence.

1. He ______ apart, for he prefers ______ to the company of others.

(A) lives—books
(B) dwells—solitude
(C) stays—throngs
(D) remains—hibernation
(E) falls—animals

Answer: (B) dwells—solitude

Reading Comprehension Questions. Reading comprehension questions test your ability to interpret the meaning of a passage and the intent of the author. The chart lists the suggested strategies to use when answering these questions.

ANSWERING READING COMPREHENSION QUESTIONS
1. Preview the questions before reading the passage. Do not read answer choices.
2. Skim the passage to get a general idea of the main idea and the author's purpose in writing.
3. Read the passage carefully keeping in mind the questions you have read. As soon as you believe you have found an answer, stop reading, go to the question, and answer it.
4. Read and answer one question at a time. Scan to check your answers or to find information needed to answer a question.

EXERCISE C: Taking Standardized Vocabulary Tests. Given below are sample questions from the three kinds of vocabulary tests. Circle the letter of the correct answer for each.

ANTONYM QUESTIONS

1. MAVERICK: (A) follower (B) dissenter (C) atheist (D) albino (E) wizard
2. BELLICOSE: (A) murky (B) skeletal (C) vegetarian (D) warlike (E) peaceful
3. MELLIFLUOUS: (A) sweetness (B) harmonious (C) sad (D) reticent (E) unpleasant

ANALOGY QUESTIONS

4. STOVE : KITCHEN : :
   (A) cone : circle (B) sink : bathroom (C) trunk : attic
   (D) television : livingroom (E) pot : pan
5. TRIANGLE : PYRAMID : :
   (A) cone : circle (B) corner : angle (C) square : box
   (D) tube : cylinder (E) pentagon : cube
6. WAVE : CREST : :
   (A) sea : ocean (B) mountain : peak (C) pinnacle : nadir
   (C) breaker : swimming (D) island : archipelago

7. BOXER : GLOVES : :

(A) swimmer : mask (B) shoes : jobber (C) fruit : peddlar (D) businessman : bills (E) bacteriologist : microscope

SENTENCE COMPLETION QUESTIONS

8. His admirers were not ______, for his essays were not widely known.
(A) respected (B) numerous (C) ardent (D) interested (E) educated

9. Great ideas have ______ youth; they are ______.
(A) no—petrified (B) eternal—immortal (C) constant—ephemeral (D) little—frivolous (E) exaggerated—wasted

10. Safe driving prevents ______ and the endless ______ of knowing you have caused others pain.
(A) recklessness—dream (B) disease—reminder (C) tragedy—remorse (D) accidents—hope (E) lawsuits—expense

EXERCISE D: Taking Reading Comprehension Tests. Read the following passage. On the basis of what is stated or implied in the passage, select the option that best completes each statement or answers each question.

Cultures have not always been dependent upon geography for their form of existence. This is evident when you look at such cultures as those of Athens and Sparta. Athens and Sparta were both city states in the same peninsula. They were exposed to the same geographic conditions; however, their cultures had little in common. Sparta was a very regimented state. It stressed the military, a highly disciplined life, and slavery. Athens, on the other hand, was a much more forward-looking and adaptable city state. It was more interested in the arts, a democratic form of government, and trade and commerce. Although Athens also conquered many smaller communities, it absorbed the inhabitants and made them citizens. It welcomed change and improvement and had a positive outlook on life. In the history of the world, there are many other instances where cultures with similar geographic conditions differ radically in respect to their politics, values, and way of life.

1. The basic idea which the passage develops is that
   (A) Sparta was not a civilized state
   (B) Athens and Sparta shared little except location
   (C) geography does not determine a culture's development
   (D) Athens and Sparta were highly civilized cultures
   (E) Athens' government was the model for modern democracy
2. According to the passage, Sparta was mostly concerned with
   (A) the arts
   (B) the military
   (C) democratic form of government
   (D) broadening their business ventures
   (E) health and physical fitness
3. The author implies that
   (A) life was more pleasant in Athens than in Sparta
   (B) Sparta was a larger city than Athens
   (C) Sparta would probably overcome Athens
   (D) democracy would eventually come to Sparta
   (E) Athens would become as militaristic as Sparta
4. The best title for the passage would be
   (A) Cultures in Ancient Greece
   (B) Greek City States
   (C) Geographic Impact on the Development of Cultures
   (D) Ancient Cultures and How They Developed
   (E) Cultural Life in Athens and Greece
5. The word "culture" in this passage means
   (A) art and music
   (B) the everyday conduct of the residents
   (C) habits formed by individuals
   (D) development of farming methods
   (E) traits for which a society is known

DEVELOPING WRITING SKILLS: Evaluating Your Test-Taking Skills. Write a paragraph about your test-taking skills including the answers to the following questions.

1. What kinds of objective test questions have you mastered?
2. How successful have you been at predicting test questions?
3. Which general test-taking strategies need improvement?
4. Which specific test-taking strategies need improvement?
5. What are your short-term goals for improving those skills?

Skills Review and Writing Workshop

Reading and Test-Taking Skills

CHECKING YOUR SKILLS

Read the following paragraph, first by skimming and then by phrase reading. Write a summary in two sentences.

The woodchuck, or groundhog is a small mammal about two feet long that belongs to the squirrel family. It lives in the northeastern and midwestern United States, and in Canada. It lives in burrows located beneath the ground. The burrow is connected to the surface by a series of tunnels leading to a main entrance. The woodchuck also digs secret entrances hidden by underbrush. If a predator, such as a fox, is blocking the main entrance, the woodchuck can still reach the safety of its burrow through a secret entrance. After hibernating most of the winter, the woodchuck leaves its burrow a few weeks before spring. This event is celebrated each year on Groundhog Day, February 2. According to legend, if the groundhog, or woodchuck, sees its shadow, winter weather will continue for another six weeks.

USING STUDY SKILLS IN WRITING:
Writing Test Questions in History

The ability to achieve superior grades on tests is essential to your success in school. How well you do depends, in part, on developing effective methods of test preparation. To prepare for an objective test in history, try to predict the questions by following these steps.

Prewriting: Review your history notes and pick out the main ideas and important details.

Writing: Turn each main idea and detail into a question. Develop multiple choice, matching, true/false, and fill-in questions. Then try to answer each question.

Revising: Make sure your questions cover all the information in your notes and develop other questions if necessary. After you have revised your questions, proofread carefully.

Chapter 34

Library and Reference Skills

Modern libraries contain many different kinds of material, from books and periodicals to microfilms and tape recordings. You may wonder how, in this mass of information, you will be able to find the specific information that you need. Libraries organize material carefully so that you can find what you need easily. In this chapter you will learn to locate and use the basic resources and reference materials of the library. You will also practice using one of the most valuable reference tools, the dictionary.

Using the Library 34.1

Whether you use the library to find a specific book or to research a topic, you need to know how to use the card catalog and how to interpret location symbols on the cards to proceed from the catalog to the shelves. Before you begin to research a topic, you need to plan ahead to get a general idea of what you want to accomplish in the library. Knowing what information you should take with you will help you use your time well.

Knowing What You Are Looking For

As part of your planning for a topic that you will research, you should gather a list of names and terms related to your topic. You should also try to determine the limits of your topic, especially in terms of time.

Begin your research by knowing basic facts about your topic.

The following suggestions should be useful in carrying out this planning stage.

Checking Your Spelling. Since the card catalogs and indexes in a library are arranged alphabetically, you must be absolutely sure of the spelling of the words that describe your topic. Incorrect spelling can defeat you before you start. For example, if you want to find informatin about the English writer Virginia Woolf, looking under *Wolf* or *Wolfe* would turn up nothing or entirely wrong information.

Considering Alternative Names and Terms. Some topics may not be listed under the name you expect. If, for example, you are looking for information about ancient Iran, you may need to look under *Persia* as well. In the course of history, this geographic area has been known by both names. Similarly, if you want information about oil, you will probably have to look under *petroleum* as well. In considering alternative names, you should also try to relate small topics to the larger fields of which they are a part. For example, if you cannot find the specific topic *gems* in a catalog or index, you might try looking under the larger, more inclusive term *minerals.*

Limiting Your Topic to a Period of Time. When information in a reference book is arranged chronologically—that is, by date—knowing the appropriate dates of your topic will help you find the proper section or volume. In addition, assigning dates to your topic will often limit the number of sources you will need to consult. Suppose, for instance, you were assigned a short oral report on the major English poets of the Romantic Period. Knowing the dates of this period (roughly 1750 to 1840) would help you limit the number of poets you research. You would not include Alexander Pope (who died in 1744) or Tennyson (who became famous in 1842).

Most of the information you need for planning will be found in your textbooks or can be learned from class discussion. The time spent in defining and limiting your topic will be saved many times over during your search for information.

EXERCISE A: Gathering Information Before You Visit the Library. Choose a topic for a research paper. Write the information you need to know in order to find the best sources by answering the following questions.

1. What is the name of your topic?
2. What alternative names, if any, are there for this topic?
3. Of what larger field is it a part?
4. Are your responses to the first three questions spelled correctly?
5. Within what span of years does your topic fall?

Using the Card Catalog

A card catalog is to a library what an index is to a book—a means of locating information quickly. The cards are filed within the card catalog according to commonly accepted standards.

Use the card catalog to find information about a library's books and other materials.

Kinds of Cards. A card catalog contains three principal kinds of cards: *title cards, author cards,* and *subject cards.* These cards and other more specialized cards will contain all the information you need to locate the materials you want.

The card below is an example of a *title card.* If you know the title of a particular book—suppose it is *A Cornish Childhood*—you would look it up in the catalog under the first main letter, *C.* (The words *a, an,* and *the* at the beginning of a title are dropped in alphabetizing.) Notice the information a title card includes.

TITLE CARD:

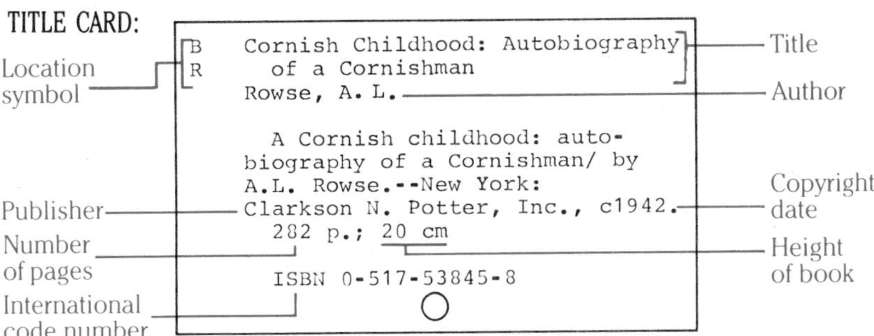

The *author card* for *A Cornish Childhood* might look like the one below. Suppose instead you cannot recall the title but remember the author's name—A. L. Rowse. Looking up the author's name (last name first) would yield several author cards for this person. Under the author's name on each card would be the title of a book written or edited by him—one title per card and all arranged alphabetically by title. Notice that the information about the book is the same as that found on the title card.

AUTHOR CARD:

B Rowse, A.L.
R A Cornish childhood: autobiography of a Cornishman/ by A.L. Rowse.--New York: Clarkson N. Potter, Inc., c1942.
282 p.; 20 cm

ISBN 0-517-53845-8

The third principal kind of card, a *subject card,* is useful when you have a topic in mind but do not know any specific titles or authors. Suppose you need information for a biology report. Looking up *Biology* in the card catalog would yield cards similar to the one below. Notice the subject is given in capital letters at the top of the card. Listed at the bottom of the card is an additional card found in the catalog: a title card.

SUBJECT CARD:

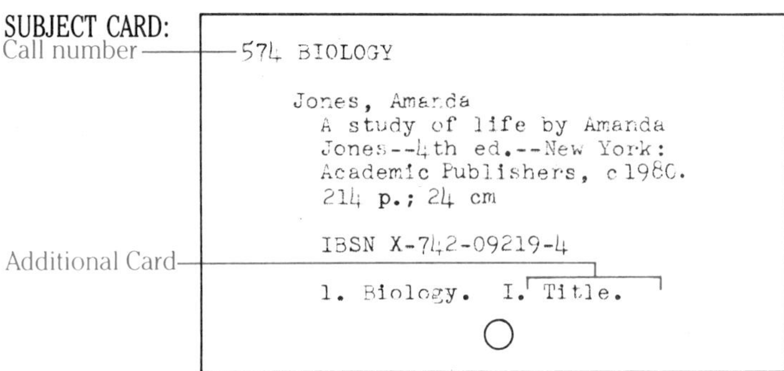

574 BIOLOGY

Jones, Amanda
A study of life by Amanda Jones--4th ed.--New York: Academic Publishers, c1980.
214 p.; 24 cm

IBSN X-742-09219-4

1. Biology. I. Title.

Besides the principal kinds of catalog cards, you should know two other kinds: *analytic cards* and *cross-reference cards.*

Analytic cards indicate *parts* of books. When using an analytic card, you must distinguish the "part" author and title from the "book" author and title. Suppose you are looking for the play *Saint Joan* by George Bernard Shaw and find the card below. It tells you that the play can be found on pages 346–391 of *Modern English Drama* by Harry Smith. First, find the book by Smith on the shelf and then the play by Shaw in the book.

ANALYTIC CARD:

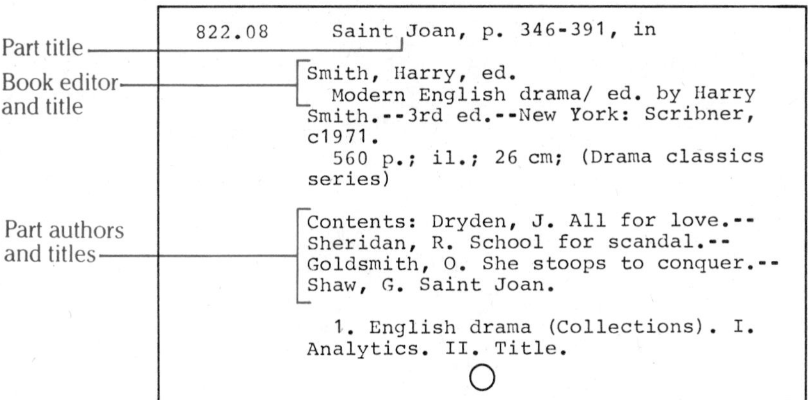

Cross-reference cards are provided when there is a chance that you will look up a term different from the one the cataloger chose to use. The cards will be marked *see* or *see also.*

A *see* card means that no information is listed under the term you have chosen. Instead, the card will direct you to another place in the catalog where the information can be found. A *see also* card will suggest additional subjects to look under.

CROSS-REFERENCE CARDS:

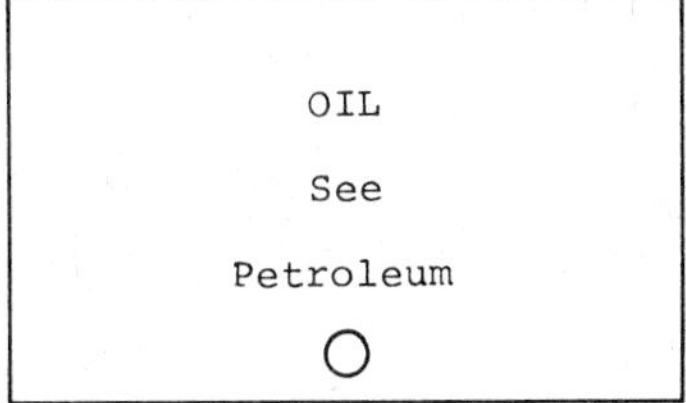

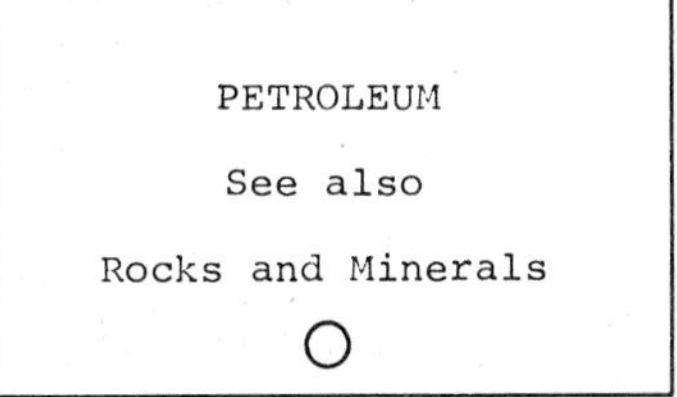

Arrangement of Cards. There are two types of card catalogs: the *dictionary* type and the *divided* type. If a library uses the dictionary type of catalog, author, title, and subject cards are filed together. If a library uses the divided type, there are separate sections for subjects and for authors and/or titles.

In either type, the cards will be alphabetized word by word, not letter by letter. In letter-by-letter alphabetizing, used in dictionaries, the order of the entries is determined by the order of the letters regardless of the number of words. In word-by-word alphabetizing, used in the card catalog, the order of the entries is determined by the order of the letters in the first word and then by the order of letters in the next word. The chart below shows the two methods of alphabetizing.

TWO METHODS OF ALPHABETIZING

Library's Method: By Word	Other Method: By Letter
To be young	To be young
To kill a mockingbird	Today in New York
Today in New York	Togetherness poems
Togetherness poems	To kill a mockingbird

In addition to knowing that the card catalog is alphabetized word by word, you need to know a few additional rules.

CARD CATALOG FILING RULES

1. Ignore *a, an,* and *the* when they are the first words of a title. *The Red Pony* is filed alphabetically under *P* for *Pony,* not *T* for *The.*
2. Treat *Mc,*and *M'* as if they were spelled *Mac* and alphabetize accordingly. The following are in correct order: *MacHenry, machine, McIntyre, M'Leod,* and *Macmillan.*
3. Treat abbreviations and numbers as if they were spelled out. *Dr.* is filed as if it were *Doctor* and *Mrs.* as if it were *Mistress; 50 Stories* would come before *Five Plays.*
4. Books *by* an author are filed before books *about* an author. *The Red Pony* by John Steinbeck comes before a biography of John Steinbeck.
5. When using subject cards, look for subdivisions of a subject before other longer terms beginning with the subject name. U.S.—FOREIGN RELATIONS is filed before U.S. ARMY.

EXERCISE B: Interpreting Information on a Catalog Card. Use the following subject card to answer the questions below.

```
398     BEES--POETRY

        Busch, Wilhelm, 1832-1908.
          The bees: a fairy tale/ by Wilhelm
        Busch: translated by Rudolph Wiemann.
        --1st ed.-- New York: Vantage Press,
        c1974.
          72 p.; il.; 21 cm

          Translation of Schnurrdiburr.

          ISBN 0-533-01215-5

          1. Bees--Poetry. 2. Stories in
        rhyme. I. Wiemann, Rudolph. II. Title.

                        O
```

1. What is the location symbol?
2. Who is the author of the book?
3. When was the author born?
4. What is the title of the book?
5. Who translated the book?
6. Where was the book published?
7. When was the book published?
8. How many pages are there in the book?
9. What was the German title of the book?
10. Under what other subjects is the book filed?

EXERCISE C: Identifying Catalog Cards. Using the information below, make an author card, a title card, and a subject card. Refer to sample cards in this section to help you place information correctly on each card.

Elizabeth Regina: The Age of Triumph, 1588–1603, by Alison Plowden. The author was born in 1947. The book was published by Times Books in New York, in 1980. It contains 214 pages, is illustrated, and has a height of 20 cm. The call number is 942.05 and the international code number is 0-686-65925-2. The book is filed under GREAT BRITAIN—HISTORY—ELIZABETH, 1558–1603.

EXERCISE D: Alphabetizing Catalog Cards. The following items are alphabetized letter by letter, as they would appear in a dictionary. Alphabetize them word by word, as they would appear in a card catalog.

1. New Amsterdam
2. Newark
3. New Deal
4. Newfoundland
5. New France
6. New Orleans
7. Newport
8. New South Wales
9. Newton
10. New York

EXERCISE E: Using Catalog Filing Rules. List each pair of catalog cards in the correct order. Four are already correct.

1. *Dr. Faustus*
   Doctors at Work
2. NEWPORT (RHODE ISLAND)
   NEW ENGLAND FOLKLORE
3. *Tales of Edgar Allan Poe*
   Biography of Edgar Allan Poe
4. *Applesauce Recipes*
   An Old Tale
5. U.S. CONSTITUTION
   U.S.—IMMIGRATION
6. *A Stone's Throw*
   Stone, Irving
7. *Mrs. Dalloway*
   Moore, Clement
8. *Eight Plays*
   80 Days to Health
9. *The Younger Set*
   Woolf, Virginia
10. *The Machine Age*
    McGregor, Ian

Going from Catalog to Shelf

Besides the title and author, the most important piece of information on a catalog card is the *location symbol.* In order to locate an item on the shelf, you must match the symbols and numbers found on the catalog card with the symbols and numbers on the material.

Use the catalog card location symbol to locate materials on library shelves.

Libraries classify books into two main groups: *fiction* and *nonfiction.* Books of fiction are stories that are created by an author. Books of nonfiction contain factual material. Nonfiction includes two smaller groups: biographies and reference books. Fiction books are shelved in a separate area from nonfiction books.

Locating Fiction. The catalog card for a work of fiction will usually have the location symbol F or Fic. Some libraries include all or the first few letters of the author's last name below the location symbol. The book you want will be arranged alphabetically by the author's last name.

The chart shows how four fiction books would be placed on the library shelf. Notice that the individual books by an author are also in alphabetical order (with *a, an,* and *the* ignored).

FICTION ARRANGED ALPHABETICALLY			
Wharton's *The Children* F Wha	Wharton's *Ethan Frome* F Wha	Wilder's *The Cabala* F Wil	Wilder's *Our Town* F Wil

Locating Nonfiction. Most high school and public libraries arrange nonfiction books by the Dewey Decimal System of classification. The location symbol on the catalog card gives you the Dewey Decimal number. This number is called a *call number.* The Dewey Decimal System divides knowledge into ten main classes, numbered from 000 to 999. Each of the classes is divided into ten divisions, and each of the divisions is divided into ten subdivisions. When necessary, the subdivisions can be divided even further.

MAIN CLASS:	600–699	Technology
DIVISIONS:	620	Engineering
SUBDIVISIONS:	621	Applied Physics
FURTHER DIVISIONS:	621.1	Steam Engineering
	621.15	Engines
	621.16	Stationary Engines
	621.165	Turbine Engines

The numbers in the call number are generally followed by the first letter or letters of the author's last name. Thus, a group of books with the same number will be arranged alphabetically according to the authors' last names. The chart on the following page shows how three books about turbine engines—one by Jones, one by Smith, and one by Young—would be organized on the shelf.

NONFICTION ARRANGED BY CALL NUMBER				
621.1 M	621.165 J	621.165 S	621.165 Y	621.2 A

To find the book by Young on turbine engines, you would go to the part of the library where the 600's are shelved, then find the 620's, the 621's, the 621.1's, and narrow it down until you come to 621.165. Then, you would find the first letter, Y, of the author's last name. Occasionally, two books will have the same call number, including the same author letters. You must check the book title to make sure you have the right book.

NOTE ABOUT ANOTHER CLASSIFICATION SYSTEM: Some libraries, especially large libraries, use a new classification system called the Library of Congress System. This system uses the letters of the alphabet—A to Z—to designate the main classes of knowledge. A combination of two letters is used to indicate divisions. Numbers under the letters indicate subdivisions.

MAIN CLASS:	B	Philosophy
DIVISION:	BC	Logic
SUBDIVISIONS:	BC 131	Early works to 1800

Books sharing the same subdivision may also be distinguished by author letters and numbers.

Locating Biographies and Special Materials. Although they can be shelved in the library's history section (the 920's of the Dewey System), biographies of individual people are often shelved in a separate area. Marked with the location symbol B (for biography) or 92 (short for 920), biographies are arranged according to the subject of the book, not according to the author of the book.

Collective biographies, books that contain chapter-length biographies about a number of people, will usually be shelved with the library's history section. They are marked with the location symbols 920 through 929.

Reference materials are usually shelved in a separate area from the other books and almost always carry the letters R or Ref above the call number.

Non-print materials will be marked with a variety of symbols to match the special format of the item. For example, FS might be used above a call number to indicate a filmstrip. Since most non-print material will be kept separate, you should ask your librarian for help in finding and using these materials.

EXERCISE F: Locating Fiction. Arrange the following works of fiction in the order in which you would find them on the library shelves.

1. *The Light in the Forest* by Conrad Richter
2. *A Tale of Two Cities* by Charles Dickens
3. *A Member of the Wedding* by Carson McCullers
4. *Memento Mori* by Muriel Spark
5. *The Outsiders* by S. E. Hinton
6. *The Mayor of Casterbridge* by Thomas Hardy
7. *Billy Budd* by Herman Melville
8. *The Lion Tamer* by Bryan MacMahon
9. *The House of Mirth* by Edith Wharton
10. *The Sun Also Rises* by Ernest Hemingway

EXERCISE G: Locating Nonfiction. Arrange the ten call numbers below in the order in which you would find them on the library shelves.

824.1 Po	824.3 Ad	825.2 Sr	824.3 Mo	823.9 L
823.6 Kh	824.3 Be	824.3 Tu	824.2 Na	824.3 Wh

EXERCISE H: Locating Biographies. Go to the biography section of your school or public library and find five biographies of people you admire. Write the location symbol, the subject, the title, and the author for each biography.

DEVELOPING WRITING SKILLS: Using Your Library Skills. Follow the steps on the next page to prepare a list of materials on a topic of your choice. Then write a brief paragraph stating how you would like to develop these materials into a research paper.

1. Use the steps in Exercise A on page 785 to plan your research for the topic you have chosen.
2. Find ten items in the card catalog related to your topic.
3. Copy the essential information from the catalog cards: title, author, and location symbol or call number.
4. Find the materials in the library.
5. Revise your list if any materials cannot be located.

34.2 Using Reference Materials

The materials in the reference section of the library fall into three categories: general reference books, specialized reference books, and periodicals. The main purpose of reference books is to help people who are doing research. Thus, most reference materials cannot be checked out of the library.

This section will help you become familiar with reference materials. It will also show you how to use them to check facts and to find the information you need for a project or report.

General Reference Books

General reference books cover broad areas of knowledge and usually do not go into great detail. They will provide you with the basic information you need to check a fact or to begin work on a topic about which you know little or nothing.

Use general reference books to check basic facts or to explore the range of a topic.

You should start with general reference works such as encyclopedias, almanacs, and atlases to guide you as you go on to more detailed sources of information.

Encyclopedias. General encyclopedias contain articles on a wide range of subjects. Usually published in sets of twenty or more volumes, they rely on alphabetical order and indexes to help readers find information quickly.

A useful way to begin your search for information in an encyclopedia is to consult the index. There you will find out whether or not your topic has an entire article devoted to it. If it does, the index will direct you to the volume and page where it can be found. Some topics may not be considered important enough to have entire articles devoted to them. Then, the index will tell you if your topic is covered within another article or in parts of several articles.

The following entry is from the index to the *Encyclopedia Americana.* The first reference indicates a main article about Queen Victoria in volume 28, page 85. Additional information about Victoria can be found in other articles on related topics.

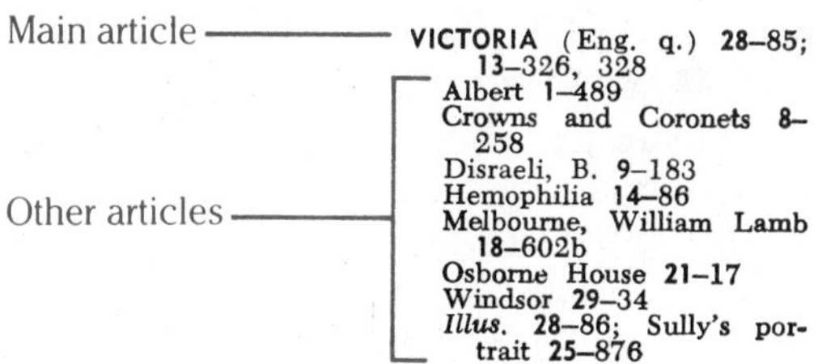

VICTORIA (Eng. q.) **28–85; 13–326, 328**
Albert **1–489**
Crowns and Coronets **8–258**
Disraeli, B. **9–183**
Hemophilia **14–86**
Melbourne, William Lamb **18–602b**
Osborne House **21–17**
Windsor **29–34**
Illus. **28–86**; Sully's portrait **25–876**

Since information about politics, economics, science, and many other subjects is constantly changing, publishers of encyclopedias continuously revise encyclopedias. They also publish yearbooks as supplements to their encyclopedias. A yearbook summarizes important events of the preceding year and describes major developments in various fields of knowledge.

The following chart lists some popular encyclopedias.

POPULAR ENCYCLOPEDIAS
Collier's Encyclopedia, in 24 volumes
Compton's Pictured Encyclopedia, in 15 volumes
Encyclopaedia Britannica, in 29 volumes
Encyclopedia Americana, in 30 volumes
Encyclopedia International, in 20 volumes
The World Book Encyclopedia, in 22 volumes.

Almanacs and Other Yearbooks. In addition to encyclopedia yearbooks, several other general reference books are published annually. Almanacs provide up-to-date statistics and other facts on such topics as government, history, geography, astronomy, economics, population, and sports. Relatively inexpensive, almanacs can be found in bookstores as well as in libraries. Among the most popular are *Hammond's Almanac,* the *Information Please Almanac,* the *Reader's Digest Almanac and Yearbook,* and *The World Almanac and Book of Facts.*

Other references that are revised yearly include *Facts on File,* a current events digest, and the *Statesman's Yearbook,* which provides basic information about international organizations and the countries of the world.

Almanacs and other yearbooks are generally arranged by topics rather than by alphabetical order. Therefore, you should use the index to locate information in these references.

Atlases and Gazetteers. Atlases and gazetteers can be very helpful when you are checking facts about geographic location. Many atlases include not only maps but also informative text. A common type of atlas is a general atlas that contains political maps, facts and charts about population distribution, seasonal temperature and rainfall, agricultural and industrial production, and natural resources. Popular general atlases are the *National Geographic Atlas of the World,* the *Rand McNally Cosmopolitan World Atlas,* the *Hammond Medallion World Atlas,* and *Goode's World Atlas*.

Other atlases are historical—that is, they show the borders of nations as they were at a particular point in history. Some historical atlases also show the movement of armies or trace the migration of different groups of people. Major historical atlases include *Shepherd's Historical Atlas,* the *Atlas of American History,* and the *Atlas of European History*

Unlike atlases, most gazetteers do not contain maps. Instead, they offer brief descriptions of places, arranged alphabetically like entries in a dictionary. In short, gazetteers are geographical dictionaries. The *Columbia-Lippincott Gazetteer* and *Webster's Geographical Dictionary* are popular gazetteers.

EXERCISE A: Selecting General Reference Books. Write *encyclopedia, almanac,* or *atlas* to identify the types of reference books you would use to find the following.

EXAMPLE: The distance between Dallas and Houston.
atlas

1. Plants that eat insects
2. Nations that border Lake Chad
3. The most populous city in the world
4. A description of The Bill of Rights

5. Three people who won the Pulitzer Prize last year
6. Major islands off the east coast of Africa
7. A description of the life of Charlotte Brontë
8. The all-time most popular television program
9. The origins of jazz
10. Three cities in Puerto Rico

EXERCISE B: Using General Reference Books. Use general reference books to find answers to the following questions. After each answer, write the name of the book you used.

EXAMPLE: What is the fourth largest city in the United States?
Philadelphia *The World Almanac*

1. In what country is South America's highest mountain?
2. What are the chief exports of Zimbabwe?
3. What holds the Milky Way together?
4. What country did Catherine the Great originally come from?
5. Who is the head of state of Canada?
6. What states border Idaho?
7. Who won the Nobel Prize for Literature in 1948?
8. What was the purpose of Hadrian's Wall?
9. How do plants and animals become fossils?
10. What was the easternmost point of the Persian Empire?

Specialized Reference Books

After you have used general reference books to learn about the broad range of a topic, your next step will often be to find more detailed information, usually on some smaller aspect of the general topic. One way to proceed is to use the card catalog to locate appropriate materials from the main collection. Another way is to use specialized reference books.

Use specialized reference books to gather detailed information about a limited aspect of a broad topic.

Specialized Dictionaries. Sometimes called glossaries, handbooks, or companions, specialized dictionaries provide brief entries describing the special terms, people, or events involved in the study of a specific topic. The entries are arranged alphabetically. Whether your topic is American slang, computer terminology, a foreign language, classical mythology, British literature, medicine, folklore, or mathematics—there is probably a specialized dictionary to suit your needs.

The information you find in these books is more detailed and informative than what you could find in a regular dictionary. For example, if you were writing a paper for English class and were unsure when to use the word *verse,* a dictionary of synonyms could explain the precise usage of the word. The entry below is from *Webster's New Dictionary of Synonyms.*

EXAMPLE: **verse 1 Verse, stanza** both mean a unit of metrical writing. **Verse** is both wider and more varied in its popular usage since it can denote a single line of such writing, such writing as a class, or, along with **stanza,** a group of lines forming a division of a poem and typically following a fixed metrical and sometimes rhythmical pattern. *Verse* may also specifically denote the part of a song preceding the refrain or chorus or a comparable part of an anthem or hymn. But in technical use and in discussion of prosody *verse* is restricted to the single line of metrical writing and *stanza* is regularly employed for the group of lines that forms a division of a poem.

Other specialized dictionaries are listed in the chart below.

SPECIALIZED DICTIONARIES
Compton's Illustrated Science Dictionary
Dictionary of Musical Terms
Mathews Dictionary of Americanisms
Webster's Geographical Dictionary
Roget's International Thesaurus

Specialized Encyclopedias. Many encyclopedias limit their coverage to one area of knowledge, such as religion, science, social science, medicine, sports, or the arts.

Some specialized encyclopedias are devoted to very limited topics. For example, *The Reader's Encyclopedia of Shakespeare* covers only William Shakespeare and information related to his works. Other well-known specialized encyclopedias you should know about are listed in the following chart.

SPECIALIZED ENCYCLOPEDIAS
Cassell's Encyclopedia of World Literature
Encyclopedia of World Art
Encyclopedia of Oceanography
Encyclopedia of Sports
International Encyclopedia of the Social Sciences
McGraw-Hill Encyclopedia of Drama
McGraw-Hill Encyclopedia of Science and Technology

Biographical Reference Books. Biographical reference books are particularly useful when no full-length biography exists about a person or when you do not have time to read an entire book. These specialized references include entries for many more persons than a general encyclopedia has room for. The coverage is also likely to be more thorough than that found in a general encyclopedia.

You will need to pay attention to the limitations each book sets on the dates, nationalities, or professions of the people they list. Pay special attention to whether the reference book covers only people still living or people already deceased.

The following chart lists some commonly used biographical reference books. The books in the left-hand column cover people still living when the volume was published. The books in the right-hand column are devoted to notable people who have died.

BIOGRAPHICAL REFERENCE BOOKS	
About Living People	**About Deceased People**
Composers Since 1900	*American Authors 1600–1900*
Congressional Directory	*The Dictionary of American Biography*
Contemporary Authors	*Dictionary of National Biography*
Current Biography	*Notable American Women*
Modern Men of Science	*Webster's Biographical Dictionary*
Who's Who in America	*Who Was Who in America*

People who are not well-known nationally or internationally can often be found in reference books devoted to a single profession. Some typical reference books emphasizing particular professions include *Contemporary Artists,* the *Biographical Dictionary of Film Directors,* and the *Biographical Encyclopedia of Science and Technology.*

Literary Reference Books. In addition to specialized dictionaries of literary terms and encyclopedias devoted to literature, a number of other useful references are available for almost every aspect of literature.

Collections of quotations and proverbs are useful if you are trying to find the source of a famous saying. Most quotation books are arranged by subject matter and contain an author index as well as a key-word or key-idea index. *Bartlett's Familiar Quotations* is different in that it is arranged chronologically by author. Standard quotations books arranged by subject include those listed in the chart below.

REFERENCE BOOKS FOR QUOTATIONS AND PROVERBS
A Dictionary of American Proverbs and Proverbial Phrases
A New Dictionary of Quotations
Dictionary of Thoughts
Hoyt's New Cyclopedia of Practical Quotations
Racial Proverbs
Stevenson's Home Book of Quotations
What They Said in 19--

Indexes to literature can help you locate works by theme or setting. They are particularly useful when an assignment calls for the comparison of two or more works. Among the indexes usually found in libraries are *Granger's Index to Poetry,* the *Poetry Index,* the *Short Story Index, Ottemiller's Index to Plays in Collections,* the *Index to Full Length Plays,* and the *Play Index.* The *Fiction Catalog,* which lists a wide range of themes and settings, and *Historical Fiction,* which is concerned only with historical times and settings, are also very useful.

Other literary indexes help you find a critical review of a specific work. The *Book Review Digest* and the *Book Review In-*

dex list entries by author, title, and subject. The *Book Review Digest* also gives a short summary of the contents of each book and quotes portions of the reviews. The *Book Review Index* gives only the location of the review, not the review itself.

EXERCISE C: Selecting Specialized Reference Books. Give the title of the specialized reference book that you would use to find each of the following.

EXAMPLE: The history of the development of computers
McGraw-Hill Encyclopedia of Science and Technology

1. Synonyms for the word *picayune*
2. A description of the musical instrument sackbut
3. A quote from Martin Luther King's "I have a dream" speech
4. Description of a Norman castle
5. The name of Laura Ingalls Wilder's best-known novel
6. A review of William Golding's *Lord of the Flies*
7. The role of satellites in modern communication
8. A biography of Jonas Salk, developer of the polio vaccine
9. Two novels with settings during the Civil War
10. An east African proverb about growing old

EXERCISE D: Using Specialized Reference Books. Use specialized reference books to find answers to the questions. After each answer, write the name of the book you used.

EXAMPLE: What was Thornton Wilder's first novel?
The Cabala *Webster's Biographical Dictionary*

1. What are three synonyms for *insignificant?*
2. What does the German word *Bahnhof* mean?
3. How did Sarah Caldwell become an orchestra conductor?
4. Which art movement did Georges Braque develop?
5. Where was soccer star Pélé born?
6. What was Clark Gable's last film?
7. Which poet wrote the line, "April is the cruelest month"?
8. What does the mathematical term *matrix* mean?
9. What are two quotations about patriotism?
10. What was Barbara McClintock's discovery in genetics that led to her being awarded a Nobel Prize in 1983?

Periodicals and Pamphlets

Periodical is a term applied to anything published regularly during the year. Periodicals include magazines and journals, but can include newspapers as well. Some periodicals, such as the magazine *Newsweek,* are of general interest, while others, such as the journal *Science,* are devoted to specialized topics. Because of their current nature, periodicals can be a valuable research aid for information that is not available in books.

Use periodicals to supplement research with specialized or current information

A number of different indexes make it possible for you to look up information in periodicals by subject or author. One index that is general in scope is *The Readers' Guide to Periodical Literature,* known generally as *The Reader's Guide.* The *Art Index,* the *Education Index,* the *Humanities Index,* the *General Science Index,* the *Business and Technology Index,* and the *Social Sciences Index* are more specialized. Because all of these indexes have the same publisher, learning to use one enables you to use the others if they are available.

The Readers' Guide to Periodical Literature. This reference, available in most libraries, indexes about 180 magazines and journals. It is issued twice a month except in February, July, and August when it is issued only once a month. A single volume containing all of these issues appears annually.

Information in *The Readers' Guide* is arranged alphabetically by author and subject. Some subjects may have various subheadings listed under them. If, for example, you looked up the subject *Arts* in the index of a recent *Reader's Guide* index, you would find the entry that begins below.

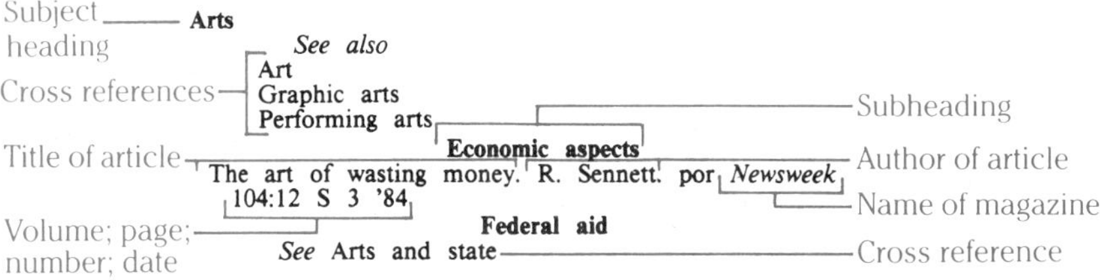

Use the key at the front of each issue for an explanation of abbreviations used in the guide.

Newspapers and Pamphlets. Major newspapers, such as *The New York Times,* the *Christian Science Monitor,* the *Wall Street Journal,* and the *National Observer,* have their own indexes. However, no general index exists for newspapers.

Since *The New York Times* is available on microfilm, *The New York Times Index* is found in many libraries. The index is arranged alphabetically by subject. Each article is then *abstracted,* or summarized. Abstracts for some articles provide enough information so that you may not need to find the newspaper at all. The following entry is from *The New York Times Index.*

Subject heading — **SPACE**

Article abstract — Five newly published geological studies indicate that several species of plants and animals became extinct at about same time 65 million years ago; researchers say that new studies add support to growing theory that an asteroid or comet smashing into earth was responsible for abrupt extinction of dinosaurs and many other creatures (S), Mr 9, I,10:5

Date — Mr 9

Short article — (S)

Section; page; column — I,10:5

Though not strictly periodicals, pamphlets are similar to magazines and newspapers in that they often contain current information. Libraries usually store pamphlets in a *vertical file,* a file cabinet with large drawers. Pamphlets can be found on such topics as welfare, Medicare, state parks, child abuse, and education. Do not hesitate to ask the librarian whether a pamphlet exists that could help you with your topic.

EXERCISE E: Using *The Readers' Guide to Periodical Literature.* Select a topic. Using *The Readers' Guide,* find three articles about your topic. Record the names and dates of the magazines and the titles and authors of the articles.

EXERCISE F: Using *The New York Times Index.* Use *The New York Times Index* to find an article on the topic you chose for Exercise E. Find the newspaper in the library and locate the article. Record the exact headline and the author (if given). Then list five facts from the article.

DEVELOPING WRITING SKILLS: Comparing General and Specialized Reference Books. Write a brief report comparing the coverage of a topic in a general reference book with the coverage of the same topic in a specialized reference book.

34.3 Using the Dictionary

Of all general reference materials, you probably use the dictionary most often. If you refer to it merely to check the meaning or spelling of words, however, you are not getting all you can out of this valuable resource. This section will describe general dictionaries and how to use them.

Recognizing Different Kinds of General Dictionaries

There are dictionaries made for almost every audience: for students to use in their studies, for adults to use at home or at work, and for scholars to use in their research. A suitable dictionary should contain all of the words you are likely to encounter in your studies and should explain them to your satisfaction in language you can readily understand.

Use the dictionary that best suits your needs.

There are two main kinds of general dictionaries that are available to you: complete *unabridged* dictionaries and shorter *abridged* dictionaries.

Unabridged Dictionaries. *Unabridged* means "not shortened." It does *not* mean that the dictionary contains all the words of a language. Unabridged dictionaries generally contain 250,000 to 500,000 words while the English language contains at least 600,000 words. Some words that might have been included are overlooked; others are intentionally excluded. Moreover, English is constantly changing. By the time an unabridged dictionary can be completed and published, thousands of new words have entered the language. Because of this flux, the editors of these dictionaries periodically publish supplements to keep their work up to date and as complete as possible.

Two well-known unabridged dictionaries found in most libraries are *Webster's Third New International Dictionary of the English Language* (published in 1966) and the *Random House Dictionary of the English Language, Unabridged Edition* (published in 1967). You should consult these books whenever you need very specific definitions and extremely detailed information about words.

The excerpt below is an example of the thoroughness of an unabridged dictionary's definitions.

[1]**but·tress** \'bətrəs\ *n* -ES [ME *butres, boterace,* fr. MF *bouterez,* fr. OF *boterez,* fr. *boter, bouter* to thrust — more at BUTT] **1 :** a projecting structure of masonry or wood for supporting or giving stability to a wall or building (as to resist lateral pressure or strain acting at a particular point in one direction) but sometimes serving chiefly for ornament **2 :** any of various things that resemble a buttress in appearance: **a :** COUNTERFORT **b :** a projecting part of a mountain or hill **c :** a horny protuberance on a horse's hoof at the heel where the wall bends inward and forward **d :** the broadened basal portion of a tree trunk or a thickened vertical part of it **3 :** something that supports, strengthens, or helps to defend ⟨a ~ of the cause of peace⟩ **4 :** an abutment built from a river bank to prevent logs in a drive from injuring the bank or jamming

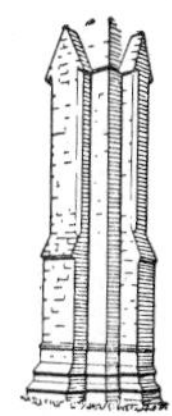

buttress 1

Another well-known unabridged dictionary is the *Oxford English Dictionary* (the OED). It is also a *historical dictionary.* The excerpt below shows how the word *pandemonium* has been used since it was first coined by John Milton in 1667.

Pandemonium (pæ:ndimōᵘ·niŭm). Also **-dæmon-**. [In form, mod.L. f. Gr. *παν-* all + *δαίμων* divinity, DEMON.]

1. The abode of all the demons; a place represented by Milton as the capital of Hell, containing the council-chamber of the Evil Spirits; in common use, = hell or the infernal regions.

1667 MILTON *P. L.* I. 756 A solemn Councel forthwith to be held At Pandæmonium, the high Capital Of Satan and his Peers. *Ibid.* x. 424 About the walls Of Pandæmonium, Citie and proud seate Of Lucifer. 1713 ADDISON *Guardian* No. 103 P 4 He would have a large piece of machinery represent the Pan-dæmonium [of Milton]. 1743 CHESTERF. in *Old England* No. 3 Misc. Wks. 1777 I. 116 'This .. is certainly levelled at us', says a conscious sullen apostate patriot to his fallen brethren in the Pandæmonium. 1831 CARLYLE *Sart. Res.* II. iii, And, in this hag-ridden dream, mistake God's fair living world for a pallid, vacant Hades and extinct Pandemonium.

2. *transf.* A place regarded as resembling Pandemonium: **a.** A centre or head-quarters of vice or wickedness, a haunt of wickedness. **b.** A place or gathering of wild lawless violence, confusion, and uproar.

1779 SWINBURNE *Trav. Spain* xlii. 367 Every province .. would in turn appear a Paradise, and a Pandaemonium. 1800 COLQUHOUN *Comm. Thames* iv. 190 The various ramifications of this Pandæmonium of Iniquity. 1813 *Examiner* 17 May 317/2 The Emperor Tiberius..wrote to the Senate from his pandæmonium at Capreæ. 1816 BYRON *Dom. Pieces* II. ii, To make a Pandemonium where she dwells, And reign the Hecate of domestic hells. 1827 LYTTON *Pelham* xlix, We found ourselves in that dreary pandaemonium,..a Gin-shop. 1876 BLACK *Madcap V.* vi. 47 She would turn the place into a pandemonium in a week. 1897 F. T. BULLEN *Cruise Cachalot* 155 Ribald songs, quarrelling, and blasphemy made a veritable pandemonium of the place.

c. Wild lawless confusion or uproar, a distracting fiendish 'row'.

1865 PARKMAN *Pioneers Fr.* I. iv. (1885) 55 When night came, it brought with it a pandemonium of dancing and whooping, drumming and feasting. 1897 *Daily News* 29 Nov. 4/5 On Saturday pandemonium again reigned in the Reichsrath.

Abridged Dictionaries. Most dictionaries for everyday use are *abridged*—that is, shortened. The ones suitable for use during and after high school usually list between 55,000 and 160,000 words. Unless you want special information about a word or need the meaning of a rare word, you will probably find all you need to know in an abridged dictionary.

The chart below lists abridged dictionaries for student use.

DICTIONARIES RECOMMENDED FOR STUDENTS

High School Dictionaries	College Dictionaries
Webster's New World Dictionary, Student Edition	*Webster's New World Dictionary*, Second College Edition
The Scott, Foresman Advanced Dictionary	*The Random House College Dictionary*
The Macmillan Dictionary	*The American Heritage Dictionary*
Webster's High School Dictionary	*Webster's New Collegiate Dictionary*

EXERCISE A: Comparing Unabridged and Abridged Dictionaries. In a library, compare an unabridged and abridged dictionary by completing the following steps.

1. Write the complete title of each dictionary.
2. Write the number of pages contained in each book.
3. Look up a common word in both dictionaries. How much longer is the coverage in the unabridged text?
4. In what other ways does the coverage of the word differ?
5. List at least three words that are in the unabridged dictionary but are not in the abridged.

Finding the Words

Looking up a word in a dictionary can be difficult if you do not know how to spell the word. Because there are several ways to spell the same sound in English, you should become familiar with a variety of spelling patterns.

Become familiar with the spelling patterns of the sounds in English words.

Some dictionaries provide a chart at the front of the book that shows the different spellings a sound may have in English. The chart below is from the beginning of one in *Webster's New World Dictionary,* Student Edition.

WORD FINDER CHART		
If the sound is like the . . .	try also the spelling . . .	as in the words . . .
a in fat	ai, au	pl*ai*d, dr*au*ght
a in lane	ai, ao, au, ay, ea, ei, eigh, et, ey	r*ai*n, g*ao*l, g*au*ge, r*ay*, br*ea*k, r*ei*n, w*eigh*, sach*et*, th*ey*
a in care	ai, ay, e, ea, ei	*ai*r, pr*ay*er, th*e*re, w*ea*r, th*ei*r
a in father	au, e, ea	g*au*nt, s*e*rgeant, h*ea*rth

Many times you will not need to determine the spelling of a word because you will have encountered it in print. When you know the spelling, you can look the word up very quickly. To do so, however, you need to make use of a dictionary's alphabetical order.

Learn to use alphabetical order to find words quickly.

The chart below lists three steps to follow in order to find a word quickly in a dictionary.

STEPS FOR FINDING WORDS QUICKLY
1. Use the four-section approach.
2. Next, use the guide words.
3. Then, follow strict alphabetical order.

First, you should first mentally divide the dictionary into the four sections at the top of the next page. Notice that the four sections are not divided equally because English words are not distributed evenly among the letters of the alphabet.

FOUR SECTIONS:	ABCD	MNOPQR
	EFGHIJKL	STUVWXYZ

When you go to look up a word, decide which section the word falls in. For example, if you were looking up *homage,* you would know that the word falls near the middle of the second section. Similarly, if you were looking up *scabbard,* you would know that the word falls near the beginning of the last section.

Second, use the *guide words* found at the top of each page. These words are printed in large, bold type. The guide word at the left tells you the first word on that page; the one on the right tells you the last word on that page. You can now narrow your search to a single page.

Third, follow strict alphabetical order to locate the word you want. Unlike the cards in a card catalog, which are alphabetized word by word, the words in a dictionary are alphabetized letter by letter. This strict alphabetical order is followed right to the end of an entry.

EXAMPLES: *sanction* before *San Diego*
sandpiper before *San Francisco*

EXERCISE B: Alphabetizing Entry Words. Put the following words in alphabetical order as you would find them in a dictionary.

1. redevelop
2. reflex
3. red light
4. Reed
5. react
6. Red Cross
7. redundancy
8. redirect
9. Redwood City
10. register

Knowing What Dictionaries Contain

As you read the following descriptions, keep in mind that all dictionaries are not the same. Apply what you learn here to your own dictionary.

Learn to recognize and use the various features of your own dictionary.

Front Matter. A good high school or college dictionary contains an introduction that explains how to use it efficiently. Here, in addition to a description of all the book's features, you will usually find instructions on how to look up a word, how to find words whose spelling you are unsure of, and how to interpret the pronunciation symbols. A complete pronunciation key and a list of all the abbreviations used in the dictionary will also be found in this part of the book.

Main Entries. In a dictionary, the words and the information about them are called *main entries.* The words themselves are called the *entry words* and are alphabetized letter by letter.

An entry word may be a single word, a compound word (two or more words acting as a single word), an abbreviation, a prefix or suffix, or the name of a special event, person, or place. (Some dictionaries do not include names of people and places. Others put them in separate alphabetical lists at the back of the book.) The following chart shows the different kinds of entry words that may be found in a dictionary.

KINDS OF ENTRY WORDS	
Single Word	old·en
Compound Word	Old Guard
Abbreviation	R.S.V.P.
Prefix	o·le·o-
Suffix	-o·ma
Person	Doug·lass
Place	Nan·tuck·et

Preferred and Variant Spellings. A dictionary is an authority for the spelling of words. Most English words have only one correct spelling, as shown by the entry word. Some words, however, can be spelled in more than one way. The spelling most commonly used is called the *preferred spelling.* Less commonly used spellings are called *variant spellings.* If the form you are looking up is a variant spelling, the entry will refer you to another entry, the one that begins with the preferred spelling. The entry for the preferred spelling will provide you with a definition.

VARIANT SPELLING: **Breu·ghel** (brü′gəl; *occas.* broi′-) *same as* BRUEGEL

PREFERRED SPELLING: **Brue·gel, Brue·ghel** (brü′gəl; *occas.* broi′-), **Pie·ter** (pē′tər) 1522?–69; Fl. painter

Sometimes a rather uncommon variant spelling or form may be listed only at the end of a main entry, as in the following.

UNCOMMON VARIANTS: **bar·bell** (bär′bel′) *n.* [BAR[1] + (DUMB)BELL] a metal bar to which disks of varying weights are attached at each end, used for weight-lifting exercises: also **bar bell, bar-bell**

Syllabification. Centered dots, spaces, or slashes in an entry word indicate where words are divided into syllables. If words are already hyphenated, hyphens will take the place of these symbols. The word *brother-in-law,* for example, has four syllables: broth·er-in-law. Most, but not all, of these divisions can be used for word breaks at the end of a line of writing. The section on hyphens (Section 16.7) gives specific rules for breaking words into syllables at the ends of lines.

Pronunciation. Pronunciations appear after most entry words, usually in parentheses or between diagonal lines. Pronunciations usually do not accompany entries that are not full words, such as abbreviations, prefixes, and suffixes. Nor are they usually found with entries that are compound words when the individual words are main entries themselves.

The dictionary indicates how to pronounce words by respelling them in a *phonetic alphabet.* This is a set of special symbols with each symbol assigned one sound. Since phonetic alphabets vary from one dictionary to another, become familiar with the one in your dictionary. A *pronunciation key* at the front or back of your dictionary explains all of the pronunciation symbols. Most dictionaries for students also provide short pronunciation keys on every other page.

Besides helping you to pronounce words correctly, the dictionary shows you which syllables are stressed. The syllable that gets the most emphasis has a *primary stress,* usually shown by a heavy mark (′) after the syllable. Words of more than one syllable may have a *secondary stress,* usually shown by a shorter, lighter mark (′) after the syllable. The syllables in a word that receive no stress when pronounced are not marked in any special way.

Sometimes, words can be pronounced in more than one way. When two or more pronunciations of a word are given, the preferred pronunciation is given first. Notice examples on the following page of how the stress marks are shown and how other pronunciation is indicated.

PRIMARY STRESS ONLY: **dwin·dle** (dwin′d'l)

PRIMARY AND SECONDARY STRESSES: **en·gi·neer** (en′jə nir′)

MORE THAN ONE PRONUNCIATION: **ei·ther** (ē′*th*ər, ī′-)

Part-of-Speech Labels. The dictionary also tells you how a word can be used in a sentence—whether it functions as a noun, a verb, or as some other part of speech. This information is given in abbreviated form, usually after the pronunciation of a word but sometimes at the end of the entry. Entries of two or more words, such as *pony express* or *bird of paradise,* have no part-of-speech labels because they are always nouns. Some dictionaries also omit part-of-speech labels for the names of people and places since these, too, are always nouns. As you can see in the following example, some words can be more than one part of speech.

out·side (out′sīd′, out′-; *for prep. & adv., usually* out′sīd′) ***n.*** **1.** the outer side, part, or surface; exterior [wash the windows on the *outside*] **2.** outward look or appearance [a man who seems jolly on the *outside*] **3.** any place or area not inside [the prisoners got little news from the *outside*] —***adj.*** **1.** of or on the outside; outer [the *outside* layer] **2.** coming from or situated beyond given limits; from some other place, person, group, etc. [to accept no *outside* help] **3.** extreme; maximum [an *outside* estimate] **4.** mere; slight [an *outside* chance] —***adv.*** **1.** on or to the outside **2.** beyond certain limits **3.** outdoors [go play *outside*] —***prep.*** **1.** on or to the outer side of [leave it *outside* the door] **2.** beyond the limits of [traveling *outside* the country] —**at the outside** at the very most —**out′side of** **1.** outside **2.** [Colloq.] other than; except for

Part-of-speech labels

A dictionary may also give additional forms of a word after the part-of-speech label. You may find, for example, the plural form of a noun, the comparative and superlative forms of modifiers, or the principal parts of a verb.

PLURAL FORM OF A NOUN: **leaf** (lēf) ***n., pl.*** **leaves**

FORMS OF AN ADJECTIVE: **ti·ny** (tī′nē) ***adj.*** **-ni·er, -ni·est**

PARTS OF A VERB: **in·fu·ri·ate** (in fyoor′ē āt′) ***vt.*** **-at′ed, -at′ing**

As the examples show, the plural of *leaf* is *leaves;* the forms of *tiny* are *tinier* and *tiniest;* and the principal parts of *infuriate* are *infuriated* and *infuriating.*

Etymologies. The origin and history of a word is called its *etymology*. The etymology of an entry word usually appears in brackets after the pronunciation and part-of-speech labels. In some dictionaries, the etymology is at the end of a main entry.

The historical information in an etymology is organized in reverse chronological order. This information is written in a code made up of symbols and abbreviations. As with pronunciation symbols, the codes for etymologies vary from one dictionary to another. It is best that you study the introduction in your particular dictionary to understand the code.

Knowing a word's etymology can often help you remember its present meaning. In the following example, see how the etymology can help you remember what *anarchy* means.

an·ar·chy (-kē) ***n.***, *pl.* **-chies** [< Gr. < *an-*, without + *archos*, leader] **1.** the complete absence of government **2.** political disorder and violence **3.** disorder or confusion in any kind of activity — Etymology

The etymology in the example above indicates that *anarchy* comes from a Greek word that came from two other Greek words, *an-* meaning "without" and *archos* meaning "leader."

Definitions. Many words in English have multiple meanings. These meanings are called *definitions*. All meanings for the same part of speech are grouped together in the dictionary and numbered consecutively. Sometimes, a definition will be broken into parts to show shades of meaning; then the different parts will be arranged by letters: *a, b, c,* and so on. One dictionary lists forty-four definitions for the word *set*, most of which are broken down into as many as eight parts.

Dictionaries sometimes help clarify the different meanings of an entry word with a phrase or sentence showing the word in use. The following entry for *render*, for example, lists eleven different definitions (one with two parts) and gives six examples of the word in use.

Definition — Example of word in use — Definition with two parts

ren·der (ren′dər) ***vt.*** [< OFr., ult. < L. < *re-*, back + *dare*, to give] **1.** to hand over, or submit, as for approval, consideration, payment, etc. [*render* an account of your actions; *render* a bill] **2.** to give (*up*); surrender [to *render* up a city to the enemy] **3.** to give in return [*render* good for evil] **4.** to give or pay as due [to *render* thanks] **5.** to cause to be; make [to *render* one helpless] **6.** *a*) to give (aid, etc.) *b*) to do (a service, etc.) **7.** to represent, as in a drawing; depict **8.** to recite (a poem, etc.), play (music), act (a role), etc. **9.** to translate [to *render* a Spanish song into English] **10.** to deliver (a judgment, verdict, etc.) **11.** to melt down (fat) —**ren′der·a·ble** ***adj.*** —**ren′der·er** ***n.*** —**ren′der·ing** ***n.***

When you are checking a word that can have more than one meaning, read each definition carefully to find the one that matches the context of the word in the sentence you are reading or writing. You should be able to substitute the correct definition for the word in the sentence. You might, for example, have to decide which definition of *render* can be substituted for the word in the following sentence.

SENTENCE: *Rendering* her poems into another language is very difficult.

Only when *render* means "to translate" (definition 9) does it make sense in the sentence above.

Usage and Field Labels. Words and meanings that are considered acceptable in formal situations by most speakers and writers of a language are said to be standard usage. Dictionaries indicate other words and meanings with *usage labels,* such as *Rare, Slang, Informal* (or *Colloquial*), *Dialect*, and *British.* The label lets you know that a particular word or meaning may be unsuitable or not understood in certain situations.

Other words or meanings are used specifically by people engaged in a particular field of knowledge, a particular occupation, or activity. Dictionaries indicate this restricted usage with *field labels,* such as *Baseball, Radio & TV,* or *Philosophy.*

Both usage labels and field labels usually appear in abbreviated form before the definitions to which they apply.

click (klik) ***n.*** [echoic] **1.** a slight, sharp sound like that of a door latch snapping into place **2.** a mechanical device, as a catch or pawl, that clicks into position **3.** *Phonet.* a sound made by drawing the breath into the mouth and snapping the tongue from the roof of the mouth **—*vi.*** **1.** to make a click **2.** [Colloq.] *a)* to be suddenly understood *b)* to work or get along together successfully *c)* to be a success **—*vt.*** to cause to click **—click′er *n.***

Field label

Usage label

Idioms. An *idiom* is an expression that has a meaning different from that which the individual words would literally suggest. Expressions such as "watch your step," "on the go," and "over and above" are idioms.

Idioms are usually found in alphabetical order near the end of a main entry or at the end of the definition for a particular part of speech. The key word in the expression determines the main entry with which the idiom appears. If the idiom seems to have two or more key words, as in "watch your step," look under the noun first (*step*). If there are no nouns in the idiom, as in "over and above," look under the first key word (*over*).

The following example shows the many idioms that one dictionary lists under the entry word *rope*.

rope (rōp) ***n.*** [OE. *rap:* for IE. base see ROW¹] **1.** a thick, strong cord made of strands of fiber, wires, etc. twisted together **2.** *a*) a noose for hanging a person *b*) death by hanging: with *the* ☆**3.** *same as* LASSO **4.** a ropelike string of things [a *rope* of pearls] **5.** a ropelike, sticky formation, as in wine —***vt.* roped, rop′ing** **1.** to fasten or tie with a rope **2.** to connect by a rope **3.** to mark off or enclose with a rope (usually with *in, off,* or *out*) [to *rope* off a statue in a museum] ☆**4.** to catch with a lasso [to *rope* steers] —***vi.*** to become ropelike and sticky [to cook candy until it *ropes*] —**know the ropes** [Colloq.] to know the details or procedures, as of a job —☆**rope in** [Slang] to trick into doing something —**the end of one's rope** the end of one's endurance, resources, etc. —**rop′er** ***n.***

Idioms

Derived Words or Run-on Entries. Words formed by adding a common suffix, such as *-ly* or *-ness,* to an entry word are called *derived words* or *run-on entries.* The suffixes are added to change words from one part of speech to another. Derived words are found at the end of a main entry and are not defined. They simply appear with their part-of-speech labels and, sometimes, with the pronunciation. If you are not sure of the meaning of a derived word, look up the meaning of the suffix and combine that with the meanings of the entry word. In the example below, the entry word *gossip* has two derived words at the end of the main entry, a noun and an adjective.

gos·sip (gäs′əp) ***n.*** [< Late OE. *godsibbe,* godparent: see GOD & SIB] **1.** [Obs. or Dial.] *a*) a godparent *b*) a close friend **2.** one who chatters or repeats idle talk and rumors, esp. about others' private affairs **3.** *a*) such talk or rumors *b*) chatter —***vi.*** to be a gossip; indulge in idle talk or rumors about others —**gos′sip·er** ***n.*** —**gos′sip·y** ***adj.***

Derived words

Synonyms and Antonyms. A *synonym* is a word closely related but not identical in meaning to another word. In some dictionaries you will see below the entry a block of words beginning with the abbreviation *SYN.* Here the differences in meaning among synonyms are explained. Such explanations are called *synonymies. Antonyms,* or words opposite in meaning, are sometimes found here, too.

The following example shows the synonymy for the entry word *large.*

large (lärj) ***adj.*** **larg′er, larg′est** [OFr. < L. *largus*] **1.** big; great; specif., *a)* taking up much space; bulky *b)* enclosing much space; spacious [a *large* office] *c)* of great extent or amount [a *large* sum] **2.** big as compared with others of its kind [a *large* mouth] **3.** operating on a big scale [a *large* manufacturer] —***adv.*** in a large way [to write *large*] —**at large** **1.** free; not confined [the runaway bull was still *at large*] **2.** in general; taken altogether [in the interests of the community *at large*] ☆**3.** representing an entire State or area rather than only a subdivision [a congressman *at large*] —**large′ness *n.***
SYN.—**large, big,** and **great** are often used interchangeably in referring to something of more than usual size, extent, etc. [a *large, big,* or *great* oak], but **large** is usually used with special reference to dimensions or quantity [a *large* studio, amount, etc.], **big** with special reference to bulk, weight, or extent [a *big* baby, a *big* difference], and **great** with special reference to size or extent that is impressive, imposing, surprising, etc. [the *Great* Lakes, a *great* success, etc.] —***ANT.*** **small, little**

Synonymy

EXERCISE C: Determining Preferred Spellings. Use your dictionary to determine whether the following words are preferred or variant spellings. If the word is considered preferred, write *preferred* on your paper; if it is a variant, write the preferred spelling.

EXAMPLE: honour
honor

1. theatre
2. gelatin
3. glamorous
4. ameba
5. hooves
6. heartsease
7. enjambement
8. interrogation mark
9. inclose
10. glamor

EXERCISE D: Determining Syllables. Find the following words in your dictionary. Then, with slashes, indicate the way each word is divided into syllables.

EXAMPLE: nationalist
na/tion/al/ist

1. handicraft
2. little
3. Mississippi
4. miserable
5. incognito
6. movement
7. misspell
8. alphabetize
9. incidental
10. demonstration

EXERCISE E: Understanding Pronunciations. Write the preferred pronunciations for each word, using the symbols in your dictionary. Pronounce each word aloud to yourself.

EXAMPLE: usual

you' zhoo wəl

1. route
2. every
3. literature
4. battery
5. surplus
6. apparent
7. February
8. temperament
9. simultaneous
10. quadruplet

EXERCISE F: Finding Part-of-Speech Labels. For each word, list the part-of-speech labels that your dictionary gives.

EXAMPLE: junket

n. vi. vt.

1. hitch
2. inside
3. range
4. run
5. sea bass
6. scruple
7. keep
8. handle
9. chime
10. probe

EXERCISE G: Interpreting Etymologies. Find the etymology for each of the following words in your dictionary. Then, write a sentence describing the origin and history of each.

EXAMPLE: snorkel

Snorkel comes from a German word that means "spiral."

1. derrick
2. radar
3. dodo
4. peninsula
5. innocuous
6. candidate
7. dandelion
8. verbose
9. melancholy
10. sophomore

EXERCISE H: Finding Usage Labels and Field Labels. Use your dictionary to answer the following questions about usage labels and field labels.

1. What is the informal or colloquial meaning of *railroad?*
2. What is the British usage of the word *boot?*

3. What is a *pass* in the field of baseball?
4. What is a *period* in physics?
5. What does *sharp* mean in music?
6. What is the colloquial meaning of *cute?*
7. What does *clear* mean in banking?
8. What is the slang meaning of *heavy?*
9. What does *sink* mean in geology?
10. What is the obsolete meaning of *gentle?*

EXERCISE I: Finding the Meaning of Idioms. Find the meaning of each idiom by looking up the underlined words.

EXAMPLE: <u>bring</u> to

bring back to consciousness

1. <u>shake</u> down
2. under one's <u>thumb</u>
3. kick the <u>bucket</u>
4. <u>have</u> it out
5. steal one's <u>thunder</u>
6. <u>down</u> and out
7. at close <u>quarters</u>
8. come to <u>terms</u>
9. make <u>do</u>
10. right off the <u>bat</u>

EXERCISE J: Finding Derived Words. For each entry word below, write the words your dictionary lists as derived words.

EXAMPLE: pale

palely paleness

1. mope
2. giddy
3. tragic
4. detect
5. stingy
6. scintillate
7. persuasive
8. circumnavigate
9. like-minded
10. miscalculate

DEVELOPING WRITING SKILLS: Using the Dictionary Efficiently. Use your dictionary to answer the questions below. Then write an evaluation of how you use the dictionary.

1. What does *satrapy* mean?
2. According to its etymology, what did *lady* originally mean?
3. What usage label is listed for the first meaning of *wight?*
4. How many syllables are in the word *meteorologically?*
5. Which is the variant spelling, *litre* or *liter?*

Skills Review and Writing Workshop

Library and Reference Skills

CHECKING YOUR SKILLS

Take notes on the following entry from an encyclopedia.

The *common cold* is a term used to describe a group of different viruses. One of these viruses is influenza, or flu. An extremely severe epidemic of influenza that broke out in 1918 killed an estimated twenty million people throughout the world. In most cases, however, colds and flu are only accompanied by coughing, sneezing, sore throat, and possibly a mild fever. The average adult catches about three colds every year. Among children, the number of colds is much higher. Women catch more colds than men, possibly because they have more contact with children. A child often catches a cold in school, and within a few days it spreads to the rest of the family.

USING STUDY SKILLS IN WRITING:

Writing a Summary of a Magazine Article

Writers know that in order to find information they must learn how to use library and reference tools. Use *The Readers' Guide* to locate a magazine article and write a summary using the steps below.

Prewriting: Look up a subject that interests you in *The Readers' Guide* and find a current magazine article on it. Read the article carefully, noting the main ideas and important details.

Writing: Write a summary that briefly states the important information in the article.

Revising: Look over your summary and add any important information that you may have omitted. After you have revised, proofread carefully.

UNIT **VIII**

Speaking and Listening

Chapter **35**

Speaking and Listening Skills

Many of the concepts you are expected to learn in school will be introduced and discussed in class. There will be times when you are called upon to participate in a group discussion or give an oral presentation to others. Similarly, there are times when you must master material that is presented orally. Then you must listen carefully and accurately to follow the speaker's train of thought.

In this chapter you will learn a variety of ways to develop your speaking skills and your listening skills.

Group Discussion 35.1

Are you a person who can talk for hours to friends but does not know what to say in a group discussion? It is not difficult to transfer your small-group skills to larger groups. The speaking skills for both groups are really quite similar. Both situations require being informed about the topic under discussion, voicing your own ideas clearly, accepting feedback on your contributions, and being a good listener.

Recognizing Different Kinds of Group Discussions

The major difference between discussions with friends and group discussions is that group discussions occur when three or more people meet for a definite purpose, to arrive at a specific goal. The group must concentrate on reaching the group's goal rather than individual goals of its members.

A group discussion is formed to achieve a specific common goal.

The goal to be achieved may be to solve a problem, arrive at a decision, or answer a question of mutual interest. Four major kinds of group discussions have been developed to reach these goals. They are committees, round-table discussion groups, panels, and symposiums.

Committees. A committee is a small group of a larger organization that has been formed to discuss specific ideas and to perform certain tasks. A leader is chosen to keep the discussion moving and on target. The leader or a recorder will take notes on the proceedings and make a report to the organization. An example could be a committee of five teachers who discuss the budget for textbooks.

Round-Table Discussion Groups. The term "round-table" comes from the legendary table around which King Arthur and his knights met to discuss their adventures. The table was round to make each knight of equal importance in the group. Today round-table discussion groups are often formed when the goal is mainly to share information. Many round-table discussions are preliminary discussions held when fact-gathering is needed before a more formal discussion can be held. An example could be a group of five students and a teacher who discuss planning an awards assembly.

Panels. A panel is a group of several informed people who hold a discussion with an audience present. The goal of a panel is to share the members' viewpoints among themselves and with the audience. Each panel member prepares his or her part of the discussion in advance. Many panel leaders hold a preliminary session with the other panel members to work out what each panel member will say, the amount of time each can speak, and whether the audience will participate. An example could be a panel of parents and members of the board of education who discuss whether or not to close a school.

Symposiums. A symposium is similar to a panel but different in that each member is an authority on one aspect of the topic under discussion and begins by giving a formal speech on that aspect. After each member gives his or her speech there may be a discussion among them and the audience may take part in the discussion. The goal of a symposium is to give a rounded, thorough picture of the problem under discussion. An example could be a symposium of four scientists who speak on careers in science to an audience of high school juniors and seniors.

EXERCISE A: Selecting Topics for Group Discussions. Review the major characteristics of a *committee,* a *round-table discussion group,* a *panel,* and a *symposium.* For each of the four kinds of groups, name two discussion topics that would be appropriate to that kind of group.

Planning a Group Discussion

Several factors affect the success of a group discussion. First, the topic must be one that is of mutual interest to all the members. Second, the topic must be one that is timely, interesting, and one that the group can manage within the discussion time. Third, the topic must be one that can be well researched by each member of the group.

A group discussion should focus on a topic that is timely, interesting, and one the members are involved with and prepared to discuss.

Most good group discussions are carefully planned. The chart below lists steps for planning a group discussion.

PLANNING A GROUP DISCUSSION
1. Hold a prediscussion meeting to determine the discussion topic. Make sure the topic is timely and interesting.
2. Define the topic precisely. After it is defined, phrase the topic as a question, not a statement.
3. Make an outline of points to be discussed. Include a history of the problem, alternatives or solutions, and possible action to be taken.
4. Research the topic by reading, thinking, and getting as much information as possible before the discussion.

EXERCISE B: Planning a Round-Table Discussion. Form a group of between five and seven students to plan a round-table discussion. Follow the four steps in the chart that appears on page 823.

Participating in a Group Discussion

Because people's personalities differ, not everyone in a group discussion will exercise the same influence or leadership. However, the effectiveness of a group discussion depends on the active participation of all its members.

Active participation is required of all members for an effective group discussion.

In all kinds of group discussion, leadership roles are needed. In less formal groups, such as a round-table discussion, the leadership roles can be assumed by several of the members. In more formal groups, such as a committee, a panel, or a symposium, leadership roles are assigned to a chairperson or a discussion leader. The chart below lists the duties of a discussion leader.

LEADING A DISCUSSION

1. Introduce members of the group to each other and to the audience, if one is present.
2. Introduce the topic. Phrase it as a question.
3. Invite and encourage all members to speak freely, especially a member who is silent.
4. Keep participation balanced by tactfully diverting discussion from a member who is talking too much to one who has said less.
5. Keep the discussion on track. Summarize for the group after they have completed major parts of the discussion.
6. Watch the time limit. Move on to a major point not yet covered to speed things up.
7. Conclude the discussion by summarizing main ideas. Allow time for other members to add their own summary points or opinions.

Since active participation is required of all members of a group discussion, the following points should be noted by those members not acting in a leadership role. First, do not monopolize the discussion. Be brief in your statements and stay on track. Second, keep the discussion goal in mind even if you may be opposed to it.

EXERCISE C: Holding a Round-Table Discussion. Using the plan your group completed for Exercise B on page 824, conduct a round-table discussion on your topic. Limit your discussion to forty-five minutes.

DEVELOPING WRITING SKILLS: Evaluating Your Round-Table Discussion. Write a paragraph that evaluates the planning and conducting of your round-table discussion.

Parliamentary Procedure 35.2

Have you ever attended a meeting at which several people were speaking at once and no one was being heard? If that meeting had been run by parliamentary procedure, it would have been run efficiently and everyone would have had a chance to be heard. Parliamentary procedure is a set of principles that were developed for the English Parliament several hundred years ago. Today the principles are used by many groups to allow decisions to be made in the most direct and democratic way. Parliamentary procedure is valuable for you to learn whether you simply participate in meetings that are conducted according to its principles, or are elected to an office that requires a full knowledge of the system.

Basic Principles of Parliamentary Procedure

Parliamentary procedure rests on five basic principles that provide for rule by the majority while at the same time guaranteeing the rights of the minority. It also guarantees that a meeting will be conducted in an orderly and efficient manner by providing rules that must be followed by everyone attending the meeting.

Parliamentary procedure guarantees that the rights of the majority and minority are respected and that a meeting is conducted in an orderly way.

The chart below lists the five basic principles of parliamentary procedure.

PRINCIPLES OF PARLIAMENTARY PROCEDURE
1. One issue at a time can be debated and voted on. If an issue is not voted on, it must be disposed of in some way before the members can go on to consider other issues.
2. The decision of the majority rules. A simple majority consists of more than one half of the people voting on an issue.
3. Minority rights are protected in part by allowing those in the minority to present their views and to change the minds of those in the majority.
4. Every member has a right to speak or to remain silent, to vote or not to vote.
5. Open discussion of every issue is protected so that members can vote in an informed way on every issue. A two-thirds vote is needed to limit debate or end it completely.

EXERCISE A: Explaining the Democratic Process. Write a paragraph explaining how the five basic principles of parliamentary procedure reflect the basis of the democratic process as we know it.

Holding a Meeting

Parliamentary procedure specifies that a meeting must be conducted in a certain way. A meeting must always be presided over by a chairperson and a specific agenda must be followed step by step.

Parliamentary procedure regulates the way the business of a meeting is conducted and the duties of the chairperson.

Quorum. After the people are assembled for a meeting, the chairperson must decide if a quorum is present. A quorum is the agreed-upon number of persons that must be present to hold the meeting. For example, an organization that has 90 members might decide that at least one third, 30 members, must be present to hold the meeting.

Order of Business. Meetings follow certain steps, generally listed in an *agenda.* The chart below shows the steps in the correct order.

STEPS FOR CONDUCTING A MEETING
1. Call to order
2. Roll call
3. Reading and approval of minutes from last meetings
4. Reading of reports of officers
5. Reading of reports of committees
6. Consideration of old (unfinished) business
7. Consideration of new business
8. Adjournment

Duties of Chairperson. The chairperson presides over a meeting. The chairperson is a voting member of the organization, usually its president. Whenever the president is unable to preside over a meeting, the vice-president presides. The chairperson prepares the agenda for a meeting and brings up each item on the agenda at the meeting. The chairperson also helps to maintain order during the meeting and sees that each member is recognized to speak and is heard impartially. When an issue is under discussion, the chairperson must not take sides on the issue.

Making of Motions. The business of a meeting is conducted through the making of motions. A motion is a formal suggestion or proposal by a member that an issue be discussed and acted upon. There are eight steps involved as shown in the following chart.

STEPS FOR CARRYING OUT A MOTION

1. A member asks to be recognized by the chairperson and introduces the motion by saying, "I move ______."
2. Some other member must second the motion, that is, agree to its introduction for discussion.
3. The chairperson restates the motion so that all members will clearly know what has been proposed for discussion.
4. Discussion of the motion begins; members may agree, disagree, explain, or attempt to change the motion.
5. When the chairperson feels that the motion has been thoroughly discussed, he or she asks the members if they are ready to vote. If two-thirds of the members agree, discussion is ended.
6. The chairperson restates the motion which may now include an amendment, a change in the original motion; such an amendment would be included only if a majority present had voted to include it during the discussion.
7. The chairperson asks the members to vote.
8. The chairperson announces the result of the vote by saying, "The motion carried" if the majority favored the motion or "The motion is lost" if the majority was against the motion.

EXERCISE B: Holding a Meeting. Assume your class is a new club devoted to community service. Elect a chairperson and hold a meeting to discuss ways of spending a donation of two thousand dollars. Omit the third to sixth steps in the chart on page 827 for conducting a meeting since this is a new club. Carry all motions, however, completely.

DEVELOPING WRITING SKILLS: Attending a Meeting. Attend a meeting such as a board of education meeting or a meeting of a local business or civic group in which parliamentary procedure is followed. Write a paragraph about the meeting, noting how faithfully the group followed the rules of parliamentary procedure, how fairly each member was treated, and in what ways, if any, the meeting could have been better run.

Public Speaking 35.3

Preparing a speech that you will give before an audience requires more preparation than an informal talk, a group discussion, or a meeting. Generally, the more time you invest in preparing and practicing your speech, the better your speech will be received by your audience.

Recognizing Different Kinds of Speeches

When you first start thinking about a speech topic, you must decide on the kind of speech you want to give. You must also consider who your audience will be.

Choose the kind of speech you will give by considering both the purpose of the speech and your audience.

Depending on the purpose of your speech you can give any one of the following. An *expository* speech is given to explain an idea, a process, or an object. A *persuasive* speech is given to try to get the listeners to agree with the speaker's position or to take some action. An *entertaining* speech is given to offer the listeners something to enjoy.

EXERCISE A: Identifying Purpose and Audience. Label each of the following speech topics as *expository, persuasive,* or *entertaining.* Then identify who might be the audience for each kind of speech.

EXAMPLE: How to drive safely

expository people learning to drive

1. The importance of voting
2. The causes of air pollution
3. How to play a guitar
4. The time I picked up the wrong date
5. Evidence that famine is increasing worldwide
6. The value of owning a watch cat
7. The history of tap dancing

8. The value of speaking a foreign language
9. The goblin who lives in our attic
10. Interviewing for a job

Giving a Speech

Once you know what kind of speech you will give and have chosen an appropriate topic, you are ready to begin the process for giving a speech. You will need to gather information, outline your speech, prepare note cards, practice, and deliver your speech.

Follow a series of steps to plan, prepare, practice, and deliver your speech.

To give a successful speech, use the following suggestions.

GATHERING INFORMATION
1. Research the subject using the library or other sources especially if the speech is expository or persuasive.
2. Conduct interviews with authorities on the subject.

After you have gathered the information you need you should write an outline that presents the information in a logical manner.

PREPARING AN OUTLINE
1. Begin with any necessary background material.
2. Arrange information in a logical sequence.
3. Include major points and supporting details.

The following outline is for an expository speech entitled "Checks and Balances in Nature" prepared for a science class.

I. Physical factors in the ecosystem
  A. Surface and subsurface differences
    1. Water
    2. Topography
    3. Geological Substrates
    4. Soil types

B. Solar and atmospheric differences
 1. Light
 2. Temperature
 3. Wind patterns
 4. Climate

II. Biological factors in the ecosystem
 A. Cycles in the ecosystem
  1. Nitrogen cycle
  2. Energy flow
  3. Water cycle
  4. Oxygen/carbon dioxide cycle
 B. Productivity of the ecosystem
  1. Food chains/food webs
  2. Colonization and succession

After you have made an outline, you should prepare note cards that you can use when you deliver your speech. A common fear among speakers is that they will forget parts of their speech or the order of the ideas. Note cards, though brief, are useful because they contain only key words that can trigger your memory if you forget any part of your speech.

PREPARING NOTE CARDS

1. Use only a few small index cards. Number each card.
2. Print neatly all of the information in the order used in the outline.
3. Copy quotations or facts you want to remember exactly.
4. Write out beginning and ending statements if helpful.
5. Rely mainly on key words and short phrases to jog your memory.
6. Letter and indent all the details under the ideas they support.
7. Use underlining and capital letters to make important information stand out.

Once you have prepared your note cards, you are ready to practice your speech. Practice your speech in front of a mirror and in front of a small audience such as your family or friends. Tape-record your speech and listen to it objectively.

PRACTICING YOUR SPEECH

1. Read over your outline and note cards until the material is familiar.
2. Be aware of the *verbal* form of language you are using. Vary the pitch of your voice. Vary the rate at which you speak. Project your voice loudly so it can be heard throughout the room. Clearly and correctly pronounce all words.
3. Be aware of the *nonverbal* forms of language you are using. The way you move, your posture, facial expressions, gestures, and appearance are language that affect your audience positively or negatively just as your words do. They can, in fact, contradict what you are saying if you use them carelessly.

When the day comes and you are ready to deliver your speech, you may still feel somewhat nervous. Being a bit nervous can work for you by making you alert and on your toes.

DELIVERING YOUR SPEECH

1. As you stand in front of your audience, try to establish eye contact with several people.
2. Briefly look over your note cards to refresh your mind one last time.
3. When delivering your speech, refer to your note cards as seldom as possible.

EXERCISE B: Preparing and Giving a Speech. Prepare a two- to four-minute speech using one of the following topics or one of your own. Research and prepare an outline of your speech. Then write note cards to use when you deliver your speech. Practice your speech at home and then give it to your class.

1. Your favorite literary character
2. The appeal of soccer (or some other sport)
3. The advantages of a personal computer for school work
4. Career opportunities in engineering (or some other field)
5. Strategies for planning a charitable function

Evaluating a Speech

When you take time to evaluate another person's speech carefully, you can accomplish two things. First, you can give the speaker constructive criticism that will be useful in improving his or her speaking skills. Second, you can apply the speaker's effective speaking skills to your own speeches.

Evaluate a speech in a way that offers benefits to the speaker and to yourself.

The checklist below lists suggestions to follow when evaluating another person's speech.

CHECKLIST FOR EVALUATING A SPEECH

What Was Said?

1. What type of speech was given—expository, persuasive, or entertaining?
2. Did the speaker introduce the topic clearly, develop it well, and end in a conclusive fashion?
3. Did the speaker support his or her main ideas with appropriate details?

How Was It Said?

1. Did the speaker approach the platform confidently and establish eye contact with the audience?
2. Did the speaker's gestures and movements confirm or contradict his or her words? Where? How?
3. Did the speaker project his or her voice loudly enough?
4. Did the speaker vary the pitch of his or her voice?
5. Did the speaker vary the rate of his or her speaking?
6. Did the speaker pronounce all of the words clearly and correctly?

EXERCISE C: Evaluating a Speech. Using the checklist above, make a detailed evaluation of a speech given in class. Then, list two or more skills that the speaker used effectively and consider using them in a speech you will give in the future.

DEVELOPING WRITING SKILLS: Evaluating Your Speaking Skills. Write a paragraph discussing the skill you are developing in giving public speeches. Mention those parts of the process you find particularly easy as well as those you find difficult. Then note the one thing you plan to work most on in the future.

35.4 Listening Skills

Listening and hearing are not the same thing. You hear simply because sound reaches your ears. Hearing is, therefore, passive. Listening, on the other hand, is an active thinking skill requiring your concentration in order to understand, analyze, interpret, and evaluate what you hear.

Listening for Important Information

If you are in a situation that requires attentive listening, such as a lecture or classroom discussion, you need to prepare yourself mentally and physically. First, get into a comfortable listening position and eliminate any distractions. Have lined paper and a pencil handy in case you need to take notes. Then give the speaker your polite and undivided attention.

When you listen to a lecture, a discussion, or a speech, it is most important that you comprehend the literal or exact meaning of the information that you hear. However, everything that a person says is not of equal value so you do not need to remember everything that is said. One of the most valuable listening skills you can acquire is to identify and remember the main ideas and major details of the material.

Learn to take mental notes of main ideas and major details as you listen.

Main Ideas. When you read material such as a chapter in a textbook, you can go back and reread to find the main ideas. However, it is not always easy to identify the main ideas when you are listening since spoken material is often more loosely organized than written material. You must be alert and try to follow the organization of the speaker's ideas.

The suggestions in the following chart are intended to guide your thinking as you listen for main ideas.

LISTENING FOR MAIN IDEAS
1. Listen carefully to the beginning statements of the speaker and to the points the speaker emphasizes, repeats, and enumerates.
2. Visualize the main ideas. Restate them in your own words.
3. Decide whether the speaker's examples, definitions, facts, and statistics support the main ideas you have in mind.

Major Details. In order to determine which details of a speech are the most important ones, you must again analyze what you hear. The next chart presents some suggestions that can help you decide which details are most important.

LISTENING FOR MAJOR DETAILS
1. As you listen, ask yourself what makes each main idea true. Keep the details that answer that question in mind.
2. Try to predict details the speaker will mention.
3. Try to link the main ideas and supporting details into some sort of visual pattern.

Imagine that you heard the following announcement on the radio. Try to determine the main idea and major details that you would make an effort to remember.

ANNOUNCEMENT: Tonight at 7 o'clock there will be a debate between the two candidates for mayor of the town. The debate will last for two hours and will take place in the high school auditorium. Everyone is encouraged to attend.

If you were interested in attending the debate, the following information would be necessary to remember.

MAIN IDEA: A debate will be held between mayoral candidates.

MAJOR DETAILS: The debate will begin at 7 o'clock tonight. It will be held in the high school auditorium.

Verbal Signals. A speaker often uses signal words and phrases to alert you to important ideas or to the way the speech is organized. These verbal signals listed in the chart are important words to watch for and remember as you listen.

VERBAL SIGNALS	
Introduction	
we will discuss	open your books to
today's lecture covers	let's look first at
Main Ideas	
a point to be made	of major importance
make note of	remember that
let me repeat	I want to stress
Change in Direction	
next	turning now to
let us move on to	however
on the other hand	even though
Major Details	
for instance	the following reasons
for example	in support of
namely	that is to say
Conclusion	
finally	in conclusion
the last point	in summation
in brief	all in all

Nonverbal Signals. A speaker may guide you at certain points in a speech or lecture with movements and gestures to reinforce verbal signals. The speaker may alert you to main ideas by speaking more loudly and more emphatically, by moving an arm, by standing up, or by moving closer to the audience. The speaker may alert you to major details by speaking more softly and slowly or by sitting down. Watch the speaker's eyes and actions to anticipate what will be said next.

EXERCISE A: Listening for Main Ideas and Major Details. Work with another student on this exercise. While one person reads aloud the first passage below, the other should listen for main ideas and major details and take written notes while listening. Then, reverse roles and repeat the steps with the second passage. Evaluate the notes for accuracy.

(1) Adult frogs lay masses of eggs in lakes and ponds in the early spring. After about fifteen days, the eggs hatch. From these eggs come small, fish-like tadpoles that use their tails to swim and get oxygen through their gills. During the next stage of tadpole growth, hind legs begin to appear on the tadpole's body. At the same time the hind legs are growing, front legs get larger, its tail becomes smaller. The last stage in tadpole development is the addition of lungs. Once the tadpole has its lungs, it is well on its way to becoming an adult frog.

(2) In the twentieth century, the United States has negotiated two treaties with Panama over the Panama Canal. Under the treaty of 1903, the United States controlled both the canal and a ten-mile zone of land on each side of the canal. This zone cut Panama in half. It has been called "the foreign flag that pierced Panama's heart." The new treaty worked out in 1979 requires the United States to turn over control of the canal to Panama by the year 2000.

EXERCISE B: Practicing Your Listening Skills. Select one teacher in whose class you will practice specific listening skills for a week. Note how lectures begin and end, how the teacher indicates a change of topic or activity, how the teacher stresses something of importance, and how the teacher uses the chalkboard. List ways in which your awareness of these techniques helps your listening comprehension.

Following Directions

Approximately fifty percent of the directions that you need to follow will be given in writing, such as the directions for the exercises in this book. The other fifty percent will be given orally, such as directions for taking a test.

Good listening skills are especially important to help you follow and remember these directions.

Learn to listen to directions by performing certain mental shapes.

The following chart lists steps to follow.

STEPS TO HELP YOU UNDERSTAND DIRECTIONS
1. Prepare to concentrate.
2. Visualize each step in the directions. Ask yourself questions about how you would carry out the assignment.
3. After hearing the directions, repeat them mentally.
4. If, after hearing the directions, any parts are not clear, ask to have the directions repeated.
5. Take notes if the directions are long or complicated.

EXERCISE C: Listening for Directions. Work with another student on this exercise. While you read the first set of directions below, your partner should take mental notes and then repeat back to you as much of the directions as possible. Then, switch roles with the second set of directions.

1. Read the textbook chapter on plants and answer the questions at the end of the chapter. Then, select a related topic and prepare a list of five books in your school library dealing with that topic.
2. Write a 200-word essay on your favorite character in Mark Twain's *The Adventures of Tom Sawyer.* Be sure to tell why the character is your favorite and how the character is important to the major theme or themes of the novel.

Listening Critically

After you have understood and analyzed the literal meaning of a speaker's words, you can then listen critically to judge the validity of those words. Listening critically does not mean that you find fault with a speaker. Listening critically is a method of asking yourself questions to help you analyze and evaluate the meaning of what is being said.

Listen critically in order to analyze and evaluate a speaker's words.

The techniques discussed below are ones that speakers and writers use to communicate their ideas to an audience. Understanding the techniques and how they can be used or misused can help you listen more critically.

Fact and Opinion. A fact is something that can be verified as true or as something that actually happened. An opinion is someone's feeling or judgment about something. If a speaker identifies something he or she says as opinion, you know that you are not expected to believe it as fact. The speaker must support the opinion with pertinent facts to make it valid or believable. However, sometimes a speaker may present information that is opinion disguised as fact. When you listen critically, you must be on the alert and ask yourself the following question. How does the speaker support the information that is presented as fact or opinion? Read the following part of a lecture given in a social studies class and ask yourself which information is fact and which is opinion.

EXAMPLE: Today we are going to learn about Pompeii, the city that slept for 1500 years. The city was discovered in the sixteenth century by workers digging an underground tunnel. Why did it sleep? The reason that it slept was that its population was frozen in time. The city was sealed under the lava and mud that covered the city after the eruption of Mt. Vesuvius. For example, even today you can see bodies from 79 A.D. preserved in the volcanic ash. Even if Pompeii were not destroyed by the eruption of Mt. Vesuvius, it surely would have been destroyed by invading armies.

The information from the lecture above contains factual information about when and how Pompeii was destroyed. You can verify these facts by checking in an encyclopedia or a history text. The last sentence that tells how Pompeii might have been destroyed is an opinion. The speaker must support this opinion with facts before you can accept it as a valid opinion.

Denotation and Connotation. The denotation of a word is its literal meaning. Connotation is a word's suggested meaning and the associations that the word has. A speaker can use the connotation of a word to make the listener feel or think a certain way. If a speaker uses the connotation of a word to distort the truth and sway the listener, this is a dishonest use of connotation. Read the following section from a speech given by a candidate for the office of student council president and ask yourself if the connotation of any words is used to distort the truth.

EXAMPLE: My opponent has a useless plan for solving the problems our school has. He wants to sit down and do a flimsy study of the problems rather than acting like a true American and getting right to work.

By calling the person's plan "useless," the study "flimsy," and the person not a "true American," the speaker has tried to persuade the listener emotionally by the use of words with unfavorable connotations rather than by a logical argument.

Euphemisms. A euphemism is a word or expression that is used to avoid speaking directly about something that is unpleasant or improper. Sometimes a speaker can use euphemism to avoid the negative reaction that the more accurate word might have on the listener. Like connotations, euphemisms can be used to distort the truth. The following quote by George Orwell shows how a euphemism can be used to conceal the real intention behind a speaker's words.

> Political speech and writing are largely the defense of the indefensible. . . . Defenseless villages are bombarded from the air, the inhabitants driven out into the countryside, the cattle machine-gunned, the huts set on fire with incendiary bullets: this is called *pacification.*

Self-Important Language. Self-important or inflated language is language that consists of scholarly, technical or scientific words and overly long phrases. Like a euphemism, inflated language conceals rather than reveals the ideas behind the words. *Jargon,* the specialized vocabulary of a profession or a hobby, can be used for this purpose. Jargon appears to be scientific or technical but actually may present ideas you could readily understand if they were stated more clearly and simply. The following passage, written by a lawyer, is a humorous illustration of the way legal language can obscure and confuse meaning.

> When a man gives you an orange, he simply says: "Have an orange." But when the transaction is entrusted to a lawyer, he adopts this form: "I hereby give and convey to you, all and singular, my estate and interest, right, title, claim and advantages of and in said orange, together with its rind, skin, juice, pulp, and pips and all rights and advantages therein and full power to bite, suck, or otherwise eat the same or give the same away with or without the rind, skin, pulp, and pips, anything hereinbefore or hereinafter or in any other means of whatever nature or kind whatsoever to the contrary in anywise notwithstanding."

EXERCISE D: Listening Critically. Choose two of the following situations to practice your critical listening skills. Analyze and evaluate what you hear for the use of the techniques you have studied. Be specific in pointing out which words or phrases are examples of each technique. Then rephrase each example to make the words reveal the intended meaning.

1. a television news program
2. a political speech
3. a class lecture
4. a school or public group discussion
5. a community meeting

DEVELOPING WRITING SKILLS: Evaluating Your Listening Skills. Write a paragraph describing ways in which your literal and critical listening skills have improved. First, explain a speaker's verbal and nonverbal signals you have learned to watch for. Then, discuss the techniques a speaker has used or misused to communicate meaning.

Skills Review and Writing Workshop

Speaking and Listening Skills

CHECKING YOUR SKILLS

Imagine that you are listening to the following lecture given by a teacher. Read through it and write down the main ideas and major details *while* you are listening.

What do the experts tell us about dogs? They were apparently the first domesticated animal. Humans probably domesticated dogs, which are descended from wolves, during the Stone Age. Dogs assisted Stone-Age humans in hunting and helped protect the caves where people lived. By the sixth century B.C., the Egyptians had successfully bred several varieties of dogs. Today there are more than two hundred different breeds. Scientists believe that dogs are probably colorblind. However, dogs hear better than humans. Their sense of smell is also far superior to ours. Although we have always known that dogs make excellent companions, recent studies show that they can help us relax too.

USING STUDY SKILLS IN WRITING: Writing a Speech

How many times have you heard a good speech? An effective speech takes proper preparation and a strong delivery. Write a speech about a funny experience by following these steps.

Prewriting: Write down everything you can recall about this experience and organize it into an outline.

Writing: Prepare note cards based on your outline. Try to make your introduction unusual so it will interest the audience. The body of your speech should present your ideas in a logical manner, and the conclusion should have strong impact.

Revising: Practice your speech. Change any words or sentences that could be more effective. After you have revised, proofread your notes carefully.

Manuscript Preparation

The following pages give suggestions for basic manuscript preparation, for dealing with a number of technical aspects of writing, for giving credit to your sources, and for understanding and using correction symbols.

Basic Preparation

Whether handwritten or typed, your manuscript should follow certain basic rules. The following chart shows the suggested procedures for each style.

PREPARING A MANUSCRIPT

Handwritten	Typed
1. Use white 8½ × 11 inch lined paper, but never pages ripped from a spiral binder.	1. Use white 8½ × 11 inch paper.
2. Use black or blue ink only.	2. Use a clear black ribbon.
3. Leave a margin of 1 inch on the right, using the paper's own rules as your margin on other sides.	3. Leave a margin of at least 1 inch on all sides.
4. Indent each paragraph.	4. Double space all lines and indent each paragraph.
5. Use only one side of each sheet of paper.	5. Use only one side of each sheet of paper.
6. Recopy if necessary to make your final copy neat.	6. Retype if necessary to make your final copy neat.

You must also identify your manuscript. For long and important papers, such as reports, you will probably want an elaborate title page, as shown on page 844. The next page and all the other pages should carry only your name and the page number, beginning with page one.

With Title Page

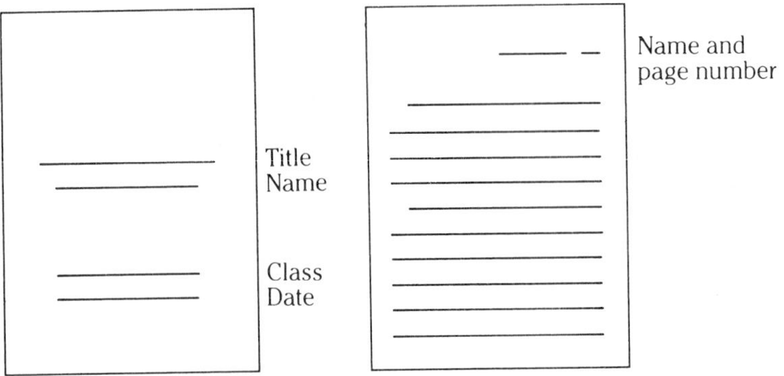

For shorter papers, use a simpler style. Basic identification appears on the first page. The second page carries your name and the page number, beginning with page two.

Without Title Page

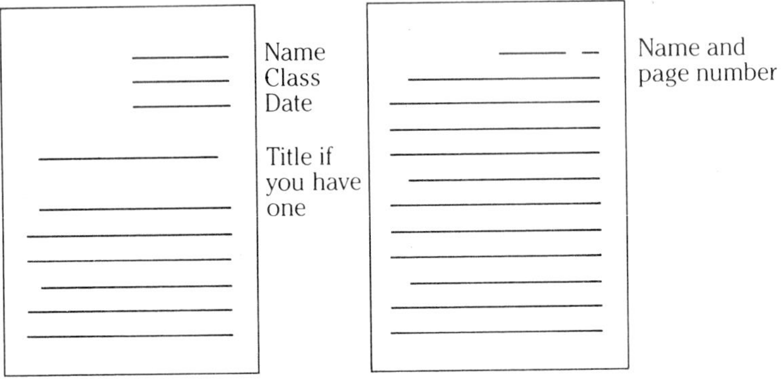

Checking Technical Matters

When preparing any manuscript, you must always check each sentence for correctness. Look for sentence errors—fragments, run-ons, and problem modifiers. Review Chapter 5, pages 73–104, if necessary. Also check the agreement of subjects and verbs. In addition, you may find it helpful to refer to the list of sixty common usage problems on pages 274–284.

Once you have checked your sentences, look for mechanical

errors such as incorrect punctuation. The following chart offers basic guidelines for using punctuation marks and other mechanical items that seem to cause most manuscript problems.

CHECKING TECHNICAL MATTERS		
Items	**Basic Guidelines**	**References**
Capitalization	Capitalize proper nouns, proper adjectives, and first words.	Section 15.1, pages 292–311
Abbreviations	Avoid most abbreviations in formal writing. Feel free, however, to use abbreviations such as Mr. and Mrs., a.m. and p.m., and well-known abbreviations for organizations such as NATO.	Section 15.2, pages 311–326
Commas	Take care not to overuse commas. Also check to make sure you are not dividing compound verbs with commas.	Section 16.2, pages 335–350
Hyphens	Check compound words in the dictionary. Hyphenate at the end of the line only when absolutely necessary and only at a syllable break.	Section 16.7, pages 385–392
Apostrophes	Avoid using apostrophes incorrectly in personal pronouns such as *its* and *theirs*.	Section 16.8, pages 392–401
Numbers	Spell out one- and two-word numbers and all numbers that begin sentences. Use numerals for lengthy numbers, dates, and addresses.	Section 15.2, pages 318–323
Spelling	Use a dictionary when in doubt.	Section 30.2, pages 731–739

Giving Credit to Sources

Whenever you are quoting the words or using the ideas of another writer, make sure you have given credit to that person. The chart in section 21.1 on page 571 shows the different forms for these kinds of citations.

Using Correction Symbols

You may find the following symbols very useful when you are proofreading your own manuscript. Your teacher may also choose to use these or similar marks when grading your papers.

USING CORRECTION SYMBOLS

Symbols	Meaning	Examples
℘	delete	The colors is red.
⁀	close up	The color is reed.
^	insert	The color is red.
#	add space	The coloris red.
∿	transpose	The colro is red.
¶	new paragraph	¶ The color is red.
no ¶	no paragraph	no ¶ The Color is red.
cap	capitalize	the color is red.
lc	use small letter	The Color is red.
sp	spelling	The colar is red.
us	usage	The colors is red.
frag	fragment	The red color and the blue.
RO	run-on	The color is red the house is blue.
mod	problem modifier	Newly painted, I saw the house.
awk	awkward	The color is, I think, kind of red.

Index

Bold numbers show pages on which basic definitions and rules can be found.

Acknowledgments

The authors and editors have made every effort to trace the ownership of all copyrighted selections found in this book and to make full acknowledgment of their use.

The dictionary of record for this book is *Webster's New World Dictionary*, Second College Edition, Revised School Printing, copyright © 1983 by Simon & Schuster, Inc. The basis for the selection of vocabulary words appropriate for this grade level is *Living Word Vocabulary: A 43,000 Word Vocabulary Inventory* by Edgar Dale and Joseph O'Rourke, copyright © 1979.

Citations follow, arranged by unit and page for easy reference.

Composition: The Writer's Techniques. Pages 432 (first item) R.A. Wilson "Jazz," *Soul* (March 1980), p. 8. **432** (second item) Christine Cannon, "Hands-on Guide to Palpatation and Ausculation," *RN* (March 1980), p. 24.

Composition: Forms and Process of Writing. Pages 474 M.L. Stein, *The Newswriter's Handbook* (New York: Cornerstone Library Publication, 1971). **475** (first item) Teresa Byrne-Dodge, "Venerable Venetians," *Americana*, Vol. 8, No. 1 (March/April 1980), p. 72. Copyright Americana Magazine, Inc. **475** (second item) Adapted from an article in *Games of the World*, Frederic V. Grunfeld, ed. (New York: Holt, Rinehart & Winston). **475** Allan C. Fisher, Jr., "Mysteries of Bird Migration," *National Geographic* Magazine (August 1979), p. 165. **476** *The New Book of Popular Science*, 1981. Published by Grolier, Incorporated, Danbury, CT. **479** Roger Tory Peterson, "An Appreciation of His Favorites from 'The King,' " *Smithsonian* (October 1979), pp. 57-59. **483** Charles N. Gaylord, "Modern Engineering," *The New Book of Popular Science*, 1981. Published by Grolier, Incorporated, Danbury, CT. **484, 488** Robert and Patricia Cahn, "Treasure of Parks for a Little Country That Really Tries," *Smithsonian* (September 1979), p. 66. **486** Adapted from J. Fritz Lanham, "The Result is Mad When Urban Wastes Become Public Art," *Smithsonian* (January 1980), p. 86. **486** Adapted from Henry Lansford, "The Frightening Mystery of the Electric Storm," *Smithsonian* (August 1979), p. 78. **487** Virginia Woolf, "Waxworks at the Abbey," in *Granite and Rainbow* by Virginia Woolf, Harcourt Brace Jovanovich, Inc. **487-488** Walter Kerr, *Tragedy and Comedy*. Copyright © 1968 by Walter Kerr. Reprinted by permission of Simon & Schuster, a Division of Gulf + Western Corporation. **488** Adapted from *The Encyclopedia Americana*. Reprinted with permission of *The Encyclopedia Americana*, copyright 1980, The Americana Corporation. **491** Judith B. Edwards, *Elements of Computer Careers*, (Englewood Cliffs, NJ: Prentice-Hall, Inc., 1977), p. 51. **519** Excerpt from p. 14 in *The Skier's Handbook* by the Editors of *Ski Magazine*. Copyright © 1965 by Universal Publishing & Distributing Corp. Reprinted by permission of Harper & Row, Publishers, Inc. **523** Adapted from Vance Packard, "The Waste Makers" (New York: David McKay Company, Inc., 1960). **525** Alice J. Hall, "Dazzling Legacy of an Ancient Quest," *National Geographic* Magazine (March 1977), p. 293. **532** From *Christy* by Catherine Marshall, (New York: McGraw Hill, Inc.). **535** Jean Kerr. Excerpt from "When I Was Queen of the May" from *The Snake Has All the Lines*, Copyright © 1959 by Jean Kerr. Reprinted by permission of Doubleday & Company, Inc. **589** Drs. Lorus J. and Margery Milne, "Will the Environment Defeat Mankind?" *The Saturday Evening Post* (September 1979), p. 103. **640-641** Excerpt from *Life Among the Savages* by Shirley Jackson, Copyright 1945, 1948, 1949, 1950, 1951, 1952, 1953 by Shirley Jackson. Copyright renewed © 1973, 1976, 1977, 1978, 1979, 1980, 1981 by Laurence Hyman, Mrs. Sarah Webster, and Mrs. Joanne Schnurer. Reprinted by permission of Farrar, Straus, and Giroux, Inc. **643-644** Helen Keller, excerpt from *The Story of My Life* (Garden City, NY: Doubleday & Company, Inc.). Copyright © 1954 by Doubleday & Company, Inc.

Study and Research Skills. Pages 745-746 *Current Events* Magazine, "Susan B. Anthony: Freedom Fighter" (January 31, 1979) Vol. 78, No. 11, p. 12. Copyright © 1979, Weekly Reader. **779-780** From *Preliminary Scholastic Aptitude Test/National Merit Scholarship Qualifying Test*, Eve P. Steinberg, used by permission of Arco Publishing, Inc. © 1980, New York,

New York. **795** *The Encyclopedia Americana*. Reprinted with permission of *The Encyclopedia Americana*, 1979 Edition, © Grolier, Inc. The Americana Corporation. **798** By permission. From *Webster's New Dictionary of Synonyms* © 1984 by Merriam-Webster Inc., publisher of the Merriam-Webster® Dictionaries. **802** *Readers' Guide to Periodical Literature* Copyright © 1984, 1985 by the H.W. Wilson Company. Material reproduced by permission of the publishers. **803** From *The New York Times Index* © 1984 by The New York Times Company. Reprinted by permission. **805** (first item) By permission. From *Webster's Third New International Dictionary* © 1976 by G. & C. Merriam Co., Publishers of the Merriam-Webster Dictionaries. **805** (second item) From the *Oxford English Dictionary* (Oxford, England: Oxford University Press, 1979). **809, 810, 811** (second, third, fourth, fifth, sixth items), **812, 813, 814** (second item), **815** With permission. From *Webster's New World Dictionary*, Students Edition. Copyright © 1981 by Simon & Schuster, Inc. **811** (first, seventh items) From the *Macmillan School Dictionary*. Copyright © 1981 Macmillan Publishing Co., Inc. **814** (first item) From *Thorndike-Barnhart Advanced Dictionary* by E.L. Thorndike and Clarence L. Barnhart. Copyright © 1973 by Scott, Foresman, and Company. Reprinted by permission.

Art Acknowledgments. **Pages 419** DPI. **516** Koren, *The New Yorker*, 1973. **517** Baron Wolman, Woodfin Camp. **538** Peabody Museum of Natural History. **539** Bridgeman, Art Resource. **540** Georg Gerster, Photo Researchers. **582** Laimute Druskis, Taurus Photos; Ellis Herwig, Taurus Photos. **583** John Chao, Woodfin Camp; Foldes, Monkmeyer Press. **584** United Feature Syndicate, Inc. © 1968. **608** Jacques Lowe, Woodfin Camp; Wide World Photos. **609** Mitchell Campbell, Photo Researchers. **610** Culver Pictures; Lehtikuva, EPU, Michal Euler, Woodfin Camp. **633** Culver Pictures. **647** Richard Wood, Taurus Photos; Susan Berkowitz, Taurus Photos; Ken Karp. **648** Culver Pictures. **649** United Feature Syndicate, Inc., © 1963. **666** Lawrence Lariar, 1966, Crown Publishers, Inc. **683** Wil Blanche, DPI. **692** Larry Downing, Woodfin Camp; Louis S. Davidson, Monkmeyer Press.

GRAMMAR USAGE MECHANICS